EMPIRE, INCORPORATED

Empire, Incorporated

Incorporated

The Corporations That Built
British Colonialism

PHILIP J. STERN

THE BELKNAP PRESS OF
HARVARD UNIVERSITY PRESS
Cambridge, Massachusetts
London, England
2023

Library of Congress Cataloging-in-Publication Data

Names: Stern, Philip J., author.
Title: Empire, incorporated : the corporations that built
British colonialism / Philip J. Stern.
Description: Cambridge, Massachusetts : The Belknap Press of
Harvard University Press, 2023. | Includes bibliographical references and index.
Identifiers: LCCN 2022038947 | ISBN 9780674988125 (cloth)
Subjects: LCSH: Colonial companies—Great Britain—History. |
Corporations—Great Britain—History. | Stock companies—Great Britain—
History. | Business and politics—Great Britain—History. | Great Britain—
Colonies—Commerce. | Great Britain—Colonies—Administration.
Classification: LCC HF485 .S74 2023 | DDC 382.0941—dc23/eng/20221128
LC record available at https://lccn.loc.gov/2022038947

For Felix

CONTENTS

Introduction: *Incorporating Empire* 1

1. Initial Public Offerings: *The Age of Discovery* 16

2. Municipal Bonds: *The Age of Crisis* 49

3. Corporate Finance: *The Age of Projects* 94

4. Hostile Takeovers: *The Age of Revolutions* 142

5. Corporate Innovations: *The Age of Reform* 193

6. Limiting Liabilities: *The Age of Imperialism* 242

Epilogue: *Winding Up* 301

ABBREVIATIONS 321

NOTES 323

ACKNOWLEDGMENTS 387

INDEX OF COMPANIES, CORPORATIONS, AND SOCIETIES 389

GENERAL INDEX 395

INTRODUCTION

Incorporating Empire

We have the romance of history, the romance of war, the romance
of geology, even the romance of the peerage; but there are tales of
the counter and the counting-house which would stir flesh and
blood with every simple telling.

𝒯HIS BOOK OFFERS A new history of British colonialism, one
that envisions empire as conceived not only by sovereigns and
statesmen but also by investors and idealists, creditors and convicts,
peers and parvenus, pirates and poets, lawyers and landowners, entrepreneurs and embezzlers. Their efforts produced what one might
call venture colonialism, a particularly prolific, if controversial, brand
of overseas expansion that was bound across four centuries by the
conviction that the public business of empire was and had always
been best done by private enterprise. While taking on many forms
across its long life, its most enduring medium was to be found in the
gradual union of two rather old concepts which, once fused together,
would transform the modern world. The one, joint stock, was a strategy
for collectively organizing, financing, and governing commercial
enterprises. The other was the notion that a group of people might
come together in law as if they were a single body—that is, the
corporation.

The story of how the joint-stock corporation came to shape British colonialism from its sixteenth-century origins through the era of decolonization may on first glance seem ripped from today's headlines, as billionaires race to colonize Mars and global technology companies have grown to the point that they look, as Mark Zuckerberg once characterized his company Facebook, "more like a government." In a world where an oil conglomerate might run what has been aptly described as a "private empire" and even insiders have come to think of the British Crown as "the Firm," understanding that the thin line between public and private governance has a deep and complex past has never been more consequential.[1] At the same time, much of this book takes place in quite distant times, places, and contexts, whose character and circumstances often shed light on those of the present through only the faintest of family resemblances. As a history of the colonial corporation, it may feel both instantly recognizable and surprisingly unfamiliar, as well-known characters appear alongside scores of others usually consigned merely to supporting or even offstage roles. As a history of corporate colonialism, it is defined as much by false starts and failed ventures as by enduring successes, as much by the torrent of companies flooding into all corners of the globe as by the constant efforts of others, not least the growing British state, to regulate, arrest, imitate, and co-opt them. Most of all, however, this history reveals that if the joint-stock corporation was well suited to empire, it was not because it was some inexorable juggernaut. Rather, like empire itself, it was—as it remains—a powerful paradox: person and group; public and private; commercial and political; mercantilist and capitalist; sycophantic and rebellious; regional and global; immortal and fragile; smugly patriotic and belligerently cosmopolitan; and the cornerstone of a British Empire never fully owned or operated by Britain as such.

* * *

Just where and when the modern joint-stock company first emerged continues to be a matter of some debate, but its echoes—in the sense of individuals engaged in some form of financial and commercial enterprise that pooled resources, risk, management, self-regulation, and rights—can be heard going back to antiquity and the Middle

Ages: the Roman *societas publicanorum;* the *commenda, maona, société, Gesellschaft, compagnia,* trust, and guild of medieval Christendom; the *waqf, qirad* or *muqarada* of the Muslim world; the South Asian *sreni;* Chinese intergenerational and lineal enterprises; the *Casa di San Giorgio* of fifteenth-century Genoa; and the English and Dutch East India Companies of early seventeenth-century northern Europe.[2] What distinguished a joint-stock company from other forms of collective finance as it traveled from the late medieval Mediterranean into the modern world was that its enterprise was divided up into portions ("dividends" or "shares") that could be purchased not only by partners but by other people, even strangers. A joint stock did not therefore rely solely on the personal resources of its own leadership, and its survival was not always solely dependent on whether it turned a profit. Rather, in theory it could draw funds from pretty much anywhere and anyone—landed wealth, other trades, foreigners—and thus amass capital, mobilize resources, tolerate risk and loss, and manage information on a far greater scale than most any self- or family-financed enterprise, and sometimes even governments.[3]

Such an ecumenical financial strategy had social and political implications. That one could become a member of a company simply by purchasing a share meant that one could also become a member of many companies at once, connecting such enterprises through various overlapping personal and institutional networks.[4] Leaders, members, and employees of one joint stock were often leaders, members, and employees of others, not to mention a wide range of commercial and civic institutions, including local government, the Crown, and Parliament. Interests, alliances, and conflicts within one forum permeated another. Company projectors and even those we might think of as "passive investors" risked their money and reputation for diverse reasons. Some were surely out for profit while others saw themselves as patriots. Some were driven by ideology and others by theology. Some bought shares because it was fashionable and others because they were compulsive gamblers.[5] Whatever the goals, promoting or joining a joint stock in early modern Europe was as much a form of "civil self-presentation" as a financial choice, where a shareholder was understood not just as an investor but also as an undertaker and an adventurer in a society, association, fellowship, brotherhood, and—in the sense the term applied to any group of people, from friends to soldiers, come together for some reason—company.[6]

What made joint stocks so appealing also made them rather unsettling. Commercial life in medieval and early modern Europe was a closed and tightly regulated world, which valued expertise enforced by elaborate rules and norms and centuries-old commercial and social associations like guilds and livery companies. A butcher was a butcher, a baker a baker, a candlestick maker a candlestick maker. In a joint stock, however, all three could also in a way become, say, East India merchants without any training or experience in the particulars of such a trade and certainly without ever having ever to set foot aboard ship. Worse still, though it would be centuries before shareholders would be thought of as owners, even at these early stages they often took some part in deciding how a company was run or at least in selecting some from among their number to do so on their behalf. Thus, not only did that candlestick maker have a say in how that East India trade was governed; he might, with enough stock and friends, become one of its governors.

In this sense, joint stock challenged traditional forms of both commerce and government. The Crown was embodied in the hereditary rule of an individual, his or her extended family, and an aristocratic, clerical, and landowning élite. A joint stock's management was drawn from among its members, usually represented in theoretically consensual and representative bodies (much like what would now be called shareholder meetings and boards of directors) whose leadership changed, in some cases annually. One might have more votes the more shares one owned, which was certainly not true of land in the House of Commons, where, of course, that unlanded candlestick maker—not to mention a woman or a foreigner—would for some time not have any vote at all. Over the years, some advocates thus came to see joint stock as a radical model for reforming both trade and politics. Others, sometimes for the very same reasons, regarded it as a dangerous if not treasonous idea.[7]

As a form of governance, however, joint-stock partnership only got you so far. On its own, it was basically a contractual relationship, which lacked any particular privileges, immunities, or guarantees of institutional permanence. For this one needed some form of legal protection. One option was a trust, by which an individual or group vested responsibility for their property in another individual or group.[8] Another not necessarily mutually exclusive option was the corporation, a discrete legal entity that could represent and work on behalf of its members. Like joint stock, the origins of the concept traced back to the medieval world, though derived less from commercial institutions than religious and civic ones: universities, municipalities, confraternities, monastic orders, bishoprics, and even concepts of the community of a universal Church incorporated in the body, *corpus,* of Christ. Yet a body that was both made up of people but also acted on its own, separate from them, posed certain inherent legal, theoretical, and even metaphysical and theological puzzles. Over time, medieval jurists had come to address these quandaries by conceptualizing the corporation as a kind of fictional or artificial person, which could act in law as an individual might—sue and be sued, possess property and privileges, contract debts, hold arms and offices—but also do things actual people could not do. It could make laws for self-government. It could amass immunities and rights that were, certainly in practice, unavailable to mere mortals. In theory, it could live forever.

Conceived as such, the corporation offered medieval jurists a powerful tool to theorize associational life. Ironically, it also provided the intellectual material these theorists would deploy to make a case for the enduring sovereignty of the Church, city-states, and kings and queens, who could now in themselves be thought of as having "two bodies": the one, the body natural, mortal and personal, the monarch; the other, the body politic, perpetual and public, the monarchy.[9] Corporate theory was so legally and philosophically robust and malleable that it would come to form the foundations for some of the most fundamental, if mutually exclusive, ideas about the origins and constitution of civil society. On the one hand, it allowed for a vision of the polity as a nesting doll of overlapping but independent corporate "commonwealths," from which followed modern notions like federalism and communalism.[10] On the other, the notion that a group of people or even a single individual could be rendered into a distinct, artificial, and perpetual body ultimately provided the key ingredients for imagining the exclusive and transcendent sovereignty at the core of the modern state.[11]

This of course raised a further question: if the state was a kind of corporation, just what was to be made of those many other corporations found within and beside it? To someone who imagined civil society as a conglomerate of concentric and intersecting corporate bodies, what later would come to be known as pluralism, such corporations were alternative and natural sites where people might choose to associate and govern themselves, produced in the first instance not by the state but rather the people that formed them. From this perspective, if the state played a role in a making a corporation, it did so somewhat in the same sense as it made a marriage: recognizing it with special legal status but hardly producing the bonds that brought the union into being in the first place.[12] Yet, if one imagined, in the tradition of those medieval Church theorists, that the corporation was a fictional or artificial person, then some other sovereign power had to be responsible for endowing it with life. In the English common law, this power was to be found, with some notable exceptions, in the royal prerogative and dispensed, like other franchises and offices, in documents known as letters patents, or what were sometimes collectively and somewhat imprecisely called "charters." Charters of incorporation would over time be unseated though never fully supplanted by Parliamentary legislation and eventually by administrative registration, but all shared the basic assumption that corporations, in the words of the seventeenth-century jurist Edward Coke, "resteth only in intendment and consideration of the Law."[13] Conceiving of corporations as "concessions" of the state, however, made for another formidable irony. As is well known, subjecting artificial persons to the law over time allowed them to claim some of the civil, international, and even human rights normally reserved for actual people by that law, affording corporations an outsize power that states could not always control and that frequently could be employed to control states.[14]

Much like with joint stock, a corporate person that was, as Coke had observed, both "invisible" and "immortal" could prove quite disturbing. By its very nature it eluded many of the tools law had for holding natural persons responsible for their actions. It could not swear an oath or be imprisoned or excommunicated. Even those who argued that the state gave birth to the corporation struggled to come up with ways the law might easily kill it. Across the political spectrum, many fretted that corporations were persons without souls, monstrosities prone to disloyalty and even rebellion. The seventeenth-century absolutist Thomas Hobbes famously likened urban corporations to "worms in the entrails" of the body politic much as critics of the royal prerogative derided chartered monopolies as "bloodsuckers of the commonwealth."[15] The godfather of modern liberalism, Adam Smith, insisted that joint-stock companies were by their very nature rife with "negligence and profusion," while Karl Marx thought of the stock market as teeming with a "new variety of parasites." Some saw them less as vermin or vampires than, like Frankenstein's creature, as a violation of nature itself, cobbled together from various parts in such a way not so much to "create life" as to "cheat death."[16] Of course, as one of the early twentieth century's leading pluralists, Harold Laski, observed, corporations also resembled the monster in another sense, namely in their "curious habit of attempting perpetually to escape from the rigid bonds in which they have been encased" and "show ingratitude to their creators," even to the point of "rebellion against the state which, in legal theory, at any rate, gave it birth."[17]

The corporation's dilemmas are thus buried deep in its DNA. Is it real or natural? Is it an extension of sovereign power, a check on sovereign power, or a sovereign power unto itself? Such quandaries were exponentially compounded in the sixteenth and seventeenth centuries, as various experiments transposed the corporate status traditionally reserved for local forms of government like cities, churches, universities, and civic associations onto far more spatially diffuse joint-stock commercial enterprises, especially those for overseas trade, exploration, predation, and settlement. Though relatively certain that the Crown gave corporations life at home, the law was far less clear on whether or how it could control them once created, especially in the world beyond the realm. On paper, charters and patents dispensed invaluable rights that many others did not have, from relief from certain duties and taxes to the prerogative to claim territory. Their most critical feature at this early stage was that they almost always, in theory, offered their holders exclusive privileges, or what critics would come to call "monopolies." In this sense then a charter did not make law so much as, as Hobbes observed, provide a "Liberty" or "exemptions from Law."[18]

Moreover, if they were laws, overseas charters were not terribly well-written ones. They were remarkably ambiguous, aspirational, and open to interpretation. Officials enforced them inconsistently. Their terms typically allowed for laundry lists of enterprises their

holders might undertake over impossibly vast and ill-defined geographical spaces insouciantly superimposed over indigenous sovereignty, rival European claims, and, often enough, other English
charters. Had these "rights" been clear, they still would have meant
little to those people and polities their holders encountered abroad
and were constantly challenged, in law and on the ground, by others,
including many of their own compatriots. If one wanted property
and sovereignty abroad, it had to be acquired abroad in treaties,
grants, contracts, and agreements of various kinds obtained of other
sovereigns and subjects through cession, purchase, pressure, conquest,
or, all too often, outright fabrication.

From the *requerimiento* sixteenth-century Spanish *conquistadores*
announced to the peoples of the Americas to the European "concession hunters" that spread themselves across nineteenth-century
Africa, the notion that indigenous peoples around the globe had
somehow dispossessed themselves of both property and sovereignty—
either voluntarily or by violating certain conditions of the law—
became one of the ideological and legal foundations of European
colonial expansion.[19] In their particular ability to exist, jurisdiction-
ally and institutionally speaking, in multiple places at once, corporations were especially well suited to such a system. Such a cobbled-
together constitution could at times admittedly render companies
doubly vulnerable, as trouble abroad reverberated at home or vice
versa. More often, however, the alleged possession of rights abroad
served as arguments for upholding corporate powers at home; in
this sense, multiple sources of authority galvanized one another,
compounding, as in an alloy or amalgam, the "jurisdictional evasive-
ness" at the core of the overseas corporation's power.[20] As Europeans imagined that chartered rights, British or otherwise, could
be bought, sold, bequeathed, disaggregated, and parceled up, corporations evinced a unique capacity for acquiring jurisdictional
rights, combining them with other legal powers, and securing both
across generations. They could also sell such rights to others or, as
joint stocks, even be bought up themselves, outright or piecemeal
through the purchase of shares. Meanwhile, any given individual,
as a stockholder in multiple enterprises, could in effect own a share
of sovereignty in various places around the world without ever
leaving home, producing the sort of portfolio colonialism that un-
derwrote so much of British overseas expansion.[21]

In time, entrenching such power in the rather mundane instruments of indentures, contracts, and share certificates had profound legal and ideological consequences. It potentially allowed even the most specious and outrageous of claims to territory or jurisdiction abroad to be normalized, routinized, and naturalized, protected in British law by a right that may arguably have been even more sacrosanct than sovereign power: private property. The colonial joint-stock corporation was adept at cultivating this form of commodified sovereignty, even if its business often looked more like a form of laundering racket mixed with what might later be called a Ponzi or pyramid scheme.[22] It thrived on its ability not only to mobilize and accumulate capital but also to forward various hypothecated financial schemes secured, circularly and tenuously, with hypothetical political rights. Like a charter, company stock was just a promissory note, which at least at a company's outset often had little (if any) assets behind it. New colonial companies offered shares of property or profits that did not yet and might never exist or whose investors, as settlers, were themselves responsible for securing. Corporations' legal status allowed them to take out loans and, in many cases, issue their own bonds and debentures, new stock issues, and subsidiary companies. Joint-stock companies could also borrow in another sense, accumulating assets—property, territories, jurisdictions, and even more debt—in exchange for shares rather than cash. Meanwhile, these "volunteer services of British pioneers," as one late nineteenth-century author called them, were commonly subsidized by assorted public and political resources.[23]

If many colonial companies thrived on the accumulation not so much of capital but of debt, their political and financial health required constant work to promote and defend their creditworthiness and credibility. Like other corporations and even actual people, colonial companies were not static entities but rather "always in the process of being enacted" with every ship and settler sent, every treaty made and battle fought, every share sold and loan taken, every letter written, lawsuit filed, and treatise or travelogue published.[24] Corporate colonialism drew in broad constituencies of stakeholders: employees, sailors, soldiers, settlers, tenants, suppliers, consumers, laborers, commercial partners, creditors, and, from the Treasury to the Admiralty, the various agents and agencies of the British state that came to rely on companies for their commercial, martial, and financial power.[25] For shareholders in particular, joint-stock companies also provided unique opportunities to participate in empire at a remove, a kind of limited moral liability to support legal and physical violence in faraway places that may have been unthinkable otherwise. "Corporate conscience is ever inferior to the individual conscience," the nineteenth-century philosopher and sociologist (and former railway company employee) Herbert Spencer lamented, such that "a body of men will commit as a joint act, that which every individual of them would shrink from did he feel personally responsible."[26]

Such a model had its fair share of critics. There were certainly those who opposed colonialism itself, but many more took issue with the notion that private bodies were the proper means for achieving it. It is hard to find any individual colonial company that escaped the opprobrium of rivals, competitors, colonists, and even its own members. Such challenges were themselves a critical part of the history of corporate empire, especially as they fueled demands to regulate, oversee, and even subsume corporate colonies into the growing British state and empire. In this sense, the British Empire proper—that is, one governed directly by the Crown, Parliament, and its agencies and bureaucracies—was also an incorporated empire, built in no small part by absorbing and assimilating those corporations and other forms of non-state enterprise that often laid the foundations of the colonial enterprise. Many, especially by the nineteenth century, came to regard such a process as natural, the logical consequence of the supremacy of the modern state and the supposed separation of public good from private interest. Yet, even then, this was a history that turned out to be far more iterative than inevitable. In every generation, new state institutions, ideologies, and legal regimes appeared to render chartered colonialism a thing of the past. Still, there colonial corporations remained, reformulated and transformed but nonetheless central to the expansion of modern empire and, eventually, its dissolution.

* * *

Over the years, corporate or venture colonialism would go by many different names: franchise and project, systematic colonization and double government, chartered colonialism and the "joint-stock principle." Its most well-known and well-studied manifestations are doubtless in what historians, myself included, have called "company-states," bodies like the East India Company or Hudson's Bay Company that came to rule millions of people over vast territorial empires.[27] Yet this dominant species thrived only within a vast and diverse eco-system of corporate enterprises big and small, enduring successes and immediate failures instituted or merely imagined for various inter-secting reasons, including trade, land, and settlement, transportation and public works, financial services and resource extraction, military and predation, philanthropy and philosophy, education and prosely-tization. They took form as commercial companies as well as churches, charities, universities, learned societies, towns, and even colonies that were themselves "Governors and Companies." Such efforts inspired, mirrored, and connected with one another and analogous enterprises across Europe. Many were joint stocks whose corporate status was questionable, while some corporations explicitly shunned the joint-stock model. Their strategies and ethos even infused supposedly al-ternative models of colonial expansion, from proprietary colonies to protectorates, not to mention the state's own empire.

Corporations thus played a leading role among the many "agents in empire" that historian Lauren Benton has shown propelled the "irregular thrust of imperial jurisdiction into extra-European space."[28] This kind of patchwork empire could certainly seem mud-dled and confused, a "chaotic pluralism" resembling, as one histo-rian has suggested, what Adam Smith had critiqued as a costly, me-diocre, and largely illusory "project of an empire."[29] From another vantage, however, chaos and anarchy proved to be quite deliberate and effective weapons of colonial expansion and violence.[30] In fact, the history of venture or corporate colonialism might suggest a chaos theory of empire, one that, when viewed at the proper scale across space and time, exposes ordered patterns in what might otherwise seem in the moment to be random and irregular, where seemingly disconnected or trivial events can end up registering dramatic if dis-tant consequences.[31] Put another way, refocusing one's gaze from a singular imperial project to the vast number of interrelated and com-peting colonial projects reveals an empire that may have been unco-ordinated but was never unintentional, acquired not in a "fit of absence of mind" but possibly in the absence of an "official mind" exclusively centered in the state.[32]

My approach to capturing this coherent chaos has been to reconstitute the story of venture colonialism as both a narrative history and an experiment in collective legal, intellectual, and institutional biography. As a narrative, it is like a novel that places an originally supporting character in the center of its story, not to replace old dominant accounts with an equally problematic new one but rather to lay bare the fundamental point that the history of empire demands many different, often conflicting narrative possibilities at once.[33] In focusing on the British Empire, I also do not mean to suggest that corporate empire is at its root a national enterprise or an especially British one. In fact, through its long history, corporate colonialism demonstrates time and again just how porous the borders of nations, empires, and companies themselves were in the first place.[34] Looking across the "long view" of several centuries also insists on a layered rather than linear story of both law and empire, one that emphasizes "disappointed expectations as often as realized ones."[35] This book's subject is not, like many histories of corporate colonialism, any particular person or company, though you will certainly find hundreds of examples of both in the pages that follow. Rather, it traces through these many vignettes the dynamic relationship between institutional and organizational structures and the arguments that fueled them, aggregating what might be thought of as "micro-intellectual" and institutional histories and projecting them, perhaps like a corporate conglomerate itself, onto a multigenerational and macro-historical scale. As a kind of intellectual biography, even if an admittedly peculiar one, this book avoids the presumption that one can or should attempt to recover any simple or "stable identity" for its subject so much as seek "to track its movements and, as nearly as possible, to witness some of the collisions that may have kept it in motion" and "situate [it] in the multiple contexts that gave shape and direction to [its] life."[36]

Trying to engage in a history of empire that does not see like a state inevitably leads as well to an account that transgresses many of the usual borders and checkpoints erected by traditional imperial history. Though organized chronologically, it offers no easy turning point in time or space when empire became especially "modern." Its broadly global scope is constituted by many particular, fragmented, and distinctly regional histories, which were simultaneously national and transnational, commercial and political, and about settler colonialism and imperial rule in equal and at times indistinguishable proportions.[37] Normally fast distinctions common to histories of the British Empire fade away: chartered, proprietary, and Crown colonies for the earlier period; protectorates and protected states, mandates, dependencies, dominions, spheres of influence, and, of course, "colonies," among others, for the later. Colonial corporations blended commercial and financial impulses with territorial, political, predatory, speculative, extractive, governmental, and even moral and philosophical ambitions. Its practitioners were well-connected "gentlemanly capitalists," felons, and foreigners alike, whose enterprises cannot be so neatly classified as mercantilist or capitalist, imperial or sub-imperial, fully part of the British Empire or exclusively partaking in the "informal," "business" or "economic" empires that have been said to lurk beneath the waterline of imperial history.[38]

Finally, what follows complicates any simple relationship between capitalism and colonialism that one might expect of a story about corporations and companies. If the core argument on behalf of venture colonialism—that public governance is best left to private and often corporate enterprise—bears a striking resemblance to the foundations of global neoliberalism, it is worth remembering that Smith himself insisted that the "corporation spirit" of chartered companies was an anachronism that undermined economy and empire alike.[39] In a way, corporations' bivalent nature helps to explain but not resolve the longstanding disputes about the role of capitalism in empire. To the early twentieth-century radical liberal John Hobson, finance capitalism was the "taproot of imperialism," while the Russian Revolutionary Vladimir Lenin envisioned imperialism as the ultimate "stage" of "parasitic or decaying" monopoly capitalism. For their contemporary, the Austrian economist Joseph Schumpeter, however, capitalism was supposed to do away with colonialism, whose persistence could only be explained away as a "social atavism" driven by impulses for glory and power deeply embedded in the minds of politicians and the public alike but belonging to a bygone world of aristocratic conquest, not modern commercial life.[40] This dilemma persists. Many would agree that companies that waged wars and dispossessed millions of their lands and livelihoods serve

as an "ominous warning about the potential for the abuse of corporate power—and the insidious means by which the interests of shareholders can seemingly become those of the state."[41] Yet, there are
those who instead see in this history the venture capitalists of their
day and the "perseverance" of the entrepreneurial spirit.[42] Somewhere between these two approaches are numerous scholars who
have looked not so much to praise or bury the modern multinational
as to locate its origins and in so doing perhaps uncover potential solutions to some of its thorniest managerial or even ethical challenges.[43]

The history of corporate colonialism can continue to represent so
many different things to different people precisely because its own
nature and history is one of contradictions. Is a corporation a person
or a society? Who holds it accountable? Should its priority be shareholder profit or social benefit? Is it best thought of as a public citizen
or a private empire? As it traveled from the sixteenth to the twentieth centuries, venture colonialism proved to be neither anathema
to capitalism nor coterminous with it, neither precisely venture
capitalism nor purely colonial venture. If it was the taproot of imperialism, it was one buried deep with centuries of offshoots and
branches; if it was an atavism, it was less a social than a legal one,
written into empire's genetics through the telling and retelling of
history through the law and vice versa. In short, a long and global
view of British venture colonialism does not suggest a solution to
such quandaries so much as reveal the debate and dilemma to be as
old as the corporation itself.[44]

This book thus makes an argument for understanding empire as
process not product and for reflecting on the present quandaries of
public and private power more through genealogy than analogy.[45]
Yet if the history of incorporated empire resists any simple answer
to what the colonial corporation was, it certainly insists on a far
more coherent and continuous story of what it did and how it did
it. The understandable preoccupation with asking the world of
early modern colonialism to explain the origins and nature of our
contemporary global predicaments has perhaps had the unintended
consequence of setting to the side somewhat more immediate questions about its legacies in shaping the history of colonialism itself.[46]
Corporations were everywhere in nineteenth- and twentieth-century
European empires, yet were neither the curious anomalies nor purely

commercial enterprises some at the time and many since took them to be. Rather, these companies turned out to have a long and at times surprisingly continuous lineage, one that their promoters and advocates often embraced and that ensured that a model of colonialism, which advanced around the globe more as a cacophony than a concert and whose story traced back centuries, would endure to exert an inordinate influence in and over the modern world.

1

INITIAL PUBLIC OFFERINGS

The Age of Discovery

Therefore generally I say unto all such
according to the old Proverb,
Nothing venture, Nothing have.

IF ELIZABETH I'S DECISION in October 1562 to offer six thousand troops and a substantial sum of money to support the Huguenot occupation of the port city of Le Havre changed the course of the history of the British Empire, it was perhaps not in the way she and her advisors had imagined. In addition to hoping to turn the French Wars of Religion toward the Protestant cause, English officials envisioned Le Havre as the first step to recovering the fourteenth-century English stronghold and staple town of Calais, itself lost just a few years earlier. "Calais must be had," Secretary of State William Cecil, later Lord Burghley, at one point scribbled in his notes, "for the honor of the realm, surety of the seas and trade of merchandise."[1]

It was not to be. Within a year, English troops had returned home defeated, along with Tudor ambitions of restoring England's medieval empire. Yet, as it turns out, the experience may have inadvertently proved to be an incubator for a different sort of overseas expansion. Many of the military leaders and soldiers who cut their teeth in the French campaigns would go on to sink them into Ireland in the coming decades.[2] Some of these men, like Sir Henry Sidney and the scholar Richard Eden, had also a decade earlier been instrumental in the establishment of an overseas English joint-stock corporation, in many ways the first of its kind, which had set out in search of a northerly maritime route to the Indies and found Russia instead. While in Le Havre, one might have struck up conversation with the cleric, explorer, and cosmographer André Thevet, who had taken part in a 1555 effort to establish a Huguenot refuge in Brazil, or the navigator Jean Ribault and supporters of his efforts in 1562 to do the same in "La Florida," along what is now coastal South Carolina. By the next year, Ribault had forged a partnership with another veteran of the French wars, the enigmatic Thomas Stukeley, to draw English investors, including the Queen, into funding a return venture to Florida. The fleet, however, never made it beyond the English Channel, where Stukeley notoriously redirected it into a more lucrative privateering mission. Ribault soon found himself in prison. Stukeley soon found himself in Ireland. Meanwhile, their names came to represent both a cautionary tale about the dangers of such speculative and potentially unscrupulous enterprises and a precedent for doing just such a thing, especially in the heart of an Atlantic world that the Iberians claimed as their own.[3]

This is certainly how Humphrey Gilbert, Stukeley's cousin and another veteran of the Le Havre expedition, saw it. It may have been at Le Havre, historians have long speculated, surrounded by the likes of Eden, Thevet, Ribault, and his future patron Sidney, that the Eton- and Oxford-educated courtier from the English West Country first developed what would become a lifelong project to explore and colonize in North America.[4] If nothing else, for someone like Gilbert, Le Havre and his later more famous colonial career were born from similar impulses. A second son who eventually married into some wealth, Gilbert nonetheless spent his lifetime on the make, looking for financial, political, and social advancement in common forms of entrepreneurial public service. Gilbert recruited and commanded troops not only in France but also later in a secret mission to Zeeland and, most infamously, under Sidney in Ireland. He served as a Justice of the Peace in Plymouth and a commissioner supervising the construction of the harbor at nearby Seaton. He volunteered his services as an advisor to the Crown, including penning an elaborate treatise for a humanist, mercantile, and military academy, anticipating by decades if not a century the better-known thought experiments of Francis Bacon and William Petty. He served briefly in Parliament, where he vigorously spoke on behalf of the Crown's prerogative against critiques of monopoly grants and, for his loyalty, was evidently rewarded with a seven-year patent to enforce and collect fines for violations of the 1541 Unlawful Games Act. He also joined with three of the Queen's most influential advisors—Burghley, the Earl of Leicester, and the Privy Councilor, diplomat, and philosopher Sir Thomas Smith—in Smith's quixotic joint-stock alchemy and mining startup, *The Society of the New Art,* all the while accumulating substantial manorial holdings in England and, like Smith and many others, looking for investors for his various and sometimes wildly ambitious plantation schemes in Ireland.[5]

Gilbert was hardly unique. Sixteenth-century England, like much of the early modern world, was a franchise government, in which offices and positions were both public service and private property, with prerogatives and perquisites meant to offer opportunities for social and financial advancement.[6] For someone like Gilbert, exploration, predation, and plantation abroad sat at the intersection of entrepreneurial enterprise and what he called "Chivallric policy and philosophie" but what more commonly might have been known as a "project."[7] Like other chartered offices and enterprises, overseas franchises could be bought, shared, sold, inherited, farmed out, and financed.[8] As they marshalled partners and investors, often including the Queen and her ministers, such projects did not easily distinguish state from individual interest and as such were less public-private partnerships than portmanteaus. Unlike their domestic brethren, however, overseas charters projected their authority into places where the Crown, legally and pragmatically, had none. Territory, jurisdiction, or trading privileges abroad had to be acquired by taking it or by negotiating for it, via grants, contracts, purchases, and agreements with the peoples and polities they found there. Even the supposed authority patents offered to govern some English subjects and to exclude others mixed and matched older legal traditions such as seigneurial lordship, martial law, the commercial guild and partnership, fellowship and confraternity, and, ultimately, the urban and associational corporation to suit this new environment. The result was a prolific if untidy set of experiments that gradually molded medieval mechanisms of civic life and government-by-franchise to fit the ambiguities and absurdities of overseas enterprise. If such models seemed to blur the lines between colony and commerce, finance and governance, and public office and private profit, it was because they arose from a world in which such fast boundaries had never existed in the first place.

FROM MOSCOW TO MUNSTER

It is often said that England was a latecomer to overseas European expansion, but that pretty much depends on what part of England one is talking about. While late fifteenth- and early sixteenth-century London and the Court were preoccupied with Continental commerce and politics, the maritime, mercantile, and seafaring communities of western England had their sights set farther afield. Bristol merchants had especially long and deep connections to southern Europe, which now kept them especially well informed of budding Iberian overseas projects. As early as the 1480s, some there had begun to develop Atlantic ambitions of their own.[9] In 1497, not long after the Genoese navigator Christopher Columbus sailed west for the Indies in the service of the Crowns of Castile and Aragon, the Venetian John Cabot and his three sons set out further north with a similar charter from the English King Henry VII and funding from a Bristol-based consortium and a number of Italian investors. Neither, of course, made it to Asia. Whereas Columbus ended up in the Caribbean, Cabot landed in present-day Canada, on an island he called somewhat obviously "New-found-land." While subsequent attempts were no more successful, investors were undeterred. In 1502, four partners—two from Bristol and two from the Azores— attempted to organize what one contemporary at least understood as "the Company adventurers into the new fownde ilondes."[10] Cabot's son Sebastian also set out on his own venture and would spend the rest of his life selling similar enterprises to Bristol merchants, the Spanish and English Crowns, and once, as rumor had it, Jean Ribault.[11]

By the mid-sixteenth century, English merchants had begun to set their sights on western Africa as well. Several terminable joint-stock *Adventurers to Guinie* drew in the London mercantile community, courtiers, and even the Crown, leading by 1562 to the first of a series of slaving operations under the leadership of the mariner and privateer John Hawkins. As war and religious turmoil in Europe led to significant disruptions in the northern European textile trade, some of those London merchants and statesmen began to take notice of what by now was over a half century of Iberian seaborne expansion into the Indian Ocean world. "Supposing the same to be a course and meane for them," in 1553, over two hundred Londoners subscribed £6,000 to fit out a fleet of three ships to head to the northeast in search of a "newe and strange Navigation." Their hope was to discover new markets, peoples, and kingdoms, and, most of all, a shorter maritime route to Asia. They called themselves *The Mysterie and Companie of the Marchants Adventurers for the discoverie of regions, dominions, islands, and places unknown.* Sebastian Cabot was their first Governor.[12]

As novel as this venture advertised itself to be, the name itself would have signaled something familiar to contemporaries. Overseas merchants, among others, routinely organized themselves into guilds and companies to maintain and control access to the special techniques and knowledge, or "mysteries," of their trades. Many only later sought out royal grants to allow them further immunities of self-government, relief from certain taxes, and, most importantly, unimpeded rights to travel from and reside beyond the realm. English merchants to the Baltic, for example, first received patents in 1408, while Henry VIII's grants to English merchants in Andalusia doubled as a trading license and authorization to maintain the chapel and confraternity of St. George in Sanlúcar de Barrameda.[13] "Merchants Adventurers" who risked themselves and their money to find new commercial markets in Europe had emerged in the fifteenth and sixteenth centuries in commercial cities across England. Exeter had one, as did Newcastle, Hull, Chester, and York. Bristol's Merchant Venturers, which dated back centuries, had recently received its first charter of incorporation from King Edward VII in 1552. The best-known of these was the London-based *Company of Merchant Adventurers of England,* which traced its origins as early as the twelfth century and to royal grants going back to 1407 but was only fully incorporated with expanded powers in 1564, governing over the textile trade to the Low Countries and northern German states.[14]

Like London's livery companies, a company of merchant adventurers was not only a commercial association but a religious enterprise, a mutual assistance society, a quasi-government council, and, like the Corporation of Trinity House, incorporated in 1514 to train ships' pilots and control traffic on the Thames, a "Guild, Fraternity, or Brotherhood."[15] Though in one sense following in that tradition, this new Company for "places unknown" was a significant departure. Unlike its more guild-like cousins, it was not a coalition of independent traders under the umbrella of a consortium but rather a single "common stocke," always to be preferred, as Cabot cautioned the first fleet, to any individual's "owne proper wares, and things."[16] As a company with its eyes on the trade to Asia, it made certain sense that it resembled less the organizational strategies of the northern European trades than it did the centuries-old practices of the *commenda* and *muqarada* of Mediterranean trade into the Indian Ocean world, with which Cabot for one, given his Italian roots and extensive Iberian experience, would have been quite familiar.[17]

The decision to organize this company as a joint stock was one made with finance and government in mind. In "so harde and difficult a matter," the author and engraver Clement Adams later noted, diffusing the funding across many adventurers ensured that no "private man should bee too much oppressed and charged" in the enterprise. Yet, it also meant that the trade would not be managed by many different competing traders but rather by a common council, "certaine grave and wise persons in maner of a Senate or companie, which should laye their heads together, and give their judgements, and provide thinges requisite and profitable for all occasions." Moreover, a common stock was a repository of knowledge and expertise, keeping accounts, journals, maps, and other materials, as Cabot put it, as a "record for the companie," not unlike an English version of the Seville *Casa de Contratación,* where Cabot had worked for many years.[18] Among its broad base of influential adventurers and their spawning networks were a panoply of authors and scholars, like Eden, Adams, Robert Recorde, and the polymath natural philosopher, mystic, and royal advisor John Dee, whose translations, travel narratives, maps, and treatises served both to advise the Company and to make its case to statesmen and the political public alike—and, of course, any potential investors among them.[19]

Still, even the great power of joint stock was no match for the sea. The Company's first fleet consisted of three ships, two of which never returned. The one that survived had not come close to "Cathay" but rather had put in at the White Sea port of Archangelsk, where its commander Richard Chancellor established trade and diplomatic relations with the Russian Empire. This was enough to justify requesting in 1555 a charter to add to the Company's joint-stock organization the more formal status of incorporation. Such patents ensured it would have a legal identity, with rights to hold property and govern itself in a manner that looked much like other municipal corporations, associations, and companies of merchants adventurers. Instead of a mayor, aldermen, and burgesses, it had a "governor," under whom were four "consuls"—possibly in imitation of the Genoese Bank of San Giorgio—and twenty-four "assistants," eventually to be elected out of its body of "adventurers," or shareholders.[20] Over the following years, the Company would receive various patents, grants, and agreements from Czar Ivan IV as well as an Act of Parliament in 1566, which gave it a new formal name—*Fellowship of English Merchants for Discovery of New Trades*—alongside its increasingly common colloquial one: the Muscovy, or Russia, Company. In addition to theoretically controlling any and all English efforts to explore and navigate the Atlantic world or forge an eastern or western passage to Asia, this Company had effectively become the English government over Anglo-Russian commerce, as well as various other trades, including Russian wax exports and, soon, English whaling and the manufacture and sale of train oil.[21] As the main conduit of relations between England and Russia, the Company had *de facto* command of Anglo-Russian diplomacy and soon attempted to extend its reach into Persia, beginning with the relatively fruitless embassy of Anthony Jenkinson in 1562 on behalf of the Company, Elizabeth, and Ivan.[22]

Inevitably, such a Company inspired rivals, emulators, and interlopers. One strategy the Company had for dealing with competitors was to use these powers and connections at home or abroad to prosecute them in England or Russia, through royal officers, customs officials, or law courts. The other was to incorporate them, offering sub-licenses, grants, buy-outs, or permission to purchase stock and become members of the company. This is what the Company agreed to do in 1566, admitting a number of independent traders to Narva as a condition of receiving its Parliamentary Act.[23] It is also, in a sense, how it handled Jenkinson's attempts the previous year to propose his own northeasterly venture to the Privy Council, sending him on another diplomatic mission to Russia just as he was forging

Sir Humphrey Gilbert, by Robert Boissard, circa
1590–1603. NPG D20541, National Portrait Gallery, London.

a potential partnership with Humphrey Gilbert, who, having returned from France, had registered a competing bid for a venture in
the opposite direction, in search of a northwest passage.[24]

Gilbert's plans were also postponed, as he soon departed to take
up a military commission under Henry Sidney, now Lord Deputy in
Ireland. However, returning to Court in late 1566 on business for
Sidney, he took the opportunity to revive his petition for letters patents authorizing him to mount an expedition for the "discooverye
of A passage to Cataya and all other the ryche partes of the worlde
as yet unfounde." His proposal was certainly ambitious. For his services, he insisted that he should be given a forty-year exclusive control of trade and government over any territories or passages he

might find. In making his case, Gilbert rehearsed what would become a familiar repertoire of arguments of the economic, social, and
strategic benefits of Atlantic plantation: establishing a "convenient"
stop *en route* to Asia, finding markets among indigenous Americans,
training seamen and increasing navigation "without the burdening
of the state," and easing poverty and crime at home.[25] The problem
was that any such grant would in theory be in violation of the Russia
Company's patents. Gilbert argued, however, that such claims were
largely moot, as for a "long tyme, there hath bin nothinge saide or
donne" to search out the passage to Asia and the recent Parliamentary Act confirming the Company's expansion into Narva suggested
it had largely abandoned its exploratory ambitions in favor of the
Russian trade. The Company's representatives saw it differently.
They were open to Gilbert's "good advise, help and conference."
They might even be persuaded to appoint him "Captaine and governour" over any discoveries he might make. Yet, to do so on his
own would be "derogatorye" to the Company's absolute rights to
"subdue possesse and occupye all manner townes Isles and mayn-
landes of Infydelytie lying northwards, northeastwards or north-
westwards which shalbe founde." The only way for Gilbert to undertake such discoveries then was with a license or commission of the
"fellyship."[26]

Gilbert apparently had little interest in such an arrangement, and
in any event, while at Court proffering his Cathay petition, he had
also been working with his uncle, Arthur Champernoun, to identify "sundry gentlemen" willing to invest and settle a plantation
closer to home in Ulster. Gilbert was hardly the first to come up with
such an idea; just a few years earlier, in 1563, a dozen former soldiers had proposed a similar enterprise in the form of a corporation
of adventurers. Elizabeth seemed to be in favor of Gilbert's proposal. She endorsed it to Sidney, who needed no persuading; as he
himself argued a couple of years later, a "body politique" that spread
that risk and effort among "sondrie mens charges" was more likely
to succeed there than a royal "Collany" that placed all the danger
and expense on the Crown.[27]

This was not to say the Crown did not have a critical role to play.
All plantation schemes were premised on the expropriation of land.
Such confiscations were justified in law in various ways. Those
who resisted the growing English presence in Ireland—and some

who did not—could be branded as rebels, which made their land subject to seizure. Others might be required to prove their ownership of land by producing deeds, which everyone knew had likely never existed in any form that would be recognized as legitimate by English officials or courts. Many Gaelic lords were cornered into arrangements by which they could "voluntarily" surrender their territory so it might be regranted back to them under more solidly English title. Some, like the Earls of Desmond in Munster, actively sold off property to English and Scottish buyers. All of this was reinforced and codified in relentless efforts to survey and map the land with an English vision of its boundaries and divisions.[28]

Not much came of Gilbert's proposals. He subsequently joined a more ambitious project, led by his cousin Richard Grenville and Henry Sidney's chief deputy in Munster, Warham St. Leger, to establish an incorporated company for governing all of Munster and its littoral, which was ultimately done in by resistance from both Desmond and the Privy Council. In 1572, Gilbert tried and failed once more, again in partnership with Champernoun, this time for a colony centered on Baltimore, aspiring to take on customs collection, a trading monopoly, mining rights, and the right to make further land seizures throughout the Cork region.[29] Around the same time, several others looked to capitalize upon English expansion in the north in the wake of the assassination of the Ulster leader Shane O'Neill in 1568, including Gilbert's partner in the Society of the New Art, Sir Thomas Smith, whose ambitious proposal to settle and fortify over 360,000 acres in the Ards Peninsula was approved by the Privy Council in October 1571.[30]

Unlike two nearly identical royal patents offered at the very same time, Smith's plan, in partnership with his son Thomas, was not to operate their colony as a personal seigneurie but to take on "associats," who for their investments would receive portions of land on which they or others would take up the work of plantation. The Crown was in turn to receive revenue in direct rent, as well as a poll tax from every English inhabitant (frankpledge) and Irish inhabitant (chiefage), fines, customs, and service, in the form of cavalry, which would be offered for several weeks per year to the Lord Deputy at no charge.[31] Smith's Ulster project was thus a creative if confounding fusion of a joint-stock company, corporation, franchise, medieval land tenure, and, as several scholars have argued, an attempt to "put into practice" the connections between the "humanism, print and colonization" embodied in his later writings, such as *De Republica Anglorum.*[32]

The Smiths laid out their arguments for the Irish project in various manuscripts, correspondence, printed materials, and a map but most explicitly detailed them in a short pamphlet, *A Letter Sent by I.B. Gentleman,* ostensibly written by the younger Smith but which many contemporaries (plausibly) took to be the work of his father. Ireland, the *Letter* argued, with its fertile lands and latent markets of consumers, offered prime terrain for plantation and settlement, in which the Crown—too distracted by France, domestic politics, and the simple fact that "hir highnesse is not bent thereto"—could never fully invest on its own. It fell to those "withoute the Queenes pay" to undertake such an "invention."[33] The plan was justified by an ecumenical assortment of historical, philosophical, and legal models, from ancient Rome and Thomas More's *Utopia* to Richard Eden's translations of European travel narratives and Ribault and Stukeley's aborted 1563 Florida project.[34] The most immediate precedent, however, could be found in the centuries of English plantation of Ireland itself, with its "many examples" of English subjects taking on such work on their own back to its very start: the twelfth-century Anglo-Norman marcher lord Richard de Clare, otherwise known as Strongbow, who planted settlers in Leinster with Henry II's license but not his "power." The Smiths simply passed over the part where King Henry II followed soon after to make claims over those territories and declare himself Lord of Ireland.[35]

What distinguished their plan from those previous efforts, the Smiths argued, was that theirs was not the work of individuals. Planters quickly "devided themselves eche to dwell uppon his own land" led to dispersed private plantations, which were hard to defend and "made not the enemie afrayed." The Smiths had something different in mind. They would take their land grant and divide it proportionally into shares. One could take up a share as a settler or stay in England, collecting rent while supporting the passage of soldiers, tenant farmers, and "Englishe families, to be planted for ever in the *Ardes.*" Key to the plan was recruiting soldiers to the plantation with such shares—120 acres for an infantry soldier, 240 for cavalry—on which they would not have to pay anything for the first four years other than their initial transport, victualling, and livery (a not insubstantial £10 for soldiers, £20 for horsemen). Soldiers could thus be recruited at no cost to the Smiths. In turn, becoming a landowner was supposed to solve the leading problems of early modern warfare: disloyalty and desertion. If soldiers would be compensated in the fruits of their own labor, becoming landowners meant soldiers would be quite literally invested in doing their job, incentivized to stay and fight. He who was "Mayster and owner of his land, to him and his heires for ever," the Smiths insisted, would "have better eye to his charge" than if he were simply in another's pay, even that of a royal garrison. Such a scheme also served the colony's goal of civilizing and social engineering, attracting Gaelicized English in Ulster back into the fold while also in theory remaking soldiers, English or Irish, into landowning planters and thus "a Gentleman, a man of livelyhode & of enheritaunce."[36]

Key to all of this was that such land be distributed and overseen by common government. The Smiths thus conceived of themselves in the mold of Roman "Coloniae ductores," an "agorum divisor" responsible for distributing land "to English men in a forein contrey" and employing the "companies stocke" to tend to "common charges" and needs. These included establishing systems of law and punishment, organizing shipping, providing victuals and ordnance, and recruiting civilians for the colony to meet its basic needs, such as artisans and artificers, doctors, and winemakers.[37] Their principal responsibility, however, was to lay out a fortified market town and urban corporation, "Elizabetha," which would not only protect the plantation physically but also by its nature "engendereth civility, policy, acquaintance, consultation, and a firm and sure seat." Such had been the case at Rome, Carthage, Venice, "and all other where any notable beginning hath been." Without it, the Smiths insisted, settlers would become nothing more than "wild beasts."[38]

Thus, a joint-stock society and an urban corporation did double work, ensuring planters and adventurers would be committed to an enterprise while also cultivating their "civility," which would ideally then spread outward into its Irish hinterlands. "The manner of man is," the elder Smith wrote his son, "the more they resort together, and have common profit or peril, the more civil and obedient they be."[39] For Smith, "a companie of Gentlemen and others that will live friendly in fellowship together" was itself what set civilization apart from the state of slavery, warfare, and barbarism of "private" men and their previous failed plantation efforts. Urban corporations reproduced English models of civility and citizenship while shareholding plantations erected a civil society based "indentures of covenants," a social compact founded not by "power of commandment" but "consent & agreement."[40] That they had to resort to publications like the *Letter Sent by I.B.* at all, Smith argued, was because they were not aristocrats with "tenants or great countries of our own" from which to draw settlers. Joint-stock projectors did not have the power of coercion. Rather, their greatest weapon was "persuasion, either by words or writing."[41]

At the same time, Smith understood how uncouth this all might look in a society tethered to chivalric notions of wealth and political power. He was clear that, though it served in one sense as a precedent, his venture was to be nothing like Stukeley's project, which many wrote off as a "lottery" that sought to be "deceivers of men and enterprisers."[42] It was not an unreasonable fear. After all, at its root, the Smiths were promising returns to investors, pay for soldiers, and revenue to support government with land they possessed merely on paper. Making matters worse, like other joint-stock ventures, many undertakers pledged subscriptions to the Smiths' scheme but never paid up. As a result, the Smiths had less cash on hand than their ledgers may have suggested. Finally, persuasion came at an ironic cost. Promoting the venture to potential adventurers also forecast the plans to adversaries, whether skeptical English officials, the Lord Deputy in Ireland, or the O'Neills in Ulster. Delays in England vastly diminished the commitment of their settlers, and when the dwindling expedition finally arrived, it was immediately met with violent resistance. Within a year, the younger Thomas had been killed and the beleaguered encampment routed out. A subsequent attempt in 1574 and again in 1579 by Thomas's nephew William Smith failed, as did overtures to sell the patent back to Elizabeth or to the Earl of Essex.[43]

In the end, the Smiths' venture resulted in little but a body of writing and an ambiguously surviving legal patent, but, as with Stukeley, this turned out to be enough for some to see it as a model. Essex received his own patents in 1573, for an association along similar lines over a jurisdiction that overlapped with Smith's grant.[44] William Piers's proposal in 1578 for a "companye" and "body pollytique" to build towns and settle and manage a commercial monopoly requested privileges "in as large and ample maner as Sir Thomas Smythe hathe graunted him."[45] Meanwhile, others insisted on returning to the seigneurial model, by which escheated and confiscated lands would be entrusted to a smaller number of large individual landowners of means and status rather than bodies of shareholding adventurers.[46] Even Sidney seemed to have had a change of heart, by the mid-1570s arguing that colonies were "no subject's enterprise" but rather required a "Prince's purse and power."[47] Essex proposed ceding his patent back to the Crown, having found that it was those settlers and soldiers "not pressed by commission but by persuasion" who turned out to be too unreliable. One proposed scheme would have had Leicester himself take personal command of a vast territory, re-granting smaller but still rather substantial portions to individuals. Henry Sidney's son, the author Philip Sidney, looked to take up such a plot, famously sending his friend, the poet and courtier Fulke Greville, as an agent to survey his lands, possibly along with another poet, Edmund Spenser, who would soon take up his own plantation in Munster.[48]

Yet, even this sharp turn by the 1570s toward a more seigneurial colonial project could not shake the joint-stock and corporate model. Spenser as much as Smith forwarded a philosophy of plantation that at the very least emphasized the centrality of central corporate market towns to territorial expansion. Meanwhile, some settlers continued to combine their resources to take up smaller plantations in the form of syndicates, collectives, sub-patents, and "colonies or companies" drawn from among the gentry, military men, artisans, and tradesmen. Robert Payne's 1589 *A Briefe Description of Ireland,* for example, served, much like the *Letter from I.B. Gentleman,* to promote a plantation with nearly two dozen investors, not under a seigneur with servants and tenants but the "better sort of under takers being many good knights & gentlemen of great worship," taking up their shares in land.[49]

NEW FOUND LANDS

Even as late sixteenth-century Irish plantation experimented with more proprietorial models of plantation, it continued to be fueled by seasoned veterans of the corporate projects of the 1560s and

1570s, men like Warham St. Leger and Richard Grenville, who converted their stakes in those earlier schemes into these new projects.[50] At the same time, many of these same men were taking up similar projects for exploration and plantation farther across the Atlantic. By the mid-1570s, Grenville had joined with several partners, possibly including Gilbert, to propose a "companie" and "corporation" for the "discovery of lands beyond the Equinoctial" via the southern Atlantic route through the Straits of Magellan. They modeled their plan to some extent on Ribault and Stukeley's 1563 Florida grant with "suche franchize and priveledge as in this case is requisite [and] in the lyke hathe been granted," including to "[e]stablishe some forme of gouernance and authorite" abroad.[51] Meanwhile, St. Leger had become involved in a murky and bizarre plot to lure Stukeley himself back from Spain. To help in this endeavor, he enlisted the services of Martin Frobisher, a navigator who had cut his teeth on slaving and trading enterprises in West Africa and had since built a career as a privateer, pirate, spy, and occasional convict. The scheme came to nothing, but for reasons that remain unclear, by 1574 Frobisher, much like Humphrey Gilbert a decade earlier, fixed his attention on an Atlantic venture of his own. As with Gilbert's initial efforts, the Privy Council referred his petition for a Northwest Passage voyage to the Russia Company, which turned him down. Unlike Gilbert, Frobisher chose to work with rather than against them. Within a couple of months, he had struck a partnership with one of the men who had denied his original petition: the Company's London agent Michael Lok, whose brother John's Guinea venture Frobisher had served two decades earlier. Together they secured a license from the Company to mount a westward expedition, funded by eighteen adventurers, including some leading political figures and members of the Russia Company, among whom was Gilbert's erstwhile competitor and collaborator Anthony Jenkinson.[52]

This voyage returned in October 1576 with an Inuit hostage, unsubstantiated claims to have seen the opening to the Northwest Passage, and a mysterious black stone that Lok was convinced—or at least tried to convince others—would prove the presence of precious metals to rival the fabled Spanish mines of Potosí. As with the Russia Company years earlier, moderate initial success encouraged Lok and the others to scale up to a more proper "Companye and corporation."[53] Articles of agreement among investors called into being the *Company of Cathay,* which in late 1576 submitted to the Privy Council a draft charter of incorporation, modeled closely on that of the Russia Company, to ensure the "good government of the Company."[54] This new company wished to have patents laying exclusive claim over any "seas, waters, iles, landes, countryes, regions, provences, and other places" it might discover, as long as they were not already in another's possession and did not infringe on the rights of the "merchants of Moscovia." Lok was to be Governor, while Frobisher would be Admiral. Meanwhile, Frobisher petitioned on his own for a personal, heritable patent, which would have commissioned him with even loftier titles and the ability to take on adventurers underneath him if he should so choose.[55]

The project, which was now in many ways more about the searching for mines in northern North America than a Northwest Passage, had reached a fever pitch. In addition to the expected Russia Company members, the venture attracted the interest, and investment, of intellectuals, writers, prominent Privy Councilors, peers, courtiers, Crown officials, and Queen Elizabeth herself, who made the largest individual adventure of £1000, including contributing her 200-ton warship *Ayde.* The Privy Council leaned on the Lord Mayor of London as well as northern corporations of Hull, Newcastle, and York to encourage more merchants to subscribe, though it is not clear how much effect this had. This venture returned largely emptyhanded, its efforts at establishing a small settlement having failed. Still, £8,000 in new subscriptions had already come in for a third voyage, which eventually took the form of an impressive fleet of fifteen ships, four owned by the Company directly and the rest leased or loaned from others, including the Queen and Lok or Frobisher themselves.[56]

Expecting the third time would be the charm, Lok committed immense sums to build mills and a furnace at Dartford for assaying and refining the ore, raising £1000 for the project by making a call for additional investment of twenty percent on existing adventurers' shares. He estimated at least six times that would eventually be required.[57] Unfortunately, the third fleet returned in 1578 with a thousand tons of rocks about as worthless as the poorly and hastily constructed Dartford works.[58] All of this had cost a lot of money, and, typically, the vast balance of subscriptions belonged

Furnaces at London and Dartford Built for the Smelting of Gold Ore Brought Back by Martin Frobisher from America, 1578. National Archives of the UK (TNA): MP 1/304.

to the thirty-one investors connected to the royal court, only two of whom—the Queen and another—were fully paid up. Nearly a quarter of the third voyage was still not paid in when the fleet weighed anchor and by its return, the Company was, according to one estimate, £5000 in debt.[59]

It was at this point the Privy Council noticed something about the scheme. When it went to pay out the Queen's obligations to the crew of the *Ayde,* it found there was "no soche Corporacion or Cumpany in lawe" to which they could disburse the money. The Company of Cathay had never received its charter. Why it had not and how it had managed to mount two massive expeditions without ever being formally incorporated have been matters of some speculation over the years. What was clear was that as an unincorporated and unchartered association, the Company was in a much weaker position to pursue its recalcitrant shareholders or repay its creditors.[60] This fact was especially apparent to Lok, who, as the Company's Treasurer, had personally signed many of its contracts and securities and was now liable for much of its debt. It turns out that Lok had also engaged in some creative bookkeeping to inflate the sense of the Company's assets, balancing its accounts by having each subsequent venture purchase the assets of the previous one at an exaggerated rate and listing the value of the Company's ore according to the highest estimate given from among a wildly varying set of assays, even as many had begun to suspect it was worth next to nothing. Without a fourth voyage on the horizon, the Company's apparent surplus was exposed as a massive deficit.[61] Drama ensued. Lok blamed Frobisher and accused him of threatening to kill the Company's assayer; Frobisher indicted Lok of being a "bankerot [*i.e.,* bankrupt] knave."[62] For his part, Lok would spend much of the rest of his life trying to put his career and reputation back together, contending with lawsuits and frequent stretches in debtors' prison through the 1610s.[63] Some would later speculate that he was the inspiration for *The Merchant of Venice*'s iniquitous Shylock, a theory especially popular among those scholars who once argued that "William Shakespeare" was Edward de Vere, the seventeenth Earl of Oxford, who had lost a lot of money in the third voyage, including £1000 of shares Lok had sold him personally (though not as much as he might have, as evidently Oxford too never fully paid up his subscription).[64]

In the end, the three ventures produced no colony, gold, or Northwest Passage. What they did leave behind, besides much debt and many unhappy investors, was a remarkable corpus of treatises, travel narratives, maps, and other material produced, in whole or in part, to promote the venture. Lok authored his own manuscript pamphlet on the state of Anglo-Russian relations, which doubled as an argument for the need to undermine Portuguese dominance in Asia, while crew member Dionyse Settle's travelogue boasted of the great potential of the 1577 voyage.[65] Others recycled even older material, such as the soldier, poet, and Le Havre veteran George Gascoigne, who published a manuscript treatise Gilbert had originally authored in support of his 1566 Cathay project, or Richard Willes, who put out a new edition of Eden's 1555 *Decades of the New World*, adding an essay on Frobisher. John Dee, who had advised the Russia Company's early expeditions and whom Lok had enlisted to train Frobisher, also produced works in support of the venture, as well as that of another privateer who had similarly had his start under Hawkins and who now was promoting a venture to circumnavigate the globe, in part to search out the Northwest Passage from its Pacific side: Francis Drake.[66]

Like the Cathay Company, Drake's ambitious and expensive expedition attracted many adventurers, including the Queen, whose investments afforded not only financial support but political imprimatur; as the story goes, once at sea, Drake was said to have quelled growing disaffection among the ranks of his crew by showing off the receipt for Elizabeth's £250 adventure as an emblem of his authority.[67] By almost any measure, however, Drake was vastly more successful than Frobisher, having navigated through the Spanish South Seas and returned with great plunder. His efforts in turn inspired more new projects still. In 1580, following the union of the Spanish and Portuguese Crowns, Francis Walsingham, the Queen's principal Secretary of State, revived the idea of a venture "beyond the equinoctial line," in the form of a Company with "like privileges" as those granted "unto her subiectes tradyng into the domynions of the Emperor of Russia"—Drake was to be governor (for life), supported by a new state agency, an English version of the Seville *Casa de Contratación*.[68] Nothing resulted immediately from this proposal, nor from the plans of Drake, Walsingham, and several others, including Leicester and John Hawkins, to outfit a large fleet of privateers with the goal of capturing Terceira in the Azores under the flag of António, the ousted rival claimant to the Portuguese throne.[69] On the heels of the failed Terceira venture, Leciester and Walsingham attempted to help Frobisher finance his own joint-stock circumnavigation, whose majority investor was to be the Muscovy Company itself. When the voyage eventually sailed, it was under the command not of Frobisher but of his former lieutenant, Edward Fenton. The voyage never made it to its intended destination of the Moluccas, staying instead in the Atlantic to prey on Iberian shipping, while Fenton briefly considered establishing his own colony in Brazil or Newfoundland.[70] By 1584, Drake had developed his own designs on an expedition to the Moluccas, which garnered nearly two dozen ships and a staggering capital stock, including substantial investment from the Queen, before it was ultimately redirected into what became an infamous privateering mission in the Spanish Caribbean.[71]

In Frobisher's wake, Humphrey Gilbert revived his Atlantic ambitions, now focused on attacking other European fisheries in Newfoundland to make way for an English plantation near the St. Lawrence River that could serve as a platform to prey on Iberian shipping in the West Indies. This, Gilbert argued, had to be done by private means. The English Crown was faced with a dilemma. Its security and prosperity rested on making itself wealthy at the expense of its enemies, especially Catholic Spain. Yet given the realities of sixteenth-century European politics, neither peace nor "open hostilytie" between the two realms was often politically, financially, or militarily appealing. The best way, then, to "annoy the King of Spayne," was to do it via a "syllie member of this Common Weale" like himself, who offered "some colorable means" and "cloake" to undertake voyages, settlement, and predation. This left the Crown free to endorse such efforts, if the outcome was agreeable, or "disavowe both them and the fact, as league breakers, leaving them to pretend [that] as done without your pryvitie."[72] The letters patent Gilbert finally received in June 1578 laid out an unthinkably vast enterprise for government, settlement, predatory, and commercial activities pretty much anywhere along coastal North America where he did not find other Europeans.[73] Though his sights were still at this point set on Newfoundland and the Northwest Passage, rumors spread about a variety of possible destinations; the Spanish ambassador, for one, insisted he intended to go to Florida to pick up where his cousin Thomas Stukeley had left off.[74]

Not everyone at Court was fond of Gilbert or his plans, and he soon ran afoul of some royal officials and found it difficult to raise money. By late 1582, he had decided to resolve this problem by looking elsewhere for support. He established a joint-stock "societie and company," based out of the borough of Southampton and called, with Gilbert's typical humility—and, one might hope, as a not-so-subtle jab at his longtime rivals in the Russia Company—*The Merchant Adventurers with Sir Humfry Gilbert*. Like those previous Marchant Adventurers as well as the Cathay Company and many others, the association was created first by a mutual compact, which was then to solicit for a charter of incorporation, especially the right to "sue and be sued" (as well as, the articles of association implied, a better name). In the meantime, it would serve as a sort of subsidiary staple company to manage the trade within the limits of Gilbert's personal charter and as a vehicle for financing his efforts to both establish his own plantation and sell territory to others. For a five-pound investment, one received a thousand acres, and double that if additionally pledging to settle in America. The joint stock also kept ten thousand acres for itself.[75]

Together, adventurers, planters, and merchants under Gilbert's company would constitute "the common Wealth of the said Sir Humfry his heyres or Successors, their Countries or Territories." Around seventy individuals were made new members, with another dozen or so pledging adventures which were not paid up and nearly fifty who were grandfathered in owing to their investments in Gilbert's 1578 venture. Gilbert and the wealthy Catholic merchant George Peckham reached out to the Merchant Adventurers of Exeter to find new subscribers, though their efforts did not yield much.[76] Walsingham and the chronicler Richard Hakluyt similarly approached the Merchant Adventurers of Bristol, though their efforts were somehow redirected to a rival and ultimately abandoned joint-stock project for a New England factory-plantation led by Walsingham's stepson, the soldier and Irish planter Christopher Carleill, in alliance rather than competition with the Muscovy Company (which his grandfather, George Barne, had helped found).[77]

In addition to the joint stock, Gilbert looked to raise money by offering separate licenses under his personal patent for exploration, fishing, and trading ventures, even though doing so for territories he had yet to "concquer and inhabite" was, the Privy Council soon fretted, of questionable legality. More lucrative still were the absurdly large proprietorial grants Gilbert offered to select supporters and allies, individually or in partnership. John Dee received, in his own words, the "royaltyes of discovery" north of 50 degrees latitude, which in theory gave the philosopher-projector jurisdiction over any future Northwest Passage scheme, despite the Russia Company's overlapping claim. A vaguely defined million and a half acres, as well as several unnamed islands of their choice, went to Peckham, Thomas Gerrard, and their "heires adventurers and associates," who intended to create their own "societie" of adventurers to plant a colony for refugee English Catholics, similar to Gerrard's previous efforts in Ireland and Ribault's Huguenot scheme. The same day Peckham received a separate five million acres, and, with his son, a year later, another fifteen thousand acres. Gilbert made a similar agreement with his former patron's son, Philip Sidney, "and his associates," granting three million acres on the condition their efforts did nothing to subvert his "Commonwealth."[78]

Gilbert's "grants" in one sense took the form of mundane legal indentures and commercial contracts, but in content, they bore a striking resemblance to royal patents, granting their holders obscene amounts of territory that Gilbert did not actually occupy or possess and in fact had never seen. They also expressed expectations of land tenure held in both soccage and knight's service, with obedience and tribute expressed in rent, precious metals, and pearls and, in some cases, armed men and ships. Thus, though Gilbert died on his way home from his first voyage, he left behind a legal legacy and a complex dispersed institutional infrastructure—part joint stock, part seigneurial—that had transformed and disseminated his wholly theoretical patent into a somewhat legally defensible, if still geographically vague, set of distributed property rights. Several assignees in turn tried to finance their own ventures under these sub-proprietorial grants by selling off shares. Peckham and Gerrard offered a tiered scheme to investors: for £100 and fifty men across two voyages, one would be considered an "Associate," with a seigneurial grant by free soccage of 10,000 acres "with as large privileges as any in England"; £50 and twenty men made one eligible to be an "Assistant" with "lordship" over 1,000 acres, held of Peckham and Gerrard by homage and fealty; and, finally, a contribution between £30 and £50 got an "adventurer" 500 acres per £5 held in knights service and, if under £30, the same terms but without rights to hold courts leet and baron. Local government officials would be selected out of the body of Associates, who together with the Assistants would form a council of state. As if this were not complicated enough, Peckham also made direct proprietorial grants out of his own estates, including one hundred thousand acres to the large Devonshire landowner William Rosewell, "to inhabit, people, and manure the same . . . in as ample manner as said Sir George might have enjoyed the same." He offered Dee five thousand acres and a promise to solicit the same from Thomas Gerrard, as compensation for Dee's services in helping counter the Spanish ambassador's attempts at Court to stop them. Peckham bought some or all of Sidney's grant and enlisted Anthony

Brigham to solicit Walsingham to help recruit adventurers for his new "Societie."[79]

Like his predecessors, Peckham and his son promoted their efforts with a treatise, drawing largely on the reports of Edward Hayes, who had been with Gilbert since 1578 and had captained the only one of the five ships that had not either absconded or sunk on the 1583 expedition. The work, which Richard Hakluyt later reprinted in his 1589 *Principall Navigations,* was framed ostensibly as a posthumous celebration of Gilbert's achievements clearly intending to establish Peckham as his self-appointed successor. Like Thomas Smith, Peckham traced the idea of colonial enterprise "done without the aide of the princes power and purse" back to Strongbow, who, "by himselfe and his allies and assistants, at theyr owne proper charges," pioneered the English colonization of Ireland. He similarly pointed to the *conquistadores* of Spanish America, such as Balboa, Cortés, and Pizarro, all "private gentlemen" who had laid the groundwork for Iberian empire.[80]

Peckham's Catholicism soon landed him in prison, and such grand plans never came to pass. Brigham's own Newfoundland voyage fizzled when one of his sailors plundered his ship. Sidney was said still by 1584 to have been "haulf perswaded" to continue in some venture but the Queen evidently would not let him go. Carleill revived his earlier scheme, but ended up instead in Ireland, then on Drake's 1585 Caribbean expedition, and then back in Ulster, where, as governor in 1588, he was involved in a plantation venture which strikingly resembled Gilbert and Peckham's schemes. In 1585, Hayes pitched his longtime patron Burghley on a joint-stock corporation for a Newfoundland settlement and fisheries trade in 1585 or 1586, which may have been the occasion on which he set about writing his own account of Gilbert's expedition. Several years later, Hayes was also the likely author, possibly with Carleill, of an even more ambitious proposal for an Atlantic settlement founded not by a "prynce of wealth & power" but rather led by few "pryvat men," who in turn might encourage others in "prosecuting & following." Only a "boddy pollitike & incorporate," they argued, could raise the capital needed for such a venture, but perhaps more importantly, it would serve as the "most indifferent and requysit above other fourmes of gover[n]ment, to the erection & advancement of thys new state & common weal."[81]

It was Adrian Gilbert who perhaps looked most explicitly to carry on this legacy. Partnering with Dee, who still theoretically held the grant from Humphrey for the Northwest Passage routes, and John Davis, he sketched out a proposal for a chartered company with "lyke privyleagues" as his brother. Unlike Humphrey, the partners were also open to cooperation with the Russia Company and met with several of their leadership, presumably to work out an agreement. Their initial ambition was to obtain exclusive rights to English settlement and travel in the parts of the world "lying (according to the earthly globe) between the aequinoctiiall line & the North Pole" with the twin goals to "wyn the people their to the knowledge of God, & to open a profitable trafficque for this realm." Originally to be called *The Collegats or the Fellowshippe of New Navigations Atlanticall and Septentrionall,* the project was eventually circumscribed to focus largely on the maritime route to Asia. In February 1584, Gilbert received, solely in his name, a five-year patent and a corporation now to be known as the *Colliges of the Discovery of the Northwest Passages.*[82] By this point, though, Dee had left for the Continent—evidently not before Davis pilfered a number of books from his library—and his place in the partnership was taken, briefly, by the Gilberts' half-brother, Walter Ralegh.[83]

Ralegh was another man of projects: soldier, Irish seigneur (which he sub-granted into proprietorships), courtier, Lord Lieutenant of Cornwall, Vice-Admiral, warden of the Cornish tin mines, and patentee for enterprises from tavern licensing to domestic cloth and wine trades. He also soon parted ways with Adrian's scheme, receiving a month or two later his own royal patents for a southerly venture that effectively took up the vast remainder of the jurisdiction that had been in Gilbert's grant. After the return of a smaller initial venture, a fleet of seven ships set out under these patents, commanded by Richard Grenville and carrying a party of colonists with Ralph Lane as Governor. Beset by attack and food shortages, the colony eventually evacuated with Drake's fleet, but like many of his predecessors, Ralegh looked to recover his losses by redoubling his efforts to organize a return venture, issuing his own patents of incorporation to a group of adventurer-settlers. Each member was to be granted a plot of land determined by the size of his investment but together they were to constitute a common government and civil body, "one Bodye pollitque and Corporate" by the name of *The Governor and Assistants of the Cittie of Raleigh in Virginia*. In 1587, John White led a group of over a hundred settlers to Roanoke Island and then sailed back to England for more supplies.[84]

This colony famously faltered. White found on his return that the colonists had mysteriously disappeared, leaving behind only a cryptic clue as to their whereabouts etched into the fledgling colony's palisade. Many lives, not to mention by some accounts £40,000, had been lost on the enterprise. Because of such vast losses, Ralegh shifted his attention more to the heart rather than the extremities of New Spain. He set out in 1593, with investment from a group of London adventurers, on a failed attempt to seize Margarita Island and then a much larger expedition to Guiana, with backing from a coterie of merchants, political figures, friends, and relatives, to reach the mythical Incan "Golden Citie," or El Dorado.[85]

The experiences of Gilbert, Drake, and Ralegh reveal that even those famous enterprises so often associated with individual exploit took a village, to use our own parlance, often many "villages" organized into companies and sometimes corporations. The same was true of the many lesser-known predatory enterprises that littered the English Atlantic in the late sixteenth century. Between 1585 and 1603, historian Kenneth Andrews estimated, at least seventy-four privateering and smuggling ventures comprising 183 ships set sail from England, a figure that gets even larger when accounting for the sundry assaults at sea that were essentially side hustles to trading ventures in north Africa, the Mediterranean, or the western Atlantic intended, as Grenville said of his voyage in Ralegh's venture, to "answer the charges of each adventurer" when commerce alone would not. Proprietors of predatory ventures often financed their voyages by borrowing on their own mortgaged property, but many took in partners and adventurers in cash and kind from ships' owners, provisioners, merchants, seamen, artisans, tradesmen—and sometimes administrators, courtiers, and even the Queen. Many of these failed to repay, yet the minority that succeeded nonetheless fed both the imagination and future investment. The plunder from Drake's circumnavigation alone was said to have seeded any number of later privateering and other commercial ventures, including Elizabeth's own subsequent investments in the Levant trade.[86]

PASSAGES TO THE INDIES

The Queen was hardly the only one with an eye on the developing English commercial and political establishment in the Mediterranean and the Ottoman Empire. As with the Northwest Passage, the Russia Company's faltering ambitions in establishing an overland route to Asia via Persia or fully exploiting the North Sea trade led to a flurry of overlapping and intersecting ventures looking to carve up its broad claim over south- and eastbound trade and traffic. England's Spanish merchants obtained a monopoly on Iberian trade in 1577 in the form of the regulated, guild-like Spanish Company. Two years later the Eastland Company did the same for Baltic merchants, which in turn became a major supplier not only of goods and spices but also of timber and other naval stores for the Crown and other overseas traders.[87] There was another round of patents for various ventures to northern and western Africa, including to the Senegal region, Benin, and the 1585 "fellowship" of the Barbary Company, a consortium of about forty merchants around the Earls of Leicester and Warwick with exclusive rights to the Moroccan and North African trade; though by all indications it never received a formal corporate charter, at least one contemporary thought of the venture as "an incorporation."[88] New enterprises emerged for the Persian trade, and twelve merchants led by Edward Osborne and Richard Staper in 1580 obtained grants from the Ottoman Sultan to settle factors and trade in Constantinople and Aleppo, followed in 1581 by patents from the Queen for a chartered "Turkey Company" with a seven-year monopoly. When that grant expired in 1588, the Company merged with the former members of a rival 1583 Venice Company, whose charter had also expired in 1589, forming the *Governor and Company of Merchants Trading into the Levant Seas,* incorporated in 1592.[89]

The Levant Company initially operated as a joint stock, though at some point before its rechartering in 1605, it was reformed as a so-called "regulated" company, a rival model of corporate trade that allowed its individual members to trade on their own account sharing common privileges, contributing to common resources, and under common regulations, much like a guild. The Company was to possess and manage the rights and privileges of English subjects in the Ottoman Empire Osborne and Staper had obtained on the Queen's

behalf from Sultan Murat III, including relief from some taxes and
duties, liberty of movement and trade, and special status under Ottoman law. It was to maintain the English ambassador, consuls, and
houses for "factors" (merchants' agents)—such trading outposts
were called "factories"—in Constantinople and elsewhere. Though
organized with monopolies over much of English Mediterranean
commerce, not least the lucrative Venetian currant trade, the Levant
Company was also like many others initially a kind of East India
venture, looking to forge overland connections through Aleppo and
Persia to Asia. Similar efforts followed by sea. That same year, Venice
Company founder Thomas Cordell led a group of adventurers to
fund two former Iberian traders and privateers, James Lancaster and
Samuel Foxcroft, on a voyage to "annoy" Portuguese shipping in the
Indian Ocean. Meanwhile, John Newbery, Ralph Fitch, and others'
abortive venture in 1583 to India and southeast Asia, backed by
Staper and Osborne, became the foundation for a Levant Company
petition for a new charter in 1592 with expanded rights into Central and South Asia.[90]

It was, however, an ostensibly unrelated joint-stock venture in the
Atlantic that same year that would unexpectedly and indirectly turn
the tide for English efforts to establish a direct trade to Asia. On the
heels of the attempted Spanish maritime invasion of England several years earlier, in 1592, a who's-who of adventurers, which included Ralegh, the City of London, and the Queen, fitted out a large
privateering expedition. Among its plunder was the richly laden
Madre de Deus captured off the Azores. Although only about
£150,000 of the Portuguese carrack's estimated value of £500,000
ever made it back to pay out the adventurers' dividends, one prize
that did return was impossible to price: a set of documents providing details on various aspects of the revenue and administration
system of the Portuguese establishment in Asia. The accuracy of
the information itself is debatable, but the ostensible treasure trove of
intelligence about the state—and limits—of Portuguese trade and
administration in the Indies found in what became known as the
"Matricola" or "Matroclia" seemed to be just the argument needed
to make the case for a competing English enterprise.[91] News in 1599
of the return from Asia of a richly laden trading fleet of one of several recently established regional Dutch companies only stoked the
fires.[92]

By late September 1599, a hundred and one investors, mostly but hardly exclusively Levant Company merchants, had subscribed over £30,000 for such a voyage in "one entire Joynt and Common Stocke" and without "private traffique & unfaithfull Dealing." Its fifteen "committees or directors" next solicited for a "priviledge in succession and to incorporate them in a Companie." Their reason was clear: "the trade of the Indias being so farre remote from hence cannot be traded but in a Joint and a unyted stock."[93] To persuade the Queen and her advisors that it was acceptable to violate what the Portuguese claimed as an exclusive right among Europeans to trade and traffic in the East Indies, they called in no less an authority than Richard Hakluyt. He constructed a brief that drew on a wide range of sources, including the Matricola, to make the case that any place the *Estado da India* did not actually possess and occupy had to be regarded as "free for anie other princes and people of the world to repayre unto, whome the soveraigne lords and governors of those territories willbee willing to admitte into there Dominions." Gilbert had made a similar form of argument against the Russia Company's hold on the Northwest Passage in 1565, and this case against the Portuguese would find its most enduring articulation in the Dutch jurist Hugo Grotius's 1609 *Mare Liberum*—a defense of the freedom of navigation which Grotius wrote at the behest of the Dutch East India Company and Hakluyt later translated into English, likely at the behest of the English East India Company to deploy against the Dutch. Here Hakluyt's brief walked through an explicit accounting of the great wealth the Portuguese earned by their East India ventures as well as the surprisingly limited list of places across the East Indies they could reasonably claim as theirs.[94] The Privy Council clearly took such arguments seriously—Walsingham reportedly referred the petition to Fulke Greville for his evaluation—but even more likely, it was the growing hopelessness of any chance of peace with the Iberians that led the Queen and the Council to finally assent to a charter.[95]

On the last day of 1600, *The Fellowship* or *Governor and Company of Merchants of London, Trading to the East Indies* was incorporated with all the trappings thereunto: a legal name and personality, succession, a seal, self-government, and, in this case, exclusive jurisdiction over all English trade, traffic, and travel "in the Countries and Parts of *Asia* and *Africa,* and into and from all the Islands, Ports, Havens, Cities, Creeks, Towns, and Places of *Asia,* and *Africa,* and *America,* or any of them, beyond the *Cape of Bona Esperanze,* to the Streights of *Magellan.*"[96] The East India Company, along with its Dutch doppelgänger, established as a union of those regional *voorcompagnieën* in 1602, represented in a sense the culmination of centuries of efforts at long-distance European trade with Asia and the convergence of joint-stock and corporate traditions, united in single chartered company.[97] Though closely tied with the Levant Company, this new company was enmeshed in the various global corporate and joint-stock projects for predation, commerce, and colonization launched across the globe in recent decades.[98] Its first governor, Thomas Smythe, a well-connected London merchant, was a Merchant Adventurer, a Skinner, and a Haberdasher, and holder across his life of numerous franchises and offices, including, like his father, the lucrative and powerful position of royal "customer," or customs collector, for the port of London. He would sit in Parliament and as governor of most of the major overseas ventures, including the Levant Company and the Muscovy Company, which his maternal grandfather helped found and for which he soon also served as ambassador to Russia.[99] What was true of its leadership was broadly true of its membership. As the East India Company's governing Court of Committees noted some two decades later, "we are a Company of merchants collected & contracted out of all sorts & ranks of men, Noble, and ignoble . . . Merchant-Adventurers . . . Turkey and Eastland Merchants . . . French Merchants . . . Spanish Merchants . . . Tradesmen . . . [and] men of other Conditions."[100]

The whole point of a joint-stock corporation was that it could be funded and directed by a wide base of individuals, regardless of whether they had experience—or even interest—in the mechanics of trade. And while the initial investors were largely merchants—there was only one peer among the original patentees—by the 1620s the Company counted among its ranks prominent courtiers, Privy Councilors, and other officeholders, as it served the Company well to "have some such their friends" at Court.[101] Moreover, even if prominent political officials had not been directly invested, they were connected to one another through the wider ecology of interlocking companies. Walsingham, Leicester, Burghley, Smith, Dee, not to mention Queen Elizabeth herself had not only backed but invested and even in some cases directed a number of ventures in the name of both public good and their own potential profit. The same was true under Elizabeth's successor, James VI of Scotland, who ascended to the English throne as James I in 1603. Prince Henry, his first son, was integral before his untimely death in encouraging a number of these early companies. The King was a bit more ambivalent about the uncertain impact overseas companies might have on foreign policy. He could, however, see advantages in working with them, including supporting the Russia Company's ultimately aborted project in 1612–1613 to seize Archangelsk and annex it as an English protectorate. Nearly all his Privy Councilors were members of at least one of Smythe's companies.[102] The East India Company, as it turns out, only drew the line at admitting the King himself, fearing the loss of independence it would entail but offering as their rationale curious legal opinions that suggested it was impossible and beneath his "dignity" for the King to enter into commercial partnerships with his subjects.[103]

As great as its ambitions were, at its origins the East India Company was, like its predecessors and contemporaries, essentially a tentative experiment fueled by a hesitant and hybrid institutional and financial structure. The "company" did not have a single permanent stock. Rather, it was organized as a series of consecutive quasi-independent stock subscriptions, at first opened on a per venture basis and later established for set terms in years. In its early days, the limited number of shareholders could "take in men under them," in theory dividing any individual share into a subsidiary, shadow joint stock. As in many other ventures, the East India Company spent its early years chasing down under- and unpaid subscriptions. By April 1601, the first joint stock was £9,000 in debt to various suppliers, leading the governing Court of Committees to issue a further call on shareholders, take out a substantial loan, and ask the Privy Council for help in leaning on recalcitrant subscribers.[104] Its initial corporate charter was similarly experimental. It was limited to a term of fifteen years, and Company leaders soon found it wanting many privileges and provisions necessary for doing their business. Over the next few decades, they solicited for numerous supplementary patents or warrants to provide the Company with rights of perpetual succession, to admit foreigners as members, to administer oaths, to execute martial law, and to arrest English interlopers abroad, among others.[105]

Even as its powers expanded, the Company's exclusive charter was in no way self-evidently secure from critics, competitors, and even the Crown that had issued it. In 1603, Sir Edward Michelbourne, disenfranchised from the Company for failing to pay his subscription, received a separate patent for his own East Indies venture. A distant Gilbert relation, Richard Penkevell, was one of those behind a kind of revival in 1607 of Adrian Gilbert's project in a new corporation similarly called the *Colleagues of the Fellowship for the Discovery of the North Passage*.[106] In 1617, King James used his authority as Scottish sovereign to grant the courtier and Ulster planter James Cunningham a competing charter with expansive rights encompassing Asia, the Mediterranean, Russia, and Spitsbergen. Even though he refused a petition the next year from the disgraced former Dutch East India Company leader Isaac Le Maire for a grant to trade via the southwestern passage, James pointed out that he certainly had the right to issue one if he so wanted; otherwise, he would be no better than "Pope Alexander, who divided and distributed the whole world" to Spain and Portugal alone.[107] In a way, the East India Company was itself a licensed interloper, at least in the sense that its explicit rights to navigate the "Ways and Passages" that "they shall esteem and take to be fittest, into and from the said *East-Indies*" allowed it to get into the Northwest Passage business. Not long after its first voyage under James Lancaster set sail eastward via the Cape of Good Hope, its leadership called on investors in that venture to contribute to a second joint stock to send out a westward expedition led by George Waymouth. The Russia Company objected "by vertue of ther previledges"; the East India Company's lawyers insisted that doing so was "expresselie in this Companie." They were both right. Negotiations for a proposed partnership fell through, and the East India Company proceeded with its plans.[108]

These two companies were hardly independent of one another, connected through shared membership and leadership, especially Governor Thomas Smythe, and their rivalry soon evolved into several attempts at partnership. Smythe had a particular interest in the Northwest Passage. In 1606, his efforts led the two Companies to cosponsor John Knight's expedition, possibly under the auspices of a separate jointly funded association. They also combined in the second English voyage of Henry Hudson, which was largely the project of men connected to both companies, like Smythe, Dudley Digges, and John Wolstenholme.[109] The shared threat posed by Cunningham's Scottish East India Company in 1617 even led the two companies to contemplate a formal union of sorts. To persuade the King to vacate his charter, they agreed to fund a large loan to the Russian Czar and an ambassador—Digges was selected—to deliver it. The Russia Company also offered to buy out Cunningham and allow him and any of his Scottish investors to join as adventurers; one contemporary observer suspected this to have been Cunningham's plan all along, even if he did in the end decline.[110] To fund all of this, the East India and Russia Companies created a separate eight-year joint stock to which each company contributed £30,000, essentially effecting a partial and temporary merger.[111] In the meantime, the combined Northwest Passage ventures had led Smythe and the others to coordinate the establishment of a separate corporation in 1612, *The Governor and Company of Merchants of London Discoverers of the Northwest Passage*, with jurisdictional rights like those previously granted to Penkevell, who, as his patent was soon to expire, was with a number of his relatives among the new company's three hundred charter members.[112]

If it is difficult to think about any company as a single entity with a coherent "charter" at home, such concepts become downright impossible abroad, where something like the East India Company was deeply entangled from its start with a wide range of other companies and polities as partners, allies, rivals, and enemies. High-level conferences intended to resolve escalating tensions with the Dutch East India Company in the mid-1610s, for example, led to a short-lived agreement to undertake joint military and commercial enterprises in Asia and even a briefly floated—not for the last time—proposal to merge the two into a single company.[113] More critical were relations with non-European sovereigns and merchants. English settlement, trade, even survival in the East Indies required active and constant work to make agreements, contracts, treaties, grants, and other similar arrangements. Moreover, companies were in many respects the vanguard of English diplomacy in the extra-European world, and from Aden to Hirado, East India Company agents blurred the lines between royal and company objectives, not least in the joint embassy of the courtier and diplomat Thomas Roe to the Mughal

Emperor in 1614.[114] The letters Lancaster carried on his first voyage to the Sultan of Aceh may have been from Queen Elizabeth, but it was the East India Company that paid the roughly £13 to the herald who prepared them.[115]

"English" overseas companies by their very nature were transnational institutions, whose rights and responsibilities were increasingly intertwined across jurisdictional and political boundaries. Companies shifted constantly, both at home and abroad, between their roles as sovereign representatives and suppliant subjects.[116] As traders, fellowships, landlords, and diplomats, sixteenth-century overseas corporations were by necessity political chameleons, whose survival and success depended on their ability to blend into systems of sovereignty in multiple places at once. The mechanisms went by various names to various parties and from various perspectives: covenant, indenture, contract, charterparty; adventure, subscription, investment; charter, patent, pass, treaty, grant, concession, *farman, shuinjō*.[117] Such instruments revealed the pervasive character of franchise government across the early modern world and just how potentially well positioned joint-stock and incorporated companies were to exploit it. Such cobbled-together forms of jurisdictional power were highly tenuous and vulnerable, requiring much supervision, vigilant defense, and, as historian Rupali Mishra has noted of English charters, "negotiation and interpretation," through the constant deployment of political, legal, ideological, financial, and, not to be forgotten, physical power.[118] As a result, any given overseas project— even the ones hindsight tells us would eventually evolve into massive empires—had fraught and tenuous beginnings, and many more outright failed. However, taken as a whole, the effervescence of joint-stock and corporate experiments of the sixteenth century had fermented by the seventeenth century into a pervasive and powerful, if controversial, model for funding and governing commercial and colonial expansion. This was, as it turned out, both the culmination of a deep legal and political history and merely the first chapter of what turned out to be a rather long story.

2

MUNICIPAL BONDS

The Age of Crisis

For then they were one corporation made,
And bent their vallour 'gainst their enemie.

IN LATE 1598, A DOZEN investors in a joint stock from the
Scottish commercial center of Fife set out to plant a colony in
the northern Hebrides. With the legal backing of King James VI and
the Scottish Parliament, several hundred settlers and soldiers soon
occupied the fort at Stornoway and drew up the "articlis for the society of Lewis," a mutual compact that governed over the means of
establishing an incorporated town, religious observance, distributing
land, collecting revenues, and conflict resolution. Underfunded and
facing violent resistance and difficult conditions, this and two further attempts to plant and fortify failed to take root. By the time
the rival Highland leader Coinneach Mackenzie of Kintail attacked
and seized their last ship in 1609, almost all of the so-called "Fife
Adventurers" had already sold off their shares, most to fellow
member George Hay. Hay and the couple of remaining shareholders
seemed now to have no choice but to cut their losses and sell their
interest to Mackenzie.[1]

As it turns out, a joint-stock colonial enterprise did not always
need to be successful to succeed. In essentially buying the company
and its pretended rights to the territory, Mackenzie fortified his

longstanding but contested hereditary claim to the lordship of Lewis, acquired legal and political recognition from the Stuart state, and established a regime that his family would command for a couple of centuries. James gained a tenuous proxy in Lewis and an indirect claim over the elusive Hebrides and its fisheries revenues. And while a great deal of money and lives were lost in the venture, Hay himself went on to a long career of commercial, infrastructural, and government projects and positions. Some evidence suggests that he and fellow adventurer James Spens, eager to sell out to Mackenzie for some time, may have conspired in his attack to seal the deal with the lowland authorities.[2]

If joint-stock corporations would come to usher in a revolution in European global expansion, in the early seventeenth century many were still quite bad at it. Most projects were underfunded and disorganized, their leadership often seemingly persuaded by their own promotional materials to overestimate their capacities and underestimate the resistance they faced at home and abroad. Yet both the joint-stock and corporate form offered resources for confronting such challenges. Companies took on debt, established subsidiaries, sought out mergers, acquisitions, and, as with Hay and Spens, divestments, establishing over time the rather bizarre idea that in buying a company, one could buy a colony. This often did not work out as well in practice as it did on paper. However, taken as a whole and over time, such efforts established not only powerful arguments for undertaking overseas trade and settlement but *de facto* tutorials in precisely how to do it.

MANIE PURCES OF THE WELL-PUBLIQUE

In 1609, the Privy Council approached the corporation of London with an offer it could not refuse to take on the task of funding and directing a large plantation in Ireland. The defeat of Hugh O'Neill in Ulster and his Iberian allies after the failed Spanish invasion of Kinsale in 1601 had once again flooded the market with newly seized estates and amplified the political pressure to populate them with loyal settlers. Two years later, the accession of James VI to the English throne as James I only added fuel to the fire. As king in Scotland, he had a proven track record of supporting similar efforts, like the Fife Adventurers, to extend lowland power into the Gaelic-speaking Highlands and the Northern Isles. Moreover, he had himself written eloquently, most notably in his 1599 *Basilikon Doron*, on the important role "answerable inland subjects" had to play in colonial enterprise, both to "reform and civilize" those who might assimilate while "rooting out or transporting the barbarous and stubborn sort, and planting civility in their room."[3] In Ireland, estates were taken up by various former English and Scottish soldiers, government officials, and other corporate institutions, such as the Irish church, Dublin's Trinity College (incorporated 1592), schools, and towns. Even the young East India Company invested £7,000 in Dundaniel, in Cork, with the goal of developing a dockyard, woodlands, ironworks, and a small settlement.[4]

London's investment was to be on a completely different scale. It was to take up forty thousand acres, managed through a separate joint-stock body and chartered as a corporation in 1613 as the *Society of the Governor and Assistants of London, of the New Plantation in Ulster, within the Realm of Ireland*. Known in Ireland as the "London Company" or "Society," and in London as the "Irish Society," the new enterprise was an object lesson in just how complex and confusing joint-stock corporate ventures could become. In its most immediate sense, the Society was like a subcommittee of the City's corporate government and simply the newest of its many guilds or livery companies, which instead of superintending, say, grocers or ironmongers was to take on Irish plantation. Crown lawyers would later maintain that the Society was in fact more like a trusteeship, holding and managing the colony on behalf of the City of London and ultimately the Crown. At the same time, it closely resembled a generation of joint-stock ventures in sixteenth-century Ireland and the Atlantic. The Society distributed out portions of its large grant to adventurers while keeping a good deal of territory, centered on the incorporated towns of Coleraine and the newly re-branded Londonderry, to govern directly. Yet, to make matters more complicated, the Society's investors were themselves corporations: fifty-five of London's livery companies were conglomerated into twelve consortia, each of which was offered large land grants by lot on which to develop and administer settlements. In turn, mirroring the parent Society, each consortium constituted both a land company and a government, farming out, licensing, or selling off some of its land

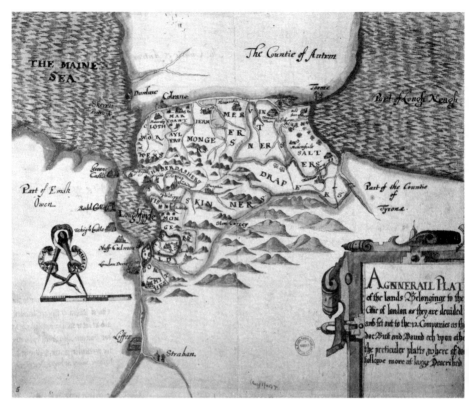

A Generall Plat of the Lands Belonging to the Cittie of London as They Are
Devided And Led Out to the 12 Companies, by Sir Thomas Phillips 1622 (1836).
Deputy Keeper of the Records, Public Record Office of Northern Ireland and the Lambeth Palace
Library / T510/1/5.

grants to others while reserving portions to themselves, especially
in order to develop their own plantations and incorporate market
towns.[5]

The livery companies were never all that enthusiastic about the
Irish enterprise; some had to be pressured, eventually compelled, by
city officials, to participate. One author, advertising a number of
other emerging opportunities for colonial investment, insisted that
already by 1611, many had grown "exceeding wearye of theyre
Ireyshe plantacion."[6] In fact, as early as 1609, all the London liveries that were to be involved in the Ulster project had already become shareholders in another chartered company with perhaps even
more ambitious plans for trade and plantation further across the

Atlantic. Scattered attempts at settlements had been made in the two decades since Gilbert and Ralegh's ventures. It was, however, the return of George Waymouth in 1605 from his second Newfoundland voyage—funded this time largely by a coterie of merchants in the naval port town of Plymouth—that seemed to spark particular enthusiasm in Plymouth and eventually London for a more sustained venture. Edward Hayes, who was becoming a rather prolific if star-crossed projector, made perhaps the most decisive pitch, reviving with his relative Thomas a version of his earlier proposals to make the case for a "Publique Stock," now with the model of the recently formed Dutch East India Company in mind, backed by Crown and Parliament but funded and directed by the "voluntary consent of manie purces of the Well-publique."[7]

The venture that emerged initially took a different form, owing to a number of factors, including difficulties between the Plymouth and London investors and possibly hesitation on the part of the relatively new King to allow either Parliament or a distinct corporate body too much latitude in affairs likely to upset a fragile but emerging peace with Spain. In 1606, a charter was issued for a royal council under which were to be two separate associations with slightly overlapping jurisdictions extending along much of coastal North America. The adventurers from Plymouth took the northern part and, after some abortive attempts, established a fortified trading post, or factory, in Sagadahoc in what is now Maine. It succumbed within a year to disease, fire, privation, a crisis of leadership, winter, and, most decisively, conflict with its would-be trading partners, the Etchemin, who had not forgotten the five of their number Waymouth had kidnapped and brought back with him to England several years earlier.[8] Meanwhile, London's company sent its own voyage to the southward both in search of a continental passage to the East Indies—they were somehow convinced North America would reveal a similar riverine network the Russia Company imagined through Central Asia—and to establish their own fortified trading colony. They never found the former but did manage to settle some colonists along the James River in the heart of Powhatan territory in what the English had come to call Virginia.

Early Jamestown was no less beleaguered than Sagadahoc, but while the Plymouth company reacted by allowing their efforts to atrophy into some scattered fishing ventures, the London adventurers

scaled up. In 1609, a charter passed for a new joint-stock company—
the one to which the liveries subscribed—with the typical rights of
a corporation (succession, legal personality, and self-government
over trade and plantation independent of any royal council) projected into an atypical jurisdictional space, offering exclusive rights
among English subjects to a four-hundred-mile stretch of the coast
of North America extending a hundred miles into the Atlantic
and a hundred miles into the South Seas, wherever that might be.
Adventurers who pledged money or to settle themselves (or both)
were to receive shares, or a dividend, of that land as well as a
promise of future revenue. It was to be called *The Treasurer and
Company of Adventurers and Planters of the City of London, for
the first Colony in Virginia,* which people came to know simply as
the Virginia Company.[9]

More setbacks soon followed, including the devastating news that
the flagship of its next Jamestown supply fleet in 1609 had run
aground in Bermuda. The wreck of the *Sea Venture* may or may not
have inspired William Shakespeare to conjure the setting for *The
Tempest,* which premiered in 1611, but it almost certainly alarmed
a number of adventurers with outstanding subscriptions into refusing
to hand over what they owed.[10] Over the next decade, Company
leadership and their surrogates aggressively attempted to promote
their venture in the hopes of winning over both current and new
subscribers with a flood of pamphlets, travel narratives, orations,
and sermons. In the same spirit, in 1616, the Company orchestrated
an elaborate tour of London society of nearly a dozen indigenous
Virginians, including Pocahontas, the daughter of the Powhatan,
now known as Rebecca Rolfe, husband to colonist John, mother to
Thomas, and, as Company leaders did not hesitate to observe, its
first indigenous convert. Despite much evidence to the contrary, the
Company maintained that its efforts were a successful experiment
in humanist ideals and an expression of divine providence. Its advocates boasted of its relations with the Powhatan and other native
peoples and establishment of effective laws and regulations. Soon
enough, they insisted the colony would not only turn a profit in
land, commerce, and domestic industries but also serve as an outlet
for the poor, a boon for naval power, and a spur to the spreading of
Christianity. Even into the 1620s, some were still convinced of the
great probability they would uncover an inland passage to India,

though the Company itself seemed to have put serious interest in the idea to the side.[11]

In 1612, the Company sought out yet another charter to clarify and expand its corporate powers. The new charter gave it now an explicit right to "expulse, disfranchise, and put out" anyone who did not pay up their pledged subscription or to sue them in the Court of Chancery or the Court of Common Pleas, two venues for the settling of private debts and contracts. It also looked to expand its shareholder base by formally allowing "Strangers and Aliens" to subscribe, and several women also now invested.[12] Still, even then, shares did not prove in themselves sufficient to raise the funds necessary for such an ambitious venture. After the *Sea Venture* wreck, Thomas Smythe, the Virginia Company's first Treasurer—what many other companies called a governor and what today might be known as a CEO or board chairman—took out a large loan on the Company's behalf, using its joint stock as collateral. The Company also borrowed smaller amounts from current adventurers in the form of "bonds" and sublicenses.[13] More lucrative still was the permission granted in the 1612 charter to put on lotteries, which, despite their dodgy reputation as scams and swindles, the Company insisted were in this instance of a different order: not for "private endes" but rather the "advancement of that most noble and Christian Plantation."[14] Over the next several years, lotteries in London and various provincial towns across England revitalized the Company's coffers, while opening up a kind of shadow revenue source drawn from individuals and corporate bodies that would or could not otherwise be subscribers. Even London's livery companies, which with the impending incorporation of the Irish Society had divested from the Company, took part, the Vintners Company for one noting in its minutes that it did so as not to "stand out" among all the others that were participating.[15]

The Virginia Company also experimented with authorizing its own subsidiary monopoly joint-stock subscriptions for specific trades or infrastructural projects. This was a common strategy, with which Smythe for one, given his polymathic connections across almost all of these major early seventeenth-century ventures, would have been quite familiar. The East India Company, for example, had organized its early Northwest Passage ventures in such a manner, and, even after the Levant Company had converted from a joint-stock to a regulated company, it nonetheless administered common stocks for specific trades. Likewise, the so-called Greenland Company was a semiautonomous venture made up of Russia Company subscribers to take on its whaling enterprise in Spitsbergen, which endured as such for a time even after its parent corporation also reformed as a regulated company in the 1660s.[16] In 1616, many among Company leadership, including Smythe, set up a joint-stock "magazine," or supply company, to which the Company gave exclusive rights to provision the colony and regulate its transatlantic trade.[17] In 1619, the Company appointed a committee to raise charitable contributions for an English college at Henrico, and, two years later, after James I withdrew the permission to hold lotteries, the Company almost immediately opened calls for investors in four additional subsidiaries: a new magazine; a company to recruit women to the colony; a fur-trading expedition into the interior; and a group of "pryvate Adventurers" who might establish a glass works for the colony, to which the Company itself would subscribe.[18]

By the second half of the 1610s, Smythe's hold on the Virginia Company began to give way to a rival coterie centered around Edwin Sandys, a well-connected member of the landed gentry—his father had been archbishop of York—and influential politician and scholar. Later in life, Sandys took a deep interest in overseas trade and colonization, including serving on the Virginia colony's original royal council at its inception in 1607.[19] Sandys and his allies, like the Earl of Southampton and the merchant John Ferrar, were as committed as Smythe to a company government. Where they seemed to disagree was on what shape that should take. (They also clashed over leadership of other companies, including the East India Company, where Sandys was less successful in unseating Smythe and his merchant allies.) One the most critical innovations under Sandys's emerging leadership was the introduction and support for joint-stock plantations. Where Smythe had imagined adventurers taking up their land shares in smaller, private estates, Sandys and others encouraged individuals to combine their individual holdings into much larger enterprises, what they called "particular plantations." These joint-stock societies, like the livery company consortia in Ulster, would then be responsible for apportioning property, recruiting settlers, managing common land, administering local justice, and, most crucially, establishing central market towns and boroughs. The idea behind this project was not only that commonly governed plantations presented certain economies of scale. As in Ireland, tethering private property to "publiq" institutions like urban corporations, advocates insisted, would encourage migration, commerce, and industry; strengthen the colony's defense and civic establishment; and presumably further longstanding Company ambitions of, as Ferrar put it, "Civilizinge of the Indians."[20]

Several groups took up the charge. Investors from Gloucestershire took on a plantation centered on Berkeley Town; another, the "Society for Martin's Hundred," combined holdings amounting to twenty thousand acres on which it established a rudimentary fort and Wolstenholme Towne. Under Sandys, the Company itself set about establishing several new incorporated towns along these same lines. Yet what would become arguably the most famous of Virginia's particular plantations did not end up in Virginia at all, when the English dissenter congregation at Leiden, along with London-based investors, formed a joint-stock association to fund their leaving the Netherlands to "live as a separate body, by themselves, under the general Government of Virginia." In 1620 the just over one hundred settler-shareholders—they thought of themselves as "pilgrims"—secured land from the Virginia Company and financed a ship, *The Mayflower,* which ultimately landed instead near Cape Cod in what would become known as New England. Well outside the general reach of Virginia or any other colonial government, like the Fife Adventurers, they instead struck a mutual compact for self-government, rendering them into a "civil body politic" called New Plymouth.[21]

By this time, the Virginia Company had established its own subsidiary joint stock for another colony outside of Virginia. Among its many other provisions, the 1612 charter confirmed claims to Bermuda that Company leadership had been making ever since the *Sea Venture* had wrecked there several years earlier. To fund and manage this new colony, 117 adventurers, all but ten of them Virginia Company shareholders, formed a separate association to which the Virginia Company sold the rights to the colony for £2,000. The move quickly infused the parent company with much-needed cash while vesting the responsibility for colonizing Bermuda in a new joint-stock enterprise, incorporated in 1615 by royal patents as the *Governor and Company of the City of London for the Plantation of the Somers Islands*—named ostensibly after the 1609 fleet's Admiral, Sir George Somers but, according to at least one contemporary, also meant to subliminally remind potential investors and settlers of its "continual temperate air."[22] Though initial plans for the colony suggested it might be owned and managed entirely by this corporation, Bermuda was instead apportioned into four hundred shares of twenty-five acres each, to be held as discrete private estates by investors and worked by sharecropper tenants. This was the vision of corporate colonization that Smythe, who unsurprisingly was made governor of the new Company, had been pushing for Virginia, conceiving of the colony not as larger, collective, and public enterprises, as Sandys and his supporters had, but instead as a collection of individual estates under Company government, or, as the directors put it several years later, "noe common-wealth but a private Inheritance inclosed to the use of the Purchasers."[23]

Meanwhile, a third model for what company colony might look like, not dissimilar to the original plans for Bermuda, began to take form around 1610 in the Bristol-based *Treasurer and Company of the Adventurers and Planters of the City of London and Bristol for the Colony or Plantation in Newfound Land*. In the wake of the now-dormant 1606 Plymouth venture, this new Company sent four dozen settlers to develop a fortified settlement for fisheries, saltworks, and mines at what they called Cupers, later transmuted to Cupid's, Cove, on the southwestern end of Newfoundland's Avalon Peninsula. The colony was quickly beleaguered by weather and pirates, as its head, the Bristol merchant, officeholder, and naval official John Guy, increasingly found himself in disputes with the Company and especially its London investors over compensation for himself and those under him. To take his place, the Company turned to the navigator and projector John Mason, just recently off a privateering venture in support of Scottish plantation efforts in the southern Hebrides and the Mackenzie plantation. In employing Mason, the Company seemed to be courting additional "Scottish undertakers of the plantations," who with the Company petitioned James I/VI in 1621 to appoint Mason as the "King's Lieutenant" in Newfoundland, appealing to his long-thwarted ambitions to unite his kingdoms more closely by insisting that the project was an expression of "England and Scotland . . . now joined together."[24]

When Cupid's Cove proved a failure, the Newfoundland Company changed tack and retreated entirely from directing colonies at all. Instead, it became a kind of land company, re-granting out its jurisdiction in the form of several ambitious proprietary patents, each of which was driven by an ecumenical alchemy of religious, national, and commercial ambition.[25] Guy led a defection of some other disgruntled Merchant Venturers and Cupid's Cove settlers, who in turn established a new colony nearby, giving it the rather unsubtle name of Bristol's Hope. The lawyer and mystic William Vaughan took up a grant, insisting that God had commanded him to establish a New Wales in the new-found-land. In turn, he sub-granted portions of his jurisdiction to men both looking to establish a Catholic refuge: one to Henry Cary, Lord Falkland, who imagined a colony of dispossessed Irish settlers, and another to Secretary of State, Virginia and East India Company investor, Irish planter George Calvert, for the first of his attempts to find a home in America for English Catholics in what he called his "Province of Avalon."[26] In 1621, the Company offered territory near Placentia Bay to Mason's friend, the Scottish courtier, poet, and future Earl of Stirling, William Alexander. Modeled on Ulster as well as ventures from Cabot, Ribault, and Gilbert to James Cunningham's Scottish East India Company scheme, Alexander's colony, like Vaughan's, was framed as a national mission; to New England, New Spain, and New France, he hoped to add a *Nova Scotia.*[27]

In form, these projects were all individual proprietorships on the model of a medieval manorial seigneurie, yet, as Alexander put it, "no one man could accomplish such a Worke by his own private fortunes."[28] Certainly state support would help. Falkland, Calvert, and Alexander all supplemented their Company grants with separate royal charters, and, for Alexander, James even created a special order of Baronets, as in Ireland and Spanish America, so that those who took up land could be further incentivized with a title.[29] "Like another *King Arthur*," Thomas Urquhart later mocked, Alexander "must have his Knights, though nothing limited to so small a number."[30] Royal support, however, hardly made this a royal project. As Alexander noted, the main goal of soliciting "publicke helps, such as hath beene had in other parts," was primarily so "that others of his subjects may be induced to co[n]curre in such common cause"—that is, to persuade more people to adventure and settle.[31]

Bristol's Hope Governor Robert Hayman compared the whole enterprise to that of Christopher Columbus, who before he could undertake his "project of his supposed Westerne Neweland" first had
to sell it to "Princes and States" for their support.[32] John Guy later
complained that "the plantation of the Newfoundland never had
penny help [from the King], but from the adventurers' purses, nor
ever had any lotteries."[33]

As in Virginia and elsewhere, such persuasion came in the form
of a rather large body of promotional literature. The Newfoundland
projectors were an especially literary bunch. Alexander was first and
foremost a man of letters; as Urquhart quipped, if King James "was
born a king, and aimed to be a poet," Alexander was "born a poet,
and aimed to be a king."[34] His treatise, unambiguously entitled *An
Encouragement to Colonies,* was joined by a flood of works from
other adventurers and sub-proprietors. Some, like Hayman's Rabelaisian set of satirical, encomiastic poems and epigrams, *Quodlibits,*
could be rather enigmatic.[35] Others, such as those from Robert
Gordon of Lochinvar and John Mason, took what was becoming
an increasingly more orthodox form of geographical and historical
treatise, travel account, and company prospectus wrapped in one,
insisting in some form that such enterprises were both for the "good
of our Common-wealth" and better for it than other options like
Virginia.[36] Mason drafted a map of Newfoundland, which included
a lengthy cartouche detailing the history of English patents for the
region going back to Cabot and Gilbert and identifying various
regions after patentees like Cary, Calvert, and Vaughan.[37] Though
it is not clear if it was intentional, it is hard not to notice that the
map's orientation, with the south to the top, allows for a framing—
with its main central territory surrounded by smaller outlying islands and inlets, Vaughan's "Cambriola" to the left, a largely offstage
"Nova Scotia" in the upper right, and "Nova Francia" separated
by a narrow channel across the map's bottom (north)—in which
Mason's Newfoundland bears a striking resemblance to England
itself.

Mason's map first appeared in two works by William Vaughan,
his *Cambrensium Caroleia* in 1625 and his equally rather eccentric
The Golden Fleece in 1626. Published under the pseudonym "Orpheus Junior," the book figured Newfoundland as a "Cambrioll

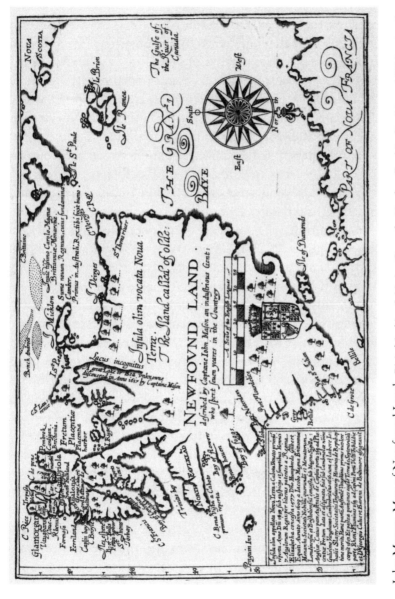

John Mason, Map of Newfound Land. Digital Archives Initiative, Centre for Newfoundland Studies, Memorial University of Newfoundland/CC BY-NC-ND 2.5 CA.

Colchos," after the destination of Jason and the Argonauts' mission in Greek mythology to steal the fleece and its political authority and power. *The Golden Fleece* begins, nearly identically to Book One of Sir Thomas More's early sixteenth-century *Utopia,* as a conversation between the author and two interlocutors, in this case William Alexander and the courtier William Elveston. Yet Vaughan makes it clear to his reader that Newfoundland was "no *Eutiopia*" but rather a very real place and very real opportunity. From there the work takes a sharp turn from More to the court of Apollo, where a pantheon of contemporary and historical figures come forward to debate the issue: Reformation luminaries making the case for the need to counter papist aggression; a debate between the political economists Gerard Malynes and Edward Misselden on the role colonies played in addressing pertinent issues like trade, shortages, and overpopulation; and finally, a pantheon of colonial projectors, from Elizabethan figures like Thomas Smith to contemporaries like John Guy, John Mason, Ferdinando Gorges, and others making a political and ideological case for plantation.[38]

By this point, Vaughan had largely retreated from his direct involvement in this enterprise, while Alexander took on a growing role. As he did, he reinforced his patents with more patents. The outbreak of hostilities with France became an opportunity to solicit the Crown to appoint him to take charge of the Admiralty's jurisdiction out of Nova Scotia, supplementing his power to confront his own new formidable rival: the Paris-based *Compagnie de la Nouvelle-France.* Also known as the *Compagnie des Cent-Associés,* it had been established that year, following several other failed company ventures, to reinforce Quebec and settle the St. Lawrence and Acadia regions. Alexander also faced competition from the Anglo-French merchant Gervase Kirke and his three sons, who had similarly seized on the conflict with France to secure English letters of marque for a privateering venture in eastern Canada. After successfully routing the French Company's squadron, the Kirkes resolved their differences with Alexander by uniting with him in a joint-stock association, securing from the King exclusive rights to trade and settle as well as the authority to "displant those who were enemies in those lands" and the "full power to treat" with them for a peace. In March 1629, the *Adventurers in the Company of Canada,* which some in England regarded simply as the "Anglo-Scotch Company," did just this, capturing the French fort at Quebec and forcing the *Compagnie*'s admiral, Samuel de Champlain, into a surrender. At the conclusion of the war, English negotiators did what early modern diplomats did, offering the territories back to France *status quo ante bellum* in their peace settlement of 1632, but not before Alexander's son, William, with James Stewart, Lord Ochiltree, managed to recruit some Scottish colonists for Acadia, Cape Breton Island, and Port Royal under the Company's auspices.[39]

Other early Newfoundland promoters, growing less sanguine about their prospects, began to look for opportunities to the south. When Gordon's New Galloway project stalled for lack of investment, he proposed "at his owne charge to procure a forraine Plantation" and privateering base off the Brazilian coast.[40] Calvert, now Baron Baltimore, indignantly blamed "other men for their private interests" for misleading him into thinking Avalon would be easy and by 1629 wanted to "shift to some other warmer climate of this new world where the winter be shorter and lesse rigourous." He died in 1632, but not before Charles I, who succeeded as King in 1625, offered him a substantial slice of land in the Chesapeake, which was taken up by his son Cecil, who agreed to name it Maryland, after the Queen.[41] Meanwhile, Robert Hayman had pulled up stakes, involving himself instead in revived projects for exploration and settlement in Guiana.[42]

Hayman was hardly alone. In the opening decades of the seventeenth century, there were many who would easily have bet—and did, in their investments—that the future of English overseas plantation lay in Guiana, including many among the *Mayflower* "pilgrims" who had argued strongly at first for going there instead of Virginia.[43] Charles Leigh, Robert Harcourt, Thomas Roe, an Anglo-Dutch syndicate out of Middelburg and Vlissingen, and a merchant group led by one Captain Budd all set out to settle in the Amazon region. Walter Ralegh, freed again from prison, mounted his own return expedition in 1617, collecting upwards of £37,000 in subscriptions. While Roe soon found himself half a world away serving as the East India Company and English Crown's ambassador to the Mughal Emperor Jahangir, his Guiana venture spawned several further attempts, one of which, led by Thomas King, the Vlissingen settler Jan Pieterse Lodewycx purportedly prophesied "will, in the course of time, be of greater benefit and consideration than that from the East Indies."[44]

It was Harcourt, however, who, upon his return, pushed forward with a vision of establishing a chartered joint-stock company for planting the territory between the Amazon and Essequibo rivers. His plan, detailed in a promotional tract in 1613, offered a pastiche of the different corporate models that were emerging in Virginia, Bermuda, and Newfoundland. Adventurers "in person, or purse" could either invest in a centrally run Company plantation or take up private estates in fee simple, which they could choose to "joyne together in severall companies or corporations of select friends and acquaintance, or else to plant apart, and single by themselves, as Lords of Mannors, or as Farmers." The Company was to be responsible for governing the colony, providing for common defense as well as managing trade, presumably in the form of a magazine company of some sort.[45] Meanwhile, Ralegh crewmember Roger North had his own ambitions. As Harcourt's efforts to raise investment faltered, North offered to buy his patent. When that failed, he petitioned the Privy Council instead to have it canceled and reissued for a new joint-stock corporation under his leadership, since something so crucial could not be "sett out for the present, or maineteined for the future" without "beinge borne by many" in "one bodye, with many large and ample priviledges that maye give encouragement, to the cheerefull proceeding in soe worthye a work." Harcourt's patent could not be so easily recalled, but North and twelve other well-connected adventurers did manage to persuade the Privy Council in 1619 simply to issue another one, with powers "as hath ben graunted to any others heretofore upon like Undertakings and Discoveries" for a corporation called *The Governor and Companie of Noblemen and Gentlemen of the Cittie of London, Adventurers in and about the River of the Amazon.*[46]

To the irate Spanish Ambassador, the Amazon Company seemed the worst of both worlds: a revival of Ralegh's predatory project in the form of a company like "that for the East Indies."[47] For his part, North argued in return that the very fact that this was a "company," governed collectively by public men "who carry no stain of dishonor," meant that it was not, and could not be, anything like Ralegh's enterprise, which was "solely his." Moreover, he insisted, its investors were nobles and gentlemen, not pirates. This claim was ironic, if not outright disingenuous. Even putting aside that Ralegh had a significant body of adventurers behind him, the Amazon Company, despite North's protests, was no doubt an aggressive move within the heart of Spanish America. In fact, the Amazon Company's first Governor was none other than the aptly named Robert Rich, Earl of Warwick, one of England's wealthiest men, who in addition to his leading role in several overseas companies maintained investments in a fleet of privateers that by the 1620s, in one historian's words, was essentially making its own "private war on Spain." In fact, even as the Amazon Company was finalizing its charter in 1619, two ships backed by Warwick had attacked a Portuguese slaving vessel *en route* to Veracruz. The *White Lion* and the *Treasurer* then made their way to Point Comfort outside Jamestown, where they sold some of the nearly sixty captive Angolans they had taken from that ship, the first known instance of the African slave trade in British North America.[48]

Fearing that King James, committed to maintaining the fragile peace with Spain he had brokered some fifteen years earlier, would side with the ambassador and decide to arrest his efforts, North and about a hundred settlers set out for Guiana. Even though the King regarded this as an open act of defiance, like with Harcourt the Privy Council could not just cancel the Company's patent. Instead, it pressured the adventurers to voluntarily surrender it. In May 1620, fifteen members did just this, returning the charter in exchange for immunity for "anie precedent Acts" they may have taken. This was still not the end of things. Some of the settlers stayed in South America. One party came back to England to organize its own company of "gentlemen adventurers" to settle at St. Kitts. Some Irish settlers arrived in the region in 1620, possibly under a subsidiary license the Amazon Company had granted to Thomas Roe. For his part, when North returned, after a brief stint in prison at the behest of the Spanish ambassador, he appealed to the House of Commons for remedy. Roe and others with connections to the Company took up his cause. Not only was it impossible to imagine that one-fifth of a company's membership could be considered capable of legally surrendering its charter, his advocates maintained, but doing so essentially on the demand of the Spanish set a very dangerous precedent. If this could happen to one corporation, as the ambassador recounted the argument to his superiors, all "the patents of the rest of the ancient companies that were in London" were in jeopardy.[49]

MUCH SUING FOR PATENTS

It was a common argument that threatening even one charter would have a chilling effect, as the Levant Company's Richard Staper had put it two decades earlier, on anyone considering "to join their stocks together to plant any trade."[50] It was, however, not enough to save North. The Crown, hardly willing to allow the Commons the power to determine the issue, stopped the proceedings and imprisoned North until he promised to never have anything to do with the Amazon again. Yet, even had royal officials not intervened, the House of Commons would have been an awkward venue in which to press the case. When called in 1621, Parliament had not sat since 1614, its longest prorogation in a century. Many members of the Commons returned especially eager to pick up on decades of attacks against, to cite Humphrey Gilbert's words in such a debate over patents from 1571, the "Prerogative Imperial."[51] The issue of monopoly charters infamously dominated Elizabeth's last Parliament in 1601, culminating in an unsuccessful effort in 1604, led by none other than future Virginia Company governor Edwin Sandys, for a "free trade" bill. Since then, the number of patents had only increased, leading to the introduction of another free trade bill in 1621, which passed as the Statute of Monopolies during Parliament's 1624 session.[52]

The debate over monopolies was not really a debate over whether monopolies were illegal—almost everyone agreed they were—so much as just what constituted a monopoly. Several landmark suits— *Davenant v. Hurdis* (1599), *Cloth Workers of Ipswich v. Sheninge* (1614), and the "Case of Monopolies" itself, *Darcy v. Allen* (1602)— had essentially maintained that exclusive grants to individual patentholders for existing trades were contrary to the common law. Yet this left much open to interpretation. What about when the patent was "many sellers," like an urban corporation or a company, or when the trade in question did not previously exist, such as with patents for inventions?[53] Even the various attempts at free trade bills over the previous decades had largely exempted corporate companies and towns. In 1601, Francis Bacon observed with some bemusement that the very distinction exposed just how "ridiculous" the question was in the first place. "If her Majesty make a patent or, as we term it, a monopoly unto any of her servants, that must go and we cry out of it," he mocked, "but if she grants it to a number of burgesses or a corporation, that must stand; and that forsooth is no monopoly."[54]

This is not to say that incorporated companies were immune to criticism. In fact, assaults on the Merchant Adventurers, arising from both within its ranks and without, had been central to the debates over the 1604 bill and had opened the door to attacks on the Levant, Spanish, Russia, Eastland, and East India Company charters as well.[55] For someone like Sandys, however, the problem was not with chartered companies *per se* but with those whose membership was so restricted as to prevent wider participation from the gentry and mercantile sorts. Moreover, even for those who were able to join, in practice many such enterprises were ultimately run by what East India Company critic Robert Kayll complained of as the "private orders" of small, uniform, and insular leadership. This "Monopoly in a Monopoly," as Sandys called it, meant that such a corporation was not in fact a collection of many sellers but rather "a whole Company, by this Means, is become as One Man, who alone hath the Uttering of all the Commodities of so great a Country."[56]

What was one to do about this? For Sandys, the solution was not to do away with companies but to enshrine the common-law proscription on monopolies in statute, compelling companies to be more open in their membership. Free trade, in this sense, was hardly incompatible with a joint stock like the East India Company, though it did call into question regulated or quasi-regulated concerns like the Merchant Adventurers. The political economist Gerard Malynes suggested that such ills had to be remedied by intervention from the King and Privy Council, the only body capable of ensuring the "Publike good," like Phoebus or Apollo, "whereby the Horses of all societies and corporations may draw a like in the course of Trade by his wise guiding and direction."[57] Others, like Kayll, insisted the company form was fundamentally irredeemable. Not only was restricting trade to some illegal and bad commercial policy, but the corporation also challenged the very sovereignty of the Crown and realm. In a company, he argued, "Subjects and equall Citizens in this great Monarke," rather than regarding themselves as "*Britaines*, all subject to one royall King, all combined together in one naturall league," were instead "tyed and subject one unto the other" in many different competing associations. In this sense, overseas companies, in his oft-quoted phrase, were akin to "the common wealth being made private."[58]

Those writing on behalf of incorporated companies largely rejected the premise that private wealth and "common-wealth" were incompatible. In the first place, Dudley Digges argued, one would be hard pressed to find anyone who undertook public office or a franchise without the hopes of some personal reward. "Perfect wisdome in all Common-wealths," he observed, "hath honors, pay and priviledges to invite the private man into such dangers, for the publique good." Similarly, Merchant Adventurer and East India Company Amsterdam agent Edward Misselden observed, merchants had the same goals as the nobility or gentry, to "advance their fortunes, renowne their names, embellize their houses, beautifie their families with the honour of this faculty: and to perpetuate the same unto posteritie, as an hereditary title of honour unto their name and blood." And like landed gentlemen, in pursuing their own advancement they served the commonwealth. Critics suggested that companies distracted labor from productive and necessary domestic industries and squandered materials, people, and money; Kayll even titled his pamphlet *The Trades Increase,* a not-so-subtle scoff at an East India ship recently lost at sea. To advocates like Digges, however, overseas merchants worked like "laborious Bees" doing "good service to the state," providing relief of the poor through employment, stimulating commercial and industrial enterprises, cultivating a ready supply of trained seamen, and supplying necessary commodities, not least those like timber that were critical for building ships and thus maritime defense. More fundamentally, Misselden asked, just what was the prosperity of the realm but the prosperity of its subjects: "Is not the publique involved in the private, and the private in the publique?" he apostrophized. "What else makes a Common-wealth, but the private-wealth . . . ?"[59]

Insisting that overseas commerce was critical to the commonwealth was not a defense of monopoly. Rather, it contributed to an argument that maintained that as public enterprises, corporate companies could not be considered monopolies in the first place. Even if they were restricted in their membership, with the imprimatur of Crown authority in the form of charters and of civil society in the form of shareholding, companies were, as Edward Hayes had put it in that early Virginia proposal, "an exploite by a publique consent, [rather] then by a private monopoly."[60] The Levant Company, the kind of guild-like regulated company of which Sandys was especially critical, could not be a "monopoly," its leadership insisted in debates over its rechartering in 1605, because all one needed to do to join was pay a fee and meet certain minimal qualifications.[61] Joint-stock corporations made a more emphatic case. There, all one needed was a single share, no qualifications necessary. That "Widows, Orphans, Lawyers, Gentlemen and others" could join the East India Company, Thomas Mun insisted, meant it was already far more public than even an unregulated trade, which was in a sense inherently restricted to traders alone.[62]

If one part of the debate over monopoly turned on just what it meant to partake in a trade, there was also the matter of the nature of overseas trade itself. Attorney-General Edward Coke's report on *Darcy* suggested that the justices had concluded that to be considered a monopoly, an enterprise had to be restricting a right to some that already existed for all. Almost all the overseas companies in this period maintained, however, that they were, as the original Russia Company had been, instituted for the "discovery of new trades." That Company still justified its exclusive rights by the fact that it both established English trade and diplomacy with Russia and had continued to maintain it for over half a century. In a sense, such companies were making an argument about commercial and chartered rights that resembled how many theorists of the *jus gentium*, or law of nations, insisted one might legitimate a claim to colonial territory: demonstrate that one had not only discovered but occupied, used, and, according to some, improved it. To Mun, the East India Company did not so much engage in trade, simply moving goods from one place to another, but produced that trade in the first place by adding "*Art* to *Nature*, our *labour* to *natural means.*" Lewes Roberts similarly observed that overseas merchants did not "preserve" goods for sale but rather gave them "*new vigour, life, strength* and *beautie.*"[63]

Seen from this perspective, overseas companies were no mere peddlers. Through the constant investment of money, effort, and expertise—not unlike an artisan, an improving landlord, or even an alchemist—such companies insisted that they took something that had no inherent or productive value and rendered it into something that did. It followed that without them, the trade itself would cease to exist. This was not some theoretical point. Companies constantly reminded their critics that they established factories, infrastructure, shipping, martial power, and diplomacy, all of which added up to perhaps their most fundamental role: the suppliers of, in Misselden's words, "Order and Government."[64] This argument was frequently inflected by spatial and racial distinctions. Companies could be justified in the world beyond Europe, as one author observed, where "the Purses of private men cannot extend to set forth Ships for making of such long, adventurous, costly, voyages," while a company like the Merchant Adventurers, trading into northern Europe, "is of another nature, for it is hard by home, and as it were at our doores."[65] Even critics like Malynes admitted that "it may bee thought convenient to have joynt Stockes for Remote places, as the *East Indies* and *Persia*." That other Europeans, especially the Dutch, did the same also suggested to many, including Sandys, that that there might be some wisdom in it.[66]

The issue was not that companies could muster greater resources than individuals, though that was hardly insignificant. It was that by engaging on their own account, private traders competed with one another, driving up prices for goods abroad and potentially upending English bargaining power, not to mention the very treaties, agreements, and contracts upon which that trade had been founded. This argument by political economy mirrored a legal and religious one, which maintained that centuries of civil and canon law envisioned Christians as in a perpetual state of war with "infidels"; under such conditions, trade could not exist at all without the protection and supervision of some form of government endowed with the capacity to make and defend treaties of peace and alliance with non-Christians.[67] According to this logic, the world beyond Christendom was still like a state of nature, where the natural law endowed individuals with a right and responsibility to protect themselves. The whole reason for coming together into civil society and abandoning those rights to a government was that such a system was ultimately insecure and unsustainable. In Europe, this took the form of Christian states; for Europeans outside Europe, however, "the law of nations," Hugo Grotius had argued on behalf of the Dutch East India Company, "places public bodies and private companies in the same category," with equal rights of just war in protection of an ally as a monarch or republic, "since whatever is right for single individuals is likewise right for a number of individuals acting as a group."[68] Outside of Christendom at least, Europeans were entitled to bind themselves into a social contract under the protection of corporations as much as states. Thus, as Grotius noted elsewhere, "It is not every kind of monopoly that amounts to a direct violation of the laws of nature."[69]

In the end, as Misselden observed, there were just "many *definitions* of *Monopolies*," and, in his opinion, those who indicted overseas companies as such were making "too loose use" of the term when what they really meant was "ungoverned trade."[70] The protean malleability and spatial flexibility of the concept made it an arena of considerable inconsistency if not hypocrisy, especially when one's own personal commitments intervened. In the 1621 Parliament alone, Sandys, for example, backed the free trade bill while defending the Virginia Company's lotteries as well as its proposal to take on exclusive control of the tobacco trade.[71] Both he and Roe championed the Amazon Company as they forwarded a bill "for the freer liberty of fishing voyages" in America, a thinly veiled attempt to defend the Virginia Company's claims in the Atlantic littoral, which only passed after John Guy and George Calvert intervened to carve out protections for Newfoundlanders' fishing stages.[72]

As it turned out, though, the Newfoundland Company was not their target. In 1620, forty adventurers, led by former military officer Ferdinando Gorges, set out to revive the patent and jurisdiction of the original 1606 "Plymouth" Virginia colony, in which Gorges had been an investor, receiving a new charter as *The Council Established at Plymouth in the County of Devon for the Planting, Ruling, Ordering, and Governing of New-England in America,* or the Council for New England. In 1621, Edward Coke, the common-law jurist and former royalist Attorney General and judge now turned opposition politician, convened a Commons committee to question the validity of the patent. Gorges was summoned and subjected to a lengthy examination, as he recalled it, to prove that the patent was not "a monopoly, and the color of planting a colony put upon it for particular ends and private gain." His defense of exclusive plantation strikingly mirrored the arguments Digges, Mun, Misselden, and others had made on behalf of exclusive trade. For one, he could not "conceive" how the Council could possibly be "esteemed a monopoly," as its aims of "the advancement of religion, the enlargement of the bounds of our nation, the increase of trade, and the employ-ment of many thousands of all sorts of people" all contributed to public, not private, ends. That some might profit along the way was hardly evidence of something illegal, and "no more in effect than many private gentlemen and lords of manors within our own coun-tries enjoyed at present." Moreover, even had he wanted to abandon the charter, Gorges observed, it was not his place to do so. The Council was a corporation, and, much like the advocates of the Am-azon Company had protested, no one could really be called to ac-count to speak for it as a whole, let alone concede its charter—"for my own part I was but a particular person, and inferior to many to whom the Patent was granted, having no power to deliver it without their assents." Besides, he told Coke and the committee, it was not clear why they thought he would have it in his personal possession in the first place.[73]

Even after summoning Gorges several more times—on subsequent occasions he made sure to bring his lawyer with him—the inquiry had no real effect on the Council or its claims. It would turn out to be Sandys and his Virginia Company, along with its near con-temporary the Irish Society, that would face the most existential threat in the coming years. Ironically, as with the New England Council, both assaults arose primarily from the personal and ideo-logical agitations of rivals—in Ulster from without, in Virginia from within—which in turn opened a space for the Privy Council and other Crown officers to make demands on the companies and inter-vene in their affairs. In both cases, the outcomes were hardly prede-termined, as opponents discovered that that trying to modify or re-possess a charter was much harder than getting one.

Resentment had been brewing against the Irish Society for some time, especially among those in Ulster who had grown exasperated for various reasons with its government. By the 1620s, one frustrated planter, the Society's former advocate and ally Sir Thomas Phillips, began a dogged campaign to convince the Crown not only that the Society itself had failed but also that Ulster would be far better off returning to a system of individual undertakers. He led a series of commissions of inquiry investigating the Society's "defects and omis-sions," which culminated in 1629 in a damning dossier, apparently assembled largely on Phillips's own initiative, detailing—and in some cases fabricating—the Society's history and its failings.[74] These efforts paid off after 1625, with the accession of Charles I to the throne. Phillips found a receptive audience among Crown officials aggressively promoting the new King's sense of his absolute and personal authority. It took ten years, but eventually yet another of his inquiries finally led the court and council of Star Chamber to conclude that the Society's charter should be withdrawn.[75]

Yet, even in a regime so convinced of its prerogative power, charters could not just be taken. At the very least, law and custom required that to annul a charter, the physical document itself needed to be repossessed and literally canceled, ceremoniously tearing or striking it through, much as one would have had to do with both sides of an indenture or contract to invalidate it. Star Chamber thus paradoxically had to demand the Society bring in its charter "voluntarily." Even then, the fate of Londonderry, as it functioned under its own charter of incorporation, remained an open question. Stoked by Bishop John Bramhall, who had designs on seizing common lands in the town for the Church, the Crown's lawyers set about withdrawing this charter by prosecuting an action of *scire facias* against the Society, London, and the twelve chief livery companies. This was a procedure that dated back at least to the thirteenth century by which the Crown could accuse a patent holder of wronging it either by virtue of some malfeasance or because for some reason the patent should never have been issued in the first place. The writ initiated a process whereby the Sheriff of London was to summon the patentee(s) to appear before the Lord Chancellor, as the Court of Chancery, literally "to make known" why their patent should be considered valid.[76]

Unsurprisingly, the case was decided in the Crown's favor and the patents for Londonderry and the titles of various landholders under the Society or the Liveries were to be recalled. Several parties came forward with proposals to take their place, each making a different case for how best to go about the task of maintaining colonies in Ulster. The Earl of Antrim and James Hamilton, Viscount Clandeboye, proposed a chartered seigneurie. Sir John Clotworthy represented a group of "now occupants," who already held subproprietorships under the Irish Society, seeking what appeared to be something akin to a joint-stock plantation. Thomas Wentworth, Earl of Strafford and Lord Deputy, proposed a plantation directly "under the dominion of [Charles's] imperial crown" to be superintended by himself. The Privy Council ultimately decided on a fourth option: keep the lands in the Crown's possession and appoint a royal commission to oversee their distribution and management. By now, however, Charles had other things on his mind. Ever closer to going to war with both his English and Scottish Parliaments and politics in his three kingdoms in utter disarray, the King simply left the status of the Irish Society and colonial Ulster in legal limbo.[77]

The same could not be said of Virginia. By the early 1620s, enthusiasm and competition for land there had perhaps never been higher, occasioning, as John Smith later recalled, "much suing for Patents for Plantations, who promised to transport such great multitudes of people" as well as "much disputing concerning those divisions, as though the whole land had been too little for them."[78] Within Company leadership and among colonists on the ground, controversy over whether Virginia should be oriented toward public particular plantations, as Edwin Sandys and his allies had promoted, or privately held estates, associated with the group around Thomas Smythe, only intensified in the wake of the Powhatan invasion that devastated Jamestown in 1622. This story of two implacable and coherent "factions"—one gentry, the other mercantile—has been often repeated over the years, but if nothing else, both sides started from the same premise: Virginia was best ruled through a chartered corporation. Each accused the other of subverting that government by preferring their private interest over the public good. Such critiques were both commercial and political in nature. Smythe came under scrutiny for his handling of the Company's finances and profiteering, especially off the magazine company. Critics also took him to task for the failures of Company government across a dozen years of his leadership, some going so far as to insist he had subjected the Company and colonists alike to oligarchy, tyranny, and, as one petition suggested of the colony's indentured laborers, "Egyptian slavery and Scythian cruelty exercised upon them by laws written in blood." Smythe and allies like Warwick and Robert Johnson similarly accused Sandys of embezzling from both his office and the tobacco monopoly, while decades of agitation in the Commons against monopolies and prerogative patents and his support for the separatist Puritan New Plymouth settlement made it especially easy for Sandys's opponents to brand him, fairly or not, as an antimonarchical republican advocating for "popular" or "Democraticall" government fueled by a pinch of dissenting Calvinist conceptions of common-wealth and a dash of situational hypocrisy.[79]

Unlike Phillips in Ireland, however, what those around Smythe wanted was not the Company's dissolution but its reformation. The King and his leading advisors were sympathetic, as they had been engaging in their own conflicts with Sandys and others over the Crown's growing demands to tobacco revenue, a battle which had in part led to the sudden and controversial withdrawal of the Company's rights to stage lotteries in March 1621. Crown legal counsel advised seeking a voluntary surrender of the charter, recalling "the case of the marchant adventurers" whose charter had been abrogated in 1614 in favor of William Cockayne's joint-stock "project" (which looked to replace the export of unfinished broadcloth with cloth dyed and dressed in England), only to be reestablished in 1617 in a sort of merger between the two rival concerns. The Crown should resort to legal proceedings, they argued, only if the Company refused, which its General Court of shareholders did, almost unanimously.[80] In this case, the Attorney General turned to a different prerogative writ, *quo warranto* ("by what warrant"). This essentially served the same purpose as *scire facias,* compelling patent holders to appear, in this case before the Court of King's Bench, to defend their grants. There was a significant technical difference between the two, however. A *quo warranto* inquiry did not question the validity of a charter but rather the right of its holders to exercise its powers. As a procedural matter, it could be taken out against not the corporation *per se* but its leadership individually and severally. Thus, when the Company responded to almost every charge with a lengthy account of the history of its various charters and rights, the Attorney General curtly dismissed each instance merely as not a "sufficient response," as the point was not whether the charter was legitimate but whether the current leadership was legitimately employing its prerogatives. Though a rather disappointing argument intellectually, it turned out to be effective.[81]

In the wake of the Court's decision against the Company, the Privy Council still seemed to be imagining not abandoning the company model but rather reverting to something like the original 1606 arrangement, a joint-stock monopoly under the government of a royal commission.[82] Discussions dragged out into 1625 when Charles I, interested in promoting "one uniform course of government through our whole Monarchy," changed course and proclaimed Virginia's government now "to depend upon ourself." An overseas plantation, he insisted in his decisive proclamation, was simply too important "to be committed to any company or corporation to whom it may be proper to trust matters of trade and commerce, but cannot be fit or safe to communicate the ordering of State affairs, be they never of so mean consequence."[83]

COSTLY AND TEDIOUS BUSINESS

Such profound and definitive language would seem to have marked a new era in the development of the state's imperial ambitions. It certainly shocked some in New England, who, especially given the Crown's increasing hostility to Puritans like themselves, feared that it might spell the same fate for them.[84] Yet, as it turned out, Charles and his advisors' aggressive interest in expressing power by undermining patents paled in comparison to their almost pathological penchant for doing so by issuing more of them. Historians have long observed a shift in this period away from corporate government toward greater assertions of Crown authority, either directly—such as the 1634 "Western Charter," asserting protections of the "ancient rights" of west country fisheries—or in the more feudal-style seigneurial proprietary grants to individual loyalists. This included Baltimore's 1632 charter for Maryland and patents granted under the Irish Crown to Sir Edmund Plowden—first in 1632 and then reconfirmed in 1634 by Wentworth—for a mid-Atlantic palatinate and earldom to be known somewhat officiously as "New Albion." By the late 1620s, Charles had also issued his Attorney General Robert Heath a patent for "Carolana," comprising what now constitutes the Carolinas, Georgia, and Florida as well as parts of the West Indies, alongside two other overlapping charters both with ostensibly exclusive rights to settle and develop Barbados among a long list of other Caribbean islands, one to the Earl of Montgomery (later Pembroke) and the other to the Earl of Carlisle.[85]

Amidst this wave of patents to individual holders, however, the Crown continued to turn, with mixed results, to the corporate form to support its ambitions. After striking a commercial treaty with the Sultan of Morocco, for example, officials tried to revive the joint-

stock Barbary Company under closer royal control but were ultimately stymied by objections from across London's commercial
community.[86] Both rival Barbados patents were also supported by
societies of adventurers. Behind Carlisle was a well-connected association of London merchants, while Pembroke was little more than
a front for a "Joint Stocke" that had already begun to settle the island. In fact, the ostensible leader of that company, the Anglo-Dutch
merchant William Courteen—one of the merchants who lobbied
against the new Barbary Company scheme—had come to Pembroke's
support after failing in his own bid to acquire a charter for Barbados
along with "all the lands in ye South parts of ye world called Terra
Australis incognita."[87] Courteen did manage soon after to persuade
Charles to issue a patent for another association by stoking growing
impulses at the Court to pressure the East India Company to allow
closer royal scrutiny and control of its trade and revenues. Despite the
Company's exclusive charter, "Courteen's Association," as it became
known, received a license to undertake a commercial and colonial
enterprise in the East Indies, though their major project focused especially on establishing a settlement on Madagascar, modeled after
Dutch Batavia. Meanwhile, the Crown backed rival Northwest Passage ventures and, in 1634, briefly flirted with a proposal for another
Scottish East India Company.[88]

Perhaps the most direct efforts at a state-sponsored corporate enterprise of the early Stuart period was found much closer to home:
the *Concilium et communitas piscationis Dominii Magne Britannie
et Hibernie,* or the *Counsell and Commountie of the Fishinge of
Great Bryttayne and Ireland,* chartered in 1632. Fisheries were in
many ways at the core of Anglo-Scottish politics, commerce, and
culture and a preoccupation of any number of company colonial ventures since the earliest efforts out of late fifteenth-century Bristol.
Not long after James's accession, an English syndicate proposed establishing a Scottish fisheries company, while an Anglo-Scottish
partnership looked to take over the failing Fife Adventure.[89] One
scheme in 1611 imagined a corporation that would purchase land
in order to develop a series of coastal "fisher towns," not only taking
charge of the coastal fisheries but also serving trade, especially in
naval supplies, from Europe, the Caribbean, and Ireland.[90] In 1623,
amidst the crisis in the Virginia Company, another group had proposed that if the Crown were willing to support the littoral fisheries

with ships and sailors, it would set about raising "voluntary contributions" to establish a new plantation in Virginia or New England to bring the domestic and colonial fisheries into a single view via a state-corporate partnership.[91]

Despite all these various English, Scottish, and self-consciously British projects, the most immediate model for something like the British Fisheries Council was no doubt its opposite number in the Netherlands, the *College van de Grote Visserij*, established about a half century earlier with exclusive charge to support, regulate, govern, and defend the Dutch herring fisheries.[92] What made such an effort seem urgently necessary in the 1630s was the news that the new Earl of Seaforth, Cailean Mackenzie, had been attempting to lure fishermen and merchants from Zeeland to Lewis, establishing his own company and offering urban and trading privileges in the hopes they might settle a factory and fisheries colony in Stornoway. Such a move could not help but stoke long-standing tensions over the fisheries. English and Dutch traders frequently clashed in Russia, Narva, and Spitsbergen, leading to violent skirmishes and even a rumored poisoning.[93] Concern, even paranoia, over Dutch ambitions ran so deep that when Hugo Grotius's *Mare Liberum* appeared in 1609, the Scottish scholar William Welwod, among others, immediately took its professed arguments defending Dutch incursions into the Portuguese East Indies to be merely a cover for a "plain proclamation of a liberty common for all of all nations to fish indifferently on all kind of seas."[94] Continued Dutch aggression in the British seas as well as the East Indies, including the "massacre" of English and Japanese merchants at Amboina in 1622, had only amplified suspicions on all sides.[95]

Mackenzie's project thus unsurprisingly sounded alarms across Britain, making strange bedfellows of the Mackenzies' rivals in the Hebrides, the Scottish Council of Royal Burghs, the English western port towns, those with interests in Atlantic plantations, and the Anglo-Scottish Crown. William Alexander, now Charles's Scottish Secretary, insisted that the project was a first step in the long-feared Dutch ambitions for universal empire. From a base in Lewis, he warned, the Dutch could exert maritime power over "any part of Chrisendome in Barbary, Asia, Affrica, East and West Indies," and "Newfoundlande."[96] The King was persuaded, sending Alexander to Scotland in 1630 to communicate his "royall and firme resolution to sett up a commoun fishing" and to have it "undertakin and ordered by commoun counsel and endeavoure."

If Charles was committed to proclaiming his sovereign rights over the British seas and beyond, he was rather less keen on paying for it. For this, "a great stocke must be raised by contributions of adventurers." At the head of this new company was Alexander's old ally, John Mason. Its other leadership was similarly drawn from those with experience in a range of company enterprises, especially those with significant maritime interests like the Fife Adventure and Newfoundland Company. William Courteen was appointed treasurer. Much like the Dutch fisheries collegium and both its East and West India Companies, the Council was initially designed to be a single joint stock made up of subsidiary, semi-independent subcompanies established in several "cheefe" cities and boroughs across the British Isles. When the urban chambers did not materialize, the Council took on a more English flavor, its subcompanies ending up instead as four joint-stock associations organized not by region but under a principal well-connected projector.[97] Meanwhile, the Council's central leadership, appointed by the Crown, was to serve as a central administrative and judicatory authority, charged to patrol the coasts, govern the fisheries trade, and "settle collonyes and plant corporations" in the Highlands, the Shetlands, the Baltic, and what one of the prime movers behind the scheme, the MP John Coke, called the "great territory" of Iceland, thought at the time to be contiguous with Newfoundland.[98] The Council was thus part joint-stock company, part royal commission, part Star Chamber for the seas. In establishing a common government over what the jurist John Selden in his 1635 *Mare Clausum* called the "Oceanus Britannicus," it was for all intents and purposes the closest thing to an Anglo-Scottish union the early Stuarts managed to accomplish. It did not escape the attention of the Scottish commissioners appointed to negotiate over the Council that its very title tended to "suppressing the name of Scotland . . . and confounding the same under the name Great Britane, alho ther be no unioun as yitt with England."[99]

The project had grand ambitions but, in the end, few investors. By 1636, fewer than half of the pledged subscriptions had been paid up, and other ideas to raise money, including a Virginia-style lottery, amounted to little.[100] Many coastal landowners, merchants, and fishermen, regarding the entire enterprise as a violation of their "ancient custom," ignored it and continued to do business with the Dutch. The Company lost several of its fleet to privateers. Yet, what really did the Council in was the Crown itself. By 1639, Charles, desperate for allies in Scotland, came to a settlement with Seòras Mackenzie, Cailean's brother and successor as Earl of Seaforth, to confirm his authority in Lewis in direct contravention of the Fisheries Council's remit. Meanwhile, the ambassador in the Netherlands and the Admiral of the Crown's ship money fleet were ordered not to repel Dutch ships but rather to sell them passes, an offer the Dutch largely disregarded. The Privy Council ordered an investigation into the Council's finances and, like many other such initiatives, it went largely dormant by the late 1630s.[101] In its wake, other fisheries-oriented projects turned back to the Atlantic, including a new patent for settlement and trade in Newfoundland issued to a group of adventurers under David Kirke.[102] One of the more quixotic of these proposals appeared in 1645, when a French projector, Hugo L'Amey, approached Scottish officials through an agent with a plan to transplant "Indian wheat" to Scotland and settle "a good plantione in the cuntrey of India," by which he presumably meant the Caribbean or continental America, in exchange for exclusive rights over the Scottish salmon fisheries.[103]

L'Amey's proposal, which did not go anywhere, was nonetheless a reminder of just how much all of these company projects, no matter how "national" their ambitions, drew on a transnational and trans-company market for financing, settlers, employees, ideas, and models.[104] East India Companies had emerged in France, Friesland, and Denmark. Upstart Swedish projects looked to expand to various points around the globe, alongside French companies for the Caribbean and Canada and several Portuguese attempts at companies in the East Indies and Brazil.[105] There was no shortage of peripatetic projectors like L'Amey, offering to sell their alleged expertise to whatever Court or company that would have them. The disgraced former Dutch East India Company director Isaac Le Maire pitched East India projects to Henri IV in France and James I in England while also proposing a union with James Cunningham's short-lived Scottish East India Company and, more successfully, funding a South Seas expedition, led by his son, through his own *Austraalse* (Southern) *Compagnie*.[106] William Usselincx was even more prolific, spending decades after leaving the Dutch West India Company he helped found trying to fulfill his vision of a colonial-evangelical company in Denmark, Prussia, Poland, and the Baltic before finally finding funding in Sweden for a host of company projects, including, along with other former West India Company employees, the New Sweden Company and its eponymous mid-Atlantic settlement.[107]

Ideas and personnel for company projects were frequently recycled and revived within Britain as well. In the 1630s, North and Harcourt struck up an uneasy alliance to resuscitate their patents in a new *Governor and Company of Noblemen and Gentlemen of England for the Plantation of Guyana,* while others established rival joint stocks to do the same; when one Captain James Duppa failed to win Charles's approval for such a scheme, he pitched the plan to King João of Portugal with equal success.[108] In 1631, a joint-stock consortium led by Nicholas Crispe petitioned to assume the charter for the defunct 1618 "Gynney or Bynney" Company, claiming that the earlier grant had been abrogated by non-use; in 1638 many of the same group became involved in the short-lived Morocco Company project.[109] Charles offered a charter to four adventurers to establish a Scottish Guinea Company fashioned after its English rival, but it only mounted one voyage.[110] Meanwhile, a Crown commission recommended bringing back the Virginia Company under closer Crown control but nonetheless "with confirmation of all their ancient Territories, rights and privileges." The plan was successfully opposed by Virginia planters in the colony's assembly, who formally and forcefully warned the King against reviving a Company that had faced *quo warranto,* in their telling, because it had become a hotbed of anti-royalist republicanism. They even attempted to prohibit voicing in Virginia itself any support for the idea of "reducing of this Colony to a Company or Corporation."[111]

The Company did not return. Its legacy, however, continued to live on in laws, policies, institutions (not least Virginia's "House of Burgesses"), and most of all enduring conflicts over plantation owners' property rights; as the Privy Council observed to the colony's leadership in 1634, it had never "intended that the interestes which men had settled when you were a Corporation should be impeached."[112] No one knew this better than William Claiborne, whose vast estate on Kent Island dated from the days of the Virginia Company; he had since acquired grants from the Virginia colony for an exclusive fur trade with the Susquehannock and a Scottish patent from Charles I for trade to New England and Nova Scotia for what has often been referred to as the "Kent Island Company." After 1632, however, Kent Island suddenly found itself no longer in Virginia but Maryland; when the new government there attempted to encroach on his territory, Claiborne sued Baltimore, arguing that the Company's dissolution did not abrogate his property and chartered rights, building his case—cleverly, speciously—around the clause in the Maryland charter, common to most all charters, prohibiting settling territory previously claimed by other Europeans. The stricture was meant to prevent patentees from creating international incidents by claiming lands under the control of other European states, companies, and proprietors. Claiborne insisted, however, that he too was another "European," and as such was essentially his own independent proprietor.[113]

As Virginia continued to hear the echoes of its corporate past, New England's commitment to joint-stock and corporate principles under the Council for New England was loud and clear. The Council had begun with a nominal capital of £100,000, but only a small portion was ever paid up. It had also at the outset established a subsidiary joint stock for fishing enterprise, which could only set sail after taking a loan from six Council members.[114] In September 1621, a complex plan was proposed to create subsidiary joint stocks in the west country port towns of Bristol, Exeter, Plymouth, Dartmouth, and Barnstaple, presumably to both raise more capital and co-opt some growing dissent among merchants there. They were to function much like the regional chambers in Dutch companies or the original plan for the later Fisheries Council, each taking on the business of trade and plantation, "uppon their owne or their friends private adventure," under the umbrella of the general Council while also contributing members to a joint council. That council was to meet periodically and decide "whether the whole shall proceed upon a jointe stock or that ev[e]ry Cittie and Towne doe proceed upon their severall adventures, w[hi]ch by al meanes is conceived to bee the worst, both for the publique and private."[115]

This model was never adopted, not least because its arguably most powerful member, the Merchant Venturers of Bristol, refused to participate and indeed became virulent opponents of the scheme.[116] Early plans to distribute land proportionally to adventurers in the form of dividends, like the Virginia Company, similarly faltered.

Thus, like the Newfoundland Company before it, the Council for New England eventually promoted settlement and plantation through sublicenses and large subordinate patents, often to its own members. In 1622 Ferdinando Gorges and John Mason took up a massive grant for what would become New Hampshire and Maine. The following year Christopher Levett, another Council member, proposed to raise money from fifty investors to send planters to settle a city and six thousand acres. In 1629, Gorges, Mason, and several others received patents from the Council for a joint-stock Laconia Company, aiming to discover and settle the "Great Lake of the Iroquois," thought to be the source and center of the northeastern fur trade. It eventually failed, although its agent Edward Hilton did sell off shares that passed through various hands, complicating later land claims in New Hampshire.[117] In 1630, Gorges granted similar rights to a joint-stock association, known as the "Company of Husbandmen" or "the Company of the Plough," which was soon abandoned and unloaded to another proprietor in 1643. He in turn divided the land and sold plots to "divers persons," some of whom ended up proclaiming themselves to be an autonomous colony which they called Lygonia, after Gorges's mother.[118] Another Council license went to a company out of Dorchester, which by 1624 had nearly 120 adventurers and had established a colony and fishing stages at Cape Ann in what is now Massachusetts, leading to several open and violent battles with colonists from nearby New Plymouth, who, having secured their own patent from another Council member, resented the incursion into what they considered their jurisdiction.[119] The Dorchester venture soon was defunct, but by 1628 several former adventurers sought to revive it as the New England Company, with grants from the Earl of Warwick, another Council member. Over the next year, joined by Warwick, Lord Saye and Sele, and another hundred-some shareholders, the New England Company sought out royal patents, so that their planned Puritan refuge and "Plantation . . . maie be the better mannaged and ordered." The new corporation was rebranded as the *Governor and Company of the Massachusetts Bay in New England.*[120]

The incorporation of the Massachusetts Bay Company and its shareholder-settlers added more urgency in the struggling New Plymouth colony to seek out a charter of its own. Its claims to jurisdiction were, admittedly but typically, ambiguous, founded as they were in a land grant from the Virginia Company, which no longer existed, and their own self-constituting "Mayflower compact" for government of a colony that now arguably fell within the jurisdiction of the Council for New England. By 1626, the London adventurers in its joint stock had divested of the enterprise, selling their interest back to the colony for £1800. Though still supporters and allies of the project, they made it clear that it would now be up to the New Englanders to forge a path forward on their own to "make a plantation, and erect a city in those remote places." As early as 1624, they had advised their brethren on the best way to do so: "Make your corporation as formal as you can, under the name of the Society of Plymouth in New England, allowing some particular privileges to all the members thereof, according to the nature of the patents."[121]

Accordingly, within a year of the chartering of the Massachusetts Bay Company, Plymouth's London agent, Isaac Allerton, had set out, as some of the erstwhile London adventurers reported, "to confirm their grant and make you a Corporation, and so to enable you to make and execute laws in such large and ample manner, as the Salem or Massachusetts plantation hath it." Allerton's efforts, however, revealed just how difficult, costly, and bureaucratic an enterprise it was to obtain a charter. The petition was referred to the Lord Keeper, who was responsible for maintaining the Great Seal, but first, a request to relieve the corporation of customs charges had to be approved by the Lord Treasurer, who then brought the issue before the Privy Council. Though Allerton "attended, day by day . . . and made great means and friends, both of Lords and secretaries," pressing business before the Council prevented Allerton from getting his petition on the agenda. It was "work by degrees" and a "costly and tedious business," filled with "many riddles which must be resolved, and many locks [which] must be opened with the silver, nay, the golden key."[122]

Allerton returned to New England before achieving his goals, but his agitations on behalf of the Plymouth colony had won him some powerful allies. Chief among these were John Mason and Ferdinando Gorges, who, locked in a battle with Massachusetts over rival territorial claims in New England, had with the assistance of the lawyer Thomas Morton (and, some in Massachusetts suspected, Allerton's encouragement) begun to lobby the Privy Council's relatively new subcommittee on New England plantations to pursue a writ of *quo warranto* against the leadership of the Massachusetts Bay Company.[123] The committee, which historian Charles Andrews likened to a Star Chamber for the colonies, albeit one that almost immediately "proved practically impotent," did not need much persuading.[124] At its helm was the Charles's chief advisor and the principal architect of the Crown's religious and political policies of "personal" rule, Archbishop William Laud. For Laud, the colony's anti-episcopal and decentralized Puritan churches was impudence enough. That they further flouted royal authority by establishing a university, Harvard College, in 1636, and incorporated their own towns with representation in a self-constituting house of deputies was only further evidence that the colony treated its charter not as a royal dispensation but, in the words of historian Mark Peterson, more like "a malleable set of guidelines" and a "license to evade the authority of the king." It needed to be brought to heel.[125]

In 1637, to no one's surprise, the Court of King's Bench decided the *quo warranto* in favor of the Crown, authorizing it to "seize their Franchises," presumably with the intention of granting it to Gorges. There was, however, a problem. Nearly a decade earlier, amidst mounting tensions between English Puritans and the Crown—in March 1629, the same month the Company received its charter, Charles had prorogued Parliament and arrested several members, partly for agitating against his religious policies—the leadership of the Massachusetts Bay Company had made the strategic decision to formally fix their government and even to transport their charter across the Atlantic.[126] Thus, the vast majority of those named in the *quo warranto* ignored the ruling, remaining, along with the charter, in New England. There was surprisingly little the Crown could or would do about this. It fell to Gorges to remedy the situation. He decided to take the remarkable step of invading Massachusetts, intending to physically repossess the charter and arrest the refractory colonial leaders. He and Mason even paid for a new ship to be built to take Gorges and a thousand troops to New England. The ship, however, fell apart just after its maiden launch, and Gorges's scheme foundered along with it. Mason died soon after and the Crown soon became distracted with more pressing matters, leaving corporate government in Massachusetts technically abrogated—and never more autonomous.[127]

Corporate life was at the heart of New England political culture, rooted in some ways in the local and community-based nature of religious life; as Roger Williams would put it in 1646, "the church, or company of worshippers, whether true or false, is like unto a body or college of physicians in a city—like unto a corporation, society, or company of East India or Turkey merchants, or any other society or company in London."[128] One did not generally hold stock in a church, and the dividends town companies paid out were almost always exclusively in land rather than share value. Still, there was at least something to the comparison. Over the next decades, colonists in Massachusetts continued to fund and organize the expansion of their own settlement through the establishment of towns that in many ways were a hybrid between urban corporations and land companies, with their founding covenants, mutual compacts, articles of association, purchases of indigenous territory, and assembly-granted exclusive rights to land and self-government distributed in proportion to investment to both resident and absentee shareholders.[129] This expansion was suborned by a range of other joint-stock companies for commerce, mutual aid, and infrastructure and public works, sometimes at the most local of levels, such as the thirteen Boston landowners who received a grant in 1652 to operate a waterworks among their properties on Conduit Street.[130] Others very much resembled the English chartered overseas corporations in their ecumenical mix of commercial, territorial, and social ambitions, like the Nashaway "undertakers," with patents from Massachusetts to settle, mine, and trade along the Nashua River.[131] *The Ancient and Honorable Artillery Company,* established in 1638, controlled a thousand acres of land and what amounted to a private militia and a mercantile, political, social, and religious fellowship, which Massachusetts Governor, John Winthrop, once compared, quite unfavorably, to a Roman Pretorian guard or the Knights Templars.[132] Many of its members were involved the 1644 Lake of the Iroquois Company, a "free company of adventurers" intending to revive the failed Laconia Company project, with rights from the assembly to occupy lands, make prize of interlopers, and undertake exclusive trade and self-government "as is granted to such companies in other parts."[133]

As Massachusetts set about its own expansion, other projects were emerging to rival and challenge it as well. In 1632, having largely displaced Gorges at the head of the relatively obsolete Council of New England, the Earl of Warwick offered a group of investors—known sometimes after its most prominent adventurers Lords Saye and Brooke as the Saybrook Company—a large tract of land for several settlements in what would eventually become the break-away colony of Connecticut and the separately governed colony-corporation of New Haven. The adventurers arranged for John Winthrop Jr., the son of the Massachusetts governor, to lead a party of settlers, some from nearby colonies in Massachusetts. Their Fort Saybrook, and the aggressive claims on indigenous territory it was meant to defend, played a central role in the devastating war with the Pequots that followed in 1636.[134] Many of these same men, including Warwick, Saye, and Brooke, had also turned their attention and purses even farther afield, to a more expansive venture to plant a colony on the island of Santa Catalina off the coast of what is now Nicaragua, which they humbly called "Providence" and which the venture's chief modern historian has pithily termed "the other Puritan colony." Chartered in 1630, *The Adventurers of the City of Westminster for the Plantation of the Islands of Providence, Henrietta and the Adjacent Islands lying upon the Coast of America* was to be a godly plantation along the lines of New England, though with the entire colony's property remaining in the corporation's hands and at its direction, settled largely by tenant farmers and slaves.[135] The enterprise was the culmination of several aborted proposals across the previous decade to establish, as John Coke put it in 1625, a "company incorporated for the West, as there is already for the East." These English West India Company projects came in various permutations, but the basic idea was for a subscriber funded joint-stock company that could "invade [the Spanish King's] countries, to fortify and plant there, and to establish government, confederacy and trade," and compete with the recently founded Dutch West India Company. As Dudley Digges had argued, such a company would also serve as a means for the Commons indirectly to conduct a war with Spain independent of the Crown, especially on the heels of the Duke of Buckingham's disastrous attempt in 1625 to invade Cadiz.[136]

The Providence Island Company lasted just over a decade, but in that time, it managed to spawn into a confounding conglomerate of ventures for settlement, commerce, predation, mining, and slave trading and trafficking. It also sought out several additional patents for various subsidiary projects and powers: to plant a "considerable colony" in Cape Gracias a Dios to support the cultivation and trade in silkgrass under the privateer Sussex Camock; to issue its own letters of marque, some of which at least were issued to ships belonging to Warwick; and, in 1637 and again in 1638, to issue new joint stocks to extend settlement elsewhere in Central America and the Caribbean. In 1638, Warwick purchased Pembroke's disputed Caribbean patent and sent his own ships out to establish a plantation at Trinidad.[137]

From its beginning, the Company had been short on cash, its subscriptions, like many of its predecessors, rarely being fully paid up. It made several additional calls on shareholders, borrowed liberally on the security of the joint stock, and eventually took on debt just to keep up with the interest payments. Nearly a decade after its abandonment of the island in 1642, its investors still owed upwards of £19,000 to various creditors, most of which was never repaid. Much of its own shipping was financed on subsidiary joint stocks, as were efforts like the Camock venture and a plan in 1638 led by Saye, Warwick, Brooke, and Henry Darley to fund their own emigration to the island. William Claiborne, who was having so much trouble at Kent Island, received a license from the Company in 1638 to establish a company for a colony at Roatán, off the coast of Honduras. Claiborne's longtime partner, the merchant Maurice Thomson, and his associates struck a number of contracts with the Company for a "magazine" company for trading with and supplying the island, privateering, shipping, and the export and sale of slaves. Also in 1638, Company leadership, which was trying to discourage slavery on the island—more out of fear of the expense and threat of rebellion rather than any abolitionist sentiment—entered into failed negotiations with another London-based joint-stock association to transport slaves off the island, presumably to sell them elsewhere in the Atlantic, and to recruit indentured English servants in their place. At the same time, another group of investors established a partnership with Anthony Hilton, the Company's governor at Association (Tortuga), to supply that island or its neighbors with slaves.[138] None of these schemes were enough to rescue the Company's fortunes. It was on the verge of collapse when the several radical options its leadership was considering—turning the plantation into a personal proprietorship under Brooke or selling it to a consortium of Dutch investors or possibly the Dutch West India Company—were rendered moot as the colony was finally lost to Spanish invasion in 1641.[139]

THE CORPORATE COMMONWEALTH

The constitutional crisis that enveloped the British Isles, which reached its apotheosis with the execution of Charles I in 1649 and the establishment of a republic and military protectorate in England, Scotland, and Ireland, proved to be a mixed experience for colonial companies. In some cases, disruptions in trade and government were not good for corporate business or politics, as the Russia Company discovered when the Czar used the occasion of the execution of a fellow monarch to suspend the Company's century-old charter of privileges.[140] At the same time, the war between the Crown and the English House of Commons over the previous decade opened up potential opportunities. When the Commons abolished Star Chamber in mid-1641, for example, it effectively voided the previous judgment against the Irish Society, reinstating the company's status in Ulster; as it turns out, when Charles returned to London in November that same year, he insisted that he had always intended to do the same, though this was too little too late.[141] In Massachusetts, officials took advantage of the uncertain political authority on the British Isles and potential support from the Puritan-dominated Commons to persuade the various plantations in New Hampshire and Maine, including Lygonia, to annex themselves to the colony and swear allegiance to its General Court. Boston also led a fundamental reorganizational experiment in New England, joining with the Connecticut, New Haven, and Plymouth colonies in a military and administrative alliance known as the New England Confederation, or the United Colonies, alongside more subtle acts of independence such as issuing a formal charter of incorporation to the *President and Fellows of Harvard College,* with typical rights to autonomy, property, and soon large land grants for its "incouragment."[142]

While both the Commons in the 1640s and the Commonwealth and Protectorate that emerged under Oliver Cromwell in the wake of Charles's execution no doubt sought to directly expand their imperial power, they in many ways continued, maybe even more than their predecessors, to draw upon the entrepreneurial tradition of colonial expansion. The Commons had declared Carlisle's Barbados patents forfeit in 1643 and took the royalist stronghold by force nine years later, but this only encouraged newly arrived landholding elites, such as Thomas Modyford and Thomas Gage, to launch their own colonial projects across the region from Guiana to Guatemala. Francis Willoughby, to whom Carlisle had leased his patents some years earlier, petitioned in 1654 to have Surinam granted him as a personal proprietorship.[143] Meanwhile, Cromwell's frequent laments at the loss of Providence Island, in historian Karen Kupperman's words, "figured heavily" in shaping his government's imperial Atlantic policy, known as the Western Design. Even its signal achievement, seizing Jamaica in 1656, was based in claims first staked by the privateer Captain William Jackson, with Warwick and Thomson's backing under the authority of the Providence Island Company.[144]

The endurance of these projects in new form should be no surprise, as several company promoters from the 1630s and 1640s, especially those with Parliamentary and Puritan connections, had now become critical figures in the new Parliamentary government of the 1640s and 1650s. Merchants like Thomson were pivotal in shaping policy through the 1650s, including the landmark protectionist Navigation Act of 1651.[145] William Claiborne was sent to receive the formal surrender of Virginia and Maryland to Parliament, likely with hopes of also reviving his claims on Kent Island along the way.[146] In 1643, the Commons appointed Warwick to be Lord High Admiral in the colonies, and, when it established its own commission for plantations, it was Warwick who was placed at its head.[147] It was from this commission that Roger Williams secured a charter in 1643 for the New England breakaway colony of Providence Plantations, later to be known as Rhode Island.[148]

More projects followed. In 1647, a group of disaffected Bermudians, led by former governor Captain William Sayle and supported by London investors, established their own rival company for planting another utopian Puritan republic in the Bahamas, calling it the *Company of Adventurers for the Plantation of the Islands of Eleutheria,* though the company itself was never able to secure a charter.[149] Many erstwhile Providence Island leaders also tried several times to revive the West India Company project. "For as much as this Commonwealth hath obtained of late years a good footing in the West India," one such proposal observed in the later 1650s, it was only by offering expansive enough immunities, powers, and "necessary encouragements and assistances to such p[er]sons as shall joyne together & incorporate themselves into a Societie or Company, by a joyntstock and subscription" that the "worke of this Commonwealth is to be donn by the means proposed [viz: A west India Compa]."[150] In 1651, Thomson and others also successfully made a case over separate traders for a west African slave trade in the form of a revived (if short-lived) corporate joint-stock Guinea Company, which had fallen apart a few years earlier when the royalist Crispe went into exile.[151] A conglomerate of varied private joint-stock whaling companies also arose in the Spitsbergen trade.[152] Martin Noell and Thomas Povey, who were involved in many of these other projects, joined with several others to propose a *Nova Scotia Company* that would capitalize on the expiration of the Kirkes' patent in 1655.[153] Meanwhile, a quite different kind of colonial corporation was established by Parliamentary Act in 1649: the *President and Society for the Propagation of the Gospel in New England,* whose corporate status allowed it to own property, elect members and officers, and collect and disburse money to be used by missionaries and other institutions in New England to support their efforts.[154]

Joint-stock colonization also proved critical to laying the foundations for the aggressive expansion of the Cromwellian state closer to home: that is, in Ireland. As the bloody conflict between Crown and its Parliaments spread to Ulster, London and the twelve liveries sent infantry troops, ordnance, and ammunition to assist the defense in the siege of Londonderry (Cromwell would later reward London in 1656 with a new formal charter for the Irish Society).[155] As Parliament declared the lands of these "rebels" forfeit, the responsibility for clearing and planting that land fell to a new joint-stock company, the *Adventure for Irish Land,* authorized by an act of Parliament in 1642. Meanwhile, an affiliated venture, the *Additional Sea Venture,* raised an expeditionary military force to dispossess nearly 2.5 million acres of Catholic land in Ulster, which would then be transferred to investors as dividends, in addition to any other profits that arose from the spoils of war. Many of these adventurers, closely tied to the Puritan establishment, had predictably long and extensive ties to various other ventures, including Atlantic commerce, slave trading,

and Providence Island and the various West India Company projects. Some had also been investors in Courteen's failed Madagascar
colony and may possibly have seen the Irish project as a chance to
make up their losses.[156]

In turn, some of these same men soon returned their attention to
Courteen's dormant project. In the 1630s, royal officials had tried
to resolve the confused mess they had made in issuing a patent to
Courteen by trying to force a merger between his company and the
East India Company, along the lines of what had been done to quell
the conflict between the Merchant Adventurers and Cockayne's
project two decades earlier. William Courteen Jr. had feebly tried
to continue the enterprise after his father's death in 1636 but had
largely gone bankrupt within several years. At this point, Noell,
Thomson, and others set up an association to buy the patent and
presented the Commons with a petition for a new charter, again centered on a proposal to establish a colony on the Madagascar island
of Nosy Be, or what they called Assada. With Barbados as its model
and Robert Hunt, former governor of Providence Island, as its first
governor, the colony was imagined to be a first step in a broad
global vision to connect the Atlantic slave trade to the Indian Ocean,
where the group also had designs on the southeast Asian island of
Run.[157]

Where the Crown had failed, the Council of State succeeded, ultimately brokering a deal whereby the East India Company would
absorb the Assada Adventure, now to be "carried on by one company and with one joint stock."[158] Over the next several years, the
onetime rival group used its position as shareholders began to colonize the East India Company from within. When its charter was allowed to lapse in 1653, Company leadership had been forced to
open a new limited joint stock to both raise money to fend off the
impending onslaught of rival traders and also essentially ensure that
some semblance of its legal identity remained intact. This led to some
predictable organizational chaos. For example, in 1654, when the
Dutch agreed at the Treaty of Westminster to compensate the Company £85,000 in reparations for Amboina, they reportedly could not
figure out which joint stock was "the Company" that should be
paid, vesting the money with trustees who perhaps uncoincidentally
promptly loaned £50,000 of it to Cromwell.[159] The arrangement
also opened further opportunity for Thomson and his "Merchant

Adventurers to the East Indies" to purchase more stock and lead what amounted to a hostile takeover of Company leadership. In the meantime, the actual trade to India by all accounts in shambles, everyone seemed agreed that there was no future for it without an exclusive company. The revitalized leadership secured a new charter from Cromwell in 1657, which, though it has not survived, reportedly set the Company out on a vastly more powerful footing than before, including for the first time matching its perpetual corporate character with a single permanent joint stock.[160]

With the rather more aggressive Thomson and his allies at its helm, the revived East India Company was now committed to expansion. It invested in the development of its port-colony at Madras in South India, which it had held since the late 1630s on grants from a nearby Vijayanagar tributary. The plan for a colony and waystation at Madagascar morphed into one for the South Atlantic island of St. Helena, occupied under proprietary patents from Oliver Cromwell's successor and son, Richard Cromwell, in 1659. The Company entered negotiations to purchase or lease the largely abandoned west African stations of the once again defunct Guinea Company and dreamed of reasserting claims to Pulo Run, ostensibly conceded by the Dutch in 1654. Much of this was put on pause in late 1659 and early 1660, as the Protectorate crumbled and General George Monck and the army under his control returned from Scotland to England, to preside over the efforts to invite King Charles II back to reassume the English, Scottish, and Irish thrones. That Monck's invasion of England had significant financial backing from many of the same men behind the Adventure for Irish Land spoke volumes about the corporate Restoration that was to follow.[161]

3

CORPORATE FINANCE

The Age of Projects

Planting is my trade.

$\mathcal{L}$IKE MUCH IN THE early Restoration, the overseas empire Charles II acquired upon his return to the English and Scottish thrones was met with great enthusiasm, which quickly turned to dashed expectations. Virginians proved surprisingly willful. The status of Barbados was ambiguous. Jamaica was quickly becoming a hotbed of pirates. The Protectorate's other major conquest from Spain, the northern European garrisoned settlement of Dunkirk and Fort Mardyck—which Charles's chief advisor, the Earl of Clarendon, regarded as one of two "jewels of an immense magnitude in the royal diadem"—was soon sold off to the French King Louis XIV.[1] Its garrison was reassigned to support the second supposed crown jewel, the north African port of Tangier, recently acquired from Portugal along with the western Indian outpost of Bombay, in a treaty of alliance sealed by the marriage between King Charles and the *infanta*, or Princess, Catarina de Bragança. Yet within two decades, Tangier would fall, hobbled by political disarray from within and Moroccan forces from without. In less than half that time, the Crown also found itself unable or unwilling to administer a colony half a world away, offering Bombay in 1668 as a proprietary colony to the only body prepared and (mostly) willing to take it: the English East India Company.[2]

For all the restored British Crown's imperial aspirations, Britons' overseas enterprise in 1660 by and large remained in private hands. Certainly among the many powers restored to Charles II was his father's prerogative—and, incidentally, penchant—for issuing patents. Many companies, from the East India Company to the Irish Society, that had weathered the political and financial chaos of the previous decades not only endured but arguably emerged on stronger footing with new charters. Meanwhile, new enterprises arose as others were revived and reformulated, all contributing to an ever-expanding scaffolding of institutions that both invested civil society at home in empire and served as the fundamental infrastructure of colonial civil society abroad. The principles of joint-stock venture colonialism alongside corporate associations and institutions infused new projects of all stripes, including the royal family's own overseas ambitions and seigneurial proprietorships such as those found in Carolina, Pennsylvania, and the Jerseys. This growth of corporate colonialism in the period inspired an equally forceful backlash. Petitions, lawsuits, pamphlets, and other protests from colonists and company rivals alike encouraged Crown, Parliament, and a number of new commissions, agents, and offices to assert their own claims over companies and other chartered bodies, even as both established and emergent corporations became ever more central to colonial expansion and to the making of Britain itself.

THE CORPORATE RESTORATION

In 1697, novelist and pamphleteer Daniel Defoe branded his era a "projecting age," and with very good reason. While the impulse for projects, Defoe observed, went back deep into human history itself—he cited Noah and his ark as perhaps the earliest example—the late seventeenth century seemed to teem with schemes, whether to maintain highways or build waterworks, dig mines or drain fenlands, open banks or offer insurance, engage in philanthropy or open trades to distant lands. To many at the time, the very mention of "projectors" conjured images of fraudsters and failures, where later generations might look back and see budding capitalist entrepreneurs. For their part, any number of projects insisted their "improving" impulses served private benefit and public good in equal proportion, refusing to draw firm lines among varied commercial, political, social, religious, and philosophical ambitions. Scams and successes alike, such projects, more and more across this period, took form as corporations.[3]

One of the most ambitious of the new enterprises to emerge in the shadow of the Restoration was also in some ways one of the most traditional. The *Royal Society of London for Promoting Natural Knowledge,* first incorporated in 1662, was the culmination of a project of gentlemen natural philosophers who had been convening for decades as a so-called "invisible college" in various venues, including another corporation, Gresham's College. One of a number of "learned projects" for new scientific societies, academies, and colleges emerging across Europe in this period, the Royal Society was primarily meant to be a forum for experimentation and communication of new scientific ideas and inventions. In a sense, it was a project for projects. Its founders imagined their role was to regulate the practices and practitioners of natural philosophy, vetting, authorizing, and profiting from their efforts and advising others, including the Crown, on their use and application. It was also, like most associations, a self-governing and restricted social space, with all of the attendant privileges, performances, and pleasures of membership. As such, the Royal Society was like a learned society, a scientific guild, an Oxbridge college, a gentleman's club, and a royal council, all in one.[4]

As a corporation, it was a city-in-a-city; as a company, it was fueled by the investment and traffic of ideas. Such was the "way to so happy a government," the architect Christopher Wren wrote in a draft of the Society's charter, "which upon mature Inspection are found to be the Basis of civil Communities, and free Governments, and which father gather Multitudes, by an *Orphean* Charm, into Cities, and connect them in *Companies;* that so, by laying in a Stock, as it were, of several Arts, and Methods of Industry, the whole Body may be supplied by a mutual Commerce of each others peculiar Faculties."[5] Much as joint-stock companies touted that they were open to "Noble-men, Clergy-men, Gentlemen, Widows, Orphans, Shop-keepers and all others" alike, the Royal Society,

Thomas Sprat insisted, had "broken down the partition wall, and made a fair entrance for *all conditions of men* to engage in these Studies"; as such, it resembled "the *Cities* themselves, which are compounded of all sorts of men, of the *Gown,* of the *Sword,* of the *Shop,* of the *Field,* of the *Court,* of the *Sea;* all mutually assisting each other."[6] And though some of these more ecumenical ambitions never came to pass, one certainly remained. As the final version of the charter put it, the Royal Society set out "to extend not only the boundaries of Empire, but also of the very arts and sciences," two enterprises that would be fused together in its activities for decades and centuries.[7]

Like other corporations, the Royal Society and many of its individual members stood at the crossroads of various intersecting networks of corporate and overseas projects, none more prolifically than one of the leading forces behind the Society, natural philosopher and philanthropist Robert Boyle. Boyle was a large Irish plantation owner, a member of the East India Company's governing court of committees, and later an adventurer in the Hudson's Bay Company. He used these various platforms to patronize what seemed to be his guiding passion of furthering proselytization efforts around the globe, including taking on the first governorship of the reincarnation of the 1649 missionary-land company, reincorporated and rechristened by royal charter in 1662 as *The Company for the Propagation of the Gospel in New England and the Parts Adjacent in America.* The New England Company—or, as it was sometimes known in New England, simply "the corporation"—was itself connected to other corporate enterprises. Many of its forty-five initial members were drawn from England's mercantile elite, including fellow East India Company leadership, as well as those engaged in land and commercial projects throughout New England.[8]

One of the most influential of the New England Company's members, Boyle's friend, Royal Society fellow, and Connecticut governor John Winthrop Jr, it turned out, was himself in London in 1662 looking to create yet another corporation: that is, Connecticut. Winthrop had come from New England in hopes of finding some traces of the Earl of Warwick's grant to the so-called Saybrook Company. Though the conveyance formed the foundations for the Connecticut colony, no one had possession of the document itself. What Winthrop could find—some have argued, fabricated—proved legally insufficient. The next option then was to seek out a confirmation of the colony's status in the form of new royal patents. Formally chartered in 1662, the resulting *Governor and Company of the English Colony of Connecticut in New England in America* was modeled in large part after the original Massachusetts Bay Company and consolidated several independent settlements, including the corporation of New Haven, into a single colony with claims to jurisdiction across southern New England into eastern Long Island.[9]

One factor that made Winthrop especially eager to formalize Connecticut's legal status was an increasingly tense border dispute with its eastern neighbor, Providence Plantations, the one major New England colony excluded from the United Colonies. Stoking the fires of this conflict was a joint-stock land company made up of several large New England landholders, including Winthrop as well as the influential military officer and politician Humphrey Atherton. The group had its eyes on an expanse of Narragansett territory, which both Rhode Island and Connecticut claimed to be at least nominally within their boundaries. In the late 1650s, the so-called Atherton Company had allegedly negotiated with sachem Cojonoquant for deeds to portions of this land, Quidnesset and Namcook (Boston Neck). The rest, however, remained out of reach until Winthrop capitalized on the opportunity of a Narragansett raid on Mohegan territory to expropriate those lands through an arrangement amounting to a protection racket. The United Colony's alliance with the Mohegan and the fact that there was an English factory in their midst provided Winthrop, as governor of the United Colonies, the pretense to levy on the Narragansett a fine of 595 fathoms of wampum. When the Narragansett sachems found themselves, quite predictably, unable to afford such an exorbitant sum, the Atherton Company conveniently stepped in to loan them the money, with their lands as collateral. The Company called in the loan in the spring of 1662, and since the sachems could still not pay, it claimed possession over the roughly four hundred square miles of territory, sanctifying the conveyance with the performance of the feudal ceremony of livery of seisin, otherwise known as "by turf and twig."[10]

Rhode Island officials saw this entire affair as a gross violation of its borders, its treaties with the Narragansett, and its own laws against making private purchases with indigenous nations. The Atherton undertakers denied that the territory was in Rhode Island

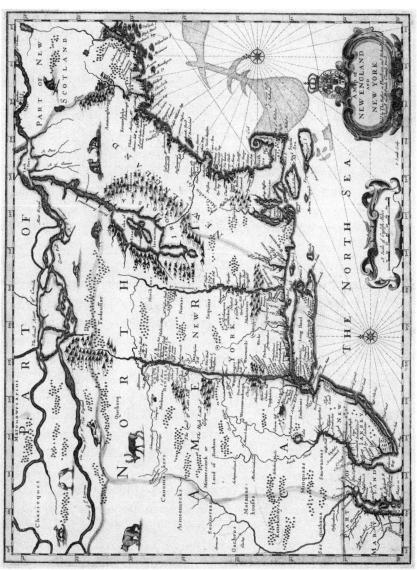

A Map of New England and New York, 1676.
New York Public Library Digital Collections.

at all but, even if it had been, they insisted that they had not actually "purchased" the lands. The initial two acquisitions, they insisted,
had been grants or gifts and the rest was merely a foreclosure on a
mortgage. Winthrop's efforts to secure a charter in London were
thus also part of a project to receive royal support for declaring the
Atherton lands to fall within Connecticut's borders. The only recourse
Providence Plantations had left, it would seem, was to secure a renewed charter of its own, though, much like Isaac Allerton decades
earlier had discovered on behalf of New Plymouth, Rhode Island
agent John Clarke complained that acquiring a charter required a
"silver key" and a "private entrance way" that the Connecticut governor seemed to have and he apparently did not.[11]

Coming to an apparent compromise with Winthrop, Clarke did
eventually get a charter for his colony, now incorporated as *The
Governor and Company of the English Colony of Rhode Island and
Providence Plantations in New England in America.*[12] There was,
however, a catch. Hoping that it would smooth the way for the
Crown to intervene in the Narragansett dispute, the Rhode Islanders
had agreed that their charter would for the first time explicitly allow
for the right to appeal intercolonial disputes to the Crown.[13] To that
point, the New England corporations had jealously guarded their
independence and autonomy from such oversight, but the move cornered Winthrop into agreeing to a royally appointed commission to
undertake a "visitation." It was a capitulation of no small consequence for a corporation, as it implied the Crown might have a say
over its internal governance and regulation, in the same sense that
a "board of visitors" might do today. The common law arguably
gave the King such rights in theory over corporations he created, but
that he held such power abroad, in willfully independent New
England no less, was hardly a matter of consensus. Whatever its implications in the long term, at the moment Winthrop found himself
compelled to make "submission to any alteration" to the border issue
that Crown deputies might command, "as if no Charter were then
passed to them."[14]

Still, even then, this was easier declared than done. The royal commission, headed by Richard Nicolls, arrived in New England in
1664 with a laundry list of objectives. It was to investigate over two
dozen affronts to royal authority allegedly committed by Massachusetts and settle possession of the newly acquired colony of New

York. The commission was also to determine a dispute between this new colony and Connecticut over eastern Long Island, where still into the 1670s, some inhabitants could be found wanting to be part of neither but rather made into a "free Corporation" unto themselves. As far as the Narragansett issue went, the commission found the Atherton purchases to be fraudulent and void and declared them to be within a royal territory of "King's Province" under Rhode Island's administration. Still, the Atherton planters had one more move to make. They simply refused to leave. Rather than escalate the conflict into violence, the Nicolls commission, at Winthrop's urging, agreed to confirm them in their private property, even if the English colonists—though certainly not the Narragansett—now agreed that the property fell within Rhode Island.[15]

This drawn-out affair was only one of the more complex and scandalous of what had become a prolific and pervasive strategy of dispossessing indigenous territories by rendering them the property of joint-stock companies and towns. Such was the effect of the New England Company's borderland "praying towns"; at one point, Winthrop went so far as to propose the creation of a large joint-stock farm that would employ and Christianize Native Americans, provide a "vending store" for commodities for sale in England, and raise revenues for further missions. "The way to raise such a stock," he argued, "may be by motion from the corporation; not, as in former transactions, by a collection of a stock in a free gift by way of charity, but only a supply for valuable consideration." To Winthrop, joint stock, not philanthropy, was the key to sustaining plantation and proselytization alike.[16]

It was not just that companies and joint-stock towns could pool resources more effectively than private individuals, though they certainly could do that. They also served to help legitimize the accumulation of indigenous lands in English and colonial law. Like in Rhode Island, almost all the North American English colonies eventually came to have some form of prohibition on "private persons" making treaties or purchases of indigenous territory without any form of authority to do so. The Atherton Company, perhaps because it was not in any formal sense a corporation, evaded the issue by insisting it had not in fact made purchases. In other cases, the public status of joint-stock land and town companies, however, were what justified their acquisition of native property in the first place. This at least was the issue at stake in a dispute that ensued in the 1680s, when several people came forward claiming to have purchased land in Connecticut and Massachusetts from the executors of the estate of one John Wompas. Wompas was a Harvard-educated Nipmuc land speculator and mariner who claimed to have received vast tracts of land through his wife, Ann Prask, the daughter of the Nipmuc sachem Romanock. Wompas had spent decades trying to make good on his claims, eventually securing patents from Charles II to such effect. When he died, he bequeathed lands to various friends and associates, including a large parcel to be managed by two executors, merchant Edward Pratt and sailor John Blake. The two men proceeded to sell off the lands to other English colonists, including portions that were located in what its current owners regarded as the town of Fairfield.[17]

When the occupants refused to yield, the purchasers sued. Before a jury in Fairfield, William Pitkin, the lawyer for two residents, insisted that they rightly held their lands by a grant from the town of Fairfield, for which they could produce deeds. The town claimed its rights, in turn, from conquest of the Pequot fifty years earlier. This was confirmed both by a treaty and purchase effected by Roger Ludlow, a veteran of the Pequot War and Connecticut's first Lieutenant Governor, and by a subsequent grant from the Connecticut General Court, which exercised its authority by virtue of the colony's charter. Thus, the Fairfield residents' private property was secured, Pitkin insisted, by layers of public corporate protections. Conversely, even if Wompas's original claims were to be considered legitimate—though he offered many arguments why they were not—as "particular Persons" Pratt and Blake could not have inherited indigenous lands, nor could the subsequent purchases from them be considered valid.[18]

The legal prohibition on private bargains with indigenous peoples was certainly intended as a pragmatic measure, a matter of policy to "prevent misunderstandings, disputes, and fraud in connection with the extinguishment of Indian title to land, and also to prevent the undue dispersion of settlers."[19] Yet it derived from legal and theoretical principles that went back to those canon law proscriptions on commercial or political interaction with "infidels" that had animated arguments for decades in favor of exclusive corporate charters for overseas ventures. As East India Company governor Josiah

Child had argued just a couple of years earlier, to give over traffic and intercourse with the non-Christian world to the "divided, various, and contrary interests" of "raw and private Persons" was "madness."[20] In fact, at the same time the Fairfield landowners were defending their territory, back in London the East India Company's lawyers were making much the same argument in their own suit against an alleged interloper, Thomas Sandys.[21] Though it is not clear if Pitkin was aware of or thinking about the case before King's Bench, he explicitly acknowledged the comparison. "In the Turkey, Guiney, East India corporations the trade is restrained to the company," he maintained, "and without such laws no bodies politic can subsist, but interlopers would ruin all." The Wompas claimants were thus transgressing Fairfield's charter in the same way that those who traded without a license violated franchises or patents for exclusive trades. In this sense, Fairfield was claiming "no more than what all corporations almost enjoy." The jury found for his clients.[22]

Colonists across the Atlantic world employed joint-stock towns and land companies to expand their own landholdings and their colonies' boundaries at their local borders and in some cases well beyond them. By the early 1660s, a lot of these efforts seemed to focus on the lands to the south of Virginia, into the territory previously encompassed in the now largely defunct patent for "Carolana." In 1663, several Massachusetts undertakers combined with English investors in a joint stock to establish a plantation on the Charles (Cape Fear) River, claiming to have purchased tracts of indigenous land there. A year earlier, Virginia's Governor William Berkeley received instructions to encourage his colony's residents to establish New England–style towns "upon every River which must tend very much to their security and in time to their profit," and various groups of "associates" took up the charge to explore, trade, and settle Virginia's indigenous borderlands, backed by large land grants and other measures.[23] Meanwhile, among many other projects across the Caribbean, including a short-lived joint stock to settle St. Lucia, in 1663, a group of Barbadians established their own joint-stock company to explore Carolina with the hopes of establishing a colony "in the forme and manner of a County or Corporation."[24]

Both the New England and Barbados Adventurers, however, soon abandoned their projects, as they faced formidable competition from a small coterie of wealthy and politically influential peers and gentlemen in England who had acquired for themselves a charter encompassing much of what is now the Carolinas, Georgia, and Florida.[25] The Lords Proprietors of Carolina were from the outset part seigneurie, part royal council, part joint-stock company headed by eight proprietors, including Clarendon, with close connections to both Court and London's mercantile elite.[26] Its "Fundamental Constitutions" of 1669, authored by the statesman and Carolina proprietor Anthony Ashley Cooper, Lord Ashley (after 1672 the Earl of Shaftesbury), and his secretary, the philosopher John Locke, established the colony's status as a form of medieval palatinate and private manor, yet one held absolutely and governed collectively by a council with delegated forms of jurisdiction and local representation. The Fundamental Constitutions, as in similar colonies, gave the proprietors the implicit power to create "towns incorporate" and described seigneurial and baronial grants as "shares." Though Carolina government and planters would resist incorporated commercial towns into the eighteenth century, Shaftesbury and others seemed hopeful they might nonetheless be introduced to the colony. Proposing a settlement in the Duke of Albemarle's portion, Virginia colonist George Milner, for one, would make the case, like Thomas Smith in sixteenth-century Ireland and Edwin Sandys in the early Virginia Company, that there was "scarce a nation in the world (though never so barbarous or remote from the more Civilized Countries) but built their Common Fabrick with these materials." Distributing lands to private persons dangerously encouraged a "disperst manner of living" and a "disjointed multitude." Even animals knew that the "common herd" enjoyed "profit, safety, or delight," while those who were outside "this Circle or line of communication are Wolves to men, & live in a perpetuall state of war & mutuall feare of each other."[27]

The Carolina proprietors were even more attuned to the value of companies. In 1670, with the encouragement of some remaining Eleutherian Adventurers, six of the Carolina proprietors acquired a royal patent to take on government of the Bahamian settlement. Shaftesbury became Governor of the Somers Isles Company the next year and, with Locke, established a subsidiary company for trade among the three colonies.[28] Back in Carolina, the proprietors each agreed to contribute £700 to create a subsidiary fund for a settlement at Port Royal, inviting previous Barbados Adventurers to redeem their shares in those ventures for land in the colony.[29] Shaftesbury was himself a partner in a short-lived 1677 joint stock with four other proprietors, who granted themselves a monopoly to organize trade with the Westo, Cusabo, "or other Indians" as well as the Spanish at Carolina's borders.[30]

Carolina was thus a proprietary colony governed by council, which relied in various ways on joint-stock and corporate forms. The now ostensibly Crown colony of Barbados presented a similarly convoluted situation. When the second Earl of Carlisle died in 1660, the Privy Council repossessed his charter, though the King evidently made a mess of things by appointing two different men as governor: Francis Willoughby, to whom Carlisle had subleased the patents in the 1640s, and the current governor, Thomas Modyford. The Attorney General also received petitions from William Courteen's heirs, renewing his original claims of discovery on the island, but seems to have ignored them. Meanwhile, the status of all the other many Caribbee Islands in the patent, sub-proprietorships in some form or another, remained ambiguous. Willoughby, who retained his personal proprietorship in the colony of Surinam, eventually emerged triumphant. He issued a proclamation on the island declaring the patents void, though one inhabitant could not help observe the irony in the fact that he had to use his authority under those patents to do so. The Privy Council had also made it clear that half the island's revenues would now be allocated to compensating Carlisle's heirs.[31] The entire arrangement proved so fraught that within a decade, the colony's assembly (as in Virginia also) would make an unsuccessful bid to obtain a new charter, several times petitioning to be restored as a "body corporate" with similar rights as had been granted originally to Carlisle. In particular, they wanted the ability to choose their own governor annually, "in the mode of a Corporation," as one islander reported it, "as New England doth."[32]

Willoughby soon lost his proprietorship in Surinam, when it was captured by Dutch invasion and ceded by the terms of the Treaty of Breda that ended the second Anglo-Dutch War. In exchange for abandoning it (along with the East India Company's claims to Pulo Run), the English Crown secured the Dutch West India Company's colony of New Netherlands, which was promptly rebranded by its new proprietor, James, Duke of York, after himself, as New York.[33] A proprietary colony that had been formerly governed by a Dutch company and whose major eponymous port and city retained the urban corporate constitution it had in its former life as New Amsterdam rendered the colony, as one historian put it, "part proprietary, part corporation, part country, and part replica of the whole of England."[34] The Duke of York also received in his grant the region to the south, formerly covered in Edmund Plowden's "New Albion" patents, which came to be known as New Jersey. He promptly sub-granted the proprietorship to two Stuart loyalists, Sir George Carteret and Lord Berkeley (who not incidentally were also Carolina proprietors). In 1674, Berkeley sold off his portion to Edward Byllinge, but a dispute between Byllinge and his agent led the two fellow Quakers to submit to arbitrators, who, as trustees for the proprietorship, agreed with Carteret formally to split the colony in two. The trustees divided their portion, West Jersey, into one hundred divisible shares, with Byllinge keeping a significant portion. When he died in 1687, his heirs sold these to the London physician, natural philosopher, and speculator Daniel Coxe, who, after a stint as absentee governor, in 1692 sold substantial his land holdings and his twenty shares in "Hereditary Government" to a London-based joint-stock land and commercial company, the *West Jersey Society*. In the meantime, when Carteret died in 1682, he left East Jersey in the hands of trustees on behalf of his widow, who promptly sold it to a dozen adventurers, mostly Quakers, who in turn split their holdings into twenty-four divisible shares.[35]

As joint-stock enterprises, the two Jerseys were distinct governments, which continued nonetheless to be intertwined with one another and other colonies. The West Jersey Society owned two shares in East Jersey, also acquired from Coxe. Meanwhile, another East Jersey share was taken up by West Jersey trustee William Penn, who in 1681 had secured his own proprietary charter for a vast colony just to the west of the Delaware River. Pennsylvania was another colony in the form of a feudal seigneurie, granted to Penn and his heirs in lieu of significant debts the Crown owed to his father, Admiral William Penn, personally as "true and absolute Proprietaries." Such "Powers," Penn would later argue, were "as much Property as Soil."[36] Still, as in Carolina, the avowedly anti-monopolist Penn leaned heavily on his power to patent corporations and associational joint-stock enterprises to put his powers into practice. In 1682, he offered a grant and twenty thousand acres to a *Free Society of*

Traders to take on recruiting settlers and laborers; to develop manufacturing, mining, and agricultural ventures; and to serve as Pennsylvania's agent for maintaining a "Constant friendship and trade" with the Native Americans within and at its borders. For all intents and purposes Penn's grant was a corporate patent, much as the Crown might have issued directly, granting the Free Society a name, a legal identity, the right to sue and be sued, self-governance, and succession, while also constituting the new corporation as sort of manorial lord in its own right, with the ability to convene a baronial court and court leet, "both to Promote the *Publique Good,* and to Encourage the *Private.*"[37]

Other similar enterprises followed. In 1686, Penn entertained a short-lived proposal from Daniel Coxe and nearly three dozen investors for a land grant of ten thousand acres, for a would-be "Governor and Company of the New Mediterranean Sea" to take on trade and settlement from the *de facto* western borders of the mid-Atlantic colony to its *de jure* chartered limits and perhaps beyond. Its immediate aims were to settle "a plantation or colony" near Lake Erie at Pennsylvania's northern border. From there, the adventurers were to be the main conduit for Pennsylvania's trade with Native Americans in the region, ideally undercutting competition from New York in the process. "Iff it proceed," Coxe noted to his agent, the Pennsylvania official and lawyer David Lloyd, "Itt will make your Country very considerable & bee beneficiall to ye Undertakers & Inhabitants."[38] The venture did not proceed in this form, but a decade and some later in 1699, Penn did sell sixty thousand acres to a group of 220 investors under the auspices of a *Pennsylvania Land Company.*[39] Likewise, in 1686, ten German adventurers, organized into a kind of corporate partnership through a "contract of society"—what they might have recognized as a *Gesellschaftsvertrag*—jointly bought from Penn twenty-five thousand acres in addition to smaller plots in and just outside Philadelphia. They divided the land among themselves into shares. All "Real Rights & Priviledges" (and public expenses) were, however, to be held and governed in common, every thousand acres entitling its holder to ten votes. Penn also a few years later granted this "Frankfort Company" patents to establish a town, aptly called Germantown, offering, as one partner and Company agent Francis Daniel Pastorius noted in 1701, "Several Considerable

Privileges to the Germans of the Said Town by making them a Corporation, by virtue of which they looked upon themselves exempted from the Jurisdiction of ye County Court of Philadelphia."[40]

Urban corporations were, like their English brethren, intended to solve any number of problems of local self-government: maintaining common jurisdictional rights, regulating commercial exchange, resolving civil disputes and administering of criminal justice, raising revenue, and guiding the development of public works.[41] The Philadelphia corporation was chartered first in 1691 and again in 1701 to take such functions, including governing its market, licensing and regulating taverns and other forms of social life, and, above all, managing the distribution of property lots and infrastructure development. In some cases, it assumed such responsibilities directly. In many others, it facilitated the work of other bodies such as a hospital and enterprises for managing ferry services. Given the relatively small population and the intimate nature of local politics, the boundaries between the town corporation and other individual and associational bodies were rather porous.[42]

Yet, unlike in England, where corporations emerged over time as an expression of local autonomy, for their part colonial authorities seemed to think of incorporation not as a check but as an extension of their central authority.[43] Penn certainly saw Philadelphia in such a light, as did Charles Calvert in Maryland, who granted St. Mary's City a charter in 1668 in the hope that spreading chartered cities across the proprietorship would generate loyalty and respect for authority.[44] Charles II and his advisors—who would by the early 1680s come to prosecute a series of *quo warranto* suits to unseat refractory leadership in a number of English corporations, including London—displayed similar ambitions at Tangier; its charter in August 1668 announced the new incorporated town as "the most likely Meanes to advance our Free-Port, diminish our Charge, and invite Inhabitants and Commerce thither."[45] The East India Company's cynicism was more explicit. It had incorporated its fortified southeastern Indian port of Madras in 1687 with "some priviledges & preheminencies by Charters under our Seal that might please them (as all men are naturally with a little power)" with the ultimate goal to "make a publick advantage of them without abating essentially any part of our own Dominion."[46]

In most cases, things did not go according to plan. Within just a few years of its chartering in 1701, Philadelphia, James Logan warned Penn, paid "too little regard" to him or his interests and constituted "too much of an *imperium in imperio* for so young a place"; Logan recommended that he "destroy or humble" it immediately.[47] In 1674, the Tangier commissioners similarly chastised the mayor and recorder that though "Civill Power and government being constituted soe independent from the Military and the Corporation dignified with a Royal Charter," the corporation would do well to respect the "Dignity of the King's Authority."[48] Soon, such recalcitrance turned to apathy, as it appeared difficult to impose corporations from above or create them, in historian Phil Withington's words, "willy-nilly," without the organic and rather long-developed civic bonds that characterized their opposite numbers in Britain.[49] Germantown's original government was essentially defunct by 1706. Not long after, the Philadelphia council similarly could barely find anyone willing to take up office and resorted to issuing fines and penalties to people for failing to do so; by midcentury, much of the day-to-day governing of civic life had fallen to voluntary associations and other corporations.[50] At both Tangier and Madras, town governments were easily infiltrated by garrison and company officials. "There are, or were, a Corporation," the interloper Alexander Hamilton reported on a visit to the South Indian colony in the 1710s, but that "scurvy way is grown obsolete" and had become a "Farce."[51]

THE CORPORATION IS DEAD, LONG LIVE THE CORPORATION

As with other colonial proprietors, the Crown—and especially the King's brother, James, Duke of York—seemed eager to embrace overseas corporate ventures, clearly imagining they could be mobilized and manipulated to both augment royal coffers and expand royal power. This did not always work out well. An attempt to revive a royal fisheries company in the form of a chartered *Governor and Company of the Royal Fishing of Great Britain and Ireland,* with James at least nominally at the helm, soon faltered and devolved into a nexus of confused and confusing lottery, mint, tax farm, and banking schemes. An attempt to bring it back in 1677 was hampered by controversy over whether it should primarily be a company of "adventurers and undertakers" or a more state-run enterprise (its first fleet was also sunk by French privateers), while its third incarnation was little more than a front for a joint-stock land bank scheme that collapsed in 1683.[52] In September 1661, James, in conjunction with several merchants and courtiers, received patents to incorporate a *Morocco Company,* likely as a joint stock, with a thirty-one-year exclusive trade and fortification on the northwestern African coast and supported in part by royal customs revenues. Despite its powerful patron, the effort was stiffly opposed by Tangier officials and merchants, who saw the company as an interloper. Nathaniel Luke, the secretary to the colony's royal governor, argued the venture represented only the "interests" of "particular men," who, if allowed, would undermine the nascent colony's efforts to expand trade and revenue and, as the merchant Thomas Povey added, to "begett a good correspondency with the Moores."[53]

The Morocco venture never materialized. It was, however, folded into an even more ambitious project chartered in 1660, *The Company of Royal Adventurers into Africa.* With the Guinea Company's patents set to expire in 1662, Nicholas Crispe, who had had his share in the older venture theoretically restored at the Restoration, seemed content to concede his supposed rights to its west African fortifications in exchange for £20,000, which, despite becoming a shareholder himself, he was apparently never fully paid. The East India Company, which had essentially been leasing them since 1657, tried to negotiate a way to remain there, but was compelled to sell off its property and abandon its claims at Fort Cormantin, Winneba, and Cape Coast Castle to the new concern.[54] The Royal Adventurers was initially closely tied to and led by members of the royal family, including James as well as Prince Rupert, who would himself soon take a great interest in the proposal of two North American fur traders for a company to revive the Kirke-Alexander Canada Adventurers, incorporated in 1670 as the *Governor and Company of Adventurers of England Trading into Hudson's Bay* and similarly empowered to make war, fortify, and establish "Colonies or Plantations" and "Compacts and Agreements w[i]th the Natives" in a vast tract of North America to be known as Rupert's Land.[55]

Even Clarendon seemed to be of the opinion that the African Company might become "a Model equally to advance the Trade of *England* with that of any other Company, even that of the *East-Indies*," but only if the "gentleman adventurers" would defer to the merchants, "who understand the Mysteries of Trade."[56] Accordingly, though James remained at its helm, it was soon restructured as a broader joint stock with a somewhat expanded subscriber base and substantially expanded commercial and political powers including explicit license for "buying and selling bartering and exchanging" African slaves. Still, this did not solve its problems. Its debts grew, compounded by losses during the Anglo-Dutch War and capital shortfalls from its subscribers, including the King, who had not fully paid for their subscriptions. The Company also sold slaves in the West Indies on credit that proved impossible to recover, not least because colonial officials and judges, themselves planters and slaveowners, often impeded its agents' attempts to collect. The turn to familiar methods for raising funds, including licenses for private trade and subsidiary ventures—among them one joint-stock company for the Gambia (in which the Company was one-fifth shareholder) and another proposed for the Gold Coast—either failed or never emerged.[57]

By May 1671, the Company's General Court had approved what was essentially another restructuring plan. The Company would open a new capital stock, offering creditors shares in the company as repayment for their loans, on the condition that they discount the loans to less than half of what they were owed. Though many of the creditors rejected the deal, the Company issued the subscription anyway. This new stock being inevitably undersubscribed and underpaid, the Company was obliged to seek political and legal remedy. Its leadership surrendered its charter and received another one, which constituted an entirely new corporation. Significantly writing down the value of the existing capital and bringing in new subscriptions, this new enterprise left creditors little option but to accept shares as compensation, along with a promise of some cash payment out of the new capital raised.[58] Joint-stock organization thus allowed the Company to discharge its debt while the new charter increased its value by again expanding its jurisdictional ambit. The *Royal African Company of England* was incorporated in 1672 with command of English affairs along much of the western African coast as well as explicit rights to possess territory, make war and peace, mine specie,

and convene courts in any of its "fort or forts plantations or factories." Though its governorship was still reserved to a member of the
royal family, in almost all other respects its organization now looked
very much like the East India Company.[59] Meanwhile, the Hudson's
Bay Company similarly retained its royal patronage but evolved over
the coming decades as an independent corporation, with similar brief
to the African and East India Companies, expanding simultaneously as a trader primarily in furs and as a military, diplomatic, and
juridical enterprise amidst the forts and factories of what was now
to be known as Rupert's Land.[60]

Royal and courtly investment in companies was not quite the same
thing as a sustained attempt at a state takeover of corporate chartered enterprises. This is not to say that both Crown and Commons
were not interested in such an intervention. That job, however, fell to
a growing bureaucracy that ironically arose out of efforts permeated
by members and leaders of London's commercial corporations.[61]
The new House of Commons subcommittee on trade, which played
a prominent role in driving the Crown toward war with the Dutch
in 1664, was initially convened to address a local dispute among
clothiers with the City of London; as it exceeded its brief and turned
to examine broader and more global commercial issues, its members,
many of whom were adventurers in the major companies, relied
heavily on advocacy and testimony from those companies' leadership.[62] Likewise, the Crown's new council for foreign plantations
and another one for trade followed on the suggestions of élite merchants like Thomas Povey looking to restore the plantations councils
of the 1650s in some form.[63]

By 1670, both councils, having largely fallen into disuse, were revived with a more circumscribed membership closely tied to the
Crown and in 1672 merged into a single Council of Trade and Foreign Plantations. This revived and reinvigorated council represented
a much more active Crown effort to supervise and regulate overseas
affairs. Its instructions, likely at Shaftesbury and Locke's instigation,
gave it a broad brief to consider "the severall Advantages that may
arise unto these Our Kingdomes by Giving way (according to the
Example of other Nations) to a more open, and free Trade then that
of Companyes and Corporations" and to investigate and recommend
proceedings against the patents of "any Person, Socyety, or Corpo-

ration of Men Whatsoever." It had the power to review appointments, instructions, and laws and became a repository of information and intelligence, including a large library of books, manuscripts, atlases, maps, and charts concerning commerce and colonies. Its day-to-day business, however, was characterized less by a coherent imperial agenda than by the many petitioners who came to see it as a potential venue for resolving complaints and disputes concerning the colonial enterprises, such as Ferdinando Gorges and John Mason's grandsons, who sought to get the Council to send a special commission to intervene in their enduring battle with Massachusetts over rights to Maine and New Hampshire.[64]

The Crown soon doubled down on its efforts to assert its power over colonial enterprises by rescinding the Council's commission and in 1674 absorbing its ambit into a parallel subcommittee of the Privy Council, known as the Committee, or Lords, of Trade and Plantations. Still, its efforts were, like its predecessor, conditioned less by proactive policymaking than by the reports, petitions, and appeals brought before it both by complainants and several of its particularly animated subordinates.[65] It was the Lords of Trade, for example, that in 1676 finally sent a special commissioner to New England to address the dispute over Maine and New Hampshire as well as Massachusetts's alleged impudence over various other matters, including coinage, trade, and revenue. Over the next several decades, that commissioner, Edward Randolph, would turn out to be the most dogged advocate for diminishing the corporate and chartered colonies, his numerous reports and lobbying largely responsible for pushing the Crown to assert its authority overseas, especially in Massachusetts, which had only incensed him by arranging to buy out Gorges, preemptively settling the conflict over Maine. Back in London, Randolph stopped it from doing the same with his cousin Mason and was vindicated when the attorney general thwarted the sale, disputing Mason's rights of government. When Randolph returned to New England in 1679, he came bearing a commission declaring the plantations of Portsmouth, Exeter, Dover, and Hampton to be united under new management: a "public-private partnership," in historian Owen Stanwood's words, that confirmed Mason's title to the land and revenues as a proprietor— over the objections of many others who claimed property there—but with government vested in a new royal colony of New Hampshire.[66]

Meanwhile, a flood of petitions from planters and tenants in Bermuda soon turned the attention of the Lords of Trade to the Somers Isles Company. In this case, the campaign was largely bankrolled and orchestrated by one of the island's largest landholders, Perient Trott, who, in a bitter feud within the Company, had been both displaced from its directorship and dispossessed of much of his property. The Lords of Trade, taking up Trott's cause, offered the Company an ultimatum: submit to their arbitration or "bee left to a Tryal at Law by a Scire facius, or Quo Warranto."[67] By this point, though, it was not clear just what the "Company" was. It seemed to have only nineteen members, questionably enough to constitute a quorum on its governing council, and few of the 150 original shareholders remained invested, having sold off their property, much of it to residents of the island. Still, this "meare Rumpe of a Companie," as one Crown advisor put it, chose to face the *quo warranto,* perhaps assuming that their connections at Court would prevail. Initially, the strategy worked. The case took four years to resolve and was at one point dismissed by the judges of King's Bench as a private dispute over which the court had no proper jurisdiction. What the Company had not anticipated, though, was the commitment of the Bermudians' lawyer. Francis Burghill, perhaps out of his ambitions to assume a role in island governance, almost singlehandedly kept the suit going, funding and prosecuting it in large part on his own account. The Company's deterioration made his job somewhat easier. By 1684, when the Court finally found against the Company, its leadership had become so enervated and distracted that no one actually appeared on its behalf.[68]

Perhaps even more than its immediate effects in rendering Bermuda to royal control, the case gave voice to several alternative legal theories that would have allowed the Crown much greater latitude in asserting royal authority over colonial enterprises. In the face of the faltering *quo warranto* prosecution, Crown lawyers contrived an argument that the King might simply replace the company's governor with his own appointment, on the grounds that the island faced a clear and present existential danger posed by disorder within and threat of invasion from without. Charles I had done much the same thing, they insisted, when in the 1630s the Crown assumed authority in Barbados by default without ever initiating a formal process against Carlisle's charter. In fact, they plumbed the archives to produce a list of instances where the King had simply ignored existing patents in order to issue new ones that overlapped with or even superseded existing jurisdictions: to the Council for New England, over the Virginia Company; to the Carolina proprietors, despite Heath's still extant Carolana patent; to New Jersey, which had technically impinged on the proprietary claims of the King's own brother. Somehow, the lawyers recast the Crown's traditionally fickle and inconsistent approach to chartering as a bold assertion of prerogative right. Even Shaftesbury, though "noe Great promoter of the Royall Prerogative," found himself agreeing that "all Plantations were Creatures of the Kings making & that he might at any tyme, alter & dispose of them at his Owne will & pleasure."[69]

Though it came about in a rather tortuous manner, the ultimate success of the *quo warranto* likewise seemed to encourage those keen on similar prosecutions elsewhere. It certainly helped Randolph make his case that "his Majesty may make short work of" Massachusetts with the same strategy.[70] As in Bermuda, though, a conviction there was hardly a *fait accompli,* even if it had already succeeded a half century earlier. Massachusetts was offered opportunities to avoid the proceedings by making financial restitution to the Crown and was allowed several postponements. In fact, Randolph's *quo warranto* never proceeded, as the Sheriff of London refused to serve summons on the corporation's members, fretting that New England was "outside his liberties." In response, the Crown's lawyers reframed the prosecution instead as a writ of *scire facias.* Unlike *quo warranto,* this action was served on the corporation itself, not its members, and before the Court of Chancery, not King's Bench. The Lord Chancellor decided in the Crown's favor in October 1684, formally dissolving, in theory at least, the Massachusetts Bay Company. Emboldened, the Crown's attorneys and the Lords of Trade and Plantations would entertain similar actions over the next few years against Connecticut, Rhode Island, Maryland, Pennsylvania, Carolina, the Jerseys, and the Bahamas. James was also evidently prepared to surrender his New York charter in service of, as William Blathwayt, the Secretary to the Lords of Trade and Plantation, put it, "that Necessary union of all the English Colonies in America which will make the King great & extend his reall Empire in those parts."[71]

Such a surrender proved unnecessary. In 1685, Charles II died without a (legitimate) heir, leaving his brother to succeed him as King James II. Given his personal experience with both proprietorships and companies, it was no surprise that James saw corporations as a means to extend the Crown's own power abroad. Though they resisted some of the Crown's more aggressive efforts to intervene in their affairs, the East India Company and the Royal African Company were certainly happy to accept the enhanced political and military support that came with royal support; with James's backing, the East India Company began a much more aggressive pursuit of interlopers in Asia, which eventually led it to prosecute a disastrous war with both Siam and the Mughal Emperor.[72] Meanwhile, in the Americas, James and his advisors set out once and for all to do away with corporate independence and place the colonies under four regional viceroyalties, on the Spanish model. Only one of these, the Dominion of New England, came to fruition, sweeping away chartered government from Maine to New Jersey and fusing them with James's own personal proprietorships into a single Crown colony.[73]

On the ground, the Dominion's governor, Edmund Andros, looked to establish the authority of this new royal colony by undermining the colonies' corporate charters and the autonomy of local town government and land companies those charters had enabled. One tactic he used was to require all landowners to prove their titles and apply for a formal reconfirmation of their property rights. Not every town or landholder had such proof, and though the Massachusetts government scrambled before his arrival to issue formal grants retroactively, in the end it was difficult if not impossible for many to meet this condition, especially since, in circular fashion, Andros did not regard grants from the New England governments as valid proof of title. As two residents of the Massachusetts town of Lynn later recalled, "our Pleas of Purchase, antient possession, Improvement, Inclosure, Grant of the General Court, and our necessitous condition . . . were insignificant, and we could have no true Title unless we could produce a Patent from the King." Andros, it was said, believed that "there was no such thing as a town in the country."[74] In effect, Andros was not so much taking over colonies in New England on behalf of James II as recolonizing them. Such tactics were similar to those that had justified colonial dispossession in Ireland, the Scottish Highlands, and the East India Company's colony of Bombay, among others: creating the legal preconditions for seizing lands by either establishing their holders as enemies or traitors, or simply creating untenable conditions for proof of prior ownership.[75] As complainants from Salem later noted, to Andros, "we should not be accounted Subjects but Rebels, and treated accordingly."[76]

With eager help from Randolph among others, Andros undertook a similar assault on corporate charters and unchartered joint-stock companies, such as arresting a scheme recently launched by John Blackwell for a note-issuing land bank, not unlike the attempt a couple years earlier to revive the British Fisheries company in which he had been involved. Yet for all his ambition, however, Andros was still limited by the pluralist tapestry of North American governance. Blackwell, for example, responded by closing up shop in Massachusetts and reintroducing his bank in Pennsylvania, where Penn made him Deputy Governor.[77] In Connecticut, one resident, as the lore goes, went so far as to hide the colony's charter in a hollow oak tree in Hartford so that Andros could not actually repossess it. Even in the royalist bastion of Virginia, the House of Burgesses openly resented the Crown's growing impulse to intercede in certain legal causes, complaining, conversely, that doing so rendered them no better than "most of the Lesser, and most inconsiderable Corporations" in England.[78]

The Dominion of New England came to as swift a conclusion as the Stuart regime, with James's ouster just a few years after his accession by his daughter Mary and her husband, the Dutch *stadholder* William of Orange in 1688–89. On its face, what became known as the Glorious Revolution promised a sea change in the American colonies' relationship with the Crown. As the Dominion crumbled, royal governors panicked for want of instructions. Bostoners arrested Andros and Randolph. Rebels in New York, under the leadership of Jacob Leisler, unseated royalist Lieutenant-Governor Francis Nicholson, who promptly fled to England. Much like what had happened at the Restoration, in the next few years each of the Atlantic colonies sent agents to London to lobby for restored rights or renewed charters, while many other overseas corporations and their critics similarly scrambled to petition for either confirmation or elimination of their status. With Parliament, especially the House of Commons, assuming a leading role at the center of the British state and new Protestant monarchs agreeing to any number of reforms from a Declaration of Rights to toleration for religious dissenters, many envisioned a stark reversal of policy across the Atlantic was soon to follow.[79]

What they found in the long run was far more continuity than they had expected. As had happened with Commonwealth figures in the early Restoration, key architects of pre-1688 colonial policy—Blathwayt, Randolph, Nicholson, even Andros—stayed or returned to similar offices. The Navigation Act was renewed, and the Committee on Trade and Plantations was reformed into an arguably more aggressive and professionalized Council, or Board, of Trade and Plantations.[80] A plan to keep East and West Jersey as part of New York was only avoided by Daniel Coxe's timely intervention with the Privy Council.[81] If it was possible, Randolph seemed even more ambitious in his efforts to press the case that corporate and proprietary governments had been guilty of "High Crimes and Misdemeanors," accusing them of suborning tax evasion, smuggling, and piracy. Over the next decade the Board of Trade and Crown lawyers began inquiries into possibly undertaking *quo warranto* or *scire facias* proceedings against Jersey, which resulted in the proprietors' preemptively abandoning their charter, Rhode Island, and Carolina. Finally, in 1701, the Commons introduced a striking bill that, had it passed, would have revoked the power of government from all chartered colonies, subsuming them into a single Crown empire.[82]

Massachusetts did get a new corporate charter, which in theory not only restored it to its former status but expanded it, confirming the colony's claims over Plymouth, Maine, and Nova Scotia and reconfirming the property rights of any "person or persons, Bodyes Politique and Corporate Townes, Villedges, Colledges or Schooles" that Andros had called into question. However, as Jeremiah Dummer, future London agent for both Massachusetts and Connecticut, would reflect a couple of decades later, this new charter was "not much more than the Shadow of the old One." It asserted an unprecedented authority for the Crown to appoint the colony's governor and other key officials, as well as to review laws passed in its assembly.[83] Soon after, in 1695, the Privy Council made good on such prerogatives by disallowing the colony's attempts to reincorporate

Harvard College, primarily on the familiar grounds that they had failed to properly reserve to the Crown the right of visitation on the college. For his part, the colony's royal governor, the Earl of Bellomont, would have preferred that they drop the issue, as it was a lot of trouble for little benefit. Moreover, he observed, Crown's ultimate right of visitation over the colony made the whole affair rather superfluous. "Whenever these people abuse the King's favour," he observed, "a writ of *Quo warranto,* or an Act of Parl[iament] will reach 'em."[84]

Most fundamentally, nothing about the Glorious Revolution resolved the question as to whether a colony's corporate status rendered it an independent, self-governing, and even sovereign body politic or, as Connecticut's Gershom Bulkeley insisted, "a corporation erected by the King's charter," whose laws could be regarded as merely by-laws, "the local private, and particular orders of a corporation" ultimately subject to Crown sovereignty. For many in New England, the mere mention of taking legal action against charters conjured immediate images of Stuart absolutism. According to Bulkeley, however, Connecticut's interpretation of its corporate status was the true despotism, tantamount to its insisting it was a "supreme government" and a "free and separate empire," which in turn had allowed it to become a "Turkish, French, arbitrary and tyrannical colony." "It is no wonder," he quipped, "they met with a *Quo warranto.*"[85]

The new political environment in the wake of the Glorious Revolution, not least given the newfound power of the House of Commons, offered ample opportunity for critics of chartered companies and monopolies in particular to marshal the state to their cause. The outcomes, however, were rather mixed. The unpopular Royal Fisheries Company ultimately succumbed.[86] The Russia Company was compelled to lower its membership fee, while the Hudson's Bay Company emerged relatively unscathed and the Levant Company's monopoly was not taken up.[87] Meanwhile, a series of decisions of the Court of King's Bench and legislation in 1698 confirmed the Royal African Company's status as a corporation but denied its right to maintain exclusive control of the trade. This resulted in a victory for independent or "separate" traders, what historian Will Pettigrew has called a "statutory deregulation" by which the Company continued to operate but was obligated to sell licenses to anyone who wanted them. A dramatic explosion in the scale and scope of the British transatlantic slave trade followed.[88]

The East India Company similarly faced no shortage of critics calling for "free trade." Its primary foes, however, were not private traders but two other corporations looking not so much to eradicate the exclusive trade as to take it on. In 1698, after nearly a decade of wrangling, a group of ex-Company leadership, interlopers, and would-be investors who had been shut out of the extant Company secured through both Crown and the English Parliament a charter for a *Governor and Company of Merchants of England*—consciously and conspicuously not "London," like the "old" Company—*Trading to the East Indies*. The new association may have secured their grant through political and financial connections to the new regime but sealed it in the best way a joint-stock company knew how: by issuing a staggering £2 million in subscriptions and offering to vest that capital stock with the Crown as a loan, much like the other newly formed corporate arm of government finance, the Bank of England. "Old" Company efforts to win favor with William and Mary at their accession by transferring King James's stock to their account and providing them with a £10,000 annual "present," much as it had the late Stuart Kings, had little effect. Even more disastrous were lobbying efforts with courtiers and members of Parliament, including offers of gifts and loans to purchase stock that Company opponents easily branded as corruption; what Company officials saw as doing business as they always had done had now developed into a bribery scandal that went all the way to the Speaker of the House of Commons. Meanwhile, the "new" English Company and the Crown exported this conflict to South Asia, sending a suite of officials to set up new factories in India and a jointly credentialed ambassador to the Mughal Court, William Norris, the first since Thomas Roe nearly a century earlier. All were met with vigilant, at times violent, opposition by the "old" Company, which continued to maintain its forts and factories and dismiss the new Company as yet another wave of interlopers that sought to undermine its authority through whatever tactics "they could invent with the assistance of hell."[89]

As all this was developing, the Scottish Parliament in 1696 offered its own charter to a new enterprise, *The Company of Scotland*

Trading to Africa and the Indies. The Company was perhaps an inevitable expression of the dilemmas and tensions that arose from
the continuing fact that England and Scotland shared a monarch but
not a state, an arrangement that had largely shut Scottish investors
and merchants out of the English East India Company but also frus-
tratingly inhibited them from having a chartered company of their
own. In shifting the balance of power from Crown to Parliament in
both England and Scotland, the Glorious Revolution had made it
possible for the legislature to take the lead in issuing such a charter
rather the monarch, who was in any event preoccupied at the time
with his European war. That Scotland was a separate dominion from
England also meant that grants there did not so much violate English patents as compete with them, like any other such European
company.

At the lead of this operation was the merchant William Paterson,
who among many other schemes had been the driving force behind
the Bank of England. After being shut out of the London and Amsterdam capital markets by the machinations of the two English as
well as the Dutch East India Companies, its leadership turned primarily to Scottish investors, framing their enterprise as a national
and patriotic project. While in spirit an East India Company, its ambitions were global in scope. Fears in England of its designs on the
west African coast, for example, factored into the decision not to
abandon the Royal African Company altogether in 1698. The project
that took up almost all of its funds and attention, however, was in a
sense an old-fashioned one: to settle a colony in the Americas with
the dual goals of invading Spanish Atlantic trade while pioneering a
westward passage to Asia. Instead of looking to sail around the continents, Paterson's idea was to truck across it at its arguably shortest
point. The result was the short-lived colony of New Caledonia in
the Darien region on the east coast of Panama, an abject failure of a
project, even if it did anticipate the canal of some two centuries later.[90]

The new centrality of the Commons, the traditional bastion of
free trade, the Crown's own imperial and warmaking ambitions, and
the commerce-friendly Whig political ascendency proved a remarkably hospitable environment for critics of exclusive corporations. Yet
doing away with such corporations was another matter. Even if dam-
aged in some way, most of the seventeenth-century chartered companies endured in some form into the eighteenth century. The 1701 bill

for consolidating the American colonies failed, primarily due to the intercession of William Penn and allies from other colonies.[91] When the Jersey proprietors succumbed to Randolph's assault and finally agreed to abandon their charter in 1702, they nonetheless insisted that they keep their private property in the "soil" and rights to make further Indian purchases.[92] Having faced threats of *scire facias* or *quo warranto* for over a decade, the Bahamas proprietors finally surrendered their government to the Crown in 1717, but the colony's territorial rights were quickly re-granted as a twenty-one-year concession to a different merchant syndicate led by Woodes Rogers, who was also appointed governor. In 1719, rebels in South Carolina demanded that the Crown take over the colony, which it did, but nearly ten years later and only after purchasing almost all of the proprietors' shares for £22,500 and, in the case of one holdout, Lord Carteret, a large land grant. The Crown thus did not so much assume power in Carolina as buy it out.[93]

Into the eighteenth century, many on both sides of the Atlantic stood firm on the question of corporate colonial autonomy, even if they did so to different degrees. Penn for one seemed open to a reformed system that would render colonies more like manors or urban corporations in England, in which chartered bodies undertook civil governance while external matters, such as military affairs and customs, fell to the Crown.[94] Jeremiah Dummer in Massachusetts, however, was having none of this. "The *American* Charters are of a higher Nature and stand on a better Foot than the Corporations in *England*," Dummer insisted. Both were in a sense corporations, but the two could not have been more constitutionally different. English borough charters, he argued, "were Acts of meer Grace and Favour in the Crown," while colonial charters were more like contracts, "given as Praemiums for Services to be perform'd; and therefore are to be consider'd as Grants upon a *valuable Consideration;* which adds Weight and Strength to the Title."[95]

Dummer possibly first composed his *Defence of the New England Charters* around 1715 but published it in 1721 just as the Board of Trade was moving again to introduce measures to render chartered and proprietary governments under the "entire, absolute & immediate dependency" of the Crown.[96] In it, Dummer struck at the core of what he regarded as a fundamental legal and historical misunderstanding. Charters did not grant sovereignty. All they provided,

essentially, was "a bare *Right of Preemption*," that is, a patent to organize, make discoveries, and claim jurisdiction exclusive of other
English subjects. In turn, colonial sovereignty in America derived
from "no other Right than what is deriv'd from the native Lords of
the Soil," that is, sale or cession from indigenous peoples, acquired
by the New England companies, which had "by vast Labour and
Expence subdu'd and cultivated" it themselves. Thus, the Crown could
not resume jurisdiction in chartered colonies as it had never had such
power in the first place. Moreover, doing so without consent and
compensation was tantamount to seizing private property without
due process. It was also questionable whether Parliament could take
such measures, Dummer argued—using logic that American revo-
lutionaries would pick up on a half century later—as the American
corporations were not represented in Parliament and thus could
not consent. Finally, even if Crown or Commons were willing to pay
for a colony, figuring its worth was nearly impossible. Not only was
it exceptionally difficult to account for the risks, expense, "Disap-
pointments, and Disasters" involved in establishing and governing
plantations; as Dummer observed, "how valuable the Charters themselves are, can never be said, Liberty being inestimable." It was, quite
literally, impossible to put a price on colonial sovereignty.[97]

It was a bold argument, but in form and content it echoed many
of the defenses of corporations' private rights in public power that
had been made over the previous century. It also in a sense reflected
generations of thinking in the law of nations, often associated with
theorists like Francisco de Vitoria or Hugo Grotius, which did not
so much deny the integrity of indigenous sovereignty as insist on it,
in order to make the case that territorial and jurisdictional rights
could be legitimately abandoned, ceded, or sold to Europeans.[98]
Dummer's case for American colonial autonomy also reflected that
made on behalf of the East India, Royal Africa, Hudson's Bay,
Russia, Eastland, and other companies over the previous decades,
which rehearsed and recycled the arguments made in the controversies of the 1620s and 1630s discussed in the previous chapter. In
some cases, this was done quite literally by reprinting or reissuing
those earlier tracts; in 1664, for example, Merchant Adventurer, East
India Company, and Royal African Company leader Sir Richard
Ford advised Sir Henry Bennet, a principal secretary of state, to have
Thomas Mun's manuscript *England's Treasure by Forraigne Trade*

published to "reclaim intelligent readers from old heresies in trade."[99] More commonly, company advocates of the late seventeenth century simply made similar if not identical arguments as those earlier writers for treating the "concerns of commerce" not only as a "matter of state" but also as a form of government unto itself.[100]

For over a century, advocates for companies had extolled the public benefits of extra-European trade in similar terms to Atlantic plantation. Corporate companies with stable and inviolable privileges were key, they insisted, to revenue, security, navigation, employment, the amelioration of poverty, and the preservation of Protestantism. The Council of Trade similarly noted in its recommendation to incorporate the Fisheries Company in 1663 that "You destroy the essence of a Corporation by lymitting it, And if you lymitt it, no man will venture their Stocke."[101] The expectation of security and institutional permanence was, however, not only a fiscal principle but a fundamental political truth. "Generally in all Human Affairs," Charles Davenant observed, "No Society of Trading Men can bring about any great Thing for the Common Good, who think themselves but in a precarious and momentary Possession of their Rights and Privileges." Like governments or great houses, estates, and titles of dignity, he noted, such institutions needed to be "render'd Immortal," otherwise "'tis a Question (notwithstanding Humane Reason), whither we should have any more Laws, Politie, Arts, Designs or Contrivance, than Flies or Summer Insects."[102]

Even if it were not the case that charters had to be sacrosanct for them to have any meaning, they would nonetheless still be protected, like Dummer's Massachusetts, as property. At the least, withdrawal or modification of a corporation would call for, as Nicholas Crispe's grandsons insisted in 1709, the company or its heirs to "receive Compensation for their Forts and Castles."[103] It was, however, perhaps just as difficult to put a value on something like the East India Company, which operated in both "Publick, as Private Capacityes," as it was for Massachusetts. The Company had ships, factories, forts, and goods. Yet the Company's assets also arguably included a "perpetuall Inheritance" in the English proprietorships of Bombay and St. Helena from the Crown and *farmans,* grants, leases, and agreements from various Asian sovereigns for Madras, Cuddalore, Bengkulu, and most recently Calcutta, not to mention government over the people that lived in all those places. All of these, the Company argued, would be lost if they were not given a "Legall existence" and "continued a Corporation."[104] "What reasonable Compensation," one East India Company author opined, "can be made for the dead Stock, the Forts, Factories, Arms, Ammunition, Phirmaunds and Priviledges, acquired, improved, recovered, and maintained by a vast Expence? And with what Equity can this be done without it?"[105] It was also hardly clear that treaties, agreements, and grants, let alone sovereign commands like a Mughal *farman*, were even transferable.[106] "For if the Companies fall," as one Eastland Company author expressed it, "their Priviledges must necessarily fall with them."[107]

This argument continued to be deeply vested in racial and spatial distinctions between the Christian and non-Christian world. "On this side of the Line," that is, in Europe, Charles Molloy wrote in 1677, exclusive rights to "voluntary Associations, or single Traders" would certainly "result into Monopolies, if incorporated."[108] But in places which by their "distance, or Barbarity, or non-Communication with the *Princes of Christendom*," as Josiah Child put it, "*Companies of Merchants* are absolutely necessary."[109] Where to locate such a "line," however, was always a matter of interpretation. Someone like Thomas Povey could thus support exclusive armed companies in the west Indies and west Africa while regarding the same in Morocco, where there was a nearby royal garrison and colony, as both unnecessary and noxious.[110] Opponents of the short-lived Canary Company— whose charter was granted in 1664 but was surrendered three years later—similarly argued for an open wine trade without opposing chartered monopolies *per se;* as they insisted, the Royal African and East India Companies might be appropriate for trade "with a barbarous People," but the same could not be said of a colony already under a European government.[111] For the Hudson's Bay Company, the threats from both the "Savage *Indians*" and "Potent Rivals the *French*" justified the kind of exceptional investment in arms and infrastructure that could only be managed "but by a *Company* in a *Joynt Stock*."[112]

The Hudson's Bay Company was not alone, as a growing number of joint-stock companies, or proposed companies, emerged in the late seventeenth and early eighteenth centuries to take on commercial and territorial expansion, especially at the southern and western boundaries of the North American colonies. Randolph warned that those in Carolina who aimed to "carry on the Government and the Indian Trade together" had rendered it "absolutely necessary to convince the world the great mischeifes which will arise to England by permitting these little Commonwealth Governments to continue distinct from the Crown."[113] Both the deposed governor of the Bahamas Cadwallader Jones and the Admiralty Judge and former Carolina Governor Robert Quary proposed to Virginia, and later Carolina, Governor Francis Nicholson the creation of exclusive chartered joint-stock companies for "Trade with the Westerne Indians that lye behind *Virginia* and *Carolina*." (Jones's "Company of Gentleman adventurers" seemed to be conceived particularly on the model of the Hudson's Bay Company.) Another proposal suggested managing the Native trade through a universal public colonial company, a "joynt stock of all Inhabitants," each contributing "according to their capacities" and sharing proportionally in the dividends.[114] "A Public Stock for the use of ye Publick," some in Carolina maintained, was critical for both prosecuting and "regulateing the Indjan Trade."[115] In 1719, the Pennsylvanian William Keith would similarly try, and fail, to acquire from King George I a patent to place lands in western Virginia "under a proper form of government" and settle them with Swiss and German protestants in a colony he proposed to call, after the King, the "Province of Georgia."[116]

The most ambitious of these projects came from none other than Daniel Coxe, who, undeterred by the failure of the New Mediterranean venture, realized that instead of the costly and uncertain process of soliciting for a charter, he could buy one that already existed; as luck would have it, there was one for sale. The vast 1629 patent for Carolana, originally granted to Robert Heath, had never been employed but neither, despite subsequent grants to others including the Carolina proprietors, had it ever been formally canceled or surrendered. In the interim, it had been sold and inherited several times and augmented along the way with the lands of one of its erstwhile owners, the Duke of Norfolk, in southern Virginia.[117] Coxe managed to buy it from its current owner, Arthur Shaen, at which point he set out to establish a joint-stock company to fund and operate a colony he imagined would be populated by Huguenots and other Protestant European refugees, the poor, and convicts somewhere in the North American interior. He envisioned this enterprise eventually blossoming into a "New Empire," which could counter French continental expansion and extend both commerce and the gospel to Native Americans, ideally in partnership with the New England Company. The initial proposal, drawn up for Coxe by James Spooner, was for an "Imperiall Compa[ny]" to manage its entire territory in common, funded by an incredible eighty thousand shares, one quarter of which were to be given to an original fourteen proprietors—it is not clear who if anyone Coxe had in mind—as well as upwards of a thousand associates of nobility, clergy, and gentlemen with 100 shares each, "the only Method that can spread it all over the Kingdome and make it exceeding Greate." The balance of the shares would be sold to anyone who wanted to invest.[118] The result was a petition to the Board of Trade in November 1699 for what he was now calling a "Florida Company," with "as ample Concessions Powers Priviledges Liberties Benefits and Advantages as have been granted to other Trading Companies and Corporations." He also proposed establishing a subsidiary London-based joint stock, much like the magazine companies in early Virginia and elsewhere, to supply the colony and profit from its commerce.[119]

Such plans seemed quixotic even by the standards of early eighteenth-century America. "By what he told me concerning his ill success of his Jersey proprietorship," Nicholson reported, "I thought he had done with all such projects; but I am afraid several people have abused the Doctor's good nature and generosity by telling him of strange countries and giving him maps thereof."[120] The Board of Trade showed equal skepticism. Apprehensive of how Spain would regard such an enterprise, it suggested to Coxe that he should instead first pursue a more modest project on his lands in Norfolk County. Coxe, protesting that this would violate his promises to his investors and planters, sent some ships to prospect for a place to establish a colony in Florida or the interior anyway. He nonetheless eventually heeded the Board's demands, focusing his subsequent efforts on raising funds for a settlement in the borderlands between Virginia and Carolina in partnership with London and the Church of England.[121]

These unfulfilled or aborted proposals did, however, finally find expression in an actual, if short-lived, company chartered by the Virginia Assembly in 1714. Supported vigorously by the colony's Lieutenant Governor Alexander Spotswood, the joint-stock *Virginia*

Indian Company was assigned territory on the colony's southwestern border and a twenty-year exclusive right over trade with the Sioux and Iroquois nations. Virginia also provided the Company use of the purpose-built Fort Christanna, on the Meherrin River, from which it was to offer "protection" to nearly three hundred Saponi and other Sioux nations that soon after settled in its environs. It was charged with building an Indian school, both to educate and convert indigenous children, as well as—using the practice of other English colleges like the College of William and Mary—to keep them, in Spotswood's word, as "hostages" to safeguard those commercial and political alliances.[122]

The Virginia Indian Company immediately met opposition from those who had competing interests or ambitions in the Indian trade, Spotswood's political enemies, or both. Spotswood and the Company mounted arguments in their defense that were remarkably similar to those made on behalf of the New England corporations and the East India, Royal African, and other companies. Spotswood insisted that the Indian Company was required to arrest the damage that had been done by trade with the Saponi and others having fallen into the "private hands" of "loose people" who had "no Stock of their own." Their "fraud," as well as unrestrained firearms trade, was undermining not only commerce but also the colony's admittedly already largely impotent attempts to exert diplomacy and control over the indigenous populations of the southwest in the wake of the Tuscarora War of the early 1710s. To opponents' complaints that the company was an illegal monopoly, Spotswood and others argued, just like their English counterparts, that private trade was the truly restricted commerce, as more colonists benefited as investing shareholders than would or could ever partake of the trade on their own. Ultimately, the Company's critics prevailed. Allies in London persuaded the Board of Trade and the Privy Council to void the company's charter. Meanwhile, when Spotswood's opponents took control of the Virginia assembly, they voted to abandon Fort Christanna altogether. Its Saponi residents were forced to disperse as far as Carolina and Pennsylvania, with some ending up on Spotswood's own estates, as the now "open" trade, much as he had predicted, ironically was soon dominated by a few unincorporated partnerships with *de facto* regional monopolies.[123]

As short-lived as it was, the Virginia Indian Company, and especially its project for an Indian college, was a present reminder of the ways in which corporations played a central role not only in managing trade and expansion into indigenous territory but also in extending Protestant religion and education among Native Americans as well. In addition to new colleges and universities like William and Mary, the Anglican *Society for the Propagation of the Gospel in Foreign Parts,* incorporated in 1701 (and funded in part by claims on Robert Boyle's endowment) sought to fund and further missionary work across the Atlantic world. The *Society in Scotland for Propagating Christian Knowledge,* incorporated by charter in 1709 to do similar work in the Scottish highlands and outer isles, similarly extended its brief after 1717 to "heathen and infidel lands."[124] Incorporation protected the endowments and self-government of such bodies, yet the events of the previous several decades had cast some light on the form's limitations. Thomas Bray and other early leaders of England's Society for the Promotion of Christian Knowledge, for example, initially thought to seek incorporation, noting the legal and political protections it offered bodies like the Royal Society and other charitable bodies, like the Sons of the Clergy, but ultimately decided to remain a "society of private gentlemen," believing that a charter would too closely define their purposes and limit their flexibility to diversify its activities over time. The strategy did turn out to be somewhat prescient. While its sibling SPG remained bound by its charter to remain in the Atlantic world, the English SPCK was able to branch out into a wide variety of enterprises at home, in Europe, and even in South India, where it cultivated partnerships at both the Danish East India Company's settlement at Tranquebar as well as English Madras.[125]

A BUNDLE OF ARROWS KNIT FAST TOGETHER

Following its near-death experience in the 1690s, both in British politics and its disastrous war with the Mughal Empire, the English East India Company entered the eighteenth century perhaps on a stronger footing than ever. It expanded its maritime establishment and reinvested in its fortified settlements, especially its newest one

at Calcutta, acquired as a Mughal *zamindari* (landholdership) in the
1690s. This recovery in Asia was reinforced by a renewed foundation for the Company in Britain. By 1702, the battle between the
two English East India Companies had largely been settled. Despite
orders to do so, the "old" Company had never actually wrapped up
its business but instead survived through a highly corporate move:
subscribing £315,000 in the new Company to become its largest
shareholder. This not only tied the companies together but also became yet another legal argument against the viability of withdrawing
its charter. After all, eliminating the "old" Company would have
been tantamount to summarily seizing the property its 1,200 adventurers held not only in their charter and possessions in Asia but
now in the "new" Company as well. These legal maneuvers—
combined with the clearly untenable and embarrassing situation of
having two exclusive English companies viciously competing in
India—demanded some kind of accommodation.[126]

After several years under a joint managerial system, in 1709 the
two corporations combined to become the *United Company of Merchants of England Trading to the East Indies*. By the terms of the
merger agreement, to which the Lord Treasurer was also party, this
United Company was, by combining their stocks and raising new
investment, to increase its capital stock to £3.2 million, still perma-
nently loaned, with a guaranteed return of five percent interest, to
the government.[127] Meanwhile, the Company of Scotland was eliminated by the terms of another treaty of union: that of England and
Scotland, whose Parliaments merged to create Great Britain in
1707—a union some historians have argued was impelled in the first
place, on the Scottish side at least, by the financial collapse that followed in the wake of the failed Darien colony scheme.[128]

An adventurer in the East India Company was now an investor
in the British national debt. This had profound effects. The public
security of the Company's capital stock ensured the continued high
price of its shares, making it arguably the most stable and valuable
stock in a bustling financial market. It also made the Company un-
assailably creditworthy, which allowed it to take on great amounts
of debt, largely in loans from the Bank of England and its own bond
issues, which reached a height of about £6 million in the early eighteenth century.[129] Both the Bank, the other great corporation managing government debt, and the Company had thus become, in the

words of one historian, "like fiscal departments of government," which, like many government departments, worked both together and in competition with one another for position, privileges, and resources.[130] At the same time, such a model of public finance, where a shadow polity mediated the relationship between the state and its people, was potentially the very problem of the commonwealth being made private about which Robert Kayll had warned a century earlier. "Monied companies," as Edmund Burke would note several decades later, proceeded "upon a principle of their own, distinct from, and in some respects contrary to, the relation between prince and subject. It is a new species of contract superinduced upon the old contract of the state."[131] At the same time, it became one critical venue in which the nation itself was being forged, as over the coming century, Scottish and Irish investors, soldiers, surgeons, merchants, and administrators famously came to "colonize" the Company in great numbers, now as "British" subjects.[132]

Though extraordinary in its reach and scope, the East India Company's early eighteenth-century expansion was part of a much larger "Financial Revolution," which in the wake of the Glorious Revolution had given rise to an active market in stock companies as well as a frenzy of opportunities for investments in loans, annuities, bonds, lotteries, and similar instruments. It was not just the number of such projects and schemes that was revolutionary but the fact that they increasingly found a market not only among the landed aristocracy, gentry, and élite overseas traders but also merchants, artisans, professionals, officeholders, and other men and many women often accounted among the "middling sorts."[133] "Shareholding," as one historian put it, "became a fact of life" by the 1690s.[134]

Especially popular among these investment instruments were the securities and debentures floated by various government departments to raise money during the Nine Years' War. Responding to growing questions over government's ability to pay its obligations, in 1700 Parliament offered debt holders an opportunity to redeem them instead for some of the nearly one million acres of Irish land confiscated of Jacobite "Rebels and Traytors" during the war. The Act retroactively vacated the nearly two-thirds of a million acres that William III had granted personally to supporters, vesting the land as the "actual and real Possession and Seisen" of thirteen trustees, empowered to restore what they determined to be legitimate claims on confiscated estates and sell off what remained "to any person or persons, Bodies Politick or Corporate," including through debt-for-land swaps.[135]

As with earlier enterprises in Ireland (among other places), several joint-stock schemes emerged with the general idea of buying up individuals' debt in exchange for company shares, exchanging that debt *en masse* for Irish estates, and then managing those estates to raise rents and revenue with which to pay out dividends to shareholders. In this way, individuals could in theory profit from their landholdings without taking them on directly, while the companies could leverage economies of scale without having to expend any actual money. Several proposals offered variations on this theme. One floated the idea of exchanging debt for stakes in a lottery. Another imagined a single "*English* Protestant Company" for the "Publick Good" that would take over all the land in the hands of the trust, "Single Purchasers being Parallel to a loose Heap of Arrows, which taken one by one can easily be all broke to pieces tho never so Numerous," while "a Company resembleth a Bundle of Arrows knit fast together, which cannot be hurt by an hundred times the Force which serveth to crush the other."[136]

Creating a new company was, however, an expensive, time-consuming, and uncertain process. Why not just repurpose an existing one? This was the idea of a group of bankers, including George Caswall, Elias Turner, and Jacob Sawbridge, and the scrivener John Blunt, who found their answer in the *Governor and Company for Making Hollow Sword Blades in England*. The obscure company had been chartered in 1691 to capitalize on a very brief bull market in domestic sword making in the wake of a ban on French imports at the outset of the Nine Years' War, but it had not done business in some time and in fact no longer even owned its foundry. The new investors, however, had no interest in swords. What they wanted was the corporation's capacities to act at law, hold property, and issue shares. Under this new leadership, the Sword Blade Company proceeded to sell £200,000 of stock, not for cash but rather in exchange for individuals' army debentures. In turn, the Company redeemed those debentures for Irish lands. By 1703, the Sword Blades Company had become, at least on paper, the seventh largest joint-stock company in England and one of the largest landlords in Ireland.

Its anticipated windfall, however, never materialized. Tenants refused to pay, titles were tied up in challenges in Irish courts, and the Company faced opposition in Ireland, especially among those justifiably concerned about the outsize political power such a shady corporation might wield. Though its leadership attempted several remedies, the Company eventually had to sell off its holdings, much to one of its own directors, reformulating into a financing operation, now known as the Sword Blade Bank. They also took a stab at a Sword Blade Coffee House, a Sword Blade Fire insurance scheme, and, in 1711, their most ambitious gambit: to convert government debt into stock in a company for commerce, colonization, and predation in the heart of New Spain.[137]

The idea for a corporation like the East India Company to secure trade in Spanish America was not especially novel. In a way, this had been the goal of the Company of Scotland, which, as it was crumbling in 1701, Paterson proposed to revive under the auspices of an English chartered company "managed by a national council of trade, or by particular undertakers, or by both." During the War of the Spanish Succession from 1702 to 1713, others, including Daniel Defoe, floated similar ideas, while the supposedly anti-monopolist Whig ministry had agreed in the 1707 Treaty of Barcelona to a secret clause that left open the possibility for a joint Anglo-Spanish monopoly company should Charles, the Hapsburg claimant to the Spanish monarchy, be successfully installed on the throne at the conclusion of the war. (Not to be outdone, his Bourbon rival Philip responded with a proposal for a south Atlantic company of his own, supported and managed by a transnational constituency of Dutch, French, Spanish, and British merchants.)[138]

What was somewhat innovative was the notion of combining this sort of Atlantic commercial and colonial corporation with government finance, which again owed much to the model established recently by the East India Company. The Sword Blade group was able to agree with Robert Harley, Queen Anne's chief minister, that the time was right for such a project. The resulting *Governor and Company of Merchants of Great Britain Trading to the South Seas and other Parts of America, and for Encouraging the Fishery,* incorporated by statute and charter in the early summer 1711, was a shrewd, indeed inspired, effort by Harley and Blunt and company to transform state finance by, in the words of historian Carl Wennerlind,

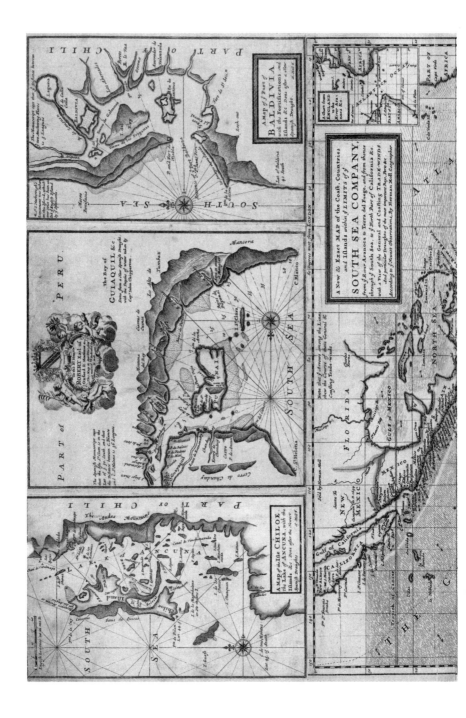

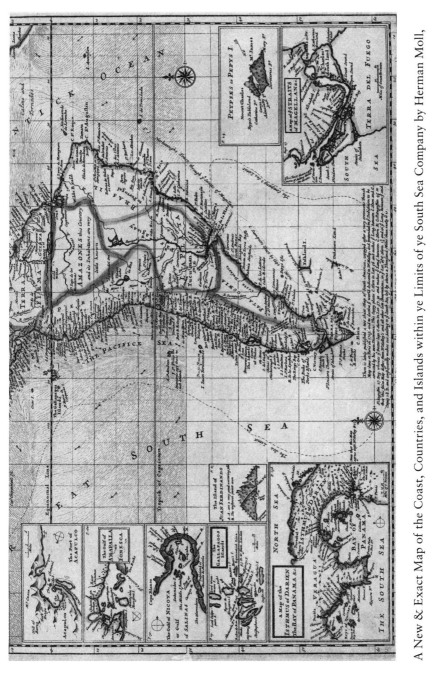

A New & Exact Map of the Coast, Countries, and Islands within ye Limits of ye South Sea Company by Herman Moll, 1736. New York Public Library Digital Collections.

"harnessing the English fascination with the Atlantic world."[139] The South Sea Company's management of state debt was directly integrated and in theory underwritten by slave trading as well as commercial enterprises including fisheries and naval supply. In time, the Company would come to express designs for colonial settlements as far afield as Minorca, St. Kitts, and Nova Scotia, not to mention continued interest in Northwest Passage ventures. Mergers were contemplated with both the Royal African and East India Companies. The most tragic irony was that the Company was also to be a licensed smuggling and predation venture in New Spain, which in 1713 became in essence a Spanish franchisee when it assumed responsibility for managing the *asiento,* a thirty-year concession for operating New Spain's slave trade that British negotiators had secured by the terms of the Treaty of Utrecht that concluded the war. The Company, in turn, subcontracted providing those slaves to the Royal African Company.[140]

Though many of these grand plans never came to pass, the South Sea Company was nonetheless provocative from the very start. First of all, its legitimately confusing and opaque consolidation of various government securities, cash purchases, loans, and other credit instruments fulfilled all the worst fears of those who had been arguing that corporations were slippery entities that could not be held responsible for their debts, let alone their actions.[141] If one traditional critique of joint-stock companies was that they compelled their members into conforming to the directions of a small directorship, this was worse, as it did the same to British subjects, compelling holders of government debt like "a High-way Man demanding Money with a Pistol in his Hand" to become shareholders in a commercial company with a business plan that seemed as plausible as a "Voyage to the *World in the Moon.*"[142] Many thought it was foolish to imagine that a trading company whose main markets were in colonies of hostile European powers would not inevitably become a colonial enterprise; as Defoe characterized the objection, "Conquering Nations is a Work which does not belong to Merchants and Companies."[143] Meanwhile, the East India Company regarded the new Company's vaguely defined jurisdiction into the Pacific as a violation of its charter, while neither it nor the Bank of England were any too happy about having this new competitor in the government debt business.[144]

If the South Sea Company was so controversial, however, it was also because it was so popular. Many welcomed the Company as a kind of one-stop shop for bolstering public credit while increasing commerce, revenue, employment, and security. To promote the enterprise, Harley enlisted figures of no small stature, from writers Defoe and Jonathan Swift to the mapmaker Herman Moll.[145] Enthusiasm for the project—and thus its share price—kept growing, as investing came to seem like not only a sure financial bet but also political and social capital across a rather broad constituency. Women took a good proportion of shares, as did colonial planters, merchants, and companies, not to mention a significant number of foreigners.[146] The frenzy for South Sea Company stock was underwritten by a general boom in company formation and speculation in the later 1710s, both in Britain and across Europe, including a number of new colonial schemes.[147] Perhaps most famous among these was the remarkably similar "Mississippi Company" project in France, stewarded by the Scottish projector John Law, which sought to combine state finance with a reformed French East and West India Company. Britain also saw its share of smaller colonial projects in the wake of Union. The pirate John Breholt, for example, with significant support among former Scottish Darien Company investors proposed a joint-stock company in 1707 with the quixotic plan of getting government to allow it to offer pardons to pirates on Madagascar if they would turn over their treasure and prizes to the company. When no patents were forthcoming, after 1711 he was similarly unsuccessful in requesting a license from the South Sea Company to do the same.[148] In 1717, the merchant and philanthropist Thomas Coram, with the merchant Joshua Gee and others, challenged Massachusetts's claims in Maine by proposing a new joint corporate-Admiralty colony in Sagadahoc.[149] Meanwhile, a charter to a new fisheries company, *The Grand Fishery of Great Britain,* prompted both a Scottish rival and English investors to acquire and open up new subscriptions under the still-existing patents for the *Company of the Royal Fishery.*[150]

New maritime enterprises also prompted several new corporate marine insurance schemes. These in turn faced powerful entrenched opposition from the dominant force in British insurance, the consortium of underwriters of Lloyd's Coffee House. Lloyd's attempted to stem the tide in corporate insurance by raising familiar concerns: corporations were not run by experts; they had no "sense of shame"; they could not be held accountable or be trusted, a particularly fatal flaw in the insurance industry.[151] The Crown's law officers, inclined to agree that marine insurance was no place for corporations, impeded these new companies in their efforts to obtain charters. In response, two would-be insurers, taking a page from the Sword Blades scheme, bought up other companies under whose name they could do business. In this case, though, they did not buy an esoteric manufacturing company but rather two of the first and oldest joint-stock corporations in England: the Mines Royal and Mineral and Battery Works companies, whose charters dated to the sixteenth century. (The governor of the Royal Lustring Company, incorporated in 1687 but whose exclusive patent had lapsed, reported he had declined similar overtures.) The Attorney General found such *ultra vires* moves to be "illegal and unwarrantable; and, if drawn into Precedent, would be of dangerous Consequence to the Publick." He recommended proceeding against them by *scire facias* and *quo warranto*.[152]

The controversy that ensued prompted the House of Commons to convene a subcommittee to investigate this proliferation of joint-stock company schemes. Its report, authored by John Hungerford, who also served as the East India Company's solicitor, painted a foreboding picture of unregulated, unchartered companies, subscription schemes, and, worst of all, a rampant market in "obsolete Charters."[153] As far as the two marine insurance corporations were concerned, the issue was settled when they offered to pay a substantial fee and loan to government in exchange for incorporating both, the *London Assurance Company* and the *Royal Exchange Assurance Company,* with a duopoly over marine insurance. As the Act of Parliament was being prepared, though, the South Sea Company, which had also become concerned about the competition for capital in all these new unregulated and unchartered joint-stock schemes, lobbied for a last-minute addition to the same bill, which now prohibited any association at all "acting or presuming to act as a Corporate Body or Bodies," even under an obsolete charter, "without Legal Authority" from the Crown or Parliament. In short, in 1720 it became, at least in theory, illegal to operate as a joint-stock company without a charter of incorporation.[154]

What happened next is well known. Between late 1719 and mid-1720, the value of the South Sea Company's stock had continued to rise precipitously and, along with it, the value of many other companies, both large and small. The Hudson's Bay Company took the opportunity to offer new stock issues, as did the Royal African Company, which under James Brydges, the Duke of Chandos, also undertook some complex but ultimately fruitless schemes to re-capitalize the Company and thus revive its fortunes. By late summer 1720, trading had become so frenzied that the South Sea Company took a hiatus from selling new subscriptions if only to catch up on the paperwork. When it reopened its books, investors scrambled to sell, sending the stock price plummeting while the Company struggled to pay as its financing arm, the Sword Blade Bank, ran out of money.[155]

It still remains a matter of debate whether the South Sea collapse—what some would come to call a "bubble"—caused an actual financial crisis. Another compelling question is whether the South Sea Company directors had schemed to drive up the stock price or if they were as caught as unawares as anyone else. What is clear is that alongside the collapse of Law's Mississippi Company, the stock crash had serious political reverberations. A flood of pamphlets seized on the opportunity to amplify the critique of joint-stock schemes and the "monied interest" in government. The crash was, critics insisted, evidence that the very foundations of state finance were at best a fraud and possibly even a Jacobite conspiracy. Something seemed broken. The House of Commons launched investigations and held company leaders to account. The ministry scrambled to come up with proposals for remedying the situation, including an aborted plan to redistribute the Company's debt to the Bank and the East India Company.[156] The scandal also resonated through North America. In Boston, pamphlets like John Higginson's *The Second Part of the South-Sea Stock* used the crisis to levy a general critique of joint-stock schemes, while the Pennsylvania Land Company's loss of £9,000 in South Sea shares rocked the Quaker mid-Atlantic in a scandal that came to be known as the "Pennsylvania Bubble."[157] The entire affair brought to the fore just how little consensus there was in this early stock market as to how to put value on a company and its stock. Was it determined by the company's actual assets and profits, its future potential, supply and demand for the stock, or more abstract factors like creditworthiness and public good? The only clear answer was that however one arrived at the value of a company involved not just economic calculations but social, political, religious, and epistemological ones as well.[158]

Still, despite such questions, the "bubble" did little to arrest the enthusiasm for joint-stock colonial projects in Britain or Europe. The terms of the "Bubble Act," as the 1720 proscriptions on unchartered companies came to be known, were exceptionally vague and largely ignored by projectors and authorities alike; for the rest of the eighteenth century, only one company was successfully prosecuted under its strictures, an unusual and obscure case in 1722 of an unchartered fisheries scheme that critics cleverly branded a "North Sea Bubble."[159] Meanwhile, other longstanding colonial companies flourished. The East India Company's commercial and financial power in both Britain and Asia continued to rise, underscored by its fateful and profitable pivot into the tea trade as well as new concessions and powers in India, especially in Bengal. This in turn encouraged the creation of several new European East India Company projects out of Sweden, Prussia, the and the Austrian Netherlands. In the 1740s, a concerted effort to pitch a Portuguese East India Company on the English model to officials in Lisbon—promoted by the former Bombay official John Cleland (best known to posterity as the later author of the ribald novel *Fanny Hill*) and Portugal's London ambassador, the later Marquis de Pombal—yielded no eastward venture but seems to have planted the seeds for several Portuguese Brazil company projects that would follow in the coming decades.[160]

With its *asiento* and exclusive jurisdiction still intact, even the South Sea Company endured, largely as a slave trader, smuggling operation, and financier of government debt. Rumors circulated of a merger with the Royal African Company, while in 1721, the Company briefly renewed their hopes of taking over a formerly French colony in the Caribbean, Canada, or elsewhere in the Atlantic "for the service of the Publick, and of this Corporation."[161] A leadership purge arrested this project, while the Company's restructuring and refinancing in the wake of the crisis led its new directors to sell about £4 million in shares to the Bank of England. With £32 million in capital stock and now partly merged into the Bank, the Company remained, in one historian's words, a "financial goliath." In 1723, it formally split its capital stock in two. One half remained shares of the commercial company, while the financing arm was converted into perpetual government-backed annuities, ensuring it would remain central, if perhaps far more quietly so, to the making of the British state and empire for more than a century to follow.[162]

4

HOSTILE TAKEOVERS

The Age of Revolutions

Wealth, as Mr. Hobbes says, is power.

ℱOR AT LEAST TWO decades after traveling to the Pacific on William Dampier's infamously disastrous 1705 *St. George* expedition, John Welbe hatched many schemes to mount a return of his own, many of them conceived while whiling away his time in one of London's several debtors' prisons. In 1707, he traveled to Copenhagen to pitch (unsuccessfully) Denmark's King and East India Company on the idea. Some years later, plans to make a similar offer to John Law were thwarted by the Mississippi Company's spectacular collapse in September 1720. In the interim, he allegedly squandered a modest inheritance on the project, while appealing for support to the very top of the English government, including George I himself. Efforts to interest the Royal Society in backing a venture and several related schemes, including the development of a cure-all "Antivenerial Water," were equally unsuccessful. By late 1720, Welbe—now in King's Bench prison, once again for debt but with some convoluted relationship to an arson and marine insurance fraud ring—finally decided to abandon his efforts to find patrons and instead turned to investors. He petitioned the Board of Trade "in behalf of himself and several others" to charter a company he called the *London Adventurers for Carrying on a Trade to (and Settling*

Colonies in) Terra Australis and began to offer "permits," which for one shilling now, would reserve a would-be adventurer the right to buy a £100 share after the company was incorporated.[1]

It is tempting to think that Welbe, by restraining himself from offering actual shares in a company that did not yet exist, was being surprisingly mindful of the prohibitions of the recently passed Bubble Act on unchartered joint-stock companies. More likely, he was looking to raise money quickly to get himself out of prison, perhaps even looking to pull off what later generations would call an advance fee scam. Still, if the *London Adventurers* project was a swindle, it was not a good one. It is possible Welbe did not manage to sell any permits by July 1721, when the Board denied his petition. Among other flaws in the scheme, his would-be company, it observed, would be illegal, as it directly contravened both the East India and South Sea Company charters. If he wanted to pursue the project, he was told to seek out licenses from one of those companies instead.[2] He does not seem to have done so, and by the next year he reappeared with an even more audacious scheme for uncovering a source of silver and gold much closer to home. Welbe now claimed to have uncovered the alchemical secrets of the Philosopher's Stone and proposed a project he insisted would bring in upwards of £100 million—if only he could get seed money from the King or Parliament to help him get going. They declined the opportunity.[3]

Outlandish in every respect as Welbe and his various get-poor-quick schemes were, they nonetheless captured something of the moment. Despite one company scandal after another, the imaginations of projectors had never been more fertile. The eighteenth century was an age of great transformation for states and empires around the globe. For the colonial corporation, it was one of both revolution and of evolution. By the century's end, the East India Company ruled a growing territorial and maritime empire, and certain of the North American colonies, having split from the British Empire, were on the verge of establishing one of their own. As old arguments and forms of corporate colonialism endured, new experiments emerged with ambitions as varied as maintaining the slave trade and abolishing it. Meanwhile, the British state continued to build an empire in no small part through merger and acquisition, a century of warfare and an expanding fiscal and imperial apparatus driving exponential growth in its ambition and power. In 1785, the political economist John Sinclair captured the character of this new state. Britain, he observed, now

> extends its views beyond the immediate events, and pressing exigencies of the moment—it forms systems of remote, as well as of immediate profit—it borrows money to cultivate, to defend, or to acquire distant possessions, in hopes that it will be amply repaid by the advantages they may be brought to yield. At one time it protects a nation whose trade it considers beneficial: at another it engages in war, lest the commerce of a neighbour and a rival should be too great: in short, it proposes to itself a plan of perpetual accumulation and aggrandizement, which, according as it is well or ill conducted, must either end in the possession of an extensive and a powerful empire, or in total ruin.

If the eighteenth century witnessed a transformation in the British Empire, it was least in part because Britain, as Sinclair put it, had finally "assumed the appearance of a great corporation."[4]

GEORGIA, LIMITED

By the mid-1720s, British joint-stock companies, mired in scandal, had never been more popular or controversial.[5] The tandem "bubbles" of the South Sea Company and the French Mississippi Company had been followed in quick succession by a number of other high-profile collapses, including the Mine Adventures Company in Wales and the York Buildings Company, a London-based waterworks concern bought by speculators, like the Sword Blades Company, in order to use its corporate character to purchase "Jacobite" estates—in this instance, Scottish lands confiscated from those who were accused of having supported the attempt in 1715 of James Francis Edward, James II's son, to invade and retake the throne—before turning to a strange combination of equally unsuccessful mining, life insurance, and lottery projects.[6] The closest rival to the South Sea scandal, though, was the failure of the so-called Charitable Corporation, a joint-stock microfinance enterprise that by the time it collapsed in 1731 had devolved into a laundry list of desperate schemes, including fire insurance, bank note issuing, and stock speculation (including in York Buildings shares) as well as, to believe its critics, usury, embezzlement, stockjobbing, popery, Francophilia, and Jacobitism.[7]

It was in this context that, in early 1730, James Oglethorpe approached his fellow member of the House of Commons, John, Viscount Perceval, with an idea for a very different sort of project. The two served together on a House of Commons committee charged with investigating the squalid state of London's prisons. On the recommendation of its several scathing reports, Parliament had ordered a large-scale release of prisoners, especially debtors, but had not quite proposed any plan of what to do with them. Oglethorpe's idea was to send them to live in a new privately funded colony, and South Carolina, which the Crown had the year before purchased from its proprietors, seemed the ideal place.[8] The idea of populating settlements with convicts and the indigent was not in itself especially original, having been part of various colonial projects from the days of Gilbert and Frobisher to the recent Transportation Act of 1717. Likewise, in the decade since its rebellion against proprietorial rule in 1719 had made a Crown takeover seem inevitable, Carolina had seemed to pose ample opportunities for projectors, such as the Swiss Jean-Pierre Pury, who finally received a favorable hearing in 1724 from the Board of Trade for his plan to settle a Huguenot plantation there, after both his erstwhile employers in the Dutch East India Company and John Law in France had turned him down.[9]

Where Oglethorpe and the others parted from tradition was in their decided opposition to undertaking this enterprise as a joint-stock company. It is tempting to imagine that their opinion of such schemes, soured by the shadow of the corporate scandals of the past decade, was only confirmed by the findings of the Gaols Committee. Eighteenth-century prisons were essentially projects: private businesses run by keepers whose positions were, like many franchises, both a kind of public office and a source of personal emolument. Such positions were routinely inherited, sold, or farmed out, which created great demands on their holders to raise revenue, both to pay off their debts and rents as well as turn a profit and thus, the committee found, perverse incentives to skimp on basic services, extort bribes and other fees from prisoners, and otherwise increase income. Their report on King's Bench Prison, for example, revealed that its marshalcy, since it had been mortgaged in the seventeenth century

The Gaols Committee of the House of Commons by William Hogarth, 1729. Oglethorpe is the first person seated on the left; Perceval sits one over. NPG 926, National Portrait Gallery, London.

as part of a land purchase, had passed through several hands until 1718, when it was purchased by a trustee on behalf of several adventurers, who divided its ownership up into twenty shares. The "great Oppression" of the prison's conditions could be directly traced, at least in part, to the large sums that the keeper owed the "proprietors" of the joint-stock trusteeship. It is hardly clear how much this experience affected Oglethorpe and others' attitudes toward joint stocks, but if nothing else, two names among the prison's one-time investors would likely have stood out: Robert Knight and Robert Surman, the disgraced former cashier and deputy cashier, respectively, for the South Sea Company, whose four shares each in the prison's keepership had since been seized with their other assets and turned over to the new South Sea Trustees.[10]

Oglethorpe wanted not investors but donors for his colonial project. By the time he approached Perceval, he had already secured a substantial bequest toward a colony, but it came with the condition that it be vested in "some Trust already in being."[11] As it turned out, Perceval already managed such a fund, a bequest the Anglican priest and philanthropist Thomas Bray had secured some years earlier from Abel Tassin, Sieur D'Allone, to establish an endowment for the Christian education of slaves, especially children, in the Americas.[12] Perceval had taken on the charge of the D'Allone fund from Bray, hoping he might be able to employ it to support his friend, the philosopher and Irish Anglican cleric George Berkeley, in his project to establish an incorporated missionary school and Indian college at Bermuda. Possibly because Berkeley had largely abandoned his endeavor by 1730, Perceval seemed open to Oglethorpe's proposal to accept the new funds into the trust and pursue a colonial project of their own.[13] They petitioned the Crown for a land grant within southwestern Carolina and, in the meantime, offered Pury a modest £200 to support his project.[14] Perceval tried to persuade Berkeley to redirect the assets remaining for his college to their project instead, but the Bishop had already pledged them to another corporation, Yale College.[15]

Oglethorpe had bigger ambitions and was set on giving the project a more permanent character through a "Patent or Charter" of incorporation so that the "miserable wretches" might be more properly "settled all together by way of colony."[16] In June 1732, the Crown provided such patents, cleaving land out of the southern portion of South Carolina and vesting it in "one body politic and corporate in deed and name, by the name of *The Trustees for Establishing the Colony of Georgia in America*."[17] Georgia was thus self-consciously a departure from precedent: a trusteeship rather than a joint stock, funded not by adventurers but philanthropists. The Georgia corporation established four different funds to which one could donate: one for the plantation itself, one for Swiss and Palatine settlers, one for the religious establishment, and one for agricultural experimentation. They also constituted a quasi-separate "Society of Associates of Dr. Bray" to manage the D'Allone fund and the other endowments Bray had left upon his death in 1730.[18]

The colony was also different in other ways. There was to be no governor, "to prevent the pride that name might instil," but rather an "overseer and council" directly responsible to the Trustees. The core of the settlement was to be made up not of landholders with shares but "colonies of poor families after the Roman method" to "fortify, build houses, clear lands, and raise provisions for themselves."[19]

Private land was entailed, held not in fee simple (which could be alienated freely) but rather fee tail-male (in which property passed indivisibly to first sons) to limit speculation and root the settlers more firmly on their property across generations. The Trustees prohibited spirituous liquors, monoculture plantations, and, most famously and controversially, slavery. Unlike in joint-stock companies, which tended to guard their records jealously, donors and the Crown's law officers could inspect the Trust's books at any time. The Trustees were also prohibited from becoming landholders in the colony or receiving any "salary, fee, perquisite, benefit or profit whatsoever." If that did not make their point clearly enough, their motto would: *non sidi sed aliis,* not for themselves but for others.[20]

At the same time, the Georgia project was not as radical an innovation as all this would have made it appear. Though run by trustees, it was still a "Corporation," a "Company," and a "Society," as Perceval referred to it interchangeably.[21] In one sense, it followed in a tradition of both incorporated charities for relief of the poor, such as Georgia trustee Thomas Coram's Foundling Hospital, or overseas philanthropic enterprises like Bray's Society for the Propagation of the Gospel or the numerous charitable endowments for the redemption of Britons captured by "Barbary Pirates" (many of which were themselves vested in companies, liveries, or other corporations).[22] Oglethorpe cited the Irish Society as "a Precedent of our own for planting Colonies, which, perhaps in Part, or in the Whole, may be worthy our Imitation," while his 1732 *Select Tracts Relating to Colonies*—one of many forms of promotional material that both resembled and drew on previous colonial enterprises—revealed a rather ecumenical case for colonial emigration, with its highly selective excerpts from William Penn and Josiah Child, alongside Francis Bacon, Machiavelli, and the Dutch republican free trader Pieter de la Court (credited as Jan de Witt).[23] It could be argued, as the historian Milton Ready did, that in its top-down structure of government executed by agents and employees on the ground, the colony looked uncannily like a Royal Africa or East India company factory or maybe a large municipality. "The key word in Georgia's charter is not 'Trust,'" Ready mused, "but more properly 'Corporation.'"[24]

Even if Georgia had as a body politic remained immune to the pull of joint-stock ventures, in an early eighteenth-century Britain filled with company schemes, it was inevitable that both its leaders and especially its donors would be wrapped up in the broader world of corporate colonialism. Just a few examples will suffice. Several colonial companies and their leadership donated; the East India Company itself evidently pledged £600 to the general fund.[25] The Trust's agricultural fund, essentially a joint enterprise undertaken with the Royal Society and the Society of Apothecaries, had for its first gardener William Houstoun, a former South Sea Company employee who took research expeditions for the colony's gardens in Spanish America under the Company's auspices.[26] Georgia's colonial secretary and second governor William Stephens had previously worked as agent in Scotland and then South Carolina for Samuel Horsey, the expelled governor of the York Buildings Company.[27] Trustee Adam Anderson, whose *The Origin of Commerce* would become one of the eighteenth century's most influential histories (and defenses of commercial empire, including the South Sea Company) had served as a secretary at the Scottish Corporation and as the longstanding clerk and accountant for the South Sea Company.[28] Coram, in addition to his foundling school, had earlier proposed a joint-stock partnership with the Admiralty for a colony in Maine and Nova Scotia (which, it turns out, he had planned to call "Georgia").[29] Oglethorpe himself was a director (1731) and then Deputy-Governor (1732) of the Royal African Company, while his right-hand man, Francis Moore, had served the Company at James Fort in what is now Ghana.[30] Not for nothing did the Scottish Highlanders recruited to settle and defend the colony's border fortification of Fort St. George quickly rename it, after the late seventeenth-century Company of Scotland scheme, Darien.[31]

In this sense, the Georgia charitable corporation and the colonial joint-stock corporation were less archenemies than alter egos. If nothing else, they shared a common premise that, one way or another, empire was something not to be governed by government. To these men, patronage, personal interest, and profit infected national politics far more than it did philanthropy. When Prime Minster Robert Walpole withdrew the promised Parliamentary support for Berkeley's Bermuda college in 1731, Oglethorpe wrote the Bishop that he was "not at all surprised," as "no private views were to be gratified, no relation served, nor pander preferred, nor no depraved opposition indulged" by the project.[32] This did not stop Oglethorpe however from lobbying Walpole for more permanent Parliamentary support for Georgia, including £10,000 from the proceeds of the sale of conquered French lands at St. Christopher—the same colony the South Sea Company had once coveted and the same money that Berkeley had originally been promised.[33]

That Georgia had in the end become largely dependent on Parliamentary subvention raised another point about the philanthropic trusteeship experiment: it did not work.[34] The Trustees were soon low on funds and faced growing opposition, especially over the colony's prohibition on slavery. By the early 1740s, the Trustees actually welcomed a Commons investigation into their affairs, hoping that their political connections would prevail and lead to a more substantial and permanent statutory support. They miscalculated. Debates in 1740 and 1741 were dominated by criticism of the enterprise. While the formal inquiry in 1742 did recommend new funding, the Commons never approved the money.[35] Short on cash and increasingly enervated by the departure or death of some of its original movers, a new generation of Trustees—from whom Oglethorpe was increasingly alienated—surrendered the charter in 1752. From this point, Georgia would develop into everything the original Trustees had insisted it would not be: a slave society and monoculture plantation economy, under neither a company nor a charity but rather the Crown.[36]

EVERY STATE IS A CORPORATION: BRITISH AMERICA

As the Georgia project revealed, the South Sea crisis inspired criticism and experimentation but, in the end, did little to stem the tide of corporate colonial projects. The Bubble Act, to the extent that it had any impact in Britain, did not apply overseas, where joint-stock enterprises proliferated without royal charters and frequently without the sanction of colonial governments. The status of such corporations continued to be a matter of great debate. In turn, the fundamental questions they raised about the nature and reach of colonial jurisdiction and autonomy would be brought into ever sharper focus as Crown, Commons, and their agents made ever greater claims to authority over colonial politics and society in the ensuing decades.

These issues may most vibrantly be seen in the virulent disputes over several New England land bank schemes in the 1730s and 1740s.[37] Though approaches differed, the idea behind such projects generally was to offer loans to individuals or groups, who would mortgage land and sometimes other forms of property as collateral. Many land banks, especially in New England where coin was in short supply, offered these loans in the form of paper notes, which to have any use would need to circulate and be accepted by others as ready money. The debate over whether money could and should be represented by such notes was one of the most controversial of the day; as in debates over the corporation, what might seem like purely economic questions about how money was to be valued in fact raised profound quandaries over the nature and location of political authority. Like the corporation, paper money was a form of credit that served as a ready solution to a shortage of capital. Also like the corporation, some advocates maintained, it derived its authority only when people mutually agreed on its validity. Paper money was thus in a sense as much a form of social compact as membership in a corporate body, acquiring value not from fiat but from "common consent" and "the Call of the People."[38] Conversely, opponents described notes much the same way others did the corporation: especially when done without royal charter or sanction, they were both a bald challenge to sovereign power and an illusory and dangerous chimera that could be neither perceived nor trusted; John Jay would later liken the concept to a kind of "political Transubstantiation" that convinced its holders that paper could be mystically willed into something of significance.[39]

It was not just, however, that the issues surrounding paper money resembled those at stake in debates over the corporation. The two frequently came together in the form of private land bank projects. *The New London Society for Trade and Commerce,* for example, was chartered by the Connecticut Assembly in 1732 to promote Connecticut's Atlantic trade and fisheries but raised great controversy when it began to allow people to become adventurers by mortgaging property to the corporation, essentially allowing its shares to serve as land-backed bank notes.[40] Critics complained not only that the Society had misled the Assembly but that as a result the joint stock did not have any real assets behind it. Eventually, they also took their case further, insisting that Connecticut, as a corporation, did not have the legal authority to make a corporation in the first place, "inasmuch as all companies of merchants are made at home by letters patents from the King, and we know not of one single instance of any government in the plantations doing such a thing."[41]

A privately funded Land Bank, or Manufactory scheme, in Massachusetts in 1740 raised the converse question as to whether such an enterprise could proceed without being a corporation. Jonathan Belcher, the colony's royalist governor and advocate for the rival Silver Bank—which as its name implied, was to issue currency backed by specie, not land—refused to approve patents for the company and then insisted that it could not proceed, as taking on so public a charge "without the Leave and Countenance of the Government" was "of dangerous Consequence to a Common Wealth." The issue nearly brought Massachusetts politics to a halt, as Belcher threatened to dismiss public officeholders who supported it and had several men arrested for planning a protest, which the governor characterized as a "rebellion."[42] Despite his defense of royal prerogative, Belcher became so unpopular in Massachusetts and with its allies in London over this issue that he was eventually replaced as governor. His concerns were heard, however, along with those of London merchants opposing the land bank, by the House of Commons. A subcommittee, whose membership included stalwart East India Company critic John Barnard and, ironically, the Sword Blade Bank and South Sea Company architect George Caswall, acted swiftly not only to restrain land banks *per se* but to prohibit forming joint-stock companies without royal or colonial patents altogether. In the matter of a few short months in 1741, they managed to pass through Parliament such a prohibition, in effect extending the 1720 "Bubble Act" to the colonies.[43]

Colonists, later Massachusetts Governor Thomas Hutchinson recalled, greeted the news "in amaze," some comparing the Act to a kind of imperial overreach not seen since the Dominion of New England.[44] Yet, like its domestic predecessor, the colonial Bubble Act was also largely ignored. Over the next decades, land bank schemes would emerge in almost all the North American colonies, structured in varying forms as corporations, trusteeships, government loan offices, and Benjamin Franklin's project in the 1760s for establishing a continent-wide bank.[45] Meanwhile, similar debates emerged in colonial North America over the incorporation of colleges and universities. As sites of religious instruction, colleges were focal points for confessional battles among episcopal Anglicans and various forms of dissenting Protestantism, which during this era translated into broad debates over the reach of royal authority. The pluralist constitutional foundations for colleges across the colonies reflected this lack of legal consensus. Harvard had received its charters, not without controversy, from the colonial assembly, while the College of William and Mary had been chartered by royal letters patent in 1693. In 1769, Eleazer Wheelock sought out the same for his New London Indian charity school, after a large donation of property from landowners in New Hampshire persuaded him to move the college there and rename it, after one of its largest benefactors, as the *Trustees of Dartmouth College*. The College of New Jersey (later Princeton University), had charters from successive royal governors, including Jonathan Belcher. *The Trustees of the Academy and Charitable School in the Province of Pennsylvania*, soon after *the College, Academy, and Charity-School of Philadelphia* (later the University of Pennsylvania), became one "community, corporation, and body politick," with patents from proprietors Thomas and Richard Penn.[46] Plans in the 1750s to incorporate King's College in New York (later Columbia) split the colony over whether such a thing could be done without royal assent. The argument for taking a charter from the Crown prevailed, since, as its President, the Anglican cleric Samuel Johnson insisted to Yale's President Thomas Clap, "a Corporation cannot make a Corporation."[47]

Back in Connecticut, this very issue had been a question with Yale from the beginning. In their initial discussions in the opening years of the eighteenth century, the founders of the Collegiate School—it would be renamed in 1718 after a benefactor, Elihu Yale, the East India Company's former governor of Madras—had debated whether they even could pursue incorporation. Some among them insisted that any college should have authority similar to towns in New York and Massachusetts, "priviledging and enabling them to dispose of Land, to sue and be sued and in many other things to act as incorporated companies." Others suggested that incorporation was too limiting and made the body too vulnerable; no doubt with the ongoing threats to other colonial charters fresh in mind, one commenter observed that it "might the better stand in wind and weather, not daring to Incorporate it, least it should be liable to be served with a

Writ of Quo Warranto." Their compromise solution was to seek patents from the Connecticut Assembly as "Trustees Partners or Undertakers"—a form of chartered but unincorporated trust that essentially protected the college's rights to property and self-government, "without," as the early twentieth-century legal scholar Frederic Maitland described the trust generally, "troubling the State to concede or deny the mysterious boon of personality."[48]

Over the years, this left Yale's status a matter of some debate. Was it, as one member of the Connecticut Assembly argued in 1717, "partners not a body politick"? Or was it a common law corporation by prescription, like "Towns, Proprietors, Owners of Shipps" which were "not bodies corporate yet as the Common law allows are as it were incorporate to do some things without which the[y] could not well mannage"?[49] Clap, who as President faced stiff opposition over his aggressively Calvinist program for the College, offered a different theory. Though leading the charge in 1745 to finally obtain a new legislative charter declaring Yale an "incorporate society," Clap nonetheless believed that Yale was already a self-constituting body politic with fundamental rights to autonomous government, without which "no Society, or Body Politick, can be *safe*, but only, in it's having, a Principle of self-Preservation, and a Power, of Providing, every thing necessary, for it's own Subsistence, and Defence."[50]

Patents guaranteed the College financial support and political protection from the legislature, which, Clap admitted, implied that the Assembly should have some right of "superintendence." Incorporation, however, had not brought the college into being in the first place. "The Common-Law is plain," he wrote, "that he is the Founder, who first erects and endows it; and not the King, who make it a Corporation by Law."[51] As legatees of the founders, the Trustees—not the Crown or the Assembly—were the corporation's proper visitors, with rights to oversee and determine its governance. In this sense, Clap insisted, Connecticut's power over the college was no more than that which it held over "all other Persons and Estates in the Colony" and perhaps a bit more as one of its "Benefactors."[52] To seal his point, Clap went back not just to Yale's origins but to that of the corporation itself. Corporate organization traced, he argued, to the ninth-century monastic *collegium and universitas*—"a Company of ministers united for the Education of ministers"—but civic charters only arose in practice some four or five hundred years later. Echoing a long tradition of Calvinist corporate and resistance theory, Clap made the case that it was not just that Yale existed prior to its charter but the very practice of incorporation predated the existence and regular use of government charters by centuries.[53]

By the mid-eighteenth century, corporate status had become a focal point for religious, political, and partisan conflict as well as unresolved questions over the nature and extent of royal authority over colonies, the civil associations within them, and inevitably those many new companies looking to expand those colonies' borders. As they had for at least a century, joint-stock associations continued to do a lot of the work of laying claim to indigenous trade and territory, while also serving to counter other Europeans and even other British colonies' efforts to do the same. The 1747 *Ohio Company* claims over half a million acres west of the Alleghanies, like those of the *Loyal Company* (1749) and *Mississippi Company* (1763), were meant as much to profit from land speculation and counter French expansion in Louisiana—itself, of course, originally the work of a company—as they were to stake a claim that those territories fell within the ambit of Virginia, not New York or Pennsylvania.[54] The Seven Years' War changed these matters significantly. The Treaty of Paris ending the war in 1763 had vested Britain with several new former French and Spanish colonies from the Atlantic to the Mediterranean as well as vast territorial claims over continental North America. Aiming both to assert its own authority and to prevent hostilities with the indigenous peoples in and at the borders of its new territory, that same year King George III issued a proclamation announcing the formation of four new royal colonies—Quebec, Grenada, and East and West Florida—and asserting the Crown's exclusive right to acquire or settle the vast tracts of North America west of the Appalachians. After the Proclamation of 1763, at least in theory, both "private persons" and colonial governments alike were prohibited from acquiring, purchasing, or surveying land of indigenous peoples, now under the Crown's direct "protection," without the license of British imperial officials.[55]

Some speculators and the several land companies were stymied by the new policy.[56] Yet in the end the proclamations' claims were just that: claims, controversially rooted in the royal prerogative,

The British Governments in Nth America: Laid Down Agreeable to the Proclamation of Octr. 7, 1763, published in the *Gentlemen's Magazine,* 1763. New York
Public Library Digital Collections.

which other colonists ignored, scorned, or mocked. Royal officials
well understood that they would be difficult to enforce.[57] Sir William Johnson, the Crown's northern superintendent for Indian affairs, complicated matters even further at a summit he convened in
1768 at Fort Stanwix. Johnson's brief was to negotiate with representatives of both the Haudenosaunee, or Iroquois Confederacy, and
those of several British colonies to settle an official demarcation of
the western boundary mentioned in the 1763 proclamation. He thus
infuriated officials back in Britain when he also facilitated an Iroquois land grant to an association of Philadelphia merchants, which
the latter demanded as compensation for attacks and losses they
claimed to have suffered during the war. Lord Hillsborough, the colonial secretary, was incensed that Johnson had vastly exceeded his

instructions especially, as the Board of Trade observed, in support of "the claims and interests of private persons . . . to mix themselves in this negotiation, and to be introduced, not as propositions submitted to your Majesty's determination, but as rights derived from the Indians."[58]

With the treaty in jeopardy of being rejected by British officials, Philadelphia merchant Samuel Wharton set out to London to try to rescue it. It turns out he arrived with more ambitious plans. The group's ranks had swelled to nearly twenty adventurers from Philadelphia and London, some of whom were influential and well-known: Benjamin Franklin and his son, the former Governor of Massachusetts Thomas Pownall, and the London banker Thomas Walpole, who had taken on a leading role in the enterprise. Infused with such financial and political clout, what soon came to be known as the *Walpole Company* now proposed not only to take up the original Iroquois grant but also to purchase from the Crown the 2.4 million acres it had acquired at Paris and Stanwix. Not only would this have been an unusually massive undertaking for a colonial land company, but, they boasted, the Company was revolutionary in another sense as the "first Adventurers" to offer to buy their land from the Crown rather than seeking it as an outright grant. They sought a charter of incorporation that would allow them to both sell off smaller shares to settlers and "form a separate Government" of a colony they called Pittsylvania, later Vandalia.

The Ohio Company predictably objected to what they saw as a Pennsylvanian conspiracy to abrogate their rights over the same region. The Walpole group tried to buy off the Virginia concern—as well as its London agent personally—with shares in the new company. The parties in London agreed on a merger, which the Virginia shareholders rejected. The Walpole Company proceeded nonetheless, and the enterprise came to be known by 1772 the "Grand Ohio Company." The group still faced considerable opposition within government, not least Hillsborough, who was not only a great skeptic of such companies but was especially unnerved by the continued (if now strategically muted) involvement of Franklin, who was emerging as a leading American critic of government policy toward the colonies. Making matters more fraught, the Company heeded its lawyers' advice that they did not technically need a corporate charter to begin to sell land and send settlers to territory they had purchased. Wharton hedged his bets by engaging in a separate private purchase of Indian lands in Ohio as well.[59]

The Grand Ohio charter never arrived, and its own efforts were largely suspended by the outbreak of the Revolutionary War in 1775. In the meantime, several similar efforts to extend company colonies into the American West had emerged in the shadow of the ostensible prohibitions of 1763. In 1768, the Mississippi Company made its own request for 2.5 million acres, that "by a union of their Councils and fortunes that may in the most prudent and proper manner explore & as quickly as possible settle that part of the Country," though the effort failed to yield results.[60] A syndicate of veterans of the British attack on Havana in 1762, most from Connecticut, sought for a decade to receive compensation for their services in the form of a grant of Florida lands. Another company solicited in 1766 to set up a government on 1.2 million acres between the Illinois and Ohio Rivers, until many of its members, including Wharton and Franklin, turned their attention to the Grand Ohio project. In the mid-1770s, a Carolina group that had been responsible for Daniel Boone's expeditions to the interior established their *Transylvania Company* to acquire Cherokee lands in what is now Kentucky with no grants or patents whatsoever.[61]

Though structured in various ways, these enterprises, with their transferable shares and collective and delegated governance, both very much looked like and often understood themselves to be, in one historian's words, "corporations in all but the technical legal sense."[62] They certainly continued in a long tradition of land companies that undertook the work of dispossessing Native territory and operating in the interstices of already fractious and ambiguous conflicts among British colonies over their own respective boundaries. There was no more striking an example of this than the so-called *Susquehanna Company*, established in Connecticut in the mid-1750s with the ambition "to enlarge his Majesty's English Settlements in North America, and further to spread Christianity, as also to promote our own temporal interest." Their specific project was to recruit settlers and purchase territory of the Haudenosaunee for a settlement in a "Howling Wilderness" on the Susquehanna River in the foothills of the Pocono Mountains in what became known as the Wyoming Valley.[63]

In one sense, the Susquehanna plan was merely one in a long line of New England joint-stock town and settlement projects that pushed at and beyond their colonies' borders. In fact, the entire scheme was premised on the assertion that the region was "within the bounds" of Connecticut. What was, as one critic put it, "wild and preposterous" about this particular scheme was that the territory in question was located on a stretch of Iroquois territory two hundred miles away in an area that most maps, "the Generality of the more knowing People," and certainly the Penn family regarded as being in Pennsylvania.[64] The problem originated in the ambiguous nature of the colonial charter itself. Connecticut's 1662 patents, like many of its sort, placed its western border somewhat optimistically at "the South Sea" and "the Islands thereunto adjoining." The speculative geography represented by such a claim was tricky enough, but since then, two new colonies arrived that complicated matters further: New York, which had its own theoretically valid designs on the Wyoming region (not to mention longstanding border conflicts with Connecticut), and Pennsylvania, whose northern border at forty-three degrees latitude encompassed the same territory.[65]

The other confusing question about the Susquehanna Company was just where it got its authority to make such a settlement in the first place. The Company began with no charter but from its outset, its leaders anticipated, or simply asserted, that they would be a "Corporation," referring in early minutes in 1754 to the "Incorporated Company Engaged in the purchase of The Susquehannah Land" (though the word "incorporated" was lined out, likely at some later date).[66] Though it initially received a favorable hearing from the Connecticut Assembly, a new royalist governor, Thomas Fitch, distanced the colony's government from the company, denying it a patent and insisting that they "act in a private Capacity, and even out of the Government, [and as such] we can do nothing only by advice relative to their Conduct under another Jurisdiction."[67] As early as 1755, the Company's leadership considered instead seeking a royal charter to become a separate colony, "in form as near as may be, of the Constitution of the said Colony of Connecticut," and again in 1761, proposed a merger with the Delaware Company—a similar enterprise with claims over territory just to the east along the Delaware River—to "be incorporated and made into one Civil Government."[68] Finally, in 1764, both companies sent an envoy to

London to petition the Crown to "constitute and erect them into a new Colony or Settlement" distinct from both Connecticut and Pennsylvania.[69] In the meantime, with no charter from either Connecticut or the Crown, the Company proceeded on its own to solicit adventurers, recruit settlers, and negotiate with Iroquois representatives for a purchase.[70] Finally, by the late 1760s, as disputes between the Company settlers and their Pennsylvania neighbors devolved into armed conflict—what historians have dubbed the Yankee-Pennamite Wars—a more sympathetic government had come to power in Hartford. Citing precedents dating back to the Saybrook Company, Connecticut now argued that it might not only issue a charter to the Company but annex the territory outright. In 1774, this is just what it did, insisting that the region was now to be known as Westmoreland County.[71]

To most Pennsylvanians, the whole thing seemed "the wild Chimera of a visionary Brain," through which "a narrow District about Connecticut River will be stretched to a stupendous Size, constituting the Governor and Company of Connecticut, into the high and mighty Lords of all South America, and the greatest part of North America too!"[72] There was a legal case to be made that the Company, since it had never been incorporated, remained a mere partnership that could not have made its land purchases with the Haudenosaunee in the first place. "I hear these Connecticut people pretend they have purchased these Lands of some Mohawk Indians," William Allen wrote Daniel Broadhead as early as 1754, "to which Pretence of theirs no Regard is to be paid, as no private persons have a Right by our Laws to purchase Lands of the Indians."[73] In 1801, as this conflict was still being fought out, the Pennsylvania politician and political economist Tenche Coxe—whose great-grandfather, Daniel Coxe, may ironically have laid the foundations for such schemes a century earlier—made the point that the Company had been illegal in two senses: first, because it had been "made for the unlawful end of purchasing property [of indigenous peoples], which no private Person could buy" and second, because "All unlawful Associations are criminal at Common Law, void, and of no effect. *Hence the Susquehanna Agreement was a nullity on the day of its execution, and at the time of their Indian Purchase.*"[74] As the argument went, without a charter or some government authority, the Company could neither be a public body politic claiming jurisdiction over indigenous lands nor a private joint-stock society legally capable of raising investment or owning those lands. Neither legal fact, though, seemed to stop it from trying to do so in practice for more than a half century.

As the proclamation of 1763 made clear, the Seven Years' War was a turning point in shaping the growing ambitions of the British state and empire. The Crown's empire now suddenly found itself directly ruling over new colonies and an unprecedented number of non-British (and non-Protestant) subjects. Moreover, the war had posed untold financial and organizational challenges, which only further highlighted the tensions between the British state's aspirations in a new age of global warfare and the traditionally decentralized and pluralist nature of British overseas settlement. Through the 1760s and 1770s, Crown and Parliament took various steps to interpose authority to resume charters, appoint governors, or introduce new revenue and disciplinary measures on the grounds of "disorder," "confusion," and colonial government's failure to keep the "peace." Such measures were hardly new but now were aided, among other things, by the great number of Crown troops lingering in British North America in the war's aftermath.[75] Moreover, frustrated by the difficulty in raising and directing troops and other wartime resources in the colonies, several military commanders and royal officials made a case for seizing remaining charters—including those of what Francis Bernard, governor of Massachusetts, in 1764 called the "two republicks" of Rhode Island and Connecticut.[76]

Finally, and perhaps most famously, the war had been incalculably expensive, and many in London expected that the colonies would at least take up the cost of maintaining their own defense in its aftermath. Laws and taxes designed to enforce this followed, some of antique vintage like the Navigation Acts and others more novel in character, facilitated by a growing imperial administrative bureaucracy represented in emerging offices like the Colonial Department and then later the War and Colonial Office. One of the first and most provocative salvos in this battle came in 1765 in the ostensibly unassuming form of new duties on paperwork and publications. When news of the Stamp Act reached the colonies, however, many on both sides of the issue immediately registered it within the context of longstanding controversies over the reach of imperial and royal authority. The Boston lawyer John Adams at one point compared the controversy to the "ferment" over the 1741 colonial Bubble Act.[77] Royalists, like the Connecticut physician Benjamin Gale, similarly saw the connection; as Gale observed to Jared Ingersoll, Connecticut's Stamp Act commissioner, the crises over the New London Society, the Susquehanna Company, and Clap's Yale could all in hindsight be seen as foreshadowing the current crisis.[78]

Given its longstanding connection to fundamental quandaries about the boundaries between colonial, royal, and parliamentary authority, the debates leading up to the American Revolution were deeply embedded in varieties of "corporate thought."[79] Many agreed that colonies were corporations, but just what kind of corporations were they? Some royalists found the model of a municipal corporation most apt. The Pennsylvanian William Keith had backed a proposal for a stamp duty decades earlier by noting that colonies were "as so many Corporations as a distance," with no power to override the "Legal prerogative" of the "Mother State."[80] By the 1760s and 1770s, it became a common refrain to observe that the colonies' laws were really more like "by-laws," instituted for convenience of local governance.[81] "An English colony is . . . a corporation," the theologian John Wesley wrote in 1775, and "as a corporation they make laws for themselves, but as a corporation subsisting by a grant from higher authority, to the control of that authority, they still continue subject."[82] Others, like Thomas Hutchinson, royalist governor of Massachusetts, compared them to "the East-India and other great companies, with powers to settle plantations within the limits of the territory, under such forms of government and magistracy as should be fit and necessary," but ultimately subject to the Crown's sovereignty.[83]

William Samuel Johnson, Connecticut's agent in London, predictably saw the matter differently. Even if colonies were like municipalities, he observed to Hillsborough in 1768, not all municipalities were created equal. Just as London was of a different order than a "petty corporation in Cornwall," colonial charters "were in several respects of a higher nature, and founded upon a better title than even that of the corporations of England."[84] A few years later, the Massachusetts House of Representatives pointed out some other differences still. Colonial corporations were able to make other corporations—admittedly still a debated point—which English mu-

nicipalities were not. Conversely, English municipalities were represented in the House of Commons, which, notoriously, American
colonies were not. Thus, if Massachusetts were a corporation, it was
so "in no other Light, than as every State is a Corporation."[85]

Johnson, however, took the point further. Just because corporate
charters derived from the King's "unlimited bounty," that did not
necessarily mean that the Crown had unlimited power over them
once established. Much in the same spirit as Jeremiah Dummer had
argued decades earlier, Johnson insisted that it was colonists, not
the King, who had purchased rights and land and settled abroad.
This kind of investment of person and purse rendered charters a
form of property and "must now be considered as grants upon
valuable consideration, sacred and most inviolable."[86] To Adams,
"the Moment the Charter and the Company were removed to
New England beyond the four Seas, out of the Realm," it had "lost all
Force, which it ever had by the Laws of England, as a legal Instrument, and became only Evidence of a Contract." Echoing Dummer,
he concluded that this meant that even if patents could be withdrawn,
the colony would not become Crown property but rather "recur to
nature."[87]

The point was that charters had not made colonies; colonists had.
The fact that they did so, as Virginia planter and lawyer Richard
Bland argued, at their own expense rendered them akin to independent "states."[88] Thus, when George III expressed indignation that
Americans could be so impudent as to rebel after Britain had spent
so "much expence and treasure" to establish their colonies, Thomas
Jefferson could not help but pen a lengthy manuscript to expose such
the "palpable untruth" of such a claim, detailing (largely through
his reading of Hakluyt) how each American colony had arisen in
some form of private enterprise. This was no doubt the inspiration
for his including among the iconic list of grievances against the King
in the Declaration of Independence that "We have reminded them
of the circumstances of our emigration and settlement here." His
original draft put an even finer point on the issue, adding a line that
did not make it into the final version: "that these were effected at
the expense of our own blood and treasure, unassisted by the wealth
or the strength of Great Britain."[89]

The dilemmas over just what kind of corporation the colonies
were endured, as debates during the rebellion evolved into debates

over the structure and sovereignty of the new United States that emerged in its wake. Scholars have shown how the corporate roots of colonial and franchise government translated into some of the more peculiar but fundamental aspects of American politics and jurisprudence, from key juridical concepts like judicial review to the somewhat novel notion of having a written constitution in the first place.[90] Charles Pinckney proposed to include among the enumerated rights of the United States government that it "shall ever be considered as one Body corporate and politic in law, and entitled to all the rights privileges and immunities, which to Bodies corporate do or ought to appertain."[91] Chief Justice John Marshall later observed that the United States was "a great corporation . . . ordained and established by the American people, and endowed by them with great powers for important purposes."[92] To John Jay, the government's structure as a federal union reflected that of a shareholder company. "It is said that 'in a multitude of counsellors there is safety,'" he noted, "because in the first place, there is greater security for probity; and in the next, if every member casts in only his mite of information and argument, their joint stock of both will thereby become greater than the stock possessed by any one single man out of doors."[93]

Such understandings of the nature of American government, however, raised more questions than answers. If a nation was like a joint stock, who were its shareholders and how was their representation to be apportioned? As Jefferson recorded it, John Witherspoon insisted that each of the colonies, and thus the states, were like individuals who had come together to make a "bargain"; this, he argued—ironically and inaccurately—rendered the federation to be like "the East India Company [in which] they voted by persons, and not by proportion of stock."[94] Conversely, James Wilson, a strong advocate for fixing representation by size of population, likened the states instead to municipal corporations; to insist they be equally "represented in their corporate capacity" would be like insisting that "old Sarum"—an infamously rotten English borough with no residents—had a right "to as many [representatives] as London."[95] Just as it had been to royalists, the analogy between states and municipal corporations was appealing to those favoring instituting a strong federal government. States in this sense were "originally nothing more than colonial corporations" (Gouverneur Morris), which as "mere corporations" (John Lansing Jr.) were limited to control of their "private & internal affairs" only (Rufus King).[96] Alexander Hamilton echoed a string of royal governors of Massachusetts when he insisted that states should be seen as "subordinate authorities" for "local purposes," even if some, like Virginia and Massachusetts, were more "formidable" than others.[97]

Some records of the constitutional debates recalled James Madison insisting similarly that states were effectively "subordinate corporations," though in his own account, Madison recorded himself as forwarding a vision of the polity more as "a gradation . . . from the smallest corporation, with the most limited powers, to the largest empire with the most perfect sovereignty."[98] In such a federal system, he insisted, there were lesser and greater corporations, but they each had little to fear from one another. He offered an analogy to Connecticut, a corporate colony that had corporate towns, and in which the legislature had never "endeavored to despoil the Townships of any part of their local authority." (Even if they had, he added, it would be tyranny, which would still be better than its alternative of "anarchy.")[99] In this sense, as corporations, states would be subordinate to federal sovereignty, but, as corporations, states had their own capacity to exert sovereignty over townships and other subordinate corporations. But Madison also observed that there were strong arguments on both sides of the question and little way to resolve it definitively. "It has been said," he noted, "that there is no similarity between petty corporations and independent states. I admit that in many points of view there is a great dissimilarity, but in others, there is a striking similarity between them."[100]

There was yet another layer to this debate still: should the federal government, corporation or not, have the same power to make corporations as the King or Parliament did? The question was debated thoroughly but, perhaps as a sign of how contentious the issue was, the final version of the Constitution contained neither such an explicit power nor a prohibition.[101] States had absorbed the lawmaking authority of their colonies and Parliament, which in theory included the capacity to establish corporations. Many American rebels, like their counterparts in Revolutionary France, had assailed corporate charters as the quintessence of royal power and privilege. After independence, however, legislatures across the early republic embraced their power to charter commercial, municipal, religious, educational, and scientific and learned corporations with a certain abandon. New corporations for insurance, for example, like the Pennsylvania-chartered Insurance Company of North America, flourished. Though in a frenzy of anti-proprietor sentiment Pennsylvania had declared the charters of both the College of Philadelphia and Philadelphia itself invalid, both were eventually reinstated by the new state legislature. Twenty new cities were incorporated across the United States in the 1780s alone, even in long-standing holdouts like Charleston and Savannah, although arguably now with more open electorates and legislative oversight.[102] Moreover, in the early republic's early days, there were attempts to establish an American analogue to no less an emblem of the "machinations of tyranny" and the "violent attack upon the liberties of America" as the English East India Company, whose tea had been so ceremoniously jettisoned into Boston Harbor in 1773. Among the many objections to the boldest and most controversial early American chartered corporate experiment—Alexander Hamilton's scheme to establish a national bank—was that it could become a precedent for just such an American East India Company.[103]

In many respects, as in so many other ways, the new American Republic did not break from the British Empire over corporations so much as pick up right where it had left off. As Hamilton observed in making a case for a bank, the power to make corporations was "inherent in & inseparable from the idea of sovereign power," because that was the way it was "in England, whence our notions of it are immediately borrowed."[104] While many in the new republic thought they should do away with charters as an *ancien regime* corruption of special privileges, state legislatures and, as Hamilton insisted, Congress nonetheless seem to have taken up the charge. Rhode Island actually continued to operate under its colonial charter until 1842, when the clamor for broader representation finally resulted in a new state constitution.[105] Meanwhile, colleges, such as Harvard and Yale, and municipalities, like New York, endured into the new republic. When the Bishop of London, as trustee for Robert Boyle's charitable endowment, sued in the English Court of Chancery in 1790 to cease payments to several American institutions on the grounds that "they are now no longer a corporation with respect to this country," the College of William and Mary's lawyers countered that but for the minor matter of "merely the relinquishment of the government of that country by this . . . every thing else remained as before."[106] Some thirty years later, U.S. Supreme Court Chief Justice John Marshall made much the same point when deciding in the landmark case *Trustees of Dartmouth College v. Woodward* that Dartmouth's charter had conveyed at the Revolution from the Crown to the state. As the charter was "as much a *contract* as a grant of land," he observed, "circumstances have not changed it. In reason, in justice, and in law, it is now what it was in 1769."[107]

Most consequentially, Congress absorbed the legal precedent represented in the proclamation of 1763, asserting its exclusive authority over continental expansion far more effectively than the Crown ever had. At the same time, the new United States as well as individual states relied just as much as their predecessors on joint-stock corporations to finance, claim, dispossess, and settle indigenous lands at and beyond those western borders. Even Hamilton had argued that land companies may have been an exception to the rule; most corporations were sovereign concessions, but in this case "something more is intended—even the institution of a government" and the "creation of a body politic, or corporation of the highest nature; one, which in its maturity, will be able to create other corporations."[108] Several colonial-era land companies survived or were revived in the 1780s and beyond. Despite a decree of the Continental Congress in 1782 settling its territory once and for all as part of Pennsylvania, the Susquehanna Company continued aggressively and at times violently to press its "right to those lands in [its] possession" well into the nineteenth century.[109] The American partners in the Walpole (including Franklin), Illinois, Wabash, and Indiana Companies all solicited Congress for some reconfirmation of their status, while some 25,000 settlers in Ohio petitioned to erect the region into a fourteenth province of Westsylvania.[110]

Meanwhile, new companies emerged, variously organized as corporations, trusts, and syndicates, to settle in Ohio, Pennsylvania, Maine, and western New York, including a couple aiming to establish refuges for royalists fleeing the revolutions in France and Saint-Domingue.[111] In 1795, Georgia sold thirty-five million acres of Choctaw, Chickasaw, Creek, and Cherokee territory—the so-called Yazoo Lands—to four new companies, which in turn flipped their stakes to investors mostly in New England, including the *Mississippi*

Land Company. Georgia's decision to rescind the original sale amidst great controversy led the Mississippi Company to contrive a suit before the Supreme Court, *Fletcher v. Peck,* which, like *Dartmouth,* became foundational in establishing the supremacy of the federal government, the sanctity of private property rights, and the power of the United States and companies under it to take on the work of colonial corporations to dispossess indigenous lands and displace their people with settlers of this new nation.[112]

QUESTIONS EQUALLY INTERESTING AND UNCERTAIN: BRITISH INDIA

One of the new issues complicating traditional questions of both corporate and colonial power in the eighteenth century was the emergence of a central role for Parliament. While in earlier periods, grants and patents by legislation were rarities, by the later eighteenth century they had become far more common, as had the role of the Commons in shaping policy of overseas expansion. This was no incidental shift, as it also had profound implications on just how much latitude government had to deal with charters once granted. While centuries of common law limited the Crown's options for modifying or withdrawing charters, Parliament's sovereignty was in theory absolute and unlimited. It followed, then, that Parliament could both make corporations as well as alter or abrogate them at will. This was a point Daniel Webster, lead counsel for the College in *Dartmouth v. Woodward,* conceded. As a practical matter, however, he observed that it was telling that in "modern times" it was a power Parliament had almost never thought fit to exercise. Webster was only able to offer one example of "a celebrated instance" in which the Commons was compelled by such "great and overruling state necessity" to introduce a measure that would have in effect nullified a corporate charter. And even in that case, he noted, the bill failed, the Ministry fell, and a more moderate regulation introduced the next year ultimately left the charter intact and passed only "with the assent of the corporation."[113]

The instance—evidently so celebrated that, even a half-century later, Webster did not think it necessary to identify it by name—was Charles James Fox's aborted India Bill of 1783. The "necessity" was the rapid expansion since the 1750s of the East India Company's territorial empire in South Asia. Fox's bill, which sought to replace the Company's government with ministry-appointed council, failed in the House of Lords. Fox was soon replaced by William Pitt, whose successful bill—developed with input, though "assent" was perhaps a stretch, from Company directors—replaced Fox's council with a "Board of Commissioners for the Affairs of India," often known as the Board of Control, made up of six Privy Councilors, including one Secretary of State and the Chancellor of the Exchequer, meant to work together and in tandem with the Company's Court of Directors, a system that would come to be known as "double government."[114]

Pitt's India Act was certainly driven by the relatively novel state of the Company's territorial expansion and the vicious partisan politics of the moment, but in a different sense it had also been a long time in the making. Since the Glorious Revolution, the Commons had taken up the business of the chartered companies, including the East India Company, with ever greater frequency. Debates over trade and manufactures, imports and protection of domestic industries, petitions and complaints from company rivals, and of course the litany of scandals that arose in the aftermath of the South Sea crisis all dramatically augmented the role the Commons had played for centuries as a venue for grievances about monopolies and corporate privileges.[115] In the case of the East India Company, Parliament was legally obligated to take up such questions periodically, as the new United Company's charter in 1709, like others now, set out the condition that it be reviewed and renewed by Parliament every twenty years. The first of these vicennial reviews in 1730, like many to follow, offered ample opportunity for critics to call the Company and chartered rights themselves into question.

Both sides of this 1730 debate rehearsed arguments that would have seemed familiar decades if not a century earlier. John Barnard led the charge against the Company, making a case not for eliminating it outright so much as to break its exclusive privilege and require it to license separate traders, much like the conditions that had been imposed on the Royal African Company in 1698. A more open trade, he argued, would bring in more revenue, mobilize more capital toward the trade, fetch higher prices abroad and sell for lower ones at home, increase navigation, and bring those Britons seeking employment in the Swedish, Ostend, and other European East India companies back into the fold. Even if none of that were true, though, he insisted bluntly that "exclusive trades are monopolies" and thus illegal. In addition to these economic and constitutional arguments, Barnard accused the East India Company leadership specifically of financial improprieties, no doubt choosing his words strategically when he complained of attempts to "bubble up" the Company's stock.[116] The Company's advocates countered that any alteration to its constitution would be a grave error. It had a proven track record and did critical public service, not least in its role as a pillar of state finance. As Solicitor General Charles Talbot reasoned, those upstart East India Companies were proof that "all nations" acknowledged the importance of corporate privileges in structuring their East India trade. Talbot added that the Company had made great investments abroad on the assumption that it possessed its chartered rights in perpetuity; changing them now would be a "breach of public faith, even Parliamentary faith." William Glanville seconded the point, insisting that the Company had as much right to their patent as if it were a "private estate." As such, Barnard's proposal was nothing more than a "pickpocket."[117]

If Barnard could be accused of trying to steal the Company's right, the Ministry was not beneath a little bit of extortion in exchange for preventing the theft. The Company received its renewal by offering a payment of £200,000 and agreeing to reduce the interest rate on the standing £3.2 million loan. In 1744, as the next renewal was looming, it repeated this strategy, adding another £1 million to its capital stock (and thus to its loan to the state), which it was to pass along to the public by taking on its own new debt in the form of bond issues, and in 1750, it again agreed to reduce the interest to three percent. All in all, by the middle of the century, these various moves left the Company holding or administering £4.2 million in public debt, over double the amount from 1709, although at just over half the interest rate.[118] The Company's growing investments in British state finance proved to be a double-edged sword, enhancing its political autonomy while also amplifying calls for intervening in its affairs. The same might be said for its growing financial, political, and martial investments across Asia. Ongoing hostilities with the French *Compagnie des Indes Orientales,* especially in southeastern India, had reached an apex with the French invasion and occupation of Madras in 1746, renewing calls in London for transforming the Company into something like the trading condominium Barnard had proposed and, some suggested, having the Crown directly assume its political and military establishment. The Company strongly and successfully resisted.[119]

While unavoidably wrapped up in the global Anglo-French conflicts known as the Wars of the Austrian Succession (1739–1748) and the Seven Years' War (1756–1763), the East India Company's military ambitions and interests were, as they had always been, neither fully allied with nor fully inimical to those of British policymakers. On the one hand, the Company had its own ambitions, which, like the French and other European companies, were determined less by European geopolitics than by the various complex commercial and political environments in which it was enmeshed around the Indian Ocean world. This was especially the case in South Asia, as the gradual decentralization of Mughal authority across the early eighteenth century had enhanced the power of regional "successor states," engaged in their own nexus of alliances, conflicts, and expectations of financial, political, and military autonomy. While hardly shying away from military engagement on its own terms, East India Company leadership did not necessarily envision the extension of European war to Asia as prudent or inevitable. From 1753, both English and French companies tried multiple times to negotiate agreements that would have made the East Indies or parts of it neutral ground in any ensuing European conflict. By 1756, those efforts had failed, allowing the Seven Years' War to reach India, layering its geopolitical ambitions onto an already complex political and martial environment.[120] Conversely, the ostensible end of the war in 1763 hardly brought an end to the political intrigue or violence with either South Asian polities or the French. Such conflicts even extended to acts of corporate espionage: in 1766, the French envoy in London—during ongoing negotiations over a postwar settlement no less—was alleged to have conspired to purchase £100,000 of English Company stock, with the plan of distributing it to allies who were to use their votes as shareholders to endorse policies that might further the rift between the Company and Government.[121]

Though extending across the Indian Ocean world, the Anglo-French company conflict was perhaps sharpest in southeastern India, where, from their fortified coastal enclaves in Madras and Pondicherry, the two Companies had through the past decades inserted themselves in the region's commercial and political dynamics. Both became especially invested in the ongoing dynastic and succession struggles in the independent Mughal successor state of Hyderabad, as the English Company put its military and financial support behind Muhammad Ali Khan's claims as ruler, or *nawab,* of Arcot. Now involved deeply in what became known as the Carnatic Wars, the Company expanded its military establishment at Madras, as both the Company and some of its employees and British private traders backed the increasingly cash-starved *nawab* with substantial loans. Such support came at a price. The *nawab* secured this credit with territory, including granting the Company a substantial *jagir* (assignment of territorial revenue) and offering it leases and what were essentially mortgages on other of his lands. As Muhammad Ali Khan's debts grew—he owed upwards of £800,000 by 1755—the Company continued to protect its investments by prosecuting campaigns on his behalf against his rivals, creating a kind of military-debt cycle that only further expanded the Company's claims over the *nawab* and his territory. Though in 1760 the Company agreed to abandon the mortgages in exchange for a fixed annual payment, the *nawab* had to continue to borrow, largely from private Europeans, to meet these demands. In what would become a pattern across Asia in the decades to come, the Company, in the name of protecting its and others' investments, continued to make ever greater claims over Arcot and its territories in southern India.[122]

On the western coast of India, where the settlement at Bombay had been dramatically expanding its naval establishment since the 1730s, the Company had come to dominate maritime affairs and project its power inland. By midcentury, the tide had turned in the Company's decades-long battle at sea with forces allied to the Maratha Empire, especially those under the command Kanhoji Angre and his son Tulaji, whom the British regarded as "pirates." The Company had also largely supplanted the Sidis of Janjira, who for generations had served the Mughal Empire as a sort of tributary naval force in the western Indian littoral. By 1759, the Company leveraged this expanding power to leave Mughal officials with little choice but to appoint it to the powerful and lucrative office of *qilidar,* or governor of the fort, and *darogha,* commander of the fleet at Surat. Meanwhile, since receiving its *farman* in 1717, the Com-

pany had been making increasingly assertive commercial and political claims in Bengal, including aggressively expanding its fortification of Fort William at Calcutta. Tensions boiled over in 1756,
leading the Mughal *nawab,* Siraj ud-Daula, to invade and occupy
Calcutta. The relief of the town the following year by troops under
the command of Robert Clive, supported by the growing presence
of Royal Naval forces, led to a decade of bloody battles and political
machinations that ultimately established the Company as a dominant
political and military power in the region. That power was formalized in 1765, when Clive accepted the Emperor's offer to appoint the
Company to another, even more powerful and lucrative Mughal office:
diwan, revenue collector and judicial administrator, in Bengal, Bihar,
and Orissa.

The East India Company's expansion in mid-eighteenth-century
Asia was determined not just by its great ability to mobilize its financial and martial resources but also, as Edmund Burke would
later fret, its political capacity as "an English Corporation" to also
become "an integral part of the Mogul empire."[123] The Company's
power was rooted in the conquest not just of territory but the offices, assignments, and jurisdictional authority—as a *jagirdar,* a *za-
mindar,* a *qilidar,* and a *diwan,* among others—that followed from
it. That the Company was a corporation allowed it to take on such
positions, which were normally assumed by individuals often with
familial and lineal claims to them. A corporation, however, was at
the same time a very strange kind of person, let alone hereditary sovereign. The point was not lost on the Bihari historian and political
theorist Ghulam Husain Khan Tabataba'i, who clearly perceived that
there was something different about this new ruler. It was "not one
individual" but rather a "numerous body" whose "constituent parts
are never permanent." Its councils and officials were constantly ro-
tating and endlessly feuding. It was, he scoffed, as if Bengal had "no
master at all."[124]

The East India Company's acquisition of the *diwani* represented,
as a Parliamentary committee in 1765 found, "a very great revolution" in both "commerce as well as dominion." It could, at least in
theory, now draw on great territorial revenues to subsidize its
commercial and military establishment, while trade served as a novel
way to transfer those territorial revenues back to Britain.[125] Meanwhile, the value of Company stock skyrocketed with the anticipated

windfall of tax and other territorial revenue, rising by nearly twenty percent between April and September 1766. More and more Britons were now literally invested in Indian empire, among them many Members of Parliament. "Stock-jobbing now makes patriots," the satirist Horace Walpole lamented. "From [Exchange Alley] to the House it is like a path of ants." It had turned out, he quipped, to be "a very South-Sea year."[126]

Walpole was hardly the only one alarmed by the Company's rapidly expanding territorial empire. Critics compared it to the despots of Catholic Europe and Mughal India and frequently warned that overextended imperial ambition in Asia threatened to bring down the British Empire much as it had the Roman one.[127] The concerns were magnified by the fact that this empire was in the hands of a company that, Edmund Burke's *Annual Register* bemoaned, "has become arbiter of kingdoms, [and] raises and deposes sovereigns by its clerks and warehouse-keepers."[128] It was not that empire was too awesome a charge for a company but that its relationship with Britain was so palpably unclear. As Burke later observed, "the East India Company in India is not the British Nation" but rather a "Republic, a Commonwealth without a people" and thus without checks, balances, or control on its power.[129] Even more concerning than an uncontrollable company were the seemingly ungovernable employees and private traders whose commercial and financial interests, such as in the *nawab* of Arcot's territories, seemed to be driving further commercial and territorial expansion.[130] "I see where all this must end!" frustrated Madras Army officer Richard Smith prophesied in 1767. "A British Parliament sooner or later will issue their Mandates."[131] Indeed, the India issue so dominated British politics in the aftermath of the *diwani* that William Samuel Johnson complained to those back home that it was impossible to get any of Connecticut's business done. "All attention is engaged by the altercations upon the subject of the immense acquisitions of the East India Company," he observed, "whether they belong to the government, or to the Company, or to both; and how they shall be divided and regulated which are truly intricate and important questions, equally interesting and uncertain in their issue."[132]

Much like the American colonies, the East India Company had accumulated centuries of charters, independent government, and claims to property in rights at home and abroad that complicated any effort to regulate or subsume it. Government had no coherent policy on the issue, not least due to, as one historian has put it, "a seemingly endless game of ministerial musical chairs" in the decade following the accession of George III in 1760. The one-quarter of the House members that were India stock owners dominated the India debates in the Commons, but this did not so much represent a Company infiltration of Parliament as project the vicious ideological and partisan debates going on in the Company over how to handle its expansion onto the floor of the Parliament, and vice versa.[133] There was also no consistent position on the question of corporate charters. George Grenville, one of the great advocates for impositions on the American colonies, defended the Company's autonomy as a matter of "public faith and private property."[134] Conversely, Thomas Walpole, who a decade later would doggedly pursue a charter for a joint-stock company for government in Ohio, insisted that an empire in India was "too unwieldy" to be governed a company of merchants. Even Robert Clive, perceiving his employers to be too reticent to support its (and his) expanding power in Bengal, made the case for more aggressive state intervention. "So large a sovereignty," he argued, "may possibly be too extensive for a mercantile company."[135]

If the state by its nature refused any decisive political position with respect to the Company's empire, so too did the law. Asked about the issue in 1757, the Crown's legal counsel—the attorney general, Charles Pratt, Lord Camden, and the solicitor general, Charles Yorke—essentially suggested that the acquisitions in India were in fact three very different kinds of enterprises. In what would become an exceptionally influential advisory opinion, they argued that any new conquests made of European or Indian powers must be considered as belonging to the Crown; the King was free to re-grant those territories to the Company but they warned, doing so "to a Trading Company" would not be "warranted by Precedent, nor agreeable to sound Policy, nor to the Tenor of the Charters which have been laid before us." However, any places previously under Company jurisdiction, such as Calcutta, should "return to the old Dominion" and remain in Company control. Finally, "Indian Grants" fell somewhere in between, with the Company assuming "Property of the

Soil" but the Crown retaining ultimate sovereignty, especially over its "English Subjects who carry with them your Majesty's Laws, wherever they form Colonies."[136]

But just what was a *diwani* (or a *qilidari*, or a *jagir*)? Did it arise from a grant, a treaty, a purchase, a plunder, or a military conquest? Company officials frequently observed that they were essentially Mughal tributaries and continued to pay the emperor handsomely for the office as revenue collector, among other costs and obligations.[137] At the same time, Crown troops and ships had played a role, as had the conflict with the French, so had the *diwani* been acquired as part of the European war or not? British officials themselves muddied these distant waters when they contradicted Pratt and Yorke's guidance toward the close of the war, telling French negotiators that they could not return captured territories in India, "the Crown of *England* having no right to interfere in what is allowed to be the legal and exclusive property of a body corporate belonging to the *English* nation." Any such dispute, they insisted, "must be settled by the Company itself."[138] Thus, while the Pratt-Yorke decision seemed definitive enough on paper, in practice, as Burke would later put it, the lawyers had "equivocated."[139] Ironically, their opinion would soon take on new life in North America, where by the early 1770s a fraudulent version, stripped of specific references to the Mughal context, was circulating—some speculated at the hands of Samuel Wharton—to persuade land company promoters that the Crown's own lawyers had rescinded the 1763 royal proclamation's prohibitions on "Indian" purchases.[140]

The issue was finally settled in 1767, not by law but politics and money. Backed by a 546–347 shareholder vote and over the strenuous objections of the Prime Minister, the Company settled with the Chancellor of the Exchequer, Charles Townshend, to pay an annual sum of £400,000 "for the use of the Public" if the Crown renounced any direct claim over Bengal, Bihar, Orissa, or their revenues. In short, the Company, as Horace Walpole put it, "laboured to their utmost to make the usurpation of three Indian provinces, or rather kingdoms, pass for private property."[141] However, neither the territorial revenues nor the Company's trade lived up to its grandiose predictions, while the Company's costs were mounting. One problem was the growing number of bills of exchange coming from Bengal. Such bills were credit notes that served as the primary means by which individuals converted and remitted money home, buying them in India and then redeeming them with the Company once back in Britain. However, despite orders to the contrary, the Bengal council had been selling far more of these than their superiors in London could now afford to redeem. As military and civil expenses exploded—rebuilding Fort William in Calcutta had alone cost more than £1.6 million by 1772—goods, especially tea, piled up in London warehouses, exacerbated by North American boycotts. A general banking crisis in 1772 left lenders, especially the Bank of England, increasingly reluctant to extend the Company's credit, while the Company owed nearly £1 million to the state in postponed payments on its annual obligation and customs duties. Meanwhile, it was paying out greater and greater dividends to shareholders even as military setbacks in southern India and famine in Bengal in 1769 and 1770 sent its stock price plummeting and analogies to the South Sea Bubble soaring.[142]

By this time, the Company was "too big to fail."[143] As Thomas Pownall lamented, it had "wrought into the very frame and composition of our finances," to the point that its collapse would prove to be "the ruin of the whole edifice of the British Empire."[144] Company leadership floated several possible solutions. Lord North, now Prime Minister, rejected proposals to enlarge its joint stock, issue new bonds, or call in a portion of the Company's share the national debt. He did ultimately agree to offer the Company a substantial £1.4 million loan. There was, however, a catch. North inverted the strategy the Company had employed in 1767: any such assistance now must be accompanied by a Parliamentary "plan of regulation." The inquiry that followed took aim at reforming the Company's governance at home and inevitably reopened the *diwani* question. The resulting 1773 "Regulating Act," among other things, introduced a new position of Governor-General and a Supreme Court in Bengal, alongside many measures modifying Company government at home and abroad.[145]

The battles over the Regulating Act were fought out on many of the same terms as previous conflicts though translated into this new context. Andrew Stuart suggested that intervention was justified by "evident public utility" and that the Company's recent territorial expansion had rendered its chartered rights as a commercial body "effectively dissolved and destroyed."[146] Where his successor Thomas

Hutchinson had suggested Massachusetts was, like the East India Company, ultimately subject to the state, Pownall argued that the East India Company should be treated like "all other like emigrations and settlements *in partibus caeteris,*" that is, the American colonies, whose territorial acquisitions were naturally "annexed" to Crown sovereignty.[147] On the other side were those like Company hydrographer Alexander Dalrymple, who observed that the Company, like both Britain and the Mughal Empire, had an "antient Constitution" that provided expertise the state did not have but that rendered the Company a "Public Concern." He insisted that it was the Company's critics, not the Company, who were driven by "particular Interest" and that it was Parliamentary intervention on corporate privileges, not Company expansion, that was proving to be the real constitutional and legal revolution.[148]

For all the controversy surrounding it, North's Act resolved little. Several more Parliamentary inquiries and smaller measures followed, until Fox, amidst the political turmoil of the end of the American war, assumed the leadership of the Commons in 1783, and, in an uneasy coalition with his old rival North, committed to a more radical intervention in the Company's affairs.[149] Among other things, the debates that ensued returned to the familiar ground of, as Burke characterized it, "private property and corporate franchise." Yet such staid legal questions missed the point. "It has been a little painful to me," Burke opined, "to observe the intrusion into this important debate of such company as *Quo Warranto,* and *Mandamus,* and *Certiorari;* as if we were on a trial about mayors and aldermen, and capital burgesses." The problem was that the Company had become more than a mere corporation, Burke insisted. As a "species of political dominion," it was "in the strictest sense a *trust.*" As a corporation it might be autonomous and entitled to look after its private interest only. As a trust, however, it had a fiduciary duty to serve the best interests of those over whom it ruled. Also as a trust, there had to be some system by which it could be held accountable, and since the Company had a charter from Parliament, it was the obvious body to take this on. Burke in essence was cleverly turning the centuries-old argument for the Company against it: the charter did not protect the Company from intervention so much as demanded it. He neither denied the Company had "bought" those rights "for valuable consideration, over and over again" nor objected "*a priori,* against the propriety of leaving such extensive political powers in the hands of a company of merchants." That the Company had paid for its rights, however, was still another reason the Commons should intercede, "lest we should be thought to have sold the blood of millions of men, for the base consideration of money." The Company might keep its charter, but, Burke contended, its empire needed to be governed by a higher law. Fox's bill, in his mind, would serve as just such "a Magna Charta of Hindostan."[150]

The Company's acquisition of vast territorial power had raised a fundamental question: when a corporation becomes an empire, who precisely were its stakeholders? To Burke, these were now, first and foremost, "the people of India," a subject which had been met by Company advocates with "total silence." The problem, Fox insisted, was that corporate government inherently lent itself to the "fleecing" of "the poor unhappy natives" of India, because it was ultimately governed by two kinds of investors: those who had "become proprietors, not for commercial, but for political purposes" and used their power to defend entrenched interests and a corrupt system, and those interested only in financial returns, who were easily placated into going along with the Company's atrocities as long as they received their high dividends. This alone would justify intervention, as Burke had suggested. Yet Fox added another point. The Company had become so critical to British commerce and finance—customs receipts alone, he insisted, had outstripped the dividends the Company paid its shareholders nearly fivefold—that at this point "the people of England therefore had a much greater stake in the business than the proprietors of the Company." Conversely, the "nation," now invested in the Company through loans, reprieves on payments, and the use of government credit, had essentially become "collateral security" on the Company's debts, which gave it "great interest" in the Company's welfare and thus the "right to take upon themselves to check and control the government of the Company's settlements."[151] In a sense, the East India Company had mortgaged itself to government, and it was time to foreclose.

The controversies over Fox's bill swept through the British press and politics, battled out not only in the Commons but in any number of pamphlets, satirical prints, and treatises. Among those keenly observing these debates for over a decade was the political economist and philosopher Adam Smith. In 1776, Smith had published the first

"A Transfer of East India Stock" (depicting Charles
James Fox) by James Sayers, published by Thomas
Cornell, 1783. NPG D9747, National Portrait Gallery, London.

edition of his *An Inquiry into the Nature and Causes of the Wealth
of Nations,* in which readers could find no shortage of critique of
monopoly corporations and of the East India Company in particular. However, in the shadow of the debates over Fox's Bill,
Smith—who had at one point had volunteered himself for an ultimately aborted Company commission of inquiry to Bengal—set
about a third edition of *Wealth of Nations* with lengthy additions
meant to make a "full exposition of the Absurdity and hurtfulness
of almost all our chartered trading companies."[152] Departing from
Burke, Smith understood the East India Company and others like it
to be inherently corrupting, both a bad form of government and a

bad form of commerce. As a chartered corporation, the Company derived a monopoly and other anachronistic protections from the same outdated "exclusive corporation spirit" as municipal governments, guilds, and some educational and religious endowments. This he called the "mercantile system" and later generations "mercantilism." Yet, the problem was not just with corporations but also joint stock. By design, joint-stock directors' very job was to traffic in "other people's money," which inevitably led them to take irresponsible risks. Where individual traders or partners in a firm would always mind their own money with "anxious vigilance," in a joint stock "negligence and profusion must always prevail." The East India Company, however, had compounded its original sins as a corporation and as a joint stock by becoming an empire, a "strange absurdity" of a "sovereign as but an appendix to that of the merchant" that inevitably perverted both. "The government of an exclusive company of merchants," Smith bluntly observed, "is, perhaps, the worst of all governments for any country whatever."[153]

Smith, however, also offered some quiet caveats to these oft-quoted pronouncements. There were, he admitted, some public charges—banks, insurance companies, infrastructure—for which charters might be appropriate. Though he did not mince words with respect to the East India or Royal African Companies, by some tortured logic Smith managed to carve out an exemption for the Hudson's Bay Company, which (he suggested) operated on a smaller scale such that, though technically a corporation, it conducted business more in the spirit of a private co-partnery.[154] In his third edition, Smith even echoed long-standing defenses of corporate privileges when he admitted that, at least at the outset, "when a company of merchants undertake, at their own risk and expence, to establish a new trade with some remote and barbarous nation," some sort of temporary monopoly joint stock—like a patent or copyright granted to an inventor—might be in order.[155]

For its part, the Company's arguments remained similar to those that had been made for over a century. It continued to maintain that its charter could not be questioned without "divesting [the Company] of their franchises and property," reminding Parliament of "the example of all former times, in which every encroachment upon the sacred rights of private property, or private franchise, has been anxiously compensated by the wisdom and justice of the Legislature."[156] In 1783, the Court of Directors sent copies of the bill to upwards of fifty counties and municipalities, some reported, with a circular exclaiming that "Our property and charter are forcibly invaded. Look to your own."[157] To Fox's argument that the Company's growing debts justified intervention, George Johnstone retorted that recovering money could hardly be a higher priority than the sanctity of chartered rights. Besides, Fox had his metaphor right but his facts wrong: "So far from being bankrupt," the Company's debts were more like "a very trifling mortgage on a very fine estate, which would soon pay it off."[158] Most of all, though, those who criticized the Company's corporate privileges, its advocates maintained, misunderstood the unique nature of Indian trade and government. "It is, according to the Doctor [Smith]," W. J. Mickle jibed, "as safe to settle in, and trade with India, as to take counting-house near London-bridge, or to buy a peck of peas at Covent-Garden."[159]

Even Burke, later prosecuting the impeachment of Company Governor-General Warren Hastings, insisted that the Company's "mercantile constitution," insofar as it introduced a government dependent upon writing, was "perhaps the best contrivance that ever has been thought of by the wit of men for the government of a remote, large, disjointed empire"; in this sense, "the Counting-house gave lessons to the State." He continued:

> It will always happen that, if you can apply the regulations which private wisdom makes for private interests to the concerns of the State, you will then find that active, awakened and enlightened principle of self-interest has contrived a better system of things for the guard of that interest than ever the droning wisdom of people looking for good and of themselves—I mean for the greater part of mankind—ever contrived for the public. And therefore I repeat it, that the regulations made by mercantile men for their mercantile interest, when they have been able as in this case, to be applied to the discipline and order of the State, have produced a discipline and order which no State should be ashamed to copy, and without which such a State cannot exist.[160]

The Company's great wrongs had thus not established a principle against mercantile government, and to Burke, there was nothing about being a merchant that necessarily prevented one from governing. "I have known merchants with the sentiments and the abilities of great statesmen," he had opined during the debate on Fox's bill, "and I have seen persons in the rank of statesmen, with the conceptions and character of pedlars."[161] Many Company advocates and even some of its more moderate critics went further, contending that the state was neither competent nor justified in taking on such an enterprise.[162] Mickle, in the historical preface to his translation of Camões's sixteenth-century epic *Os Lusíadas,* offered a thinly veiled comparison to current circumstances when he excoriated the *Estado da India* as "the worst of all MONOPOLIES, a *Regal one.*"[163] There was no particular reason, Pitt noted in objecting to Fox's bill, to think a Prime Minister would be more responsible in charge of the "power and patronage" of Indian government than Company directors. As he observed in forwarding his own bill a year later, the prevailing sentiment that "commercial companies could not govern empires" was mere "speculation," a "theory" that had not been borne out "in practice."[164]

In the end, Pitt's India Act set out, in the words of historian P. J. Marshall, to "refurbish" rather than revoke the Company's "ancient form of government." The "price of financial aid," in this sense, was not the withdrawal of a charter but the establishment of a new principle of government oversight, or what North and George III had called a right of "constant inspection."[165] The introduction of some form of regulation served to naturalize and sanitize the whole idea of a Company empire in India, not to mention the notion of a British Empire in India. Moving forward for the next few decades, the question would be not whether the Company should govern India but rather how much it should be supervised and whether it should or could trade while doing so. The introduction of the Board of Control, not to mention the power over patronage that it entailed, also ensured that government ministries would now be invested in maintaining the new form of status quo. Thus, by the time of the next vicennial charter renewal in 1793, it was Henry Dundas at the head of the Board who repeated Pitt's argument that corporate rule might be "in opposition to established theories of government and commerce," but with proper supervision of the Board, it had become an indispensable "organ." Moreover, Dundas made the familiar case that Company rule rested on settlements, treaties, and territorial rights that traced to its "original and perpetual charters." Taking them would at best require a "complicated investigation & adjustment of the Claims," which the "Public" would owe it as compensation for its property. At worst, doing so at this point could jeopardize the entire foundation of British sovereignty in India.[166] The Company thus escaped yet again, though the cost of the twenty-year renewal this time was to agree to cancel the entirety of the state's £4.2 million debt, increase the Company's annual payment obligations to £500,000, and agree to various other obligations, such as wartime demands for use of soldiers, ships, and supplies. Dundas—who after all was also War Minister—reminded the Company that its monopoly did come at a price. Of course, the same was true of saltpeter, grain, rice, and all the other provisions the Company supplied, for which it managed to be paid handsomely.[167]

ABOLITION, INC.

One often underappreciated point about the controversy over the East India Company is how much it arose in the context of a "very great outcry against companies of all kinds," as the Duke of Bedford had put it, that had emerged by the 1740s.[168] When Jamaican planter and historian James Knight proposed reviving the Darien scheme in 1739, for example, he insisted that it should be a Crown project; "Companys," he wrote, "are too Subject to Errors and miscarriages through the Avarice or Sinister designs of the managers or their Agents."[169] Inquiries into the Levant Company in 1744 and 1753 resulted in further diminishments of its autonomy, including lower barriers of entry and the possibility of appeals on its policies to the Board of Trade. In 1750, the South Sea Company abandoned its *asiento*, rendering it largely a state debt servicing company.[170]

The Hudson's Bay Company similarly faced a wave of assaults, largely prompted by Arthur Dobbs, a large Irish landowner and colonial theorist and projector—he was one of the promoters of Virginia's Ohio Company—who had his own ambitions to establish a joint-stock corporation for trade, settlement, and exploration especially with the goal of reviving a venture to uncover a northerly westward route to Asia. Dobbs's efforts resulted in a review of the Company's charter by the Crown's law officers, a House of Commons inquiry, and a new £20,000 prize to incentivize anyone (or any company) that might uncover the Northwest Passage. For its part, the Hudson's Bay Company responded with what was by now an extremely familiar set of arguments: only an exclusive "Society or Company of Men" could bear the costs and difficulty of both governance and indigenous trade and maintain both profit and public interest; a charter was property and therefore could not be summarily withdrawn; and doing so would not only ruin British Canada but lead to a general "outcry" among all other colonists, boroughs, cities, colleges, and churches, who worried that their "properties" would be likewise "invaded, taken away or laid open and common."[171]

While the Hudson's Bay Company ultimately survived, the already beleaguered Royal African Company was not so lucky. When it was finally dissolved in 1752, however, its property and fortifications were bought and vested in a new consortium of Liverpool, London, and Bristol slave traders established by Parliament in 1750, known as *The Company of Merchants Trading to Africa*. More like a regulated company than a joint stock, this new Africa Company was to be much more actively supervised by the Board of Trade. The Board also insisted on taking direct responsibility for the new royal colony of Senegambia in 1765, as the Africa Company was, in its opinion, "in no respect qualified" to manage it.[172]

Yet even as the state and private traders were playing a greater role in West Africa, some in Britain were on the verge of developing one of the most radical corporate colonial experiments to date: not for promoting the slave trade but rather to abolish it. As with many aspects of the eighteenth-century British colonial world, this story also began, indirectly, with India. Through the second half of the eighteenth century, the volume of East India Company maritime traffic had increased dramatically, and with it the number of Asian sailors who served as crew on London-bound voyages. Often unable to return on eastbound ships, now replenished by European crew, many of these lascars, as they were known, ended up resident in London's docklands. By the 1780s, a self-appointed group of philanthropists set out to raise funds to provide relief for what they perceived to be an exploding crisis. The "Committee for the Relief of the Black Poor," however, soon discovered that this Asian community was not nearly as immense or as indigent as they had imagined.

Thus, they turned their attention to a new cause: the growing number of individuals of African descent arriving from across the Atlantic, especially the swelling number of black Loyalist refugees who ended up in London in the wake of the American war.[173]

Urged on by Harry Smeathman, a longtime advocate for west African colonization, the Committee soon reformulated its strategy from raising money for providing alms in London to attempting to export the "Black poor" to a colony in Africa. At this point, the philanthropic aims of the committee began to intersect with what had become a rapidly growing movement in Britain for abolishing the slave trade. By mid-1786, with the abolitionist Granville Sharp now leading the charge, the committee had secured support from the Treasury and Navy and fitted out ships with supplies and settlers for its new "Province of Freedom." Their plans centered on a main settlement, Granville Town, at what they called St. George's Bay in Sierra Leone, on land purchased from a Temne chieftain, known to the British as "King Tom." Sharp imagined this colony much as his close friend James Oglethorpe had Georgia: not only as an outlet for needy settlers but also as a utopian project that could remake the very nature of colonial property while also serving as a beacon of anti-slavery. He rejected the model of seigneurial proprietorship or dividing land into shares, favoring instead to base the property arrangements of the colony on the medieval legal principle of frankpledge, a kind of combined trusteeship and joint stock in which every member of the community paid tithings into a common fund.[174] Though the initial settlement succumbed to disease as well as conflict with European slavers and their allies among the Temne, Sharp remained undeterred.[175] In 1789, he wrote to the remaining inhabitants of Granville Town announcing a new plan to "form a *Company*, in order to carry on an *honourable trade* with the coast of Africa; and I have at last great hopes of success."[176]

Behind the *St. George's Bay Company* were some of the late eighteenth century's leading evangelicals and abolitionists, men such as Sharp, Thomas Clarkson, Charles Grant, and William Wilberforce, for whom the enterprise was, in the words of one historian, "an explicit experiment in moral mercantilism."[177] At the same time, it might also be thought of as an experiment in explicit mercantile morality, a colonial and humanitarian venture that insisted that private profit and public good were not only reconcilable but the best way to both run a successful colony and put an end to the slave trade and slavery. As a commercial body, a company could help to replace the profits of the slave trade with Sharp's "honourable" trade, what later generations of abolitionists would think of as "legitimate" commerce. As Grant put it, "Large profits are not indeed so much the object of the Company as the establishment of a fair progressive trade, and of the benefits of just government, arts and civilization among the Natives."[178] Meanwhile, incorporation would structure investment, order government, defend against rivals and critics, protect against "fraud or mismanagement," and "secure the separate property of the several Members from any claims upon them, beyond the amount of their respective subscriptions to the joint stock of the Company"—limited liability, *avant la lettre*.[179]

By 1790, Sharp and others set out to obtain a charter for their abolitionist resettlement experiment. There was, however, a legal conundrum. Defenders of corporate rights from Jeremiah Dummer to John Adams had long held that charters did not give sovereignty so much as make it possible for some British subjects to go out to try to obtain it for themselves. This time it was the opponents of the scheme that mobilized the same point: the Crown could not give a charter for St. George's Bay because it was not the Crown that had obtained sovereignty or property in the region. The Committee for the Black Poor had only occupied the colony on a sort of lease from the Temne, the validity of which, now that the colony had been routed by the same people, was questionable.[180] Sharp contended, however, that unlike the Royal African Company and its successors, these territories had not been acquired as leases but "actually *purchased,* [. . .] given up by the native Chiefs (under a ratified Charter) from themselves and their Heirs for ever to the Crown of England, for the use of the Settlers and their successors for ever." Thus, the colony was "not only an *English Settlement,* but an *English Territory,*" and as such was "the *most valuable Inheritance* of the present Free Settlers, and of all honest and orderly People, who shall hereafter seek an Asylum therein."[181] In other words, his contention was that the Committee had secured from the Temne an inviolable property right—through a charter and contract of sale—under Crown sovereignty, which, once vested in a British corporation, would serve as a perpetual foundation for a company colony.

This question over the nature of the Company's sovereignty was only one of several arguments made by a broad coalition of opponents. West Indian plantation owners, the Africa Company, and their allies all worked to forestall the effort, objecting to it both as an abolitionist project and a corporate one.[182] When, with the help of Attorney General Archibald Macdonald, they succeeded in rendering the attempts for a royal charter a dead letter, the would-be Company turned to Parliament, where many of their number were members and the humanitarian movement had growing support. Slave owners and slave traders remained fervent. Petitions poured into the Commons, ironically making much the same arguments for free trade and against an abolitionist "monopoly" that had been used to bring down the slave-trading Royal African Company.[183] The Merchant Venturers of Bristol reminded Parliament of "the Mischiefs which at former periods the Public has felt" from the creation of corporate bodies for overseas plantations; the Africa Company similarly recalled that "this Country derived little or no benefit" before 1698, when the slave trade and West African commerce were in the hands of a Royal African Company monopoly. Perhaps even more ironically, or cynically, arguments looking to preserve a commerce in human beings did so in part by insisting that coastal West Africa was no longer one of those "remote and barbarous nations," as Adam Smith called them, that had long justified corporate privileges. As the Bristol merchants continued, "exclusive Companies, if necessary or politic in any Point of View, can only be so where the Commerce proposed is of too great Magnitude or Extent to be undertaken by Individuals," but after more than a century of commercial and diplomatic exchange, West Africa was infused with "the free Spirit of Trade."[184]

Of course, no debate on such a colonial scheme would be complete without someone reaching to the early eighteenth century for a comparison to even greater corporate scandals. "The continent of Africa is certainly an object of speculation," one critic of the St. George's Bay project insisted, "not inferior to the *South-Sea*, or the *River Mississippi*; and nobody can deny that the present age abounds with *visionaries*, no less romantic, though perhaps inferior in abilities to a Knight or a Law." The political lesson of the past, however, was as important as the commercial one. This same polemicist alleged that much like those earlier "bubbles," the public abolitionist agenda of this Company would ultimately be revealed as a "mask" for their real objectives of personal enrichment and territorial expansion.[185] Another pamphleteer warned that a British territorial colony in west Africa would violate the terms of free trade in the Treaty of Paris and create such "alarm" with other Europeans as to set off a scramble for their own colonies. Some worried that a company authorized by Parliament would draw Great Britain into obligations to protect the colony while at the same time raising another version of the perennial omnipotence paradox: could Parliament make a company that, in making laws for itself and treaties with other nations, was "out of the controul of Parliament"? In this case, the problem was compounded by the idea of a perpetual body driven by the moral principles of mortal men. The current founders might indeed be trustworthy

> men of humanity, conscience, and good faith, and may make proper bye-laws and regulations; but their children or their assignees may be of a very different stamp, and interest may lead them to alter these bye-laws;—and where is then the humanity—where is the protection to be found?—not in the Parliament of this country; for they have given away the power from them to the St. George's Bay Company.[186]

The critics ultimately succeeded in their commercial but not political arguments. By the time it came to debate, the bill had abandoned any assertion of a commercial monopoly but instead focused on rendering the Company as a colonial government. This had, after all, been Sharp's vision all along. In May 1791, Parliament passed legislation authorizing the creation of the corporation and calling on the Crown to issue a charter for what was now being called the *Sierra Leone Company,* to exercise government over its territory for an initial term of thirty-one years. The new Company sent its first ship, under the command of Clarkson's brother John, to Nova Scotia, where, using the promise of land grants, he recruited over a thousand settlers for its new colony, ambitiously named Freetown.[187]

In many respects the Sierra Leone Company was a clear descendent of a long history of corporate colonies, yet it also reflected significant shifts in thinking over the century. Though it had commercial interests, it in essence began where the East India Company had recently ended: a corporation made to govern first and trade second. Moreover, once rare and exceptional or even oppositional in matters involving joint-stock companies, Parliament had now become central to the process of issuing "charters." Owing to their close ties to the Commons, the directors of the Sierra Leone Company did not jealously guard their independence from government as the East India Company or Massachusetts colony and many others once had. And, once again, it did seem, whether explicitly or not, that the Sierra Leone project had Georgia on its mind, as the Company soon became similarly reliant on government subventions for its civil and military establishment. It even approached the ministry about the possibility of sharing power, with the Crown taking over governance and martial matters and the Company overseeing commerce and civilizing missions.[188] In any event, the experiment was rather brief. By 1807, the year Parliament abolished the slave trade, the Company had largely collapsed, voluntarily surrendering its assets and authority, by means of more Parliamentary legislation, to a new Crown colony of Sierra Leone.[189]

Even in its demise, however, the Sierra Leone Company had set the stage for several more settlement experiments on the west African coast. The colony had been an object lesson in legal pluralism: a free port under English sovereignty, subsidized with British state funds, deeply reliant on the Royal Navy, but under company rule.[190] While the colony's administration was now in government hands, the Company's call to cultivate "civilization" in Africa was taken up by an unincorporated subscription society, the African Institution.[191] Meanwhile, a number of individuals who had left the Sierra Leone venture in 1791 conjured another abolitionist scheme, with significant partnership from several leading members of London's Sephardic Jewish community.[192] The aim of the *Bulama Island Association* was to establish a colony on Bolama, the former Portuguese fort and port off the coast of what is now Guinea-Bissau. Though it also aimed to contribute to the cause of abolition, this association forwarded an alternative vision of such a colony, rooted in cultivation rather than commerce. Its approach focused not on the relocation of freed slaves and promotion of legitimate trade but attracting European settlers who would instead use the colony as a base from which to spread "letters and religion" in the African interior. It was organized not as a corporation but a partnership and trust. Land was not to be held jointly, as in Sierra Leone, but sold to each adventurer as freehold property, at the rate of £15 per 125 acres, up to five hundred acres; the price was halved for those who would also settle in the colony. One could also acquire land by recruiting other settlers, while laborers, farmers, and indentured servants upon their freedom would receive smaller plots. These conditions, along with a plan for a legislative, judicial, and executive establishment, were formalized in a contract executed by the Society's founding members on March 9, 1792, which was to serve as a "Constitution of Government."[193]

Though it did organize some initial ventures, the Bulama Association did not last long. It faced stiff political opposition, having managed to antagonize both the Sierra Leone Company and the West Indian planters. By 1793, most of the initial investment had been spent and subsequent attempts to raise further capital failed.[194] A couple of years later, C. B. Wadström, the Swedish traveler active in English abolitionist circles, proposed reviving the Bulama enterprise in the form of a more formal company, one that would, more like Sierra Leone, be operated by a court of directors empowered to: "sell land; to engage colonists; to receive money or commodities; to pay money, and dispose of commodities; to appoint their own officers and agents, both in Europe and in the colony; to send out vessels, to trade wherever it may be found beneficial for the whole concern &c. and to lay a proper and satisfactory account of their proceedings, before a general meeting of the subscribers, every year." One of his more original ideas was to propose that such a company should explicitly separate responsibility for the different aspects of its government among two "classes" of directors. The first would be responsible for tending to the moral and social health of the colonists; the second would supervise commercial and political concerns, itself split into one division for the production of raw materials, internal trade and manufacture, and managing imports and exports and another to administer defense, finance, and political and diplomatic affairs "(1) with its government or direction, (2) with other companies or colonies, (3) with it's neighbouring African nations." He also proposed that the colony have its own court of directors, to manage the "active, practical, or executive" affairs on the spot.[195]

Not least because of the resumption of war with France, Wadström's proposals remained just that. However, all of these experiments taken together revealed that corporate plantation models had endured but also evolved in the face of the equally enduring and evolving opposition ideology, which picked up on the ideas of Smith and others and carried them into the nineteenth century. And as always, those arguments remained highly fungible and situational. The slave-trading African Company, for example, insisted its problem was not the Sierra Leone Company's "civilizing" mission *per se* but that it was not warranted in a place like coastal West Africa. Its representatives snidely suggested that the evangelicals' efforts would be better served elsewhere, like New Zealand.[196] As it turned out, they were not the only ones with that idea.

5

CORPORATE INNOVATIONS

The Age of Reform

There can be no excuse for the founders of New colonies who neglect
to profit by the sad experience which history affords them.

IN 1834, THE EAST INDIA Company invaded the nominally independent princely state of Kodagu and seized the territory,
goods, and person of its erstwhile ally, the Maharajah Virarajendra Wadiar. The "Rajah of Coorg," as the British knew him,
remained the Company's prisoner and pensioner for nearly two
decades, until, pleading for his health and his daughter's education, he received permission to travel briefly to Britain. Once there,
he refused to leave and instead petitioned the Queen and sued the
Company in the Court of Chancery to recover his "territory and
public revenue, together with private treasure." This included two
government securities—so-called "Company paper"—that the
East India Company held it had rightly repossessed as spoils of
war. Virarajendra and, after his death, his executors countered
that, as sovereign debt, the bonds were "property resting on the
faith of nations" which were exempted by the law of conquest
from seizure.[1] Both sides thus seemed to share a common premise:
whether as a military power or a public borrower, the East India
Company was a form of government. The Court agreed, dismissing
the case in 1860—as it had in several similar suits for over a half

century, including one brought by the *nawab* of Arcot in 1791—not on its merits but because the legal action fell outside its jurisdiction as a commercial court. The Company, it found, had acted not in a "mercantile character" but rather "in the exercise of their sovereign and political power."[2]

By the 1830s, the idea that companies might still be considered colonial sovereigns seemed to many simply "preposterous." It was bad enough that anachronisms like the East India Company endured, but by that time "no one would ever dream of asking for a Charter to govern," the journalist and MP James Buckingham insisted, "as that was the business, not of private individuals but of the Government and the State."[3] The late eighteenth century had introduced many models—"double government," Sierra Leone, Adam Smith—that suggested that even if such companies did exist, they should be rare and much more closely regulated by Crown and Parliament. In the meantime, the British state now asserted its own direct imperial authority from New South Wales to Canada, the Caribbean, and the Cape of Good Hope, through reformulated and newly emerging institutions, such as the Colonial Office, the Foreign Office, and legal commissions of inquiry fanning out across the globe. In short, many colonial subjects and imperial agents alike were making a gradual but persuasive case for a more "single, if flexible, imperial legal order," in which something like *the* British Empire might begin to emerge.[4]

Yet, alongside all this, it turned out that people still did dream of asking for charters to govern and were in fact doing so with an exuberance perhaps not seen since the early seventeenth century. The 1820s and 1830s, long thought to be a period either of imperial doldrums caught between the tempests of the first and second British empires or connected to them only by the "informal" empires of capital and trade, turned out to be fertile with corporate projects from South America to South Australia. As older enterprises like the East India Company persisted, newer ones drew on their legacies, continuing to blur the lines between public and private interest and indeed to make a virtue of that blurring. These companies were in many ways quite different than their forebears, but, in an age of reform that was also another age of speculation, they continued to make the powerful case that corporations should do the work of colonialism, not least because they had always done so.

THE COMPANIES RAJ

In 1813, the East India Company's charter was up for another of its vicennial renewals. It was a controversial one, even by the Company's standards. The Company's vast and rapid territorial expansion—and vast debts accumulated in the process—introduced novel and complex concerns, from granular if divisive questions about the proper methods of land tenure and revenue collection to the highly politicized issue, taken up by many of the same evangelicals who had driven the Sierra Leone experiment, of the extent to which missionaries should be free to do their work in India. Yet, despite all that had changed, much about the debate that ensued would not have seemed out of place twenty, or even two hundred, years earlier. Company critics assailed monopoly and the notion of commercial sovereignty, now better armed with the odd sentiment or digested wisdom from *The Wealth of Nations* in their quiver. Meanwhile, advocates defended the deep history of the Company's constitution, its long experience, and, above all, the critical necessity of maintaining its exclusive privilege.[5] The lawyer and economic writer Joshua Montefiore (who had taken part in the Bulama Company expedition among other colonial adventures) rehearsed a common refrain when he made the case that the Company's trade and its settlements were "actual and patrimonial possessions" that could not simply be seized, even by Parliament.[6] David Macpherson reminded his readers that the Crown in 1762 had contended to French negotiators that British territory in India was the Company's "undoubted property."[7] John Bruce, Dundas's ally now at the head of both the State Papers Office and the East India Company's new Historiographers Office, drove this point home in his two-thousand-plus-page *Annals of the Honourable East India Company,* which made the case for the "progressive aspects of Company's Rights" going back to its origins.[8] Montefiore summed it up it in his 1803 *Commercial Dictionary,* as Dundas and many others had before: the idea of the Company might be "contrary to the best esteemed theories respecting trade, monopolies, and free merchants, but in this, as in all other cases, experience should be preferred to even the most plausible theory."[9]

The most "esteemed" of such theories were those of Adam Smith. "Some persons had bolstered up their own sentiments by quoting the authority of Dr. Adam Smith," the political economist Hutches Trower observed, but, quoting the equally venerable Edmund Burke, he insisted that no "established form of government" should be destroyed "for a theory however perfect." Moreover, "the present question was more nearly connected with their *duties* as *sovereigns*," and not about, as he noted it was in Smith's day, "their *privileges* as merchants."[10] Montefiore, whose nephew Moses would become one of the most influential financiers and philanthropists in Victorian Britain, blamed "the Theory of Adam Smith," along with the French Revolution, for having set in motion a "[s]torm which has been gathering these thirty years," enabling an assault on the Company that arose from the "clamours of fashion, or the interest of individuals," not sound principles.[11] "Dr. Adam Smith, the great oracle of the advocates for the extension of trade, but who, like other oracles, is not always understood by his own priests," Company director Robert Grant argued, was "considerably mistaken in all this business."[12] Macpherson concluded that Smith's "erroneous" conclusions were founded in a "deficiency of knowledge of the facts."[13] At the same time, Company officials observed, current critics were in many ways more extreme and unyielding. "The ablest writers on political economy, and the most strenuous against monopolies have not condemned them simply and universally, as most of the petitions now in question do"—"Even Dr. Adam Smith."[14]

The Company eventually got its renewed charter in 1813, though, with the notable exception of China, it had now been stripped of much of its commercial monopoly as well as its exclusive jurisdiction over some selected places and people, most notoriously the missionaries. The law made subtle but substantial reforms as well. In particular, the "Territorial and Political" branch was now to be separated from its "Commercial" revenue in its account books and those books were to be made available to Parliament for annual inspection.[15] Turning the Company into two distinct enterprises, at least on paper, was a concession to those who, with Smith, thought it was time to cease the "strange absurdity" of combining the merchant and the sovereign in a single body. Yet in practice, the measure tended to have the opposite effect. The commercial business continued to do what it had been doing for years, only more transparently, as if the Company now owned a subsidiary trading company to help fund and facilitate running its territorial government.

The commercial department even charged the political department interest on its loans as if it were a separate business. When in 1825 Crown lawyers questioned whether this was legal, the Company's solicitor, J. B. Bosanquet, insisted that doing so was completely proper "according to all mercantile principles." As he continued, "It appears to me to be reasonable and consistent with the true intent of the statute to state the account as it would be stated if the transaction had occurred between the Indian government on the one hand and a private merchant on the other."[16]

The issue was rendered moot in 1834, when, in the next routine charter renewal, Parliament finally stripped the Company of its trading functions and for the first time formally asserted that the Company held its territorial government not in its own right but "in trust" for the British Crown. The legal scholar Frederic Maitland would later rightly call this "no idle proposition but the settlement of a great dispute," which set a precedent for the concept of imperial trusteeship' for generations to come.[17] At the time, however, it left much unsettled. Though liberalizing the India trade, the measure had managed to reinscribe illiberal Company government and strengthen its authority in various ways. The Governor-General, one Indian newspaper lamented, now had "the same despotic power as the Czar of Russia."[18] Moreover, as the Company's advocates had insisted for centuries, divesting it of its commercial business was no simple task. To effect it, the Company had to sell off over £15 million worth of assets, and some claims, such as the money still owed from the territorial revenues, were never fully or adequately accounted. Moreover, shareholders needed to be compensated for the sudden loss of a substantial aspect of the company in which they had invested. The solution was to offer them an option either to redeem their stock immediately for double its nominal value or to hold onto it as a forty-year annuity secured by £2 million taken out of the sales of Company assets. That endowment would be vested with the government's national debt commission, an ironic twist given that a century earlier the Company had basically served as such a commission.[19]

Divesting the Company of its commercial business did not so much sharpen the lines between colonial commerce and government as redraw them. Joint stock, with its capacity to allow people to participate in trade quietly and at a remove, continued to encourage a slippery relationship between state officials and commercial enterprises. Since 1793, Company government, revenue, and judicial officers had been expressly prohibited from direct involvement in private commercial transactions but not from holding shares in companies that might do so on their behalf.[20] There was certainly nothing stopping former Company employees from capitalizing on their experience and connections, investing both money and connections made in private trade in finance, shipping, and manufacturing enterprises both in Britain and India.[21] Some went on to found or work for the growing number of "agency houses" that served as local managers, bankers, and insurers for a range of other commercial concerns, many of which themselves would in time become Company shareholders.[22]

The Company's government continued, as it had in the eighteenth century, to employ and support other companies that took on different aspects of colonial development and governance, such as banking, insurance, infrastructural and territorial development, and local administration.[23] As its territorial and governmental power expanded, the Company encouraged some enterprises with grants of land, relief from certain financial obligations, and forms of exclusive patent. This ran up against another centuries-old legal question: Could the East India Company, a corporation, make a corporation? In a strict interpretation of the common law, the answer was no, but in 1839, the Crown's legal advisors and the Company's counsel found that, in its legislative capacity derived from the Crown's letters patent—that is, as a form of government—the Company did have the power to make corporations and limit liability much as a royal charter might do.[24] The Company had been doing this for some time anyway. In 1824, for example, Thomas Munro, the otherwise professedly anti-monopolist governor of Madras, had recommended that the Company offer exclusive patents to a civil servant, Josiah Marshall Heath, for an ironworks company. Munro had thought of the enterprise as "not only a public but as a national object," though its collapse soon after had left it merely what Charles Dickens later called "a great To Be."[25] Following the reforms to the Company in 1813 and 1833, many companies took the opportunity to branch into services that had once been under its purview, such as the *Marine Insurance Company,* established in 1836 and formally incorporated a half century later, and the *Assam Company,* founded in 1839, backed by land grants, laws, and regulations to take on Company tea plantations and their attendant responsibilities for local administration, policing, services, and development.[26]

As the Company evolved into a primarily and then exclusively governing body, various other private or corporate enterprises not only took over many of its previous commercial roles but also assumed many of the arguments the Company had once made on its own behalf. This was clearest in the case of the railways. Both the *East Indian Railway* (EIR) and the *Great Indian Peninsular Railway* (GIPR) were incorporated by Parliament in 1849, though the extent of their powers and rights in India were largely defined by laws, regulations, and contracts made subsequently by and with the East India Company.[27] Like the East India Company before them, the railway concerns were assailed by critics as monopolies, as too large, as too powerful, as doing work more properly suited to government, and as prone to corruption, all the more so in India, which allegedly lacked Europe's civic infrastructure for "checking the abuses to which monied institutions are so liable."[28] Advocates likewise responded in familiar terms. "For reasons common to all countries, Governments do not, and cannot manage such affairs nearly as well as private persons can," argued John Chapman, chairman of the GIPR. "The principles on which the Government, as a Government, must necessarily proceed"—here "government" ironically meant the East India Company—"are incompatible with the shrewdness of observation, the freedom of thought, the quickness of resolve, the energy of action, the exactness of arrangement, the completeness of supervision, and the fulness of individual responsibility which give to private interests their customary success." Moreover, companies were in themselves a critical vanguard of the colonial civilizing mission, as their "principle of association" would transform a place like India, where "the energy of individual thought has long been cramped by submission to despotic governments, to irresponsible and venal subordinates, to the ceremonies and priesthood of a highly irrational religion, and to a public opinion, founded not on investigation, but traditional usages and observances."[29]

The racialist political argument for companies mirrored an economic one. As Louis Mallet later observed, any notion that "strict rules of economic and financial science" applied in India was "impossible and illogical." Liberal political economy might have been fine for Europe, but, outside it, undertaking business without some kind of hedge against risk was simply the "venture of a gambler."[30] In this sense, corporations might have served colonial enterprise better than the state but could not do that work without the backing of the state. "Private capitalists," the EIR's managing director Rowland Macdonald Stephenson insisted, would never invest without the security of the "cooperation and support of the Government" in the form of charters, land grants, and subsidies.[31] And this is precisely what they got. The East India Company offered land to the EIR on a ninety-nine-year leasehold and promised to "promote the passing" of further Acts by the Indian government necessary to "fulfil, in India, the objects of their undertaking." As if to make the analogy between the two companies complete, as security, the EIR was to deposit its £1 million capital stock in the East India Company's treasury, which in return guaranteed it earnings of five percent interest, an arrangement that was uncannily similar to the one the Company had reached with the British state in 1709.[32]

Guaranteed returns on shares became a standard requirement for the development of colonial railways, in India and elsewhere, alongside other subsidies, such as rent and tax abatements, land grants, rights of way and eminent domain, and other powers over local property and people "for public objects."[33] In turn, the railways became vital to the expansion and preservation of empire, facilitating the construction of civic infrastructure and the transportation of troops, travelers, supplies, commodities, food, and information, especially as telegraph lines often paralleled, quite literally, the expansion of rail. Railways also took on forms of local administration, and over time came to assert great influence over property, people, labor regimes, and the very culture of colonial India.[34] A similar dynamic played out at sea, as the increasing number of British steamship companies in the Indian Ocean sought charters, subsidies, and exclusive contracts, such as for mail service, on the grounds, as James Mackillop argued at an East India Company shareholder meeting in 1853, that they undertook matters of "great importance" while "suffering by the part they have taken in a great public enterprise."[35]

New commercial initiatives were perhaps no more central to East India Company government than the emergence of what one later observer called "Public Banks, or Banks of a corporate character."[36]

The East India Company's government in Calcutta, with a twenty-percent stake, was the largest shareholder in the Bank of Bengal, incorporated in 1809. Similar arrangements emerged in Bombay in 1840. In Madras, a joint-stock bank replaced the government bank in 1843, since, as officials argued, it made little sense to leave banking to civil servants and political appointees "to whom the business of Banking is utterly strange."[37] The presidency banks managed government debt and pay and issued bank notes, much as the East India Company once had. They did not, however, undertake foreign exchange and remittances of revenue back to Britain that had once been handled by the Company's commerce. Agency houses were more than happy to fill that void through their own system of hypothecation bills sold to the East India Company and redeemable on their London houses. Meanwhile, a new generation of "managing" agency houses, which arose after a string of established Calcutta houses failed in the wake of a widespread commercial and credit crisis in India (spurred on in part by high levels of Company borrowing during the Burmese war of 1824–26), sought to avoid repeating what they regarded as the mistake of combining commercial and financial functions. Instead, they used suites of subsidiary joint-stock companies to do business in a range of fields, including insurance, banking, shipping, infrastructure, and trades such as tea and opium. The sometimes labyrinthine nexus of firms and corporations tracing back to powerful parent agency houses like Jardine Matheson & Co. and Dent & Co. in turn came to insinuate themselves into government and imperial concerns, of which the mid-nineteenth century attacks on China, known generally as the Opium Wars, were the most notorious but hardly the only outcome.[38]

George Larpent, a partner in the London agency house of Cockerell, Trail, & Co.—later chairman of both *The Peninsular & Oriental Steam Navigation Company* (P&O) and the EIR—proposed a different solution for the problem of Indian colonial finance: a single, London-based, chartered central joint-stock bank. It was to have £5 million in capital, handle remittances, and ultimately substitute for the East India Company as a venue for determining colonial economic policy and governance. Despite the support of nearly a hundred individuals and firms and a manifesto penned by the political economist John Ramsay McCulloch, the scheme met with stiff resistance from other agency houses, Calcutta merchant circles, and Company government, which derided it as what Governor-General Lord Auckland called a "swaggering interloper."[39]

Larpent's project may have failed, as did several more similar attempts over the following decade, but it was a reflection of a much broader and enduring phenomenon: the rise through the 1830s and 1840s of several joint-stock foreign investment banks looking to take on exchange, deposit, remittance services, mortgage financing, and commercial and property investment within and across colonial boundaries.[40] Around the globe, "colonial banks" became institutional investors and in some cases took controlling interests in foreign financial institutions, public works, transportation, communication, and even local politics, territory, and other aspects of governance.[41] Such banks capitalized on westward expansion in British Australia and North America and infiltrated the revolutions occurring across early nineteenth-century Central and South America, not to mention the new nations that emerged in their wake. The beginning of the end of slavery in 1833 turned out to be a big business, as joint-stock banks clamored to take on the management of the large amounts of capital represented by the government's lavish offer of compensation to slaveholders: the *Bank of Jamaica*, established in Kingston in 1836 and operating until 1865; the *Colonial Bank*, chartered in London that same year and persisting into the twentieth century; the *West India Bank*, founded in 1839 in Barbados; and the short-lived *Planters Bank*, established the same year.[42]

Many colonial officials were rather skeptical of these joint-stock banks. The East India Company dismissed them as being of a "novel and peculiar character."[43] Company secretary James Cosmo Melvill, among others, ironically suggested that their joint-stock character and mixture of public enterprises like note-issuing with commercial investments would lead to "improper and reckless management."[44] The Company especially resented the ways in which these independent banks threatened to impose on its jurisdiction. Its officials intervened, for example, to compel the projectors of a would-be *Bank of Asia* to exclude India from their charter, while the *Chartered Bank of India, Australia, and China* similarly attempted to avoid the issue by restricting its India business to subsidiaries. The Company was not alone in its concern. James Wilson at the Treasury worried that proposals to allow the *Oriental Bank* to issue legal tender at Ceylon and its own attempts to forestall charters for the Bank of Asia and other competitors were signals of its ambition to mobilize its charter to "establish a monopoly in the hands of a single Company."[45] Worse still, John Montagu, the colonial secretary of Van Diemen's Land—the island colony off the southeastern coast of Australia later known as Tasmania—warned that the chartered *Bank of Australasia* threatened nothing less than to "obtain an ascendancy in all the British possessions abroad . . . and raise up an *imperium in imperio* which may in time look to higher ends than the profits of Banking Establishments."[46]

To the advocates of joint-stock banks, however, this was precisely the reaction one might have expected from entrenched and established interests. As national debates raged over widening the franchise, and the very concept of the "middle class" was emerging as a political force, joint-stock banks were to some a model of political reform, one constituted by "representatives of the people" rather than the aristocratic and affluent Bank of England and the privileged private banking houses.[47] Colonial banks may have rejected the suggestion that they aimed at monopoly but did agree they were far more than simple financial institutions. "If they promote their interest, they promote the interest of the Colonies," George Reny Young argued on behalf of the *Bank of British North America* in 1838. Moreover, by investing in bank shares, "local capitalists are bound up as part of the body-politic."[48] G. M. Bell observed in 1840 that joint-stock banking forged "a chain of connection" through urban, national, and provincial and colonial jurisdictions, "supported by the extended and diversified business and commercial resources of a numerous proprietary." They thus served not only commercial but moral, religious, and national ends in the "character of public institutions."[49]

THE ROARING '20S

The East India Company was hardly the only chartered company that faced challenges in the early nineteenth century. For some, it again seemed that the era of colonial companies was coming to an end. The Levant Company, especially strained in the wake of the Napoleonic War, had largely devolved into a set of regionalized

trading interests when, in 1825, the Crown finally subsumed its diplomatic functions, part of an effort to centralize British diplomacy
globally.[50] In 1821, the Africa Company, hobbled by the end of the
slave trade in 1807 and financially and politically exhausted from
its ongoing military conflicts with the Ashanti, was divested of its
responsibilities in West Africa, though it would be another two decades before the Crown took them in directly.[51] The South Sea Company still hobbled along, servicing its annuities as an arm of government finance; at its headquarters, the essayist Charles Lamb
lamented, "some forms of business are still kept up, though the soul
be long since fled."[52] In 1822, the Irish Society ordered that a collection of its history, records, and charters be published to prove its
"powers could neither be alienated nor discontinued," but while it
continued on as large landholder, several lawsuits and Parliamentary interventions from the 1830s through the 1850s would eventually transform it into a philanthropic trust.[53]

The Hudson's Bay Company faced stiff competition as well, from
both the new Crown colonies of Lower and Upper Canada, formally
established by statute in 1791, and the Montreal-based commercial
consortium known as the *North-West Company,* or *Sociétés.* First
emerging around the 1780s, the North-West Company had by the
early nineteenth century begun aggressively to challenge the Hudson's Bay Company's charter and territorial government. An ingenious partnership which merged its subsidiary joint-stock *Michilimackinac* (later *Montreal-Michilimackinac*) *Company* with John
Jacob Astor's New York–chartered *American Fur Company* and its
two subsidiaries allowed the Montreal partners to effectively pursue
both westward expansion and ultimately a Pacific trade as an American company unrestricted by either the Hudson's Bay Company or
East India Company's jurisdictions.[54] When Astor cut ties with his
Canadian partners after the United States prohibited foreign fur
traders following the War of 1812, the North-West Company refo-
cused on breaking into Hudson's Bay Company territory more directly. An escalating set of confrontations, legal challenges, and violent conflicts followed, culminating in a bloody battle in 1816 at
the 116,000-square-mile Red River or Assiniboia colony, which the
Hudson's Bay Company had granted as a proprietary concession to
its largest shareholder, the Earl of Selkirk.[55]

Though the Company was not technically party to the conflict, the controversy was tailor-made for the airing of longtime grievances against it. The North-West Company protested that it was only acting in the defense of its Métis allies against Selkirk's aggression, while also insisting that his proprietorship, whose authority ultimately rested on a Hudson's Bay Company that dated to the days of the Stuarts, could not possibly still be considered legitimate in their day and age.[56] The attorney general of Upper Canada, John Beverly Robinson, brought criminal charges against Selkirk, who promptly fled to England and died.[57] W. B. Coltman, appointed as commissioner to investigate the affair, accused the Company of having failed both as a government, for allowing a private war to unfold in its jurisdiction, and as a joint-stock company, in allowing "so complete controul to be obtained over their Company by an Individual" in Selkirk. Though "the test of experience" might still suggest a monopoly company was the best way to manage trade and relations with First Nations, the Company's infractions, he argued, amounted to an offense "of nonuser and misuser" that would have justified taking out an action against its charter.[58]

Persuaded, Henry Goulburn, the permanent colonial undersecretary, began the first steps of a legal challenge by collecting evidence, which included reports from the previous Commons inquiry in 1749. Whether Goulburn and others intended to follow through or simply leverage the threat to force the companies to come to some truce, it worked. In a moment reminiscent of the union of the two warring East India Companies in 1709, by 1818, the North-West and Hudson's Bay Companies had agreed to a merger of sorts, which was to be effected by allowing North-West Company members to trade in their shares for Hudson's Bay stock. Also much like the East India Company, the Hudson's Bay Company, which in the late eighteenth century had largely rested on its trading enterprises, emerged reinvigorated as a territorial government.[59] Though continuing on the foundations of its 1670 charter, the Company's authority was reinforced by an Act of Parliament in 1821 and vastly expanded, in the form of a twenty-one-year grant to manage trade and settlement on all the territory from the Company's western boundaries to the Pacific. The Company absorbed the Red River settlement at Selkirk's death in 1820, and placed it under a corporate government, the

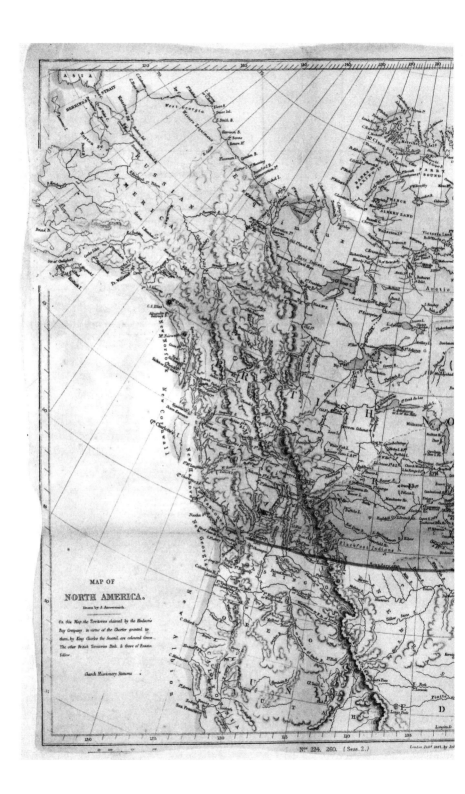

MAP OF

NORTH AMERICA.

Drawn by J. Arrowsmith.

On this Map the Territories claimed by the Hudsons
Bay Company in virtue of the Charter granted to
them by King Charles the Second are coloured Green.
The other British Territories Pink & those of Russia
Yellow.

Church Missionary Stations

Nº 224. 260. (Sess. 2.)   London Publ 1857 by John

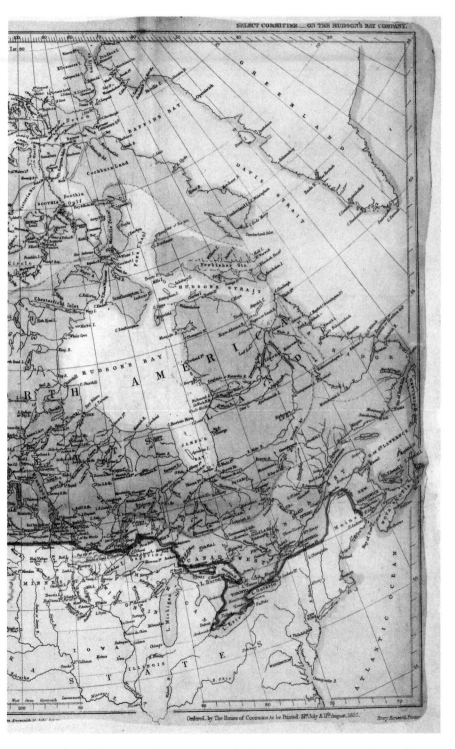

Map of North America by J. Arrowsmith, showing the Territories claimed by the Hudson's Bay Company, 1857. National Archives of the UK (TNA): MPK 1/386 (6).

Council of Assiniboia. Finally, in 1839, it expanded its territory further when it leased the territory along the West Coast to the south of Cape Spencer in Alaska from the Russian-chartered American Company.[60]

As the East India and Hudson's Bay Companies were defending themselves from their critics, many new projects for colonial companies emerged, some clearly inspired by their predecessors. In 1821, the geographer James MacQueen proposed a chartered company for West Africa "after the manner of the East India Company," calling on centuries of similar arguments to advance this as the only way to ensure the "Unity of action and design . . . such as has been done in India, against which no native power shall be able to raise its head."[61] The proposal did not proceed. MacQueen himself would become involved in a number of other projects over the next decade, including as agent for the Colonial Bank, whose roots traced to yet another company project of the period: a proposal in 1824 for a West India Company with broad interests in marine insurance, government lending, plantation projects, and mortgage banking for West India planters. Such an ambitious enterprise, its projectors insisted, must be a joint-stock company, as it was "a business which cannot be advantageously carried on by a small Capitalist."[62]

The proposal was deeply controversial. William Wolryche-Whitmore decried it as a misguided attempt to "renew the experiment" of the South Sea Company and, channeling Adam Smith, was skeptical of the very idea of establishing a joint-stock company for such purposes. "How could a company," he asked, "carry on the business of plantations better than expert individuals?"[63] Abolitionists were particularly incensed. As debates continued over when, how, or if to abolish slavery through the British Empire, it was becoming clear that any such settlement would almost inevitably require granting compensation to slaveholders. While the new West India Company was in one sense ostensibly anticipating great revenue from managing the windfall of money that would come to plantation owners, critics objected that the scheme was not meant to profit from emancipation but to prevent it. One concern was that the company, either as a plantation owner or through its mortgage holdings on others' lands, could come to claim slaves as a form of perpetual mortmain property of a corporation, making the emancipation of slaves much harder to legislate than if they were claimed by individuals. There was also a moral issue. A corporation by its nature had no mercy and worked through agents who, as mere employees, would inevitably prove crueler in general than individual slaveholders; as Henry Brougham put it, "those who had been ill-used before, would be ten thousand times worse off now, and be sacrificed to a joint-stock company, trafficking in the property of human flesh."[64] (For their part, advocates maintained that they would be less prone to such "acts of oppression" precisely because their enterprise would be a London-based corporation "whose proceedings must necessarily be known to the public."[65]) It was certainly questionable logic to rest one's argument on the morality of individual slave owners, but even if one believed a corporation would act with more compassion, it was still inherently offensive to establish any new institution that would perpetuate slavery. The abolitionist Thomas Fowell Buxton, for one, made it clear he did not "object to this Company because it was a Joint-Stock Company, but because its object was to deal in men."[66]

James Stephen Jr., legal counsel at the Colonial Office, did, however, have several "weighty objections" to the rather confused nature of the company being proposed. Its projectors had requested it be chartered by act of Parliament so that it might be given "legal existence recognized by the Legislature" but did not seek evidently for that legislation to formally incorporate it. Instead, they imagined that, as a private partnership, its status in the West Indies could be secured by Crown "Proclamations" giving it the "same legal rights for the Company as are already Secured to individuals." This was both strangely convoluted and legally nonsensical. If granting a company the same rights held by individuals did not make the company a corporation, Stephen scoffed, "I do not understand the expression." Making matters more confusing was the fact that the projectors then set out to secure a royal charter that would have rendered the company a corporation after all. By Stephen's math, such a charter would be "repugnant" to the antecedent legislation and "ipso facto" render it and the rights it had already granted "obsolete and inoperative." Worse still was the constitutional paradox raised by the Company's ecumenical business plan. "The objects for which the Company is to be incorporated are so large and indefinite," Stephen objected, "that I scarcely know what species of Trade or Business they might not lawfully undertake." The clause that would have allowed the Company to lend money to its own members seemed especially noxious to him. Putting that into the charter, he feared, "would make the King directly Accessary to this delusion."[67]

For some, the problem was not the West India Company *per se* (it did eventually get its charter) but that it was yet another example of the disturbing fervor in company speculation that had emerged by the mid-1820s. Some estimates put the number of new companies at over six hundred, a good number of which were driven by speculation in the newly independent nations of Latin America, including at least twenty-eight for mines alone.[68] In theory, many of these companies, as unchartered joint-stock associations, were illegal by the terms of the 1720 "Bubble Act." However, as the Court of King's Bench observed in *Rex v. Dodd* in 1808, the statute had been largely ignored for nearly a century.[69] In the following years, there were several more attempts to revive the law, perhaps no more boldly than in a suit that concerned one of those new mining companies, *The Company of Adventurers in the Mines of Real del Monte*. Established largely under the direction of engineer and company promoter John Taylor, its project was to invest in and manage the Count of Regla's mines in the Pachuca–Real del Monte district in what would later become the Mexican state of Hidalgo. The company had no charter or act authorizing it, yet its deed of settlement outlined a governance structure that was strikingly corporation-like, with rules governing shareholding and governance, including establishing courts of directors and proprietors. It even had a well-connected (if largely honorary) chairman: Thomas Fowell Buxton.[70]

Real del Monte might have remained one of the many failed and forgotten enterprises of the period had one of its original promoters not sued Taylor in the Court of Chancery over being cut out of a subsidiary venture. The Lord Chancellor, Lord Eldon, took the ensuing case, *Kinder v. Taylor,* as an opportunity to address the joint-stock problem writ large. Though neither litigant had really raised the issue, in his decision he made it clear that he had "strong doubts" as to whether Real del Monte, having taken "upon themselves to act as a corporate body," had ever been a legal association. Its articles of association, Eldon insisted, essentially served as self-constituting patents for an overseas enterprise, detailing an organization and powers that looked much like a chartered corporation. "If the Bank of England, the East India Company, or the South Sea Company wanted a new charter," Eldon scoffed, "they could not do better than copy the deed of the regulation of the Real del Monte Company." Having raised such emphatic objections, Eldon felt compelled ultimately to dismiss them. Not unlike in *Rex v. Dodd,* his reasons were procedural. The 1720 law, he admitted, had been too "ill drawn" and ill-enforced and the lawyers in the current case too silent on the question to allow him to decide on that basis. Yet, while he found for Taylor and Real del Monte, the arguments he laid out were nonetheless meant as a shot across the bow and a potential precedent for breathing new life into the Bubble Act.[71]

The issue soon became moot. The growing possibility that the Bubble Act might indeed make a return had already led projectors to overwhelm Parliament with some four hundred petitions for private bills of incorporation. Even as Eldon was handing down his decision, the Commons was already considering a range of solutions to what was beginning to seem like a crisis. Some advocated for a return to royal charters. Others suggested a system of incorporation by general registration. In the end it was the MPs with significant investments in joint-stock companies who prevailed in their desire to be rid of the 1720 Act altogether, which one contemporary dismissed (like Eldon had) as "a string of *non sequiturs* from first to last." One of those non sequiturs, the original parts of the Act providing for the London Assurance and Royal Exchange Assurance Companies' duopoly, had already been annulled the year before, in response to a petition from a powerful coalition of financiers to allow their *Alliance British and Foreign Fire and Life Insurance Company* to branch into marine insurance. In 1825, Parliament repealed the rest of the Act, freeing promoters to form companies, charter or not.[72]

Parliament had thus not stemmed the tide of company formations so much as opened its floodgates. And, while companies like Real del Monte had no territorial ambitions on the scale of something like the East India Company, many of these new companies for land, mining, railways, agriculture, and various other overseas enterprises were inevitably enmeshed in some form of control over territory, people, politics, policing, and other assertions of jurisdiction, if sometimes only at a local level. Moreover, while they may not have had British charters, such ventures frequently relied on various forms of grants, concessions, treaties, or contracts acquired abroad to secure those rights, even if such instruments were often (and at times deliberately) misrepresented, misinterpreted, or outright fabricated.

No one was more attuned to this possibility than the enigmatic Gregor MacGregor. MacGregor, whose father had been a military officer with the East India Company, was one of many British soldiers who, finding themselves unemployed at the end of the war with France in 1815, sought out opportunities as mercenaries in the ongoing rebellions from Spanish authority unfolding across Latin America. Raising and commanding troops for Simon Bolívar, among other revolutionary leaders, opened an opportunity for MacGregor to attempt his own conquests of coastal enclaves, supported by a number of newly befriended West Indian merchants and financiers. After several misfired attempts, in 1820, he secured a grant of some nearly eight million acres along the Nicaraguan coast from the Miskito King George Frederic, who himself had close ties to Jamaica and British officials in the nearby colony of Honduras (Belize). On the strength of these indigenous patents—which afforded rights of governance such as to make laws and collect taxes, though explicitly not "sovereignty" itself—MacGregor declared his own independent republic. He called it Poyais (and sometimes "Indiada" or "Indialand"), and himself at various times Inca, Prince, *Cacique*, General, King, and, somehow most bizarrely, Sir Gregor. While many dismissed such claims as either quixotic or fraudulent, others clearly bought them—literally. In the flush capital market in England and Scotland and with his assumed sovereignty as collateral, Mac-Gregor managed to issue £200,000 in bonds and to print money from his "Bank of Poyais." He recruited fellow Scottish soldiers and settlers, pitching the project as a revival of the Darien Company's scheme of the 1690s. Though George Frederic—under pressure from the British in Honduras and ostensibly insisting MacGregor had broken his agreement by asserting himself as sovereign—had actually withdrawn his patents by 1823, from "his office in Edinburgh," one contemporary noted, MacGregor "distributed out his territory and . . . exercised sovereign power" despite being "a Sovereign without territory, a ruler without subjects, a Captain without an army, and a land-agent without land to sell."[73]

To some extent, such critics had a point. Poyais was undoubtedly to some extent a scam, and MacGregor ultimately ended up in a

Paris prison for trying to swindle investors by reviving his scheme under the auspices of a French company. Yet, what was more remarkable was just how typical his ambitions were at the time. Contemporaries in Britain clearly seemed less troubled about his claims to be the head of a new colonial state than his failure to follow through with it. He was hardly alone among Europeans looking to make money off the revolutions in Latin America. Yet, it was impossible to distinguish such bald financial objectives from what was also an ideological and almost idealist experiment; MacGregor was, from a certain perspective, working to establish a kind of postcolonial authoritarian-republican state whose basic contours were not all that dissimilar from Bolívar's regime.[74] Moreover, even though the scheme proved disastrous—most of its settlers either died or were looking to flee—there still seemed to be some hope it might endure. Upon his return from France, after an unsuccessful attempt to make more bond issues, MacGregor managed to sell his land and interest in his existing bonds in 1828 to a newly formed *Black River Commercial and Agricultural Company*. Its efforts to revive the venture similarly failed.[75]

Many of those working hard to discredit MacGregor did so, either themselves or through hired pens, to highlight the legitimacy of their own rival projects, competing for settlers, labor, investors, and creditors, especially amidst the rampant speculation in Latin American finance and mining enterprises. This was almost certainly the case for the promoter, financier, and occasional arms dealer John Diston Powles. Powles and his partners had established lucrative provisioning businesses during the wars for independence and as credit brokers in their aftermath, including facilitating a £2 million loan to the newly independent republic of Gran Colombia. Among many other ventures, including a copper mining company in partnership with the Chilean envoy to London, by the early 1820s, Powles and the others were now looking to extend those connections and investments in Colombia into territorial and mining settlements through the auspices of two connected joint-stock enterprises, the *Colombian Mining Association* and the *Columbian Agricultural Association*.[76] Their first settlement, at Lake Maracaibo in what is now Venezuela, collapsed, as did a second attempt to establish a colony of about two hundred Scottish emigrants from Aberdeen and Inverness at Topo near Caracas.[77]

Soon the Agricultural Association went bankrupt, like many others when the company bubble came crashing down on London financial markets in 1826. With some help from British government officials, the Topo settlers were relocated some 2,500 miles away to Guelph in a colony in Upper Canada which was, it turned out, the project of yet another corporation.[78] With early leadership drawn from various prominent London overseas companies, especially Hudson's Bay and former North-West Company directors, this group set out to establish what many might have assumed at this point was an anachronism: a chartered colonial land company. The *Canada Company,* chartered in 1826, was designed as a kind of vertically integrated, almost one-stop shop colonial enterprise. In 1791, when Parliament established the colony of Upper Canada, it had also created "reserves" of vast tracts of land for the Crown and the Anglican Church, both of which had since remained largely unexplored and unexploited. The Canada Company's plan, backed by a £1 million capital stock, was to purchase those lands and then sell and lease them to others who would develop and settle them. At the same time, the Company was also a development company charged with building infrastructure such as roads, canals, churches, and schools, a transportation company to facilitate the migration of European settlers to the colony and to help employ them upon arrival, a finance company to make small loans to those settlers to help them acquire their lands, and an advertising company to promote the entire enterprise in Britain. Its original prospectus suggested that it might engage in commerce and agriculture, though Company directors decided largely against doing so.[79] Crown officials were on board but persuading the Church to part with the so-called "Clergy Reserves"—already held in trust by another body, the *Clergy Reserves Corporation*—proved impossible.[80] The Government offered instead to sell to the Company—for the same price of just over £145,000—one million acres out of what became known as the Huron Tract, which Crown officials had spent the previous several years negotiating to purchase from the Anishinaabe (Chippewa). The Company was then reimbursed one-third of the price to spend on "public works and improvement."[81]

The Canada Company enterprise was central to one of the most hot-button issues concerning early nineteenth-century colonial policy and political economy: emigration. The end of the war in 1815 had ushered in a major economic slump, exploding the national debt and reintroducing three hundred thousand demobilized soldiers and sailors into a labor market already glutted by population growth. Some saw the answer to this "surplus" population, as many had for centuries, in colonies. Even Thomas Malthus, best known for his theory that overpopulation naturally corrected itself through inevitable catastrophe such as famine, disease, and war, noted in the 1817 edition of his *Essay on the Principle of Population* that in extraordinary situations, some intervention to encourage emigration might be the only "real relief" available. By the early 1820s, the case was being made for doing so through the sale of the Crown and Clergy reserves, both by self-proclaimed Malthusian Robert Gourlay and by Robert Wilmot-Horton, Malthus's friend and fellow member of the recently founded Political Economy Club. Adding his voice to the chorus was Wilmot-Horton's friend John Beverley Robinson, who would become one of the key figures behind the Canada Company. The question was: Who should be responsible for this? Malthus for one had long been of the opinion that emigration was best left in private hands, though the recent crisis—and possibly Wilmot-Horton, who as undersecretary of state for the colonies was convinced this was a job for government—may have softened him on the issue.[82]

That the Canada Company project took the form it did, however, was primarily due to the relentless efforts of a more inscrutable figure in this debate. John Galt was best known as a novelist and poet but came to have a long and varied career as a frustrated businessman, law student, lobbyist, traveler, and fixer. (Among his many claimed accomplishments, Galt maintained he had been responsible for smuggling Lord Elgin's marbles out of Athens.) Most recently, Galt had become the London agent for frustrated colonists in Upper Canada seeking compensation for damages suffered during the war, which had opened his eyes to the "ample sums" that could be raised by selling off Crown Reserves. The idea of doing so through a chartered company, though, seems to have been years in the making. Galt had published his own "statistical account" of Canada in 1807 and such companies appear in various forms in many of his novels and other writings. As a fellow Scot, he seemed especially inspired by the Darien Company and later set about writing a biography of William Paterson, who, Galt insisted, had intended "to project the plantation of a state, in its design, as described in the Act of Incorporation, worthy of the greatest Kings." He similarly admired the contemporary frenzy of land companies in the United States, pointing to the scramble to settle western New York as both a model and a threat; after all, the vast tracts of untapped territory in Upper Canada, he argued, had sparked the American invasions in 1812 in the first place. For his part, Robinson was convinced that Galt, a "shrewd scheming man," had taken the whole concept from him, having "conceived the idea of getting up a company & making a grand speculation" only after reading a paper he wrote on the subject in 1823.[83]

It has long been assumed that Galt and the Canada Company took inspiration from a near-simultaneous project for an *Australian Agricultural Company,* or simply the Australian Company, though historian Matthew Birchall has shown that the evidence suggests otherwise. Playing the role of John Galt in the Australian Company was John Macarthur Jr., the wealthy and well-connected son of the army officer frequently credited with pioneering the wool industry in the British colony of New South Wales, established in 1788. Like the Canada Company, the Australian Company's first meeting attracted many from among London's company establishment— including the chairman of the Bank of England and four East India Company directors, with many more East India Company shareholders among its early investors.[84] The cross-pollination was clearly on the mind of the East India Company leadership. They consulted their lead counsel—whose brother Charles was the first chairman of the Canada Company—for an official opinion on whether investing in the Australian Company might be construed as violating centuries-old by-laws prohibiting members from supporting "interlopers." The answer Bosanquet gave was a definitive no, as long as the Australian Company largely stuck to being a land company and did not branch into overseas commercial enterprises.[85]

Like the Canada Company, the Australian Company was premised on the idea that there were vast tracts of "wasteland" in the environs of a recently established British colony that government and individual enterprise failed to exploit. The Company was to have one million pounds in capital and one million acres to buy up and in turn sell and lease, encouraging European settlement and investing in infrastructure. It received a Parliamentary Act and a Charter of Incorporation in 1824, which, Macarthur insisted—citing the opinion in *Rex v. Dodd* as precedent—was critical to allowing it not only to "hold lands, to have a common Seal, and enjoy the other privileges of a Corporation" but also to "limit the risk of the Partners" and encourage investment.[86] There were significant differences between the Canadian and Australian projects as well. Encouraged by John Bigge's recent report as royal commissioner of inquiry in New South Wales, the Australian Company intended to develop its own land and invest heavily in manufacturing and agricultural cultivation, primarily sheep for wool but also olive, flax, tobacco, hemp, silk, and opium. Specific to its context, the Company was also to rely on convict labor and claimed that doing so would not only save the government up to £30,000 annually but encourage "industrious & moral habits" among the New South Wales settlers. Its leadership soon developed an interest in mining, especially coal, which highlighted yet another advantage of incorporation. To those concerned that mining was not specifically provided for in its charter, the Company's leadership maintained that it could nonetheless pursue such projects since, as a property owner, it essentially was free to do whatever a "private Individual with an Estate in fee simple" or "Landed Proprietor would do in England" on his land.[87]

Whatever their relationship to one another, both the Canada and Australian Companies were followed by, and even became models for, similar projects. One group of merchants and investors soon after requested a grant of half a million acres for a *Van Diemen's Land Company* to establish an enterprise in Tasmania "upon the same terms which we understand are to accompany the Grant which is now about to be made to the Australian Company."[88] The wealthy radical John George Lambton, later the first Earl of Durham, proposed a *New Zealand Company* with broad ambitions for settlement, sheep farming, mining, whaling, banking, and infrastructure development; it had already sent out agents allegedly to "purchase" the rights to over a million acres of Māori land before it went dormant when Durham failed to acquire a charter.[89] In 1826, a group of investors rebranded their failed 1824 *General South American Mining Association* as the *General Mining Association* to take up a lease on mineral and coal resources in Nova Scotia that the Duke of York had offered two of its proprietors, the royal jewelers Phillip Rundell and John Bridge, as partial repayment for a massive debt (in exchange for which he took a quarter share in the enterprise). Ostensibly this was a mining company, but the development and settlement projects that came with it, two historians have observed, gave it "many of the hallmarks of a proprietary land company."[90] It was joined in 1831 by the *Nova Scotia Mining Company*—only one of thirty applicants since the abolition of the Bubble Act to which the Board of Trade had granted full rights of limited liability—and the *New Brunswick and Nova Scotia Land Company,* incorporated by charter and act of Parliament to purchase and develop over five hundred thousand acres of Crown lands in those regions.[91]

Both Nova Scotian enterprises found that they faced an extremely mysterious and forceful opponent in a certain Alexander Humphreys, who emerged seemingly from nowhere complaining that he was the rightful owner of all the territory they were looking to develop. His claim was based on his assertion that he had inherited the entire colony, along with the title of the Earl of Stirling, from his alleged seventeenth-century ancestor, William Alexander. Among the proof he produced were copies of the 1621 charter and various other documents, some of which were peculiarly scrawled on the back of a copy of Guillaume de l'Isle's 1703 map of Canada. Humphreys lobbied, published, petitioned, and sued in defense of his supposed rights, though whether the ultimate aim was to take on a settlement project of his own or get a payoff from the new companies was unclear. He did issue a call to "encourage and give every countenance to individuals who might be disposed to form a Company," offering land rights in exchange for ten percent of any shares it might offer. His efforts were soon arrested, however, by an Edinburgh jury, which took only five hours to determine several of his claims to both his lineage and the Canadian territories to be forgeries. It did not in the end find enough evidence to convict Humphreys of having knowingly perpetrated the fraud.[92]

Among those to whom Humphreys had sent cease and desist letters for "trespassing and encroaching" on his rights was an even larger enterprise that, after nearly a decade of efforts, had finally in 1832 drafted a prospectus for a *British American Land Company.* Explicitly aiming to "follow up the principles and purposes of the existing Canada Company, which have proved so eminently beneficial to that Corporation, the Colony, and the Emigrant," its plan was to take up nearly 850,000 acres of Crown lands and reserves in the colony of Lower Canada.[93] The proposal received a relatively warm reception at the colonial office, where the only serious concern seemed to be that it should not be granted a commercial monopoly. After much negotiation, in 1834, it received its charter. Like its opposite number in Upper Canada, the Company eventually evolved into a sprawling conglomerate of rail, telegraph, and commercial and agricultural projects, some of which came to be operated by several subsidiary joint-stock companies. It chose John Galt—recently recalled from North America by the Canada Company under accusations of financial impropriety and imprisoned for debt—as its first secretary.[94]

A PENNSYLVANIA ON THE SOUTH COAST OF NEW HOLLAND

That Galt, a writer by profession, was central to such enterprises was not incidental. As it had been for centuries, any company project, as one scholar has put it about the Canada Company, "was as much a literary endeavor as a colonial one."[95] Galt looked to stimulate interest in his enterprises through his connections with, for example, the influential publisher William Blackwood and the novelist and former West Indian merchant Andrew Picken. Another friend and fellow investor was the colorful surgeon, army officer, and journalist William "Tiger" Dunlop, a man described by his relation, the author Thomas Carlyle, as "one of the strangest men of the age."[96] Likewise, Powles and his partners published their own periodical in support of their enterprises in Colombia and elsewhere, cultivating relationships with the publisher John Murray and a suite of pamphleteers and journalists—and calling on them on at times to author damning critiques of their rivals like Gregor MacGregor. Among Powles and Murray's hired pens was fellow investor, up-and-coming novelist, and future prime minister Benjamin Disraeli, who, though he would eventually become a critic, lauded the South American mining project as exhibiting the wisdom of "our forefathers" and the sixteenth-century companies "whose enterprise was the foundation of our present glory."[97]

There was probably no more canny, slippery, or influential a member of this cohort of nineteenth-century company promoters than Edward Gibbon Wakefield. To his extensive network of friends and allies, Wakefield was one of the most incisive economic and colonial theorists of his day. To his enemies, he was the epitome of everything that was wrong with this new age of speculation. Both sides had a point. The first salvo in his protracted battle to establish a company for colonization in South Australia, which purported to be a "letter from Sydney," was in fact a pamphlet written from Newgate Prison, where he was serving out a sentence for kidnapping a fifteen-year-old heiress and forcing her into marriage in hopes of purloining her fortune—not, it should be mentioned, the first time he had tried such a thing. James Stephen claimed to know immediately upon meeting him that he "was in the presence of a man whose society was dangerous"; the *Times* once warned that "Nature does not often produce such a monster."[98] Wakefield often published anonymously, cleverly tending to cite his own previous work as if it was an independent authority.[99] He also borrowed liberally from others. Robert Gouger, likely a *Letter from Sydney* coauthor, and Major Anthony Bacon—both of whom Wakefield met in prison—made major early contributions. Wakefield drew on the ideas of Robert Torrens, who had been a member of Durham's 1825 New Zealand Company, as well as Bigge, Gourlay, Wilmot-Horton, and others influential in shaping the earlier Canadian and Australian ventures.[100]

Wakefield repackaged a lot of these arguments into a theory he called "systematic colonization." Its core tenet was to insist that colonies not be thought of as outlets for "surplus" population—the poor, convicts, and others—or as a resource to aggrandize the holdings of the landed elite. For colonies to be successful, Wakefield held, they needed builders, scientists, surveyors, lawyers, printers, teachers, merchants, financial professionals, clerks, doctors, artists, performers, clergy, artisans, and authors—"even reviewers" and "at least, one good Political Economist." Settlers should not just be men but families that could create more settlers. They also needed to be free, not slaves or convicts, but did not necessarily need to be Europeans. Wakefield imagined South Australia as a natural magnet for labor from the Pacific and Indian Ocean worlds, and especially the East India Company's growing empire. "The poorest class of Hindoos," he imagined, would rush "to labour and enjoy in Australasia, rather than drown their children in the sacred stream, or die of misery near their own temples" while "a few thousand Chinese emigrants would be of more advantage than a rich gold mine."[101]

At the core of Wakefield's theory was the radical notion that British class relations could and should be reproduced abroad; for this vision of remaking capitalist society in the colonies, Karl Marx would later label Wakefield the "most notable political economist of that period."[102] The key to all this was another self-conscious break from the past in insisting that land in colonies should not be granted but rather sold at a fair market price. This would ensure that colonial populations were properly stratified among landowners and laborers alike and would become not just producers but consumers. Such an approach also reversed the dangerous trend, as Wakefield and his acolytes saw it, of absurdly large land grants going to dispersed and distanced plantations. His model instead encouraged concentration of populations in towns and cities, which—just as some seventeenth-century theorists had maintained—would facilitate the cultivation of both markets and institutions of self-government. Meanwhile, revenues raised from land sales could fund what Wakefield called a "toll-free bridge" for emigrant settlers to the colonies, a concept known more generally as "assisted emigration."[103]

The best means to do all this, Wakefield and his allies insisted, was through a corporation. Gouger took the lead by establishing the National Colonisation Society in 1831 as a voluntary association which, in the next year, petitioned for a charter as the *South Australian Land Company*.[104] As the Society's proposal passed through several iterations, it reiterated extremely familiar arguments on behalf of company colonization. First and foremost, such a company was supposed to relieve government of any financial or political responsibility while leaning on the imprimatur of a charter or Colonial Office support, as Bacon put it, to "induce the capitalists who admire the plan in the abstract, to put their names down for subscriptions."[105] The joint-stock corporation was, as Wakefield later put it, "a contrivance for the combination of capital in particular works, which is used only in the most advanced societies" to mobilize resources for large investments. Moreover, any colony governed "from a distance," as the British state's apparatus inevitably was, was certain to be wasteful and bloated. Chartered settlements were inherently more "local" in their government, "moderate" in their expenditure, and, most importantly, immune to those statesmen tempted to use them as sites of patronage and taxation. As both a financial and political enterprise, the work of building such a colony was "peculiarly suited to companies."[106]

For as much as Wakefield and his allies represented their South Australian project as a capitalist innovation, it turned out that what they had in mind was not at all new.[107] Torrens cited cases of such a form of colonial government going back to the city-states of Greece, Italy, and the Dutch.[108] Closer to home, the lawyer Richard Davies Hanson testified to a Commons Select Committee in 1836 that since the sixteenth-century the British empire had almost exclusively been the work of chartered individuals and companies, with the "whole power of disposing of the land."[109] The many enterprises leading American westward expansion, as well as the Canada Company, stood as further testimony that colonies were to be pioneered in the first instance by companies, which should give way only when colonial society was ready for local self-governance.[110] Wakefield had a particular affinity for William Penn and envisioned South Australia as "a Pennsylvania on the south coast of New Holland," though at one point also flirted with modeling the enterprise after what he called the "joint stock company for founding Carolina."[111]

The South Australian promoters clearly had no time for the finer distinction others might have drawn between corporate and proprietary models. There was rather a single continuous tradition of the "chartered colony" that suggested their project "instead of being distinguished by novelty, is founded on precedent." Indeed, they argued that "every Colony, properly so called, founded by this Country" had arisen from a "compact amongst the first settlers, which led to the foundation of the Colony; a compact of which the essence was, that the Colonists should govern themselves in local matters and provide for the expenses of local government." Government's job was to give "sanction" and binding force to that "compact into which these individuals are desirous to enter." More often than not, this "sanction" came in the form of a charter.[112] That colonial corporations were, as Wakefield wrote, "not founded by government," and most were "not even aided by any government," was not only historical fact but a sound principle of both economics and government. "Would such a man as William Penn have crossed the Atlantic," he asked, "knowing that, when in America, he should be

subject to a minister like Horace Twiss"—the colonial undersecretary superintending the recent catastrophic attempt to establish a
colony at Swan River in Australia—"residing in England?"[113]

The South Australian Company represented the apotheosis of the
new breed of colonial company emerging in the wake of the East
India Company's transformations, whose business was more about
government than commerce. Its promoters argued, as many "free
trade" advocates might have, that something like sheep farming was
better done by private persons on their own land and with their own
money. "In the production of almost any commodity whatsoever, a
Company can scarcely hope to compete successfully with individuals managing their own capital." What individuals could or would
not do on their own, especially in a colonial context, was invest in
or govern over public infrastructure; thus "in the formation of roads,
bridges, docks, &c., on the contrary, individuals cannot compete
with companies." It was not that the company was uninterested in
making money. It would achieve this, however, through investment
in development, and that would increase the market for land and
thus revenue from land sales and rents. The Company also in a sense
planned its own obsolescence. From the start, it was designed to per-
sist as the "supreme power" only until population reached a sufficient level—it originally proposed five thousand but doubled that on
the advice of the Colonial Office—at which point the settlers were
supposed to take on self-government, convening a legislative assembly with a Crown-appointed governor.[114]

Stephen, who in addition to his personal disdain for Wakefield
had emerged as one of the government's most consistent and vocal
critics of company colonial projects, was unmoved. The plan was
"wild and impracticable" and "pregnant . . . with republican principles," which sought to steal away what he regarded as the core of
royal prerogative by erecting courts, raising militias, and issuing laws
and ordinances, bound only by the strictures in its charter that such
measures not be "repugnant" to British law. Stephen rightly observed
that similar clauses could be found in charters going back centuries,
but still had no precise legal meaning or effective means of enforcement. The proposed charter, meanwhile, claimed "Sovereignty over
a Territory exceeding in extent the Kingdoms of Spain & Portugal"
and "a more unlimited authority than is enjoyed by the Legislatures
of Canada and Jamaica." Worse yet, he complained, no doubt with

Wakefield in mind, it was to be run not by government or even gentlemanly capitalists but by men "who certainly are but little known to society at large." That they pledged to do so in "avowed imitation of that which prevailed over the first settlement of the British North American Colonies" was hardly persuasive, as such arrangements were "wholly unfit to be adopted as models in the present day."

Stephen further observed that Wakefield, Torrens, and others misunderstood or (what he probably suspected) misrepresented their own history. The East India Company, he argued, was a prime example of why such a grant to a private body made for bad public policy, while many of the seventeenth-century grants they so admired were not corporate but palatinate charters, granted to particular individuals with no sense of public interest. The plan was "an imitation of those of the seventeenth century," he concluded, only insofar as "like them it proposes a surrender of all the Crown has to yield, and offers no equivalent or compensation in return." It did not help that the Company slipped into its request the right to expand into other jurisdictions "elsewhere soever" and, like the West India Company to which Stephen had so strenuously objected a decade earlier, did not specify what businesses it might undertake there. Such a company, he fretted, might become "Bankers, merchants, Whale-fishers, shipbuilders, Founders of Colleges or any thing else they might think proper." This might arguably be fine for individuals, but a powerful corporation without specific and definite objects was dangerous if not outright illegal.[115]

Stephen's arguments seem to have moved Lord Goderich, the colonial secretary. Initially favorable, he now upbraided Torrens for a proposal that would "virtually transfer to this company the sovereignty of a vast unexplored territory, equal in extent to one of the most considerable kingdoms in Europe." Moreover, the colony was open to foreigners "upon complete equality," was unaccountable to government, divested the Crown of its prerogative, and, worst of all, because it tended to popular government, "would be to erect within the British monarchy a government purely republican."[116] In the face of such objections, the South Australian promoters were willing to concede or compromise on many points. This, however, only made things worse since, as Robert Hay informed Torrens, "the very readiness with which the objectionable parts have been abandoned, contrasted with their prominent appearance in the plan as fundamental principles, unavoidably induces in the mind of the Secretary of State a serious misgiving as to the maturity of their knowledge and counsels on the very important subject which they have submitted to his consideration." By August, the enterprise seemed "virtually abandoned."[117]

If the group had retreated, however, it was only to recover and rearm. Soon, they had a new plan. Many of the same men now formed another voluntary society, the *South Australian Association,* with the goal of obtaining a charter not for a land company but rather an incorporated trusteeship to facilitate government and land sales over what would now be considered the "Province" of South Australia. This *South Australian Commission,* they maintained, would remedy the ills of earlier company projects, which had been tainted by "some private object." Their new corporation was instead to be "entirely of a public nature." As if responding to Stephen's concerns, the project's leaders now argued that private interest had been the root problem with all earlier phases of colonial settlement and emigration. In fact, they mused, had early Atlantic promoters and proprietors had such wisdom, the United States might well still be part of the British Empire.[118]

This would have been a stunning and suspicious about-face had it not also been clear that not much had changed in their argument. The Association was still committed to a core project of systematic colonization, assisted emigration, and, eventually, devolution to local government. Most importantly, though in one sense they suggested the public trust was a departure from the past, their central tenet still seemed to be that it followed on a long tradition of how the British Empire did business. "In former times the government of England never undertook the formation of colonies," their prospectus announced. "Every old colony planted by the English seems to have been projected by one or more private persons." Citing a long if selective list of chartered colonial projects, beginning with Humphrey Gilbert and ending at the Sierra Leone Company, the group now made the case that charters, more than just sanctifying a mutual compact, "erected a kind of sovereignty, bestowing upon a single person, or several persons, incorporated as one, a degree of authority which was supreme, so far as related to the country about to be colonized." It was a point, they admitted, that "may, at first sight, appear anomalous, and inconsistent with the principles of government; but upon reflection it will be seen that the exercise of such powers by somebody was absolutely necessary."[119] Private colonization, recast as an extension of royal sovereignty, could now continue to "endeavor to follow the example of the London and Plymouth Companies which founded Virginia; of William Penn and his companions, who founded Pennsylvania; of Lord Baltimore and his associates, who founded Maryland; and of Lord Percival and his cotrustees, who established the colony of Georgia."[120] The key point was that even as a public enterprise it was not one governed directly by the state. "A Colony founded by Charter is one example of that delegation of authority which in perpetual succession has for ages been a leading principle of the British government," wrote one association member, the ancient historian and political economist George Grote, "while a Colony founded by the Crown is an example of that central authority . . . which is a leading principle of the French government."[121]

This proposal was intriguing and controversial in equal proportion. Its first meeting and debate at Exeter Hall reportedly attracted two thousand interested observers.[122] Some dismissed the economic foundations as vague and ill-conceived, claiming that its promoters never explained how settlement would end up as "systematic" or how they would arrive at the elusive "sufficient price" for land.[123] Edward Stanley, who had briefly taken over as colonial secretary, worried that there was little mechanism to hold the commission responsible to either government or the settlers and concluded, as Gouger recalled, that the entire venture still amounted to a "republic" and an *"imperium in imperio."*[124] Stephen continued to fret that the venture was, in so many words, asking the Crown to use its prerogative power to diminish its prerogative power. In fact, the whole proposal was worse than when it took the form of a company. The only advantage of the previous iteration had been that it would relieve government of the responsibility to foot the bill. Now, not only had that advantage been eliminated but there was "no joint stock—no proprietary Body—no chartered Company" that could be comprehended and controlled by the law. He pointed specifically to the plan to raise money on bonds and securities, which constituted a more opaque and unaccountable body of stakeholders than joint-stock shareholders. "The South Australian revenue Bond Holders or the South Australian land Bond Holders will be just so many Speculators at the Stock Exchange," Stephen observed, "a Class of Persons whose interference in Government, either metropolitan or colonial, can never be vindicated upon the simple ground that they are possessed of a certain amount of the national or colonial debt."[125]

It was not just government that was opposed. The Australian Agricultural Association saw the new scheme as a potential violation of its charter.[126] The financier and politician Alexander Baring, concerned that the project might divert capital from North American land investments, rose to speak against it in the House of Commons. The record of the debate shows him asserting that "the real object of the colony was, to realize the views of a set of gentlemen, whom he hoped he should not offend by calling experimental philosophers," who might do better to attempt a more modest proof of concept, perhaps in the "wastes of Pennsylvania" or "some moderate-sized cabbage-garden." He was deeply skeptical the Commission would ever step aside from government, pointing out that intertwined loans and land sales would leave it "so tied up by mortgages" that government would not in practice be able to revert to the Crown.[127] Other critics took to the press to decry it as a "South Australian Swindle," a "Whig Humbug Colonization Scheme," a "joint-stock juggle for getting British paupers scalped by Bushmen in Southern Australia," and the familiar "bubble."[128] "The Cacique of Poyais," one wrote, "never put forth a more impudent prospectus, or one calculated to dupe in the most flagrant way a nation susceptible of gullibility."[129]

South Australian promoters fired back. No one denied that profit was possible, but Grote and Torrens protested that they were never in this for "personal advantage." Rather, their promise was to "strive in all our power to erect this society on a broad and deep foundation, without any view of lucre or gain."[130] Thomas Maslen thought that behind all this agitation would be found the machinations of the recently emerged *Edinburgh Australian Company*.[131] Others claimed the real self-interested philosophers were "those professors and writers," most notably John Ramsay McCulloch, whose outdated ideas were threatened by the "heresies" of the Wakefield system.[132] There was some truth to the accusation that the Association's project was driven by political and philosophical impulses and the social networks of utilitarian and radical reformers. Wakefield no doubt intended his own multi-volume (but ultimately unfinished) edition of *The Wealth of Nations*—published a year later as the work of the "Author of 'England and America'"—to be an intervention in this debate, envisioning Smith's writings, he told the poet and essayist Leigh Hunt, to be "the best statement of that principle of the *Combination* of Labour which forms the base of the System of colonization."[133] Torrens was a cofounder of the Political Economy Club, while decades later Grote's widow Harriet still blamed James Mill, whom Grote had met through their mutual friend David Ricardo, for having inculcated "acquired convictions" and "antipathies" in her once gentle and charitable husband.[134]

Wakefield had somehow insinuated himself into the inner circles of Utilitarian political economists, some of whom, like Charles Buller, were now among the leadership of the South Australian Association.[135] John Stuart Mill was taken with his ideas and supported his projects when he became editor of the *Westminster Review,* especially after it was bought in 1834 by the radical Sir William Molesworth, another South Australia committee member and Wakefield devotee.[136] Yet, of all his famous philosopher friends, Wakefield seemed most proud of having seemingly won Jeremy Bentham over to his cause.[137] Bentham may have already been a receptive audience, having considered in his work a range of imperial questions, including ones pertaining to the American rebellion and penal colonies; he was, after all, famously the man who coined the word "international."[138] He was also no stranger to corporations, having, for example, composed his earlier poor-relief plan around a proposed "National Charity Company," modeled after the East India Company and premised on the notion that joint-stock companies were an older and more advanced form of management than national government.[139]

Bentham was energized enough by his acquaintance with Wakefield and the proposals of the National Colonization Society in August 1831 that he was driven to explore the ideas in a short manuscript, written in about a week and a half, making a case for a joint-stock "Colonization Society" or "Company" for Australian colonization. Translating systematic colonization into Benthamese—"the Vicinity-maximizing or Dispersion-preventing principle"—he refigured the enduring argument about the homology of public and private interest in Utilitarian principle terms, with the goals of government, "the greatest happiness of all the inhabitants," being entirely compatible with the goals of a company, "the greatest profit, or say benefit in a pecuniary shape." Private bodies, not nearly as prone to "the sweets of patronage" as government officials and unencumbered by traditions of aristocracy, might lead to the establishment of "the very chimaera of chimaeras—a Commonwealth." Where Wakefield looked to North America for his models, Bentham found inspiration in other sources, including the East India Company and the recent efforts in the United States by the *Society for the Colonization of Free People of Color of America*, a philanthropic trust that designed to plant a colony of free blacks and manumitted slaves in West Africa after the model of the Sierra Leone Company and African Institution. Liberia, Bentham believed, exemplified the fundamental virtues of a colony where "Government will not intermeddle with the business of Government."[140]

In 1834, the Association got its charter, which established a colony in South Australia overseen by a board of "Colonization Commissioners."[141] One critic later reflected that the whole thing seemed like an "Australian 'Board of Control'" that would result in "the same mischief of double government which were before exhibited in India."[142] By now, Wakefield, frustrated and insulted over the drawn-out affair, had moved on, while those who remained from the South Australian Company project quietly tried to recover in this new scheme some of its original joint-stock principles. Torrens convinced the commission that colonial officers should be required to purchase land in South Australia—at least five hundred acres per £100 salary—to invest themselves in the colony.[143] The Association successfully lobbied for the power to incorporate land companies, "many combining to do that in the best way, which separated individuals could not do at all."[144] Gouger, the colony's first colonial secretary, and Hanson floated one such company, while Osmond Gilles, South Australia's first colonial treasurer, suggested a land bank. Meanwhile, George Fife Angas, an early enthusiast, proposed a new joint-stock company to buy up the commission's remaining land at a discount and to manage its surveying, sale, and distribution, with side businesses in commerce, agricultural development, whaling, naval provisioning, and banking. It was to be called the *South Australian Company*.[145]

GLOBAL WAKEFIELD

Like Wakefield, Angas was fascinated with William Penn, though for a different reason. For him, emigration and settlement in South Australia were part of a vision of colonies as religious and moral enterprises, not just for proselytization but, like Pennsylvania, as a kind of nonconformist utopian experiment. The symbolism of having the ship *Prince George,* carrying two hundred German settlers he recruited for the colony, depart in 1838 from Plymouth, just like the early New England "Pilgrim Fathers," was not lost on him or his supporters. Like those early Puritans, Angas was also a prolific businessman. He started his own shipping firm, G. F. Angas & Co., during the 1824 company speculation bubble and went on to be instrumental in the founding of the National Provincial Bank, the Union Bank of Australia, and the South Australian Company's own subsidiary South Australian Banking Company. He was what one might call a typical philanthropreneur of his era, perceiving no contradiction between Christian and capitalist enterprise, leaving him much in demand as an advisor, investor, and director of many overseas schemes.[146]

Among these was an offer to become chairman of a new *Eastern Coast of Central America Commercial and Agricultural Company,* a venture that had grown out of the short-lived Black River scheme and the related *Río Tinto Commercial and Agricultural Company,* another in a long line of efforts to assume the land rights and securities of the defunct Poyais scheme. Angas declined the invitation, and the position was ultimately taken by Peter Harris Abbott, an accountant who, ironically or appropriately, was one of Britain's leading authorities on public debt and bankruptcy (and who, not for nothing, himself went bankrupt by the early 1840s). Abbott was also invested in several company projects, including the British American Land Company.[147] Meanwhile, a rival group of Poyais bondholders acquired their own grant from the Miskito king, vesting it in an ill-fated *British Central American Land Company* and, by 1838, an affiliated *Yorkshire and Lancashire Central American Land and Emigration Company.* They too set out to revive MacGregor's dream of a colony, but also claimed by virtue of their land grant to be the King's envoy to London, even petitioning, unsuccessfully, for the right to join Queen Victoria's coronation parade as a foreign dignitary under the Miskito flag.[148]

Though this venture eventually collapsed, it was enough to help turn the Eastern Coast Company's attention away from Miskito to a more ambitious plan to establish settlements in the Verapaz region of Guatemala. Eastern Coast's project was not so much about extending the boundaries of the British Empire as about investing in the "internal" colonization characteristic of state building across early nineteenth-century Central and South America.[149] José Felipe Mariano Gálvez, the governor of the state of Guatemala from whom the new Company received its grants, stated the point succinctly to his Legislative Assembly: "Colonizations are the first interest of the State." That this happened when it did was no coincidence. Gálvez, who had keenly watched the debate over the East India Company's charter renewal in 1833, was convinced that the elimination of its commerce would create a flood of former shareholders in search of similar opportunities.[150]

Before he could send representatives to London, however, Gálvez agreed with agents for the Eastern Coast Company to offer it a concession for the port of Santo Thomás, rights to establish self-governing settlements in the interior (they would call these Abbotsville and New Liverpool), and to assume twenty-year monopolies on timber, steam navigation, indigenous trade, mines, and fisheries in the region. In return, the Company promised to import a hundred families as well as to develop infrastructure, including roads and a bridge over the Montagua River. By 1835, the Company had become fully invested in the colonial project, pressing the Colonial Office, the Privy Council, the Foreign Secretary, and the public via pamphlets, books, maps, and news items, to support a Guatemalan colony made up of "British subjects."[151] It explicitly touted Central America as a much closer alternative for settlement than Australia, offering similar "virgin soil," fresh water, and a situation in a "free and independent state under a constitutional and representative government; in which no convict or penal settlement is to be found; and the natives are a civilized and professing Christian community." There was supposedly something for everyone: for the capitalist, "an ample field for safe and profitable investment"; for the philanthropist, a prime location for promoting the emigration of the "industrious" poor; for settlers, a chance for investment, employment, and affluence "far more productive than their means with a life of laborious employment could provide for them at home." The colony, its promoters claimed, was a natural destination for emancipated slaves from the West Indies.[152]

The British Government was not quite sure what to do with this. Foreign Secretary Lord Palmerston attempted, at least at first, to make it the Colonial Office's problem, while Colonial Secretary Lord Glenelg and the Privy Council suggested the best course of action was just to ignore it. Career officials were somewhat more circumspect. Henry Taylor, then a clerk in the Colonial Office, doubted that the Guatemalan grant was valid, ironically arguing that this British company could not establish a colony because the territory had not devolved to the Central American Federal Republic from Spain at independence and actually belonged to Britain. Other critics feared that the scheme only intended to recruit Jamaicans as settlers to re-enslave them through an apprenticeship system. James Stephen, along with Taylor and Francis Cockburn, the superintendent for the British colony at Honduras, thought the whole scheme was another Poyais in the making. It did not help matters that it was difficult even to figure out who the Company's leaders and officers were. The *Morning Herald* suspected that this was deliberate, as the names "would not look well in print."[153]

Eventually, however, the venture was undone by the controversy it caused not in Britain but in Guatemala, where many were reasonably skeptical that it would never follow through on its obligations. Complaints about the deal with the Company, in fact, were among the grievances that eventually led to the overthrow of Gálvez's regime. The Company also had new competition in a Dutch company's possible interest in colonization contracts as well as in the British government, which in 1836 looked to expand the authority of its colony of British Honduras by asserting a formal claim to San Juan del Norte.[154] Facing insurmountable obstacles, the Company ended up selling its remaining rights to the newly formed Belgian joint-stock *Compagnie belge de colonisation*, which, as it turned out, had been busy searching the world for a colony on behalf of King Léopold I, largely through the efforts of the colonial promoter and former Eastern Coast Company agent Louis Henri-Charles Obert.[155]

Léopold had spent much of the 1820s in England witnessing the ongoing company frenzy, and since his accession in 1831 had been a monarch in search of a colony in very much the same spirit. At various points he entertained the possibilities of purchasing Guinea, Ethiopia, Cozumel, Cuba, the newly created Texan Republic, and even the Philippines.[156] Eventually the Belgian Colonization Company focused on acquiring land in the newly and nominally independent Sandwich, or Hawai'ian, Islands, primarily by buying up shares of another company, Peter Allan Brinsmade's New England–based Ladd & Co. The effort was arrested by George Paulet's ill-fated occupation of Hawaii, and subsequent attempts at a "purely commercial company" from Belgium amounted to little. While Ladd & Co. entered a protracted arbitration with King Kamehameha III to determine the fate of its assets, Brinsmade looked to recover his fortunes with several new ambitious projects, including proposing a partnership with George Simpson, the Hudson's Bay Company governor in Rupert's Land, to form a joint-stock land company for the whole of Hawai'i. Simpson declined, regarding the notion as a "thing too visionary to be entertained for a moment."[157]

That said something. Simpson had been the architect—a "little emperor," some called him—of the Hudson's Bay Company's westward expansion and especially of its growing ambitions on the West Coast and the Oregon territory.[158] This too took the form of several subsidiary company schemes. A prospectus floated by John McLoughlin and several other Company shareholders for a joint-stock *Oragon Beef & Tallow Company* prompted Simpson to have the Hudson's Bay Company establish a subsidiary enterprise of its own, the *Puget's Sound Agricultural Company,* to take on agriculture, cattle farming, settlement, and assisted emigration in the disputed Oregon Territory. McLoughlin was aggrieved but eventually mollified by his appointment as the Company's manager. The experiment was short-lived. Most of the few settlers it seemed to attract came from other Hudson's Bay Company colonies, like Red River. Many seemed put off by both its anti-Wakefieldian model of offering tenancy rather than freehold land purchases, and the escalating conflicts with competing American migrants to the region. Finally, after the British government conceded much of this territory to be under US sovereignty in the 1846 Oregon Treaty, the Company cut its losses by trying to sell its rights to the American government, a deal that was fraught with twists and turns and took twenty-five years to settle.[159]

The Hudson's Bay Company, now effectively evicted from the Oregon territory and anxious to reinforce its position north of the treaty's dividing line, became interested in acquiring a charter to develop a colony to the north, at Vancouver Island and the region known at the time as New Caledonia.[160] To its advocates, Vancouver would be "a recognition of the principle that colonization can be most effectually conducted by corporate bodies," especially by an established "association, who have given solid proofs of sound policy, by maintaining a difficult position with honour and profit to themselves and their country since the reign of Charles II."[161] Stephen dismissed the idea for precisely the same reason, as akin to the "ancient proprietary" colonies of a bygone era.[162] Colonial Secretary Earl Grey sought out a variety of opinions, including from Wakefield, and entertained several rival proposals for a Scottish settlement, a Mormon settlement, and a whaling station. The leading contender was a mining-centered joint-stock *Company of Colonists of Vancouver's Island,* led by the Wakefieldian James Edward Fitzgerald. Like Arthur Dobbs in the eighteenth century and the North-West Company several decades earlier, Fitzgerald looked to promote his company by going after the Hudson's Bay Company's very foundation, its charter. The question was taken up in the House of Commons by the fervent (if inconsistent) anti-monopolist and future prime minister William Gladstone, who was incredulous, as he later reflected, that it could possibly be "legally in the power of Charles II to mark off a vast portion of a continent, and invest a handful of his subjects with power to exclude from those territories all subjects of the Crown."[163]

Fitzgerald, in the end, just could not come up with the money. The Company's arguments and political connections won the day. It was granted a charter for a subsidiary colony at Vancouver, ostensibly to be settled on principles of systematic colonization, though critics complained that it invested little in the project, could not compete with the California and Western Australia gold rushes, set the price of land too high, and kept all the best land for itself and its Puget Sound subsidiary. Still, as the Hudson's Bay Company continued to hold out against the Wakefield "system," many others were converted. Wakefield's ideas were translated into other contexts and languages, applied by various writers to situations ranging from the expanding French empire to Mexico to emigration and land tenure policies in British Ceylon and British Jamaica.[164] "Systematic colonization" even inspired arguments for reconceiving of India as a colony of British and Asian settlement.[165]

Inevitably, many of these projects sought to apply its principles, as Wakefield had, through joint-stock companies. In 1834, Gouger reported that he had "persuaded" the projectors of a company in Natal to "adopt greatly the 'Wakefield system' of colonization."[166] The London-based *Western Australia Company* followed in 1840, buying up the rights to a land grant in the Swan River Colony to establish a colonial conduit between Australia and India (to be called, perhaps a little too on the nose, Australind); it was chaired by the liberal MP and South Australia commissioner William Hutt with Wakefield as one of its founding directors.[167] In 1847, John Robert Godley and other projectors proposed a chartered company for facilitating assisted emigration from Ireland to Canada, to be funded by subscribed capital and a large loan financed by a tax in Ireland. This *Irish Canada Company* was also to issue its own loans to local Canadian governments, purchase land, and undertake infrastructural investments and development. "Official management has never colonized very successfully," its proponents suggested, in what had now become the nineteenth century's version of a meme: "Nearly all the very successful colonial enterprises of this nation have been managed by companies," which unlike "members of a public office" were meritocracies, immune to the lure of patronage or status, and unimpeded in management by the pretention of rank and "dignity." In other words, companies represented the middle class.[168]

New West India projects emerged in the wake of emancipation, compensation, and the advent of the "apprenticeship" system. Following on a failed proposal in late 1836 for a joint-stock plantation and migration company under the name of the *West India Agricultural Company*, a decade later the London-based West India merchant John Innes "with other Capitalists and Merchants" received a charter for a *British West India Company*, with £500,000 in capital, to set up parochial sugar factories and distilleries and build out the infrastructure, including roads, to support them across the Caribbean.[169] A couple of years later, an anonymous author proposed another, far more elaborate West India Company scheme. Though it seems not to have gone anywhere and may never have been intended to do so, its contours exemplified, even caricatured, the extent to which projectors continued to find solutions to colonial problems in joint-stock forms of colonial governance. The idea here was to bring about a kind of quasi-decolonization of the British Caribbean by turning administration over to an autonomous joint-stock government modeled after the East India Company. Its directors were to be drawn from both shareholders and landowners, with some appointed by the Crown, and the corporation would be represented in Parliament. The Colonial Office would cease to have direct authority over the colonies, becoming, "so far as *those* Colonies are concerned," something like "a mere office or *Board of Control.*" The Company's capital was to be managed by a separate "West-India Joint Stock Association," with shares sold for cash or for property on the islands. All the land was then to be combined in hotchpot, "in one unencumbered estate" and rented back to the erstwhile landowners, while a permanent stock of £2 million, drawn from unallocated emancipation compensation funds, would function as an endowment to fund government, infrastructure, and "*permanent* improvements" in the united colonies. Labor and settlement would be handled as a department of the Joint Stock Association, by individuals, or by a subsidiary company "formed for that purpose," eventually also serving the "philanthropic" goals of ending slavery by revealing, especially to the Spanish and Brazilians, the benefits of voluntary over forced migration.[170]

As Wakefield's model was taking root in admittedly sometimes weird ways around the globe, Wakefield himself had not gone anywhere. In addition to taking part in similar projects as in Western Australia, he had joined Lord Durham's Canadian mission, influencing his subsequent report and thus policy and politics in Lower Canada until the mid-1840s. Most famously, he soon turned his attention to New Zealand. As with previous efforts, this one began with a voluntary New Zealand Association, created in 1837, to lobby Parliament to "apply to New Zealand the peculiar system of colonization which has proved so eminently successful in South Australia." As a foundation, the Association also purchased the specious land rights of the defunct 1825 New Zealand

Company, whose head, Lord Durham, was now at the center of Association leadership.[171]

For Wakefield, joined by many old allies and former promoters of the South Australia scheme, New Zealand was an ideal opportunity to try out his philosophical program.[172] As in previous efforts, these promoters insisted that their plan proposed nothing more than, as Wakefield's son Edward Jerningham Wakefield observed, "the supreme government of this country has very frequently delegated to a corporation in like cases." He proposed that "a special authority should be created" along the same lines that, "with only two recent exceptions," characterized all British colonies—especially the East India Company, especially since it had been "now divested of [its] trading character." It was a pedigree, like the Australian companies, that reached back to Ralegh, Penn, Baltimore, and the proprietors and directors of Virginia, Massachusetts, Carolina, Georgia, and others, examples "sufficient to justify the assertion, that it was once a practice with the leading men of this country to take an active part in the colonization of distant lands. And the fashion was a good one for England."[173]

The Colonial Office, under the leadership of Lord Glenelg, was under pressure from the ministry to grant a charter but was also reticent. Glenelg was no stranger to the debates over company colonization. Born Charles Grant in Bengal in 1778, he was the eldest son and namesake of Charles Grant, the former East India Company governor, Clapham Sect evangelical, and Sierra Leone Company director. His brother, Robert, was made Governor of Bombay in 1834. Before becoming colonial secretary and Baron Glenelg in 1835, Grant had headed the Board of Control during the 1833 charter renewal that stripped the Company of its commercial functions. He offered to support the New Zealand Association proposal but with conditions that would have made the project into something else entirely. Glenelg objected to the establishment of the company by Act of Parliament, which he regarded as "unusual and unnecessary," but did seem ready to consent to a royal charter, "framed with reference to the precedents of the colonies established in North America by Great Britain in the sixteenth and seventeenth centuries."[174]

The Association found the model of "delegation" quite acceptable but regarded a coincident Parliamentary endorsement as essential

and "according to the modern law and practice of the constitution."
More problematic, however, was the implication of Glenelg's model,
which as they took it was a demand that the project be remodeled
to be "founded on a private pecuniary interest." As Durham noted,
echoing the kinds of arguments the promoters of the South Australia
Association had made, the corporation was conceived so as not to
compel its leadership to risk its own capital, which would create a
potential conflict. "Although the old colonial charters were founded
on a private interest," he argued, "a better knowledge of political
economy in modern times has condemned the practice of placing in
the same hands a private interest and public duty, incompatible with
each other, as has been conspicuously shown by the recent reform
of the East India Company, whereby they are divested of their
trading character." Instead of a privately interested "speculating"
corporation, such an effort would be better structured like a "public
corporation," along the lines of another enduring sixteenth-century
example: Trinity House.[175]

Government's position did not yield. As Stephen had urged several years earlier with respect to the South Australian Association,
the Colonial Office now seemed to be of the opinion that if one
was going to establish a corporate colony, better it be founded on
joint-stock than on philanthropic principles, as the former had more
precedent and were easier to understand, limit, and control. Finding
itself unable to consent to Glenelg's version of the charter, the Association decided instead to try its luck with the Commons, and the
Colonial Office withdrew its offer.[176] The bill the Association proposed did not quell the objections. The *Asiatic Journal* noted that it
would have delegated "the perpetual sovereignty of the country . . .
to the Commissioners, almost without control"; the *Times,* calling
it an "attempt at establishing a monopoly conceived in the most
sordid spirit, and only maintainable by the most peremptory despotism," repeatedly dismissed Wakefield as a "philosophical emigrationist" and his projects as "Newgate-born schemes."[177] "It is one
thing," the *Edinburgh Review* opined much later in 1850, "to spread
into vast commercial firms, and another thing to consolidate into
nations."[178] Given the many strong objections, not least of the
missionary societies and now even from parts of Government,
the measure failed by a shocking margin of 92 to 32.[179]

The drama over the incorporation of the New Zealand Association represented the culmination of the subtle and gradual shift in ideas surrounding company colonization. The Association wished to be a corporation, self-consciously sailing in the wake of its seventeenth-century forbears, yet it resisted, perhaps even more than the South Australia Association, being reduced to a commercial joint stock. Seeing no other alternative, however, the Association's principal leaders regrouped and reformulated their plan, in essence calling the Colonial Office's bluff. In August 1838, they issued a prospectus for a joint-stock *New Zealand Land Company,* with £400,000 in capital and Durham as its governor.[180] Charles Buller drafted its charter.[181] Since it in theory owned Durham's former New Zealand Company's territorial rights, by May of the following year the Company sent out a ship on its own accord, which in August 1839 made landfall in Queen Charlotte Sound, and the next month planted its flag in Port Nicholson, just as another four ships took sail from Gravesend with more surveyors and settlers.[182]

Now somewhat of a *fait accompli,* the Association finally succeeded in securing its first charter, as the *New Zealand Company,* on a forty-year term in February 1841. It sponsored a range of promotional enterprises, including publishing its own periodical, *The New Zealand Journal,* which unsurprisingly offered positive reviews of travelogues, Company proceedings, and articles from the Wakefields and others that continued to make the case that "all experience," as William Fox phrased it in one such piece, "is against the fitness of governments to carry out the first details of colonization." The arguments were awfully familiar: government was too slow, too uninterested, too distracted by other business, and too fickle in its changes of ministries, while the New Zealand Company—with its financial interest, efficient system of management, consistent policy, and leadership with "no 'other business' to attend to"—was well suited to the task.[183]

Despite such theory, in its earliest days, New Zealand was not exactly a single coherent company. In addition to several modest missionary settlements and "lawless Europeans" engaging in sealing and whaling around the south island, the Company's own government was a kind of federation of quasi-subsidiary companies, corporate governments, and associations that managed local development and settlement of its territory. A *Plymouth Company* was founded in 1840 by a subset of the New Zealand board of directors to purchase, manage, and finance the settlement of fifty thousand acres that became the city of New Plymouth, acquired by the New Zealand Company in 1841.[184] *The Canterbury Association*, incorporated in 1849 with Wakefield, John Robert Godley, and the Anglican Church behind it, bought land from the New Zealand Company, which it resold to settlers, using the profits to fund assisted migrants; this eventually folded into the Canterbury provincial council, created in the New Zealand Constitution Act of 1855.[185] The New Zealand Company tried to sell the Chatham Islands to the *German Colonization Company*, founded in February 1842, and to promote a German colony, but the plan was done in by opposition in the British government.[186] It launched a range of other subsidiary operations, such as the 1842 *Whale Fishery and Steam Communication Company*, in which the South Australian Company also invested.[187] Meanwhile, both Australia and New Zealand were being overrun with independent or semi-independent corporate projects in fields including meat preserving, canning, and, most famously, a great speculative fervor in mining brought on by the gold rush between 1845 and 1848.[188] Some of these, like similar enterprises elsewhere, blurred the lines between commercial and territorial power. The *South Australian Mining Association*, for example, having purchased the land and monopoly rights to the Burra Burra mine outside Adelaide in 1845, over the next fifteen years produced nearly five percent of the global copper supply while undertaking significant public works and planning projects, including its ultimately neglected company town of Kooringa, present-day Burra.[189]

Company projects had growing competition, not least from the British Government, which had essentially taken charge of assisted emigration as the South Australian Commission project was merged into a new Colonial Land and Emigration Commission—later simply the Emigration Commission—that put emigration, and ultimately South Australia itself, firmly under the Colonial Office's control.[190] At the same time, imperial expansion had given rise to a new suite of popular voluntary and charitable societies, which also posed an alternative vision to Wakefield's political economy of company colonization but not to its central tenet that such work was best done outside the state. "A new bond of union is now required," the report of the Society for the Promotion of Colonization put it in 1848; companies were not the solution, but neither was "the unchallenged arbitration of one Minister" distracted by "all their complicated interests and duties" and prone to "bold and irresponsible despotism."[191]

These new enterprises took various forms. Leading the charge were missionary societies and humanitarian efforts like the Aborigines Protection Society, founded in 1837, and the British and Foreign Anti-Slavery Society, created in 1839. Some took the form of parochial or region-based bodies, such as the Petworth Emigration Committee, formed in Sussex in 1838 to facilitate migration to Upper Canada. Others focused on women, such as the Colonization Society's British Ladies' Female Emigrants Society or Sidney Herbert's Society for the Promotion of Female Emigration, with close ties to the Church, and especially the SPG. Caroline Chisolm promoted a Family Colonization Loan Society to offer interest-free loans for emigration to Australia, so that the laboring poor might "obtain a passage to that Colony, not as a pauper—not as a criminal; but in the more worthy position of a borrower." This brand of self-reliant benevolence was anathema to the "assisted" form of emigration, but it was no less a paradox than the company colonial model, premised as it was on the notion, as Chisolm put it, that "Nothing but what is voluntary is deserving of the name national." As she added, "A Society such as that contemplated would commence its labours with many advantages over those which Her Majesty's Commissioners have enjoyed or a mercantile House can command."[192] It turned out, if there was one thing that charitable societies and joint-stock companies could agree on, it was, as Bentham had concluded, that colonial expansion was no business for government.

6

LIMITING LIABILITIES

The Age of Imperialism

> Depriving me of my Government, you consign me to History; and
> History is my best friend. I feel in my heart, brother, that when
> I become a tradition, my real glory will commence.

FOR THEIR TRIUMPHANT RETURN to the Savoy Theatre stage in October 1893, the recently reunited impresario team of W. S. Gilbert and Arthur Sullivan chose to put on a comedic opera about, of all things, the limited liability corporation. Audiences were sung the story of a South Pacific island whose Cambridge-educated Princess Zara returns home from Britain with six men, each offering different proposals for "remodeling" the island's "political and social institutions." She and her father, King Paramount, become enthralled by the clever English company promoter, Mr. Goldbury, who quickly persuades the monarch to convert the kingdom into a joint stock. Enthusiasm for the idea spreads, and by the time the curtain lifts on the second act "every man, woman, and child" has made him- or herself "a Company Limited."[1]

Gilbert had mocked the fashion for joint-stock companies before, but in its moment, *Utopia, Limited, or, The Flowers of Progress* resonated. The opera was an obvious homage to Thomas More's early sixteenth-century *Utopia*, a satire on the tales of extra-European exploration of the day that had been experiencing its own passionate revival of interest in the late nineteenth century.[2] Gilbert and Sullivan's version was also ripped from the headlines, from the adoption of Western "modernizing" practices at Hawai'i beginning under King Kamehameha III in the 1840s to the recent trial in France of Suez Canal Company promoter Ferdinand de Lesseps for fraud and bribery in raising money for a new canal company in Panama.[3] Most of all, however, the joke was supposed to be on their own countrymen and their seemingly boundless appetite for new company schemes and new company scandals.[4] All of this was enabled, the opera made clear, by more than a half century of legislation and practices that had democratized the means of forming a corporation. Instead of the laborious, uncertain, and expensive process of acquiring a charter or act of Parliament, all one needed now were seven signatories and some paperwork and fees filed with a registry office. "It's shady," *Utopia*'s Chorus observed, "but it's sanctified by custom."[5]

New "companies acts" in Britain and various colonies provided the legal conditions necessary for the rapid proliferation of incorporated, limited-liability joint-stock banking, transportation, communication, land, and mining companies, and many others that were critical to late nineteenth-century imperial expansion. Along with the final death blows struck to the remaining seventeenth-century company colonies in India and Canada, it seemed to many that modern capitalism and the modern state had finally triumphed over the lingering relics of Adam Smith's "exclusive corporation spirit." Yet, in places as far afield as the Falkland Islands and Borneo, and most famously and pervasively in colonial Africa, the idea of the corporate colony endured, often now in partnership rather than competition with this new species of limited company. Together they ushered in hybrid and labyrinthine financing and organizational schemes that worked both in tandem and tension with Britain's own expanding empire and its burgeoning administrative, military, and diplomatic apparatus. As they had for centuries, advocates for such enterprises touted their efforts as both quintessentially modern and rooted in history, finding exemplars, arguments, precedents, and models in corporate colonialism's distant and recent past alike. The result was a "new" imperialism that at times could look quite old indeed.

THE BLOWING UP IN LEADENHALL STREET

In June 1850, George Lyall Jr. joined the Hudson's Bay Company directors to see their annual fleet off from Gravesend. Despite the "splendid dinner," Lyall, whose father had been one of the founding directors of the New Zealand Company, could not bring himself to enjoy the moment. "My heart was sad," he reported, "to think that they after a flourishing career of 180 years were as prosperous as ever & that we in only our 12th year would probably soon be annihilated."[6] As it turned out, the New Zealand Company did abandon its charter later that year, facing intense financial and political pressures as well as an uprising among shareholders, former director Edward Gibbon Wakefield among them, over proposals to introduce convict labor into the colony.[7] What Lyall had not foreseen, however, was that the Hudson's Bay Company would also soon find itself under mortal threat.

The collapse of the Vancouver colony experiment and growing tensions with and atrocities committed against the First Nations and Métis at Red River had brought the question of the legality and legitimacy of the Company's charter front and center. News of the failed attempt to effectively prosecute Pierre-Guillaume Sayer and other Métis interlopers in an Assiniboia court in 1849 only added fuel to the fire. Some within the Colonial Office and other agencies wished simply to do away with the Company. Such efforts, however, were stymied in part by government lawyers, who argued that officials could not actually initiate such an action on their own. They first needed a complainant and a petition. The Company had no shortage of critics, and still Earl Grey could find no one willing to take it on. Alexander Ibister, the Métis Red River resident lobbying in London on behalf of the colonists' grievances, politely excused himself, as he had never intended his complaints to rise to the "far higher grounds" of a constitutional challenge. John McLoughlin was more direct. He just did not have a chance against "a great public corporation" that "where the very existence of their monopoly of trade is at stake, would naturally resort to every legal subterfuge, entailing an amount of expense which no private individual would be justified in incurring." Besides, the government's legal position was perplexing. As he reminded Grey, "numerous precedents are on record, in the case of the charters of the early American colonies, in which the Sovereign, by writs of *quo warranto,* had repealed such of them as contained powers inimical to the rights and liberties of the subject."[8]

While the Hudson's Bay Company narrowly escaped this attack, this principle could not save the East India Company, as its vicennial renewal approaching in 1853 became yet another opportunity to put the Company and the whole concept of corporate colonial government—as more than one MP put it—"on trial."[9] Many in the Commons took the occasion to argue for the removal of what they regarded as the "fiction" or "sham," indeed the "ridiculous and childish" idea and "monstrous delusion," of continuing to govern India by a corporation.[10] The anti-imperialist radical Richard Cobden made the case that the system had drawn Britain into an empire in "tropical countries" that neither "public opinion" nor Parliament needed or wanted.[11] For most, though, the question was once again about how to rescue Britain's Indian Empire from a dangerous and corrupt anachronism. Company government had created a despotism, John Blackett argued, akin to "the most barbarous buccaneer that ever cleared a jungle" and perhaps worse than George III in America.[12] To Thomas Phinn, company rule was "the most repulsive form of government that could be devised, because it was not the government of a Sovereign tempered by an aristocracy, but was the government of a plutocracy"—a board of directors.[13]

That the system was tempered by state supervision in the form of the Board of Control did not satisfy the radical John Bright, who contended that the "theory" of double government had no place in "a constitutional and Parliamentary Government," as it had been born not from sound political principles but contingencies and compromises: factional battles between Fox and Pitt in 1783–84; the exigencies of war in 1813; and, in 1833, "the hurricane which carried the Reform Bill."[14] Nor did it quell the concerns of Henry Baillie, a conservative politician and recent joint secretary to the Board of Control. He derided the Company as a plutocracy whose shareholder elections were dominated by "London bankers" in command of a "system of bribery and corruption" that looked conspicuously like the rotten corporate boroughs supposedly swept away by the Reform Acts.[15] Baillie's cabal of bankers conjured a common specter of financial conspiracy infected with the anti-Semitism, xenophobia, and misogyny pervasive on all sides of this debate. An examiner for the Commons special committee preparing evidence for the ensuing debate made the point explicit when he pressed one East India Company administrator to account for how nearly four hundred "ladies" and a suspiciously incalculable number of "English and foreign Jews" holding Company stock could possibly be trusted to "exercise a sound discretion" in choosing the government of India.[16]

The witness—the philosopher and political economist John Stuart Mill—mostly evaded the question. Mill was, however, more unequivocal over several days of testimony, in which his arguments echoed many made over previous generations in advocacy of the Company and its system of government.[17] "Many bad, and few good consequences would result" from government intervention, he insisted, while a colonial government vested in a secretary of state would be "the most complete despotism that could possibly exist."[18] This was typical of Mill's brand of liberalism; elsewhere he would later argue that government was to intervene in companies only as was necessary to "watch, and superintend, and if need be, to regulate" them to prevent a descent into monopoly and "dictatorship."[19] Yet Mill also recognized the East India Company as something more than just another aspect of autonomous economic and civic life. Like many before him, he saw how its illiberal government served, to borrow one historian's metaphor, as a necessary "vaccine" to inoculate Britain from the moral and political infections that ruling an empire consistently threatened.[20] Where critics like Phinn and Baillie made the case that the directors and electorate of a company were too self-interested to govern justly, Mill countered that, in the case of India and indeed most colonies, it was the English public and their representatives in Parliament who were too fickle, disconnected, and distracted to make reasoned and informed decisions about empire. Professional, "philosophical legislators," like Company directors, conversely, were guided by expertise and experience and not patronage or politics.[21] It might not be a bad idea, Mill suggested, for every colony to have something like a court of directors, but such a system was especially indispensable in places deemed to be incapable of self-rule.[22]

Mill's arguments resonated through the Company's defense strategy in 1853. "The best government of a great dependency that the world had ever seen," former New Zealand Company director and soon-to-be East India Company chairman Ross Mangles argued before the Commons, was to have an "intermediate body standing between India and the strong political action of the Home Government."[23] As the financier Thomas Baring put it, Indian government required "all the powers of the Crown" but "independent of the Crown" and free from the "vortex of party politics."[24] A joint stock, to such individuals, was hardly a plutocracy. Rather it was the very model of middle-class government, which was, as Mill observed, "generally unconnected with the influential classes in this country, and out of the range of Parliamentary influence."[25] Others echoed the essayist, historian, and former India government lawyer Thomas Babington Macaulay, who in his prominent essay on Robert Clive a decade earlier had suggested that the system of double government had transformed Company government from "a nuisance" to a "beneficial anomaly."[26] Macaulay, now speaking as MP for Edinburgh, pronounced the debate about directorship to have missed the point entirely. The Company's true contribution to Indian government was its development of a professionalized—and middle-class—colonial civil service. These were the men who did the real ruling of British India. "Three or four or six incompetent Directors," he contended, "would cause far less evil to the people of India than a single incompetent [district revenue] collector."[27]

A common premise among these arguments was that Company government worked and had for some time. Charles Wood, president of the Board of Control, echoed arguments made in the 1833 debates when he suggested that, while no one now "would dream of constructing a Government upon such a system for so mighty an empire," it was the system that had "grown up along with the growth of our Indian empire" and as such was, with some modest reforms, worth keeping.[28] Robert Jocelyn, also a former secretary to the board, took the point even further, suggesting that Company government in India worked better than that of Crown-governed colonies. Since 1833, while there had been rebellions in Canada, the Cape, Ceylon, and New Zealand, not "a single arm had been raised against British rule and authority in India."[29]

The 1853 Government of India Act passed, confirming Company government "in trust" for the Crown while making some concessions to critics, such as reducing the size of its board of directors and providing for the appointment of some of them by the British government.[30] Yet arguments like Jocelyn's soon proved tragically ironic. Just a few years later, in March 1857, a rebellion did break out in an East India Company garrison in Meerut, which soon cascaded into a general uprising among the Company's Indian soldiers (*sepahi*, or "sepoys") and eventually landholders, peasants, and others throughout northern India. As news of the Sepoy Mutiny, as the Company would reductively call it, spread across the world through the summer and autumn of 1857, Company critics seized on the opportunity to finally remove the Company from power. "The commercial monopolists in whose name the conquest was made," one article opined, "hoodwinked the nation and the legislature, and made them believe that India was safe only in their hands, and those of their creatures."[31] The government under Lord Palmerston was on board and, like much of the public discourse, eager to lay blame for the rebellion at the Company's feet. As Palmerston wrote the Queen, the crisis was the final proof that "the government of a vast country on the other side of the globe by means of two Cabinets, the one responsible to your Majesty and to Parliament, the other responsible only to a mob of Holders of Indian stock," had to come to an end.[32] Charles Wood excused the Act he had supported five years earlier and touted the wisdom of government-appointed directors, now insisting that "a more absurd mode of selecting a Council than by the votes of the Proprietors of Stock, who have no knowledge of or interest in India, cannot well be conceived."[33] Nothing captured the mood better than the illustration in the August 1857 issue of the satirical magazine *Punch*, which featured a cannon destroying the East India Company's famed headquarters in the City of London, and along with it bundles of paperwork representing "avarice," "blundering," "nepotism," "supineness," and "misgovernment." Its title: "Execution of 'John Company;' Or, The Blowing up (there ought to be) in Leadenhall Street."[34]

The image proved to be prophetic. In the wake of the rebellion in late 1858, Parliament finally succeeded in removing the Company from its role as the Government of India; a few years later, its city-block-long headquarters in Leadenhall Street was razed and, in advance of moving the newly formed India Office to Whitehall, about three hundred tons of Company documents were destroyed, sold to paper makers "to be boiled, bleached, and bashed into low class paper pulp."[35] As critics aimed to make the Company a thing of the

EXECUTION OF "JOHN COMPANY;"

The Blowing up (there ought to be) in Leadenhall Street.

The Execution of "John Company;" Or, The Blowing up (there ought
to be) in Leadenhall Street. Reproduction from *Punch, Or the London Charivari*
(15 August 1857), provided by Duke University Libraries.

past, its advocates returned to time-tested arguments on its behalf
in these final debates and their aftermath. The Company, some still
maintained, was a preferable form of colonial government, driven
by expert *"middle-class* energy and intelligence" and thus immune
to "the tempests of parliamentary strife, or the intrigues of political
office."[36] One author judged the "suppression of the East India

Company" to be the "soundest box on the ears ever administered to the middle and mercantile classes."[37] Former Company chairman William Sykes sneered that the bill being debated in 1858 made Fox's 1783 India Bill seem "a gentle measure" by comparison, and, if passed, would mean "no charter or rights of any corporation whatever will be safe."[38] As Mill reflected several years later, "It has been the destiny of the government of the East India Company to suggest the true theory of the government of a semibarbarous dependency by a civilized country, and after having done this to perish."[39] Conversely, many advised, pointing to recent catastrophes in the Crimean War, against being so quick to assume that Government would have done any better a job putting down the Indian rebellion.[40] After all, "America was once a colony," historian and East India Company administrator John Kaye acerbically reminded his readers, and "it was lost to you by parliamentary government."[41]

Even those who looked to place India in the hands of the British government were not necessarily sure how it should be done. Queen Victoria had for decades regarded it as a "quite absurd" idea that the Company might so impinge on her imperial prerogative, yet now when faced with the reality of Crown rule in India had to admit the precise structure and form it should take was not entirely clear.[42] The Company itself might be removed from power, but not everyone was willing to part with its system of government entirely. Many, including Mill, pushed for a reformation that would keep the old structure but change its name, a suggestion the jurist Henry Maine likened to a "re-baptism." Palmerston envisioned replacing double government with a Cabinet-level "president" or secretary of state appointed by the ministry, but supported by a Crown-nominated governing council serving longer terms and comprised of men who either had been East India Company directors or had otherwise served or resided in India.[43] The Queen was skeptical, as such an approach did not in her mind give enough direct control to the Crown. Worse still were William Gladstone's designs to vest power more centrally in Parliament, which she scoffed would to leave her with "less authority than the President of the American Republic."[44]

Not everyone was all that comfortable with the hasty manner in which this business was being dispatched. The once and future prime minister Lord John Russell, who in 1853 had favored getting rid of the Company entirely, cautioned that one must be careful not to abandon "any materials which formed the strength of the old building & might be adapted to the uses of the new," observing that "the real ground for change is that the machine is worn out & as a manufacturer changes an excellent engine of Watt & Bolton made 50 years ago for a new modern engine with modern improvements, so it becomes us to find a new machine for the government of India. The task is not an easy one."[45] He favored the proposal to replace the Court of Directors with an eight-member committee made up of former Company leadership and others who had lived and worked in India for at least a decade. "The choice," he noted, "is between the danger of making India a party question & the creation of an anomaly."[46] The Earl of Minto, Russell's longtime ally—and father-in-law—agreed, worrying that "we must discover another system which avoiding Scylla does not drift upon Charybdis." Whatever was done, he warned, one must "beware of a leaf out of the bill of 1783."[47]

Not long after proposing his bill, Palmerston's ministry fell to a Conservative government, headed by the Earl of Derby and the erstwhile mining company propagandist Benjamin Disraeli, which managed in August to pass the Government of India Act—albeit, even then, only after months of negotiation and compromise measures. British India would no longer be governed in trust but rather by the Crown directly. Responsibility for its administration in Britain was placed under a new Cabinet minister, a secretary of state for India, and a larger council than Palmerston had envisioned; in India, a viceroy replaced the old post of governor-general. Some twenty years later, Disraeli would complete the process, having Queen Victoria declared Empress of India, though evidently some had already been using the phrase for some time. Meanwhile, new coins, bank notes, and postage stamps announced the Crown's direct rule, as did a formal proclamation which was declared in hastily organized ceremonies across India by late October. In a way, the government had accomplished precisely what Minto had feared; J. M. Ludlow, a lawyer, Christian socialist, and son of a former East India Company employee, even echoed the words Edmund Burke had used to describe Fox's bill some three-quarters of a century earlier when he styled the 1858 proclamation "British India's Magna Charta."[48]

The Company, however, did not disappear that quickly. In the first place, the transition especially in India was hardly seamless. Perhaps

most striking were the protests that arose among European soldiers in several garrisons—beginning in May 1859, in Meerut of all
places—objecting to being forced from Company into Crown service.[49] In a legal sense, the Company also still lingered on constitutionally in the secretary of state for India, who was still responsible
for its debts, legal causes against it, and other obligations; in its legal
capacity as the Company's successor, the secretary's office, India
counsel Courtenay Ilbert later argued, constituted a sort of "juristic
person" and a "body corporate."[50] The Company's legacy could still
be seen in the continuing work of those many other joint-stock corporations, discussed in the previous chapter, that had taken on the
management of finance, transportation, infrastructure, natural resources, and territory in the wake of the Company's transformations across the first half of the nineteenth century.[51] Finally, the
Company had not actually been abolished. It lingered on, even if,
as the Duke of Argyll later reflected, it was now merely a "shadow
of a shade" of its former self. It was neither a merchant nor a sovereign, but it was a corporation, and its shareholders were entitled
above all to their annuities from the 1833 settlement. It was only
in March 1873, at the expiration of the forty-year term of that
agreement, that Parliament took up its option to buy out the Company, finally bringing, as Argyll put it, "an end to the last purpose
of its existence."[52]

Despite the all-consuming nature of India issues in 1857, Parliament had managed to turn some attention that year back to
the Hudson's Bay Company charter, as its twenty-year license for the
western territories, last renewed in 1838, was due to expire. The
Company had effectively been unable to enforce its monopoly since
the Sayer trial, and many in its leadership, including George Simpson,
had come to believe they should cut their losses and strike a deal to
sell the Company's charter to the British or Canadian government.
As Donald Ross, an official at Red River, sized up the options years
earlier, it would be "far better to make a merit of necessity than to
await the coming storm, for come it will." The Company's new governor, however, dug in. A former East India Company chairman,
John Shepherd chose instead to maintain the Company's claim to
government and pursue a renewal of its grant. Things did not go
quite as planned. The Company's government west of Rupert's Land
was allowed to lapse. Meanwhile, the proprietary patent for Van-

couver had been withdrawn, with the Company receiving £57,500 in compensation from the British government. The region was now to be a Crown colony called British Columbia.[53]

For the moment, the Company and its 1670 charter remained secure; at the same time, the experience had emboldened a number of formidable opponents. Many in the Canadian colonial government seemed all too happy to encourage corporate competitors with charters for fur trading, rail, telegraph, mining, and other companies in the suddenly ambiguous western territories.[54] A Toronto-based *North-West Transportation Land Company* succeeded in obtaining a charter from the Canadian Assembly to oversee roads, maritime traffic, and a railroad from Lake Superior to the Pacific, complaining that the Hudson's Bay Company's "odious monopoly, the entire fabric of which has been built upon utterly false and fictitious grounds," had somehow become understood as "rights."[55] Meanwhile, Sir Richard Broun advanced a decade-long attempt to obtain a Parliamentary incorporation for a transcontinental steam-and-rail line from Halifax to Vancouver, citing not only contemporary analogues in Canada and the United States but also a panoply of historical precedents including "the method by which several of the United States of America were originally colonized and their wild lands reclaimed"; eighteenth-century land bank schemes with their capacity for "coining their land into money"; and the seventeenth-century Irish Society's strategy of raising capital out of the "corporations of cities and large towns in Great Britain and Ireland." He proposed that Queen Victoria convert the entire territory to "an hereditary Vice-Royalty," on the model of James I/VI's grants to William Alexander.[56]

Appropriately enough, when the Hudson's Bay Company's government finally fell, it was to a buyout. In January 1862, a group of Anglo-Canadian financiers and merchants in the form of a *British North American Association* set out to revive plans for a trans-Canadian Grand Trunk telegraph and railway company. Its representative, the railway magnate Edward Watkin, petitioned for a large territorial grant for the project but the Company refused, telling Watkin that the only way his group could receive such territory was by purchasing the Company outright. It even named a price: £1.5 million. Whether he was meant to or not, Watkin called its bluff. He proposed to secure the money as a loan from the British government and to finance that loan through two subsidiary joint-stock companies (one for fur trading and one for land). The territory itself would become a Crown Colony, as in British Columbia, which he suggested naming "Hysperia," as the ancient Greeks called their western colony of Italy. As Watkin later recalled, he received "all sorts of moral support" from government officials but was told that if he wanted to pursue such a plan, it would have to be done with "private resources." So he turned to a recently founded capital group, the *International Financial Society,* whose members included major banks and several men already involved in the British North American Association. It floated a joint stock to serve as a sort of holding company and offered three times the nominal value for any Hudson's Bay Company shares. Most Company directors and other shareholders took the opportunity, leaving the Society the controlling owner of the Company and thus of vast amounts of Britain's Canadian empire.[57]

It turned out that the International Financial Society had little interest in territorial government. Over the next several years, it gradually sold off much of what it now controlled for a hefty profit. The Company's directors at this point began protracted negotiations to sell its charter back to the British government. They faced significant obstacles. A number of shareholders revolted, wishing to continue the Company as a colonial enterprise. It also proved impossible to settle on a value of its assets, which included the government of Rupert's Land, significant property in British Columbia, and outstanding claims against the United States. The Company estimated that, all told, it was worth over £1 million. The Ministry offered £250,000. Meanwhile, American westward expansion and especially the creation of the Montana Territory in 1864, the financial crisis of 1866, and the creation of the Dominion of Canada in 1867 made some kind of settlement ever more urgent. The directors entertained an offer from the United States government but ultimately came to terms with the British ministry to cede its rights in Rupert's Land to the Crown for £300,000. Government was to be vested in Canada, while the Company would remain a commercial enterprise with significant property in its former territories. The Company formally surrendered Vancouver in 1867 and gave up its last holdings on the West Coast, its Russian-American Company leases, when Alaska was sold to the United States that same year.[58]

Many cheered this turn of events, but there were some that greeted them with lament. Robert Brown composed a kind of eulogy in 1870:

> The last of the old proprietary governments, they saw the gorgeous career of the East India Company, and its decline and fall; they witnessed Louisiana ceded by his Most Christian Majesty of Spain, and the Seigneurs of Canada become subjects of Great Britain and again of the new-born Dominion of Canada: the Darien enterprise come to ruin, the South Sea Bubble burst, and a dozen rivals brought to naught: they remembered when all of North America was the plantation of his Majesty, themselves remaining loyal and attached when the colonies broke from the mother country: they survived eleven sovereigns and died in the reign of the twelfth.

The Hudson's Bay Company would remain a trading company. It still had its charter. However, as Brown wrote, recalling Charles Lamb's requiem for the South Sea Company a half-century earlier, its "soul be long since fled." As he put it, "those who remember the old times cannot but feel some regret at the decease of the great Corporation," but it just turned out that "the world is too advanced for monopolies."[59]

THE REIGN OF REGISTRATION

"Time was," Leone Levi observed, also in 1870, "when the foreign and colonial trade of the country was, in a great measure, monopolised by chartered companies, such as the Russian and the Levant, the East and the West Indies Companies, the Hudson Bay and the African." The Anglo-Italian economist and lawyer noted the evolution since: "All such monopolies have long ago been abolished, yet the reign of companies is as undisputed as ever."[60] The largely unregulated field of company formation inaugurated by repeal of the Bubble Act nearly a half-century earlier had predictably led to a flood of company promotion and, with it, growing anxiety about the company "promoter," the nineteenth century's answer to Daniel Defoe's "projector." To some, he was the embodiment of capitalist enterprise; to many others, he was embodied in a figure like Montague

Tigg, the ne'er-do-well of Charles Dickens's *Martin Chuzzlewit*, "burnished, lacquered, newly-stamped" into Tigg Montague after refashioning himself as the promoter of a pyramid scheme in the form of an "Anglo-Bengalee Disinterested Loan and Life Insurance Company."[61]

In 1844, the same year Dickens issued his final installment of the serial novel, Parliament passed the first of what turned out to be a string of joint-stock companies laws, culminating in (though not ceasing with) the Companies Act of 1862. These new laws formalized critical aspects of what it meant to be a joint-stock company, such as limiting shareholders' liability, and introduced relatively streamlined mechanisms for both creating a company and "winding up," or liquidating, one. Most importantly, these measures brought into being a new office, the Registrar of Joint Stock Companies, which would superintend this new system.[62] In theory regulated by statute and a government agency, incorporation had now become a bureaucratic process not a political one. Companies and their promoters once again proliferated, perhaps even more than in Tigg Montague's day. After 1862, there was apparently, as Goldbury touted to the Utopians, "no schemes too great and none too small For Companification."[63]

Dickens's sardonic choice for the specific business in which Montague's company engaged was no accident. Company speculation had thrived not only in India but across the Anglophone world since the 1820s and ever more so after the advent of the companies acts.[64] Still, it remained an open question how much the 1862 Act obtained to companies formed in or by colonies themselves.[65] Thus, through the second half of the nineteenth century, the legislatures or governing councils of many British colonies adopted some form of companies law of their own. The East India Company introduced registration in 1850 and limited liability in 1857; similar measures followed over the next decades in the Cape, Canada, Australia, and elsewhere. Along with complementary laws regulating taxation, banking, philanthropy, and trusts, the private registered corporation was over the later nineteenth century enshrined in colonial law as a primary means of public association not only for commercial companies but also a range of other forms of civic enterprise, from colleges and charities to chambers of commerce.[66]

Yet, while they no longer needed patents to be protected in British or colonial law, registered companies could still acquire special privileges, grants, concessions, and contracts abroad, which continued to blur if not erase the line between commercial and territorial enterprises. For example, the mahogany logging interests of the *British Honduras Company, Limited* (registered 1858) led it to develop plantations and actively recruit settlers to work them; part of its outreach was in the United States where, in competition with two short-lived American companies, it advertised its proposed "Townships of Colored People" to entice emigrants from Black communities in the early days of the Civil War. The project faltered when the Lincoln administration failed to provide subsidies. Ironically, the company recruited much more successfully after the war by enticing former Confederate soldiers to settle instead.[67] *The Central Argentine Land Company,* a subsidiary of the *Central Argentine Railway,* and the *Santa Fe Land Company* similarly facilitated immigration and the settlement of "agricultural colonies," on the strength of Argentine government grants and guarantees. The 1888 *Mexican Land and Colonization Company, Limited* obtained its rights by buying the Connecticut-chartered *International Company of Mexico* and its concessions from the Mexican government in Baja California, and soon spun off a development company, a bank, and railway and telegraph companies.[68]

Meanwhile, British charters had apparently not lost their value or prestige either. According to the modern Privy Council's reckoning, between 1844 and 1914 the Crown approved at least 267 corporate charters to associations, just over seventy fewer than it had in the previous six centuries since the incorporation of Cambridge University in 1231.[69] For charities, learned societies, and other associations, charters still offered special privileges, protections, and a public imprimatur, including sometimes the "royal" name; the still flourishing Royal Society of 1662 was joined by several others with deep connections to colonial expansion: the *Royal Asiatic Society* (1824); the *Royal Geographical Society* (1859); and the *Royal Colonial Society,* incorporated in 1882 though originally established over a decade earlier to address the "want [of] some medium by which we may form our scattered colonies into a homogenous whole."[70] The commissions of the imperial exhibitions of 1851, 1862, and 1886 were likewise incorporated by charter.[71]

Despite the introduction of registration, charters remained appealing for a wide range of overseas commercial enterprises, such as joint-stock banks, mining, and steamship companies, as well as the most globally transformative late nineteenth-century imperial business of telegraphy. Between 1846 and 1856, a Parliamentary Act, a Royal Charter, or both incorporated thirteen new British telegraph companies, six of which were simultaneously registered under the Companies Act.[72] Like rail and steam, international telegraph companies called on British government agencies from the Admiralty to the Post Office for support in other ways, including subsidies, guarantees, contracts, diplomatic and political backing, maritime surveys, monopoly protections, and, above all, use of their services: by the dawn of the twentieth century, one report found that government had spent nearly £3 million over the years on telegraphy.[73] Even as these companies turned to British charters with less frequency after the 1860s, they nonetheless continued to depend on agreements with colonial and foreign governments for rights to run lines through their territory, to acquire land and other property of their own, security, and for other forms of support. Such agreements were in turn often used as leverage to extract further backing from home. For example, once the *Red Sea Telegraph Company* had negotiated a concession from the Ottoman Government to connect Alexandria to Aden and Karachi, the British Treasury seemed compelled to support it with a 4.5 percent guaranteed return for its investors to keep the company from failing; the arrangement cost the British government £36,000 per year for a line that soon broke and never sent a single message.[74]

Telegraphy seemed to offer a new vision of global order, with its twinned promises to "utterly annihilate distance" and, as Rudyard Kipling put it, to kill "father Time."[75] That early transnational and transmarine telegraphy was unevenly distributed, unreliable, slow, expensive, and vulnerable to interception and interruption hardly stopped those, like the governor of the Australian colony of Victoria, from seeing its potential, as a "great Imperial binding force," to forge connections across time and space that would strengthen centralized imperial government.[76] "As all roads led to Rome," the MP and Australian journalist John Henniker Heaton mused, "so do all the great ocean telegraph routes lead to London" and there "link together, like so many pearls on a single string, the scattered dependencies of the

British Crown."[77] To John Kaye, it was precisely the illusion that "nearness of time" could overcome "remoteness of place" that had deluded people into thinking there could be a British India without the East India Company. "I shudder," he lamented in the wake of the 1858 India Act, "when I think of the not very distant period when India will be governed by the electric telegraph."[78]

International telegraphy was thus a paradoxical intervention into the world of company colonialism: a technological innovation that seemed to promise a new, centrally governed British Empire but that was almost wholly dependent upon regionalized incorporated companies for its establishment and operation. Confusing matters further, by the 1870s, much of that singular global British communication network had come under the control of the very thing that registration and the elimination of the East India Company were supposed to have eradicated: a "private monopoly," in the form of the *Eastern Telegraph Company,* which, Henniker Heaton complained, "like a huge octopus, has fastened its tentacles upon almost every part of the eastern and southern world."[79] If Eastern Telegraph was a monopoly, it was one built much like the British Empire, first created in 1872 as a conglomerate of several existing ventures and then growing through the acquisition or creation of subsidiary companies, each with its own regional focus, such as the *Eastern Extension Australasia and China Telegraph Company,* the *Brazilian Submarine Telegraph Company,* the *Western and Brazilian Telegraph Company,* and, in 1885, the *African Direct Telegraph Company.* Its longtime chairman, John Pender, led the Company to invest heavily in manufacturing lines through its *Gutta Percha Company,* which through a later merger with *Glass Elliott* became *Telegraph Construction & Maintenance.* All told, by the turn of the century, Eastern Telegraph owned and operated nearly 45 percent of the global telegraph network, while its affiliate TC&M was responsible for making nearly two-thirds of the world's telegraph cable. Three other British-owned companies made up about another twenty percent of the share. Thus, while from one perspective it might be said that "Britain" owned nearly two-thirds of the global telegraphic network, only three percent of it belonged to or was administered directly by British or colonial authorities.[80]

Pender worked hard to sell his companies to the state and public as imperial goods, while cultivating relationships with various government agencies, especially through strategic appointments to various companies' directorships. Overall, the strategy worked, though there were those, especially in the Colonial Office, who were skeptical of Pender's influence within their and other agencies; John Anderson, for one, reproved the Post Office, which managed Britain's domestic telegraph, for its support of a company for which "the interest of their shareholders, not that of the public, is always paramount." Moreover, for all the promotion of its national character, telegraphy was an inherently transnational business. For example, the Danish financier Carl Frederik Tietgen's 1869 *Great Northern Telegraph Company*, which may have done as much as any company since the Opium Wars to facilitate European penetration of China, was effectively a Pender subsidiary, relying heavily on TC&M for its infrastructure and receiving substantial funding from Pender and other London banks.[81]

The ability to create subsidiary companies by registration profoundly muddied any sense that these were somehow inherently national enterprises. Pender's great rival to connect India to European telegraph service, the *Indo-European Telegraph Company*, though registered under the Companies Acts with an office in London, was owned by the German conglomerate *Siemens und Halske*. One of Eastern Telegraph's great rivals in the Atlantic was a partnership of the US-based *Commercial Cable Company* and the French *Cable Company*. Their two subsidiaries, the *Halifax and Bermudas Company* in 1890 and the *Direct West India Company* in 1898—both registered in Britain with boards populated by British and Canadian directors—managed to beat out Eastern Telegraph's *West India and Panama Telegraph Company* for British government subsidies to create a Canada-to-Caribbean line. Conversely, British-based competitors like *India Rubber, Gutta Percha, and Telegraph Works Company's* subsidiary *West African Telegraph* worked around Pender's hold on government support by obtaining concessions from France and striking up a partnership with the Spanish *National Telegraph Company*.[82] Most emblematic of this transnational traffic in imperial identity was *Reuter Telegram Company Limited*, which by the late nineteenth century had become the virtually exclusive purveyor of news across the British empire. It promoted itself as an "imperial" service even as both it and its founder, the German-Jewish-born, British-Protestant convert Paul

Julius Reuter, maintained financial investments in other European telegraphs, and in January 1875 led an attempt to formally merge with the French *Agence Havas* and the German *Wolffs Telegraphisches Bureau*.[83]

The contests over controlling international telegraphy reflected the debates that had prevailed for centuries over rival company models for colonial expansion. This was most evident in the great battles between Eastern Telegraph and the *Pacific Telegraph Company*, established in 1886 to try to break its rival's firm grip over the Indian Ocean route by connecting to Australasia via the western United States or Canada. Its colorful chairman, Sandford Fleming, formerly a Hudson's Bay Company director and once chief engineer for the *Canadian Pacific Railway*, was another in a long line of polarizing company promoters. Fleming was connected to numerous civic and private institutions; he also had been dismissed from the CPR for alleged financial misdealing, and the Canadian Prime Minister John Thompson once called him "the greatest example which Canada presents of successful dishonesty and deceit." Fleming promoted the transpacific telegraph as a public-private partnership that was key to the making of Greater Britain, while aggressively pursuing his own ambitions, most notoriously when he and some partners mounted an imprudent expedition to seize Necker Island for themselves after the British government had actually ceded the island to Hawai'i.[84] Like many a company promoter looking to break in on monopolies, Fleming somehow managed to position himself as a critic of companies, insisting that what he was proposing was more closely tied to the interests of government and the public. "Is the peace of the world," the joint-stock promoter asked rhetorically, "to be endangered at the bidding of a joint stock company?" Pender's response was equally typical: not only was the current system less expensive and more strategically valuable but "it has been the rule of all Governments, or of all honest Governments, that they never attempt to compete with private enterprise." John Downer, the Australian premier, could not resist pointing out Fleming's hypocrisy: "It is not the case of the Eastern Extension Telegraph Company seeking to maintain a monopoly," he observed, but rather "the case of the Pacific Telegraph Company asking for assistance from the Government to initiate an enterprise which would be in competition with what he is pleased to call a monopoly."[85]

EMPIRE (CHARTERED AND LIMITED)

By the later part of the nineteenth century, company-driven colonialism seemed alive and well. For overseas enterprises at least, company registration had not supplanted patents so much as begun to work in tandem with them. Registered companies deployed tactics and arguments honed over years by chartered corporations, while chartered companies deployed registration to support, protect, diversify, finance, obscure, and reinforce their enterprises. This was certainly the case for the Liverpool-born merchant Samuel Fisher Lafone as he looked in the 1840s to establish a colony in East Falkland, the largest of nearly eight hundred islands in an archipelago off southern Patagonia, which Charles Darwin, who sailed there on the HMS *Beagle* in 1833 and 1834, dismissed as "miserable islands" with "a population, of which rather more than half were runaway rebels and murderers."[86] Despite their reputation, the Falklands, or Malvinas, had been a point of contention among Spain, France, Britain, the United States, and Argentina for over a century, with their strategic location near the Straits of Magellan and potential agricultural and commercial benefits, especially for lucrative whaling and sealing enterprises. In 1833, Britain had asserted control over East Falkland, and the recently established Colonial Land and Emigration Commissioners soon entertained various proposals to make it into an agricultural, convict, or a naval colony. On the Commissioners' recommendation, Britain declared the territory to be a Crown Colony in 1840, though did little to develop it.[87]

Samuel Lafone saw this as an opportunity. Lafone was one of the most financially and political powerful merchants in Uruguay, and the Falklands seemed ideally placed to act as a key link in a commercial empire he imagined reaching from Punta del Este to the Pacific.[88] With the assistance of his brother (and attorney) Alexander, Lafone purchased the lands as well as a cattle monopoly in the Falklands from the British Crown in 1846. Like in many similar deals, the payments were to be spread out over installments, so to finance both the debt and future operations, the Lafones provisionally registered a joint-stock company, the *Royal Falkland Land, Cattle, Seal and Whale Fishery Company* in 1850 "to purchase a grant of the Southern Peninsula of the Falkland Islands with the Cattle & Stock thereon and to trade with the produce thereof and of the adjacent territories." Lafone had the company buy the Falklands concession from him, along with his obligations to Government, compensating himself in both cash and stock. The Company then solicited for a royal charter, which was granted in 1852. The registered company was now converted into a chartered colonial enterprise known as the *Falkland Islands Company*.[89] The Company in theory controlled the 600,000 acres of East Falkland—now renamed "Lafonia"—as well as 200,000 acres in 138 small neighboring islands.[90] In another relatively common arrangement, the Colonial Office allowed the Company to reinvest the annual payments it owed the British government for Lafone's original purchase toward developing local infrastructure rather than repay them to the Crown. Finally, in 1859, the Company received a more "absolute grant" in the form of a perpetual charter, with its annual payments now formally reduced to the symbolic centuries-old amount of a single peppercorn.[91]

By the second half of the nineteenth century, this had become a familiar story. An individual or group of partners, having purchased or otherwise making to claim concessions, grants, patents, or the like—from either a British or a foreign sovereign—could register a joint-stock company to raise investment and purchase those rights from their original holders, also assuming whatever debt they owed. Sometimes these companies stopped there, allowing promoters to divest themselves of their debts and even to make an immediate and handsome profit. In some cases, they became more ambitious, looking to finance the purchase of more property or further grants and companies, facilitating sub-licenses of concessions, securing government or other contracts and subsidies, and diversifying into new commercial, governmental, or other enterprises. A huge advantage a corporation had over individuals was that it could not only sell shares to pay for all this but also pay others with shares rather than cash. As corporate investors, rather than private projectors, company leaders were limited in their liability and could raise further sums by borrowing, including issuing bonds. Finally, in some cases, like the Falkland Islands Company, the registered company could solicit for a charter, which offered additional political protections and privileges, and then either liquidate the registered company or keep it, ensuring that the enterprise would survive in law even if its chartered rights were taken away.

This was the sort of strategy James Brooke, a former East India Company soldier turned mercenary, considered in 1841 when Muda Hashim, the heir to the sultan of Brunei, offered him a territorial fiefdom as a reward for putting down an insurgency on the Sultan's behalf in the coal- and antimony-rich region of Sarawak on Borneo. Early on, the so-called "White Rajah of Sarawak" entertained various possibilities for capitalizing on his territorial sovereignty, including selling the grant outright, granting concessions to a syndicate or firm (what he called a "primitive society"), or creating a joint-stock company to manage development, immigration, and mineral extraction. "Such speculations are in fashion," he wrote his mother, "and here it would certainly succeed."[92] To advance any such plan, Brooke also needed the British government to recognize him as a legitimate head of state. The East India Company came readily to mind as a model, both to Brooke and lawyers at the Foreign Office.[93] By 1842, Brooke found himself strategizing with Henry Wise, a fellow former East India Company sailor, about floating a "public company" in Britain. Their plan was recognizable: "Get Government recognition, and form a company with a capital of from 300,000*l* to 500,000*l*. Let them have plantations, diamond mines, &c. and a monopoly of antimony and opium, to help their expenditure till the country yields a revenue."[94]

Brooke soon had a bitter falling out with Wise and the London investors, leading him to an abrupt about-face not only on these company plans but on the very question of company colonialism. He now—and, he averred, always had—believed that involving himself in any such scheme, "which is puffed up and tricked out like a saint, and which like a saint promises much in future, for a small present contribution," to be too far beneath his exalted status as an hereditary sovereign.[95] Brooke argued, as Adam Smith might have, that smaller firms and partnerships might be respectable, but "vast schemes backed by millions never did, and never will, open a new country properly. The one is a natural growth from the tender seedling to the noble monarch of the forest; the other the forced plant of the hot-house, the Prophet's gourd running up to the sky, but withering as fast as it grew."[96] Wise clearly did not feel the same way. He and his partners secured a British charter in 1847 for an *Eastern Archipelago Company*, to which he promptly sold the concession for mining rights at Labuan he claimed to have obtained from Brooke.

With the Glasgow MP John MacGregor as its chairman, the Company had its eye on cornering the lucrative market in supplying coal for Indian Ocean steamships, for customers including the Admiralty, the East India Company, and the P&O.

Things did not go as planned. The Company faced formidable opposition not only from Brooke but also from various critics of its monopoly. The financial crisis of 1847, technical obstacles, and disorganized leadership generally made the entire enterprise an uphill battle. Worse still, the Company failed to satisfy the conditions the Board of Trade had placed on its charter. Eastern Archipelago was required, within one year, to have subscribers to at least one-half of its £200,000 capital stock and to have taken in at least half of that in actual payments, yet by that time only £5,000 of the necessary £50,000 had been paid up. The Company tried to make up the difference with some desperate if clever bookkeeping, purchasing Wise's Labuan mine for deferred salary and shares and representing the mine as worth the outstanding required balance of £46,000 in shares. In somehow converting a debt liability into paid-up capital, *The Times* sneered, the directors had made "a contribution towards the history and philosophy of joint-stock Companies," revealing "two codes of law and morality, the one for Directors of joint-stock Companies, and the other for the public."[97] Brooke agreed. The Company was a "bubble" and Wise a swindler who had tried to sell him a "golden prize" that turned out to be a "golden calf," promising to make him a "second Arkwright"—as renowned, that is, as the eighteenth-century inventor Richard Arkwright, who many thought of as the father of the Industrial Revolution—if he would do something Brooke had once contemplated but now insisted he never had once considered: sell Sarawak out to a company.[98] Brooke's British attorneys, with the cooperation of the Attorney General, sued in the Court of Queen's Bench for a writ of *scire facias* against Eastern Archipelago, which was granted and subsequently held up on appeal in the Court of Exchequer.[99]

By now, however, a charter was not the only way one might make a corporation. Wise, along with partners—Royal Naval Admiral Charles Bethune, former East India Company officer and East India Railway director Captain Alexander Nairne, and former East India Company official and China merchant Hugh Hamilton Lindsay, who was to serve as chairman—registered a new *Eastern Archipelago Company, Limited,* with the same overly ambitious £200,000 capital stock and a registered address just a block and change away from the East India House. (MacGregor, though taking fourteen shares in the new project, was no longer deeply involved, and was soon indicted for his role in a high-profile fraud scandal surrounding another joint-stock scheme, the British Royal Bank. He died soon after.)[100] When that Company failed, Wise, who was wrapped up in the Royal Bank collapse, disappeared from the project, but the other three, along with some old and new investors, re-registered as the *New Eastern Archipelago Company* in 1858. This repeat effort seems also to have stalled; in 1882 it was dissolved by the registry office for failing to carry on business or even to respond to inquiries about its status.[101]

If Brooke was inconsistent on the issue of corporate concessions— he offered a grant to some friends and allies who had formed the *Borneo Company, Limited* in 1856, and a subsidiary *Borneo Jute Company* three years later—his much-romanticized example set off a transnational scramble of imitators in sovereignty speculation, not only in Borneo but also as far away as Patagonia and Nicaragua.[102] One such concession hunter in Borneo was the new, and first, United States consul to Brunei, Charles Lee Moses. Without any apparent authority from Washington to do so, Moses struck a deal with the Sultan of Brunei for a ten-year lease in North Borneo on similar terms to Brooke at Sarawak. He then promptly sold these rights to an American merchant in Hong Kong, Joseph Torrey. Torrey, largely with funding from Chinese opium traders, secured them in his *American Trading Company of Borneo* and sailed to Borneo to obtain from the Sultan his own titles as Raja of Ambong and Marudu and Marharaja of Sabah.

Torrey had grand ambitions for a plantation colony and made equally grand promises, including pitching the colony to the US Secretary of State in 1866 as a potential destination for slaves freed in the American Civil War. Such plans never came to fruition. A US tour, complete with a royal entourage, to try to raise shareholders failed to meet expectations, and Torrey soon went bankrupt. He finally found an investor to help rescue the venture in an old business associate named Gustavas von Overbeck, the Austrian Consul-General in Hong Kong and employee of the agency house Dent & Co. Overbeck's plan was not to develop the colony but to sell the rights quickly for a profit, but his overtures to governments in Austria-Hungary, Germany, Italy, and the United States all fell through. Finally, in 1875, Overbeck convinced Alfred Dent, now at the head of his family's firm, and his two brothers to invest in the scheme. The Dents and Overbeck offered the Sultan of Brunei, his son, and the Sultan of Sulu an annual tribute of twenty thousand dollars in exchange for a confirmation of proprietary rights over 28,000 square miles along the northern coast of Borneo as well as their own titles: Maharaja of Sabah, Raja of Gaya and Sandakan, Datu Bandahara, and Raja of Sandakan.[103]

The British government was split on what to do about all this. Officials in the ministry, the Colonial Office, and the Dutch and Spanish governments objected, as did Charles Brooke, who had succeeded his uncle as the Raja of Sarawak. While Overbeck was still evidently intent on finding a buyer, even managing to draft a contract for sale with the Japanese ambassador in Berlin, the Dents seemed interested in taking actual possession of the concession and establishing a company, in Overbeck's words, "after the manner of the late East India Company." Advised by their lawyer that a charter would be more politically feasible if they shed their non-British partners, the brothers bought out Torrey and Overbeck and, gathering up scores of influential supporters in Britain, proposed to establish a company of "British subjects under a Charter of Incorporation." Such an arrangement, they insisted, would secure for the British Empire an invaluable commercial and strategic colony—and, specifically, a critical landing point for Eastern Extension Telegraph Company lines—while shielding the Crown and ministry from the inevitable criticisms of anti-imperialists at home and from diplomatic imbroglios with European and American governments.[104]

The Dents' approach followed a pattern. They first registered the *North Borneo Provisional Association, Limited,* "for convenience of common action and for limitation of liability," to purchase the "interests and powers" in Borneo and Labuan from the partners, who were thus immediately compensated and were no longer personally liable.[105] The Association could then invest in operations in Borneo while it did the political work necessary to acquire a charter. That charter finally came in November 1881, renaming the Association as *The British North Borneo Company.* The measure won

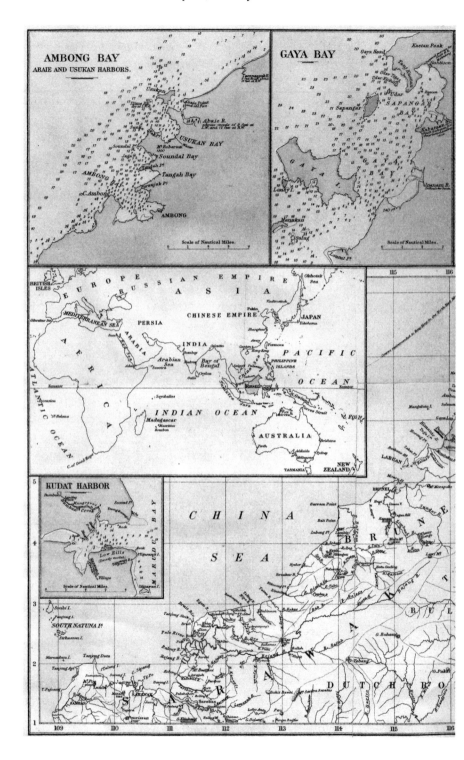

Borneo, Shewing the Lands Ceded by the Sultans of Brunei & Sulu to the British North Borneo Company, Published by Edward Stanford for the British North Borneo Company, 1881. National Archives of the UK (TNA): C0700/LABUA NANDBORNEO6.

the unlikely support of the liberal anti-imperialist prime minister, William Gladstone, who was somehow persuaded, or at least argued, that a charter was the only means the government had to rein in "British enterprize" and its "irrepressible tendency" to expand trade by settlement "beyond the limits of the Empire." Moreover, he observed, companies had been undertaking efforts like this "during all my life," going back at least forty years to the "controversy" over the Falkland Islands Company (though at that moment Gladstone claimed not to be able to remember the Company's name). Some, like the New Zealand Company, he added, had on "balance" managed to do work "for the happiness of mankind."[106]

In any event, there were few other legal remedies. Seizing the North Borneo Company's territories was not an option, as it would be tantamount to what Henry James, the attorney general, called a "confiscation of their property." Criminalizing activities half a world away was impractical. The most feasible way to prevent abuses or excesses in the Company, he suggested like Gladstone, was to have a company voluntarily submit to the terms and conditions of a charter. Besides, he added, the charter was not proactively offering anything the Company did not already possess. Such an instrument was not required to incorporate the company, which already existed in law, nor did it provide it its sovereignty. It certainly would not encourage the Company to do anything it had not already done. "What it got was restraint," James argued, "not privilege." This was, in effect, a "new system" of charters that was nothing like the "old system" of the East India Company, as critics continued to insist.[107]

What the North Borneo Company got out of a charter was political imprimatur and protection that served to bolster its position with international rivals and potential investors. The Company was able to raise more capital, with which it immediately bought out the assets of the erstwhile Provisional Association—including its Bornean concessions—for £300,000 in a combination of cash and shares.[108] Dent then went looking for a formidable figure to serve as chairman, so that "the British government and British public would be well satisfied that the new government would be inaugurated in our territory on sound principles." When the former colonial secretary Lord Carnarvon turned him down, he looked to the former diplomat and Royal Geographical Society President, Rutherford

Alcock.[109] Now duly constituted and recognized as the government of the "State of North Borneo," the Company then entered into a treaty with the British government to constitute North Borneo as a British-protected state, like Brunei and Sarawak. Such an arrangement placed responsibility for its defense and foreign policy under the command of the British Foreign Office but left its internal governance, in theory, autonomous.[110]

Borneo was thus in theory an independent state, governed as a colony by a British chartered company in the name of the Sultans of Brunei and Sulu, whose external affairs were managed by the British Empire and its naval power. Incorporation allowed the Company an expectation of institutional permanence, vastly preferable to the hereditary sovereignty of someone like Brooke, as his "succession is personal & the present Rajah cannot live forever, whereas the Company is impersonal and may survive as did the East India Company for centuries"—that is, "until H.M. Government may see fit to take over its succession."[111] On these foundations, the Company set about establishing an administrative and judicial apparatus, a small police force, and investments in railway, telegraph lines, and public infrastructure. It looked to attract Chinese settlers and merchants, boasting of its "liberal form of government," whose revenue was to come not from commercial enterprises directly but rather from taxes, opium and alcohol licenses, government fees, and land grants and mineral concessions for developing mines, commerce, and plantation agriculture, especially the "veritable gold mine" of tobacco cultivation.[112]

Many of those grants and concessions went to companies. Before the end of the Company's first decade, about twenty joint-stock companies out of the Netherlands, Britain, Hong Kong, and Germany owned over forty percent of the seventy-eight plantation lots within the Company's jurisdiction, representing some sixty-five percent of the nearly 700,000 acres under cultivation.[113] Many of these companies were independent, but some were clearly quasi-subsidiaries or projects of prominent Company leadership and investors. One of the largest, the *London and Amsterdam Borneo Tobacco Company*, with forty thousand acres across six plantations, was chaired by Alfred Dent; financed by the banks Martin & Co. (same as the North Borneo Company) and the *Chartered Bank of India, Australia, and China* (of which Dent was a director); and represented by the same

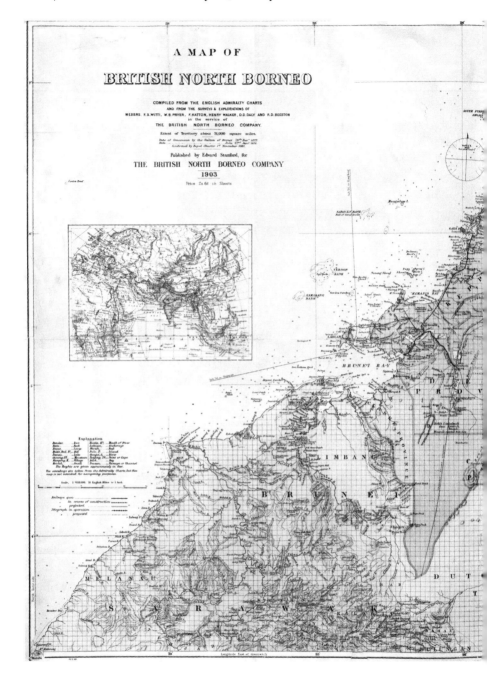

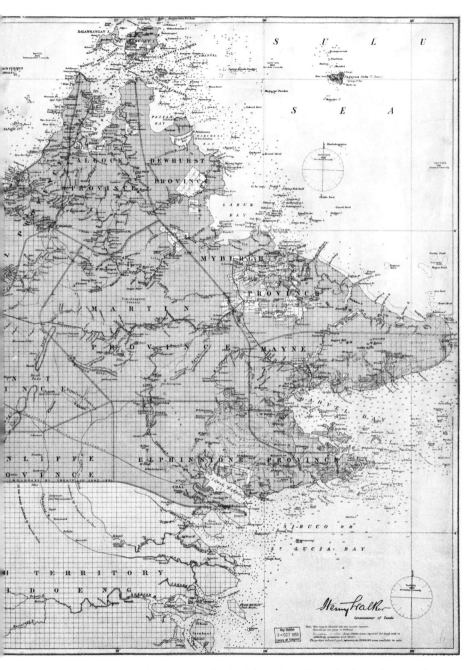

A Map of British North Borneo, Published by Edward Stanford for the British North Borneo Co., 1903. The territories in white represent nearly 500,000 acres of land sold by the Company "to subsidiary companies and others." (See following figure for detail.) Library of Congress, Geography and Map Division.

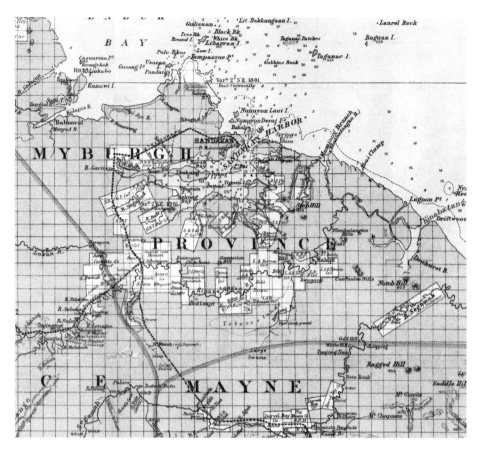

Closeup of a Map of British North Borneo, Published by Edward Stanford for the British North Borneo Co., 1903, showing the area of concentration of subsidiary company estates. Library of Congress, Geography and Map Division.

legal firm, Harwood and Stephenson, as the North Borneo Company, among other colonial companies.[114] The Borneo Company eventually branched into commerce and infrastructure itself, becoming especially involved by the early twentieth century in rubber cultivation, mostly through subsidiary corporations and agency houses.[115] Meanwhile, the competing *Central Borneo Company (Limited)* appeared in 1887, claiming its own concessions for mineral rights in Labuan from the Sultan of Brunei and the British Crown Agents. Its apparent intention was to seek its own charter from the British Crown and to establish its own subsidiaries to exploit the grant, neither of which ever materialized.[116]

Dent, like many successful company promoters, soon became a sought-after chairman in his own right. Among other positions, he was appointed to head the *Peruvian Corporation,* established to put into operation the terms of an agreement between the Peruvian and Chilean governments and several British creditors, led by Grace Brothers & Co., after the two states had defaulted on their bond debts. In what was essentially a debt-for-equity swap, the Corporation bought up bad government bonds in exchange for shares and then used its leverage to exact further concessions from the Peruvian state, diversifying into railway and guano monopolies. Though this was not a territorial enterprise in any straightforward sense, at least one contemporary boasted that the scheme was akin to "one of the greatest of joint-stock companies ever organised to carry on operations in a foreign country," the East India Company.[117]

While the East India–North Borneo chartered company model continued to influence colonial projectors and projects around the globe, it took root most prolifically in late nineteenth-century Africa.[118] The Berlin West Africa Conference in late 1884 and early 1885 famously carved up Africa among various European "spheres of influence," setting off a European "scramble" for colonies in which companies would play the prominent role. The most infamous example was the Belgian Congo Free State, a colony run by a corporation whose single shareholder was an unincorporated philanthropic organization, which in turn was the sole personal property of King Léopold II of Belgium. Like his father, Léopold seemed interested in having a colony. It mattered less to him where it was. To that point, he had attempted to acquire various footholds around the world, including having previously negotiated with Overbeck to purchase North Borneo. In fact, Léopold's ambitions were profoundly influenced by both the distant and recent history of colonial companies. He admired Brooke and had studied up on the East India and Hudson's Bay Companies. One could draw a rather straight line from the long history of colonial companies and early modern theorists of the law of nations, like Hugo Grotius, to the arguments Léopold's legal team, especially the British international lawyer Travers Twiss, made for why corporations could be considered legitimate actors in international law capable of acquiring alienable forms of indigenous sovereignty. A chance encounter in 1876 with Verney Lovett Cameron—who had been the first European to cross the entirety of equatorial Africa, and had been suggesting a chartered company for Africa on the model of the East India Company—may have been formative in stoking the King's imagination. Léopold certainly followed the debates over the North Borneo Company closely in 1882, and later instructed his agent, Henry Morton Stanley, to use Dent's concessions as his model for drafting similar agreements in Africa.[119]

Léopold's Congo soon became either inspiration or competition for further British companies in Africa. In 1885, Cameron floated another proposal for a "powerful chartered Company" for the Sudan, to secure an Ottoman *farman* and, with an outlandish £10 million capital stock and £2 million in government subsidies, to take on both sovereign and commercial monopolies: "powers," Cameron wrote, "similar to those possessed by the Honourable East India Company."[120] When the Foreign Office declined to support the proposal, Cameron turned into an advocate for other company projects, especially William Mackinnon's efforts to acquire a territorial concessionary colony in East Africa from Seyyid Barghash bin Said Al-Busaid, the Sultan of Zanzibar.[121]

Mackinnon had built his fortune in India as a partner in the agency house Mackinnon Mackenzie; by the 1850s he fatefully turned the firm to steam shipping with the incorporation of the *Calcutta & Burmah Steam Navigation Company* and then its reincorporation and expansion in 1862 as the *British India Steam Navigation Company*. By the 1870s, the Company had come to rival P&O, with which it merged in 1914, and acquired lucrative British mail contracts for the eastern Indian Ocean. (One of its ships was the first to navigate northward through the newly opened Suez Canal in 1869.) By 1882, Mackinnon's nexus of companies included four other steamship companies spread across the Indian Ocean world, a contract with Portugal for mail service between Lisbon, Goa, and Mozambique, and subsidiary projects that connected to inland river navigation and railway development. All told, Mackinnon ran a conglomerate which at its height was worth somewhere in the neighborhood of £2.5 million.[122]

Mackinnon's Indian and Indian Ocean interests, combined with his religious and ideological commitments to the colonial "civilizing" mission, had led him to involve himself in various attempts through the 1870s and 1880s to acquire from the aforementioned Sultan of

Zanzibar a concession for governmental and commercial rights over his territories along the mainland East African coast. This was the first step of extending that maritime network far inland. Mackinnon eventually struck up a collaboration with Léopold, which included buying £800 in shares of the Belgian *Comité d'Etudes du Haut Congo*. From early on, the idea was to vest such control in a concessionary company of the sort Cameron had been proposing, on foundations, as the missionary Horace Waller had proposed to Mackinnon in 1877, "nothing less than those of the East India Company." Given Zanzibar's status under a British sphere of influence, Mackinnon had to persuade not only the Sultan but also the India Office and the Foreign Office. The concessions from the Sultans of Sulu and Brunei, as well as the royal charter, to the North Borneo Company—Alfred Dent was Mackinnon's longtime friend and associate—helped the case along, as did, for different reasons, the establishment of the rival *Deutsch-Ostafrikanische Gesellschaft,* or German East Africa Company, in 1885.[123]

Mackinnon followed a version of the North Borneo Company's strategy, though in this case the concessions were acquired directly by a company newly registered in London for that purpose, the *East African Association*. Having secured its main concession from the Sultan, with assistance from the British consul in Zanzibar, agents for the Association, both on its and the Sultan's behalf, then made over twenty further treaties and contracts for territory and concessions along the mainland coast. Mackinnon flirted with various other arrangements, including partaking in the establishment of a *Companhia Africana* under Portuguese charter in 1884 and entertaining a merger with Carl Peters's German company in 1886. The arrangement he and others involved in the Association preferred, however, was a royal charter, which was finalized in 1888. This new *Imperial British East Africa Company* took command of rights to customs revenues and postal services as well as "promoting trade, commerce, and good government" on a nearly thousand-mile stretch of coast along what is now Tanzania, Kenya, and Somalia and reaching into the interior lake districts.[124]

As in North Borneo, the new chartered company bought out the previous Association's rights and assets. In a somewhat novel arrangement, the IBEAC reserved half of its capital stock for five nontradable "founders' shares," each of which was set aside to ensure a particular stream of revenue for various Company obligations, including additional emoluments for its leadership. One share was dedicated to paying out the Company's concessionary tribute to the Sultan. Though taken in his name, it was held in trust and could not be sold or transferred; it was also, as a founder's share, in second position, to be paid only after dividends on ordinary shares had been satisfied.[125] The Company pursued further concessions to establish a monopoly state bank and acquired more territory to the north of Kismayo, which it then sold to the Italian government. It failed in its efforts to purchase Wituland from the German *Tana Company.*[126] Most famously, the Company's agent, Frederick Lugard, set out in late 1890 on an inland mission to visit King Mwanga of Buganda and, from there, various other kingdoms in the region. Over the next year, he secured several treaties and a military presence effectively establishing IBEAC territorial and administrative authority in Uganda. The process was so reiterative and *pro forma* that the Company had its treaties printed up as lightly customizable forms, though Lugard, regarding these to be a "fraud," evidently made up his own. Years later, he would reflect on the entire system as a "naked deception." Still, he added, it was one which governments back in Europe were all too happy to accept "without too close scrutiny, and to persuade themselves that the omelette had been made without breaking any eggs."[127]

One reason the IBEAC had a relatively easy time obtaining its charter was that one had recently been granted to a similar enterprise in west Africa, modeled on North Borneo, driven by the one-time engineer and soldier Sir George Dashwood Taubman Goldie (born, perhaps reminiscent of Dickens's Tigg Montague, George Dashwood Goldie-Taubman). Like the others, Goldie's enterprise began with a registered company. The infiltration of British trade in west Africa, he believed, had been hampered by "incessant inter-tribal wars and slave raids" as well as the "want of unity of action" among "private firms" and their agents. Several of these concerns, including the Manchester-based *West African Company, Limited,* and the London-based *Central African Company, Limited*—which Goldie had taken over from his brother's father-in-law—agreed in 1879 to merge into a privately held conglomerate, the *United African Company, Limited.* Soon, however, their combined capital of about £125,000 proved too modest for their lofty goals not only to extend

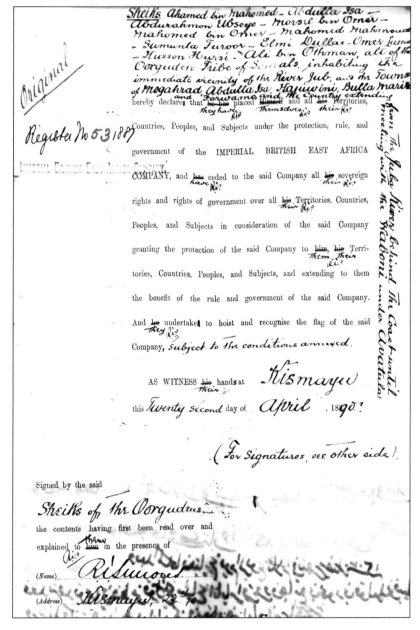

Treaty between Imperial British East Africa Company and Sheikhs of the
Ogaden, 22 April 1890. These treaties, by which the signatories were said to
be placing their "Countries, Peoples, and Subjects Under the Protection, Rule,
and Government" of the Company, were printed up as brief reproducible
legal forms. Translations were rendered on the reverse. National Archives of the
UK (TNA): FO 2/14/0/53.

their trade but also to exert, as Goldie later recalled, "political influence over as many of these heterogeneous tribes, and to weld them together (so far, at any rate, as their intertribal relations were concerned) into a single and homogenous State."[128]

Goldie's solution was to establish a new "great public company," registered in 1882 as the *National African Company* with £1 million in capital to be raised in a public stock offering. Lord Aberdare, the president of the Royal Geographical Society and former home secretary, was to be nominally at its helm while Goldie would do much of its political and intellectual work as deputy governor. The new company was to purchase the "commercial assets and the political good will" of its predecessor, entirely for deferred shares, for up to double the value of the United Company; like many others, its articles of association detailed a vast range of potential legal fields of business: commerce, finance, transportation, mining, land, and "all other things whatsoever, whether of the like or other nature." Among these enumerated "objects" was "to apply for, acquire, and hold any Charters, Acts of Parliament, privileges, monopolies, licenses, concession, patents, or rights or powers from the British Government, or any other Government or State, or any potentate or local or other authority in Africa or elsewhere" and to "constitute or incorporate the Company as an anonymous or other society in any foreign country or state."[129]

This question of foreign grants and incorporation was not an idle one. Goldie deliberately branded the concern as a "National" one, and was intent on pursuing a royal charter. He seemed open, however, to the possibility—or at least willing to leverage the threat—that the Company could seek such protections elsewhere if efforts in Britain failed. As Goldie later recalled, had the Company succeeded in its protracted negotiations to purchase two rival companies, one based in Paris and the other in Marseilles, it was entirely conceivable the "amalgamated" venture would have ended up "passing under the French flag"; doing so, he added, would probably have been advisable from a "pecuniary point of view" and might have come to pass "had the shareholders acted as investors rather than Englishmen."[130] Yet more immediately important than powers from other European states were those the Company claimed from African ones. Along the same lines as the North Borneo Company, the National African Company sought a charter not to provide but rather to protect jurisdiction it claimed it already had by virtue of twenty-nine "Acts of Cession" struck with west African principalities, mostly between August and November 1884.

Of course, such treaties—in its various iterations, the Company would ultimately go on to acquire 237 such agreements—were, as in other places and times, highly suspect. To what exactly African polities imagined they were agreeing is an open question. Some were certainly coerced or defrauded by mistranslation or differences between what was said and what was written. Others no doubt imagined the Company as submitting itself as a tributary, offering protection or weapons, or engaging in some sort of commercial exchange or contract. It was hardly clear whether such treaties were secured with individuals authorized to make them, or on terms that resembled the ones later represented. Doubtless there were many who believed that they were making a treaty with Britain and its fellow monarch.[131] For their part, Company officials were equally slippery. At times Goldie represented these agreements as having rendered "sovereign and territorial" power and at other times he insisted, as in Borneo, that actual sovereignty remained in African hands. At one point he offered to sell these rights to the Crown while defending them as the inalienable property of the Company. One way or the other, though, the National African Company had made itself into a government in west Africa, making the charter, which Goldie primarily regarded as needed to secure "international recognition" from other Europeans, not so much a request as a *fait accompli*.[132]

The immediate model for such a charter adopted by Goldie, and by Treasury counsel R. S. Wright, who was charged with drafting it, was the North Borneo Company, though Goldie also leveraged other contemporary exemplars, such as Léopold's Congo and the German concessionary company in Cameroon, the *Deutsch-Westafrikanische Gesellschaft*. He explicitly drew on the East India Company and also somehow managed at different times to invoke the Hudson's Bay Company's erstwhile power as a territorial government as precedent for vesting in "a private Company the government of a Crown Colony" (as the Crown's lawyers described it), and to use the process by which it was dispossessed of that government as an argument for why the Company should be compensated for agreeing to government demands that it give up monopolies supposedly granted in its various concessions. The analogies were not without complications. Julian Pauncefote at the Foreign Office pointed out that the powers of both the Hudson's Bay and East India Companies had both been "hotly contested" at the time and that controversies over both Companies eventually led them to be regulated by Parliamentary statute. Meanwhile, the Crown's lawyers observed that the example was outdated, once again drawing a distinction between the older model represented in the Hudson's Bay Company and that of the Borneo Company, which derived its territorial power not from the Crown but from the Sultans of Sulu and Brunei. In fact, they could think of "no instance in modern times, in this country, of the grant by Royal Charter to a private Association of sovereign rights and powers of government, including the administration of civil and criminal justice over territories situated within or without the British dominions," which was not to say the Queen could not do so if she wished.[133]

The Company did obtain its charter in the summer of 1886, after which, instead of dissolving the registered National African Company, Goldie petitioned to have its articles of association amended, rebranding the concern in a rather unorthodox style that highlighted its reinforcing sources of authority in Britain. It was now to be called the *Royal Niger Company (Chartered and Limited).*[134] This arrangement in turn became a model for imitators and competitors. One of Goldie's most vociferous critics, a consortium of companies and firms known as the Liverpool African Association, after failing to persuade Goldie to buy them out, registered itself as the *African Association, Limited,* and solicited, unsuccessfully, for their own charter for taking on the nearby Oil Rivers Protectorate. After years of protesting against the National African and Royal Niger Companies, they now they believed a colony in such a place "could not be satisfactorily carried out under a Colonial Government."[135] The Association also unsuccessfully demanded subsidies or reimbursement for its expenses in establishing relationships in west Africa— "handshakes," it called them—without which, its leadership claimed, "the natives would never have accepted the Protectorate." The merchant Donald Mackenzie's 1879 *North-West Africa Company,* having already purchased the Moroccan town of Tarfaya, similarly sought out a charter modeled on the RNC. This "plucky experiment," as one later account called it, faltered when the Foreign

Office and Admiralty determined that it was not wealthy or large enough to be viable. Mackenzie instead enlisted the Foreign Office to help it sell the town and nearly three hundred miles of coastline back to the Sultan of Morocco for £50,000.[136]

HOW TO MAKE MONEY BY STARTING A NEW EMPIRE

Two decades before Goldie had conceived of his own "African Sarawak," many, like the Duke of Newcastle in 1861, were already fretting that it would be in southern Africa that events would take "much the same course as during the last century in India."[137] Much of this dated to the formal annexation of Natal to the British Cape Colony in 1843. The ensuing speculative land grab inspired the establishment of a joint-stock company—modeled, in its projectors' minds at least, on the Canada Company—to purchase its members' landholdings in exchange for shares, vesting them in a single corporation to serve as landlord, land broker, and mortgage lender all in one. To that end, the *Natal Land and Colonisation Company Limited* was registered in Britain in December 1860 and was subsequently confirmed by a special act of the Natal Legislative Council. The Company attempted to secure a territorial concession from the Zulu leaders Mpande kaSenzangakhona and Cetshwayo kaMpande, while also spawning a network of connected subsidiaries for railways, cotton, coal, and mining.[138]

Most of these subsidiaries, like the concession gambit, ultimately failed. Meanwhile, soon after the Company's founding, many of the original landholders sold off their shares to British-based investors for a healthy profit, while the Company expanded its own landholdings by buying up other estates and foreclosing on settlers who had defaulted on their Company loans during the war and financial crisis in Natal in the mid-1860s. By the 1870s and 1880s, most of the Company's lands were occupied by African tenants, from whom it was extracting increasingly extortionate rents. White settlers began to leave farming for new opportunities in transport, war provisioning, and, most of all, mining during the gold and diamond rush of the late 1860s and early 1870s. These new speculative industries produced their own web of partnerships, corporations, and intercompany cartels, including the Natal Company's own subsidiary *South*

Africa Gold Fields Exploration Company; many of the resultant companies pursued their own treaties and concessions from African states to secure or expand their access to territory, mines, and other resources.[139]

This was, in a sense, the program taken up by one former Natal Company tenant turned diamond speculator, Cecil Rhodes. Rhodes, using financing from the Rothschilds and working with various partners, proceeded to set up several companies, including *De Beers Consolidated Mines* and the *Consolidated Gold Fields of South Africa Company, Limited.* In 1888, on his behalf, a business partner, Charles Rudd, the lawyer James Rochfort Maguire, and the planter and administrator Francis Thompson reached an agreement—or so they said—with the Ndebele leader Lobengula for exclusive territorial and mining rights over his entire territory in Matabeleland in exchange for the low price of £100 per month, plus firearms and other considerations. Lobengula would soon insist that he had been defrauded and had never agreed to the terms of what became known as the "Rudd concession." There was some question as to whether he himself had the absolute authority Rudd and others assumed he did to grant all the rights and territory it contained. Certainly the deal led to unrest among his leadership, stoked by rivals, from the Transvaal, the Portuguese, and a host of British competitors and critics.[140] At the same time, a rival *Bechuanaland Exploration Company* had been seeking its own concessions in the region. The Company's lead directors—the former colonial administrator, Edric Frederick, Lord Gifford, and the enterprising if slippery lawyer, stockbroker (some said "stockjobber"), and amateur geographer George Cawston— had established the Company in partnership with Francis Ricarde-Seaver to acquire a concession, originally from Khama III, King of the Ngwato in present-day Botswana, which Ricarde-Seaver had bought on behalf of his employer, the *Caisse des Mines de Paris,* from the Cape Town–based *Northern Gold Fields Exploration Company.* Through a subsidiary, the *Exploring Company, Limited,* Gifford and Cawston sent their own agent to Lobengula and set their ambitions on Matabeleland.[141]

By mid- to late 1888, both rivals had been talking to government officials about obtaining charters for their companies, as in North Borneo and west and east Africa; with a nod to Mackinnon, the

Exploring Company had proposed calling their venture the "Imperial British Central South Africa Company." Yet, with Lobengula disavowing the Rudd Concession in a letter to Queen Victoria and planning a deputation to London to press the case, the two sides began to talk merger in the form of a new "powerful British Company" to implement their "concessions, agreements, grants, and Treaties," with all the "powers necessary for the purposes of government."[142] As Maguire put it a few years later, the goal was "to found a company that would become to South Africa what the East India Company had been to India." *The British South Africa Company*— or the "Chartered Company," as it was known to many—received its charter in late 1889.[143]

In addition to the new chartered company, the new partners established a separate subsidiary, the *Central Search Association Limited*. Given the unreasonable and vague list of potential businesses listed in its articles of association, one could be excused for not having any real idea what this company was intended to do. As it turned out, it had only one purpose: to serve as a sort of holding company to acquire from Rudd, Rhodes, and Consolidated Gold Fields the "mineral rights and interests in the Principalities and Dominions of Lo Bengula King of Matabeleland Mashonaland and adjoining territories"—that is, the Rudd concession—and then lease it back to the British South Africa Company. Its £120,000 in shares were not publicly traded but were owned mostly by the prime movers behind the BSAC and other allies and supporters such as the financier Nathan Rothschild and the high commissioner and governor of the Cape Colony (and De Beers and later BSAC director) Hercules Robinson. The next year, £1000 in shares were added for the physician Leander Starr Jameson, whose efforts as Rhodes's agent to Lobengula would pave the way for the Company's occupation of Mashonaland in 1890. Its two largest shareholders were other companies—Gold Fields of South Africa Limited and the Exploring Company—which together held £48,000 in fully paid-up stock. For 2,400 shares, the new company purchased the *Austral Africa Exploration Company* to extinguish its claims to have a rival concession. Finally, in 1890, the group registered yet another company, the *United Concessions Company*, with a nominal £4 million capital stock. It bought Central Search, compensating its shareholders

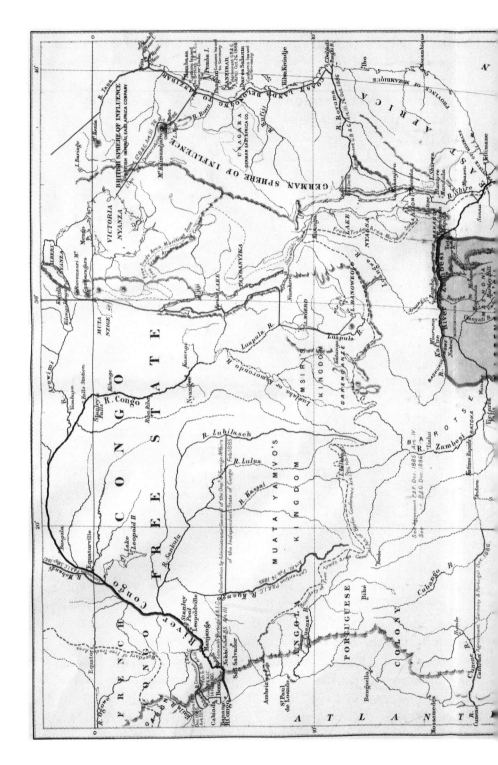

286

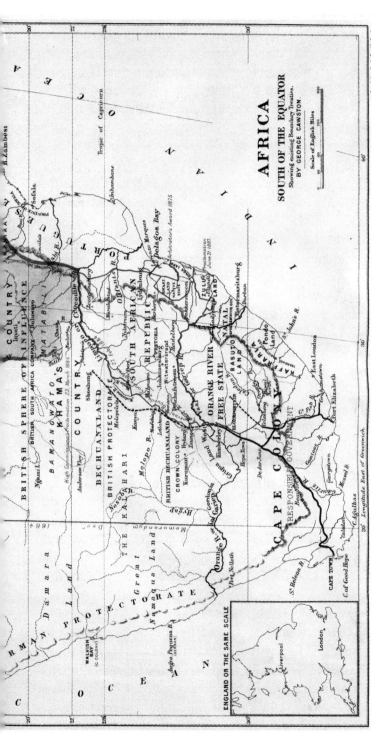

Africa South of the Equator Showing Existing Boundary Treaties, by George Cawston, published by Edward Stanford. 1889. Cawston's map, published a few days after the BSAC received its charter, was reproduced several times, sometimes with radically altered shading and highlighting depending on audience and purpose. This version emphasizes "Lobengula's Country." National Archives of the UK (TNA): FO 925/468.

proportionally while folding in others—including an American with a specious claim to his own concession—in fully paid-up shares. With no money changing hands, Rhodes, Cawston, and the others had in a single stroke made a ten- to thirteenfold profit, bought out several competitors, and quietly sheltered the concession in a limited holding company, distinct from the more politically visible and potentially vulnerable BSAC.[144]

If such a scheme seems suspect, that is because it was. Plenty of these companies purchased their "rights" with shares rather than cash, but in this case many were none too pleased to discover that the British South Africa Company did not own its concession. The *Matabeleland Company*—which held five thousand shares in the BSAC, offered to Rhodes's longtime rival A. O. Ochs and others to quell their opposition to the charter—sued unsuccessfully in the Court of Chancery to stop the directors from even bringing the issue before the shareholders for a vote. Some in the British government insisted they would never have approved the charter if they had truly understood the extent of the scheme. As one financial writer reflected, it was "a most interesting exhibition of 'how to make money by starting a new empire.'"[145]

Ultimately, under political pressure, the BSAC ended up directly purchasing United Concessions in 1893 (for £1 million in shares), but this represented just the tip of the iceberg. The "Chartered Company" was in fact not really a single company but such a labyrinthine network of subsidiaries, partnerships, and concessionaries that, as one critic observed in 1899, it was "difficult to obtain land of any real value from the Chartered Company direct."[146] In addition to numerous land and mining companies, it created or controlled three banks, Rhodes's pet "Cape-to-Cairo" telegraph project in the *African Transcontinental Telegraph Company,* and several subsidiary railway services—among them, the *Bechuanaland Railway Company* (later *Rhodesia Railways, Limited*), which was fully owned by the BSAC, De Beers, and a holding company, *Bechuanaland Railway Trust, Limited,* created by the Bechuanaland Exploration Company.[147] In one typical if extreme instance in 1891, a would-be "Shashi-Mcloutsie Exploration and Mining Company" contracted to provisionally purchase a concession from its current owners—the Bechuanaland Exploration Company, the Exploring Company, the United Concessions Company, and a syndicate that claimed to have first obtained it from Lobengula—in exchange for its full £500,000 capital stock. The problem was that British officials had prohibited concession purchases in the region; though the group had it on good authority that those restrictions were soon to be lifted, the Shashi-Mcloutsie Company could not be registered, and the sale could not be effected, until its objects were technically legal. Thus, Gifford and the merchant Bernard Henry Schroder were to act as "trustees" for this "Intended Company" to execute the agreement and a second one with the BSAC to place the territory under its police and administration once incorporated. This was a poignant example of what the Matabeleland Company had in its suit grumbled was "an agreement made by one party with itself." Gifford, for example, was signatory in the first contract on behalf of three of the five parties, while his longtime partner George Cawston represented the Bechuanaland and Exploring Companies in the first contract and the BSAC in the second.[148]

Schemes like this served various purposes, sheltering legal claims in separate companies, channeling profits back to individuals, and expanding options for financing various enterprises. Many of these companies were especially valued for their ability to borrow, especially in the form of bond issues. Unlike public shares, bonds infused a company with capital without having to offer any say in company governance.[149] Such a system was backed ultimately by the BSAC's credit and collateral, supported by the Company's armed police, aggressive military-fiscal state, and immense regional political influence, especially after Rhodes became prime minister of the Cape Colony in 1890. Protecting those concessions and subsidiaries served as justification for periodic expeditionary invasions of its neighbors, including an attack that led to the suspicious disappearance of Lobengula and, most infamously, Jameson's bungled attempt in 1895 to stoke a rebellion in the South African Republic (Transvaal). Despite great controversy—in the wake of Jameson's raid, the Company was brought before Queen's Bench and one member of Parliament suggested an investigation on "the precedent" of the 1772 inquiry into the East India Company—the power of the Company's government nonetheless continued to reinforce its capacities on the battlefield, in the boardroom, and in the courtroom alike.[150]

More than outright conquest, the Company secured its financial power with political power and vice versa. Substantial amounts of shares were sold below market at face value ("at par") or given as fully paid up to politicians and allies in Britain, the Cape, and beyond; Léopold II and his chief advisor owned three thousand shares purchased in proxy on their behalf by William Mackinnon, in his own hopes of facilitating the relationship between British East Africa and the Congo Free State. The Company or its subsidiaries could buy up concessions and buy out potential competitors using what seemed like an endless supply of shares, rather than cash. Some of these rival concerns, such as the *Tati Company*, went back decades to the concessions rush of the 1870s, while others, like those of Eduard Lippert, a German financier in the South African Republic, were of a more recent vintage. (There is no doubt that at least some of the boom in concession hunting was owing to those who hoped for just such a buyout, or what Company and Government officials referred to as "black-mail.") When amicable terms could not be reached, the BSAC or its subsidiaries could use such techniques to effect what one might now call a hostile takeover, absorbing a company by buying a controlling share of it. This is, for example, what the BSAC did after protracted talks for a merger with the *African Lakes Company* and its concessions in Nyasaland—which at one point involved a plan to recreate the Company in cooperation with William Mackinnon—broke down.[151]

As in other cases, the Company's deep roots and sprawling tendrils drove new projects that aspired either to imitate its success or to link up with its expanding empire in some way. In 1902, for example, Eugene Sharrer acquired a concession from the British government to build a railway through the Central African Protectorate, in what is today Malawi, with additional promises from the British South Africa Company of both mining concessions and railway connections. Sharrer's scheme followed a familiar pattern: vesting the concession in the *Shire Highlands Railway Company* and combining his own estates and his steamer operator *Zambezi Traffic Company* into the new *British Central Africa Company*. The Central Africa Company then contracted with Shire Highlands to undertake the railway construction in exchange for debentures, shares, and the land grant itself. The result was a conglomerate with £1 million in nominal capitalization, £400,000 in debenture issues, over 640,000 acres of property, and enterprises ranging over the following decades into settlement, mining, land sales, transportation, tobacco, cotton, coffee, tea, and other agricultural products.[152]

Like elsewhere in Africa, this competition for territory and concessions had little respect for national identities or boundaries. The "German" *South-West Africa Company, Limited (Südwestafrikanische Gesellschaft)*, was in fact a company registered and headquartered in London—George Cawston was one of its directors—established to acquire vast land, mineral, and railway rights in the German concessionary territories of Damaraland and Great Namaqualand in present-day Namibia, as well as from the German concessionary *Damaraland Company* and the Hamburg-based *Hanseatic Land, Mining, and Trading Company*.[153] Meanwhile, Rhodes, Cawston, and others in the BSAC, especially keen to connect their developing railway lines to the eastern coast, increasingly turned their attention to territory held and governed by three Portuguese chartered companies, all established in part on the model of the BSAC: the *Mozambique Company* (Companhia do Moçambique), the *Nyassa Company* (Companhia do Niassa), and in Angola, the mostly French-owned *Moçâmedes Company*.[154]

The Mozambique Company, which was largely financed by British, French, German, and South African shareholders, including Ochs, granted monopoly concessions to Rhodes's ally Henry Theodore van Laun, who vested them in a British-registered *Beira Railway Company, Limited*. Along with its subsidiary, *Beira Junction Railway (Port Beira to Fontesville) Limited*, the Company undertook to develop the railway connection to the coast that the British South African Company so desperately wanted; it also in the process acquired ten thousand acres of territory per mile and associated rights over telegraphy, taxation, and other services. Beira's sixty thousand shares had no nominal valuation and were not sold publicly but rather were fully offered as compensation to representatives of the Mozambique Company (49 percent) and the BSAC (51 percent), with each shareholder's liability limited by the articles of association to £1.

What Beira did offer the public was £250,000 worth of thirty-year bonds, promising six percent interest and the revenue of one company share for every pound invested. Bondholders did not, however, receive those Company shares. Instead, they were given "coupons" representing the value of the shares, with the actual shares held "in trust" by the BSAC. Thus, once again, the Company raised large amounts of capital without diluting voting shares. (A second issue in July 1895 for a further extension of the line raised another £210,000.) Meanwhile, the Anglophone identity of the enterprise was plainly evident to Portuguese officials on the ground, who complained of its English-speaking employees flouting Catholic holidays, flying the Union Flag, and issuing their own postage stamps. "There can be no doubt," the *African Review* suggested, "that Beira is the natural port of the Mashonaland province of Southern Rhodesia, even if it be not of the whole of that territory."[155]

The Nyassa Company similarly came to be owned largely by British and South African investors, including the powerful firm Lewis and Marks, which, through its subsidiary *the Ibo Syndicate, Limited* (later *Ibo Investment Trust, Limited*), as one contemporary observed, had rendered the Portuguese Company its "tributary." The Trust corporation's £300,000 in investment shares and £112,600 in bond debentures flushed the enervated Nyassa Company with capital but, as venture capital is wont to do, also imposed new pressures to find revenue. This exacerbated the already brutal regime of underpaid and underfunded employees, exorbitant hut taxes, and extraction of labor and natural resources, all of which culminated in a "civil and military" expedition in 1899 to expand its territory into the Great Lakes region led by Major Albert Spilsbury.[156]

Spilsbury was a strange and revealing choice for such a post. He had just returned from a spectacularly failed venture to establish concessionary rights and sell firearms in Morocco on behalf of an outlet known as the *Globe Venture Syndicate,* a successor after a fashion to Mackenzie's failed North-West Africa Company. Even by the dubious standards of a late nineteenth-century European colonial project in Africa, the Syndicate was shady. In the mid-1890s, an enigmatic man calling himself Abd-al Karim Bey—he was most likely an Austrian adventurer named Geyling who for years had been peddling various schemes in Europe and Africa—appeared in London claiming to own concessions in Sus. He insisted that local rulers were primed to rebel against the Sultan in Fez, and would reward a British invasion by making its sponsors "sole masters of the place." At some point "Abdul Karim" befriended Spilsbury, and the two persuaded the Syndicate to back the two of them on just such an expedition.[157]

Unsurprisingly, things did not go as he had promised. Once in Africa, the two men went their separate ways. When he arrived at Sus, Spilsbury was greeted not with gratitude but gunfire and quickly retreated. He nonetheless returned to London claiming, as one contemporary recorded, that he had acquired concessions for a "splendid trading monopoly" in a territory "far superior to what obtains in the territory of the British South Africa Company or that of the Royal Niger Company." All he needed was more money to secure it.[158] Many seemed to buy the story. "But for an accident," the journalist and traveler Cunninghame Graham noted, "Spilsbury might have been Emperor of Agadhir, the Lord Protector of the Sus, or Rajah of Tamagrut."[159]

The Globe Syndicate touted the venture as a crowning success. To the Foreign Office, however, it had been a crime, both against Britain and Morocco. Several of the more reputable leaders of the Syndicate evidently backed off and distanced themselves from the project. What happened next becomes, if it is possible, even murkier. One account suggests that some remaining members of the Syndicate continued to raise funds through another subsidiary known as the "Mauritania Syndicate."[160] What is clear is that Spilsbury eventually returned to Africa, where he was now met by the Sultan's troops and gunboat. He never left his ship. The "invasion" turned out to consist of landing five hundred rifles and other goods, one English subordinate, a German accountant, a Jewish interpreter, and a Portuguese sailor to which one French-Algerian witness reportedly reacted by exclaiming "voilà un bouillabaisse!"[161] For critics, the entire affair was prime evidence of the ill effects of "private war" that had been spread by "Mr. Rhodes's example."[162] To another practiced observer of corporate empire, Joseph Conrad, the whole thing looked "like a wretched fizzle." The later author of *Heart of Darkness,* who among his many company investments and employments had himself once dabbled in African gun running, wrote to Graham, "the whole business seems to have been managed in a mysteriously silly manner. I've done better in my time but then I didn't act for a syndicate."[163]

STATESMAN, ECONOMIST, PHILANTHROPIST

Like the East India Company before them, the African chartered companies in the closing decades had clearly inspired a sizeable body of critics. For the anti-imperialist *Manchester Guardian* journalist John Hobson, writing in the shadow of the catastrophe of the second Boer War, such companies were "little else than private despotism rendered more than usually precarious in that it has been established for the sake of dividends."[164] The "joint-stock system of exploitation and government," *The Spectator* put it in 1886, had been "glorified into a religion by prophets who are carried beyond the bounds of reason by their zeal in the cause of a powerful group of financiers."[165] Blurring those lines, another wrote, suborned "unscrupulous acts performed for the purpose of furthering financial speculation."[166] Even ardent imperialists like Hugh Oakeley Arnold-Foster fretted that the whole system had revived the "curse and danger of the East India Company" in "mixing up the duty of government with the love of gain."[167] One resident in the Lagos colony seemed to echo the general apprehension over the Royal Niger Company when he suggested that "he had no faith in private Companies being clothed with governmental authority, as they generally ruled only to the interests of the monopolists by shutting out competition, as illustrated by the East India Company."[168] With their monopolies, private armies, territorial power, and mix of commerce and administration, Charles Harrison similarly commented, the African companies acted "as if they held an old East India Company charter," something he thought had been happily "terminated" after it had "proved a failure."[169]

It would be tempting to see in these critiques, as with the East India debates several decades earlier, the final blows against the notion of government by corporate joint stock, yet even as late as 1893 Charles Dilke could still note with some accuracy that "there is as yet no settled policy with regard to chartered companies themselves. We are still in an era of indecision with regard to them."[170] There were certainly some, like Lugard, who came to see the "chartered company experiment" as a "bad form of government, which may be said to have been justified by its results for the Empire."[171] Those theorists, commentators, and promoters that actively defended such enterprises had different personal, political, or intellectual commitments, but the basic contours of the arguments they deployed resembled those that had been made on behalf of similar enterprises going back centuries.

In the first place, there was nothing, company advocates claimed, that made companies somehow in themselves worse than other forms of government. Mobilizing the power of commerce to support the primary work of "pacifying, civilizing, and crystallizing into one body politic the heterogeneous tribes of the Territory" was, George Goldie insisted, "an object commending itself to the statesman, the economist, and the philanthropist" alike. "I am not blind to the skepticism with which *les esprits forts* will regard any profession of philanthropy by a Board of Directors," Goldie opined, but "there is not, after all, any inherent impossibility in a body of Englishmen having, in dealing with a population of many millions, some views beyond that of earning a dividend."[172] Just because chartered companies "are instituted for the purposes of commercial gain," Verney Cameron argued, did not necessarily mean they would not "ensure an enlightened and just administration in the areas confided to their control."[173] Conversely, the writer Edward Dicey was convinced that it was "a matter of absolute indifference" to the British public whether the BSAC turned a profit, as long as they took actions "conducive to the interests of the British public."[174] Even Hobson, it turned out, did not assume that private despotism was "necessarily bad in its direct results," or any worse than any other sort of despotism; thus, Rhodes might have abused his power to establish an "unchecked tyranny," but Goldie stood out for him as the counterexample of a "scrupulous and far-sighted" director.[175]

For advocates, though, it was not just that profit did not necessarily make companies bad governments. It actively made them good ones. The Royal Niger Company, Goldie argued, was a "vast cooperative public Association" that only persisted because of the "confidence" investors had in their "important private rights."[176] James Rochfort Maguire repeated arguments made for generations when he observed that all public servants—from a bishop or a schoolteacher to a civil servant or even a Member of Parliament—were motivated by some form of personal incentive, whether it be professional advancement, political influence, or simply a "comfortable income." The "British Empire" itself, he insisted, was like "a gigantic Company, of which the Imperial Executive Is the Board of

Directors," which made dividends both in money and "reputation and power." One did not go to all the expense and risk of colonial expansion "for the childish vanity of painting as much of the atlas red as is in our power." It was "the love of money" that "lies at the root of Empire," and as such, no institution was better positioned to undertake it than the company. "After all," Maguire quipped, "is it not our boast that we are a nation of shop-keepers?"[177]

That companies were self-funded and profit-driven enterprises frequently served as an argument for how their responsibilities as governments called for special consideration. Goldie liked to point out that since Britain did not have a "philanthropic Monarch" like Léopold II, it needed companies to take on the "cost and risk" of colonial government.[178] Because companies were not agents of the state, they were owed extraordinary accommodation for their efforts and extraordinary compensation whenever asked to give them up. A charter was not a "grant" that could simply be withdrawn, but, as Justice Coleridge put it when deciding the Eastern Archipelago case, it was "in its essence a compact" that had to be respected by both parties.[179] Charters also backed companies, as Goldie argued, with an "international status" and offered, as Leopold's lawyer Travers Twiss noted, certain rights of jurisdiction over British subjects.[180] The one thing they did not give was sovereignty in places like Africa and elsewhere, since, as the Lord Chancellor observed in 1892, "The Crown could not grant to the Company what it did not itself possess."[181]

The entire point of colonial companies was that they were not coterminous with the state. "The important principle that a chartered flag does not involve the national flag is, I admit, somewhat illogical," Goldie wrote in defense of the IBEAC's expansion into Uganda, but it was necessary for the progress of colonial expansion. Unlike states, which were "governed by sentiment," Goldie continued, "a chartered company has no dignity to humiliate, no national flag to avenge. It can stoop to conquer and can redeem defeat by diplomacy and money where the prestige of great Power would compel a crushing display of force."[182] Echoing points made by Mill, he maintained that companies were immune from the "intermittent or spasmodic policy" determined by the political demands of Parliament, party, and public opinion.[183] Maguire argued similarly that companies were not limited by the short-term thinking of ministries worried about keeping power, balancing budgets, or managing complex agencies. "In Charterland," he observed, government was unburdened by superfluous traditions and characterized by "the absence of unnecessary red-tape"—or what Goldie had called a "rough-and-ready" sort of rule. "The task of developing the resources of a new country is not one for which Governments are adapted," Maguire contended, "and it is one which the genius and traditions of the Anglo-Saxon race have always left to private enterprise."[184]

For centuries, this line of logic had been inseparable from racialized assumptions about the people and polities of the non-European world. Where early modern advocates for chartered corporations thought that such bodies were justified by the "uncivilized" and "barbarous" nature of the world beyond Christendom, Goldie was convinced that for African "Chiefs," political and military power was inextricable from "commercial supremacy." A chartered company could apply its "strong and disinterested ambition" to governance, so that its territories would "grow under their auspices from barbarism to civilization, from anarchy to order, from slavery to freedom, and from universal poverty to a source of wealth both to the natives of the country and to the overcrowded working classes of Great Britain."[185] Or, as he put it elsewhere, "many years must elapse before [Africans] become sufficiently civilized to understand the advantages, or even the justification, of an Administration which does nothing but govern." To act otherwise would prove a "radical vice in the system of government."[186]

It was not just, however, that arguments in favor of these new chartered companies resembled those made in the past. History was itself an argument on their behalf. Lugard later reflected on the African companies as "the modern adaptation of the instrument by which the Hudson's Bay company had added the Dominion of Canada, and the East India Company had secured India to the Empire, and to which some of our American colonies had owed their origin."[187] The journalist and author Flora Shaw—later Lady Lugard—cited J. R. Seeley's recent meditations on the East India Company's history in his *Expansion of England* (1882) when she noted one of the British South Africa Company's distinct advantages was that it had "the immortality of a corporation" and "can neither be killed in battle nor die of fever."[188] As Lionel Decle, an Anglo-French traveler in sub-Saharan Africa and a self-proclaimed convert to the BSAC's cause, later fawned, "The shareholders were all men who could afford to wait for a return on their money, and their idea was to found a great undertaking that would rival the old East India Company."[189]

Some took matters back even further. "All experience has shown that the work of developing new possessions in remote savage countries cannot well be performed by the direct action of governments, and especially of parliamentary governments," Dicey argued; such efforts had only been successful when ruled "indirectly by British adventurers, to use the good old English word for the men who have made our Empire."[190] As Joseph Thomson opined in 1889, what "Liberal politicians who have so little read their national history . . . utterly failed to grasp" was that "in chartered companies alone is there hope for the development of British influence, commerce and civilization in Africa."[191] Cameron predicted that the African companies would produce "equally beneficial results, not only to our country, but also to the native races with whom they will come in contact" as in America, Canada, and India.[192] Lugard labeled them the "modern 'Merchant Adventurers.'"[193] Twiss similarly observed in 1884 that "Colonization by private entities has been the predominant form of western expansion since the sixteenth century and for this purpose chartered companies and philanthropic associations had often been vested with sovereign rights."[194] As noted in an 1890 promotional tract for the North Borneo Company (which had recently taken offices at 15 Leadenhall Street, just a few doors down from where the East India House once stood), the East India Company and Hudson's Bay Company had been responsible for making "the smallest of European States in the 16th century the greatest of maritime and commercial powers," revealing in the process the more general principle: "where mercantile associations and companies have succeeded in forming important Colonies and permanent settlements, Governments have signally failed."[195]

In this sense, when the editor of the *Pall Mall Gazette,* W. T. Stead, quipped that Cecil Rhodes appeared to be "an Elizabethan statesman born out of time," it was no idle observation.[196] As if almost to prove it, Maguire authored a lengthy study on the "pioneers of empire," tracing the origins of the South Africa Company all the way back to the medieval charter, through Portugal's "Chartered African Company" under Henry the Navigator in 1444 and eventually the

English Merchant Adventurers, the Muscovy Company, the Eastland Company, the Turkey Company, the Hudson's Bay Company, and, of course, the East India Company. The Spanish Armada, he pointed out, had been repelled by ships that were "mostly the property of private persons."[197] The civil servant and historian Alfred Lyall—whose cousin, George, had seen off that Hudson's Bay Company fleet a half-century earlier—made a similar case in a lecture before the Society of Arts in June 1898. Companies, he suggested, had "played a very great part in founding, extending, and consolidating the vast dominion of Great Britain beyond the seas"; in language that could almost have been written three centuries earlier, he boasted that they had extended "our commerce, our language, our manners, and, I hope, our civilisation." The East India Company's rule in Bengal, he noted, was founded on similar principles "under which a governor and company had taken possession, a century or more earlier, of Massachusetts." The late Victorian charters in Africa "differ very little" from those Elizabethan ones. As Lyall argued,

> The history of these associations shows how much could be done by private effort, when that effort is judiciously backed by the State—that is, when private enterprise receives public sanction. There are some things which a Government cannot do officially, and which are best accomplished when the people take the lead, while the State lends its support, remaining in the background until it is required to interfere. *Colonisation* is certainly one of those things. *Commerce* is another.

The state had always been "a kind of sleeping partner," only awaking if its political interests were at stake; otherwise, "companies carried on a kind of private war among themselves," a fact "almost forgotten now in these days of international law, of diplomats, and of quick intelligence sent to headquarters by wire from the uttermost parts of the earth."[198]

A couple of years earlier, George Cawston gave his own lecture on the subject, which he expanded and published with the historian A. H. Keane as an extended history of *Early Chartered Companies* in 1896. The book, which remains a ubiquitous if rarely interrogated resource for historians of early companies today, had the explicit goal of "awakening public interest in our great historical Chartered Companies" and proving that "most of the colonial possessions of this Empire were in the first place settled through the agency of Chartered Companies." The one authority cited for this claim was an anonymous pamphlet "written about the year 1820," a reference, though he had the date off by fourteen years, to the proposal for the South Australian Association.[199] Like Maguire and Lyall, Cawston and Keane traced the history of colonial companies back to the Merchant Adventurers, through the American colonies, the Royal African Company, and many others, reserving two chapters for the East India Company. All of this seemed to prove a point. "Individuals whose public spirit, prudence, and resolution were not otherwise assisted by the Government of their country" and "the companies they founded" had indeed "secured the fairest lands of the earth for our race, laying the foundations of our great Colonial Empire."

Yet, to them, the real significance of something like the East India Company was "not so much the inheritance itself, as the discipline and great qualities developed in its acquisition, and the inspiring memories which must survive even should the 'pageant' itself dissolve." More than colonies themselves, such companies had left behind a legacy of what Cawston and Keane called the "joint-stock principle," which was anything but a thing of the past. In the book's final appendix, after offering transcriptions of various "specimens" of sixteenth- and seventeenth-century charters, the authors quietly and without comment concluded with just one last example: the charter of the British South Africa Company.[200] The implication was clear: the BSAC was, as Dicey had remarked more explicitly, "simply the latest page in the long series of transactions to which our worldwide empire owes its existence."[201]

EPILOGUE

Winding Up

You may wind up a Limited Company,
You cannot conveniently blow it up!

I N M I D - 1 9 0 6, the renowned legal scholar Frederic Maitland invited Cecil Carr to meet up with him in Cambridge. The Selden Society, which Maitland had helped found some two decades earlier, was interested in publishing a volume on the history of early chartered companies, and Maitland had Carr, a young lawyer who had just written a well-regarded book on corporation law, in mind for the job. Presumably to illustrate how he planned *not* to approach the task, at one point Carr led Maitland on an ultimately unsuccessful search through the university library for what he regarded as a "not very impressive book": George Cawston and A. H. Keane's *Early Chartered Companies*.[1] When Carr's own *Select Charters of Trading Companies* appeared some seven years later, it was certainly more impressive, offering a sweeping and erudite history on the origins of incorporated companies that one reviewer ranked with Maitland's own contributions to the field of legal history. Yet, despite his disdain for Cawston's book—and one might think Cawston himself—Carr had come to at least one similar conclusion: "Turn from the Elizabethan grants to the Victorian," he observed, "in the incorporations of British North Borneo, of Nigeria, of British East Africa, and Rhodesia, the modern grant follows the old."[2]

By the dawn of the twentieth century, it seemed to many that such an era had become history. Modern empire was, as even Gilbert and Sullivan's Utopians decided in the end, "no longer a Monarchy (Limited), but, what is a great deal better, a Limited Monarchy!"[3] Many celebrated the coming demise of a "device tolerable enough in a less developed age" but that was now a "barbarous anachronism" and hopelessly "out of date."[4] If the imperial historian John Seeley and imperial critic John Hobson could agree on one thing, it was that company colonialism seemed to be a relic of the age of Hernán Cortés and Robert Clive, a history that exposed, as Seeley put it, the "general principle" that "whatever conquests they made by their own unassisted audacity and effort were confiscated at once and as a matter of course" by the "supreme control" of the state.[5] Stalwart imperialists like the Earl of Cromer saw the scandal of the Belgian Congo as a self-evident case that companies should not be governments, something "we tried ourselves years ago with the old East India Company," to only "very modified success."[6] When Alfred Lyall concluded his long encomium to company colonization by predicting that such an era was "very near its close" and "not suited to modern circumstances," the explorer Henry Morton Stanley, Léopold II's former agent, admitted that it left him "melancholy." Still, he had to agree.[7]

On all sides of the issue, people seemed to expect that those colonial companies that still existed would soon disappear. Even for as ardent an advocate of company colonialism as James Maguire, the East India Company's history suggested there would come a time when the British South Africa Company would "have reached the limits that Nature had marked out for it" and need to be taken over by the state.[8] British and colonial officials had long looked to past examples to call for at least the greater regulation of this system. Proposals for something like a Board of Control for the North Borneo or Royal Niger Companies went back to those companies' beginnings in the 1880s.[9] Others suggested compelling chartered companies to rigidly segregate their political and commercial administrations, something "not accomplished till the East India Company was of much older standing."[10] This would have made the distinction between trade and sovereignty more transparent, but as

Verney Cameron observed, doing so would have another benefit: making it easier to calculate the cost to the state "when the time came for administration under the charter to be succeeded by another form of government."[11]

* * *

Cameron had a point. By the mid-1890s, both the Imperial British East Africa Company and the Royal Niger Companies had entered into talks to surrender their charters. Neither could consider capitulating, however, without what the IBEAC's former chairman called their "undeniable moral if not a legal right to compensation."[12] After all, as P. L. McDermott, the Company's assistant secretary, argued, they had not done their work for "private enterprise" but rather "on behalf of Empire"; to fail to offset (at the very minimum) the great costs they had undertaken in doing so was to make the "specious," "groundless," and "illogical and unjust" assumption that the "immediate interests of the Company were identical with those of the nation." Paying, however, was not the primary problem. First, there was the "considerable difficulty," as the Earl of Rosebery put it with respect to Uganda in 1892, "inherent in the situation"—that is, it was hardly clear that the state could legally assume treaties and contracts with scores of rulers that had been taken in the Company's name and on its behalf.[13] Even if that could be resolved, the "bill of costs," as Frederick Lugard observed, for a chartered company whose commercial and political enterprises were interwoven, "could be checked by no satisfactory standard."[14] Even though it was essentially bankrupt and had made little revenue in its short tenure, the IBEAC accounted among its assets both its treaties and expenditures in acquiring and implementing them, not to mention its significant real estate and movable property, railways, telegraph, wharves, and roads, including the still fairly rudimentary route from the coast to Kibwezi that technically belonged not to the Company but to the now deceased William Mackinnon's estate. It also claimed mortgages it held on 159 east African properties, rights to future customs returns, and, most inscrutably and incalculably, its services in suppressing the slave trade, protecting British interests on the coast, extending its influence into Uganda, and its political and social standing—or what it called "Good-will."[15]

The Royal Niger Company listed a similarly ambiguous and complex suite of assets, including its 237 treaties and diplomatic and administrative expenditures, such as losses from the recent French invasion of its territories. Government officials were bemused. To Thomas Sanderson in the Foreign Office it seemed that Goldie was trying to get paid twice for the same thing: "If we pay for the expenses incurred in acquiring these rights," he asked rhetorically, "are we also to pay for the rights themselves?" G. L. Ryder, a Treasury official, and Clement Hill, also of the Foreign Office, conversely noted that the Company had already been compensated for its administrative expenses through the extraordinarily high dividends shareholders had received, which could be credited to the de facto trading monopoly the Company enjoyed because it was also the colony's government.[16] Michael Hicks-Beach, the Chancellor of the Exchequer, seemed especially exasperated that the Company would be compensated for an illegal monopoly at all, merely because a previous ministry "had been so careless" as to allow it to come into being. He reserved special indignation for the Company's claims against losses from the French, since, he suggested, they might not have happened if the Company had lived up to its responsibilities defending its borders in the first place.[17]

Unsurprisingly, the estimates as to what all this should add up to varied wildly. Goldie asked for £1.5 million. Sanderson, Ryder, and Hill proposed about half of that, sweetened by other concessions, such as rights to continued royalties from mines and land.[18] Hicks-Beach rejected the premises of such calculations. He was still skeptical that Government could buy up the Company's treaties and concessions without invalidating them in the process, but even if that had not been an issue, it was still "impossible to base such a proposal on any calculation of the value of the Company's rights." A cleaner solution, he argued, would not be to buy the Company's assets but rather buy the Company itself, purchasing its shareholders' stock, which, at the current price plus an added premium, he estimated would cost £600,000, just under a third of what Goldie was asking.[19] Goldie countered, however, that this was not as straightforward as one might think, since "the selling value of Nigeria" should be accounted not by what it would cost to buy the Company in Britain but rather its "international value," that is, what Germany or France might pay to have it. This, he somehow reckoned, could be as much as £2 million.[20]

Negotiations with both companies became increasingly tense. Career bureaucrats complained that East Africa Company leadership were obfuscating and uncooperative, while McDermott reproved state officials for "chaffering like a furniture broker over the details of a valuation."[21] In both cases, settlements took several years. In 1895, the IBEAC finally surrendered its charter for £250,000—£200,000 of which was money belonging to the Sultan of Zanzibar held in trust by the British government—through a series of contracts involving, in various combinations, the Crown, the executors of William Mackinnon's estate, and the Sultan, who, as the head of a British Protectorate, was "represented" in the entire affair by the Marquess of Salisbury, the Prime Minister. The Foreign Office assumed the Company's assets and territorial responsibilities in the guise of the two new Protectorates of Uganda and East Africa, as the Company's directors liquidated its limited company.[22]

The Niger Company delivered up its charter in December 1899 for the considerably greater sum of £865,000, and the Northern Nigeria and Southern Nigeria Protectorates were established the following month. Unlike in East Africa, it continued to do business as a commercial concern, the *Niger Company Limited,* earning rents on mining concessions, an arrangement, Lugard later observed, that was quite like the settlement made with the Hudson's Bay Company decades earlier. Meanwhile, Company leadership haggled for at least another year over the interpretation of the settlement, including disputing with government just which property in Nigeria it had agreed to sell off.[23] Though still technically a form of indirect rule, the Protectorates that emerged out of the purchase of the two chartered companies began a process by which the British Empire formally expanded its authority in sub-Saharan Africa. The Southern Nigerian Protectorate merged with the Crown colony of Lagos in 1906 and then in 1914 with Northern Nigeria to create the Colony and Protectorate of Nigeria. Responsibility for the East Africa Protectorate was soon transferred from the Foreign to the Colonial Office, which in 1920 re-established it, with the exception of a small part of Zanzibar's territory that remained under "protected" status, as the colony of Kenya.

The British government's empire by merger and acquisition was not merely reserved for British companies. Most infamously, in 1875, Disraeli's government, financed by a £4 million loan from N. M. Rothschild & Sons, acquired control of the Suez Canal by purchasing the Egyptian Khedive Ismail Pasha's forty-four percent stake in the joint-stock *Compagnie Universelle du Canal Maritime de Suez.* "The Khedive," the *Manchester Guardian* observed at the time, "was willing to sell just what the Government required, not territory, but a sufficient interest in the Canal to enable us, in the capacity of shareholders, to keep control over our most important highway."[24] In the Suez, Britain continued to exert its influence through an ostensibly Egyptian-French company. In other cases, such as when it seized the large number of German-owned shares of the Nyassa Company's financing arm, Nyassa Consolidated, and arranged for them to be purchased by the British-based *Union Castle Mail Steamship Company,* it could work through client corporations. In that instance, the company's chairman, Owen Cosby Philipps, later Lord Kylsant—who would soon end up in prison for fraud relating to Union Castle's parent the *Royal Mail Steam Packet Company*—left the colony so indebted, chaotic, and brutally extractive that the Foreign Office in 1929 supported Portugal's nationalization of the colony.[25] Government could also absorb companies outright into new agencies, as in 1919, when, in partnership with Australia and New Zealand, it purchased the British-based *Pacific Phosphate Company* and vested its formerly German mining concession on the Pacific island of Nauru, now a British mandated territory, in a new British Phosphate Commission.[26]

By 1914, the old system of company colonization seemed to be such a relic that, when asked if the British government still chartered or subsidized overseas companies, one Colonial Office clerk was surprisingly cautious in his response: "Empire building in the past was largely developed by means of Chartered Companies," he replied, "but of the many that were formed there are I think now only two with administrative jurisdiction—the B.S.A.Co. and the B N Borneo Co."[27] Soon, even these two would see their end. The British government had been gradually extending its influence over the British South Africa Company through oversight, regulation, and revisions to its charter. In 1918, the judicial committee of the Privy

Council set the stage for a further acquisition when, in a suit brought against the BSAC by the Aborigines Protection Society on behalf of the natives of Southern Rhodesia, it sided with neither party but instead declared all unalienated lands in Rhodesia to belong to the Crown. With the Company's charter set to expire in 1924, talks began soon after for a surrender. Any transfer, of course, would require compensation—again, as Arthur Keith observed as early as 1911, "somewhat analogous," to the Hudson's Bay Company in 1870.[28] The Company proposed £10 million. It ultimately got £3.75 million, an amount Sydney Buxton, former Governor-General of South Africa, described as the Company having been "cut to the bone." Like the Royal Niger Company, the BSAC continued to do business as a corporation, as did a number of its subsidiaries, with large holdings of property, railway investments, and proceeds on land sales and mines, which were later sold to Southern Rhodesia for another £2 million.[29]

Leadership of the British North Borneo Company held out even longer, despite the Colonial Office's growing impatience. Their concerns ranged from critical matters of policy to petty questions of precedence; for example, as early as 1900, officials had not only come to insist that the person the Company called the colony's "Governor" be officially referred to as "Principal Representative," but internally they evidently assigned him the far less flattering codename of "Stoopingly."[30] Of course, government's attitude only got them so far. As the Company's lawyers reassured their clients in the early 1920s, their charter could never be "put an end to by a mere stroke of the pen," and the measures government might take, like *quo warranto,* were "somewhat mediaeval & obscure."[31] What was more, the Company was not just a British chartered corporation but a Bornean government. Thus, even though they could rest assured that "at Common Law a Charter once granted cannot be revoked," the lawyers advised that if the Company wanted to hedge against the withdrawal of its charter, it could very well charter its own company in Borneo, transfer to it rights of government, and thereby "vest in itself the sovereignty and soil of the State" in a subsidiary. The directors seem to have declined to follow counsel's advice.[32]

The Company endured for another two decades, until the Japanese occupation of the island during World War II decimated the island and its recovery left a British caretaker regime in charge. By 1946, Borneo was _de facto_ a British colony, but legally, there remained the matter of compensation. Unable to come to terms, the Company and the Government agreed to submit the matter to arbitration. As with the other chartered companies, the accounting firm hired to assess the Company's books complained that their job was "by no means easy," what with its assets consisting of both its sovereign grants from the Sultans of Brunei and Sulu and a dizzying complex of holdings. As a government, its property included infrastructure like railway and telegraph lines and even note issues of the State Bank. As a company, it owned shares in various other corporations, from its own concessionaries like the _British North Borneo Timber Company_ to bond issues of a private golf club.[33] The Company's directors further believed it was owed reparations from the War Damage Commission, but the board rejected its claims, arguing that, unlike other governments that had received funds, the Company "exercised its sovereignty with a view to making profits."[34] Three years later, the arbitrator, Lord Uthwatt, finally issued his ruling: the company was to receive £1.4 million, somewhat less than the £2.1 million government had originally offered.[35] British North Borneo would thus become a Crown colony, though not, one administrator later reflected, because "the administration of the State had been otherwise than good, but rather that the administration of a state by a Company had come to be in the nature of an anachronism."[36]

* * *

It was certainly becoming clear that "chartered companies," as Buxton put it, were no longer "as a rule, in very good odour."[37] On the one hand, it appeared to many in hindsight that company colonization in Africa had been a disaster. A Colonial Office report in the late 1940s, written as Nyasaland looked to acquire the territory of the British Central Africa Company, concluded that the Company had done an "incalculable disservice" to the Protectorate, its "extreme parsimony" and neglect leading it to become one the most exploitative and violent examples of shareholder-driven development companies, which was a low bar indeed.[38] On the other hand, charters themselves seemed to be increasingly irrelevant, as "modern traders," one government official observed in 1933, "prefer the Companies Acts to the creaking of its obsolete machinery."[39]

Yet, the machinery remained. Its imprints could certainly be felt in the constitutional echoes it had left behind. "We may miss the old words that were used of Connecticut and Rhode Island: 'one body corporate and politic in fact and name,'" Maitland observed, "but 'united in a Federal Commonwealth under the name of the Commonwealth of Australia' seems amply to fill their place."[40] There were also still plenty who sought out charters, either for their protection or their cachet. In 1933, for example, the Australian Prime Minister's plan to offer charters for the development of the Northern Territory easily conjured memories of the Australian Agricultural Company and the Van Diemen's Land Company.[41] Some projectors even skipped the step of getting the charter at all and just attempted (it seems unsuccessfully) to register their companies with "chartered" as part of their names. Their defenses for doing so varied, from claiming distant lineal connections with nineteenth-century chartered companies to, as in the 1910 would-be "Chartered Company of Mexico," insisting it was indeed "chartered"—not by Britain but rather the Mexican government, which had granted it a concession "to purchase large tracts of land for colonization purposes."[42]

Even if something like an East India or British South Africa Company was increasingly unthinkable, the smaller company-concessionary with grants from foreign or colonial governments was alive, well, and proliferating through the opening decades of the twentieth century. From Malaya to the Middle East, corporations continued to take charge not only of land and settlement but various enterprises for transportation, communication, manufacturing, energy, and the control and extraction of natural resources—not least oil—that intertwined company and government authority over people, places, and infrastructure on both grand and local scales.[43] In the wake of the dissolution of the IBEAC, for example, individuals and groups flooded into the East Africa Protectorate with concessions for making land purchases, insisting that such efforts were better done on a larger scale by groups "with capital" than by an ungovernable cacophony of "Cockatoos or small men."[44] Despite the objections of his superiors, the high commissioner Charles Eliot made several such grants before he was forced from his office, including 320,000 acres to an *East African Syndicate, Ltd.*, facilitating the removal of the Masasi and fatefully laying the ground for the white settlers and landowners that would flood into Kenya in coming years.[45] British mandate Palestine seemed an especially open field, where companies like Edmond de Rothschild's *Palestine Jewish Colonisation Association*, in the business of purchasing land for Jewish settlement, sat alongside development concessions in fields ranging from electrification to citrus plantations.[46] While in many cases such work was done with the cooperation of government, some, like the suspiciously ambitious "Pan-Arab Corporation," with professed operations in banking, mortgage, land, insurance, and fruit exports, raised alarms in the Colonial Office, as did their projectors: in this case, Henry James Hardy, whose previous gambits included a "Latino-American Corporation" for "trading, mining and plantation operations on a vast scale," and one Colonel J. L. O'Connor, a "concession hunter who appears to have some means."[47]

For expanding empires across the globe, corporate colonialism seemed as critical as ever, whether in the *South Manchuria Railway Company* furthering Japanese ambitions in China or American concerns in Latin America, most notoriously, but hardly exclusively, the *United Fruit Company*.[48] Chartered companies remained central to administering and imagining the late British Empire as well, though, by the 1920s and 1930s had come to take a much different form than in the past: genuinely "public" corporations, responsible to state agencies, regulated by statute, and in many cases, part- or fully owned and governed by the British government. Even though the debates surrounding them resembled arguments that had been made for centuries, this new generation of colonial corporation by and large contributed to overseas expansion and governance not through large-scale territorial enterprises but the management of the more elusive arenas of communication, transportation, commerce, and finance. As such, these state-owned or -affiliated enterprises generally evinced a different spatial and jurisdictional vision of empire than their predecessors. In place of corporate empire's federated, regionally specific jurisdictional patchwork, this new brand of imperial corporatism was mobilized in service of a more integrated, global, coherent, and finally singular "British" Empire.[49]

Likely the best-known and earliest of these experiments was the *British Broadcasting Corporation,* which began as a private subsidized company but was converted into a chartered public corporation in 1927. From its start, largely through the efforts of its long-time chairman, Sir John Reith, the BBC responded by aggressively selling itself as a national cultural institution, a critical national service, and, with the launch in 1932 of its empire service, the key to "maintaining a consolidated British Empire" against the twin threats of anticolonial nationalism and communism, not least in the form of Radio Moscow. The birth of the BBC was mirrored in colonial spaces by the emergence of other companies with similar ambitions, though in some places under very different structures. Not long after the BBC received its public charter, for example, the Government of India licensed the *Indian Broadcasting Company, Ltd.*, not, as Reith had hoped, as a public corporation but as a five-year private commercial monopoly, subsidized by the revenue generated from wireless licensing fees, just as the BBC had started its life several years earlier. By 1930, IBC had gone bankrupt and was acquired by the Government of India, later remade into All India Radio.[50]

A similar process unfolded with radiotelegraphy. By the 1940s, *Cable & Wireless*—born from a merger of Eastern Telegraph with Guglielemo Marconi's radiotelegraphy company—was proposing to fold in telephone services to become an ambitious single chartered "Empire Corporation," backed by royal charter and government-purchased shares.[51] The controversy this proposal produced, especially in Australia and New Zealand, led to the appointment of a "mission" to India and the Commonwealth in 1945 led by John Reith, which resulted in a compromise proposal to have independent national and colonial companies coordinated by a central board. In 1947, the British government acquired C&W outright, part of what Hugh Dalton, the Chancellor of the Exchequer, called a "united Empire policy," putting it under the direct control in Britain of the Post Office and respective colonial postal ministries.[52]

Meanwhile, communication over the airwaves—as well as corporations that had connected the empire for decades, such as enduring steamship and telegraph companies—found a new rival in air travel. Initial government policy in the 1920s had been summed up in a typically pithy way by then Secretary of State for War and Air Winston Churchill: "Civil aviation must fly by itself; the Government cannot possibly hold it up in the air."[53] These experiments did not, however, prove particularly successful, and by 1923, a committee under the Air Ministry was calling for proposals for a subsidized commercial monopoly company for overseas and imperial air travel. The result was the formation of *Imperial Airways* in April 1924.[54] Continental travel was taken on by another company, *British Airways, Ltd.*, while colonies developed their own airline services, such as *Indian National Airways* and *Qantas* in Australia, which promoted itself as "a national enterprise playing an important part in the development of the Commonwealth and the Empire."[55]

Great expectations soon turned to faltering fortunes. By 1938, the future of both Imperial Airways and British Airways were topics of high-level and wide-ranging debate within the Ministry. One option would have been to allow air travel to be taken up by an "ordinary" company, but some feared that this would be too suspect as a "private profit-making concern." A chartered enterprise, like the BBC or the London Passenger Transport Board, conversely, might produce insufficient commercial incentives, resulting in something "artificial and inapprop[r]iate" as well as "archaic."[56] The compromise government settled on was a "not-profit-making public corporation" established through Parliament, which as the Secretary of State for India put it, would be neither "a limited liability company which must, of course, quite properly watch its shareholders' interests" nor "a Government Department" but rather an institution that could combine the "stimulus to enterprise" characteristic of private concerns with the centralization, financial guarantees, and oversight and control of government.[57]

As Churchill might have put it, not everyone was on board. Colonial governments were especially skeptical. The Government of India, for example, feared that a new public airline would throw "into the melting pot so much of the previous negotiations" over the for-profit Indian National Airways and especially its joint airmail venture with Imperial Airways, *Indian Trans-Continental Airlines*. Concerned that in "the development of Empire Air Services by a Public Corporation political and other aspects may overshadow the commercial side," INA proposed to sell its stake in the subsidiary directly to the Government of India.[58] In the Dominions, as with telecommunications, the controversy mirrored the anxiety over the structure of authority in the late British empire and commonwealth. One solution, Treasury official Henry Wilson Smith proposed, was to set up a decentralized system of subsidiary companies "to run individual services," like ITCA or Qantas.[59] Another, which had been suggested by the Government of India, was to constitute its board with representatives from various colonial and commonwealth governments or otherwise, which would, as Reith endorsed it, render the company an "Imperial body, Empire-owned and Empire-managed."[60] What emerged from these debates in November 1939 was a nationalized airline, the *British Overseas Airways Corporation*, chartered by Parliamentary statute, overseen by government, funded by bond issues vested in the national debt commission, and chaired by Sir John Reith.[61]

As the Marquess of Londonderry observed in 1939, "the whole world evolution runs along the lines of vast State-aided corporations, and we have to accept this modern development"; like the BBC, the BOAC was evidence that "if we consider the whole field of international life, we would see that the world is resolving itself into great national corporations."[62] The British Government similarly created and subsidized a number of commercial and agricultural enterprises over the beginning of the twentieth century. In response to the disruptions to American and Egyptian cotton supplies in 1921, the government-subsidized British Cotton Growing Association was chartered as the *Empire Cotton Growing Corporation*, with nearly £1 million in government investment but also, in theory, support from industry. The project, Tory MP Gerald Hurst observed, "will bring nearer to realisation that long-cherished ideal of a self-sufficing Empire which ever since the days of Queen Elizabeth has inspired so many of the pioneers and pathfinders of Great Britain."[63]

If Empire Cotton was to Hurst a throwback to a vaunted imperial past, the *United Kingdom Commercial Corporation, Ltd.,* established in 1940, was a self-proclaimed "new conception in trading," a multinational commercial corporation that was a fully owned subsidiary of the Exchequer.[64] After German occupation rendered moot its initial design as a wartime measure to undermine Axis supply lines by infiltrating the Balkans, Greece, and Turkey, the corporation began to take on commercial enterprises in the Soviet Union, Iberia, the Middle East, Africa, South America, and Asia both directly and through a dozen subsidiary companies.[65] When confronted by a member of Parliament on whether the UKCC was a monopoly, Hugh Dalton, then President of the Board of Trade, offered a time-tested response: "No Sir," he replied, "they are agents of the Government."[66] In India, some saw it differently, the entire enterprise appearing, at least to Muthiah Chettiar, the President of the Federation of Indian Chambers of Commerce, like "another *Avatar* of the East India Company."[67]

Though the UKCC was wound up in 1946, a number of its functions lived on in some of its subsidiaries or various government ministries.[68] Meanwhile, a new form of colonial enterprise emerged in the form of development corporations.[69] Some of these efforts were led by banks, most notably Barclays Bank and its subsidiary, *Barclays Bank (Dominion, Colonial and Overseas)*, which in 1946 established its own *Overseas Development Corporation*. The effort, the Vice-Chairman of Barclay's (DCO) at the time, William Goodenough, noted, raised obvious if difficult questions about "what are the respective fields of Government and private enterprise."[70] In 1948, the Government also inserted itself into this field with two new fully owned statutory public development corporations: the *Overseas Food Corporation*, which collapsed soon after an ill-designed project in Tanganyika, and the *Colonial Development Corporation*, later the *Commonwealth Development Corporation*, which was empowered to take on direct investment, establish partnerships, and make loans to both private bodies and government departments. In 1950, who would be selected to lead it but John Reith.[71]

* * *

These varied attempts at integrating the British Empire through new forms of global communication and investment were short-lived. The continued failures of implicit promises of citizenship and inclusion in a global system soon gave way, whether through devolution or revolution, to the "national-territorial space" of postcolonial states and international order.[72] Unsurprisingly, the many European and American concessionary companies that did so much of the work of managing colonial territory, people, and resources served as a focal point for anti-colonial protests, labor actions, raids, and revolutions: a wave of protests beginning in the 1930s against the *Belize Estate and Produce Company*, formerly the British Honduras Company; boycotts and riots targeting the *United Africa Company* (the corporate descendent of the Royal Niger Company) or the *Ashanti Goldfields Corporation* in Ghana in the late 1940s; strikes against the *Anglo-Iranian Oil Company* in Abadan in 1951; and many, many more still.[73] Renegotiating relationships with such corporations, up to and including a wave of nationalizing efforts across the globe, was key to decolonization and postcolonial state building. Egyptian President Gamal Abdel Nasser's appropriation of the Suez Canal Company in 1956 stands out among countless other examples.[74] More quietly but more pervasively, a number of postcolonial national state institutions emerged from colonial-era corporate enterprises, such as the State Bank of India, created in 1955 when India's central bank acquired the *Imperial Bank of India,* which had been created in the merger of the joint-stock banks of Bengal, Bombay, and Madras in 1921.[75] State-run or affiliated corporations proliferated in India after independence in 1947 as models for public commercial and development projects as well, such as the *National Textile Corporation* and regional analogues like the *Gujarat State Textile Corporation.*[76]

Just as there was no single form of corporate empire, there was no single corporate reaction to the impending end of empire. Certainly, anxieties over nationalist and socialist ideologies and policies, compounded by racialist fears of nonwhite regimes and nonwhite workers, led many companies (and their investors) and trade groups to attempt to forestall or impede decolonization, whether through lobbying or recalcitrance at home or active support of anti-nationalist movements abroad.[77] At the same time, new nationalized companies, in need of capital and commercial partners, were frequently recolonized, if not by British investors and companies then by other European, American, Japanese, Soviet, or Chinese enterprises. Many British-based companies or their subsidiaries also profited directly from anti-colonial rebellion and decolonization, as happy to supply violent counterinsurgency efforts as they were to find they could now pay their new non-European employees substantially less.[78] In time, the postcolonial world became famously fertile ground for myriad European and American companies, from oil to tobacco, to expand their "private empires," a story that is well known and has been well told.[79]

Amidst all the tumult and transformation of the era of decolonization, though, a good number of formerly colonial corporations still endured in some shape or form. Certainly, countless noncommercial corporate bodies—cities, churches, universities, and learned societies—across the globe can trace their roots, if not their actual charters, to colonial origins. Among commercial companies, the Hudson's Bay Company is no doubt the most famous survivor; though now largely an American-owned retail, technology, and real estate conglomerate, it nonetheless still boasts its status as "North America's longest continually operating company."[80] As of this moment at least, the Australian Agricultural and Van Diemen's Land Companies are still in business, as is De Beers, which, perhaps like the diamond, as its slogan goes, may "live forever." In 2010, the East India Company even returned, revived as a high-end retail shop, selling foodstuffs from chocolates to chutneys, gold and silver, gin, and, "history-infused tea & coffee" out of its flagship off London's fashionable Regent Street, a "timeless shop with a history dating back to 1600."[81]

Even more companies lived on through conglomeration and diversification, surviving largely unrecognized and unrecognizable in the DNA of their corporate progeny.[82] Many mergers and subsidiaries later, P&O, the company Margaret Thatcher reportedly once called "not just a company but the very fabric of the empire," was bought for £3.3 billion by the Emirates-based conglomerate *DP World* in 2006.[83] In 1965, De Beers's erstwhile parent company, the British South Africa Company, along with its concessions, merged into the appropriately if coincidentally named *Charter Consolidated, Ltd.*—which in 2008 re-domiciled in Ireland as *Charter International plc* until it was bought by an American company in 2012. The British soap company *Lever Brothers* merged in 1930 with the *Dutch Margarine Unie,* to create *Unilever,* which built its West Africa business through an acquisition of the United Africa Company.[84] Glaxo Laboratories, the core of the pharmaceutical giant *GlaxoSmithKline,* originally started life as a subsidiary of a New Zealand–based company, Joseph Nathan and Co., in 1873.[85] The Hongkong Bank had merged into four hundred related and subsidiary enterprises by the time it renamed itself in 1989 *The Hongkong and Shanghai Banking Corporation Limited,* or HSBC.[86]

Naturally, as it did in many other fields, colonialism left behind its webs of corporate laws and practices, including various iterations of joint-stock company laws, that echoed through these new national states and economies as they navigated the murky boundaries between public and private, governance and the market—and governance of the market—in the postcolonial world. The infusion of Western companies in the nineteenth century and the introduction of British-style company law to China in 1904 laid foundations that continue to reverberate in the structure of Chinese corporate enterprise today. In India, the corporation became a "model for public association" that drew lines between legitimate and illegitimate forms of political, commercial, financial, and other enterprises.[87] Both colonial rule and anticolonial nationalism gave rise in some cases to new centers of corporate power, like the multinational conglomerate *Tata* in India, that both helped make postcolonial national states and also challenged them, as historian Mircea Raianu has shown, "fashioning themselves as sovereigns on par with the state, with workers, consumers and citizens as their subjects."[88] At the same time, colonialism left in its wake a legacy of any number of new nations that now serve multinationals as lightly regulated or entirely unregulated free trade zones and tax shelters. From the Caribbean to Tangier, erstwhile colonies became corporate havens, sheltering assets of companies, states, and strongmen alike, occluding the activities of global ownership, and asserting an influence on government that, in historian Vanessa Ogle's phrase, turned "private investors into virtual suzerains" and turned venture colonialism into what historian Raymond Craib has called "adventure capitalism."[89]

Into the late twentieth-century, of the scattered places around the globe where the British empire still endured, several could trace their roots to corporate origins. Bermuda had once been a company colony; so too had St. Helena. By the early 1980s, though, one still, in a sense, was. As *The Tribune* noted in October 1982, there remained in Britain's overseas territories, off the coast of Argentina, "a classical colonial enclave, with a monopolist trading company," The Falkland Islands Company, still controlling nearly half its land as well as the major newspaper, television, and commercial enterprises with interests as well in Antarctic exploration.[90] Attempts since the 1960s, including intervention of the United Nations, had failed to reach an amicable settlement of sovereignty between Britain and Argentina over the Malvinas. This was not least due to the interventions of the none-too-stealthily named Falkland Islands Pressure Group, created in London in 1967 as a shadow lobbying arm of the century-old Company, and which, by inserting the Company's interests into these negotiations, according to one scholar, turned what should have been "bi-lateral" talks between Britain and Argentina into "tri-lateral" ones. One attempt by an Argentine company, in concert with French and British investors, to buy out the Falkland Islands Company in 1977 might have helped settle the issue had it not been arrested under political pressure by the British government. The continued failure to reach a settlement hit a boiling point by 1982, when it provided the context for an Argentine invasion of the island.[91] The short, notorious, and controversial conflict—which despite Britain's victory arguably marked the final battle in four centuries of British imperial expansion—was known as the Falklands War to Britons and the *Guerra de las Malvinas* in Argentina. Within the British military, however, the expedition was given a more obscure code name. They called it "Operation Corporate."[92]

ABBREVIATIONS

NOTES

ACKNOWLEDGMENTS

INDEX

ABBREVIATIONS

APDE	Adams Papers, Digital Edition, Massachusetts Historical Society, https://www.masshist.org/publications/adams-papers/
BJHS	*British Journal for the History of Science*
BL	British Library, Manuscripts Department
BT	Board of Trade Series, TNA
CO	Colonial Office Series, TNA
CUP	Cambridge University Press
DUP	Duke University Press
FO	Foreign Office Series, TNA
FONA	Founders Online, National Archives (U.S.), https://founders.archives.gov
HC Deb	Hansard, House of Commons Sittings, https://api.parliament.uk/historic-hansard/commons/index.html
HJ	*The Historical Journal*
HL Deb	Hansard, House of Lords Sittings, https://api.parliament.uk/historic-hansard/lords/index.html
HMSO	His/Her Majesty's Stationary Office
HSP	Historical Society of Pennsylvania
HUP	Harvard University Press
IOR	India Office Records, Asia, Pacific & Africa Collections, British Library
JBS	*The Journal of British Studies*
JHUP	The Johns Hopkins University Press
NYUP	New York University Press
OIEAHC	Omohundro Institute of Early American History and Culture

OUP	Oxford University Press
PMHB	*The Pennsylvania Magazine of History and Biography*
PUP	Princeton University Press
SLNSW	Mitchell Library, State Library of New South Wales, Australia
SP	State Papers Series, TNA
TNA	The National Archives (U.K.)
UNCP	University of North Carolina Press
UPenn	University of Pennsylvania Press
VCE	D. B. Quinn, ed., *The Voyages and Colonising Enterprises of Sir Humphrey Gilbert* 2 vols. (London: Hakluyt Society, 1940)
VMHB	*The Virginia Magazine of History and Biography*
WMQ	*The William and Mary Quarterly*
YUP	Yale University Press

NOTES

Introduction

Epigraph: Charles Dickens, "Patent Wrongs," *Household Words: A Weekly Journal* 154 (5 March 1853), 229.

1. Steve Coll, *Private Empire: ExxonMobil and American Power* (New York: Penguin, 2012); Zuckerberg quoted in David Kirkpatrick, *The Facebook Effect: The Inside Story of the Company That Is Connecting the World* (New York: Simon & Schuster, 2010), 254; Janet McLean, *Searching for the State in British Legal Thought: Competing Conceptions of the Public Sphere* (Cambridge: CUP, 2012), 135-139; Kenneth Chang, "Two Companies Aim to Beat SpaceX to Mars with 'Audacious' Landing," *The New York Times* (19 July 2022); Mark Landler, "In Royal 'Firm,' The Family Business Always Comes First," *The New York Times* (9 March 2021, updated 18 March 2021).

2. Ron Harris, *Going the Distance: Eurasian Trade and the Rise of the Business Corporation, 1400–1700* (Princeton: PUP, 2020); Philip J. Stern, "Corporations in History," in *The Critical Corporation Handbook,* ed. Grietje Baars and André Spicer (Cambridge: CUP, 2017); Carlo Taviani, *The Making of the Modern Corporation: The Casa di San Giorgio and Its Legacy (1466–1720)* (Abingdon: Routledge, 2022). The classic study is William Robert Scott, *The Constitution and Finance of English, Scottish and Irish Joint-Stock Companies to 1720,* 3 vols. (Cambridge: CUP, 1912).

3. Harris, *Going the Distance,* 95–96, 369-370.

4. Edmond Smith, *Merchants: The Community that Shaped England's Trade and Empire* (New Haven: YUP, 2021).

5. K. R. Andrews, "Sir Robert Cecil and Mediterranean Plunder," *English Historical Review* 87, no. 344 (1972): 531.

6. Lauren Working, *The Making of an Imperial Polity: Civility and America in the Jacobean Metropolis* (Cambridge: CUP, 2020); Phil Withington, *Society in Early Modern England: The Vernacular Origins of Some Powerful Ideas* (Cambridge: Polity, 2010).

7. Timothy L. Alborn, *Conceiving Companies: Joint-Stock Politics in Victorian England* (London and New York: Routledge, 1998); Mark Freeman, Robin Pearson, and James Taylor, *Shareholder Democracies? Corporate Governance in Britain and Ireland Before 1850* (Chicago: University of Chicago Press, 2012).

8. Frederic William Maitland, "Trust and Corporation," in *The Collected Papers of Frederic William Maitland,* Volume III, ed. H.A.L. Fisher (Cambridge: CUP, 1911), 321–404; Ron Harris, *Industrializing English Law: Entrepreneurship and Business Organization, 1720–1844* (Cambridge: CUP, 2000), 21–22, 137–67; John D. Morley, "The Common Law

Corporation: The Power of the Trust in Anglo-American Business History" *Columbia Law Review* 116 (2016): 2145–97.

9. Ernst Kantorowicz, *The King's Two Bodies: A Study in Mediaeval Political Theology* (Princeton: PUP, 1957); J. P. Canning, "Law, Sovereignty, and Corporation Theory, 1300–1450," in *The Cambridge History of Medieval Political Thought, c. 350–1450,* ed. J. H. Burns (Cambridge: CUP, 1988), 454–76; Brian Tierney, *Foundations of the Conciliar Theory: The Contribution of the Medieval Canonists from Gratin to the Great Schism* (Leiden: Brill, 1998), 98–140; Amanda Porterfield, *Corporate Spirit: Religion and the Rise of the Modern Corporation* (New York: OUP, 2018), 9, 31, 38.

10. Thomas O. Hueglin, *Early Modern Concepts for a Late Modern World: Althusius on Community and Federalism* (Waterloo: Wilfrid Laurier University Press, 1999); Henry Turner, *The Corporate Commonwealth: Pluralism and Political Fictions in England, 1516–1651* (Chicago: University of Chicago Press, 2016); Phil Withington, *The Politics of Commonwealth: Citizens and Freemen in Early Modern England* (Cambridge: CUP, 2005).

11. Quentin Skinner, "A Genealogy of the Modern State," *Proceedings of the British Academy* 62 (2009).

12. Frederic William Maitland, "Introduction," in Otto Gierke, *Political Theories of the Middle Age,* translated and introduction by Frederic William Maitland (Cambridge: CUP, 1900), xxxviii; David Million, "Theories of the Corporation," *Duke Law Journal* 201 (1990): 201–62.

13. Edward Coke, "The Case of Sutton's Hospital (1612), Michaelmas Term, 10 James I," in *The Selected Writings and Speeches of Sir Edward Coke,* ed. Steve Sheppard (Indianapolis: Liberty Fund, 2003), I:371.

14. Adam Winkler, *We the Corporations: How American Businesses Won Their Civil Rights* (New York: W. W. Norton, 2018); Turkuler Isiksel, "The Rights of Man and the Rights of the Man-Made: Corporations and Human Rights," *Human Rights Quarterly* 38, no. 2 (2016).

15. Thomas Hobbes, *Leviathan; or, The Matter, Forme, and Power of a Common Wealth, Ecclesiastical and Civil* (London, 1651), 174; David Harris Sacks, "The Countervailing of Benefits: Monopoly, Liberty, and Benevolence in Elizabethan England," in *Tudor Political Culture,* ed. Dale Hoak (Cambridge: CUP, 1995), 275.

16. I. Maurice Wormser, *Frankenstein, Incorporated* (New York: McGraw-Hill, 1931), 85; Paddy Ireland, "Efficiency or power? The Rise of the Shareholder-oriented Joint Stock Corporation," *Indiana Journal of Global Legal Studies* 25, 1 (2018), 296, 308.

17. Harold J. Laski, "The Personality of Associations," *Harvard Law Review* 29, no. 4 (1916): 407.

18. Hobbes, *Leviathan,* 150; Joshua Barkan, *Corporate Sovereignty: Law and Government Under Capitalism* (Minneapolis: University of Minnesota Press, 2013), 20, 37–38.

19. Saliha Belmessous, ed., *Empire by Treaty: Negotiating European Expansion, 1600–1900* (Oxford: OUP, 2015); Andrew Fitzmaurice, *Sovereignty, Property, and Empire, 1500–2000* (Cambridge: CUP, 2014), 8–9; Steven Press, *Rogue Empires: Contracts and Conmen in Europe's Scramble for Africa* (Cambridge, MA: HUP, 2017).

20. William A. Pettigrew and David Veevers, "Establishing the Field: Global History," in *The Corporation as a Protagonist in Global History, c. 1550–1750,* ed. William A. Pettigrew and David Veevers (Leiden: Brill, 2019), 25–26; Vicki Hseuh, *Hybrid Constitutions: Challenging Legacies of Law, Privilege, and Culture in Colonial America* (Durham, NC: DUP, 2010), 84.

21. A concept inspired here, by way of analogy, by Sanjay Subrahmanyam and C. A. Bayly, "Portfolio Capitalists and the Political Economy of Early Modern India," *Indian Economic and Social History Review* 25, no. 4 (1988): 401–24.

22. See and compare Charles Tilly's classic formulation of state formation as a form of protection scheme. Charles Tilly, "War Making and State Making as Organized Crime," in *Bringing the State Back In,* ed. Peter B. Evans, Dietrich Rueschemeyer, and Theda Skocpol (Cambridge: CUP, 1985), 169–91.

23. Edward James Stephen Dicey, "The Work of the Chartered Company," *Fortnightly Review* 59 (June 1896): 985.

24. Marina Welker, "Notes on the Difficulty of Studying the Corporation," *Seattle University Law Review* 39, no. 397 (2016): 408–9; Welker, *Enacting the Corporation: An American Mining Firm in Post-Authoritarian Indonesia* (Berkeley: University of California Press, 2014).

25. Regina Grafe and Alejandra Irigoin, "A Stakeholder Empire: The Political Economy of Spanish Imperial rule in America," *Economic History Review* 65, no. 2 (2012): 609–51.

26. Herbert Spencer, *Railway Morals & Railway Policy: Reprinted from the Edinburgh Review with Additions and a Postscript by the Author* (London: Longman, Brown, Green & Longmans, 1855), 10.

27. Philip J. Stern, *The Company-State: Corporate Sovereignty and the Early Modern Foundations of the British Empire in India* (New York: OUP, 2011); Andrew Phillips and J. C. Sharman, *Outsourcing Empire: How Company-States Made the Modern World* (Princeton: PUP, 2020); Edward Cavanagh, "A Company with Sovereignty and Subjects of Its Own? The Case of the Hudson's Bay Company, 1670–1763," *Canadian Journal of Law and Society* 26, no. 1 (2011): 25–50.

28. Lauren Benton, *A Search for Sovereignty: Law and Geography in European Empires, 1400–1900* (Cambridge: CUP, 2010) 3, 6; Helen Dewar, "Agents, Institutions, and French Empire/State Formation," *Canadian Historical Review* 102, no. 1 (2021): 85–108; Christopher Tomlins, "Law's Empire: Chartering English Colonies on the American Mainland in the Seventeenth Century," in *Law, History, Colonialism: The Reach of Empire*, ed. Diane Kirkby and Catherine Coleborne (Manchester: Manchester University Press, 2001), 27–28.

29. John Darwin, *The Empire Project: The Rise and Fall of the British World-System, 1830–1970* (Cambridge: CUP, 2009), xi, 3, 20; E. A. Benians, "Adam Smith's Project of an Empire," *Cambridge Historical Journal* 1, no. 3 (1925): 249–83.

30. William Dalrymple, *The Anarchy: The East India Company, Corporate Violence, and the Pillage of an Empire* (London: Bloomsbury, 2019); Jon Wilson, *India Conquered: Britain's Raj and the Chaos of Empire* (London: Simon & Schuster, 2016).

31. C. Dyke, "Strange Attraction, Curious Liaison: Clio Meets Chaos," *Philosophical Forum* 21, no. 4 (1990): 369–92; D. N. McCloskey, "History, Differential Equations, and the Problem of Narration," *History and Theory* 30, no. 1 (1991): 21–36.

32. On "absence of mind," see J. R. Seeley, *The Expansion of England: Two Courses of Lectures* (London: MacMillan and Co., 1883, repr. 1895), 10. On "official mind," see most famously, Ronald Robinson and John Gallagher, with Alice Denny, *Africa and the Victorians: The Official Mind of Imperialism* (London: Macmillan, 1961). On projects, see, among others, Vera Keller and Ted McCormick, "Towards a History of Projects," *Early Science and Medicine* 21, no. 5 (2016): 423–44.

33. Jeremy Rosen, *Minor Characters Have Their Day: Genre and the Contemporary Literary Marketplace* (New York: Columbia, 2016), 5–6.

34. On the importance of comparative histories of corporate colonialism, see, e.g., Phillips and Sharman, *Outsourcing Empire*, 1; Pettigrew and Veevers, "Establishing the Field," 13. On the cosmopolitanism and porousness of corporate and commercial empire, see, for example, Alison Games, *The Web of Empire: English Cosmopolitans in an Age of Expansion, 1560–1660* (New York: OUP, 2008); Felicia Gottmann and Philip Stern, "Introduction: Crossing Companies," *Journal of World History* 31, no. 3 (2020): 1–12; David Veevers, *The Origins of the British Empire in Asia, 1600–1750* (Cambridge: CUP, 2020).

35. Paul D. Halliday, *Habeas Corpus: From England to Empire* (Cambridge: Belknap, 2010), 6; Halliday, "Legal History: Taking the Long View," in *The Oxford Handbook of Legal History*, ed. Markus D. Dubber and Christopher Tomlins (Oxford: OUP, 2018), 326–29, 331–32.

36. Andrew Fitzmaurice, *King Leopold's Ghostwriter: The Creation of Persons and States in the Nineteenth Century* (Princeton: PUP, 2021), 24 ("micro-intellectual"); Malachi Hacohen, "Rediscovering Intellectual Biography—and its Limits," *History of Political Economy* 39, Suppl. 1 (2007), 17 ("stable identity"); Kimberly J. Stern, *Oscar Wilde: A Literary Life* (Cham: Palgrave Macmillan, 2019), 18 ("track . . . motion"); Dane Kennedy, *The Highly Civilized Man: Richard Burton and the Victorian World* (Cambridge, MA: HUP, 2005), 7 ("situate").

37. Krishan Kumar, "Colony and Empire, Colonialism and Imperialism: A Meaningful Distinction?" *Comparative Studies in Society and History* 63, no. 2 (2021): 280–309.

38. Classically, John Gallagher and Ronald Robinson, "The Imperialism of Free Trade," *Economic History Review,* Second Series, 6, no. 1 (1953): 1; on "gentlemanly capitalism," see P. J. Cain and A. G. Hopkins, *British Imperialism, 1688–2015,* 3rd ed. (Abingdon: Routledge, 2016).

39. Sankar Muthu, "Adam Smith's Critique of International Trading Companies: Theorizing 'Globalization' in the Age of Enlightenment," *Political Theory* 36, no. 2 (2008): 185–212; Emma Rothschild, "Adam Smith in the British Empire," in *Empire and Modern Political Thought,* ed. Sankar Muthu (Cambridge: CUP, 2002).

40. J. A. Hobson, *Imperialism: A Study* (London: James Nisbet & Co., 1902), 86; Vladimir Il'ich Lenin, *Imperialism: The Highest Stage of Capitalism, A Popular Outline* (1917, trans and repr. New York: International Publishers, 1939), 124; Joseph Schumpeter, "The Sociology of Imperialism," (1919) in Schumpeter, *Imperialism and Social Classes,* trans. Heinz Norden (New York: A. M. Kelly, 1951).

41. Dalrymple, *Anarchy,* 397.

42. John Butman and Simon Targett, *New World, Inc.: The Making of America by England's Merchant Adventurers* (New York: Little Brown and Company, 2018), xxv.

43. There is so much to digest here that it would be impossible to try to adequately cite in the space allowed. A lot of examples, but hardly close to all, can be found in the citations elsewhere in this book. I have also tried to capture these themes more extensively elsewhere. Philip J. Stern, "The English East India Company and the Modern Corporation: Legacies, Lessons, and Limitations," *Seattle University Law Review* (2016): 423–45; Stern, "The Google of its Time? The English East India Company and the Modern Corporation," in *The Oxford Handbook of the Corporation,* ed. Thomas Clarke et al. (Oxford: OUP, 2019).

44. Lisa Siraganian, *Modernism and the Meaning of Corporate Persons* (Oxford: OUP, 2020), 3.

45. Barkan, *Corporate Sovereignty,* 17.

46. There are notable and important recent exceptions. See, for example, Press, *Rogue Empires;* Matthew Birchall, "Company Colonisation and the Settler Revolution, 1820–1840," unpublished PhD thesis, Cambridge University, 2021.

1. Initial Public Offerings

Epigraph: George Peckham, *A True Report of the Late Discoveries, and Possession Taken in the Right of the Crowne of England of the Newfound Lands, By that Valiant and Worthy Gentleman, Sir Humfrey Gilbert Knight* (London: J.C. for John Hinde, 1583).

1. Wallace T. MacCaffrey, "The Newhaven Expedition, 1562–1563," *HJ* 40, no. 1 (1997): 15.

2. Neil Murphy, *The Tudor Occupation of Boulogne: Conquest, Colonisation, and Imperial Monarch, 1544–1550* (Cambridge: CUP, 2019), 238; John Patrick Mantaño, *The Roots of English Colonialism in Ireland* (Cambridge: CUP, 2011), 136.

3. Stephen Alford, *London's Triumph: Merchants, Adventurers, and Money in Shakespeare's City* (New York: Bloomsbury, 2017), 69, 136–37; John Butman and Simon Targett, *New World, Inc.: The Making of America by England's Merchant Adventurers* (New York: Little, Brown and Company, 2018), 39; Jonathan Decoster, "'Have You Not Heard of Florida?': Jean Ribault, Thomas Stukeley, and the Dream of England's First Overseas Colony," *Itinerario* 43, no. 3 (2019): 404, 410; Andrew Fitzmaurice, *Humanism and America: An Intellectual History of English Colonisation, 1500–1625* (Cambridge: CUP, 2003), 39; David B. Quinn, *Explorers and Colonies: America, 1500–1625* (London: The Hambledon Press, 1990), 261; Juan E. Tazón, *The Life and Times of Thomas Stukeley (c. 1525–78)* (Aldershot: Ashgate, 2002), 62–93.

4. *VCE,* I:3–6, 9–10; J. A. Williamson, *The Age of Drake* (London: A&C Black, 1938), 40; Butman and Targett, *New World, Inc.,* 39; Nathan J. Probasco, *Sir Humphrey Gilbert and the Elizabethan Expedition: Preparing for a Voyage* (Cham: Palgrave Macmillan, 2020), 41.

5. *VCE*, I:19–22; David Beers Quinn, "Sir Thomas Smith (1513–1577) and the Beginnings of English Colonial Theory," *Proceedings of the American Philosophical Society* 89, no. 4 (1945): 545, 558; Rory Rapple, *Martial Power and Elizabethan Political Culture: Military Men in England and Ireland, 1558–1594* (Cambridge: CUP, 2009), 62; Henry Turner, *The Corporate Commonwealth: Pluralism and Political Fictions in England, 1516–1651* (Chicago: University of Chicago Press, 2016), 87–89.

6. Mark Knights, "Explaining Away Corruption in Pre-Modern Britain," *Social Philosophy and Policy* 35, no. 2 (2017): 94–117; Kenneth R. Andrews, *Elizabethan Privateering: English Privateering during the Spanish War, 1585–1603* (Cambridge: CUP, 1964), 23, 30; Lawrence Stone, "The Fruits of Office: The Case of Robert Cecil, First Earl of Salisbury, 1596–1612," in *Essays in the Economic and Social History of Tudor and Stuart England*, ed. F. J. Fisher (Cambridge: CUP, 1961), 89–116.

7. F. J. Furnivall, ed., *Queene Elizabethes Achademy (by Sir Humphrey Gilbert)* (London: N. Trübner, 1869), 12; Rapple, *Martial Power*, 81–82; Vera Keller and Ted McCormick, "Towards a History of Projects," *Early Science and Medicine* 21, no. 5 (2016): 423–44; Koji Yamamoto, *Taming Capitalism before Its Triumph: Public Service, Distrust, and "Projecting" in Early Modern England* (Oxford: OUP, 2018).

8. Robert Ashton, *The City and the Court, 1603–1643* (Cambridge: CUP, 1979), 30–31.

9. Kenneth R. Andrews, *Trade, Plunder, and Settlement: Maritime Enterprise and the Genesis of the British Empire, 1480–1630* (Cambridge: CUP, 1984), 43–44; Evan T. Jones, "Henry VII and the Bristol Expeditions to North America: The Condon Documents," *Historical Research* 83, no. 221 (2009): 444–54; David Harris Sacks, *The Widening Gate: Bristol and the Atlantic Economy, 1450–1700* (Berkeley: University of California Press, 1991), 34–36.

10. J. A. Williamson with R. A. Skelton, ed., *The Cabot Voyages and Bristol Discovery under Henry VII* (Cambridge: CUP for the Hakluyt Society, 1962), 68, 150–52, 186, 204–24, 250–63 (quote on 263); Andrews, *Trade, Plunder, and Settlement*, 49.

11. Williamson, *Cabot Voyages*, 248–52; Joyce Lorimer, *English and Irish Settlement on the River Amazon, 1550–1646* (London: Hakluyt Society, 1989), 3–4, 8–9; Andrews, *Trade, Plunder, and Settlement*, 65, 79; Butman and Targett, *New World, Inc.*, 29–31, 37; Decoster, "'Have You Not Heard of Florida?'" 400; Alison Sandman and Eric H. Ash, "Trading Expertise: Sebastian Cabot Between Spain and England," *Renaissance Quarterly* 57 (2004): 817, 820, 826, 829–32; Francesco Guidi-Bruscoli, "John Cabot and His Italian Financiers," *Historical Research* 85, no. 229 (2012).

12. Richard Hakluyt, *The Principall Navigations, Voyages, and Discoveries of the English Nation, Made By Sea or Over Land, to the Most Remote and Farthest Distant Quarters of the Earth at Any Time Within the Compasse of these 1500 Yeares* (London: George Bishop and Ralph Newberie, 1589), 280; William Robert Scott, *The Constitution and Finance of English, Scottish, and Irish Joint-Stock Companies to 1720* (Cambridge: CUP, 1912), I:21, 34, II:3–11; Andrews, *Trade, Plunder, and Settlement*, 7–8, 58–62, 101, 105, 117–34; Robert Brenner, *Merchants and Revolution: Commercial Change, Political Conflict, and London's Overseas Traders, 1550–1653*, 2nd ed. (London: Verso, 2003), 14; Keith Wrightson, *Earthly Necessities: Economic Lives in Early Modern Britain* (New Haven: YUP, 2000), 145–49; T. S. Willan, *The Muscovy Merchants of 1555* (Manchester: Manchester University Press, 1953).

13. Cecil T. Carr, ed., *Select Charters of Trading Companies, A.D. 1530–1707* (London: Bernard Quaritch, 1913), xxii–xxiv, 1–3; Michael E. Williams, "The English Hospice of St. George at Sanlucar De Barrameda," *British Catholic History* 18, no. 3 (1987): 263–76; Ron Harris, "Trading with Strangers: The Corporate Form in the Move from Municipal Governance to Overseas Trade," in *Research Handbook on the History of Corporate and Company Law*, ed. Harwell Wells (Cheltenham and Northampton, MA: Edward Elgar Publishing, 2018), 93.

14. Carr, ed., *Select Charters*, xxii; E. M. Carus-Wilson, *Medieval Merchant Venturers: Collected Studies*, 2nd ed. (London: Methuen & Co, 1967), xv–xxxiv; Thomas Leng, *Fellowship and Freedom: The Merchant Adventurers and the Restructuring of English Commerce, 1582–1700* (Oxford: OUP, 2020), 13–18; Miller Christy, "Attempts towards Colonization: The Council for New England and the Merchant Venturers of Bristol,

1621–1623," *American Historical Review* 4, no. 4 (1899): 678–79; Anne F. Sutton, "The Merchant Adventurers of England: The Place of the Adventurers of York and the North in the Late Middle Ages," *Northern History* 46, no. 2 (2009): 219–29.

15. Joseph Cotton, *Memoir of the Origin and Incorporation of the Trinity House of Deptford Strond* (London: J. Darling, 1818), 33.

16. Hakluyt, *Principall Navigations*, 261; Turner, *Corporate Commonwealth*, 100.

17. Robert K. Batchelor, *London: The Selden Map and the Making of a Global City, 1549–1689* (Chicago: University of Chicago Press, 2014), 37–38.

18. Hakluyt, *Principall Navigations*, 251, 280; Sandman and Ash, "Trading Expertise," 836–37.

19. J. McDermott and D. W. Waters, "Cathay and the Way Thither: The Navigation of the Frobisher Voyages," in *Meta Incognita: A Discourse of Discovery: Martin Frobisher's Arctic Expeditions, 1576–1578*, 2 vols., ed. Thomas H. B. Symons, with Stephen Alsford and Chris Kitzan (Hull, Quebec: Canadian Museum of Civilization, 1999), II:357; Andrews, *Trade, Plunder, and Settlement*, 69.

20. Robert Lemon, ed., *Calendar of State Papers, Domestic Series of the Reigns of Edward VI, Mary, Elizabeth, 1547–80* (London: Longman, Brown, Green, Longman & Roberts, 1856), 65 (26 February 1555); Scott, *Constitution and Finance*, I:7, 19–20, 36–37, II:40–42.

21. Mary Anne Everett Green, ed., *Calendar of State Papers Domestic Series, Of the Reign of Elizabeth, Addenda, 1566–1579* (London: Longman & Co and Trübner & Co., 1870), 39 (22 September 1567); Carr, ed., *Select Charters*, 28–30; Scott, *Constitution and Finance*, I:18, 35; Butman and Targett, *New World, Inc.*, 49–62; Martti Koskenniemi, "Sovereignty, Property, and Empire: Early Modern English Contexts," *Theoretical Inquiries in Law* 18, no. 2 (2017): 364.

22. *VCE*, I:6; Kurosh Meshkat, "The Journey of Master Anthony Jenkinson to Persia, 1562–1563," *Journal of Early Modern History* 13 (2009): 209–28.

23. Scott, *Constitution and Finance*, I:56–57, II:40–42; T. S. Willan, "The Russia Company and Narva, 1558–81," *Slavonic and East European Review* 31 (1952): 405–19.

24. *VCE*, I:7, 105–7.

25. *VCE*, I:10–13, 108–10, 137–39, 161–62; Margaret Small, "From Thought to Action: Gilbert, Davis, And Dee's Theories behind the Search for the Northwest Passage," *Sixteenth Century Journal* 44, no. 4 (2013): 1055.

26. *VCE*, I:13, 108–14.

27. *VCE*, I:13, 118–19; Sidney quoted in Quinn, "Sir Thomas Smith," 544; Robert Dunlop, "Sixteenth Century Schemes for the Plantation of Ulster, Part 1," *Scottish Historical Review* 22, no. 85 (1924): 55–57; Hiram Morgan, "The Colonial Venture of Sir Thomas Smith in Ulster, 1571–1575," *HJ* 28, no. 2 (1985): 263; Turner, *Corporate Commonwealth*, 94; Robert A. Williams, Jr., *The American Indian in Western Legal Thought: Discourses of Conquest* (New York: OUP, 1992), 140.

28. Annaleigh Margey, "Representing Plantation Landscapes: The Mapping of Ulster, c. 1560–1640," in *Plantation Ireland: Settlement and Material Culture, c. 1550–c.1700*, ed. James Lyttleton and Colin Rynne (Dublin: Four Courts, 2009).

29. *VCE*, I:13–20, 122–28, II:491, 493, 495; Robert Dunlop, "Sixteenth Century Schemes for the Plantation of Ulster, Part II," *Scottish Historical Review* 22, no. 86 (1925): 116; Annaleigh Margey, "Plantations, 1550–1641," in *The Cambridge History of Ireland*, ed. Jane Ohlmeyer (Cambridge: CUP, 2018), 562; Quinn, "Sir Thomas Smith," 545; Peter Piveronus, "Sir Warham St. Leger and the First Munster Plantation, 1568–69," *Éire-Ireland* 14, no. 2 (1979): 19–33.

30. Morgan, "Colonial Venture," 261–78.

31. C. L. Kingsford, ed., *Historical Manuscripts Commission: Report on the Manuscripts of Lord de L'Isle & Dudley Preserved at Penshurst Place* (London: HMSO, 1934), II:12–13; Dunlop, "Sixteenth Century Schemes, II," 116–19; Quinn, "Sir Thomas Smith," 547–50; Morgan, "Colonial Venture," 263; Margey, "Plantations, 1550–1641," 567.

32. Fitzmaurice, *Humanism and America*, 36 ("humanism, print, and colonization"); Quinn, "Sir Thomas Smith," 552–53; Turner, *Corporate Commonwealth*, 91 ("put into practice").

33. [Thomas Smith], *A Letter Sent by I.B. Gentleman Vnto His very Frende Maystet [Sic] R.C. Esquire* (London, 1572), [9].

34. Nicholas Canny, *Making Ireland British, 1580–1650* (Oxford: OUP, 2001), 121–22; Decoster, "'Have You Not Heard of Florida?'" 404; David Gwyn, "Richard Eden Cosmographer and Alchemist," *Sixteenth Century Journal* 15, no. 1 (1984): 34; Christopher McMillan, "A Letter from I.B. Gentleman: Sir Thomas Smith's Ulster Scheme and Its Scottish Context," *Prose Studies*, 39, 2/3 (2017): 87–88; Morgan, "Colonial Venture," 261, 269–70; Quinn, "Sir Thomas Smith," 545–47; Phil Withington, "Plantation and Civil Society," in *The Plantation of Ulster: Ideology and Practice*, ed. Éamonn Ó Ciardha and Micheál Ó Siochrú (Manchester and New York: Manchester University Press and Palgrave Macmillan, 2012), 61.

35. [Smith], *Letter Sent by I.B. Gentleman*, [10, 12].

36. [Smith], *Letter Sent by I.B. Gentleman*, [14, 17–18, 36]; *The Offer and Order Given Forth by Sir Thomas Smyth Knight, and Thomas Smyth his sonne, unto suche as be willing to accompanye the sayde Thomas Smyth the sonne, in his voyage for the inhabiting some partes of the Northe of Irelande* ([London, 1572]).

37. [Smith], *Letter Sent by I.B. Gentleman*, [37].

38. Arthur John Butler and Sophie Crawford Lomas, eds., *Calendar of State Papers Foreign: Elizabeth, Volume 17, January–June 1584 and Addenda* (London: HMSO, 1913), 493 (18 May 1571).

39. Butler and Lomas, eds., *Calendar of State Papers Foreign*, 17: 493 (18 May 1571).

40. Withington, "Plantation and Civil Society," 59–62, 71–72; Quinn, "Sir Thomas Smith," 547, 550–51, 553–44, 557; McMillan, "Letter"; Turner, *Corporate Commonwealth*, 91–93; Koskenniemi, "Sovereignty, Property, and Empire," 371.

41. Butler and Lomas, eds., *Calendar of State Papers Foreign*, 17:457, 469 (10 April 1572, 16 April 1572); Quinn, "Sir Thomas Smith," 551; Morgan, "Colonial Venture," 265; McMillan, "Letter," 87–88.

42. Audrey Horning, *Ireland in the Virginian Sea: Colonialism in the British Atlantic* (Chapel Hill: OIEAHC, 2013), 114; Nicholas Canny, *Kingdom and Colony: Ireland in the Atlantic World, 1560–1800* (Baltimore: JHUP, 1988), 1–2; Decoster, "'Have You Not Heard of Florida?'" 411.

43. Quinn, "Sir Thomas Smith," 547–51, 555, 559–60; Margey, "Plantations, 1550–1641," 566; Morgan, "Colonial Venture," 265; Henry Turner, "Corporations: Humanism and Elizabethan Political Economy," in *Mercantilism Reimagined: Political Economy in Early Modern Britain and its Empire,* ed. Philip J. Stern and Carl Wennerlind (New York: OUP, 2014), 160–63.

44. Dunlop, "Sixteenth Century Schemes, II," 124–26; 70; Morgan, "Colonial Venture," 263; Margey, "Plantations, 1550–1641," 567.

45. Kingsford, ed., *Historical Manuscripts Commission*, II:87–90; Turner, *Corporate Commonwealth*, 94.

46. Canny, *Making Ireland British*, 130; Margey, "Plantations, 1550–1641," 568–69.

47. Kingsford, ed., *Historical Manuscripts Commission*, II:28; Canny, *Making Ireland British*, 119; Robert Dunlop, "Sixteenth Century Schemes for the Plantation of Ulster," Part III, *Scottish Historical Review* 22, no. 87 (1925): 211.

48. Walter Bourchier Devereux, *Lives and Letters of the Devereux, Earls of Essex in the Reigns of Elizabeth, James I, and Charles I, 1540–1646* (London: John Murray, 1853), 45–46, 52; Dunlop, "Sixteenth Century Schemes," III, 199–202; Canny, *Making Ireland British*, 109, 119–20, 121–64.

49. Robert Payne, *A Briefe Description of Ireland: Made in this Yeare, 1589* (London: Thomas Dawson, 1589), 11; Canny, *Making Ireland British*, 130–32, 135–37; Withington, "Plantation and Civil Society," 62.

50. Canny, *Making Ireland British*, 143, 147.

51. Richard Collinson, ed., *The Three Voyages of Martin Frobisher, In Search of a Passage to Cathaia and India by the North-West, A.D. 1576–8* (London: Hakluyt Society, 1868), 4–8; Andrews, *Elizabethan Privateering*, 189; Decoster, "'Have You Not Heard of Florida?'" 404; Rupali Mishra, *A Business of State: Commerce, Politics, and the Birth of the East*

India Company (Cambridge, MA: HUP, 2018), 20; *VCE*, I:29; Probasco, *Sir Humphrey Gilbert*, 23–24.

52. Butman and Targett, *New World, Inc.*, 88–101; David B. Quinn, "Frobisher in the Context of Early English Northwest Exploration," in *Meta Incognita*, ed. Symons, Alsford, and Kitzan, I:14–15; James McDermott, *Martin Frobisher: Elizabethan Privateer* (New Haven: YUP, 2001), 89–92, 103–19; McDermott, "Michael Lok, Mercer and Merchant Adventurer," in *Meta Incognita*, ed. Symons, Alsford, and Kitzan, I:130–32; McDermott, "The Company of Cathay: The Financing and Organization of the Frobisher Voyages," in *Meta Incognita*, I:149–55; Robert Baldwin, "Speculative Ambitions and the Reputations of Frobisher's Metallurgists," in *Meta Incognita*, II:401–76.

53. Collinson, ed., *Three Voyages*, 111; McDermott, "Company of Cathay," 156, 159; Butman and Targett, *New World, Inc.*, 108–9.

54. Quoted by McDermott, "Company of Cathay," 157.

55. Collinson, ed., *Three Voyages*, 102–3, 111–15; McDermott, "Company of Cathay," 155–56.

56. McDermott, "Company of Cathay," 159–62, 164–65, 166–69.

57. James McDermott, "The Construction of the Dartford Furnaces," in *Meta Incognita*, ed. Symons, Alsford, and Kitzan, II:507, 519n13.

58. McDermott, "Construction of the Dartford Furnaces," 516–17; Butman and Targett, *New World, Inc.*, 132; Ann Savours, "A Narrative of Frobsher's Arctic Voyages," in *Meta Incognita*, ed. Symons, Alsford, and Kitzan, I:49.

59. McDermott, "Company of Cathay," 164–65, 169, 173; Ian Friel, "Frobisher's Ships: The Ships of the North-Western Atlantic Voyages, 1576–1578," in *Meta Incognita*, ed. Symons, Alsford, and Kitzan, I:301–2; Carole Shammas, "The 'Invisible Merchant' and Property Rights: The Misadventures of an Elizabethan Joint Stock Company," *Business History* 17 (1975): 98.

60. John Roche Dasent, ed., *Acts of the Privy Council of England Volume 11, 1578–1580* (London: Her Majesty's Stationery Office, 1895), 64–65 (6 March 1578[/9?]); Butman and Targett, *New World, Inc.*, 134; Carr, ed., *Select Charters*, xxxiv; McDermott, "Company of Cathay," 157–59, 171–72; McDermott, "Financing and Organization," 148–49, 174; Scott, *Constitution and Finance*, I:75.

61. McDermott, "Michael Lok," 133; McDermott, "Construction of the Dartford Furnaces," 505; McDermott, "Company of Cathay," 161; Shammas, "'Invisible Merchant,'" 101–2.

62. Collinson, ed., *Three Voyages*, 361–63; Baldwin, "Speculative Ambitions," 445.

63. McDermott, "Company of Cathay," 171; Butman and Targett, *New World, Inc.*, 134; Baldwin, "Speculative Ambitions," 442, 445.

64. Alford, *London's Triumph*, 152, 180; Theodore K. Rabb, *Enterprise and Empire: Merchant and Gentry Investment in the Expansion of England, 1575–1630* (Cambridge, MA: HUP, 1967), 152; McDermott, "Michael Lok," 133; McDermott, "Company of Cathay," 165, 171.

65. Dionyse Settle, *A True Reporte of the Laste Voyage into the West and Northwest Regions &c. 1577, Worthily Atchieved by Capteine Frobisher of the Sayde Voyage the First Finder and General* (London: Henrie Middleton, 1577); McDermott, "Michael Lok," 130.

66. *VCE*, I:8–9, 29–30, 129–64; Butman and Targett, *New World, Inc.*, 94–96, 100–101, 110–11; Nicholas Clulee, *John Dee's Natural Philosophy: Between Science and Religion* (London: Routledge, 1988, repr. 2013), 181–82; Claire Jowitt, "'Monsters and Straunge Births': The Politics of Richard Eden. A Response to Andrew Hadfield," *Connotations* 6, no. 1 (1996/97): 238; Ken MacMillan, "Discourse on History, Geography, and Law: John Dee and the Limits of the British Empire, 1576–80," *Canadian Journal of History* 36, no. 1 (2001); R. W. Maslen, "Sidneian Geographies," *Sidney Journal* 20, no. 2 (2002): 53; McDermott, "Company of Cathay," 150–55; McDermott, "Michael Lok," 132; Quinn, "Frobisher," I:14, 17; Savours, "Narrative of Frobisher's Arctic Voyages," 36–37; Scott, *Constitution and Finance*, I:21; Probasco, *Sir Humphrey Gilbert*, 7.

67. Scott, *Constitution and Finance*, I:80.

68. Zelia Nuttall, *New Light on Drake: A Collection of Documents Relating to his Voyage of Circumnavigation, 1577–1580* (London: Hakluyt Society, 1914), 430; Lemon, ed., *Calendar of State Papers*, 689.

69. John Sugden, *Sir Francis Drake* (New York: H. Holt, 1990), 165–68.

70. Lemon, ed., *Calendar of State Papers*, 656; Andrews, *Elizabethan Privateering*, 15, 203–4; Brenner, *Merchants and Revolution*, 20–21.

71. Mary Frear Keeler, ed., *Sir Francis Drake's West Indian Voyage, 1585–86* (London: Hakluyt Society, 1981); Scott, *Constitution and Finance*, I:73–88.

72. *VCE*, I:34, 170–72.

73. John Dee, *The Private Diary of Dr. John Dee*, ed. James Orchard Halliwell (London: J. B. Nicholas and Son, 1842), 8; *VCE*, I:35–36, 49.

74. Martin A. S. Hume, *Calendar of Letters and State Papers Relating to English Affairs Preserved Principally in the Archives of Simancas, Volume III. Elizabeth, 1580–1586* (Cambridge: CUP, 1896), 349.

75. *VCE*, II:313–26 (2 November 1582).

76. *VCE*, I:60–62, 92–93, II:328, 480–82 (12 December 1582; January 1584); R. P. Bishop, "Lessons of the Gilbert Map," *Geographical Journal* 72, no. 3 (September 1928): 237.

77. Carr, ed., *Select Charters*, xxxvi; Christy, "Attempts towards Colonization," 679; Scott, *Constitution and Finance*, I:156; Andrews, *Trade, Plunder, and Settlement*, 15.

78. *VCE*, I:58–59, II:242 (22 October 1581), 245–50 (6 June 1582, 28 February 1583), 260–66 (7 July 1582), 483; Dee, *Diary*, 8; Andrews, *Trade, Plunder, and Settlement*, 32; Decoster, "'Have You Not Heard of Florida?'" 410; Roger Kuin, "Ou-topia or, the Road Not Taken: Florida, Its Narratives, and Sir Philip Sidney," *Sidney Journal* 36, no. 2 (2018): 98–99; Richard D'Abate, "On the Meaning of a Name: 'Norumbega' and the Representation of North America," in *American Beginnings: Exploration, Culture, and Cartography in the Land of Norumbega*, ed. Emerson W. Baker et al. (Lincoln: University of Nebraska Press, 1994); Fulmer Mood, "Narragansett Bay and Dee River, 1583," *Rhode Island Historical Society Collections* 28, no. 4 (1935): 97–100.

79. *VCE*, I:64, 75, 90–94; II:256–60 (9 June 1582), 359–73 (15 May 1583); 375–76 (1583); W. Noel Sainsbury, ed., *Calendar of State Papers, Colonial, America and West Indies: Volume 9, 1675–1676 and Addenda 1574–1674* (London: HMSO, 1893), 29–30 (July 1583 and [November?] 1583).

80. Peckham, *True Report*; Fitzmaurice, *Humanism and America*, 45–46.

81. *VCE*, I:93–96; Edward Hayes to Lord Burghley, 10 May 158[6] and [Edward Hayes and Christopher Carleill], "A Discourse Concerning A Voyage Intended for the Planting of Chrystyan Religion and People in the North West Regions of America in Places Most Apt for the Constitution of Our Boddies, and the Speedy Advauncement of a State," [1592], in *New American World: A Documentary History of North America to 1612*, ed. David B. Quinn, Alison M. Quinn, and Susan Hillier (New York: Arno Press and Hector Bye, Inc., 1979), III:124, 165; Scott, *Constitution and Finance*, I:156; Philip Edwards, "Edward Hayes Explains Away Sir Humphrey Gilbert," *Renaissance Studies* 6, no. 3 (1992): 286; Alexander B. Haskell, *For God, King, and People: Forging Commonwealth Bonds in Renaissance Virginia* (Chapel Hill: UNCP/OIEAHC, 2017), 156–57.

82. *VCE* I:97–100, II:486–89 (1583?, September 1583?, and January 1584); Baldwin, "Speculative Ambitions," 453.

83. Small, "From Thought to Action," 1054–55.

84. Andrews, *Trade, Plunder, and Settlement*, 214; Butman and Targett, *New World, Inc.*, 188–95, 197–201; Haskell, *For God, King, and People*, 120; Paul Musselwhite, *Urban Dreams, Rural Commonwealth: The Rise of Plantation Society in the Chesapeake* (Chicago: University of Chicago Press, 2018), 19; *VCE*, I:96.

85. Andrews, *Trade, Plunder, and Settlement*, 287; John W. Shirley, "Sir Walter Raleigh's Guiana Finances," *Huntington Library Quarterly* 13, no. 1 (1949): 56–57.

86. Andrews, *Elizabethan Privateering*, 45–50, 62, 69–70, 79–80, 98, 100–123, esp. 102–4, quoting Grenville on 192; Andrews, *Trade, Plunder, and Settlement*, 18, 282–83; Scott, *Constitution and Finance*, I:82, 103.

87. Harris, "Trading with Strangers," 93; Edmond Smith, "Corporate Naval Supply in England's Commercial Empire, 1600–1760," *International Journal of Maritime History* 31, no. 3 (2019): 579–80.

88. Hakluyt, *Principall Navigations*, 235, 237; Carr, ed., *Select Charters*, xlii; Scott, *Constitution and Finance*, II:10–11.

89. CO 77/1 no. 6 (f. 8); Andrews, *Trade, Plunder, and Settlement*, 84, 88–93, 98; Carr, ed., *Select Charters*, xxxix; T. S. Willan, "Some Aspects of English Trade with the Levant in the Sixteenth Century," *English Historical Review* 70, no. 276 (1955): 399–410.

90. Clements R. Markham, ed., *The Voyages of James Lancaster, Kt.* (London: Hakluyt Society, 1877); Andrews, *Elizabethan Privateering*, 209–16; Brenner, *Merchants and Revolution*, 21; Gerald Maclean and Nabil Matar, *Britain and the Islamic World, 1558–1713* (Oxford: OUP, 2011), 66–68; Mishra, *Business of State*, 25; Despina Vlami, "Corporate Identity and Entrepreneurial Initiative: The Levant Company in the Eighteenth and Nineteenth Centuries," *Journal of European Economic History* 39, no. 1 (2010): 71–72.

91. Andrews, *Trade, Plunder, and Settlement*, 70–74, 261; Sanjay Subrahmanyam, *Empires Between Islam and Christianity* (Albany: State University of New York Press, 2019), 223–30.

92. Mishra, *Business of State*, 25.

93. Henry Stevens, *The Dawn of British Trade to the East Indies as Recorded in the Court Minutes of the East India Company, 1599–1603* (London: Henry Stevens & Son, 1886), 5–6, 8, 130, 132 (24 September, 25 September 1599, and 10 February 1600/01); Mishra, *Business of State*, 6.

94. CO 77/1 no. 17, ff. 26–27 [1599 or 1600?]; Heidi Brayman Hackel and Peter C. Mancall, "Richard Hakluyt the Younger's Notes for the East India Company in 1601: A Transcription of Huntington Library Manuscript EL 2360," *Huntington Library Quarterly* 67, no. 3 (2004), 433; John Bruce, *Annals of the Honorable East-India Company from their Establishment by the Charter of Queen Elizabeth, 1600, to the Union of the London and English East-India Companies, 1707–8* (London: Black, Parry, and Kingsbury, 1810), I:115–21; Peter C. Mancall, *Hakluyt's Promise: An Elizabethan's Obsession for an English America* (New Haven: YUP, 2007), 237–43.

95. Bruce, *Annals*, I:121–26.

96. John Shaw, ed., *Charters Relating to the East India Company from 1600 to 1761, Reprinted from a Former Collection with Some Additions and a Preface* (Madras: R. Hill at the Government Press, 1887), 6–7.

97. Ron Harris, *Going the Distance: Eurasian Trade and the Rise of the Business Corporation, 1400–1700* (Princeton: PUP, 2020), especially 289.

98. Andrews, *Elizabethan Privateering*, 113–18, 198–99, 213–38; Harris, "Trading with Strangers," 101–2; Edmond Smith, "The Global Interests of London's Commercial Community, 1599–1625: Investment in the East India Company," *Economic History Review* 71, no. 4 (2018).

99. Basil Morgan, "Smythe [Smith], Sir Thomas (c.1558–1625)," *Oxford Dictionary of National Biography* (23 September 2004, updated 3 January 2008), https://doi.org/10.1093/ref:odnb/25908.

100. W. Noel Sainsbury, ed., *Calendar of State Papers, Colonial Series: East Indies, China and Japan, Volume 4, 1622–1624* (London: Longman, Green, Longman & Roberts, 1878), 490 (17 June 1624?).

101. Quoted in K. N. Chaudhuri, *East India Company: The Study of an Early Joint-Stock Company, 1600–1640* (London: Frank Cass, 1965), 36; Mishra, *Business of State*, 63 and ch. 3.

102. Lauren Working, *The Making of an Imperial Polity: Civility and America in the Jacobean Metropolis* (Cambridge: CUP, 2020), 41; Chester Dunning, "James I, the Russia Company, and the Plan to Establish a Protectorate over North Russia," *Albion* 21, no. 2 (1989): 219.

103. Chaudhuri, *East India Company*, 31, 36; Mishra, *Business of State*, 73.

104. Stevens, *Dawn of British Trade*, 156–57, 160–61 (6 March 1600/1 April 1601); W. Noel Sainsbury, ed., *Calendar of State Papers, Colonial Series, East Indies, China and Japan, 1513–1616* (London: Longman, Green, Longman & Roberts, 1862), 156 (22 and 24 July 1607); Carr, ed., *Select Charters*, xliii n4; Chaudhuri, *East India Company*, 28; Mishra, *Business of State*, 32; Scott, *Constitution and Finance*, I:146, 200.

105. Mishra, *Business of State*, 152–53; Shaw, ed., *Charters*, 19; Mary Anne Everett Green, ed., *Calendar of State Papers Domestic Series, Of the Reign of James I, 1603–1610* (London: Longman, Brown, Green, Longman & Roberts, 1857), 647 (27 November 1610).

106. Stevens, *Dawn of British Trade*, 178 (6 July 1601); Sainsbury, ed., *East Indies, 1513–1616*, 146 (9 January 1607); Green, ed., *State Papers, 1603–1610*, 344 (9 January 1607); Ashton,

City and the Court, 90; Carr, ed., *Select Charters,* xxxvii; Mishra, *Business of State,* 156–61; Scott, *Constitution and Finance,* II:100.

107. Mishra, *Business of State,* 149–50, 162–77 (James I quotation on 150); K. N. Chaudhuri, *The Trading World of Asia and the English East India Company* (Cambridge: CUP, 1978), 417; Joseph Wagner, "The Scottish East India Company of 1617: Patronage, Commercial Rivalry, and the Union of the Crowns," *Journal of British Studies* 59 (2020): 591, 593, 596n85.

108. Stevens, *Dawn of British Trade,* 183–86, 196, 197–201, 211–14, 217–18, 236–37 (7 August, 1 September, 2 September, 13 September 1601, 5 January 1601/2, 11 January 1601/2, April 1602, 30 April 1602, 4 January 1602/3); Sainsbury, ed., *East Indies, 1513–1616,* xxviii–xxxi, 127–28, 131–33, 135–38.

109. [Samuel Purchas], *Purchas His Pilgrimes in Five Bookes* (London: William Stansby, 1625), III:827; "Journal of the Voyage of John Knight to Seek the North-West Passage, 1606," in Markham, ed., *The Voyages of James Lancaster, Kt.,* 341–47.

110. Norman Egbert McClure, ed., *The Letters of John Chamberlain* (Philadelphia: American Philosophical Society, 1939), II:135 (31 January 1618); Mishra, *Business of State,* 163–70.

111. W. Noel Sainsbury, ed., *Calendar of State Papers, Colonial Series, East Indies, China and Japan, 1617–1621* (London: Longman & Co. and Trubner & Co., 1870), 142–43 (26–27 March 1618); Maria Salomon Arel, *English Trade and Adventure to Russia in the Early Modern Era: The Muscovy Company, 1603–1649* (London: Lexington Books, 2019), 27–33.

112. Sainsbury, ed., *State Papers East Indies, 1513–1616,* 238–40 (July 26 1612); Andrews, *Trade, Plunder, and Settlement,* 348–49; Miller Christy, ed., *The Voyages of Captain Luke Foxe of Hull, and Captain Thomas James of Bristol* (London: Hakluyt Society, 1894), I:xl.

113. Andrew Van Horn Ruoss, "Competitive Collaboration: The Dutch and English East India Companies and the Forging of Global Corporate Political Economy," PhD dissertation, Duke University, 2017, 60–97.

114. Alison Games, *The Web of Empire: English Cosmopolitans in an Age of Expansion, 1560–1660* (New York: OUP, 2008), 102–3; Miles Ogborn, *Indian Ink: Script and Print in the Making of the English East India Company* (Chicago: University of Chicago Press, 2007), 34, 58–60; Guido Van Meersbergen, "The Diplomatic Repertories of the East India Companies in Mughal South Asia, 1608–1717," *HJ* (2019): 1–24; Rupali Mishra, "Diplomacy on the Edge: Split Interests in the Roe Embassy to the Mughal Court," *Journal of British Studies* 53 (2014): 5–28.

115. Stevens, *Dawn of British Trade,* 139 (12 February 1600/1).

116. Guido van Meersbergen, *Ethnography and Encounter: The Dutch and English in Seventeenth-Century South Asia* (Leiden: Brill, 2021); David Veevers and William Pettigrew, "Trading Companies and Business Diplomacy in the Early Modern World," *Diplomatica* 2, no. 1 (2020): 39–47.

117. Derek Massarella and Izumi K. Tytler, "The Japonian Charters: The English and Dutch *Shuinjō,*" *Monumenta Nipponica* 45, no. 2 (1990): 189–205.

118. Mishra, *Business of State,* 156.

2. Municipal Bonds

Epigraph: Thomas Gainsford, *The Vision and Discourse of Henry the Seventh Concerning the Unitie of Great Brittaine* (London, 1610), 18.

1. See Aonghas MacCoinnich, *Plantation and Civility in the North Atlantic World: The Case of the Northern Hebrides, 1570–1639* (Leiden: Brill, 2015), esp. chap. 3. On the Mackenzie plantation, see chaps. 4–5.

2. MacCoinnich, *Plantation and Civility,* 140–41, 164, 181; Jane Ohlmeyer, "'Civilzinge of Those Rude Partes': Colonization within Britain and Ireland, 1580s–1640s," in *The Oxford History of the British Empire, Volume I: Origins of Empire,* ed. Nicholas Canny (Oxford: OUP, 1998), 132–33.

3. Ohlmeyer, "'Civilzinge,'" 135.
4. C. W. Russell and John P. Prendergast, eds., *Calendar of the State Papers Relating to Ireland of the Reign of James I, 1611–1614* (London: Longman & Co., 1877), 704–5, 710 (July 1613); Audrey Horning, *Ireland in the Virginian Sea: Colonialism in the British Atlantic* (Chapel Hill: UNCP, 2013), 177–79; MacCoinnich, *Plantation and Civility,* 170; Annaleigh Margey, "Plantations, 1550–1641," in *The Cambridge History of Ireland,* ed. Jane Ohlmeyer (Cambridge: CUP, 2018), 572–74; William O'Reilly, "Ireland in the Atlantic World: Migration and Cultural Transfer," in *Ireland,* ed. Ohlmeyer, 394; Edmond Smith, "The Global Interests of London's Commercial Community, 1599–1625: Investment in the East India Company," *Economic History Review* 71, no. 4 (2018): 582–84.
5. *Concise View of the Origin, Constitution, and Proceedings of the Honorable Society of the Governor and Assistants of London, of the New Plantation in Ulster, within the realm of Ireland, commonly called The Irish Society* (London: Gye and Balne, 1822), 17–18, 32, 35–39, 57; Ian Archer, "The City of London and the Ulster Plantation," in *The Plantation of Ulster: Ideology and Practice,* ed. Éamonn Ó Ciardha and Micheál Ó Siochrú (Manchester: Manchester University Press, 2012), 82–83; T. W. Moody, *The Londonderry Plantation 1609–41: The City of London and the Plantation in Ulster* (Belfast: W. Mullan and Son, 1939), 35–37, 82–84, 130–33; Phil Withington, "Plantation and Civil Society," in *Plantation of Ulster,* ed. Ciardha and Siochrú, 69.
6. David B. Quinn, "Advice for Investors in Virginia, Bermuda and Newfoundland, 1611," *WMQ* 23, no. 1 (1966): 145; Moody, *Londonderry Plantation,* 97–98.
7. Alexander Brown, *The Genesis of the United States* (Boston: Riverside Press, 1890), 37–42; Karin A. Amundsen, "Thinking Metallurgically: Metals and Empire in the Projects of Edward Hayes," *Huntington Library Quarterly* 79, no. 4 (2016): 561–90; Andrew Fitzmaurice, "The Company-Commonwealth," in *Virginia 1619: Slavery and Freedom in the Making of English America,* ed. Paul Musselwhite, Peter C. Mancall, and James Horn (Chapel Hill: UNCP, 2019), 196–201; Alexander B. Haskell, *For God, King, and People: Forging Commonwealth Bonds in Renaissance Virginia* (Chapel Hill: UNCP/OIEAHC, 2017), 156–64.
8. Christopher J. Bilodeau, "The Paradox of Sagadahoc: The Popham Colony, 1607–1608," *Early American Studies* 12, no. 1 (2014): 1–35; Bernard Bailyn, *The New England Merchants in the Seventeenth Century* (Cambridge, MA: HUP, 1955), 2–5, 201n7; Fitzmaurice, "Company-Commonwealth," 201–2.
9. Wesley Frank Craven, *The Virginia Company of London, 1606–1624* (Williamsburg, VA: Virginia 350th Anniversary Celebration Corporation, 1957), 10–20; Cecil T. Carr, *Select Charters of Trading Companies, A.D. 1530–1707* (London: Bernard Quaritch, 1913), lxxxiv.
10. Kenneth R. Andrews, *Trade, Plunder, and Settlement: Maritime Enterprise and the Genesis of the British Empire, 1480–1630* (Cambridge: CUP, 1984), 349.
11. Andrew Fitzmaurice, *Humanism and America: An Intellectual History of English Colonisation, 1500–1625* (New York: CUP, 2003); Haskell, *God, King, and People,* esp. ch. 3; Karen Ordahl Kupperman, *Pocahontas and the English Boys: Caught Between Cultures in Early Virginia* (New York: NYUP, 2019), esp. ch. 3. For the passage to Asia, see Edward Waterhouse, *A Declaration of the State of the Colony and Affaires in Virginia* (London: Robert Mylbourne, 1622); Craven, *Virginia Company of London,* 48.
12. Francis Newton Thorpe, ed., *The Federal and State Constitutions, Colonial Charters, and Other Organic Laws of the States, Territories, and Colonies Now or Heretofore Forming the United States of America* (Washington: Government Printing Office, 1909), VII: 3802–10.
13. Misha Ewen, "Women Investors and the Virginia Company in the Early Seventeenth Century," *HJ* 62, no. 4 (2019): 859, 870; William Robert Scott, *The Constitution and Finance of English, Scottish, and Irish Joint-Stock Companies to 1720* (Cambridge: CUP, 1912), II:251–52.
14. Robert C. Johnson, "The Lotteries of the Virginia Company, 1612–1621," *VMHB* 74, no. 3 (1966): 279–84; E. M. Rose, "The 'Bewitching Lotteries for Virginia,' 1616–21: A List of Sites and Charitable Donations," *Huntington Library Quarterly* 81, no. 1 (2018): 107–119;

Peter Walne, "The 'Running Lottery' of the Virginia Company: In Reading, 1619, and in Chester, 1616," *VMHB* 70, no. 1 (1962): 30–34.

15. Ewen, "Women Investors," 855; Horning, *Ireland*, 277–80; Moody, *Londonderry Plantation*, 97–98; Johnson, "Lotteries," 263–66, 276–78; Kupperman, *Pocahontas*, 129.

16. Maria Salomon Arel, *English Trade and Adventure to Russia in the Early Modern Era: The Muscovy Company, 1603–1649* (Lanham: Lexington Books, 2019), 38n59; Scott, *Constitution and Finance*, I:200; Alfred C. Wood, *A History of the Levant Company* (London: Frank Cass & Co., 1935, second ed., 1964), 70–71; Despina Vlami, "Corporate Identity and Entrepreneurial Initiative: The Levant Company in the Eighteenth and Nineteenth Centuries," *Journal of European Economic History* 39, no. 1 (2010): 75.

17. Susan Myra Kingsbury, ed., *The Records of the Virginia Company of London* (Washington, DC: Government Printing Office, 1906), I:95–96; Paul Musselwhite, *Urban Dreams, Rural Commonwealth: The Rise of Plantation Society in the Chesapeake* (Chicago: University of Chicago Press, 2018), 33; Robert Brenner, *Merchants and Revolution: Commercial Change, Political Conflict, and London's Overseas Traders, 1550–1653* (Princeton: PUP, 1993; 2nd ed., London: Verso, 2003), 98.

18. Kingsbury, ed., *Records*, I:512–15 (16 July 1621); Lauren Working, *The Making of an Imperial Polity: Civility and America in the Jacobean Metropolis* (Cambridge: CUP, 2020), 52.

19. On Sandys, see Theodore K. Rabb, *Jacobean Gentleman: Sir Edwin Sandys, 1561–1629* (Princeton: PUP, 1998).

20. Kingsbury, ed., *Records*, 1:267–68 (17 November 1619); Paul Musselwhite, "Private Plantation: The Political Economy of Land in Early Virginia," in *Virginia 1619*, ed. Musselwhite, Mancall, and Horn, 150–72; Musselwhite, *Urban Dreams*, 30–55. Ferrar quoted in Working, *Making of an Imperial Polity*, 64.

21. William Bradford, *Of Plymouth Plantation*, ed. Samuel Eliot Morison (New York: Alfred A. Knopf, 1952, repr. 2002), 29, 76; Andrews, *Trade, Plunder, and Settlement*, 329–30; Carla Pestana, *The World of Plymouth Plantation* (Cambridge, MA: HUP, 2020).

22. W. Nöel Sainsbury, ed., *Calendar of State Papers Colonial Series, 1574–1660* (London: Longman, Green, Longman & Roberts, 1860), 12 (12 February 1612); Michael J. Jarvis, *In the Eye of All Trade: Bermuda, Bermudians, and the Maritime Atlantic World, 1680–1783* (Chapel Hill: UNCP, 2010), 11–20, 478n12; Scott, *Constitution and Finance*, II:252, 254.

23. J. H. Lefroy, *Memorials of the Discovery and Early Settlement of the Bermudas or Somers Islands 1515–1685, Vol. I: 1515–1652* (London: Longmans, Green, and Co., 1877), 357; Jarvis, *In the Eye*, 20–24.

24. Sainsbury, ed., *Calendar of State Papers*, 25–26 ([16 March] 1621); Gillian T. Cell, *English Enterprise in Newfoundland, 1577–1660* (Toronto: University of Toronto Press, 1969), 61, 71, 76, 87; Peter Pope, *Fish into Wine: The Newfoundland Plantation in the Seventeenth Century* (Chapel Hill: UNCP, 2004), 50–51; George Pratt Insh, *Scottish Colonial Schemes, 1620–1686* (Glasgow: Maclehose, Jackson & Co., 1922), 32–39; MacCoinnich, *Plantation and Civility*, 299–303; Joseph Wagner, "The First 'British' Colony in the Americas: Interkingdom Cooperation and Stuart-British Ideology in the Colonisation of Newfoundland, 1616–1640," *Britain and the World* 15, no. 1 (2022): 1–23.

25. Brenner, *Merchants and Revolution*, 110; Cell, *English Enterprise*, 81; Pope, *Fish into Wine*, 51.

26. Richard Whitbourne, *A Discourse Containing a Loving Invitation: Both Honourable and Profitable to All Such as Shall Be Adventurers, Either in Person or Purse, for the Advancement of His Majesties Most Hopefull Plantation in the New-found-land Lately Undertaken* (London: Felix Kyngston, 1622); T. C., *A Short Discourse of the New-Found-Land* (Dublin: Society of Stationers, 1623); Mark Netzloff, "Writing Britain from the Margins: Scottish, Irish, and Welsh Projects for American Colonization," *Prose Studies* 25, no. 2 (2002): 12; Cell, *English Enterprise*, 81–94; Pope, *Fish into Wine*, 92–94.

27. Cell, *English Enterprise*, 95; Insh, *Scottish Colonial Schemes*, 39, 48–49; MacCoinnich, *Plantation and Civility*, 304; David Armitage, "Making the Empire British: Scotland in the Atlantic World, 1542-1707," *Past and Present* 155, no. 1 (1997): 50; Joseph Wagner,

"The Scottish East India Company of 1617: Patronage, Commercial Rivalry, and the Union of the Crowns," *Journal of British Studies* 59 (2020): 588.

28. Sir William Alexander, *An Encouragement to Colonies* (London: William Stansby, 1625), 46.

29. Working, *Making of an Imperial Polity*, 41; Insh, *Scottish Colonial Schemes*, 68.

30. [Thomas Urquhart], *Ekskybalauron: or, The Discovery of a Most Exquisite Jewel, More Precious than Diamonds Inchased in Gold, the Like Whereof Was Never Seen in Any Age* (London: Ja. Cottrell, 1652), 208.

31. Alexander, *Encouragement*, 46–47; Insh, *Scottish Colonial Schemes*, 62; Netzloff, "Writing Britain," 7–8.

32. Quoted in Vera Keller and Ted McCormick, "Towards a History of Projects," *Early Science and Medicine* 21, no. 5 (2016): 427.

33. Quoted in Cell, *English Enterprise*, 57.

34. [Urquhart], *Ekskybalauron*, 208.

35. R[obert] H[ayman], *Quodlibets, Lately Come Over from New Britaniola, Old Newfoundland* (London: Elizabeth All-de, 1628); Anne Lake Prescott, "Rabelaisian Apocrypha and Satire in early Canada: The Case of Robert Hayman," in *Éditer et traduire Rabelais à travers les âges*, ed. Paul J. Smith (Amsterdam: Rodopi, 1997), 104–5.

36. John Mason, *A Brief Discourse of the New-found-land, with the situation, temperature, and commodities therof, inciting our Nation to goe forward in that hope-full plantation begune* (Edinburgh: Andro Hart, 1620), [10]; [Robert Gordon], *Encouragements for such as shall have intention to bee Under-takers in the new plantation of Cape Briton, now New Galloway, in America, By Mee Lochinvar* (Edinburgh: John Wreittoun, 1625).

37. Ken MacMillan, "Centers and Peripheries in English Maps of America, 1590–1685," in *Early American Cartographies*, ed. Martin Brückner (Chapel Hill: UNC/OIEAHC, 2011), 70–84.

38. Orpheus Junior, *The Golden Fleece, Divided into Three Parts* (London: Francis Williams, 1626); Netzloff, "Writing Britain," 15–17.

39. Sainsbury, ed., *Calendar of State Papers*, 128 (26 February 1631); Insh, *Scottish Colonial Schemes*, 68–78, 106–10.

40. *Royal Letters, Charters, and Tracts Relating to the Colonization of New Scotland and the Institution of the Order of Knight Baronets of Nova Scotia* (Edinburgh: G. Robb, 1873), 108; Insh, *Scottish Colonial Schemes*, 99–104.

41. Baltimore to Charles I, 19 August 1629, in *Report and Accompanying Documents of the Virginia Commissioners Appointed to Ascertain the Boundary Line Between Maryland and Virginia* (Richmond, VA: R. F. Walker, 1873), 97.

42. Wagner, "First 'British' Colony," 23n99.

43. Bradford, *Of Plymouth Plantation*, 28, 39; Melissa N. Morris, "Virginia and the Amazonian Alternative," in *Virginia 1619*, ed. Musselwhite, Mancall, and Horn, 257–81.

44. Joyce Lorimer, *English and Irish Settlement on the River Amazon, 1550–1646* (London: Hakluyt Society, 1989), 37–53, 159.

45. Robert Harcourt, *A Relation of a Voyage to Guiana* (London: John Beale, 1613), 67–68, 71; Andrews, *Trade, Plunder, and Settlement*, 297; Lorimer, *English and Irish Settlement*, 41.

46. Lorimer, *English and Irish Settlement*, 61, 190–91, 193, 195; Andrews, *Trade, Plunder, and Settlement*, 299; Morris, "Virginia and the Amazonian Alternative," 258, 264–65, 277–78; Working, Making of an *Imperial Polity*, 40, 168.

47. Lorimer, *English and Irish Settlement*, 202–03, 204, 206–07; Morris, "Virginia and the Amazonian Alternative," 278–79.

48. W. Frank Craven, "The Earl of Warwick, a Speculator in Piracy," *Hispanic American Historical Review* 10, no. 4 (1930): 468; Philip D. Morgan, "Virginia Slavery in Atlantic Context 1550 to 1650," in *Virginia 1619*, ed. Horn, Mancall, and Musselwhite, 85–86.

49. Sainsbury, ed., *Calendar of State Papers*, 23–24 (15 May 1620); Lorimer, *English and Irish Settlement*, 67, 215n3, 216, 219–20, 222; Andrews, *Trade, Plunder, and Settlement*, 301; Morris, "Virginia and the Amazonian Alternative," 278–79, 281; Theodore K. Rabb, *Enterprise amd Empire: Merchant and Gentry Investment in the Expansion of England, 1575–1630* (Cambridge, MA: HUP, 1967), 382; Paul Slack, *The Invention of Improvement:*

Information and Material Progress in Seventeenth-Century England (Oxford: OUP, 2015), 78–79.

50. Quoted in Carr, *Select Charters,* xl.
51. Simonds D'Ewes, *The Journals of All the Parliaments During the Reign of Queen Elizabeth Both of the House of Lords and House of Commons* (London: John Starkey, 1682), 168.
52. Chris R. Kyle, "'Wrangling Lawyers': Proclamations and the Management of the English Parliament of 1621," *Parliamentary History* (2015); Chris R. Kyle, "'But a New Button to an Old Coat': The Enactment of the Statute of Monopolies, 21 James I cap.3," *Legal History* 19, no. 3 (1998): 203–23; Thomas B. Nachbar, "Monopoly, Mercantilism, and the Politics of Regulation," *Virginia Law Review* 91, no. 6 (2005): 1313–1379; David Harris Sacks, "The Countervailing of Benefits: Monopoly, Liberty, and Benevolence in Elizabethan England," in *Tudor Political Culture,* ed. Dale Hoak (Cambridge: CUP, 1995); Scott, *Constitution and Finance,* I:119–22.
53. Kyle, "'But a New Button,'" 206, 207, 211–14; Carr, *Select Charters,* lxvii, lxxii; Nachbar, "Monopoly, Mercantilism," 1327, 1349, 1351, 1355; Jacob I. Corre, "The Argument, Decision, and Reports of Darcy v. Allen," *Emory Law Journal* 45, no. 4 (Fall 1996): 1261–1327, A1–A8; D. Seaborne Davies, "Further Light on the Case of Monopolies," *Law Quarterly Review* 48, no. 3 (July 1932): 394–414; William L. Letwin, "The English Common Law Concerning Monopolies," *University of Chicago Law Review* 21, no. 3 (Spring 1954): 360–62, 364–67.
54. James Spedding, ed., *The Letters and the Life of Francis Bacon* (London: Longmans, Green, Reader, and Dyer, 1868), III:27.
55. Thomas Leng, *Fellowship and Freedom: The Merchant Adventurers and the Restructuring of English Commerce, 1582–1700* (Oxford: OUP, 2020), 195–99.
56. *Journal of the House of Commons: Volume I, 1547–1629* (London: HMSO, 1802), 214–15 (19 May 1604), www.british-history.ac.uk/commons-jrnl/vol1/pp214-215; [Robert Kayll], *The Trades Increase* (London: Nicholas Okes, 1615), 51.
57. Gerard Malynes, *The Center of the Circle of Commerce. Or, A Refutation of a Treatise, Intituled The Circle of Commerce, or The Ballance of Trade, Lately Published by E.M.* (London: William Jones, 1623), 138; Rabb, *Jacobean Gentleman,* 92–97.
58. [Kayll], *Trades Increase,* 51–55.
59. [Dudley Digges], *The Defence of Trade in a Letter to Sir Thomas Smith Knight, Governour of the East-India Companie, &c.* (London: William Stansby, 1615), 1–2, 32; E[dward] M[isselden], *The Circle of Commerce; Or, the Ballance of Trade in Defence of Free Trade* (London: John Dawson, 1623), 17–18.
60. Brown, *Genesis,* 38; Fitzmaurice, "Company-Commonwealth," 198–99; Haskell, *God, King, and People,* 154–64.
61. Alfred C. Wood, *A History of the Levant Company* (London: Frank Cass & Co., 1935), 39–41.
62. Thomas Mun, *England's treasure by forraign trade, or, The ballance of our forraign trade is the rule of our treasure* (London: J.G., 1664), 145.
63. Mun, *England's treasure,* 26, 219; Lewes Roberts, *The Merchants Mappe of Commerce Wherein the Universall Manner and Matter of Trade, Is Compendiously Handled* (London: R.O., 1638), 19–20.
64. Edward Misselden, *Free Trade, Or, the Meanes to Make Trade Flourish* (London: John Legatt, 1622), 53–54.
65. [Thomas Johnson], *A Discourse Consisting of Motives for the Enlargement and Freedome of Trade* (London: Richard Bishop for Stephen Bowtell, 1645), 6.
66. Gerard Malynes, *The Maintenance of Free Trade* (London: J.L., 1622), 72; [Kayll], *Trades Increase,* 55; Rabb, *Jacobean Gentleman,* 95.
67. James Muldoon, *Popes, Lawyers, and Infidels: The Church and the Non-Christian World, 1250–1550* (Philadelphia: UPenn, 1979); Richard Tuck, "Alliances with Infidels in the European Imperial Expansion," in *Empire and Modern Political Thought,* ed. Sankar Muthu (Cambridge: CUP, 2012); Edward Cavanagh, "Infidels in English Legal Thought: Conquest, Commerce and Slavery in the Common Law from Coke to Mansfield, 1603–1793," *Modern Intellectual History* 16, no. 2 (2019): 375–409.

68. Hugo Grotius, *Commentary on the Law of Prize and Booty,* ed. Martine Julia van Ittersum (Indianapolis: Liberty Fund, 2006), 158–59, 302.

69. Hugo Grotius, *The Rights of War and Peace, Including the Law of Nature and Nations,* trans. A. C. Campbell (New York: M. Walter Dunne, 1901), 152.

70. Misselden, *Free Trade,* 55, 57, 73.

71. Robert Ashton, *The City and the Court, 1603–1643* (Cambridge: CUP, 1979), 115; Johnson, "Lotteries," 288–92.

72. *Proceedings and Debates of the House of Commons in 1620 and 1621* (Oxford: Clarendon Press, 1766), 258; William Brigham, ed., *The Compact with the Charter and Laws of the Colony of New Plymouth* (Boston: Dutton and Wentworth, 1836), 1–18; Charles Deane, "New England," in *Narrative and Critical History of America,* ed. Justin Winsor (Boston: Houghton, Mifflin and Company, 1881), III:296–99; Lorimer, *English and Irish Settlement,* 220–21.

73. Ferdinando Gorges, *A Briefe Narration of the Originall Undertakings of the Advancement of Plantations Into the Parts of America* (London: E. Brundell, 1658), in *Collections of the Massachusetts Historical Society,* 3rd ser. (Boston: American Stationers' Company, 1837), 66–68; Deane, "New England," III:300.

74. Sir Thomas Phillips, *Londonderry and the London Companies, 1609–1629: Being a Survey of and other Documents Submitted to King Charles I* (Belfast: HMSO, 1928); Moody, *Londonderry Plantation,* 114–18; Archer, "City of London," 92; Thomas Moody, "Sir Thomas Phillips of Limavady, Servitor," *Irish Historical Studies* 1, no. 3 (1939): 258–59; Jane Ohlmeyer, "Strafford, the 'London Business,' and the 'new British history,'" in J. F. Merritt, *The Political World of Thomas Wentworth, Earl of Strafford, 1621–1641* (Cambridge: CUP, 2003), 211; Horning, *Ireland,* 270, 276.

75. Privy Council to Lords Justices of Ireland, 7 August 1631, in *Concise View,* 53; Archer, "City of London," 92; Moody, "Sir Thomas Phillips," 267.

76. William Blackstone, *Commentaries on the Laws of England* (Oxford: Clarendon Press, 1765–1769), III, chap. 17.

77. *Concise View,* 53–57; Archer, "City of London," 92; Moody, "Sir Thomas Phillips," 267–69; Horning, *Ireland,* 265, 275; Ohlmeyer, "Strafford," 219–22, 224–25, 229; Withington, "Plantation and Civil Society," 78, 92.

78. John Smith, *The Generall Historie of Virginia, New-England, and the Summer Iles* (1629) (Richmond: Franklin Press, 1819), II:61.

79. Sainsbury, ed., *Calendar of State Papers,* 39 ([February] 1623); Musselwhite, "Private Plantation," 166–70; Fitzmaurice, "Company-Commonwealth," 206–12; Working, Making of an *Imperial Polity,* 88; Alison Games, *The Web of Empire: English Cosmopolitans in an Age of Expansion, 1560–1660* (New York: OUP, 2008), 145.

80. Kingsbury, ed., *Records,* IV:256, 290; Leng, *Fellowship and Freedom,* 202–27; Wesley Frank Craven, *Dissolution of the Virginia Company: The Failure of a Colonial Experiment* (New York: OUP, 1932); Emily Rose, "The End of the Gamble: The Termination of the Virginia Lotteries in March 1621," *Parliamentary History* 27, no. 2 (2008): 175–97.

81. Kingsbury, ed., *Records,* IV:295–398; Herbert Osgood, *The American Colonies in the Seventeenth Century* (New York: Macmillan & Co., 1926), III:47–54; Horning, *Ireland,* 15, 172; Fitzmaurice, "Company-Commonwealth," 212; J. Mills Thornton, III, "The Thrusting out of Governor Harvey: A Seventeenth-Century Rebellion," *VMHB* 76, no 1 (1968): 13–14.

82. Brenner, *Merchants and Revolution,* 102; Ken MacMillan, *Sovereignty and Possession in the English New World: The Legal Foundations of Empire, 1576–1640* (Cambridge: CUP, 2006), 103–4; Osgood, *American Colonies,* III:52–53; John Gorham Palfrey, *History of New England During the Stuart Dynasty* (Boston: Little, Brown, and Company, 1864), III:392.

83. "Proclamation by Charles I in Regard to Virginia," 13 May 1625, in *VMHB* 7, no. 2 (1899): 133.

84. John C. Kemp, ed., *Governor William Bradford's Letter Book Reprinted from the Mayflower Descendant* (Bedford, MA: Applewood Books, 2001), 20–21.

85. Alexander Moore, "Marooned: Politics and Revolution in the Bahamas Islands and Carolina," in *Creating and Contesting Carolina: Proprietary Era Histories,* ed. Michelle LeMaster and Bradford J. Wood (Columbia: University of South Carolina Press, 2013), 258; Lindley S. Butler, "The Early Settlement of Carolina: Virginia's Southern Frontier," *VMHB*

79, no. 1 (1971): 20–21; MacMillan, *Sovereignty and Possession*, 101; Paul E. Kopperman, "Profile of Failure: The Carolana Project, 1629–1640," *North Carolina Historical Review* 59, no. 1 (1982): 1–23; L. H. Roper, "New Albion: Anatomy of an English Colonisation Failure, 1632–1659," *Itinerario* 32, no. 1 (2008): 39–57.

86. Edmond Smith, *Merchants: The Community that Shaped England's Trade and Empire* (New Haven: YUP, 2021), 91–93, 183–84.

87. James A. Williamson, *The Caribbee Islands under the Proprietary Patents* (London: OUP, 1926), esp. 38–47; William Courteen to James I, n.d., repr. *The Torch and Colonial Book Circular* 1, 3 (March 1888), 90; Sarah Barber, *The Disputatious Caribbean: The West Indies in the Seventeenth Century* (New York: Palgrave Macmillan, 2014), 67–69; Andrews, *Trade, Plunder, and Settlement,* 301–2; MacCoinnich, *Plantation and Civility,* 317.

88. Alison Games, *The Web of Empire: English Cosmopolitans in an Age of Expansion, 1560–1660* (New York: OUP, 2008), 183; Rupali Mishra, *A Business of State: Commerce, Politics, and the Birth of the East India Company* (Cambridge, MA: HUP, 2018), 24, 272–301.

89. MacCoinnich, *Plantation and Civility,* 313–14.

90. Smith, "Global Interests," 579.

91. Kingsbury, ed., *Records,* IV:294.

92. Erik Odegard, *Patronage, Patrimonialism, and Governors' Careers in the Dutch Chartered Companies* (Boston: Brill, 2022), 33, 44, 56.

93. Arel, *English Trade and Adventure to Russia,* 27.

94. William Welwod, "Of the Community and Propriety of the Seas" (1613) in *The Free Sea, trans. Richard Hakluyt, with William Welwod's Critique and Grotius's Reply,* ed. David Armitage (Indianapolis: Liberty Fund, 2004), 65.

95. Alison Games, *Inventing the English Massacre: Amboyna in History and Memory* (New York: OUP, 2020); Adam Clulow, *Amboina, 1623: Fear and Conspiracy on the Edge of Empire* (New York: Columbia University Press, 2019).

96. MacCoinnich, *Plantation and Civility,* 266, 272–73, 343–44, 462–68, 475–79, Alexander quoted at 280.

97. *Acts of the Parliament of Scotland, Vol. V* ([London]: House of Commons, 1817), 221 (30 July 1630); John R. Elder, *The Royal Fishery Companies of the Seventeenth Century* (Glasgow: James Maclehose and Sons, 1912), 35–39, 55–56, 62, chaps. 3–4; MacCoinnich, *Plantation and Civility,* 312n81, 313, 317, 324–25, 502–4; Allan I. Macinnes, *Union and Empire: The Making of the United Kingdom in 1707* (Cambridge: CUP, 2007), 141n12.

98. John Bruce, ed. *Calendar of State Papers, Domestic Series, of the Reign of Charles I 1631–1633* (London: Longman, Green, Longman & Roberts, 1862), 482 ("great territory"); Sainsbury, ed., *Calendar of State Papers,* 166–71; Elder, *Royal Fishery Companies,* 37–39, 49–51, 55–56; MacCoinnich, *Plantation and Civility,* 321, 325, 490, 491 ("settle collonyes"); Cell, *English Enterprise,* 112; Scott, *Constitution and Finance,* I:203.

99. P. Hume Brown, ed., *The Register of the Privy Council of Scotland, A.D. 1630–1632,* 2nd ser., Vol. IV (Edinburgh: H.M. General Register House, 1902), 57; David Armitage, *The Ideological Origins of the British Empire* (Cambridge: CUP, 2000), 115; Elder, *Royal Fishery Companies,* 70–71; Thomas Wemyss Fulton, *The Sovereignty of the Sea: An Historical Account of the Claims of England to the British Seas, and of the evolution of the Territorial Waters* (Edinburgh: Blackwood, 1911), 19–20.

100. Elder, *Royal Fishery Companies,* 71, 83.

101. MacCoinnich, *Plantation and Civility* 323–25, 333, 346–47; Elder, *Royal Fishery Companies,* 51, 58–76, 63–64, 77–83.

102. Cell, *English Enterprise,* 114–15; Miller Christy, "Attempts towards Colonization: The Council for New England and the Merchant Venturers of Bristol, 1621–1623," *American Historical Review* 4, no. 4 (1899): 699–700n1; Rabb, *Enterprise and Empire,* 224; MacMillan, *Sovereignty and Possession,* 83.

103. "Reference in favour of Seignior L'Amey anent the fishinge," 7 March 1645, in *The Records of the Parliaments of Scotland to 1707,* ed. K. M. Brown et al. (St. Andrews, 2007–2021), 1645/1/174, www.rps.ac.uk/trans/1645/1/174; Elder, *Royal Fishery Companies,* 84.

104. Felicia Gottmann and Philip Stern, "Introduction: Crossing Companies," *Journal of World History* 31, no. 3 (2020): 1–12.

105. L. J. Coornaert, "European Economic Institutions and the New World; the Chartered Companies," in *The Cambridge Economic History of Europe from the Decline of the Roman Empire: Vol. 4, The Economy of Expanding Europe in the Sixteenth and Seventeenth Centuries,* ed. E. E. Rich and C. H. Wilson (Cambridge: CUP, 1967), 227–28, 234–46.

106. Martine van Ittersum, *Profit and Principle: Hugo Grotius, Natural Rights Theories and the Rise of Dutch Power in the East Indies, 1595–1615* (Leiden: Brill, 2006), 151–53; J. G. Van Dillen, "Isaac le maire et le commerce des actions de la compagnie des indes orientales," *Revue d'histoire moderne* 10, no. 16 (1935): 5–21; Lodewijk Petram, *The World's First Stock Exchange,* trans. Lynn Richards (New York: Columbia University Press, 2014), ch. 4.

107. Mark L. Thompson, *The Contest for the Delaware Valley: Allegiance, Identity, and Empire in the Seventeenth Century* (Baton Rouge: Louisiana State University Press, 2013), ch. 2; Coornaert, "European Economic Institutions," 246.

108. *Publication of Guiana's Plantation Newly undertaken by the Right Honble. The Earle of Barkshire* ([London]: William Jones, 1632); Lorimer, *English and Irish Settlement,* 101–3, 116–17.

109. Brenner, *Merchants and Revolution,* 163–64, 174; Carr, *Select Charters,* xliv.

110. Robin Law, "The First Scottish Guinea Company, 1634–9," *Scottish Historical Review* 76, no. 202, pt. 2 (1997): 185–202.

111. Sainsbury, ed., *Calendar of State Papers,* 135–36; Warren M. Billings, *Sir William Berkeley and the Forging of Colonial Virginia* (Baton Rouge: Louisiana State University Press, 2004), 17, 86–88; J Thornton, "Thrusting out,", 14–17; Musselwhite, *Urban Dreams,* 66–67;

112. W. L. Grant and James Munro, eds., *Acts of the Privy Council of England, Colonial Series, Vol. I: A.D. 1613–1680* (Hereford: HMSO, 1908), 204 (22 July 1634).

113. W. N. Sainsbury, "Virginia in 1631," *VMHB* 8, no. 1 (1900): 28–29; Brenner, *Merchants and Revolution,* 121–24; Antoinette Sutto, "The Borders of Absolutism: Restoration Politics, Royal Authority, and the Maryland-Pennsylvania Boundary Conflict, 1681–1685," *Pennsylvania History: A Journal of Mid-Atlantic Studies* 76, no. 3 (2009): 280–81.

114. Scott, *Constitution and Finance,* II:302–3.

115. Christy, "Attempts," 686–90; Insh, *Scottish Colonial Schemes,* 58.

116. Bailyn, *New England Merchants,* 8.

117. R. A. Preston, "The Laconia Company of 1629: An English Attempt to Intercept the Fur Trade," *Canadian Historical Review* 31, no. 2 (1950): 125–44; Bailyn, *New England Merchants,* 49–51; Insh, *Scottish Colonial Schemes,* 39; John Frederick Martin, *Profits in the Wilderness: Founding of New England Towns in the Seventeenth Century* (Chapel Hill: UNCP/OIEAHC, 1991), 102.

118. Frances Farnham, ed., *Documentary History of the State of Maine, Vol. VII: Containing the Farnham Papers, 1603–1688* (Portland: Thurston Print, 1901), 135; Hannah Farber, "The Rise and Fall of the Province of Lygonia, 1643–1658," *New England Quarterly* 82, no. 3 (2009): 490–513; Victor C. Sanborn, *Stephen Bachiler and the Plough Company of 1630* (Exeter: William Pollard & co., 1903).

119. Daniel C. Beaver, "'Fruits of Unrulie Multitudes': Liberty, Popularity, and Meanings of Violence in the English Atlantic, 1623–1625," *Journal of British Studies* 59 (2020): 372–95; Andrews, *Trade, Plunder, and Settlement,* 332–33; Scott, *Constitution and Finance,* II:304.

120. "The Charter of Massachusetts Bay—1629," in *The Federal and State Constitutions, Colonial Charters, and Other Organic Laws of the States, Territories, and Colonies Now or Heretofore Forming the United States of America,* ed. Francis Newton Thorpe (Washington, DC: Government Printing Office, 1909), III:1851; Andrews, *Trade, Plunder, and Settlement,* 333.

121. James Sherley, William Collier, Thomas Fletcher, and Robert Holland to The General Society of Plymouth in New England, 18 December 1624, in *Bradford's Letter Book,* ed. Kemp, 8.

122. James Sherley and Thomas Hatherley to Plymouth in New England, 19 March 1629 [or 1630], in *Bradford's Letter Book,* ed. Kemp, 51–52; Bradford, *Of Plymouth Plantation,*

184–85; Haig Z. Smith, *Religion and Governance in England's Emerging Colonial Empire, 1601–1698* (Cham: Palgrave Macmillan, 2022), 79–81.

123. Peter Mancall, *The Trials of Thomas Morton: An Anglican Lawyer, His Puritan Foes, and the Battle for a New England* (New Haven: YUP, 2019), 123–30; Cynthia J. Van Zandt, *Brothers among Nations: The Pursuit of Intercultural Alliances in Early America, 1580–1660* (New York: OUP, 2008), 102–3.

124. Charles MacLean Andrews, *British Committees, Commissions, and Councils of Trade and Plantations, 1622–1675* (Baltimore: JHUP, 1908), 14–18.

125. Mark Peterson, *The City-State of Boston: The Rise and Fall of an Atlantic Power, 1630–1865* (Princeton: PUP, 2019), 85, 139.

126. Ronald Dale Karr, "The Missing Clause: Myth and the Massachusetts Bay Charter of 1629," *New England Quarterly* 77, no. 1 (2004): 89–107.

127. BL Egerton MS 2495 fols. 27–29; CO 1/9 f. 127; Mancall, *Trials*, 129; Evan Haefeli, *Accidental Pluralism: America and the Religious Politics of English Expansion, 1497–1662* (Chicago: University of Chicago Press, 2021), 173.

128. Roger Williams, *The Bloudy Tenet of Persecution, for Cause of Conscience Discussed, in A Conference Betweene Truth and Peace* (London, 1644), ed. Edward Bean Underhill (London: J. Haddon, 1848), 46.

129. Martin, *Profits*, 59, 131–32, 137–49; Richard Bushman, *From Puritan to Yankee: Character and the Social Order in Connecticut, 1690–1765* (Cambridge, MA: HUP, 1967), 44–45.

130. Simeon E. Baldwin, "American Business Corporations Before 1789," *American Historical Review* 8, no. 3 (1903): 451–52.

131. Margaret Ellen Newell, *From Dependency to Independence: Economic Revolution in Colonial New England* (Ithaca, NY: Cornell University Press, 1998), 56–58; Newell, "Robert Child and the Entrepreneurial Vision: Economy and Ideology in Early New England," *New England Quarterly* 68, no. 2 (1995), 235, 239–40; Martin, *Profits*, 19.

132. Louise A. Breen, *Transgressing the Bounds: Subversive Enterprises Among the Puritan Elite in Massachusetts, 1630–1692* (New York: OUP, 2001), 3–4, 11; Louise A. Breen, "Religious Radicalism in the Puritan Officer Corps: Heterodoxy, the Artillery Company, and Cultural Integration in Seventeenth-Century Boston," *New England Quarterly* 68, no. 1 (1995): 3–43.

133. James Kendall Hosmer, ed., *Winthrop's Journal "History of New England," 1630–1649* (New York: Charles Scribner's Sons, 1908), II:164; Nathaniel B. Shurtleff, ed., *Records of the Governor and Company of Massachusetts Bay in New England* (Boston: William White, 1853), II:60; Breen, *Transgressing the Bounds*, 129–30; Newell, "Robert Child," 234; Bailyn, *New England Merchants*, 51–52.

134. Charles J. Hoadly, *The Warwick Patent* (Hartford: Hartford Press, 1902), 8–12, 15–24; Kupperman, *Providence Island*, 325–32; Sabine Klein, "'They Have Invaded the Whole River': Boundary Negotiations in Anglo-Dutch Colonial Discourse," *Early American Studies* 9, no. 2 (2011): 324–47. Ronald Dale Karr, "'Why Should You Be So Furious?': The Violence of the Pequot War," *Journal of American History* 85, no. 3 (1998): 897.

135. Kupperman, *Providence Island*, 21, 28–29, 33, 55–57, 118–29; Musselwhite, "Private Plantation," 160.

136. Barber, *Disputatious Caribbean*, 67; Brenner, *Merchants and Revolution*, 67, 256–68, Coke quoted at 257; John C. Appleby, "An Association for the West Indies? English Plans for a West India Company 1621–29," *Journal of Imperial and Commonwealth History* 15 (1987): 213–41; Smith, *Merchants*, 221–22.

137. Sainsbury, ed., *Calendar of State Papers*, 317–20; Brenner, *Merchants and Revolution*, 302; Kupperman, *Providence Island*, 94–100, 103, 109, 169–73, 296, 307–9, 314–15; Craven, "Earl of Warwick," 470; Jarvis, *In the Eye*, 45.

138. Brenner, *Merchants and Revolution*, 158–59, 301–2; Kupperman, *Providence Island*, 70, 98, 174, 167, 173–74, 199, 201, 281–82, 295, 297–99, 302, 309, 311, 314–19, 323, 335, 367–69; Scott, *Constitution and Finance*, I:201.

139. Sainsbury, ed., *Calendar of State Papers*, 305 (9 December 1639); Kupperman, *Providence Island*, 299, 304.

140. Geraldine M. Phipps, "The Russian Embassy to London of 1645–46 and the Abrogation of the Muscovy Company's Charter," *Slavonic and East European Review* 68, no. 2 (1990): 257–76.

141. *Concise View,* 60–61; Archer, "City of London," 79–80, 93; Ohlmeyer, "Strafford," 209, 224–27.

142. Peterson, *City-State,* 140–45; "Charter of 1650" (1650), Harvard University Archives UAI 15.100, http://id.lib.harvard.edu/via/olvwork368905/catalog; "An Act for Incorporating of Harvard College, At Cambridge, New England," 27 June 1692, *The Acts and Resolves, Public and Private, of the Province of Massachusetts Bay,* ed. A. C. Goodell (Boston: Wright & Potter, 1869), I:39; *Records of the Governor and Company of the Massachusetts Bay in New England, Vol. III: 1644–1657* (Boston: William White, 1854), 299.

143. Sainsbury, ed., *Calendar of State Papers,* 414 (16 March 1654); Vincent T. Harlow, *A History of Barbados, 1625–1685* (Oxford: Clarendon Press, 1926), 28.

144. Kupperman, *Providence Island,* 347, 350–51, quotation at 319; Alfred D. Chandler, "The Expansion of Barbados," *Journal of the Barbados Museum and Historical Society* 13, no. 3 (1934): 112.

145. John Donoghue, *Fire Under the Ashes: An Atlantic History of the English Revolution* (Chicago: University of Chicago Press, 2013), 221–22.

146. Wesley Frank Craven, *The Southern Colonies in the Seventeenth Century, 1607–1689* (Baton Rouge: Louisiana State University Press, 1949), 254, 258.

147. Billings, *Sir William Berkeley,* 105–06; Andrews, *British Committees,* 21.

148. Ruth Moynihan, "The Patent and the Indians: The Problem of Jurisdiction in Seventeenth Century New England," *American Indian Culture and Research Journal* 2, no. 1 (1977): 11–13.

149. Brenner, *Merchants and Revolution,* 523–24; Jarvis, *In the Eye,* 45, 49; Moore, "Marooned," 258.

150. BL Egerton MS 2395, f. 87; Sainsbury, ed., *Calendar of State Papers,* 257 (September? 1637), 475 (26 August 1659), Brenner, *Merchants and Revolution,* 301; Kupperman, *Providence Island,* 343.

151. L. H. Roper, *Advancing Empire: English Interests and Overseas Expansion, 1613–1688* (Cambridge: CUP, 2017), 80–84.

152. Carr, *Select Charters,* xlv; Scott, *Constitution and Finance,* I:246–50.

153. Andrews, *British Committees,* 53.

154. Alden T. Vaughan, *New England Frontier: Puritans and Indians, 1620–1675,* 3rd ed. (Norman: University of Oklahoma Press, 1995), 270–71.

155. *Concise View,* 61–62.

156. David Brown, "The Sea Venture to Munster and Connacht, July and August 1642," in *Ireland in Crisis: War, Politics and Religion, 1641–50,* ed. Patrick Little (Manchester: Manchester University Press, 2020); David Brown, *Empire and Enterprise: Money, Power, and the Adventurers for Irish Land During the British Civil Wars* (Manchester: Manchester University Press, 2020), 116–17; Brenner, *Merchants and Revolution,* 400–410; Kupperman, *Providence Island,* 344; Horning, *Ireland,* 266–67.

157. Robert Hunt, *The Island of Assada Neere Madagascar Impartially Defined* ([London]: Nicholas Bourne, 1650); Brenner, *Merchants and Revolution,* 170–71, 177–78; Donoghue, *Fire Under the Ashes,* 213–21; Games, *Web of Empire,* 208–18; Kupperman, *Providence Island,* 342; Mishra, *Business of State,* 301; Roper, *Advancing Empire,* 146–49.

158. Ethel Bruce Sainsbury, ed., *A Calendar of Court Minutes etc., of the East India Company, 1644–1649* (Oxford: Clarendon Press, 1912), xxv.

159. John Shaw, ed., *Charters Relating to the East India Company from 1600 to 1761, Reprinted from a Former Collection with Some Additions and a Preface* (Madras: R. Hill at the Government Press, 1887), v.

160. Sainsbury, ed., *Calendar of Court Minutes,* 78, 335; Brenner, *Merchants and Revolution,* 178–81, 516–17, 610–12; William A. Pettigrew and Tristan Stein, "The Public Rivalry Between Regulated and Joint Stock Corporations and the Development of Seventeenth-Century Corporate Constitutions," *Historical Research* 90, no. 248 (2017): 349.

161. Brown, *Empire and Enterprise,* 213–16.

3. Corporate Finance

Epigraph: Peter Colleton to John Locke, 28 May 1673, in Langdon Cheves, ed., *The Shaftesbury Papers and Other Records Relating to Carolina and the First Settlement on Ashley River Prior to the Year 1676, Collections of the South Carolina Historical Society, Volume V* (Charleston: South Carolina Historical Society, 1897), 423.

1. Edward Hyde, *The Life of Edward Earl of Clarendon, Lord High Chancellor of England and Chancellor of the University of Oxford,* Vol. I (Oxford: Clarendon, 1817), 282.

2. Philip J. Stern, *The Company-State: Corporate Sovereignty and the Early Modern Foundations of the British Empire in India* (New York: OUP, 2011), 21–27.

3. [Daniel Defoe], *An Essay Upon Projects* (London: R.R. for Tho. Cockerill, 1697), 20; Vera Keller and Ted McCormick, "Towards a History of Projects," *Early Science and Medicine* 21, no. 5 (2016): 425–29, 435; Paul Slack, *The Invention of Improvement: Information and Material Progress in Seventeenth-Century England* (Oxford: OUP, 2015), 173–74; Koji Yamamoto, *Taming Capitalism before Its Triumph: Public Service, Distrust, and "Projecting" in Early Modern England* (Oxford: OUP, 2018).

4. Mordechai Feingold, "Projectors and Learned Projects in Early Modern England," *Seventeenth Century* 32, no. 1 (2017); Noah Moxham, "Natural Knowledge, Inc.: The Royal Society as a Metropolitan Corporation," *BJHS* 52, no. 2 (2019): 250, 253, 254, 255–62, 266–70; Phil Withington, *Society in Early Modern England: The Vernacular Origins of Some Powerful Ideas* (Cambridge: Polity, 2010), 121, 237.

5. Christopher Wren (Jr.), *Parentalia: or, Memoirs of the Family of the Wrens* (London: T. Osborn and R. Dodsley, 1750), 196–97.

6. [Robert Ferguson], *The East-India-Trade. A Most Profitable Trade to the Kingdom. And Best Secured and Improved in a Company, and a Joint-Stock* (London, 1677), 25; Thomas Sprat, *The History of the Royal-Society of London for the Improving of Natural Knowledge* (London, J. Martyn, 1667), 76; Moxham, "Natural Knowledge, Inc.," 263.

7. Moxham, "Natural Knowledge, , Inc." 253.

8. Gabriel Glickman, "Protestantism, Colonization, and the New England Company in Restoration Politics," *HJ* 59, no. 2 (2016): 365–91; William Kellaway, *The New England Company, 1649–1776: Missionary Society to the American Indians* (London: Longmans, Green and Co., 1961), 46, 50; Alden T. Vaughan, *New England Frontier: Puritans and Indians, 1620–1675,* 3rd ed. (Norman: University of Oklahoma Press, 1995), 274–75.

9. Richard S. Dunn, *Puritans and Yankees: The Winthrop Dynasty of New England, 1630–1717* (Princeton: PUP, 1962), 130, 142, 143–44; Richard S. Dunn, "John Winthrop, Jr., and the Narragansett Country," *WMQ* 13, no. 1 (1956), 74–76.

10. J. Hammond Trumbull, ed., *The Public Records of the Colony of Connecticut, from 1665 to 1678* (Hartford: F.A. Brown, 1852), II:541–42; III: Appendix VII; Dunn, "John Winthrop, Jr.," 69–70, 82; Julie A. Fisher and David J. Silverman, *Ninigret, Sachem of the Niantics and Narragansetts: Diplomacy, War, and the Balance of Power in Seventeenth-Century New England and Indian Country* (Ithaca, NY: Cornell University Press, 2014); John Frederick Martin, *Profits in the Wilderness: Founding of New England Towns in the Seventeenth Century* (Chapel Hill: UNCP/OIEAHC, 1991), 62; James A. Warren, *God, War, and Providence: The Epic Struggle of Roger Williams and the Narragansett Indians against the Puritans of New England* (New York: Scribner, 2018), 192–93.

11. Quoted by Dunn, *Puritans and Yankees,* 134.

12. Dunn, *Puritans and Yankees,* 141; Dunn, "John Winthrop, Jr.," 78–82; Cecil T. Carr, *Select Charters of Trading Companies, A.D. 1530–1707* (London: Bernard Quaritch, 1913), lxxxix.

13. Mary Sarah Bilder, *The Transatlantic Constitution: Colonial Legal Culture and the Empire* (Cambridge, MA: HUP, 2004), 48–49; Bilder, "Salamanders and Sons of God: The Culture of Appeal in Early New England," in *Many Legalities of Early America,* ed. Bruce H. Mann and Christopher L. Tomlins (Chapel Hill: UNCP/OIEAHC, 2001), 59–60, 66–67.

14. John Romeyn Brodhead, ed., *Documents Relative to the Colonial History of the State of New-York* (Albany: Weed, Parsons, and Company, 1853), III:55; Dunn, *Puritans and Yankees*, 142.

15. W. L. Grant and James Munro, eds., *Acts of the Privy Council of England, Colonial Series, Vol. I: A.D. 1613–1680* (Hereford: HMSO, 1908), 580 (3 July 1672); Richard S. Dunn, "John Winthrop, Jr., Connecticut Expansionist: The Failure of His Designs on Long Island, 1663–1675," *New England Quarterly* 29, 1 (1956): 3–26; Dunn, "John Winthrop, Jr. and the Narragansett Country," 84–85; Mark Peterson, *The City-State of Boston: The Rise and Fall of an Atlantic Power, 1630–1865* (Princeton: PUP, 2019), 149–52.

16. *Collections of the Massachusetts Historical Society, Vol. IX, Fifth Series: The Trumbull Papers* (Boston: Massachusetts Historical Society, 1885), 47; Richard L. Bushman, *From Puritan to Yankee: Character and the Social Order in Connecticut, 1690–1765* (Cambridge, MA: HUP, 1967), 29–30, 42–43; Glickman, "Protestantism, Colonization," 377; Martin, *Profits*, 33, 71, 81, 151.

17. *Trumbull Papers*, 123–27 (5 March 1683/4); Trumbull, ed., *Public Records*, 281–82; Jenny Hale Pulsipher, *Swindler Sachem: The American Indian Who Sold His Birthright, Dropped Out of Harvard, and Conned the King of England* (New Haven: YUP, 2018), 210–14, 222–33.

18. *Trumbull Papers*, 129–31 (16 June 1684).

19. Herbert Levi Osgood, *The American Colonies in the Seventeenth Century* (New York: Macmillan & Co., 1904), I:530.

20. Philopatris, *A Treatise Wherein is Demonstrated That the East-India Trade is the Most National of Foreign Trades* (London, 1681), 33.

21. Stern, *Company-State*, 51–54

22. *Trumbull Papers*, 129–31 (16 June 1684).

23. "Instructions to Berkeley, 1662," *VMHB* 3, no. 1 (1895): 15, 17, 19–20 (12 September 1662).

24. William L. Saunders, ed., *The Colonial Records Of North Carolina* (Raleigh: P. M. Hale, 1886), I:39 (12 August 1663); Nicholas Blake to Charles II, 5 January 1671, CO 1/26 fols. 8–9; Wesley Frank Craven, *The Southern Colonies in the Seventeenth Century, 1607–1689* (Baton Rouge: Louisiana State University Press, 1949), 316–18, 329–30; Justin Roberts and Ian Beamish, "Venturing Out: The Barbadian Diaspora and the Carolina Colony, 1650–1685," in *Creating and Contesting Carolina: Proprietary Era Histories,* ed. Michelle LeMaster and Bradford J. Wood (Columbia: University of South Carolina Press, 2013), 52–54; Simon P. Newman, *A New World of Labor: The Development of Plantation Slavery in the British Atlantic* (Philadelphia: UPenn, 2013), 251–52.

25. Saunders, ed., *Colonial Records,* I:36–42 (6 August 1663); *Trumbull Papers,* 55–59 (6 August 1663); Alfred D. Chandler, "The Expansion of Barbados," *Journal of the Barbados Museum and Historical Society* 13, no. 3 (1934), 123–24; Craven, *Southern Colonies,* 329–33.

26. Vicki Hsueh, *Hybrid Constitutions: Challenging Legacies of Law, Privilege, and Culture in Colonial America* (Durham, NC: DUP, 2010), 55–82.

27. George Milner, "Proposals in order to the improvement of the county of Albemarle in the Province of Carolina in point of Townes, Trade, and Coyne," BL Egerton MS 2395 ff. 661–65; Paul Musselwhite, *Urban Dreams, Rural Commonwealth: The Rise of Plantation Society in the Chesapeake* (Chicago: University of Chicago Press, 2018), 4, 139–40.

28. David Armitage, "John Locke: Theorist of Empire?" in *Empire and Modern Political Thought,* ed. Sankar Muthu (Cambridge: CUP, 2012), 89; Craven, *Southern Colonies,* 324, 343–44; Michael J. Jarvis, *In the Eye of All Trade: Bermuda, Bermudians, and the Maritime Atlantic World, 1680–1783* (Chapel Hill: UNCP), 45; Alexander Moore, "Marooned: Politics and Revolution in the Bahamas Islands and Carolina," in *Creating and Contesting Carolina,* ed. LeMaster and Wood, 259–60.

29. Craven, *Southern Colonies,* 334–36; Chandler, "Expansion," 128–30.

30. Verner W. Crane, *The Southern Frontier, 1670–1732* (Durham, NC: DUP, 1928), 118, 140; Daniel W. Fagg Jr., "St. Giles' Seigniory: The Earl of Shaftesbury's Carolina Plantation," *South Carolina Historical Magazine,* 71, no. 2 (1970): 117–23.

31. W. Noel Sainsbury, ed., *Calendar of State Papers, Colonial Series, America and the West Indies, 1661–1668* (London: HMSO, 1880), vol. 5, 13 (20 February 1661), 26–27 (1 April 1661), 541–42 (23 January 1668); Larry Gragg, *"Englishmen Transplanted": The English Colonization of Barbados, 1627–1660* (Oxford: OUP, 2003), 56.

32. Nicholas Blake to Charles II, 28 February 1669, CO 1/67 fol. 327v; W. Noel Sainsbury, *Calendar of State Papers, Colonial Series, America and the West Indies, 1669–1674* (London: HMSO, 1889), 134 (17 November 1670); Richard Dunn, "The Glorious Revolution and America," in *Oxford History of the British Empire, Vol. I: The Origins of Empire*, ed. Nicholas Canny (Oxford: OUP, 2001), 447.

33. Hendrik Hartog, *Public Property and Private Power: The Corporation of the City of New York in American Law, 1730–1870* (Chapel Hill: UNCP, 1983), 14; Simon Middleton, *From Privileges to Rights: Work and Politics in Colonial New York City* (Philadelphia: UPenn, 2006), 76, 153–54.

34. Daniel J. Hulsebosch, *Constituting Empire: New York and the Transformation of Constitutionalism in the Atlantic World, 1664–1830* (Chapel Hill: UNCP, 2005), 43.

35. Maxine N. Lurie, "New Jersey: The Long Lived Proprietary," in *Constructing Early Modern Empires: Proprietary Ventures in the Atlantic World, 1500–1700*, ed. L. H. Roper and B. Van Ruymbeke (Leiden: Brill, 2007), 330–35; John E. Pomfret, *The Province of East Jersey, 1609–1702: The Rebellious Proprietary* (Princeton: PUP, 1962), 130–33; G. D. Scull, "Biographical Notice of Doctor Daniel Coxe, of London," *PMHB* 7, no. 3 (1883): 335; Frederick R. Black, "The West Jersey Society, 1768–1784," *PMHB* 97, no. 3 (1973): 379–80; John Strassburger, "Our Unhappy Purchase: The West Jersey Society, Lewis Morris and Jersey Lands, 1703–36," *New Jersey History* 98, no. 1 (1980): 98; William McClure, "The West Jersey Society, 1692–1736," *Proceedings of the New Jersey Historical Society* 74, no. 1 (1956): 3–4.

36. William Penn, *The Case of William Penn, Esq; Proprietary-Governor of Pensilvania; and of Joshua Gee, Henry Gouldney, Silvanus Grove, John Woods, and others, mortgagees under the said William Penn* (London, 1720).

37. "Charter of Incorporation for Free Society of Traders and the Grant of a Manor of Franke" [copy], Society Miscellaneous Collection, HSP 0425, box 6B, folder 11, p. 3; Gary Nash, "The Free Society of Traders and the Early Politics of Pennsylvania," *PMHB* 89, no. 2 (1965): 154, 163.

38. Crane, *Southern Frontier,* 50–54; Owen Stanwood, *The Global Refuge: Huguenots in an Age of Empire* (New York: OUP, 2020), 128; Albright G. Zimmerman, ed., "Daniel Coxe and the New Mediterranean Sea Company," *PMHB* 76, no. 1 (1952): 89, 94.

39. Kristen Beales, "Commercial Theologies and the Problem of Bubbles: The Pennsylvania Land Company and the Quaker Debate on Financial Ethics," *Eighteenth-Century Studies* 53, no. 1 (2020): 126.

40. *Minutes of the Provincial Council of Pennsylvania* (Harrisburg: Theophilus Fenn, 1838), II:8 (5 January 1701); Francis Daniel Pastorius, "The Case of the Frankfort Company's Business Briefly Stated," n.d., Francis Daniel Pastorius Papers, HSP 0475, Vol. 2; "A Translation of the Francfort Companies Contract of Society," Francis Daniel Pastorius Papers, HSP 0475, Vol. 2, C.

41. Howard Lee McBain, "The Legal Status of the American Colonial City," *Political Science Quarterly* (June 1925): 186–87; Jon C. Teaford, *The Municipal Revolution in America: Origins of Modern Urban Government, 1650–1825* (Chicago: University of Chicago Press, 1975).

42. Judith Diamondstone, "The Philadelphia Corporation, 1701–1776," PhD thesis, University of Pennsylvania, 1969.

43. Philip J. Stern, "The Corporation and the Global Seventeenth-Century English Empire: A Tale of Three Cities," *Early American Studies* 16, no. 1 (Winter 2018): 41–63.

44. Musselwhite, *Urban Dreams,* 131–32.

45. Quoted in Tristan Stein, "Tangier in the Restoration Empire," *HJ* 54, no. 4 (2011): 999.

46. London to Madras, 28 September 1687, IOR E/3/91 f. 213.

47. Mary Maples Dunn and Richard Dunn, eds., *The Papers of William Penn* (Philadelphia: UPenn, 1981–1987), 1:139, 2:119, 146.

48. Tangier Commissioners to Mayor and Recorder of Tangier, 4 May 1674, BL Sloane 3512 f. 46v.

49. Phil Withington, *The Politics of Commonwealth: Citizens and Freemen in Early Modern England* (Cambridge: CUP, 2005), 18–19.

50. Jessica Choppin Roney, *Governed by a Spirit of Opposition: The Origins of American Political Practice in Colonial Philadelphia* (Baltimore: JHUP, 2014); "The Humble Petition of the Inhabitants of Germantownship to the Honourable Thomas Penn Esquire one of the Proprietors of the Province of Pensilvania &c.," [n.d.], HSP 0425, box 6A, folder 10.

51. Petition of Freemen of Tangier [1676], BL Sloane 3512, f. 271; Alexander Hamilton, *A New Account of the East Indies*, 2 vols. (Edinburgh: J. Mosman, 1727), 1:361.

52. F. H. Blackburne Daniell, ed., *Calendar of State Papers Domestic Series, March 1st 1676 to February 28th 1677* (London: HMSO, 1909), 154–55 (12 June 1676), 574 (28 February 1677); Carr, *Select Charters*, cvi, 183–86; Charles MacLean Andrews, *British Committees, Commissions, and Councils of Trade and Plantations, 1622–1675* (Baltimore: JHUP, 1908), 84; John R. Elder, *The Royal Fishery Companies of the Seventeenth Century* (Glasgow: James Maclehose and Sons, 1912), 98–106, 110–15; 127–28; J. Keith Horsfield, "The Origins of Blackwell's Model of a Bank," *WMQ* 23, no. 1 (1966): 127–29.

53. "Mr Lukes reasons against the erecting of a Morocco Company," "Reasons against the erecting of a Morocco Company by Mr. Povey," and "The Merchants Reasons Against the Morocco Company," Sloane MS 1956 fols, 45, 50v–51v, 61v–64v; Sainsbury, ed., *Calendar 1661–1668*, 56 (11 September 1661); E. M. G. Routh, *Tangier: England's Lost Atlantic Outpost* (London: John Murray, 1912), 20–21; Stein, "Tangier," 990–94.

54. Ethel Bruce Sainsbury, *A Calendar of the Court Minutes of the East India Company, 1660–1663* (Oxford: Clarendon Press, 1922), 250–51 (3 September 1662), 260–63 (11, 15, and 16 October 1662); *The Case of Sir John and Mr. Charles Crisp, Grandsons of Sir Nicholas Crisp, in Relation to the Forts and Castles of Africa* (London, 1709).

55. "His Majest. Royall charter to the Governor and Company of Hudson's Bay," CO 135/1 ff. 7-19; Hudson's Bay Company to King Charles II, [November 1682], CO 135/1 f. 20v; Edward Cavanagh, "A Company with Sovereignty and Subjects of Its Own? The Case of the Hudson's Bay Company," *Canadian Journal of Law and Society* 26, no. 1 (2011): 29-30.

56. Hyde, *Life*, III:144.

57. Mary Anne Everett Green, ed., *Calendar of State Papers, Domestic Series, October 1668 to December 1669* (London: HMSO, 1894), 459 (25 August 1669); Andrews, *British Committees*, 68; Carr, *Select Charters*, xlv–xlvii, 172–77; 180; Steven C. A. Pincus, *Protestantism and Patriotism: Ideologies and the Making of English Foreign Policy, 1650–1668* (Cambridge: CUP, 1996), 247; Paul Seaward, "The House of Commons Committee of Trade and the Origins of the Second Anglo-Dutch War, 1664," *HJ* 30, no. 2 (1987): 440; William Robert Scott, *The Constitution and Finance of English, Scottish and Irish Joint-Stock Companies to 1720* (Cambridge: CUP, 1912), II:18–19; George Frederick Zook, "The Company of Royal Adventurers of England Trading Into Africa, 1660–1672," *Journal of Negro History* 4, no. 2 (1919): 144, 149–51, 156–58, 196–97, 209–10, 218–19; K. G. Davies, *The Royal African Company* (London: Longmans, Green, 1957), 47–79; Holly Brewer, "Creating a Common Law of Slavery for England and its New World Empire," *Law and History Review* 39, no. 4 (2021): 782–83.

58. "At a Generall meeting of the subscribers to the stock of the Royal Company, holden at Drapers-Hall the 19th of December 1671," TNA PRO 30/24/49 no. 18; Zook, "Company of Royal Adventurers," 158–62; Scott, *Constitution and Finance*, I: 283, II:19–20.

59. Carr, *Select Charters*, xlvii, 191–92; Scott, *Constitution and Finance*, I:283, II:20–21.

60. Cavanagh, "A Company with Sovereignty and Subjects of Its Own?," 30–34.

61. Andrews, *British Committees*, 68; Elizabeth Mancke, "Chartered Enterprises and the Evolution of the British Atlantic World," in *The Creation of the British Atlantic World*, ed. Elizabeth Mancke and Carole Shammas (Baltimore: JHUP, 2005), 250–52.

62. *The History and Proceedings of the House of Commons from the Restoration to the Present Time* (London: Richard Chandler, 1742), I:76; Andrews, *British Committees*, 86, 88–92; Seaward, "Committee of Trade," 445–47.

63. *The History and Proceedings of the House of Lords from the Restoration in 1660, to the Present Time* (London: Ebenezer Timberland, 1742), 19, 65; Andrews, *British Committees,* 64, 68–71, 82–83.

64. Andrews, *British Committees,* 67, 79–80, 91, 106–9, 128, 131; Ralph Paul Bieber, *The Lords of Trade and Plantations, 1675–1696* (Allentown, PA: H. Ray Haas, 1919), 40–43; Asheesh Kapur Siddique, "Governance through Documents: The Board of Trade, Its Archive, and the Imperial Constitution of the Eighteenth-Century British Atlantic World," *JBS* 59 (2020): 270–73.

65. Bieber, *Lords,* chap. 5; Bilder, *Transatlantic Constitution,* chap. 4.

66. Owen Stanwood, *Empire Reformed: English America in the Age of the Glorious Revolution* (Philadelphia: UPenn, 2011), 3; Andrews, *British Committees,* 104–5, 110; Ralph Paul Bieber, "The British Plantation Councils of 1670–4," *The English Historical Review* 40, no. 157 (1925): 104–5; Peterson, *City-State,* 153–58.

67. J. H. Lefroy, *Memorials of the Discovery and Early Settlement of the Bermudas or Somers Islands, 1514–1685,* 2 vols. (London: Longman, Green, and Co., 1877), II:477; W. L. Grant and James Munro, eds., *Acts of the Privy Council of England, Colonial Series, Vol. I: A.D. 1613–1680* (Hereford: HMSO, 1908), 869 (10 November 1679).

68. "Memorandum Concerning the Bermuda Company," [30 May 1683], CO 1/51 fol. 349; Jarvis, *In the Eye,* 52–61, 492n79–81, 494n84; Philip S. Haffenden, "The Crown and the Colonial Charters, 1675–1688: Part I," *WMQ* 15, no. 3 (Jul., 1958): 302–5; Richard S. Dunn, "The Downfall of the Bermuda Company: A Restoration Farce," *WMQ* 20, no. 4 (1963): 487–512.

69. "Memorandum Concerning the Bermuda Company," [30 May 1683], CO 1/51/118 f. 348; "State of the Proceedings Against the Bermuda Company," 1 November 1683, CO 1/53/57; "Opinion of the Attorney-General on the Petition of the Inhabitants of Bermuda," 7 June 1683, CO 1/51/59 fol. 347; "Sir George Jeffreys' opinion on the clause of the Bermuda Charter for choosing the Governor," 1 May 1683, CO 1/51/125 fol. 364.

70. W. Noel Sainsbury and J. W. Fortescue, eds., *Calendar of State Papers, Colonial Series, America and the West Indies, 1677–1680* (London: HMSO, 1896), 489 (11 February 1680); Craven, *Southern Colonies* 395; Jarvis, *In the Eye,* 60; Glickman, "Protestantism, Colonization," 382–83; Haffenden, "Charters, I," 305; Martin, *Profits,* 266.

71. Attorney-General to Mr. Wynne, 13 May 1684, CO 1/54/95; J. W. Fortescue, *Calendar of Colonial State Papers, Colonial Series, America and West Indies 1681–1685* (London: HMSO, 1898), 631 (13 May 1684); Blathwayt quoted in Robert M. Bliss, *Revolution and Empire: English Politics and the American Colonies in the Seventeenth Century* (Manchester: Manchester University Press, 1990), 236; Haffenden, "Charters, I," 304–10; Philip S. Haffenden, "The Crown and the Colonial Charters, 1675–1688: Part II," *WMQ* 15, no. 4 (1958): 452–66; Moore, "Marooned," 261–62; Peterson, *City-State,* 159–60.

72. William Pettigrew, *Freedom's Debt: The Royal African Company and the Politics of the Atlantic Slave Trade, 1672–1752* (Chapel Hill: UNCP, 2013), 29–31; Stern, *Company-State,* 59, 79–83.

73. Dunn, "The Glorious Revolution and America," 452.

74. Jeremiah Shepard and John Burrill, 3 February 1689/90, in *Exploring the Bounds of Liberty: Political Writings of Colonial British America from the Glorious Revolution to the American Revolution,* ed. Jack P. Greene and Craig B. Yirush (Indianapolis: Liberty Fund, 2019), I:167.

75. Brendan Bradshaw, *The Irish Constitutional Revolution of the Sixteenth Century* (Cambridge: CUP, 1979), esp. chs. 7–8; Christopher Maginn, "'Surrender and Regrant' in the Historiography of Sixteenth-Century Ireland," *Sixteenth Century Journal* 38, no. 4 (2007): 955–74; Jane Ohlmeyer, "Eastward Enterprises: Colonial Ireland, Colonial India," *Past and Present,* 240, no. 1 (2018): 83–118.

76. John Higginson and Stephen Sewall, 24 December 1689, in *Exploring,* ed. Greene and Yirush, 163.

77. *A Model for Erecting a Bank of Credit with a Discourse in Explanation Thereof* (London: J.A., 1688); Andrew McFarland Davis, "The Fund at Boston in New England,"

Proceedings of the American Antiquarian Society 15, no. 3 (1903): 368–84; Andrew Mc-Farland Davis, "Was it Andros?" *Proceedings of the American Antiquarian Society* (1907): 352–61; Dror Goldberg, "Why Was America's First Bank Aborted?" *Journal of Economic History* 71, no. 1 (March 2011): 214–15, 218; J. Keith Horsfield, "The Origins of Blackwell's Model of a Bank," *WMQ* 23, no. 1 (1966): 122–25, 129, 133; Newell, *Dependency*, 123–26; Mark Valeri, "William Petty in Boston: Political Economy, Religion, and Money in Provincial New England," *Early American Studies* 8, no. 3 (2010): 559–60.

78. H. R. McIlwaine, *Journals of the House of Burgessses of Virginia 1659/60–1693* (Richmond, 1914), 229.

79. Dunn, "Glorious Revolution," 445, 455–61; Peterson, *City-State,* 166–73.

80. Dunn, "Glorious Revolution," 461.

81. Eugene Sheridan, "Daniel Coxe and the Restoration of Proprietary Government in East Jersey, 1690—A Letter," *New Jersey History* 92, no. 2 (1974): 107.

82. Dunn, "Glorious Revolution," 460–65; I. K. Steele, "The Board of Trade, The Quakers, and Resumption of Colonial Charters, 1699–1702," *WMQ* 23, no. 4 (1966): 602–6.

83. A. C. Goodell, ed., *The Acts and Resolves, Public and Private, of the Province of Massachusetts Bay* (Boston: Wright & Potter, 1869), I:1, 7–8, 10; Jeremiah Dummer, *A Defence of the New-England Charters* (London: W. Wilkins, 1721), 4.

84. Goodell, ed., *Acts and Resolves,* I:39n, 290n, 308 (27 June 1692, 4 June 1697, 15 July 1700)

85. Gershom Bulkeley, "Will and Doom, or The Miseries of Connecticut by and under an Usurped and Arbitrary Power" (1692), in *Collections of the Connecticut Historical Society, Vol. III,* ed. Charles J. Hoadly (Hartford: Connecticut Historical Society, 1895), 103, 131–32, 192; Thomas W. Jodziewicz, "A Stranger in the Land: Gershom Bulkeley of Connecticut," *Transactions of the American Philosophical Society* 78, no. 2 (1988): 31–33, 46–49.

86. Elder, *Royal Fishery,* 115.

87. William A. Pettigrew and George W. Van Cleve, "Parting Companies: The Glorious Revolution, Company Power, and Imperial Mercantilism," *HJ* 57, no. 3 (2014): 617–38; Michael Wagner, "The Levant Company under Attack in Parliament, 1720–53," *Parliamentary History* 34, no. 3 (2015): 295–313; Michael Wagner, "Managing to Compete: The Hudson's Bay, Levant, and Russia Companies, 1714–1763," *Business and Economic History Online* 10 (2012): 8–9, www.thebhc.org/publications/BEHonline/2012/wagner.pdf.

88. Pettigrew, *Freedom's Debt,* 13, 31–39.

89. Stern, *Company-State,* 154–56, 164–68 ("they . . . hell" on 164).

90. K. N. Chaudhuri, *The Trading World of Asia and the English East India Company* (Cambridge: CUP, 1978), 432–35; Pettigrew, *Freedom's Debt,* 37.

91. Dunn, "Glorious Revolution," 464.

92. Pomfret, *East Jersey,* 357–62.

93. Moore, "Marooned," 256–57, 263–68.

94. *The Case of William Penn;* Steele, "Board of Trade," 609, 614–15.

95. Dummer, *Defence,* 7–8.

96. Siddique, "Governance through Documents," 284; Craig Yirush, *Settlers, Liberty, and Empire: The Roots of Early American Political Theory, 1675–1775* (Cambridge: CUP, 2011), 97–98.

97. Dummer, *Defence,* 7–8, 14–15, 76, 78.

98. Andrew Fitzmaurice, *Sovereignty, Property, and Empire, 1500–2000* (Cambridge: CUP, 2014), especially chapter 4.

99. Thomas Mun, *England's Treasure by Forraign Trade, or, The Balance of our Forraign Trade is the Rule of our Treasure* (London: Printed by J.G. for T. Clark, 1664); Mary Anne Everett Green, *Calendar of State Papers Domestic Series, of the Reign of Charles II, 1663–1664* (London: Longman, Green, Longman & Roberts, 1862), 525 (22 March 1664), 527 (24 March 1664); Seaward, "Committee of Trade," 443.

100. Charles Davenant, *Discourses on the Public Revenues, and on the Trade of England* (London, 1698), 2:174

101. Quoted by Andrews, *British Committees,* 85.

102. Davenant, *Discourses,* II, 422–23.

103. *Case of Sir John and Mr. Charles Crisp.*

104. Stern, *Company-State*, 156–58.

105. William Langhorne, *Considerations Humbly Tendred, Concerning the East India Company* ([London, 1688]).

106. [Josiah Child], *A Supplement, 1689, to a former Treaties, concerning the East-India Trade, Printed 1681* ([London, 1689])

107. *Reasons Humbly Offered By the Governour, Assistants, and Fellowship of Eastland Merchants Against the giving of a General LIBERTY to all Persons whatsoever to Export the English Woollen-MANUFACTURE Whither they PLEASE* (London, 1689), 9.

108. Charles Molloy, *De jure maritime et navali, or, A treatise of affaires maritime and of commerce in three books* (London, 1677), 434.

109. Josia Child, *A New Discourse of Trade* (London, 1694), 103, 105; Davenant, *Discourses* II, 399, 401.

110. "Reasons against the erecting of a Morocco Company by Mr. Povey," Sloane MS 1956 fols. 50v–51v; Stein, "Tangier," 992.

111. Caroline A. J. Skeel, "The Canary Company," *English Historical Review*, 31, no. 124 (1916): 542; Stein, "Tangier," 992n25.

112. *The Case of the Hudsons-Bay-Company* ([London, 1690]).

113. Thomas Scrope Goodrick, ed., *Edward Randolph; Including His Letters and Official Papers From the New England, Middle, and Southern Colonies in America, and the West Indies, 1678–1700, Vol. VII* (Boston: Prince Society, 1909), 554–55; Crane, *Southern Frontier*, 142.

114. Cecil Headlam, ed., *Calendar of State Papers Colonial Series, America and West Indies, Jan.–Dec. 1 1702* (London: HMSO, 1912), 198 (7 April 1702); H. R. McIlwaine, ed., *Journals of the House of Burgesses of Virginia* (Richmond, 1913), 169 (19 May 1699), 178 (25 May 1699); Cadwallader Jones, "Louissiania and Virginia Improved" (17 January 1698/9), in Fairfax Harrison, "Western Explorations in Virginia between Lederer and Spotswood," *VMHB* 30, no. 4 (1922): 331; Crane, *Southern Frontier*, 61–62, 143.

115. A. S. Salley, Jr., ed., *Journals of the Commons House of Assembly of South Carolina for the Two Sessions of 1698* (Columbia, SC: Historical Commission of South Carolina, 1914), 22 (4 October 1698); A. S. Salley Jr., ed., *Journals of the Commons House of Assembly of South Carolina for 1703* (Columbia: Historical Commission of South Carolina, 1934), 15 (20 January 1702/3); Crane, *Southern Frontier*, 142–43, 149.

116. Milton Ready, "The Georgia Concept: An Eighteenth Century Experiment in Colonization," *Georgia Historical Quarterly* 55, no. 2 (1971): 162–63.

117. Thomas Trevor to the Lords Commissioners for Trade and Plantations, 12 December 1699, CO 5/1259, pp. 507–9.

118. [James Spooner], "Draught of the Scheme I drew for Dr Daniel Cox many years since for the settlemt of New which wee called the New Empire," Rawl A 305 fol. 3r–7v, Bodleian Library, Oxford University; G. D. Scull, "Biographical Notice of Doctor Daniel Coxe, of London," *PMHB* 7, no. 3 (1883): 323–24. Thanks to Owen Stanwood for sharing of his transcription of the Spooner manuscript.

119. "The Humble Petition of Daniel Coxe," [November 1699], CO 5/1259 p. 449; Verner W. Crane, *The Southern Frontier, 1670–1732* (Durham, NC: DUP, 1928), 50–58, 58n33; Owen Stanwood, *The Global Refuge: Huguenots in an Age of Empire* (New York: OUP, 2020), 128–29.

120. Cecil Headlam, ed., *Calendar of State Papers, Colonial Series, America and West Indies, 1700* (London: HMSO, 1910), 497 (27 August 1700).

121. Daniel Coxe to Board of Trade, 8 January 1699/1700, CO 5/1529 p. 523; Crane, *Southern Frontier*, 59; Stanwood, *Global Refuge*, 133.

122. Cecil Headlam, ed., *Calendar of State Papers, Colonial Series, America and the West Indies, Jan. 1716–July 1717* (London: HMSO, 1930), 73–74 (9 May 1716); Stephanie Gamble, "A Community of Convenience: The Saponi Nation, Governor Spotswood, and the Experiment at Fort Christanna, 1670–1740," *Native South* 6 (2013): 81, 83–84.

123. Spotswood quoted in Gamble, "Community of Convenience," 76 ("fraud" and "no stock"), 82 ("loose people"), also 82–83, 88–95, 103n55; Crane, *Southern Frontier*, 126–27.

124. Glickman, "Protestantism, Colonization," 388–89; Frederick V. Mills, "The Society in Scotland for Propagating Christian Knowledge in British North America, 1730–1775," *Church History* 63, no. 1 (1994): 15–30.

125. Brent S. Sirota, *The Christian Monitors: The Church of England and the Age of Benevolence, 1680–1730* (New Haven: YUP, 2014), 105–9, 120–21, 139, 142.

126. Stern, *Company-State*, 156–58; on the Company's expansion in Asia, see also David Veevers, *The Origins of the British Empire in Asia, 1600–1750* (Cambridge: CUP, 2020).

127. K. N. Chaudhuri, *The Trading World of Asia and the English East India Company* (Cambridge: CUP, 1978), 436.

128. David Armitage, "The Scottish Vision of Empire: Intellectual Origins of the Darien Venture," in *A Union for Empire: Political Thought and the British Union of 1707*, ed. John Robertson (Cambridge: CUP, 1995), 97–118; Allan I. Macinnes, *Union and Empire: The Making of the United Kingdom in 1707* (Cambridge: CUP, 2007), esp. 30–50, 88–95, 172–81; Douglas Watt, *The Price of Scotland: Darien, Union, and the Wealth of Nations* (Edinburgh: Luath Press, 2006).

129. H. V. Bowen, *The Business of Empire: The East India Company and Imperial Britain, 1756–1833* (Cambridge: CUP, 2005), 30–35.

130. John Brewer, *The Sinews of Power: War, Money, and the English State, 1688–1783* (Cambridge, MA: HUP, 1988), 120, 122, 126; Bruce Carruthers, *City of Capital: Politics and Markets in the English Financial Revolution* (Princeton: PUP, 1996), chap. 6.

131. [Edmund Burke], *Observations on a Late State of the Nation,* 3rd ed. (London: J. Dodsley, 1769), 94.

132. Andrew Mackillop, "Locality, Nation, and Empire: Scots and the Empire in Asia, c.1695–1813," in *Scotland and the British Empire*, ed. John M. Mackenzie and T. M. Devine (Oxford: OUP, 2011), 63; Linda Colley, *Britons: Forging the Nation, 1707–1837* (New Haven: YUP, 1992).

133. Margaret Hunt, *Middling Sort: Commerce, Gender, and the Family in England, 1680–1780* (Berkeley: University of California Press, 1996), 25; Amy M. Froide, *Silent Partners: Women as Public Investors During Britain's Financial Revolution, 1690–1570* (Oxford, 2016), esp. 8–9, 65–66; P. G. M. Dickson, *The Financial Revolution in England: A Study in the Development of Public Credit, 1688–1756* (London: Macmillan, 1967).

134. Yamamoto, *Taming Capitalism,* 235.

135. *An Act for Granting an Aid to His Majesty, By Sale of the Forfeited and Other Estates and Interests in Ireland &c.,*11&12 Wil. III (Dublin: Andrew Crook, 1700), 1–2, 3–14; Frances Nolan, "The Representation of Female Claimants Before the Trustees for the Irish Forfeitures, 1700–1703," *HJ* 63, no. 4 (2019): 836–61; Julia Rudolph, "A Broker's Advice: Credit Networks and Mortgage Risk in the Eighteenth-Century Empire," in *Networks and Connections in Legal History*, ed. Michael Lobban and Ian Williams (Cambridge: CUP, 2020), 200–201.

136. J.H., *An Argument proving that it is more the interest of the government and nation of England, that the forfeited estates in Ireland be purchased by an incorporated company, than by single purchasers* (London, 1701), 5, 7, 10, 12; Stuart Bell, "'A masterpiece of knavery'? The Activities of the Sword Blade Company in London's Early Financial Markets," *Business History* 54, no. 4 (2012): 625–29.

137. Bell, "'Masterpiece," 624, 628–45; Patrick Walsh, *The South Sea Bubble and Ireland: Money, Banking, and Investment, 1690–1721* (Woodbridge: Boydell, 2014), 29–31.

138. William Paterson, "A Proposal to Plant a Colony in Darien to Protect the Indians Against Spain; and to Open the Trade of South America to All Nations" (1701), in *The Writings of William Paterson, Founder of the Bank of England*, ed. Saxe Bannister, 2 vols. (London: Effingham Wilson, 1858), I:149; Srinivas Aravamudan, "Defoe, Commerce, and Empire," in *The Cambridge Companion to Daniel Defoe*, ed. John Richetti (Cambridge: CUP, 2008), 53; Shinsuke Satsuma, *Britain and Colonial Maritime War in the Early Eighteenth Century: Silver, Seapower, and the Atlantic* (Woodbridge: Boydell, 2013), 164–67; John Shovlin, *Trading with the Enemy: Britain, France, and the 18th-Century Quest for a Peaceful World Order* (New Haven: YUP, 2021), 84–97.

139. Carl Wennerlind, *Casualties of Credit: The English Financial Revolution, 1620–1720* (Cambridge, MA: HUP, 2011), 198.

140. Carr, *Select Charters,* cxxix; Aaron Graham, "The British Financial Revolution and the Empire of Credit in St. Kitts and Nevis, 1706–21," *Historical Research* 91, no. 253 (2018): 701–2; Pettigrew, *Freedom's Debt,* 160–62; Shovlin, *Trading with the Enemy,* 97–102; Helen Paul, *The South Sea Bubble: An Economic History of Its Origins and Consequences* (London: Routledge, 2011), 47–48.

141. William Deringer, "For What It's Worth: Historical Financial Bubbles and the Boundaries of Economic Rationality," *Isis* 106, no. 3 (2015): 654.

142. *Some queries, which being nicely answered may tend very much to the encouragement of the South-sea company, and to forwarding that laudable undertaking to our greater satisfaction* ([London], 1711).

143. Daniel Defoe, *An Essay on the South-sea Trade* (London: J. Baker, 1712), 10; Deringer, "For What It's Worth," 653.

144. *Journals of the House of Commons, From November the 16th 1708 in the Seventh Year of the Reign of Queen Anne to October the 9th 1711, in the Tenth Year of the Reign of Queen Anne* ([London]: House of Commons, 1803), 671 (18 May 1711); Satsuma, *Britain,* 167–68.

145. Wennerlind, *Casualties,* esp. 203–12.

146. Beales, "Pennsylvania Land Company," 121–41; Anne M. Carlos and Larry Neal, "Women Investors in Early Capital Markets, 1720–1725," *Financial History Review* 11, no. 2 (2004): 197–224; Froide, *Silent Partners,* 9, 155–63; Graham, "British Financial Revolution," 695–97; Larry Neal, *The Rise of Financial Capitalism: International Capital Markets in the Age of Reason* (Cambridge: CUP, 1990), 71.

147. Stephano Condorelli and Daniel Menning, "Chartering Companies: A Dialogue about the Timeline and the Actors of the Pan-European 1720 Stock Euphoria," in *Boom, Bust, and Beyond: New Perspectives on the 1720 Stock Market Bubble,* ed. Stefano Condorelli and Daniel Menning (Berlin: De Gruyter, 2019), 45–66.

148. Arne Bialuschewski, "Greed, Fraud, and Popular Culture: John Breholt's Madagascar Schemes of the Early Eighteenth Century," in *Money, Power, and Print: Interdisciplinary Studies on the Financial Revolution in the British Isles,* ed. Charles Ivar McGrath and Chris Fauske (Newark: University of Delaware Press, 2008), 106–12.

149. Ready, "Georgia Concept," 157–59; Crane, *Southern Frontier,* 315.

150. *Journals of the House of Commons from November the 11th 1718 in the Fifth Year of the Reign of King George the First to March the 7th 1721, in the Eight Year of the Reign of King George the First* (London: House of Commons, 1803), 341–43 (27 April 1720); Bob Harris, "Scotland's Herring Fisheries and the Prosperity of the Nation, c. 1660–1760," *Scottish Historical Review* 79, no. 1 (2000), 49–50; Patrick Walsh, "The Bubble on the Periphery: Scotland and the South Sea Bubble," *Scottish Historical Review* 91, no. 231, pt. 1 (2012): 122–23.

151. Frederick Martin, *The History of Lloyd's and of Marine Insurance in Great Britain* (London: Macmillan and Co., 1876), 91–92.

152. *Journals of the House of Commons, 1718–1721,* 345 (27 April 1720); Carr, *Select Charters,* cci–cxiii, cxxx.

153. *Journals, 1718–1721,* 341 (27 April 1720).

154. Michael Aldous and Stefano Condorelli, "An Incomplete Revolution: Corporate Governance Challenges of the London Assurance Company and the Limitations of the Joint-Stock Form, 1720–1725," *Enterprise and Society* 21, no. 1 (2020), 247–53; Anastasia Bogatyreva, "England 1660–1720: Corporate or Private?" in *Marine Insurance: Origins and Institutions, 1300–1850,* ed. Adrian Leonard (London: Palgrave Macmillan, 2015), 179–204; Ron Harris, *Industrializing English Law: Entrepreneurship and Business Organization, 1720–1844* (Cambridge: CUP, 2000), chap. 3.

155. Ann Carlos and Larry Neal, "The Micro-Foundations of the Early London Capital Market: Bank of England Shareholders during and after the South Sea Bubble, 1720–25," *The Economic History Review* 59, no. 3 (2006): 501–2; Matthew David Mitchell, "'Legitimate Commerce' in the Eighteenth Century: The Royal African Company of England Under the Duke of Chandos, 1720–1726," *Enterprise and Society* 14, no. 3 (2013): 544–79; Pettigrew, *Freedom's Debt,* 165–69; Scott, *Joint-Stock Companies,* I:436.

156. Ron Harris, "The Bubble Act: Its Passage and Its Effects on Business Organization," *Journal of Economic History* 54, no. 3 (1994): 610–27; Julian Hoppit, "The Myths of the South Sea Bubble," *Transactions of the Royal Historical Society* 12 (2002): 141–65; Abigail Swingen, "The Bubble and the Bail-Out: The South Sea Company, Jacobitism, and Public Credit in Early Hanvoverian Britain," in *Boom, Bust, and Beyond: New Perspectives on the 1720 Stock Market Bubble*, ed. Stefano Condorelli and Daniel Manning (Berlin: De Greuter, 2019), 147–58.

157. Beales, "Commercial Theologies," 121–41; Mark Valeri, "William Petty in Boston: Political Economy, Religion, and Money in Provincial New England," *Early American Studies* 8, no. 3 (2010): 564–65.

158. Deringer, "For What It's Worth," 652–55.

159. Harris, "Bubble Act," 623; A. B. Levy, *Private Corporations and their Control* (London: Routledge, 1950), 43.

160. Edward Jones Corredera, *The Diplomatic Enlightenment: Spain, Europe, and the Age of Speculation* (Leiden: Brill, 2021); Felicia Gottman, "The Social Networks of Cosmopolitan Fraudsters: The Prussian Bengal Company as a Transnational Corporation," in *Commercial Cosmopolitanism: Cross-Cultural Objects, Spaces, and Institutions in the Early Modern World*, ed. Gottman (Abingdon: Routledge, 2021), 161–80; Hal Gladfelder, *Fanny Hill in Bombay: The Making and Unmaking of John Cleland* (Baltimore: JHUP, 2012), 39–45, 245–47; Andrew Mackillop, "Accessing Empire: Scotland, Europe, Britain, and the Asia Trade, 1695–c. 1750," *Itinerario* 29, no. 3 (2005): 7–30; Nicholas D. Nace, "The Curious Case of the Unfortunate John Cleland," *Eighteenth Century*, 56, no. 1 (Spring 2015): 137–43; Gabriel Paquette, "Views from the South: Images of Britain and Its Empire in Portuguese and Spanish Political Economic Discourse, ca. 1740–1810," in *The Political Economy of Empire in the Early Modern World*, ed. Pernille Røge and Sophus Reinert (Basingstoke: Palgrave Macmillan, 2013), 91–92; Lucia Lima Rodrigues and Russell Craig, "English Mercantilist Influences on the Foundation of the Portuguese School of Commerce in 1759," *Atlantic Economic Journal* 32, no. 4 (2004): 334, 337–38; Ofélia Pinto and Brian West, "Accounting, Slavery, and Social History: The Legacy of an Eighteenth-Century Portuguese Chartered Company," *Accounting History* 22, no. 2 (2017): 147–50; Kenneth Maxwell, *Conflicts and Conspiracies: Brazil and Portugal, 1750–1808* (New York: Routledge, 2004), 62–65, 70–71; Lúcia Lima Rodrigues and Alan Sangster, "'Public-Private Partnerships': The Portuguese General Company of Pernambuco and Paraíaba (1759)," *Business History* 54, no. 7 (2012): 1149–50; Stern, *Company-State*, 196.

161. Cecil Headlam, ed., *Calendar of State Papers, Colonial Series, America and West Indies, March 1720 to December 1721* (London: HMSO, 1933), 229–30 (3 January 1721); Graham, "British Financial Revolution," 701–3.

162. Froide, *Silent Partners*, 14, 130–31; Neal, *Rise of Financial Capitalism,* 53 ("financial goliath"), 116–17.

4. Hostile Takeovers

Epigraph: Adam Smith, *An Inquiry into the Nature and Causes of the Wealth of Nations,* 3rd ed., 3 vols. (London, 1784), I:45.

1. John Welbe to Hans Sloane, 1716, with enclosures, BL Sloane MS 4044 ff. 212–17; John Welbe to Captain Mandell, 16 February 1719/20, SP 35/20 f. 152; "Captain John Welbe's Proposals," [c. 1720?] Bibliothèque nationale de France, FOL-NT-666. Immense gratitude to Sasha Pack for helping me acquire an image of this. Glyndwr Williams, *The Great South Sea: English Voyages and Encounters* (New Haven: YUP, 1997), 184–89.

2. K. H. Ledward, ed., *Journals of the Board of Trade and Plantations: Volume 4, November 1718–December 1722* (London: HMSO, 1925), 296–307 (6, 13, and 14 July 1721), www.british-history.ac.uk/jrnl-trade-plantations/vol4/pp296-307.

3. Joseph Redington, ed., *Calendar of Treasury Papers, 1720–1728* (London: HM Stationary Office, 1889), 156–57 (27 August 1722), www.british-history.ac.uk/cal-treasury-papers/vol6/pp142-176.

4. John Sinclair, *The History of the Public Revenue of the British Empire* (London: W. and A. Strahan for T. Cadell, 1785), I:5, 14.

5. Paul Slack, *The Invention of Improvement: Information and Material Progress in Seventeenth-Century England* (Oxford: OUP, 2015), 208.

6. Amy M. Froide, *Silent Partners: Women as Public Investors During Britain's Financial Revolution, 1690–1570* (Oxford: OUP, 2016), 13, 132–33; Christine Gerrard, *Aaron Hill: The Muses' Projector, 1685–1750* (Oxford: OUP, 2003), 122–23; David Murray, *The York Buildings Company: A Chapter in Scotch History* (Glasgow: James Maclehose & Sons, 1883).

7. Peter Brealey, "The Charitable Corporation for the Relief of Industrious Poor: Philanthropy, Profit and Sleaze in London, 1707–1733," *History* (2013): 708–29; Amy M. Froide, "The Long Shadow of the South Sea Bubble: Memory, Financial Crisis, and the Charitable Corporation Scandal of 1732," in *Boom, Bust, and Beyond: New Perspectives on the 1720 Stock Market Bubble*, ed. Stefano Condorelli and Daniel Manning (Berlin: De Greuter, 2019); Froide, *Silent Partners*, 167–75; Harold E. Raynes, *A History of British Insurance* (London: Sir Isaac Pitman & Sons, 1948), 90; Scott, *Joint-Stock Corporations*, I:364, III:380.

8. Alan Taylor, *American Colonies: The Settling of North America* (New York: Penguin, 2002), 226.

9. *Historical Manuscripts Commission, Manuscripts of the Earl of Egmont: Diary of Viscount Percival, Afterwards First Earl of Egmont, Vol. I: 1730–1733* (London: HMSO, 1920), 99 (30 July 1730); Popple to Shelton, 11 June 1724, CO 5/400 pp. 185–87; Verner W. Crane, *The Southern Frontier, 1670–1732* (Durham, NC: DUP, 1928), 319; Owen Stanwood, *The Global Refuge: Huguenots in an Age of Empire* (New York: OUP, 2020), 207–08; Milton Ready, "The Georgia Concept: An Eighteenth Century Experiment in Colonization," *Georgia Historical Quarterly* 55, no. 2 (1971): 161–62.

10. *A Report of the Committee Appointed to Enquire into the State of the Goals [sic] of this Kingdom, Relating to the King's-Bench Prison* (London: Richard Williamson, 1730), 4–10, 13–14.

11. *Diary of Viscount Percival*, 45 (13 February 1729/30), 90 (1 April 1730).

12. William Webb Kemp, *The Support of Schools in Colonial New York by the Society for the Propagation of the Gospel in Foreign Parts* (New York: Teachers College, Columbia University, 1913), 15n58; Crane, *Southern Frontier*, 305–9, 318.

13. *Diary of Viscount Percival*, 45 (13 February 1729/30); Berkeley to Percival, 10 February 1725/1726, in *Berkeley and Percival*, ed. Benjamin Rand (Cambridge: CUP, 1914), 230; Scott Breuninger, "Planting an Asylum for Religion: Berkeley's Bermuda Scheme and the Transmission of Virtue in the Eighteenth-Century Atlantic World," *Journal of Religious History* 34, no. 4 (2010); Brent S. Sirota, *The Christian Monitors: The Church of England and the Age of Benevolence, 1680–1730* (New Haven: YUP, 2014), 247–48.

14. *Diary of Viscount Percival*, 99 (30 July 1730); Crane, *Southern Frontier*, 319.

15. Rand, ed., *Berkeley and Percival*, 283–84 (14 March 1731/2); *Diary of Viscount Percival*, 256 (5 April 1736).

16. *Diary of Viscount Percival*, 45 (13 February 1729/30), 90 (1 April 1730).

17. *Documents and Other Papers Relating to the Boundary Line between the States of Georgia and Florida* (Washington, DC: Beverly Tucker, 1855), 116; Cecil Headlam, *Calendar of State Papers, Colonial Series, America and West Indies 1730* (London: HMSO, 1937), 383 (7 December 1730); K. H. Ledward, ed., *Journals of the Board of Trade and Plantations: Volume 6, January 1729–December 1734* (London: HMSO, 1928), (8 December 1731), www.british-history.ac.uk/jrnl-trade-plantations/vol6/pp250-261; James Ross McCain, *Georgia as a Proprietary Province: The Execution of a Trust* (Boston: Richard G. Badger, 1917), 22.

18. See accounts for 1732 in Allen D. Candler, ed., *The Colonial Records of the State of Georgia* (Atlanta: Franklin Printing and Publishing Co., 1905), III:18–19; *Diary of Viscount Percival*, 43 (4 March 1733/4), 192 (3 September 1735); Crane, *Southern Frontier*, 320, 322–23.

19. Oglethorpe to Berkeley, May 1731, in *Berkeley and Percival*, ed. Rand, 277.

20. Karen Auman, "'Give Their Service for Nothing': Bubbles, Corruption, and their Effect on the Founding of Georgia," *Eighteenth-Century Studies* 53, no. 1 (2020): esp. 109; Ready, "Georgia Concept," 157–72.

21. *Diary of Viscount Percival*, 286 (20 July 1732), 327 (11 February 1733).

22. Milton L. Ready, "Philanthropy and the Origins of Georgia," in *Forty Years of Diversity: Essays on Colonial Georgia*, ed. Harvey H. Jackson and Phinizy Spalding (Athens: University of Georgia, 1984), 47–48, 50, 53–54; Ruth K. McClure, *Coram's Children: The London Foundling Hospital in the Eighteenth Century* (New Haven: YUP, 1981); Catherine M. Styer, "Barbary Pirates, British Slaves, and the Early Modern Atlantic World, 1570–1800," unpublished PhD dissertation, University of Pennsylvania, 2011, 296–97.

23. [James Oglethorpe], *A New and Accurate Account of the Provinces of South-Carolina and Georgia* (London; J. Worrall, 1733), iv–v; Rodney M. Baine, ed., *Publications of James Edward Oglethorpe* (Athens: Georgia, 1994), 168; Julie Anne Sweet, "'The Natural Advantages of This Happy Climate': An Analysis of Georgia's Promotional Literature," *Georgia Historical Quarterly* 98, no. 1/2 (2014): 1–25.

24. Ready, "Georgia Concept," 165–66.

25. *Diary of Viscount Percival*, 292 (14 September 1732).

26. See Zachary Dorner, "From Chelsea to Savannah: Medicines and Mercantilism in the Atlantic World," *Journal of British Studies* 58 (2019): 28–29, 29n3, 32, 39, 42, 45, 57.

27. Thomas Stephens, *The Castle-Builders, or the History of William Stephens, of the Isle of Wight, Esq., Lately Deceased* (London: William Stephens, 1759), 91; Gerrard, *Aaron Hill*, 124; Julie Anne Sweet, *William Stephens: Georgia's Forgotten Founder* (Baton Rouge: Louisiana State University Press, 2010), 19–20.

28. Crane, *Southern Frontier*, 321; Paul Tonks, "British Union and Empire in the *Origin of Commerce:* Adam Anderson as Eighteenth-Century Historian and Scottish Political Economist," *History* 105, no. 364 (2020): 60–81.

29. Ready, "Georgia Concept," 161–62.

30. Robert Wright, *A Memoir of General James Oglethorpe* (London: Chapman and Hall, 1867), 81, 97.

31. Anthony W. Parker, *Scottish Highlanders in Colonial Georgia: The Recruitment, Emigration, and Settlement at Darien, 1735–1748* (Athens: University of Georgia Press, 1997), 53.

32. Oglethorpe to Berkeley, May 1731, in *Berkeley and Percival,* ed. Rand, 276.

33. Thaddeus Mason Harris, *Biographical Memorials of James Oglethorpe, Founder of the Colony of Georgia in North America* (Boston: For the Author, 1841), 336–37; Breuninger, "Planting an Asylum," 429n77; Richard S. Dunn, "The Trustees of Georgia and the House of Commons, 1732–1752," *WMQ* 11, no. 4 (1954): 559.

34. Dunn, "Trustees of Georgia," 551–55.

35. Dunn, "Trustees of Georgia," 562–63.

36. Auman, "'Give Their Service for Nothing,'" 113; Dunn, "Trustees of Georgia," 563–65; Watson Jennison, *Cultivating Race: The Expansion of Slavery in Georgia, 1750–1860* (Lexington: University Press of Kentucky, 2012), ch. 1; Randall M. Miller, "The Failure of the Colony of Georgia Under the Trustees," *Georgia Historical Quarterly* 53, no. 1 (1969): 13–14.

37. Mark Peterson, *The City-State of Boston: The Rise and Fall of an Atlantic Power, 1630–1865* (Princeton: PUP, 2019), 183–88.

38. *New England Weekly Journal*, 23 September 1740, quoted in Elizabeth E. Dunn, "'Grasping at the Shadow': The Massachusetts Currency Debate, 1690–1751," *New England Quarterly* 71, no. 1 (1998): 70; T. H. Breen and Timothy Hall, "Structuring Provincial Imagination: The Rhetoric and Experience of Social Change in Eighteenth-Century New England," *American Historical Review* 103, no. 5 (1998): 1432–48. On land banks in seventeenth-century English political economy, see Carl Wennerlind, *Casualties of Credit: The English Financial Revolution, 1620–1720* (Cambridge, MA: HUP, 2011), 73–75, 114–21.

39. John Jay to John Adams, 1 November 1786, APDE, www.masshist.org/publications/adams-papers/index.php/view/ADMS-06-18-02-0264.

40. Charles J. Hoadly, ed., *The Public Records of the Colony of Connecticut, Volume 7: From May 1726, to May 1734, Inclusive* (Hartford: Case, Lockwood & Brainard, 1873), 419–

23; George Athan Billias, "The Massachusetts Land Bankers of 1740," *University of Maine Bulletin* 61, no. 17 (1959): 3, 8; Andrew MacFarland Davis, "A Connecticut Land Bank of the Eighteenth Century," *Quarterly Journal of Economics* 13 (1898): 70–85; Bruce P. Stark, "The New London Society and Connecticut Politics, 1732–1740," *Connecticut History* 25 (January 1984): 1–21; Richard L. Bushman, *From Puritan to Yankee: Character and the Social Order in Connecticut, 1690–1765* (Cambridge, MA: HUP, 1967), 123–27.

41. Hoadly, ed., *Public Records,* 449; Davis, "Connecticut Land Bank," 78–79.

42. *Journals of the House of Representatives of Massachusetts: Volume 18, 1740–1741* (Boston: The Massachusetts Historical Society, 1942), 132; Billias, "Massachusetts Land Bankers," 13, 34–36; Breen and Hall, "Structuring Provincial Imagination," 1422–23, 1432–48; Dunn, "'Grasping at the Shadow,'" 64, 70; Stephen Foster, "Another Legend of the Province House: Jonathan Belcher, William Shirley, and the Misconstruction of the Imperial Relationship," *New England Quarterly* 77, no. 2 (2004): 181, 195, 206–10, 212, 214–15, 219–21; Peterson, *City-State,* 210–11, 267–69.

43. *An Act for Restraining and Preventing Several Unwarrantable Schemes and Undertakings in His Majesty's Colonies and Plantations in America,* 14 Geo II. c. 37 (1741); Shaw Livermore, *Early American Land Companies: Their Influence on Corporate Development* (New York: Commonwealth Fund, 1939), 58, 61, 66; Foster, "Another Legend," 180–81, 221–22.

44. Billias, "Massachusetts Land Bankers," 36.

45. Theodore Thayer, "The Land-Bank System in the American Colonies," *Journal of Economic History* 13, no. 2 (1953): 145–59.

46. *Charters and Statutes of the University of Pennsylvania* (Philadelphia: Crissy & Markley, 1853), 7 (13 July 1753).

47. Johnson to Clap, 15 February 1754, quoted in Christopher Grasso, *A Speaking Aristocracy: Transforming Public Discourse in Eighteenth-Century Connecticut* (Chapel Hill: UNCP/OIEAHC, 1999): 173; Elisha Williams to Timothy Woodbridge, 2 July 1728, in *Documentary History of Yale University Under the Original Charter of the Collegiate School of Connecticut 1701–1745,* ed. Franklin Bowditch Dexter (New Haven: YUP, 1916), 276; Daniel Hulsebosch, *Constituting Empire: New York and the Transformation of Constitutionalism in the Atlantic World, 1664–1830* (Chapel Hill: UNCP, 2005), 88–90.

48. Dexter, ed., *Documentary History,* 12–14, 16, 21; Frederic Maitland, "The Unincorporate Body," in *The Collected Papers of Frederic William Maitland, Volume III,* ed. H.A.L. Fisher (Cambridge: CUP, 1911), 283.

49. Dexter, ed., *Documentary History,* 129–30.

50. Thomas Clap, *The Religious Constitution of Colleges* (New London: T. Green, 1754), 12.

51. Thomas Clap, *The Annals or History of Yale-College* (New Haven: John Hotchkiss and B. Mecom, 1766), 4.

52. [Thomas Clap], *The Answer of The Friend in the West to A Letter from A Gentleman in the East, Entitled, The Present State of the Colony of Connecticut Considered* (New Haven: James Parker, 1755), 16.

53. Grasso, *Speaking Aristocracy* 169–70, 173 (quoting Clap, "Company of ministers"); Richard J. Ross and Philip J. Stern, "Reconstructing Early Modern Notions of Legal Pluralism," in *Legal Pluralism and Empires,* ed. Lauren Benton and Richard Ross (New York: NYUP, 2013), 109–42.

54. Herbert T. Leyland, *The Ohio Company: A Colonial Corporation* (Cincinnati: The Abingdon Press, 1921), 15–16; Erin M. Greenwald, *Marc-Antoine Caillot and the Company of the Indies in Louisiana* (Baton Rouge: LSU, 2016).

55. *By the King. A Proclamation* (London: Mark Baskett, 1763); Allan Greer, *Property and Dispossession: Natives, Empires, and Land in Early Modern North America* (Cambridge: CUP, 2018), 383; Hannah Weiss Muller, *Subjects and Sovereign: Bonds of Belonging in the Eighteenth-Century British Empire* (New York: OUP, 2017).

56. Eugene M. Del Papa, "The Royal Proclamation of 1763: Its Effect upon Virginia Land Companies," *VMHB* 83, no. 4 (1975): 406–11.

57. Andrew Fitzmaurice, *Sovereignty, Property, and Empire, 1500–2000* (Cambridge: CUP, 2014), 185–86; P. G. McHugh, "Prerogative and Office in Pre-Revolutionary New York: Feudal Legalism, Land Patenting, and Sir William Johnson, Indian Superintendent

(1756–1774)," in *Empire and Legal Thought: Ideas and Institutions from Antiquity to Modernity,* ed. Edward Cavanagh (Leiden: Brill, 2020), 455–56.

58. Quoted by Peter Marshall, "Lord Hillsborough, Samuel Wharton and the Ohio Grant, 1769–1775," *English Historical Review* 80, no. 317 (1965): 719.

59. *Report of the Lords Commissioners for Trade and Plantations on the Petition of the Honourable Thomas Walpole, Benjamin Franklin, John Sargent, and Samuel Wharton, Esquires, and their Associates for a Grant of Lands on the River Ohio, in North America; for the Purpose of Erecting a New Government* (London: J. Almon, 1772); "The Formation of the Grand Ohio Company [June? 1769], *FONA,* https://founders.archives.gov /documents/Franklin/01-16-02-0083; "Endorsement of Legal Opinions on Land Titles Obtained from the Indians, 12 July 1775," *FONA,* https://founders.archives.gov/documents /Franklin/01-22-02-0061; Thomas Walpole, *To the King's Most Excellent Majesty in Council* ([London?], [1774?]), 2; Eric Hinderaker and Peter C. Mancall, *At the Edge of Empire: The Backcountry in British North America* (Baltimore: JHUP, 2003), 146–50; Leyland, *Ohio Company,* 17–18; Marshall, "Lord Hillsborough," 720–25, 735–37.

60. Clarence E. Carter, "Documents relating to the Mississippi Land Company, 1763–1769," *American Historical Review* 16, no. 2 (1911): 311–19; "Mississippi Land Company's Memorial to the King, 9 September 1763," *FONA,* https://founders.archives.gov/documents /Washington/02-07-02-0150; "Mississippi Land Company's Petition to the King, December 1768," *FONA,* https://founders.archives.gov/documents/Washington/02-08-02-0116.

61. Livermore, *Early American Land Companies,* 74–132.

62. Livermore, *Early American Land Companies,* 74.

63. Julian P. Boyd, ed., *The Susquehannah Company Papers, Volume I: 1750–1755* (Wilkes-Barre, PA: Wyoming Historical and Geological Society, 1930), 1–2; *Minutes of the Susquehanna Company, Claiming Lands in Wyoming: Documents Relating to the Connecticut Settlement in the Wyoming Valley* (Harrisburg, 1890), 3.

64. Report of John Armstrong, 11 December 1754, HSP 0485A, NV-005, 39.

65. "Address of the Mayor and Corporation of New York to the King," May 17, 1687, CO 1/62/45 fol. 157.

66. Minutes, 9 January 1754, in *Susquehannah Company Papers,* ed. Boyd, I:43.

67. *Minutes of the Provincial Council of Pennsylvania* (Harrisburg: T. Fenn, 1851–52), 8:627; Moyer, "Contest for the Wyoming Valley," 224.

68. Boyd, ed., *Susquehanna Company Papers,* I:283, II:72.

69. Petition of Eliphalet Dyer, 9 June 1764, HSP 0485A, NV-184 (Connecticut Claims), no. 16.

70. *Minutes of the Provincial Council,* 32–33; Patrick Spero, *Frontier Country: The Politics of War in Early Pennsylvania* (Philadelphia: UPenn, 2016), 202–3; Kevin Kenny, *Peaceable Kingdom Lost: The Paxton Boys and the Destruction of William Penn's Holy Experiment* (Oxford: OUP, 2009), 220.

71. William Samuel Johnson to Jonathan Trumbull, 26 February 1770, in *Collections of the Massachusetts Historical Society, Vol. IX, Fifth Series: The Trumbull Papers* (Boston: Massachusetts Historical Society, 1885), 413–16.

72. [William Smith], *An Examination of the Connecticut Claim to Lands in Pennsylvania, With an Appendix, Containing Extracts and Copies Taken from Original Papers* (Philadelphia, 1774), 1, 26, 32, 35; Paul B. Moyer, *Wild Yankees: The Struggle for Independence Along Pennsylvania's Revolutionary Frontier* (Ithaca: Cornell, 2007).

73. William Allen to Daniel Broadhead, 16 March 1754, in *Susquehannah Company Papers,* ed. Boyd, I:68.

74. Tenche Coxe, *An Important Statement of Facts; Relative to the Invalidity of the Pretensions formerly Made upon the Pennsylvania Lands, by the unincorporated Companies of Connecticut Claimants, and by those who claimed under those Companies . . .* ([Lancaster, Pa.], W&R. Dickson, May 1801), 10.

75. Lisa Ford, *The King's Peace: Law and Order in the British Empire* (Cambridge, MA: HUP, 2021), 18–20, 54–55.

76. P. J. Marshall, *The Making and Unmaking of Empires: Britain, India, and America, c. 1750–1783* (Oxford: OUP, 2005), 109–10, 117–18, 165.

77. "To the Inhabitants of the Colony of Massachusetts-Bay," 13 February 1775, APDE, www
.masshist.org/publications/adams-papers/index.php/view/ADMS-06-02-02-0072-0005.

78. *The Historical Magazine and Notes and Queries Concerning the Antiquities, History and
Biography of America* (New York: Charles B. Richardson & Co., 1862), VI:139; Bushman,
From Puritan to Yankee, 259; Grasso, *Speaking Aristocracy,* 168–69, 180.

79. Hulsebosch, *Constituting Empire,* 88.

80. William Keith, "A Short Discourse on the Present State of the Colonies in America with
Respect to the Interest of Great Britain," CO 5/4 fols. 170–71.

81. See, for example, Edward Channing and Archibald Cary Coolidge, eds., *The Barrington-
Bernard Correspondence and Illustrative Matter, 1760–1770* (Cambridge, MA: HUP, 1912),
96 (23 November 1765); Hulsebosch, *Constituting Empire,* 88.

82. John Wesley, *A Calm Address to Our American Colonies* (London, 1775).

83. Thomas Hutchinson, *The History of the Colony of Massachusetts-Bay, From the First Settlement Thereof in 1628, Until its Incorporation with the Colony of Plimouth, Province
of Main, &c. By the Charter of King William and Queen Mary in 1691* (Boston: Thomas
and John Fleet, 1764), 14; Ronald Dale Karr, "The Missing Clause: Myth and the Massachusetts Bay Charter of 1629," *New England Quarterly* 77, no. 1 (2004), 94.

84. William Samuel Johnson to William Pitkin, 13 February 1768, in *Trumbull Papers,*
257–58.

85. "Reply of the House to Hutchinson's First Message," 23 January 1773, APDE, www
.masshist.org/publications/adams-papers/index.php/view/ADMS-06-01-02-0097-0002.

86. *Trumbull Papers,* 257–58.

87. APDE (April 1775), www.masshist.org/publications/adams-papers/index.php/view/ADMS
-06-02-02-0072-0015; APDE (13 March 1775), www.masshist.org/publications/adams
-papers/index.php/view/ADMS-06-02-02-0072-0009.

88. Alexander B. Haskell, *For God, King, and People: Forging Commonwealth Bonds in Renaissance Virginia* (Chapel Hill: UNC/OIEAHC, 2017), 353–54, 363–66.

89. Henry Augustin Washington, ed., *The Writings of Thomas Jefferson, Being His Autobiography, Correspondence, Reports, Messages, Addresses and other Writings, Official and
Private* (New York: J. C. Riker, 1857), I:21; FONA (after 19 January 1776), https://founders
.archives.gov/documents/Jefferson/01-01-02-0147.

90. Mary Sarah Bilder, "The Corporate Origins of Judicial Review," *Yale Law Journal* 116,
no. 3 (2006): 502–66; David Ciepley, "Is the U.S. Government a Corporation? The Corporate Origins of Modern Constitutionalism," *American Political Science Review* 111, no. 2
(2017): esp. 423–24, 428–30; Nikolas Bowie, "Why the Constitution was Written Down,"
Stanford Law Review 71, no. 6 (2019).

91. Gaillard Hund and James Brown Scott, eds., *The Debates in the Federal Convention of
1787, Which Framed the Constitution of the United States of America, Reported by James
Madison, a Delegate from the State of Virginia* (Oxford: OUP, 1920), 20 August 1787,
https://avalon.law.yale.edu/18th_century/debates_820.asp; Mary Sarah Bilder, *Madison's
Hand: Revising the Constitutional Convention* (Cambridge, MA: HUP, 2015), 133.

92. "The United States v. Maurice, et al.," *The Writings of John Marshall, Late Chief Justice
of the United States Upon the Federal Constitution* (Washington, DC: William H. Mor-
rison, 1890), 477; Ciepley, "Is the U.S. Government a Corporation?" 432.

93. John Jay, "An Address to the People of the State of New-York on the Subject of the Constitution, Agreed Upon at Philadelphia, the 17th of September 1787, [c.12 April 1788],"
FONA, https://founders.archives.gov/documents/Jay/01-04-02-0324.

94. Washington, ed., *Writings,* I:32.

95. *Debates,* 28 June 1787, https://avalon.law.yale.edu/18th_century/debates_628.asp.

96. *Debates,* 7 July 1787, https://avalon.law.yale.edu/18th_century/debates_707.asp; Bilder,
Madison's Hand, 92 (Lansing), 98 (King), 107 (Morris).

97. "Madison Debates," 18 June 1787, 19 June 1787, https://avalon.law.yale.edu/18th_century
/debates_618.asp; https://avalon.law.yale.edu/18th_century/debates_619.asp; Bilder, *Madison's Hand,* 93; Hulsebosch, *Constituting Empire,* 223.

98. "Rule of Representation in the First Branch of the Legislature," [29 June] 1787, FONA,
https://founders.archives.gov/documents/Madison/01-10-02-0049; Bilder, *Madison's Hand,*

89, 98–100, 226–27; Ciepley, "Is the U.S. Government a Corporation?" 433. For other versions of Madison's position: James Madison to Joseph Gales Jr., 26 August 1821, FONA, https://founders.archives.gov/documents/Madison/04-02-02-0317; "Madison Debates," 29 June 1787, https://avalon.law.yale.edu/18th_century/debates_629.asp; Charles C. Tansill, ed., *Documents Illustrative of the Formation of the Union of the American States* (Washington, DC: Government Printing Office, 1927), https://avalon.law.yale.edu/18th_century /king.asp.

99. "Madison Debates," 21 June 1787, https://avalon.law.yale.edu/18th_century/debates_621 .asp.

100. "Power to Levy Direct Taxes; the Mississippi Question," (12 June 1788), FONA, https:// founders.archives.gov/documents/Madison/01-11-02-0076.

101. Biilder, *Madison's Hand*, 206–7; Baldwin, "American Business Corporations," 464–65.

102. Hart, "City Government," 195–211; Pauline Maier, "The Revolutionary Origins of the American Corporation," *WMQ* 3rd Series, 50, no. 1 (1993): 63; Jesssica Choppin Roney, *Governed by a Spirit of Opposition: The Origins of American Political Practice in Colonial Philadelphia* (Baltimore: JHUP, 2014), 185; Hannah Farber, *Underwriters of the United States: How Insurance Shaped the American Founding* (Chapel Hill: UNCP/ OIEAHC, 2021), 89–113.

103. Francis S. Drake, ed., *Tea Leaves: Being a Collection of Letters and Documents Relating to the Shipment of Tea, to the American Colonies in the Year 1773 by the East India Tea Company* (Boston: A. O. Crane, 1884), xliii, 297; James Fichter, *So Great a Profit: How the East Indies Trade Transformed Anglo-American Capitalism* (Cambridge, MA: HUP, 2010), 42–43.

104. Alexander Hamilton, "Final version of an Opinion on the Constitutionality of an Act to Establish a Bank," 23 February 1791, FONA, https://founders.archives.gov/documents /Hamilton/01-08-02-0060-0003.

105. Joseph Stancliffe Davis, *Essays in the Earlier History of American Corporations,* 2 vols. (Cambridge, MA: HUP, 1917), I:41.

106. "Attorney General at relation of Bishop of London v. College of William and Mary in Virginia, the City of London, and Others" (1790, November 12 S.C. Bo. C.C. 171), in *Reports of Cases Argued and Determined in the High Court of Chancery,* ed. Francis Vesey, 20 vols. (Boston: Charles C. Little and James Brown, 1844), I:244; Herbert Lawrence Ganter, "Some Notes on 'The Charity of the Honourable Robert Boyle, Esq., of the City of London, Deceased (Second Installment)" *William and Mary Quarterly* 15, no. 3 (1935): 216, 218.

107. The Trustees of Dartmouth College v. Woodward (1819), in Henry Wheaton, *Reports of Cases Argued and Adjudged in The Supreme Court of the United States, February Term, 1819* (New York: R. Donaldson, 1819), IV:592, 643.

108. Hamilton, "Final version," https://founders.archives.gov/documents/Hamilton/01-08-02 -0060-0003.

109. William Henry Eagle, ed., *Documents Relating to the Connecticut Settlement in the Wyoming Valley* (Harrisburg, 1893), 105–6; Fredrick W. Gnichtel, "The 'Pennamite Wars' and the Trenton Decree of 1782," *Proceedings of the New Jersey Historical Society* 6, no. 1 (1921).

110. "Endorsement of Legal Opinions on Land Titles Obtained from the Indians, 12 July 1775," FONA, https://founders.archives.gov/documents/Franklin/01-22-02-0061; "Virginia Delegates to Thomas Nelson, 16 October 1781," FONA, https://founders.archives.gov /documents/Madison/01-03-02-0140; J. M. Toner, "Colonies of North America and the Genesis of the Commonwealths of the United States," *Annual Report of the American Historical Association for the Year 1895* (Washington: Government Printing Office, 1896), 612–14.

111. Livermore, *Early American Land Companies*, 133–213.

112. See Charles Hobson, *The Great Yazoo Lands Sale: The Case of* Fletcher v. Peck (Lawrence: University of Kansas Press, 2016); Hobson, "The Yazoo Lands Sale Case: Fletcher v. Peck (1810)," *Journal of Supreme Court History* 42, no. 3 (2017): 239–55; Lindsay G. Robertson, *Conquest by Law: How the Discovery of America Dispossessed Indigenous Peoples of their Lands* (New York: OUP, 2005).

113. *Dartmouth v. Woodward*, 558–59.

114. William Foster, "The India Board (1784–1858)," *Transactions of the Royal Historical Society* 11 (1917): 61–85.

115. Jonathan P. Eacott, "Making an Imperial Compromise: The Calico Acts, the Atlantic Colonies, and the Structure of the British Empire," *WMQ* 69, no. 4 (2012): 731–62; Michael Wagner, "The Levant Company under Attack in Parliament, 1720–53," *Parliamentary History* 34, no. 3 (2015): 295–313; Michael Wagner, "Managing to Compete: The Hudson's Bay, Levant, and Russia Companies, 1714–1763," *Business and Economic History On-Line* 10 (2012), www.thebhc.org/publications/BEHonline/2012/wagner.pdf.

116. *Journals of the House of Commons, From June the 15th 1727, In the First Year of the Reign of King George the Second, to December the 5th, 1732, In the Sixth Year of the Reign of King George the Second* ([London], 1803), 538; *Diary of Viscount Percival*, 65–70 (26 February 1729/30).

117. *Journals of the House of Commons, 1727–1732*, 538; *Diary of Viscount Percival*, 65–70 (26 February 1729/30).

118. Francis Russell, *A Short History of the East India Company, exhibiting a state of their affairs, abroad and at home, political and commercial*, 2nd ed. (London, 1793), 5–8; P.G.M. Dickson, *The Financial Revolution in England: A Study in the Development of Public Credit, 1688–1756* (London: Macmillan, 1967), 205, 217; H. V. Bowen, *The Business of Empire: The East India Company and Imperial Britain, 1756–1833* (Cambridge: CUP, 2005), 33–34.

119. James M. Vaughn, *The Politics of Empire at the Accession of George III: The East India Company and the Crisis and Transformation of Britain's Imperial State* (New Haven: YUP, 2019), 80–84.

120. Etrait des Articles du Projet de Neutralité, n.d. (May 1753), IOR H/93 f. 110–11; John Shovlin, *Trading with the Enemy: Britain, France, and the 18th-Century Quest for a Peaceful World Order* (New Haven: YUP, 2021), 232–44.

121. Richard Arthur Roberts, ed., *Calendar of Home Office Papers of the Reign of George III, 1770–1772* (London: Longman's & Co, 1881), 244–46; H. V. Bowen, *Revenue and Reform: The Indian Problem in British Politics, 1757–1773* (Cambridge: CUP, 1991), 72.

122. Marshall, *Making and Unmaking*, 140–46; Jessica Hanser, "From Cross-Cultural Credit to Colonial Debt: British Expansion in Madras and Canton, 1750–1800," *American Historical Review* 124, no. 1 (2019): 87–107.

123. Edmund Burke, "Speech on the Opening of Impeachment" (15 February 1788) in *The Writings and Speeches of Edmund Burke, Volume VI: India: The Launching of the Hastings Impeachment, 1786–1788*, ed. P. J. Marshall (Oxford: Clarendon Press, 1991), 281.

124. Seid-Gholam-Hossein-Khan, *A Translation of the Sëir Mutaqherin; or View of Modern Times* (Calcutta, 1789, repr. Calcutta and Madras: R. Cambray, 1926), III:185. Much gratitude to Robert Travers for drawing the reference to my attention.

125. Bowen, *Business of Empire*, 219–59 (quotation on 219).

126. Walpole to Horace Mann, 19 March 1767 in *The Letters of Horace Walpole, Earl of Oxford*, ed. Peter Cunningham (London: Henry G. Bohn, 1861), 43; Bowen, *Revenue and Reform*, 16.

127. Marshall, *Making and Unmaking*, 197–98.

128. *Annual Register*, 7 (1764), 34.

129. Marshall, ed., *Writings and Speeches of Edmund Burke*, VI, 285–86.

130. P. J. Marshall, *East Indian Fortunes: The British in Bengal in the Eighteenth Century* (Oxford: Clarendon Press, 1976).

131. Richard Smith to Robert Orme, 7 January 1767, and 15 March 1767, BL OIOC EurMSS O.V.37 fols. 16, 79–80.

132. William Samuel Johnson to William Pitkin, 19 March 1767, and Johnson to Jonathan Trumbull, 14 March 1767 in *Trumbull Papers*, 218, 485–86.

133. Bowen, *Revenue and Reform*, 1, 32–33.

134. Marshall, *Making and Unmaking*, 209.

135. William Stanhope Taylor and John Henry Pringle, eds., *Correspondence of William Pitt, Earl of Chatham* (London: John Murray, 1839–40), I:389–90, III:62.

136. "Copy of His Majesty's Advocate, Attorney, and Solicitor Generals Report," 16 August 1757, BL AddMS 18464 fol. 1; "Copy of the Attorney and Solicitor Generals Report," 24 December 1757, fols. 5–7.

137. Bowen, *Revenue and Reform*, 53–63; Edward Cavanagh, "The Imperial Constitution of the Law Officers of the Crown: Legal Thought on War and Colonial Government, 1719–1774," *Journal of Imperial and Commonwealth History* 47, no. 4 (2019): 626–31.

138. *The Debates and Proceedings of the British House of Commons, From April 1772 to July 1773* (London: J. Almon, 1774), 240 (9 March 1773), 139.

139. Bowen, *Revenue and Reform*, 55.

140. Livermore, *Early American Land Companies*, 106–7n69; Cavanagh, "The Imperial Constitution," 633, 641; J. M. Sosin, "The Yorke-Camden Opinion and American Land Speculators," *PMHB* 85, no. 1 (1961): 38–49.

141. IOR A/2/8, no. 38: "Proposal to the Offers to Administration," 16 December 1766; *The Parliamentary Register: Or History of the Proceedings and Debates of the House of Commons* (1766), Vol. 4 (London: Printed for J. Almon, 1766), 471–72; Walpole to Horace Mann, 21 January 1767, in Cunningham, ed., *Letters*, 34; Bowen, *Revenue and Reform*, 21, 58–66.

142. Bowen, *Revenue and Reform*, 116–20, 128–32; Bowen, *Business of Empire*, 17, 35–36, 76–77.

143. Timothy Reuter, "Bad Economics and Bank Bailouts were the Norm Long Before TARP: A Retrospective On the East India Company," *Forbes*, 14 April 2013; Nick Robins, "East India Company: The Original Too-Big-to-Fail Firm," *Bloomberg News*, 12 March 2013; William Dalrymple, "The Original Evil Corporation," *The New York Times*, 4 September 2019.

144. Thomas Pownall, *The Right, Interest, and Duty of Government as Concerned in the Affairs of the East Indies* (London: J. Almon, 1773), 4.

145. Bowen, *Revenue and Reform*, 130, 153–86.

146. Andrew Stuart, *Considerations on the Present State of East-India Affairs and Examination of Mr. Fox's Bill, Suggesting Certain Material Alterations for Averting the Dangers and Preserving the Benefits of that Bill* (London: J. Stockdale, 1784), 6, 8; *The True Alarm* (London, 1770), 6–7, 15.

147. Thomas Pownall, *The Right of the State as Concerned in the Affairs of the East Indies* (London: S. Bladon, 1773), 14–15, 27–28, 43–44.

148. Alexander Dalrymple, *Considerations on a Pamphlet, Entitled "Thoughts on our Acquisitions in the* East-Indies, *particularly respecting Bengal"* (London, 1772), 19; *Retrospective View of the Antient System of the East-India-Company with a Plan of Regulation* (London, 1784), 14.

149. Marshall, *Making and Unmaking*, 215–16.

150. P. J. Marshall, ed., *The Writings and Speeches of Edmund Burke, Volume V: India: Madras and Bengal, 1774–1785* (Oxford: Clarendon Press, 1981), 381, 384–87 (1 December 1783).

151. *The Parliamentary Register; or History of the Proceedings and Debates of the House of Commons*, Vol. XII (London: J. Debrett, 1784), 34, 36–37 (18 November 1783).

152. Ernest Campbell Mossner and Ian Simpson Ross, eds., *The Correspondence of Adam Smith* (Oxford: OUP, 1987), 266; Emma Rothschild, *Economic Sentiments: Adam Smith, Condorcet, and the Enlightenment* (Cambridge, MA: HUP, 2001), 275n77; Nicholas Phillipson, *Adam Smith: An Enlightened Life* (London: Penguin, 2010), 264; Sankar Muthu, "Adam Smith's Critique of International Trading Companies: Theorizing 'Globalization' in the Age of Enlightenment," *Political Theory* 36, no. 2 (2008): 198–99.

153. Smith, *Wealth of Nations* (1784), II:191, 367, 479, III:124; Adam Smith, *Additions and Corrections to the First and Second Editions of Dr. Adam Smith's Inquiry into the Nature and Causes of the Wealth of Nations* ([London], 1784), 60; Rothschild, *Economic Sentiments*, 27, 32, 88–89; Andreas Ortmann, "The Nature and Causes of Corporate Negligence, Sham Lectures, and Ecclesiastical Indolence: Adam Smith on Joint-Stock Companies, Teachers, and Preachers," *History of Political Economy* 31, no. 2 (1999): 297–315.

154. Smith, *Wealth of Nations* (1784), III:127–28, 132, 144.

155. Smith, *Wealth of Nations* (1784), III:143–44; Smith, *Additions and Corrections*, 47–48.

156. *The Parliamentary Register; Or History of the Proceedings and Debates of the House of Lords, Vol. XIV* (London: J. Debrett, 1784), 36 (9 December 1783).

157. Sir N. William Wraxall, *Historical Memoirs of My Own Time,* edited and introduction by Richard Askham (London: Kegan Paul, Trench, and Trubner, 1904), 652; C. H. Philips, "The East India Company 'Interest' and the English Government, 1783–4," *Transactions of the Royal Historical Society* 20 (1937): 88, 91.

158. *The Parliamentary Register; or History of the Proceedings and Debates of the House of Commons,* Vol. XII (London: J. Debrett, 1784), 54 (18 November 1783).

159. [W. J. Mickle], *A Candid Examination of the Reasons for Depriving the East-India Company of its Charter* (London: J. Bew, 1779), 17; Emma Rothschild, "Adam Smith in the British Empire," in *Empire and Modern Political Thought,* ed. Sankar Muthu (Cambridge: CUP, 2002), 194–95.

160. Marshall, ed., *Writings and Speeches of Edmund Burke,* VI, 295–96.

161. Marshall, ed., *Writings and Speeches of Edmund Burke,* V, 387.

162. P. J. Marshall, "The East India Company's 'Ancient Form of Government' and the Exigencies of Empire: Bengal 1765 to 1773," in *Envisioning Empire: The New British World from 1763 to 1773,* ed. Robert A. Olwell and James M. Vaughn (London: Bloomsbury, 2020), 175, 189; H. V. Bowen, "British India, 1765–1813: The Metropolitan Context," in *The Oxford History of the British Empire, Vol. II: The Eighteenth Century,* ed. P. J. Marshall (Oxford: OUP, 1998), 532–33.

163. William Julius Mickle, *The Lusiad; or, The Discovery of India. An Epic Poem. Translated from The Original Portuguese of Luis de Camöens,* 2nd ed. (Oxford, 1778), lxxix.

164. *The Parliamentary Register; or History of the Proceedings and Debates of the House of Commons,* Vol. XII (London: J. Debrett, 1784), 51 (18 November 1783); *The Parliamentary Register; or History of the Proceedings and Debates of the House of Commons,* Vol. XVI (London: J. Debrett, 1784), 6 (17 July 1784).

165. Marshall, "Ancient Form," 185–86, 189; Marshall, *Making and Unmaking,* 214.

166. *Annual Register, or a View of the History, Politics and Literature for the Year 1793* (London, 1793), 119–21, 127–28; Henry Dundas to East India Company, 16 February 1793, IOR A/2/11a f. 361–62.

167. Bowen, *Business of Empire,* 36, 48–52.

168. Quoted by Michael Wagner, "The Levant Company," 303.

169. AddMS 32694 f. 9.

170. Wagner, "Levant Company," 295–313; John Carswell, *The South Sea Bubble* (London: Alan Sutton, 1960), 240.

171. Mr. O'Connor, *Considerations on the Trade to Africa, Together with A Proposal for Securing the Benefits thereof to* this *Nation* (London, 1749), 33 ("Society"); Glyndwr Williams, "The Hudson's Bay Company and Its Critics in the Eighteenth Century," *Transactions of the Royal Historical Society* 20 (1970): 157–58 ("outcry . . . common"), 162; Marie Peters, "State, Parliament, and Empire in the Mid 18th Century: Hudson's Bay and the Parliamentary Enquiry 1749," *Parliamentary History* 29, no. 2 (2010): 173, 176–80, 181–82, 187–88; Wagner, "The Levant Company," esp. 309, 312; David Chan Smith, "The Hudson's Bay Company, Social Legitimacy, and the Political Economy of Eighteenth-Century Empire." *WMQ* 75, no. 1 (2018): 79–108.

172. Christopher Leslie Brown, "1763 and the Genesis of British Africa," in *Envisioning Empire,* ed. Olwell and Vaughn, 115–16; Smith, "Hudson's Bay Company," 97–99; Williams, "Critics," 159–60, 164.

173. Michael H. Fisher, *Counterflows to Colonialism: Indian Travellers and Settlers in Britain, 1600–1857* (Delhi: Permanent Black, 2004), 65–71; Rozina Visram, *Asians in Britain: 400 Years of History* (London: Pluto Press, 2002), 18–33; Maya Jasanoff, *Liberty's Exiles: American Loyalists in the Revolutionary World* (New York: Alfred A. Knopf, 2011), 128–29.

174. Granville Sharp, *A Short Sketch of Temporary Regulations (Until Better Shall Be Proposed) for the Intended Settlement on the Grain Coast of Africa, Near Sierra Leona,* 3rd ed. (London, 1788); Prince Hoare, ed., *Memoirs of Granville Sharp, Esq.* (London: Henry Colburn and Co., 1820), 155–65; Christopher Leslie Brown, *Moral Capital: Foundations of British Abolitionism* (Chapel Hill: OIEHC, 2006), 188–89.

175. Jasanoff, *Liberty's Exiles,* 285.

176. Hoare, ed., *Memoirs,* 347.

177. Jasanoff, *Liberty's Exiles,* 287.

178. Quoted by Stephen J. Braidwood, *Black Poor and White Philanthropists: London's Blacks and the Foundation of the Sierra Leone Settlement, 1786–1791* (Liverpool: Liverpool University Press, 1994), 227.

179. [Granville Sharp], *Free English Territory in Africa* (London, [1790?]), 10–12; Hoare, ed., *Memoirs,* 358; Braidwood, *Black Poor and White Philanthropists,* 226–27.

180. Braidwood, *Black Poor and White Philanthropists,* 231.

181. [Sharp], *Free English Territory,* 9.

182. Braidwood, *Black Poor and White Philanthropists,* 234.

183. See, for example, the arguments of Bamber Gascoyne, MP for Liverpool, in *Parliamentary Register of History of the Proceedings and Debates of the House of Commons, Vol. XXIX* (London, 1791), 316 (3 May 1791).

184. *Journals of the House of Commons, from August the 10th 1790, in the Thirteenth Year of the Reign of King George the Third to December the 20th, 1791 In the Thirty-second Year of the Reign of King George the Third* ([London]: House of Commons, 1791), 454 (3 May 1791), 457 (4 May 1791).

185. Detector's Letter, II, in *Heads of the Speeches Delivered On the 18th and 19th April, 1791, in a Committee of the House of Commons, On A Motion Made By Mr. Wilberforce, for the Abolition of the Slave-Trade, with Detector's Letters, &c.* (Liverpool, 1791), 88.

186. *Reasons against giving a Territorial Grant to a Company of Merchants to Colonize and Cultivate The Peninsula of Sierra Leona on the Coast of Africa* (London, 1791), 2–6, 10, 13.

187. "Heads of a Bill for Incorporating Certain Persons Therein Named and Described, and their Successors, by the name and stile of the St. George's Bay Company," in *Heads of the Speeches Delivered On the 18th and 19th April, 1791, in a Committee of the House of Commons, On A Motion Made By Mr. Wilberforce, for the Abolition of the Slave-Trade, with Detector's Letters, &c.* (Liverpool, 1791), 79–80; Braidwood, *Black Poor and White Philanthropists,* 244–45; Jasanoff, *Liberty's Exiles,* 289.

188. Hoare, ed., *Memoirs,* 306.

189. 47 Geo III cap 44 (8 August 1807)

190. Tim Soriano, "The White Ensign on Land: The Royal Navy and Legal Authority in Early Sierra Leone," in *Networks and Connections in Legal History,* ed. Michael Lobban and Ian Williams (Cambridge: CUP, 2020), 171–78.

191. *Report of the Committee of the African Institution Read to the General Meeting on the 15th of July, 1807, Together with the Rules and Regulations Adopted for the Government of the Society* (London, 1811), 35–36.

192. Albert M. Hymanson, *The Sephardim of England: A History of the Spanish and Portuguese Jewish Community, 1492–1951* (London: Methuen, 1951), 201–2.

193. Captain Philip Beaver, *African Memoranda: Relative to an Attempt to Establish a British Settlement on the Island of Bulama, On the Western Coast of Africa, in the Year 1792* (London: C. and R. Baldwin, 1805), appendix 2, 421 (9 March 1792).

194. Philip D. Curtin, *Image of Africa: British Ideas and Action, 1780–1850* (London: Macmillan & Co., 1965), 111–12.

195. C. B. Wadstrom, *An essay on colonization, particularly applied to the Western Coast of Africa, with some free thoughts on cultivation and commerce* (London, 1794), 108–11, 114.

196. Braidwood, *Black Poor and White Philanthropists,* 240.

5. Corporate Innovations

Epigraph: Information Respecting the Settlement of New Plymouth, in New Zealand, From the Testimony of Eye-Witnesses (London: Smith and Elder, 1841), 4.

1. *Copy of the Correspondence which has passed between Sir J. S. Login and Robert Montgomery Martin, Esq.* (House of Commons, 22 July 1863), 3–4, 26; Robert Aldrich,

Banished Potentates: Dethroning and Exiling Indigenous Monarchs Under British and French Colonial Rule, 1815–1955 (Manchester: Manchester University Press, 2018), 78–79, 82.

2. Charles Beavan, ed., *Reports of Cases in Chancery* (London: V&R Stevens, Sons & Haynes, 1862), 29, 310; *The English Reports, Volume XXIV: Chancery XXIV* (Edinburgh: William Green & Sons, 1904), no. 182, 364; HL Deb 21 July 1856 vol. 143, cc. 1065–1067; Philip J. Stern, "The English East India Company and the Modern Corporation: Legacies, Lessons, and Limitations," *Seattle University Law Review* (2016): 434.

3. HC Deb 10 July 1833 vol. 19 c. 479.

4. Lauren Benton and Lisa Ford, *Rage for Order: The British Empire and the Origins of International Law, 1800–1850* (Cambridge, MA: HUP, 2016), 18.

5. Timothy L. Alborn, *Conceiving Companies: Joint-Stock Politics in Victorian England* (London and New York: Routledge, 1998), 27–28; Anna Gambles, *Protection and Politics: Conservative Economic Discourse, 1815–1852* (Woodbridge: The Boydell Press, 1999), 158–59.

6. J[oshua] Montefiore, "Vindication of Chartered Companies" n.d., [c. 1810], BL APAC MssEur B/27.

7. David Macpherson, *The History of the European Commerce with India* (London: Longman, Hurst, Rees, Orme, and Brown, 1812), iv, 348, 393, 410.

8. John Bruce, *Annals of the Honorable East-India Company from their Establishment by the Charter of Queen Elizabeth, 1600, to the Union of the London and English East-India Companies, 1707–8*, 3 vols. (London: Black, Parry, and Kingsbury, 1810), I:vi–vii.

9. Joshua Montefiore, *Commercial Dictionary: Containing the Present State of Mercantile Law, Practice, and Custom intended for The Use of the Cabinet, The Counting-House and the Library* (London: For the Author, 1803), s.v. "East-India Company"; Stanley Mirvis, "The Trial of Joshua Montefiore and the Limits of Atlantic Jewish Inclusion," in *From Catalonia to the Caribbean: The Sephardic Orbit from Medieval to Modern Times*, ed. Frederica Francesconi, Stanley Mirvis, and Brian Smollett (Brill, 2018), 249.

10. *Debates at the General Court of Proprietors of East-India Stock, on the 17th and 23d February 1813, On a Petition to Parliament for a Renewal of the Company's Charter as Far as it Regards Their Exclusive Privileges* (London: Black, Parry & Co., 1813), 9.

11. Montefiore, "Vindication," 27.

12. *Debates at the East-India House, During the Negotiation for a Renewal of the East-India Company's Charter* (London: Black, Parry & Co., 1813), 1:94; Robert Grant, *A Sketch of the History of the East-India Company from its First Formation to the Passing of the Regulating Act of 1773* (London: Black, Parry & Co., 1813).

13. Macpherson, *History*, 192–93.

14. *Debates at the General Court*, 170.

15. *An Act for Continuing in the East India Company for a Further Term, the Possession of the British Territories in India, Together with Certain Exclusive Privileges*, 53 Geo 3 c. 155 cc. 64–65.

16. *Minutes of Evidence Taken Before the Select Committee on the Affairs of the East India Company, Also an Appendix and Index, Volume II. Finance and Accounts—Trade* (House of Commons, 1832), 317–19.

17. F. W. Maitland, "Trust and Corporation," in *The Collected Papers of Frederic William Maitland, Volume III*, ed. H.A.L. Fisher (Cambridge: University Press, 1911), 404.

18. Quoted by Joshua Ehrlich, "The Crisis of Liberal Reform in India: Public Opinion, Pyrotechnics, and the Charter Act of 1833," *Modern Asian Studies* 52, no. 6 (2018): 2033.

19. Examination of James Cosmo Melvill, 3 May 1852, *Report from the Select Committee of the House of Lords Appointed to Inquire in to the Operation of the Act 3 & 4 Will. 4, c. 85, for the better Government of Her Majesty's Indian Territories* ([London], 1852), 3–4; Courtenay Ilbert, *The Government of India, Being a Digest of the Statute Law Relating Thereto* (Oxford: Clarendon Press, 1898), 84–85.

20. Ilbert, *Government of India*, 259.

21. H. V. Bowen, *The Business of Empire: The East India Company and Imperial Britain, 1756–1833* (Cambridge: CUP, 2005), 288–94.

22. Anthony Webster, *The Twilight of the East India Company: The Evolution of Anglo-Asian Commerce and Politics, 1790–1860* (Woodbridge: Boydell, 2009), 106; Geoffrey Jones,

Merchants to Multinationals: British Trading Companies in the Nineteenth and Twentieth Centuries (Oxford: OUP, 2000), 32.

23. C. A. Bayly, *Rulers, Townsmen, and Bazaars: North Indian Society in the Age of British Expansion, 1770–1870* (Cambridge: CUP, 1983), 229, 421, 449; David Kimche, "The Opening of the Red Sea to European Ships in the Eighteenth Century," *Middle Eastern Studies* 8, no. 1 (1972): 67; A. B. Leonard, "Underwriting British Trade to India and China, 1780–1835," *HJ* 55, no. 4 (2012): 992–94, 997–98, 1005.

24. Opinion of J. Campbell, R. M. Rolfe, R. Spankie, "The Case for the East India Company," 6 June 1839, IOR F/4/1752/71530 fol. 53.

25. Alexander J. Arbuthnot, ed., *Major-General Sir Thomas Munro, Bart., K.C.B., Governor of Madras, Selections from his Minutes and Other Official Writings* (London: C. Kegan Paul & Co., 1881), 12; Charles Dickens, "Patent Wrongs," *Household Words: A Weekly Journal*, New Series, 1, no. 35 (1853): 230; Tirthankar Roy, *India in the World Economy: From Antiquity to the Present* (Cambridge: CUP, 2012), 151–53.

26. *The Marine Insurance Company, Ltd., 1836–1936* (London: Hazell, Watson and Viney, 1936); Sarah Palmer, "The Indemnity in the London Marine Insurance Market, 1824–50," in *The Historian and the Business of Insurance*, ed. Oliver M. Westall (Manchester: Manchester UP, 1984), 76; Erika Rappaport, *A Thirst for Empire: How Tea Shaped the Modern World* (Princeton: PUP, 2017), 104–5; Michael Aldous, "Avoiding 'Negligence and Profusion': The Ownership and Organization of Anglo–Indian Trading Firms, 1813–1870," *Enterprise and Society* 17, no. 4 (2016): 661–62.

27. Deeds and Settlements of the East Indian Railway Company, IOR L/AG/46/11/1.

28. R. Macdonald Stephenson, *Report upon the Practicability and Advantages of the Introduction of Railways into British India* (London, 1845), 25; Edward Watkin, HC Deb 17 July 1857 vol. 146 c. 1718.

29. Chapman quoted in *A Letter to the Right Honourable Lord John Russell, M.P., &c. &c. &c. On the Subject of Indian Railways by an East Indian Merchant* (London: Smith, Elder, 1848), 121; Daniel Thorner, *Investment in Empire: British Railway and Steam Shipping Enterprise in India, 1825–1849* (Philadelphia: UPenn, 1950), 151–52; Manu Goswami, *Producing India: From Colonial Economy to National Space* (Chicago: University of Chicago Press, 2004), 49.

30. Quoted in Goswami, *Producing India*, 52–53.

31. Stephenson, *Report*, 21–22, 44; W. J. Macpherson, "Investment in India Railways, 1845–1875," *Economic History Review*, New series, 8, no. 2 (1955): 180; James Belich, *Replenishing the Earth: The Settler Revolution and the Rise of the Anglo-World, 1783–1939* (Oxford: OUP, 2009), 228.

32. "Indenture between the East India Company and the East Indian Railway Company," 17 August 1849, L/AG/46/11/1 pp. 169–87.

33. Stephenson, *Report*, 22.

34. Laura Bear, *Lines of the Nation: Indian Railway Workers, Bureaucracy, and the Intimate Historical Self* (New York: Columbia University Press, 2007); Ian Kerr, *Building the Railways of the Raj: 1850–1900* (Delhi: OUP, 1995); Ritika Prasad, *Tracks of Change: Railways and Everyday Life in Colonial India* (Cambridge: CUP, 2015).

35. East India Company, *Collection of Debate at the East-India House*, March 19, 1845–Aug. 25, 1858 (London, 1848–58), 217 (28 September 1853); "Examination of Alexander Rogers," 2 June 1840, *Report from the Select Committee on East India Produce* (21 July 1840), 302; Freda Harcourt, *Flagships of Imperialism: The P&O Company and the Politics of Empire from Its Origins to 1867* (Manchester: Manchester University Press, 2006), 70; Glen O'Hara, "New Histories of British Imperial Communication and the 'Networked World' of the 19th and Early 20th Centuries," *History Compass* 8, no. 7 (2010): 615.

36. Charles Northcote Cooke, *The Rise, Progress, and Present Condition of Banking in India* (Calcutta: P.M. Cranenburgh, 1863), 8.

37. James Oucherlany to Chief Secretary of Madras Government, 4 July 1840, IOR F/4/1895/80482, p. 56.

38. Jones, *Merchants to Multinationals*, 32–33; Aldous, "Avoiding 'Negligence and Profusion,'" 681, 752–53; Leonard, "Underwriting British Trade," 1005; Anthony Webster, "The Strategies and Limits of Gentlemanly Capitalism: The London East India Agency Houses,

Provincial Commercial Interests, and the Evolution of British Economic Policy in South and South East Asia, 1800–50," *Economic History Review* 59, no. 4 (2006): 748–49, 754–55.

39. Webster, "Strategies," 751–54, 757, Auckland quoted on 753.

40. P. J. Cain and A. G. Hopkins, *British Imperialism, 1688–2015,* 3rd ed. (New York: Longman, 2016), 173–74, 315; Goswami, *Producing India,* 94–95; Webster, "Strategies," 759–61; Webster, *Twilight,* 108–9.

41. "Banks in Colonies and Dependencies: Charters etc.," TNA T 64/381A; S. J. Butler, *Australia and New Zealand Bank: The Bank of Australasia and the Union Bank of Australia Limited* (London: Longmans, 1961), 21–27; Charles Jones, "Commercial Banks and Mortgage Companies," in *Business Imperialism, 1840–1930: An Inquiry Based on British Experience in Latin America,* ed. D.C.M. Platt (Oxford: Clarendon Press, 1977), 22, 40–41, 49–50, 52; Geoffrey Jones, "Competitive Advantages in British Multinational Banking Since 1890," in *Banks as Multinationals,* ed. Jones (London: Routledge, 2012), 33; D. T. Merrett, "Paradise Lost? British Banks in Australia," in *Banks as Multinationals,* ed. Jones, 65. I am so grateful to Lauren Jackson and Ted Leonhardt, two former students and research assistants, whose stellar work on this subject was indispensable in shaping my approach here. Lauren Jackson and Theodore Leonhardt, "Financing British Empire: Banking, Insurance, and the Rise of the Modern Corporation on a Continuum of Empire," unpublished paper, 1 May 2020.

42. Kathleen Mary Butler, *The Economics of Emancipation: Jamaica and Barbados, 1823–1843* (Chapel Hill and London: UNCP, 1995), 133–38.

43. Draft Despatch, Financial Department, 20 November 1850, IOR E/4/807 pp. 165–71.

44. Quoted by Webster, *Twilight,* 139.

45. James Wilson to Herman Merivale, 15 August 1853, Harry George Gordon to George Arbuthnot, 4 August 1853, SLNSW ML A2367 pp. 273–74, 279–82.

46. Montagu quoted in A. S. J. Baster, *The Imperial Banks* (London: P.S. King & Son, 1929), 60.

47. Alborn, *Conceiving Companies,* 85–86; Dror Wahrman, *Imagining the Middle Class: The Political Representation of Class in Britain, c.* 1780-1840 (Cambridge: CUP, 1995).

48. George R. Young, *Upon the history, principles, and prospects of the Bank of British North America and of the Colonial Bank* (London: Wm. S. Or and Co., 1838), 29.

49. G. M. Bell, *The Philosophy of Joint Stock Banking* (London: Longman, Orme, Brown, Green and Longmans, 1840), 22, 43.

50. HC Deb 25 March 1825 v. 12 cc.1220–27; Despina Vlami, *Trading with the Ottomans: The Levant Company in the Middle East* (London: I.B. Tauris, 2015), 278–82.

51. Arthur Mills, *Colonial Constitutions: An Outline of the Constitutional History and Existing Government of the British Dependencies* (London: John Murray, 1856), 170; *Report from the Select Committee on the West Coast of Africa Together with Minutes of Evidence, Appendix and Index, Part II* (Shannon: Irish University Press, 1968), 10; *Parliamentary Accounts and Papers* 31 (2 February–24 August 1843), 5; Inge van Hulle, "British Protection, Extraterritoriality and Protectorates in West Africa, 1807–80," in *Protection and Empire: A Global History,* ed. Bain Attwood, Lauren Benton, and Adam Clulow (Cambridge: CUP, 2017), 195–97.

52. [Charles Lamb], "The South Sea House," in *Elia, Essays Which Have Appeared under that Signature in the London Magazine* (London: Taylor and Hessey, 1823), 2.

53. *A Concise View of the Origin, Constitution and Proceedings of the Honorable Society of the Governor and Assistants of London, of the New Plantation in Ulster, within the realm of Ireland, commonly called The Irish Society* (London: Gye and Balne, 1822), 187; *The Skinners' Company Versus The Honourable The Irish Society and Others* (London: Richard Clay, 1836).

54. John S. Galbraith, *The Hudson's Bay Company as an Imperial Factor, 1821–1869* (Berkeley: University of California Press, 1957), 51; Allan K. McDougall, "Eastern Games, Western Lives, 1793–1846," in Allan K. McDougall, Lisa Philips, and Daniel L. Boxberger, eds., *Before and After the State: Politics, Poetics, and People(s) in the Pacific Northwest* (Vancouver and Toronto: UBC Press, 2018), 50–51; James R. Fichter, *So Great a Profit: How the East Indies Transfomed Anglo-American Capitalism* (Cambridge, MA: HUP, 2010), 216–17; Lawrence B. A. Hatter, *Citizens of Convenience: The Imperial Origins of American*

Nationhood on the U.S.-Canadian Border (Charlottesville and London: University of Virginia Press, 2017), 151–56.

55. Coltman to Sherbrooke, 14 May 1818, CO 42/181 f. 4v; Galbraith, *Hudson's Bay Company*, 48.

56. Michael Hughes, "Within the Grasp of Company Law: Land, Legitimacy, and the Racialization of the Métis, 1815–1821," *Ethnohistory* 63, no. 3 (2016): 528–31.

57. C. W. Robinson, *Life of Sir John Beverly Robinson* (Toronto: Morang & Co., 1904), 140–41.

58. Coltman to Sherbrooke, 14 May 1818, CO 42/181 f. 7–7v, 16v; Galbraith, *Hudson's Bay Company*, 6.

59. Tolly Bradford and Rich Connors, "The Making of a Company Colony: The Fur Trade War, the Colonial Office, and the Metamorphosis of the Hudson's Bay Company," *Canadian Journal of History* 55, no. 3 (2020): 171–96.

60. Galbraith, *The Hudson's Bay Company*, 5–9, 48, 114–15, 154–74, 186; Dale Gibson, *Law, Life, and Government at Red River, Volume I: Settlement and Governance, 1812–1872* (Montreal and Kingston: McGill-Queen's University Press, 2015), 21; R. M. Martin, *The Hudson's Bay Territories and Vancouver's Island* (London: T. and W. Boone, 1849), 5, 19–21, 46, 53–54; Ilya Vinkovetsky, *Russian America: An Overseas Colony of a Continental Empire, 1804–1867* (New York: OUP, 2011), 105–6.

61. James M'Queen, *A Geographical and Commercial View of Northern Central Africa* (Edinburgh: Blackwood, 1821), 267–68, 269–72; David Lambert, *Mastering the Niger: James MacQueen's African Geography and the Struggle over Atlantic Slavery* (Chicago: University of Chicago Press, 2013), chap. 3.

62. "Heads of a Charter," and "Prospectus," TNA CO 318/100, pp. 1–2; Butler, *Economics of Emancipation*, 131–32.

63. HC Deb 10 May 1824, cc. 611–12.

64. HC Deb 16 May 1825 vol. 13, cc. 608–9.

65. HC Deb 16 May 1825, c. 610.

66. HC Deb 29 March 1825, c. 1278–79; Thomas Fowell Buxton, *Observations on the West-India Company Bill* (London: Ellerton and Henderson, 1825).

67. James Stephen Jr. to Robert Wilmot Horton, 16 April 1825 and 9 August 1825, CO 318/100.

68. Robert W. Randall, *Real del Monte: A British Mining Venture in Mexico* (Austin: University of Texas Press, 1972), 34.

69. James Taylor, *Boardroom Scandal: The Criminalization of Company Fraud in Nineteenth-Century Britain* (Oxford: OUP, 2013), 11–12.

70. Randall, *Real del Monte*, 37–38, 42–44, 65–85.

71. *The Law Journal Reports for the Year 1825*, Vol. 3 (London: J.W. Paget, 1825), 75, 78, 81, 82; Ron Harris, "Political Economy, Interest Groups, Legal Institutions, and the Repeal of the Bubble Act in 1825," *Economic History Review* 50, no. 4 (1997): 687–88.

72. John George, *A View of the Existing Law, Affecting Unincorporated Joint Stock Companies* (London: S. Sweet, 1825), 53; Bishop Carleton Hunt, *The Development of the Business Corporation in England 1800–1867* (Cambridge, MA: HUP, 1936), 41–42; Ron Harris, *Industrializing English Law: Entrepreneurship and Business Organization, 1720–1844* (Cambridge: CUP, 2000), 243–47; Frederick Martin, *The History of Lloyd's and of Marine Insurance in Great Britain* (London: Macmillan and Co, 1876), 229–52; Palmer, "Indemnity," 76; James Taylor, *Creating Capitalism: Joint-Stock Enterprise in British Politics and Culture, 1800–1870* (Woodbridge: Boydell, 2006), 109.

73. "MacGregor (and 'Ingenious' Counsel)," *Bells Life in London and Sporting Chronicle* 3, no. 99 (18 January 1824), 18; "The Court of Poyais: A New Song for the New World," *John Bull* 4, no. 11 (15 March 1824), 93; Matthew Brown, "Inca, Sailor, Soldier, King: Gregor MacGregor and the Early Nineteenth-Century Caribbean," *Bulletin of Latin American Research* 24, no. 1 (2005): 44, 48, 53, 55; Damian Clavel, "What's in a Fraud? The Many Worlds of Gregor MacGregor, 1817–1824," *Enterprise and Society* 22, no. 4 (2021): 997-1036; Douglas Pike, *Paradise of Dissent: South Australia, 1829–1857*, 2nd ed. (London and New York: Melbourne University Press, 1967), 33.

74. "Sir Gregor McGregor v Lowe," *John Bull* 4, no. 17 (26 April 1824), 142; Brown, "Inca, Sailor, Soldier, King," 55-56; Clavel, "What's in a Fraud?," 1027-28.

75. Robert A. Naylor, *Penny Ante Imperialism: The Mosquito Shore and the Bay of Honduras, 1600–1914, A Case Study in British Informal Empire* (Rutherford: Farleigh Dickinson, 1989), 120.

76. John Woodland, *Money Pits: British Mining Companies in the Californian and Australian Gold Rushes of the 1850s* (London: Routledge, 2016), 17–20; Clavel, "What's in a Fraud?," 1017-18.

77. *Report from the Select Committee on Emigration from the United Kingdom* (House of Commons, 26 May 1826), 101; Robert Grant, *Representations of British Emigration, Colonisation, and Settlement: Imagining Empire, 1800–1860* (Basingstoke: Palgrave, 2005), 51; John Fox, *Macnamara's Irish Colony and the United States Taking of California in 1846* (Jefferson, NC and London: McFarland & Company, 2000), 27–28; Woodland, *Money Pits*, 17, 22.

78. Nigel Leask, "Robert Burns and Latin America," in *Robert Burns and Transatlantic Culture*, ed. Sharon Alker, Leith Davis, and Holly Faith Nelson (London and New York: Routledge, 2002), 135; Fox, *Macnamara's Irish Colony*, 28.

79. Robert C. Lee, *The Canada Company and the Huron Tract, 1826–1853: Personalities, Profits, and Politics* (Toronto: Natural Heritage Books, 2004), 42, 51.

80. William Morris, *A Letter on the Subject of the Clergy Reserves, Addressed to the Very Rev. Principal Macfarlan and the Rev. Dr. Burns* (Toronto, 1838), appendix 1, i–ii; Curtis Fahey, *The Anglican Experience in Upper Canada, 1791–1854* (Ottawa: Carleton University Press, 1991), 63–64; Lee, *Canada Company*, 30.

81. Minutes, 23 May 1826, CO 42/407 fols. 47–54; *Indian Treaties and Surrenders* (Ottawa: Brown Chamberlin, 1891), I:71–75; Lee, *Canada Company*, 39.

82. Alison Bashford and Joyce E. Chaplin, *The New Worlds of Thomas Robert Malthus: Rereading the Principle of Population* (Princeton: PUP, 2018), 208–12.

83. John Galt, "Biographical Sketch of William Paterson," *The New Monthly Magazine and Literary Journal, Part II* (London: Henry Colburn, 1832), 176; John Galt, *The Autobiography of John Galt* (London: Cochrane and M'Crone, 1833), 158–60, 296–97; Matthew Birchall, "History, Sovereignty, Capital: Company Colonization in South Australia and New Zealand," *Journal of Global History* (2020), 81–83, 107–9; Lee, *Canada Company*, 16–31, 42–48, 240n30 (Robinson quoted on 19); Angela Esterhammer, "Galt the Speculator: *Sir Andrew Wylie*, *The Entail*, and *Lawrie Todd*," in *International Companion to John Galt*, ed. Gerard Carruthers and Colin Kidd (Glasgow: Scottish Literature International, 2017), 49.

84. Birchall, "History, Sovereignty, Capital," 54, 62–63; Zoë Laidlaw, *Colonial Connections, 1815–45: Patronage, The Information Revolution, and Colonial Government* (Manchester: Manchester University Press, 2005), 132.

85. Opinion of J. B. Bosanquet, 29 July 1824, IOR L/L/6/2, p. 608 no. 682.

86. Brief, n.d. [1826], TNA CO 280/2 ff. 315–16; *Australian Agricultural Company* (London: Ruthven and Whitcomb, 1826), 7–8, 10–11; Opinion of J. B. Bosanquet, 29 July 1824, IOR L/L/6/2, p. 608 no. 682.

87. J. Strettell Brickwood, "Statement," TS 25/2039/52, p. 497; *Proposed Plan for Australian Agricultural Company*, n.d. [1824], CO 28/2 fols., 7–8; *Proposals for a charter for an Australian Agricultural Company* (1824), CO 280/2 fols., 22–24.

88. Proposed Subscribers to Earl of Bathurst, 22 May 1824, CO 280/1 fol., 6.

89. Belich, *Replenishing the Earth*, 276.

90. Donald Nerbas, "Empire, Colonial Enterprise, and Speculation: Cape Breton's Coal Boom of the 1860s," *Journal of Imperial and Commonwealth History* 46, no. 6 (2018): 1070; Daniel Samson and Danny Samson, "Industrial Colonization: The Colonial Context of the General Mining Association, Nova Scotia, 1825–1842," *Acadiensis* 29, no. 1 (1999): 6–9, 18 ("proprietary").

91. Hunt, *Development of the Business Corporation*, 58; Robert Montgomery Martin, *Statistics of the Colonies of the British Empire* (London, 1834), 76; Lucille H. Campey, *With Axe and Bible: The Scottish Pioneers of New Brunswick, 1784–1874* (Toronto: National Heritage Books, 2007), 105.

92. *Case of the Right Hon. Alexander Earl of Stirling and Dovan* (London: Hatchard and Son, 1833), 39, 55–56; Simon Macgregor, *The Stirling Peerage: Trial of Alexander Humphrys*

or *Alexander, Styling Himself Earl of Stirling* (Edinburgh: William Blackwood and Sons, 1839), lxxv, lxxxii, 14–15; Archibald Swinton, *Report of the Trial of Alexander Humphreys Or Alexander, Claiming the Title of Earl of Stirling* (Edinburgh, 1839), 355.

93. Prospectus, 25 February 1832, Report, 6 April 1832, and Nathaniel Gould to Howick, 17 September 1832, CO 42/248 fols. 9, 28, 166; "Report of the Provisional Committee of the British American Land Company," 6 April 1832, CO 42/328 fols. 28.

94. Minutes of Meeting, 9 February 1832, Galt to Howick, 24 February and 28 April 1832, "Minutes of Agreement," n.d. [1832], and CO 42/248 fols. 4–5, 8, 44, 52.

95. Jennifer Scott, "Reciprocal Investments: John Galt, the Periodical Press, and the Business of North American Emigration," *Victorian Periodicals Review* (Fall 2013): 369.

96. David E. Latané, *William Maginn and the British Press: A Critical Biography* (London: Routledge, 2013), 65. [William Dunlop], "Upper Canada By A Backwoodsman," *Blackwood's Magazine*, 238; [William Dunlop], *Statistical Sketches of Upper Canada, for the Use of Emigrants, by A Backwoodsman* (London: John Murray, 1832); Tiger-Galt-Picken, "Canada," *Fraser's Magazine* 5, 30 (July 1832); [Andrew Picken and John Galt], *The Canadas as They Now Are* (London: James Duncan, 1833).

97. [Benjamin Disraeli], *Lawyers and Legislators: Or Notes on the American Mining Companies* (London: John Murray, 1825), 24; [Benjamin Disraeli], *An Inquiry into the Plans, Progress, and Policy of the American Mining Companies*, 3rd ed. (London: John Murray, 1825); Clavel, "What's in a Fraud?," 1018.

98. Stephen quoted in Bernard Semmel, *The Rise of Free Trade Imperialism: Classical Political Economy and the Empire of Free Trade and Imperialism* (Cambridge: Cambridge, 1970), 120; *Times* (7 June 1827) quoted in Tony Ballantyne, "Remaking the Empire from Newgate: Wakefield's A Letter from Sydney," in *Ten Books That Shaped the British Empire: Creating an Imperial Commons*, ed. Antoinette Burton and Isabel Hofmeyr (Durham, NC: DUP, 2014), 33, 38–39; Pike, *Paradise of Dissent*, 54.

99. Tony Ballantyne, "The Theory and Practice of Empire-Building: Edward Gibbon Wakefield and 'Systematic Colonisation,'" in *The Routledge History of Western Empires*, ed. Robert Aldrich and Kirsten McKenzie (Routledge, 2013), 93–94; Ballantyne, "Remaking the Empire," 42.

100. Semmel, *Rise*, 76–77, 103–9; Pike, *Paradise of Dissent*, 42; Peter Burroughs, *Britain and Australia, 1831–1855: A Study in Imperial Relations and Crown Lands Administration* (Oxford: Clarendon Press, 1967), 35–75; Belich, *Replenishing the Earth*, 146–47; Bashford and Chaplin, *New Worlds*, 234; "Torrens, Robert (1780–1864)," *Australian Dictionary of Biography* (1967), http://adb.anu.edu.au/biography/torrens-robert-2740.

101. [Edward Gibbon Wakefield], *A Letter from Sydney, the Principal Town of Australia, Together with the Outline of a System of Colonization*, ed. Robert Gouger (London, 1829), 186–87, 201–4, *Rise*, 78, 83; Angela Woollacott, *Settler Society in the Australian Colonies: Self-Government and Imperial Culture* (Oxford: OUP, 2015), 41–43.

102. Karl Marx, *Capital: A Critique of Political Economy*, ed. Friedrich Engels (New York: Modern Library, 1936), I:742; Ballantyne, "Theory and Practice," 90.

103. [Edward Gibbon Wakefield], *England and America: A Comparison of the Social and Political State of Both Nations* (London: Richard Bentley, 1833), II:184.

104. *Plan of a Company to be established for the purpose of founding a colony in Southern Australia* (London: Ridgeway and Sons, Piccadilly, 1832), CO 13/1; Pike, *Paradise of Dissent*, 58.

105. Anthony Bacon to [Thomas Frederick Elliot], 1 November 1831, CO 13/1 ff. 72–73; Bashford and Chaplin, *New Worlds*, 205–8.

106. Wakefield, *England and America*: 1:18, 2:234, 251–53.

107. Birchall, "History, Sovereignty, Capital," 5.

108. Semmel, *Rise*, 63–64.

109. *Report from the Select Committee on The Disposal of Lands in the British Colonies* (London: House of Commons, 1836), 239–303.

110. "South Australian Land Company Prospectus," (1832) CO 13/1 f. 79, 82; Wakefield, *England and America*, 118–19; Birchall, "History, Sovereignty, Capital," 141; Pike, *Paradise of Dissent*, 81, 111.

111. "Carolina" quoted in Birchall, "History, Sovereignty, Capital," 7; Wakefield, *England and America,* 1:308.

112. Whitmore, Torrens, et al., to Goderich, 4 June 1832, CO 13 / 1 fol. 103v–104, 108.

113. Wakefield, *England and America,* 2:241, 253.

114. *Plan of a Company,* ff. 10–11, 27, 32–36; Memorandum, 31 October 1831 CO 13 / 1 ff. 69–71.

115. J. Stephen, 14 July 1832, CO 13 / 1 f. 265, 268, 270, 271, 273–75, 283–84; Birchall, "History, Sovereignty, Capital," 9–10; Burroughs, *Britain and Australia,* 172.

116. R. W. Hay to R. Torrens, 17 July 1832, CO 13 / 1 f. 179.

117. R. W. Hay to R. Torrens, 6 August 1832, CO 13 / 1 ff. 180; Torrens to Goderich, 19 July 1832, CO 13 / 1 f. 179.

118. Provisional Committee to E. G. Stanley, 21 February 1834, CO 13 / 2 f. 7v–7r; "Draft of a Proposed Charter for the South Australian Commission, with some Introductory Remarks," CO 13 / 2 f. 9r–10; Pike, *Paradise of Dissent,* 64–65, 81; Birchall, "History, Sovereignty, Capital," 155–56, 160–63.

119. *Draft of a Proposed Charter for the South Australian Commission* (London: William Nicol, 1834), TNA CO 13 / 2 fol. 57.

120. *Outline of the Plan of a Proposed Colony to be Founded on the South Coast of Australia; With An Account of The Soil, Climate, Rivers, &c, With Maps* (London: Ridgway and Sons, 1834), 3–4; "The South Australian Association," *The Spectator,* 11 January 1834, 10.

121. George Grote to John Lefevre, 21 March 1834 CO 13 / 2 fol. 117v–118r.

122. "New Colony of South Australia," *The Asiatic Journal,* 1 August 1834, 307; "South Australian Association for Emigration," *The Times,* 1 July 1834, 4.

123. Semmel, *Rise,* 117.

124. John Lefevre to W. W. Whitmore, 17 March 1834, CO 13 / 2 f. 13r; Robert Gouger, *The Founding of South Australia as Recorded in the Journals of Mr. Robert Gouger, First Colonial Secretary,* ed. Edwin Hodder (London: Sampson Low, Marston, and Company Ltd., 1898), 88, 97.

125. James Stephen, 4 July 1834, CO 13 / 2, f. 214r, 215v. Robert Foster and Paul Sendziuk, *A History of South Australia* (Cambridge: CUP, 2018), 11.

126. Pike, *Paradise of Dissent,* 64, 71–72.

127. HC Deb 29 July 1834 vol. 25 c. 701.

128. "The Whig Humbug Australian Scheme," *The Age,* 3 August 1834, 243; "The South Australian Swindle," *The Age,* 20 March 1836, 96; "The New Province of South Australia," *The Spectator,* 19 July 1834, 682.

129. "Full Exposure of the Whig Colony Bubble," *The Age,* 7 September 1834, 282.

130. *The New British Province of South Australia,* 2nd ed. (London: C Knight, 1835), 150, 183–84.

131. T. J. Maslen to Goderich, 19 March 1831, TNA MPG 1 / 681.

132. "The New Province of South Australia," *The Spectator,* 19 July 1834, 682.

133. Adam Smith, *An Inquiry into the Nature and Causes of the Wealth of Nations by Adam Smith, LL.D., With a Commentary by the Author of "England and America,"* 4 vols. (London: Charles Knight, 1835–39); Wakefield quoted by Tim Causer and Philip Schofield, eds., *Panopticon versus New South Wales and Other Writings on Australia* (London: UCL Press, 2022), xcix–c.

134. Harriet Grote, *The Personal Life of George Grote* (London, 1873), 23–24, 36–37.

135. Pike, *Paradise of Dissent,* 90; H. J. Spencer, "Buller, Charles (1806–1848), politician and wit," *Oxford Dictionary of National Biography,* 23 September 2004, rev. 3 January 2008, https://doi.org/10.1093/ref:odnb/3913.

136. Pratap Bhanu Mehta, "Liberalism, Nation, and Empire: The Case of J. S. Mill," in *Empire and Modern Political Thought,* ed. Sankar Muthu (Cambridge: CUP, 2012), 257n65; Semmel, *Rise,* 119.

137. Pike, *Paradise of Dissent,* 91–92.

138. David Armitage, "Globalizing Jeremy Bentham," *History of Political Thought* 32, no. 1 (2011); R. N. Ghosh, "Bentham on Colonies and Colonization," *Indian Economic Review* 6, no. 4 (1963): 64–80.

139. Jeremy Bentham, "Pauper Management Improved," *The Collected Works of Jeremy Bentham: Writings on the Poor Laws, Vol. 2*, ed. Michael Quinn (Oxford: OUP, 2010); L. J. Hume, *Bentham and Bureaucracy* (Cambridge: CUP, 1981), 134–35, 138; Gertrude Himmelfarb, *Victorian Minds: A Study of Intellectuals in Crisis and Ideologies in Transition* (New York: Knopf, 1968), 74.

140. Jeremy Bentham, "Colonization Society Company Proposals," 11 August 1831, Bentham (Jeremy) Papers, Special Collections, University College London, Bentham MS Box 008, 171, 177, 179–80, 183; Barbara Arneil, "Jeremy Bentham: Pauperism, Colonialism, and Imperialism," *American Political Science Review* 115, no. 4 (2021): 1153; Causer and Schofield, eds., *Panopticon versus New South Wales*, c-ciii (I regrettably only became aware of Causer and Schofield's publication of Bentham's treatise too late to make better use of it here); Bronwen Everill, *Abolition and Empire in Sierra Leone and Liberia* (Basingstoke: Palgrave Macmillan, 2013), 1; Philip Schofield, "Jeremy Bentham on South Australia, Colonial Government and Representative Democracy," in *Jeremy Bentham and Australia: Convicts, Utility, and Empire,* ed. Tim Causer, Margot Finn, and Philip Schofield (London: UCL, 2022); Semmel, *Rise*, 94.

141. 4–5 William IV cap. 95 (15 August 1834).

142. C. B. Adderley, *Review of "The Colonial Policy of Lord J. Russell's Administration," by Earl Grey, 1853; and of Subsequent Colonial History* (London: Edward Stanford, 1869), 116.

143. Pike, *Paradise of Dissent*, 98–99.

144. "Draft of a Proposed Charter," f. 9r, 12v; *Outline of the Plan*, 6–8.

145. Birchall, "History, Sovereignty, Capital," 163–86; Burroughs, *Britain and Australia*, 178–79; Pike, *Paradise of Dissent*, 87, 121.

146. Birchall, "History, Sovereignty, Capital," 7; Edwin Hodder, *George Fife Angas, Father and Founder of South Australia* (London: Hodder and Stoughton, 1891), 181–82; Pike, *Paradise of Dissent*, 127–30; P. A. Howell, "Angas, George Fife (1789–1879)" *Oxford Dictionary of National Biography* (23 September 2004), https://doi.org/10.1093/ref:odnb/537.

147. William J. Griffith, *Empires in the Wilderness: Foreign Colonization and Development in Guatemala, 1834–1844* (Chapel Hill: UNCP, 1965), 69n29; Hodder, *George Fife Angas,* 125; Naylor, *Penny Ante Imperialism,* 120–21; "Peter Harriss Abbott," Centre for the Study of the Legacies of British Slavery, www.ucl.ac.uk/lbs/person/view/43811.

148. Naylor, *Penny Ante Imperialism,* 123–24.

149. A. Eugene Havens and William L. Flinn, eds., *Internal Colonialism and Structural Change in Colombia* (New York: Praeger, 1970); Ana Carolina Teixeira Delgado, *Internal Colonialism and International Relations: Tracks of Decolonization in Bolivia* (Abingdon: Routledge, 2021).

150. Griffith, *Empires in the Wilderness*, 8 (quoting Gálvez), 17–19.

151. *Mr. Anderson's Report* (London: Manning and Mason, 1839), 14–33; *Brief Statement Supported By Original Documents of Important Grants Conceded to the Eastern Coast of Central America Commercial & Agricultural Company by the State of Guatemala* (London: Manning and Mason, 1840), 169; Griffith, *Empires in the Wilderness, 19–22,* 32, 64–65, 67–68; Craig S. Revels, "Concessions, Conflict, and the Rebirth of the Honduran Mahogany Trade," *Journal of Latin American Geography* 2, no. 1 (2003): 4; Revels, "Timber, Trade, and Transformation: A Historical Geography of Mahogany in Honduras," unpublished PhD dissertation, Louisiana State University, 2002, 106; Ralph Lee Woodward, *Rafael Carrera and the Emergence of the Republic of Guatemala, 1821–1871* (Athens: University of Georgia Press, 1993, repr. 2008), 132, 374.

152. "Emigration to Vera Paz," [n.d.], BL Add MS 40510 fol. 274–77; Griffith, *Empires in the Wilderness,* 22, 129–30.

153. Griffith, *Empires in the Wilderness,* 24–27, 65, 68, 71–72, 187.

154. Griffith, *Empires in the Wilderness,* 112, 122–23, 152–53, 155, 160, 224.

155. Ora-Westley Schwemmer, "The Belgian Colonization Company, 1840–1858," unpublished PhD dissertation, Tulane University, 1966, 23–27, 31–33; Woodward, *Rafael Carrera,* 132.

156. Joseph Blocher and Mitu Gulati, "Transferable Sovereignty: Lessons from the History of the Congo Free State," *Duke Law Journal* 69, no. 6 (2020): 1227–28; Schwemmer, "Belgian Colonization Company," 9–11, 13–22.

157. *Report of the Proceedings and Evidence in the Arbitration between the King and Government of the Hawaiian Islands and Messrs. Ladd & Co.* (Honolulu, Oahu: Charles E. Hitchcock, 1846), 123; Manley Hopkins, *Hawaii: The Past, Present, and Future of Its Island-kingdom* (London: Longmans, Green, and Co, 1866), 304–9.

158. John S. Galbraith, *The Little Emperor: Governor Simpson of the Hudson's Bay Company* (Toronto: Macmillan, 1976), 121.

159. Martin, *Hudson's Bay Territories*, app. C, 166–67; Galbraith, *Hudson's Bay Company*, 192–217, 247–82, 455n35.

160. Galbraith, *Hudson's Bay Company*, 283–84.

161. Martin, *Hudson's Bay Territories*, 47, 111, 148; "Statement of the Rights, as to Territory, Trade, Taxation and Government Claimed and Exercised by the Hudson's Bay Company on the Continent of North America," [13 September 1849], in *Papers relating to the Legality of the Powers in respect to Territory, Trade, Taxation and Government claimed or exercises by the Hudson's Bay Company, on the Continent of North America, under the Charter of Charles the Second, or in Virtue of any other Right or Title* ([London]: House of Commons, 12 July 1850), 4–6.

162. Quoted by Barry M. Gough, "Crown, Company, and Charter: Founding Vancouver Island Colony—A Chapter in Victorian Empire Making," *BC Studies* 176 (2012/13).

163. Gladstone quoted in Jeremy Mouat, "Situating Vancouver Island in the British World, 1846–49," *BC Studies* 145 (2005); Galbraith, *Hudson's Bay Company*, 288–90, 294–300; Richard Mackie, "The Colonization of Vancouver Island, 1849–1858," *BC Studies* 96 (1992–93), 3–40; Stephen Royle, *Company, Crown, and Colony: The Hudson's Bay Company and Territorial Endeavour in Western Canada* (London: I. B. Tauris, 2011).

164. Ballantyne, "Theory and Practice," 93, 96–98; Gregory Dening Taylor, *The Law of the Land: The Advent of the Torrens System in Canada* (Toronto: University of Toronto Press, 2008), 31.

165. Onur Ulas Ince, "Deprovincializing Racial Capitalism: John Crawfurd and Settler Colonialism in India," *American Political Science Review* 116, no. 1 (2022): 146–47, 153–56.

166. Robert Gouger to John Lefevre, 1 April 1834 CO 13/2 f. 137v.

167. *Western Australia, Containing a Statement of the Condition and Prospects of that Colony, And Some Account of the Western Australian Company's Settlement of Australind, With a Map of the Colony* (London: Smith, Elder & Co., 1842), 165; Woollacott, *Settler Society*, 50–56.

168. "A Plan of Colonization for Ireland," *Supplement to The Spectator* 979 (3 April 1847), 6; Hilary M. Carey, *God's Empire: Religion and Colonialism in the British World, c. 1801–1908* (Cambridge: CUP, 2010), 351–52.

169. Petition of John Innes, 24 September 1846, BT 1/463/14 [p. 5ff.]; *Observations Relative to the Establishment of the West India Agricultural Company* (London: J. Peters, 1836).

170. *Suggestions for an United West-India Government and Joint Stock Company* (Jamaica: For the Author, 1849), 18–20, 25–30, 36, 39.

171. Peter Adams, *Fatal Necessity: British Intervention in New Zealand, 1830–1847* (Auckland: Auckland University Press, 1977, repr., Wellington: Bridget Williams Books, 2013), 83.

172. New Zealand Land Company prospectus, 2 May 1839 TNA C 184 f. 36; Adams, *Fatal Necessity*, 83, 94.

173. [Edward Jerningham Wakefield], *The British Colonization of New Zealand; Being an Account of the Principles, Objects, and Plans of the New Zealand Association* (London, 1837), 2, 64, 66.

174. *Report from the Select Committee on New Zealand* (House of Commons, 1840), 148–49; Adams, *Fatal Necessity*, 79–81, 99; Birchall, "History, Sovereignty, Capital," 13.

175. *Report from the Select Committee on New Zealand* (House of Commons, 1840), 149–50.

176. Adams, *Fatal Necessity*, 82.

177. "The New Zealand Bill," *The Asiatic Journal and Monthly Register for British and Foreign India, China, and Australasia, Volume XXVI* (May–August 1838) (London, 1838), 240; *The Times* ("attempt . . . despotism") quoted in J. A. Harrop, "The Companies and British Sovereignty, 1825–1850," in *The Cambridge History of the British Empire, Volume VII, Part II: New Zealand*, ed. J. Holland Rose, A. P. Newton, and E. A. Benians (Cambridge: CUP, 1933), 70 and ("philosophical . . . schemes") by Semmel, *Rise*, 113.

178. "Colonization," *The Edinburgh Review, or Critical Journal* 91 (1850): 37.

179. Adams, *Fatal Necessity,* 87.

180. "New Zealand Land Company" (2 May 1839) TNA C 184 ff.36–38.

181. Spencer, "Buller."

182. Bain Attwood, "Protection Claims: The British, Maori and the Islands of New Zealand, 1800–40," in *Protection and Empire,* ed. Attwood, Benton, and Clulow, 165–66; Harrop, "Companies," 72, 78.

183. *New Zealand Journal* 3, no. 56 (5 March 1842), 57; Lydia Wevers, *Country of Writing: Travel Writing and New Zealand, 1809–1900* (Auckland: Auckland University Press, 2002), 128; Grant, *Representations,* 104.

184. *Information Respecting the Settlement of New Plymouth in New Zealand, From the Testimony of Eye-Witnesses* (London: Smith and Elder, 1841), 3–4; Adams, *Fatal Necessity,* 21–22, 24, 30, 99.

185. "An Act Empowering the Canterbury Association to Dispose of Lands in New Zealand," 13 Vic cap. 60.

186. Harrop, "Companies," 77.

187. "Whale Fishery and Steam Communication Company," *New Zealand Journal* 3, no. 74 (12 November 1842), 267; *Letters from Settlers & Labouring Emigrants in the New Zealand Company's Settlements of Wellington, Nelson & New Plymouth* (London, 1843), 23–24.

188. Belich, *Replenishing the Earth,* 366; Aaron Graham, "Incorporation and Company Formation in Australasia, 1790–1860," *Australian Economic History Review* 60, no. 3 (2020): 322–45.

189. Mel Davies, "Copper and Credit: Commission Agents and the South Australian Mining Association 1845–77," *Australian Economic History Review* 23, no. 1 (1983): 58–77; Woodland, *Money Pits,* 57.

190. Burroughs, *Britain and Australia,* 221.

191. Society for the Promotion of Colonization, "Report of the Committee," *Report of the General Committee, February 1849* (London, 1849), 9–10.

192. Caroline Chisolm, *The A.B.C. of Colonization* (London, 1850), 6, 28, 35; Janet C. Myers, *Antipodal England: Emigration and Portable Domesticity in the Victorian Imagination* (Albany: State University of New York Press, 2009), 30; Wendy Cameron and Mary McDougall Maude, *Assisting Emigration to Upper Canada: The Petworth Project* (Montreal & Kingston: McGill-Queen's University Press, 2000); Robin Haines, *Emigration and the Labouring Poor: Australian Recruitment in Britain and Ireland, 1831–60* (Basingstoke: Macmillan, 1997), 170, 192–93, 212–17, 220–49.

6. Limiting Liabilities

Epigraph: Sir John William Kaye, "A Familiar Epistle from Mr. John Company to Mr. John Bull," *Blackwood's Edinburgh Magazine* 83 (February 1858), 257.

1. W. S. Gilbert and Arthur Sullivan, *An Original Comic Opera in Two Acts entitled Utopia Limited or, The Flowers of Progress* (London: Chappel & Co., 1893), 34.

2. Gregory Claeys, *Searching for Utopia: The History of an Idea* (London: Thames and Hudson, 2011).

3. Albert Borowitz, "Gilbert and Sullivan on Corporation Law: Utopia, Limited and the Panama Canal Frauds," *Legal Studies Forum* 29, no. 2 (2005): 941–56; Rob McQueen, "The Flowers of Progress: Corporations Law in the Colonies," *Griffith Law Review* 17, no. 1 (2008): 384–87; Jeffrey Richards, *Imperialism and Music: Britain, 1876–1953* (Manchester: Manchester University Press, 2001), 34–36. On Hawaii, see Sally Engle Merry, *Colonizing Hawai'i: The Cultural Power of Law* (Princeton: PUP, 2000).

4. James Taylor, *Boardroom Scandal: The Criminalization of Company Fraud in Nineteenth-Century Britain* (Oxford: OUP, 2013), esp. chs. 8–9.

5. Gilbert and Sullivan, *Utopia Limited,* 30–31.

6. G. Lyall Jr. to T. C. Harrington Esq., 9 June 1850, CO 208/305 f. 476.

7. Notice of Special General Court of Proprietors, 7 April 1849, *The London Gazette,* 13 April 1849, 1219.

8. *Papers relating to the Legality of the Powers in respect to Territory, Trade, Taxation and Government claimed or exercises by the Hudson's Bay Company, on the Continent of North America, under the Charter of Charles the Second, or in Virtue of any other Right or Title* ([London]: House of Commons, 1850), 7–14; HC Deb 13 July 1848, vol. 100, cc. 469–70; John S. Galbraith, *The Hudson's Bay Company as an Imperial Factor, 1821–1869* (Berkeley: University of California Press, 1957), 322–25, 328-30.

9. HC Deb 3 June 1853, vol. 127 c. 1194; 9 June 1853 vol. 127 c. 1305; 23 June 1853 vol. 128 c. 611; 27 June 1853 vol. 128 c. 816.

10. HC Deb 27 June 1853 vol. 128 c. 832.

11. HC Deb 3 June 1853 vol. 127 c. 1174, 23 June 1853 vol. 128 c. 669, 27 June 1853 vol. 128 c. 821.

12. HC Deb 09 June 1853 vol. 127 c. 1304-5.

13. HC Deb 23 June 1853 vol. 128 c. 645.

14. HC Deb 03 June 1853 vol. 127 c. 1173–74.

15. HC Deb 23 June 1853 vol. 128 c. 665, 893–94.

16. Examination of John Stuart Mill (21 June 1852), *The Sessional Papers Printed By Order of the House of Lords, Or Presented by Royal Command in the Session 1852 (15 & 16 Victoriae),* Vol. XIX (1852), 310–11.

17. Douglas M. Peers, "Imperial Epitaph: John Stuart Mill's Defence of the East India Company," in *J. S. Mill's Encounter with India,* ed. Martin I. Moir, Douglas M. Peers, and Lynn Zastoupil (Toronto: University of Toronto Press, 1999), 1198–1220; Mark Tunick, "Tolerant Imperialism: John Stuart Mill's Defense of British Rule in India," *Review of Politics* 68 (2006): 586–611.

18. Examination of John Stuart Mill (21 June 1852), 300–301, 314.

19. John Stuart Mill, *Centralisation* (1862), in *The Collected Works of John Stuart Mill,* ed. J. M. Robson (Toronto: University of Toronto Press, 1977), 19:592; J. S. Mill, *On Liberty* (1859), in *Collected Works,* ed. Robson, 18:306.

20. Timothy L. Alborn, *Conceiving Companies: Joint-Stock Politics in Victorian England* (London and New York: Routledge, 1998), 46, 48.

21. John Stuart Mill, *Principles of Political Economy, with Some of their Applications to Social Philosophy* (1848), ed. J. M. Robson, introduction by V. W. Bladen (London: Routledge and Kegan Paul, 1965), 963; Duncan Bell, "John Stuart Mill on Colonies," in Bell, *Reordering the World: Essays on Liberalism and Empire* (Princeton: PUP, 2016), 220–21; David Williams, "John Stuart Mill and the Practice of Colonial Rule in India," *Journal of International Political Theory* (2020): 8–10; Bernard Semmel, *The Rise of Free Trade Imperialism: Classical Political Economy and the Empire of Free Trade and Imperialism* (Cambridge: CUP, 1970), 96.

22. Examination of John Stuart Mill (21 and 22 June 1852), 309, 313.

23. HC Deb 24 June 1853 vol. 128 c. 777.

24. HC Deb 09 June 1853 vol. 127 c. 1321.

25. Examination of John Stuart Mill, 303; HC Deb 03 June 1853 vol. 127 c. 1139, 1157.

26. Thomas Babington Macaulay, "Lord Clive," (1840) in *Critical and Historical Essays Contributed to the Edinburgh Review,* 3 vols. (London: Longman, Brown, Green and Longmans, 1848), III: 173; HC Deb 03 June 1853 vol. 127 c. 1134-35; HC Deb 27 June 1853 vol. 128 c. 842, 845-46.

27. HC Deb 24 June 1853 vol. 128 c. 745.

28. HC Deb 03 June 1853 vol. 127 c. 1148.

29. HC Deb 24 June 1853 vol. 128 c. 767.

30. "An Act to Provide for the Government of India," 16&17 Vic c. 95, 20 August 1853.

31. "How to Establish Our Empire in India," *The Examiner,* no. 2595 (24 October 1857), 1.

32. Brian Connell, *Regina v. Palmerston: The Correspondence Between Queen Victoria and her Foreign and Prime Minister, 1837–1865* (London: Evans Brothers Limited, 1962), 227–28; Miles Taylor, *Empress: Queen Victoria and India* (New Haven: YUP, 2018), 74.

33. HC Deb 18 February 1858 vol. 148 c. 1642.

34. *Punch, Or the London Charivari* 33 (15 August 1857), 65.

35. Birdwood, *Report on the Old Records of the India Office,* 71n; Henry Yule, "Preface," in *The Diary of William Hedges, Esq.* (London: Hakluyt Society, 1887), I:vii; Antonia Moon, "Destroying Records, Keeping Records: Some Practices at the East India Company and at the India Office," *Archives* 33, no. 119 (2008): 114–25.

36. George Trevor, "The Company's Raj," *Blackwood's Edinburgh Magazine* 82, no. 505 (November 1857), 618, 641.

37. "The Middle Classes and the Abolition of the East India Company," *Saturday Review of Politics, Literature, Science and Art* 5, no. 115 (9 January 1858), 31.

38. HC Deb 18 February 1858 vol. 148 c. 1616, 1618, 1632, 1633.

39. John Stuart Mill, *Considerations on Representative Government* (1861), in *Collected Works,* ed. Robson, 19:523, 573–74, 577.

40. Trevor, "Company's Raj," 616–18, 641–42; HC Deb 18 February 1858 vol. 148 c. 1652.

41. Kaye, "Familiar Epistle," 256.

42. Taylor, *Empress,* 36; Arthur Christopher Benson and Viscount Esher, eds., *The Letters of Queen Victoria: A Selection from Her Majesty's Correspondence Between the Years 1837 and 1861* (London: John Murray, 1911), 3:127–28, 258.

43. HC Deb 12 February 1858 vol. 148 c. 1284–86; Connell, *Regina v. Palmerston,* 228; Alborn, *Conceiving Companies,* 49 (quoting Maine); Taylor, *Empress,* 75.

44. Benson and Esher, eds., *Letters,* III:295.

45. John Russell to Vernon Smith, 5 December 1857, TNA PRO 30/22/13D f. 277.

46. John Russell to Vernon Smith, 4 December 1857, TNA PRO 30/22/13D f. 275–76.

47. Minto to Russell, 9 December 1857, TNA PRO 30/22/13D fol. 285.

48. Taylor, *Empress,* 76–78, 86–116 (Ludlow quoted on 87).

49. Peter Stanley, *White Mutiny: British Military Culture in India, 1825-1875* (London: Hurst, 1998); Taylor, *Empress,* 101-02.

50. Courtenay Ilbert, *The Government of India, Being a Digest of the Statute Law Relating Thereto* (Oxford: Clarendon Press, 1898), 99, 114, 172–73.

51. Mircea Raianu, *Tata: The Global Corporation that Built Indian Capitalism* (Cambridge, MA: HUP, 2021), 6; Ritu Birla, *Stages of Capital: Law, Culture, and Market Governance in Late Colonial India* (Durham, NC: DUP, 2009); David Sunderland, *Financing the Raj: The City of London and Colonial India, 1858–1940* (Woodbridge: Boydell, 2013).

52. HL Deb 29 April vol. 215 c. 1115; HC Deb 26 March 1873 vol. 215 c. 217.

53. Galbraith, *Hudson's Bay Company,* 304–6, 338–39, 347–53, Ross quoted at 331–32.

54. *Resolutions to be Proposed by the Hon. Mr. Loranger, in Reference to Rupert's land, the Indian Territory and the affairs of the Hudson's Bay Company* ([Toronto]: S. Derbishire & G. Desbarats, 1858).

55. *Memoranda and Prospectus of the North-West Transportation and Land Company* (Toronto: Globe Office, 1858), BL Add MS 60781, fol. 162r; Galbraith, *Hudson's Bay Company,* 333, 359–62.

56. *European and Asiatic Intercourse Via British Columbia by Means of a Main Through Trunk Railway from the Atlantic to the Pacific* (London: Robert Hardwicke, 1858), BL AddMS 60781 fol 82r., 89v, 90–92.

57. E. W. Watkin, *Canada and the States: Recollections, 1851 to 1886* (London: Ward, Lock & Co., 1887), 120–33; Galbraith, *Hudson's Bay Company,* 369–90.

58. Galbraith, *Hudson's Bay Company,* 23, 114–15, 154–74; John S. Galbraith, "The Hudson's Bay Land Controversy, 1863–1869," *Mississippi Valley Historical Review* 36, no. 3 (1949): 463–72.

59. Robert Brown, "The Story of a Dead Monopoly," *Cornhill Magazine* 22 (August 1870), 159, 176.

60. Leone Levi, "On Joint Stock Companies," *Journal of the Statistical Society of London* 33, no. 1 (1870): 1–2.

61. Charles Dickens, *The Life and Adventures of Martin Chuzzlewit,* ed. Patricia Ingham (London: Penguin, 1999), 408; Bishop Carleton Hunt, *The Development of the Business Corporation in England, 1800–1867* (Cambridge, MA: HUP, 1936), 90–94.

62. Michael Lobban, "Joint Stock Companies," in *The Oxford History of the Laws of England: Volume XII: 1820–1914 (Private Law),* ed. William Cornish et al. (Oxford: OUP, 2010), 619–31; John D. Turner, "The Development of English Company Law Before 1900," in *Re-*

search Handbook on the History of Corporate and Company Law, ed. Harwell Wells (Cheltenham: Edward Elgar, 2018), 132–39.

63. Gilbert and Sullivan, *Utopia Limited,* 28.

64. P.J. Cain and A.G. Hopkins, *British Imperialism, 1688-2015,* 3rd ed. (New York: Longman, 2016), 271.

65. Opinions of William Atherton and Roundell Pamer, 2 December 1862, TNA TS 25/1216.

66. Birla, *Stages of Capital,* 39–52, 48, 105, 199–200; Manu Goswami, *Producing India: From Colonial Economy to National Space* (Chicago: University of Chicago Press, 2004), 77–78; McQueen, "Flowers of Progress," 383–412; Tirthankar Roy and Anand V. Swamy, *Law and the Economy in Colonial India* (Chicago: University of Chicago Press, 2016), 147–52.

67. Janet L. Coryell, "'The Lincoln Colony': Aaron Columbus Burr's Proposed Colonization of British Honduras," *Civil War History* 43, no. 1 (1997): 9, 15; Phillip W. Magness, "The British Honduras Colony: Black Emigrationist Support for Colonization in the Lincoln Presidency," *Slavery and Abolition* 34, no. 1 (2013): 42–44, 54; Paul J. Scheips, "Lincoln and the Chiriqui Colonization Project," *Journal of Negro History* 37, no. 4 (1952): 418–53; Donald C. Simmons Jr., *Confederate Settlements in British Honduras* (Jefferson, NC and London: McFarland & Company, 2001), 37, 96.

68. "The Santa Fé Land Company, Limited," *The Economist,* 8 July 1883, 810; "Argentine Land and Investment Co. Ltd.," *The Argentine Year Book* (London: The South American Journal, 1903); *Commercial Relations of the United States with Foreign Countries during the year 1902,* vol. I (Washington, DC: Government Printing Office, 1903), 517–18; Dale L. Morgan and James R. Scobie, eds., *William Perkins' Journal of Life at Sonora, 1849–1852* (Berkeley: University of California Press, 1964), 53–54; Lawrence D. Taylor, "The Mining Boom in Baja California from 1850 to 1890 and the Emergence of Tijuana as a Border Community," in *On the Border: Society and Culture Between the United States and Mexico,* ed. Andrew Grant Wood (Lanham: SR Books, 2001), 16–17.

69. The list is certainly incomplete and seems to be periodically updated. "List of Charters Granted," https://privycouncil.independent.gov.uk/royal-charters/list-of-charters-granted/.

70. *Proceedings of the Royal Colonial Institute,* Vol. I (London: Royal Colonial Institute, 1870), 2.

71. See, for example, *First Report of the Commissioners of for the Exhibition of 1851 to the Right Hon. Spencer Horatio Walpole* (London: W. Clowes and Sons, 1852), x–xiii, xv–xvii.

72. "Returns of the Names of All Companies, incorporated either by Act of Parliament or Royal Charter, or otherwise, with power to establish and manage Lines of Electric Telegraph," 6 July 1860, *House of Commons Papers* 434, Vol. 62 (1860), 2.

73. P. M. Kennedy, "Imperial Cable Communications and Strategy, 1870–1914," *The English Historical Review* 86, no. 341 (1971): 738–39; James Smithies, "The Trans-Tasman Cable, the Australasian Bridgehead and Imperial History," *History Compass* 6, no. 3 (2008): 698.

74. "Telegraphic Communication with India: Red Sea Telegraph Company. Copy of Treasury Minute Granting Certain Concessions to the Company," 17 July 1858, BTA POST 30/2395C, file 2, BT Digital Archives, www.digitalarchives.bt.com/; Daniel R. Headrick and Pascal Griset, "Submarine Telegraph Cables: Business and Politics, 1838–1939," *Business History Review* 75, no. 3 (2001): 547–49.

75. Rudyard Kipling, "The Deep Sea Cables," in *The Seven Seas* (London: Methuen and Co., 1896), 9–10; Examination of F. J. Halliday, 9 May 1853, *Second Report of the Select Committee on Indian Territories* (House of Commons, 12 May 1853), 46; James Smithies, "The Trans-Tasman Cable, the Australasian Bridgehead and Imperial History," *History Compass* 6, no. 3 (2008): 701.

76. Daniel Headrick, *Invisible Weapon: Telecommunications and International Politics, 1851–1945* (New York: OUP, 1991), 68; Duncan Bell, *The Idea of Greater Britain: Empire and the Future of World Order, 1860–1900* (Princeton: PUP, 2009), 76–91; Robert W. D. Boyce, "Imperial Dreams and National Realities: Britain, Canada and the Struggle for a Pacific Telegraph Cable, 1879-1902," *English Historical Review* 115, no. 460 (2000): 39; Glen O'Hara, "New Histories of British Imperial Communication and the 'Networked World' of the 19th and Early 20th Centuries," *History Compass* 8, no. 7 (2010): 618.

77. John Henniker Heaton, "Postal and Telegraphic Communication of the Empire" (13 March 1888), *Proceedings of the Royal Colonial Institute*, Vol. 19 (London: Sampson Low, Marston, Searle & Rivington, 1888), 183.

78. Sir John William Kaye, "John Company's Farewell to John Bull," *Blackwood's Edinburgh Magazine* 84 (September 1858), 341–42.

79. Henniker Heaton, "Postal and Telegraphic Communication," 185.

80. "Curiosities of Ocean Cables," *Scientific American* 46, no. 25 (24 June 1882), 393; Headrick and Griset, "Submarine Telegraph Cables," 549, 553, 560–61; John A. Britton, "International Communications and International Crises in Latin America, 1867–1881," *Latin Americanist* 52, no. 1 (2008): 135–36.

81. Boyce, "Imperial Dreams," 58 (quoting Anderson); Headrick and Griset, "Submarine Telegraph Cables," 562–63; Headrick, "Double-Edged Sword," 57; Ariane Knuesel, "British Diplomacy and the Telegraph in Nineteenth-Century China," *Diplomacy and Statecraft* 18, no. 3 (2007): 523; O'Hara, "New Histories," 616.

82. Charles Bright, *Submarine Telegraphs: Their History, Construction, and Working* (London: Crosby Lockwood and Son, 1898), 134; Headrick, "Double-Edged Sword," 55–56; Headrick and Griset, "Submarine Telegraph Cables," 560–62; Dwayne R. Winseck and Robert M. Pike, *Communication and Empire: Media Markets, Power, and Globalization, 1860–1930* (Durham, NC: DUP, 2007), 86–88.

83. Simon J. Potter, *News and the British World: The Emergence of an Imperial Press System* (Oxford: OUP, 2003), 87–89; Headrick and Griset, "Submarine Telegraph Cables," 551; Headrick, "Double-Edged Sword," 57; Alex Nalbach, "'Poisoned at the Source?': Telegraphic News Services and Big Business in the Nineteenth Century," *Business History Review* 77, no. 4 (2003): 583–84, 591; Gordon M. Winder, "London's Global Reach? Reuters News and Network, 1865, 1881, and 1914," *Journal of World History* 21, no. 2 (2010): 271–96; Dwayne R. Winseck and Robert M. Pike, "Communication and Empire: Media Markets, Power and Globalization, 1860–1910," *Global Media and Communication* 4, no. 1 (2008): 10.

84. Boyce, "Imperial Dreams," 46, 55, 60–61; Potter, "Communication," 195.

85. *Proceedings of the Colonial Conference at London in 1887 in Relation to Imperial Postal and Telegraphic Communications through Canada* (Ottawa: Brown Chamberlain, 1888), 30, 48–50, 59–60, 72, 76–80.

86. Charles Darwin, *The Voyage of the Beagle* (New York: P. F. Collier & Son, 1909), 193; Fritz L. Hoffmann and Olga M. Hoffmann, *Sovereignty in Dispute: The Falklands/Malvinas, 1493–1982* (Boulder: Westview, 1984, repr. Routledge, 2019).

87. Stephen A. Royle, "The Falkland Islands, 1833–1876: The Establishment of a Colony," *Falkland Islands Journal* 5, no. 1 (1987): 17–18.

88. Lauren Benton and Lisa Ford, *Rage for Order: The British Empire and the Origins of International Law, 1800–1850* (Cambridge, MA: HUP, 2016), 173; David Rock, *The British in Argentina: Commerce, Settlers, and Power, 1800–2000* (Cham: Springer International, 2019), 115; Stephen Bell, "New Frontiers and Natural Resources in Southern South America, c. 1820–1870: Examples from Northwest European Mercantile Enterprise," in *Trading Environments: Frontiers, Commercial Knowledge, and Environmental Transformation, 1750–1990*, ed. Gordon M. Winder and Andreas Dix (New York: Routledge, 2016), 55–58.

89. "Royal Falkland, Land, Cattle, Seal and Whale Fishery Company," 16 February 1850, BT 41/601/3312; *Some Account of the Falkland Islands to Which is Added a Preliminary Sketch for the Formation of a Chartered Company to be Called The Falkland Islands Company*, 2nd ed. (London: Cuthbert and Southey, 1851), 16.

90. *Some Account of the Falkland Islands*, 14–15, 26.

91. "Falkland Islands Co. v. Reg [1863]," *The English Reports, Volume XV, Privy Council IV* (Edinburgh and London: William Green & Sons and Stevens & Sons, 1901), 714–15.

92. John C. Templer, ed., *The Private Letters of Sir James Brooke, K.C.B., Rajah of Sarawak*, 3 vols. (London: Richard Bentley, 1853), I:141–42, 223; Rodney Mundy, *Narrative of Events in Borneo and Celebes down to the Occupation of Labuan: From the Journals of James Brooke, Esq., Rajah of Sarawak and Governor of Labuan* (London: John Murray, 1848), 337.

93. Steven Press, *Rogue Empires: Contracts and Conmen in Europe's Scramble for Africa* (Cambridge, MA: HUP, 2017), 13–16, 24–35.
94. Templer, ed., *Private Letters*, I:240, 250.
95. Templer, ed., *Private Letters*, II:120, 122–23.
96. Mundy, *Narrative*, II:55 (Journal, 24 October 1845).
97. *The Queen on the Prosecution of Sir James Brooke, KCB against the Eastern Archipelago Company* (London: William Clowes and Sons, 1853), 4–5; Robert Bickers, "The Challenger: Hugh Hamilton Lindsay and the Rise of British Asia, 1832–1865," *Transactions of the RHS* 22 (2012), 157–65.
98. Templer, ed., *Private Letters*, II:182, 266, 308–9, III:2, 12–13, 28–29.
99. "Disputes Between Sir James Brooke and the Eastern Archipelago Company," 15 June 1852, CO 882/1/21; "The Eastern Archipelago Company v The Queen," 22 November 1853, TNA KB 28/599/6; Templer, ed., *Private Letters*, III:119, 133.
100. "Eastern Archipelago Company Ltd.," TNA BT 41/212/1202; Paul Johnson, *Making the Market: Victorian Origins of Corporate Capitalism* (Cambridge: CUP, 2010), 133–34; Taylor, *Boardroom Scandal*, 108–15.
101. "New Eastern Archipelago Company," TNA BT 31/368/1350; H. H. Lindsay to Sir E. B. Lytton, 19 November 1858, Papers of Sir Edward Bulwer Lytton, National Library of Australia, M1177–1178, 1836–1876, Vol. 025/Item319/2, available at https://nla.gov.au/nla.obj-1224177637/view; "Appendix No. 52, Labuan: Lease of Coal and Hereditaments to the Labuan Coal Company, Limited," *Twenty-Fourth General Report of the Emigration Commissioners* (London: George E. Eyre and William Spottiswoode, 1864), 201–2.
102. Stanley Chapman, "British Free-Standing Companies and Investment Groups in India and the Far East," in *The Free-Standing Company in the World Economy*, ed. Mira Wilkins and Harm Schröter (Oxford: OUP, 1998), 206–7; Geoffrey Jones, *Merchants to Multinationals: British Trading Companies in the Nineteenth and Twentieth Centuries* (Oxford: OUP, 2000), 40–41; Press, *Rogue Empires*, 47–49.
103. John S. Galbraith, "The Chartering of the British North Borneo Company," *Journal of British Studies* 4, no. 2 (1965): 104–10; Press, *Rogue Empires*, 39–45, 50–51, 53–57, 61–68.
104. "Memorandum," [October 1884], CO 874/137 pp. 90–91; Rutherford Alcock to Robert Herbert, 24 October 1884, CO 874/137 p. 88–89; Galbraith, "North Borneo Company," 108–16, 119–22; Press, *Rogue Empires*, 68–71 (Overbeck quoted on 69).
105. "British North Borneo Provisional Association Ltd.," TNA BT 31/2766/15069; Agreement for Sale, 4 April 1881, CO 874/31; Conveyance, 6 July 1881, CO 874/32.
106. HC Deb 17 March 1882 vol. 267 c. 1191–1195.
107. HC Deb 17 March 1881 vol. 267 c. 1177; Press, *Rogue Empires*, 76, 79.
108. Conveyance, 19 July 1882, CO 874/35; Agreement for Sale, 19 April 1882, CO 874/34.
109. Alfred Dent to R. G. W. Herbert, 16 November 1881, Alfred Dent to Carnarvon, 21 November 1881, Carnarvon to Dent, 8 December 1881, BL Add MS 60810 fols. 150–53.
110. Agreement Between Her Majesty's Government and the British North Borneo Company, 28 April 1888, CO 874/105 fol. 83.
111. British North Borneo Company to R. Herbert, 23 October 1884, CO 874/137 pp. 95.
112. *Handbook of British North Borneo* (London: William Clowes & Sons, 1890), 106, 165–66, 168–70, 177.
113. *Handbook*, 15, 17, 92–94, 178–82; *Views of North Borneo with a Brief History of the Colony* (London: William Brown & Co., 1899), 53.
114. "The London & Amsterdam Borneo Tobacco Company Limited," *The Money Market Review*, 16 February 1889, 383.
115. Amarjit Kaur, *Economic Change in East Malaysia: Sabah and Sarawak Since 1850* (Basingstoke: Macmillan, 1998), 10, 29, 41–42.
116. Prospectus, "The Central North Borneo Company, Limited," 4 May 1889; A. W. Florance to Foreign Office, 22 April 1890, CO 874/105 fol. 7; P. Currie to Central Borneo Company, 3 May 1890, CO 874/105 fol. 6v.; HC Deb 26 August 1887 vol. 320 cc. 7–8; John Anderson, *The Colonial Office List for 1896* (London: Harrison and Sons, 1896), 141.
117. *South American Journal* quoted by Rory Miller, "The Making of the Grace Contract: British Bondholders and the Peruvian Government, 1885–1890," *Journal of Latin American*

Studies 8, no. 1 (May 1976): 96; Rory Miller, "The Grace Contract, The Peruvian Corporation, and Peruvian History," *Ibero-amerikanisches Archiv* 9, no. 3/4 (1983), 331.

118. See also Press, *Rogue Empires*, ch. 5.

119. Andrew Fitzmaurice, *King Leopold's Ghostwriter: The Creation of Persons and States in the Nineteenth Century* (Princeton: PUP, 2021), part 4; Joseph Blocher and Mitu Gulati, "Transferable Sovereignty: Lessons from the History of the Congo Free State," *Duke Law Journal* 69, no. 6 (2020): 1228, 1236; Press, *Rogue Empires*, 88, 91, 116–19, 234–35; John S. Galbraith, *Mackinnon and East Africa, 1878–1895: A Study in the "New Imperialism"* (Cambridge: CUP, 1972), 5.

120. V. Lovett Cameron and Francis Wm. Fox to the Marquis of Salisbury, 19 December 1885, TNA CAB 37/46 no. 1; V. Lovett Cameron and Francis Wm. Fox to Julian Pauncefote, 4 January 1886, TNA CAB 37/46 no. 4; "Draft for a Soudan Charter," [January 1886], TNA CAB 37/46 no. 4 (encl).

121. Pauncefote to Cameron, 3 February 1886, TNA CAB 37/46 no. 11; J. Forbes Munro, "Shipping Subsidies and Railway Guarantees: William Mackinnon, Eastern Africa and the Indian Ocean, 1860–93," *Journal of African History* 28, no. 2 (1987): 216, 220; Press, *Rogue Empires*, 91.

122. Jones, *Merchants to Multinationals*, 38–39; Stephanie Jones, *Merchants of the Raj: British Managing Agency Houses in Calcutta Yesterday and Today* (Basingstoke: Macmillan, 1992), 14; Munro, "Shipping Subsidies," 211–14, 214, 218; E. I. Carlyle and John S. Galbraith, "Mackinnon, Sir William, baronet (1823–1893), shipping entrepreneur and imperialist," *Oxford Dictionary of National Biography*, 23 September 2004, https://doi.org/10.1093/ref:odnb/17618.

123. Galbraith, *Mackinnon*, 54 (quoting Waller), 73, 93, 106; Munro, "Shipping Subsidies," 216, 220.

124. P. L. McDermott, *British East Africa or IBEA: A History of the Formation and Work of the Imperial British East Africa Company* (London: Chapman and Hall, 1895), 12; F. Lugard, *Dual Mandate in British Tropical Africa* (Edinburgh and London: William Blackwood and Sons, 1922), 20; Galbraith, *Mackinnon*, 38, 89, 93, 106, 127, 134–35, 152.

125. Edward Hertslet, *The Map of Africa By Treaty* (London: HMSO, 1896), I:119; McDermott, *IBEA*, 12, 470–74.

126. "Terms of Agreement with Sultan for Establishment of Imperial East Africa Company's Bank, Zanzibar," 5 March 1891, FO 2/57 fol. 36; McDermott, *IBEA*, 46, 99–103; P. W. Currie to IBEAC, 15 June 1893, in "Report of the Court of Directors to the Shareholders," 31 July 1893, FO 2/58 fol. 235v.

127. Lugard, *Dual Mandate*, 17; Saadia Touval, "Treaties, Borders, and the Partition of Africa," *Journal of African History* 7, no. 2 (1966): 282–83. For variations of treaty forms, see FO 2/140.

128. "Concise History by the Deputy Governor," [1887], FO 403/75 P. 144; John Flint, "Goldie, Sir George Dashwood Taubman," *Oxford Dictionary of National Biography*, 23 September 2004, https://doi.org/10.1093/ref:odnb/33441.

129. Memorandum and Articles of Association of the National African Company (Limited), FO 403/75 p. 13; George Taubman-Goldie, "The International Struggle for the Niger," 17 February 1888, FO 403/76 pp. 50.

130. G. D. Goldie-Taubman to Marquis of Salisbury, 27 January 1886, FO 403/75 p. 208–9; Taubman-Goldie, "International Struggle," 51.

131. Touval, "Treaties," 280–87; Lugard, *Dual Mandate*, 15; Press, *Rogue Empires*, 6, 204–5.

132. Aberdare to Granville, 13 February 1885 and Julian Pauncefote to C. Russell, H. Davey, and J. Parker Deane, 14 July 1886, FO 403/75 p. 1–2, 12; Petition of the National African Company, 25 May 1886, FO 881/5270X p. 9; Royal Niger Company to Foreign Office, 21 February 1888, FO 403/76 p. 57; Goldie, "Britain's Priority on the Middle Niger" (1897), in D.J.M. Muffett, *Empire Builder Extraordinary: Sir George Goldie, His Philosophy of Government and Empire* (Isle of Man: Shearwater Press, 1978), 96.

133. J. Pauncefote to C. Russell, H. Davey, and J. Parker Deane, 13 March 1886, G. D. Goldie-Taubman to the Earl of Iddesleigh, 18 August 1886, G. D. Goldie-Taubman to Julian Pauncefote, 20 December 1886, The National African Company (Limited) to the Marquis of Salisbury, 27 January 1886, Foreign Office (T. V. Lister) to Board of Trade, 29 De-

cember 1887, 237, FO 403/75, p. 6, 30, 63–67, 205, 237; 26 July 1888, FO 403/76 p. 172; J[ulian] P[auncefote], Minute, 13 April 1888, "Memorandum by Vice-Consul Johnston on the British Protectorate of the Oil Rivers, with Suggestions as to its future Government," George Taubman-Goldie, 24 September 1888, FO 403/76 p. 172, 228–29; R. E. Webster, J. E. Gorst, and J. Parker Deane to Salisbury, 8 August 1885, FO 84/2275 f. 76; Galbraith, "British North Borneo Company," 125; Press, *Rogue Empires,* 81–82.

134. G. D. Goldie-Taubman to the Earl of Rosebery, 13 July 1886, FO 403/75 pp. 10–11.

135. H. P. Anderson, "Minutes," 5 July 1888, FO 403/76 p. 147; T. Stanley Rogerson to Marquis of Salisbury, 7 January 1890, FO 403/149 p. 3; E. A. Ditchfield to the Marquis of Salisbury, 23 August 1888, FO 403/76 p. 205; T. Stanley Rogerson (African Association) to Foreign Office, 6 October 1888, FO 403/76 p. 235–36; T. Stanley Rogerson and George Taubman-Goldie, 12 October 1888, "Confidential Memorandum on the Niger and Oil Rivers," FO 403/76 p. 242; Petition of the African Association, Ltd., FO 403/149 p. 3–6; HC Deb 07 March 1890 vol. 342 cc. 253–54.

136. W. B. Stewart, "Appendix on South-West Barbary As a Field for Colonisation," in Albert Gibbon Spilsbury, *The Tourmaline Expedition* (London: J.M. Dent & Co., 1906), 239; Hertslet, *Map of Africa By Treaty,* 1064–66; F. V. Parsons, "The North-West African Company and the British Government, 1875–95," *HJ* 1, no. 2 (1958): 136–53; John D. Hargreaves, "The Chronology of Imperialism: The Loaded Pause," *Journal of the Historical Society of Nigeria* 7, no. 2 (1974): 236–37.

137. Goldie quoted in Press, *Rogue Empires,* 82; Newcastle quoted in John Darwin, "Imperialism and the Victorians: The Dynamics of Territorial Expansion," *English Historical Review* 112, no. 447 (1997), 623–24.

138. Charles Fitzwilliam Cadiz, *Natal Ordinances, Laws, and Proclamations* (Pietermaritzburg, 1879), 390–91; Deputation from the Natal Land and Colonization Company (Limited)," 14 June 1877, CO 879/11 fols. 201r–202v; Henry Slater, "Land, Labour, and Capital in Natal: The Natal Land and Colonisation Company, 1860–1948," *Journal of African History,* 16, no. 2 (1975): 265–67, 267–70.

139. *Further Correspondence Respecting the Affairs of Bechuanaland and Adjacent Territories* (London: Eyre and Spottiswoode, April 1888); Arthur Keppel-Jones, *Rhodes and Rhodesia: The White Conquest of Zimbabwe, 1884–1902* (Kingston and Montreal: McGill-Queen's University Press, 1983). 16; David E. Torrance, *The Strange Death of the Liberal Empire: Lord Selborne in South Africa* (Montreal: McGill Queen's University Press, 1996), 20, 45.

140. John S. Galbraith, *Crown and Charter: The Early Years of the British South Africa Company* (Berkeley: University of California Press, 1974), 31–33, 71–79, 83; Slater, "Land, Labour, and Capital," 271–72.

141. Robert I. Rotberg, *The Founder: Cecil Rhodes and the Pursuit of Power* (New York: OUP, 1988), 252; Galbraith, *Crown and Charter,* 57–74.

142. Sir Edward Hertslet, ed., *A Complete Collection of the Treaties and Conventions and Reciprocal Regulations at Present Subsisting Between Great Britain and Foreign Powers* (London: Butterworths, 1893), 134, 136; Galbraith, *Crown and Charter,* 63–64, 80–88, 114.

143. [James Rochfort Maguire], *The Pioneers of Empire: Being a Vindication of the Principle and a Short Sketch of the History of Chartered Companies, with Especial Reference to the British South Africa Company/by an Imperialist* (London: Methuen, 1896), 88.

144. "Central Search Association," BT 31/4451/28988; Galbraith, *Crown and Charter,* 67, 84–86; Keppel-Jones, *Rhodes,* 291–95.

145. A. J. Wilson, *An Empire in Pawn: Being Lectures and Essays on Indian, Colonial, and Domestic Finance, "Preference," Free Trade, etc.* (London: T. Fisher Unwin, 1909), 240; The Matabeleland Company (Limited) and Others v. The British South Africa Company and Others, 16 November 1893, in *Annual Digest of the Times Law Reports* (London: George Edward Wright, 1893–94).

146. Harry Craufuird Thomson, "The Rule of the Chartered Company," *The National Review* 31 (February 1899), 903; Galbraith, *Crown and Charter,* 126.

147. "Director's Report and Accounts" (31 March 1891), FO 881/5847X p. 11; Marquess of Ripon to H. B. Loch, 20 December 1892, C. J. Rhodes to Colonial Office, 16 November 1892,

and John Bramston to C. J. Rhodes, 30 December 1892, CO 879/37/9 f. 348, 356, 358; Charles Sydney Goldmann, *South African Mines; their Position, Results & Developments, Volume II: Miscellaneous Companies* (London: Effingham Wilson & Co, 1895–96), 62, 172–73; Neil Parsons, "The 'Victorian Internet' Reaches Halfway to Cairo: Cape Tanganyika Telegraphs, 1875–1926," in *The Social Life of Connectivity in Africa*, ed. Mirjam de Bruijn and Rijk van Dijk (New York: Palgrave Macmillan, 2012), 103; Jon Lunn, *Capital and Labour on the Rhodesian Railway System, 1888–1947* (Basingstoke: MacMillan, 1997), 28.

148. CO 879/37/9 fols. 367v–368r, 383v–384; *Times Law Reports*, 78.

149. Lunn, *Capital and Labour*, 28–29.

150. HC Deb 21 May 1896 vol. 41 c. 71; Edward Cavanagh, "Crown, Conquest, Concession, and Corporation: British Legal Ideas and Institutions in Matabeleland and Southern Rhodesia, 1889–1919," in *Empire and Legal Thought: Ideas and Institutions from Antiquity to Modernity*, ed. Edward Cavanagh (Leiden: Brill, 2020), 536.

151. CO 897/37/9 fols. 357v, 369–369v; 371v–372, 378v–380v; FO 881/5847X p. 16; HC Deb 04 May 1893 vol. 12 cc70–72; Gailbraith, *Crown and Charter*, 118–19, 124–25; Galbraith, *Mackinnon*, 157.

152. "History of the Blantyre and East Africa Company," and "History of the British Central Africa Company," [1949], CO 525/208/2 [pp. 93–132]; *Issues, 1903: A Reprint of the Prospectuses of Public Companies &c., Advertised in The Times* (London: George Edward Wright, 1903); 26; *The Statist* (1 November 1902), 793; John McCracken, *A History of Malawi, 1859–1966* (Woodbridge: James Currey, 2012), 92.

153. Skinner, *Mining Manual for 1894*, 565–66; Walter R. Skinner, *Mining Manual for 1895, Containing the Full Particulars of Mining Companies Together with a List of Mining Directors* (London: [The Financial Times], 1895), 646–47.

154. Leroy Vail, "Mozambique's Chartered Companies: The Rule of the Feeble," *Journal of African History* 17, no. 3 (1976): 391–93; Barry Neil-Tomlinson, "The Nyassa Chartered Company: 1891–1929," *Journal of African History* 18, no. 1 (1977): 111–12; W. G. Clarence-Smith, *The Third Portuguese Empire, 1825–1975: A Study in Economic Imperialism* (Manchester: Manchester University Press, 1985), 103.

155. *The African Review* 20 (23 September 1899), 495; "The Beira Railway Company, Limited," *The Railway News* (29 October 1892), 656; Goldmann, *South African Mines*, 175; Vail, "Mozambique's Chartered Companies," 393–94; Landeg White, *Bridging the Zambesi: A Colonial Folly* (Basingstoke: MacMillan, 1993), 32.

156. "Ibo and Nyassa Corporation, Limited," *The Statist* (31 May 1902), 1115–16; "Opening up the Nyasa District," *African Review* (16 September 1899), 458; Zachary Kingdon, *A Host of Devils: The History and Context of the Making of Makonde Spirit Sculpture* (London: Routledge, 2002), 21–22.

157. R. Cunninghame Graham, "The Voyage of the 'Tourmaline, II" *The Saturday Review* (18 June 1898), 811.

158. Henry M. Grey, *In Moorish Captivity: An Account of the "Tourmaline" Expedition to Sus, 1897–98* (London: Edward Arnold, 1899), 5–6.

159. Graham, "Voyage," 811; R. B. Cunnighame Graham, *Mogreb-el-Acksa: A Journey in Morocco* (London: William Heinemann, 1898), 40–42.

160. Major A. Gibbon Spilsbury, *The Tourmaline Expedition* (London: J.M. Dent & Co, 1906), 213; Henry M. Grey, *In Moorish Captivity: An Account of the 'Tourmaline' Expedition to Sus, 1897–98* (London: Edward Arnold, 1899), 5–6.

161. Graham, "Voyage," 812.

162. "The Raid on the Moorish Coast," *The Spectator* (5 February 1898), 192.

163. *Joseph Conrad's Letters to R. Cunninghame Graham* (Cambridge: CUP, 1969), 81; Maya Jasanoff, *The Dawn Watch: Joseph Conrad in a Global World* (New York: Penguin, 2017), 163–66; Stephen Donovan, "'Figures, Facts, Theories': Conrad and Chartered Company Imperialism," *The Conradian* 24, no. 2 (1999): 34.

164. J. A. Hobson, *Imperialism: A Study* (London: J. Nisbet & Co., 1902), 243n1.

165. "Sir H. Johnston and Chartered Companies," *The Spectator* 77, no. 3558 (5 September 1896), 296.

166. Francis Reginald Statham, "The Chartered Company: The Other Side," *The National Review* 17 (March 1896), 49.

167. Mary Lucy Story-Maskelyne Arnold-Forster, *The Right Honourable Hugh Oakeley Arnold-Forster: A Memoir* (London: E. Arnold, 1910), 119–21.

168. "Extract from the 'Lagos Observer' of May 26, 1888," FO 403/76 p. 156.

169. Charles Harrison, "South Africa and the Chartered Company," *Contemporary Review* 69 (March 1896): 339–40, 346.

170. Charles W. Dilke, "The Uganda Problem," *Fortnightly Review* 53, no. 314 (1 February 1893).

171. Lugard, *Dual Mandate*, 25.

172. G. D. Goldie-Taubman to Marquis of Salisbury, 28 December 1885 and 27 January 1886, FO 403/75 p. 198, 211.

173. V. Lovett Cameron, "Chartered Companies in Africa," *The National Review* 15, 88 (1890), 466.

174. Edward James Stephen Dicey, "The Work of the Chartered Company," *Fortnightly Review* 59 (June 1896), 985.

175. Hobson, *Imperialism,* 243n1.

176. G. D. Goldie-Taubman to Marquis of Salisbury, 28 December 1885 and 27 January 1886, FO 403/75 p. 197, 205.

177. Maguire, *Pioneers,* 7–8, 10, 12, 19, 121.

178. The National African Company (Limited) to the Marquis of Salisbury, 27 January 1886, FO 403/75 pp. 209; George Taubman-Goldie, "Memorandum," 20 August 1888, FO 403/76 p. 202.

179. *Prosecution of Sir James Brooke,* 30.

180. George Taubman-Goldie, "The International Struggle for the Niger," 17 February 1888, FO 403/76 pp. 50–51; Travers Twiss, "Opinion," 25 August 1886, TNA FO 403/75 pp. 62–63.

181. "Memorandum," 5 November 1892, FO 881/6401 p. 1.

182. George Taubman Goldie, "How to Govern Uganda," *The Times* (8 November 1892), 10.

183. George Goldie, "France and England on the Niger" (1891), in Muffett, *Empire Builder,* 66, 68.

184. Goldie, "How to Govern Uganda," 10; Maguire, *Pioneers,* 25, 119–21.

185. G. D. Goldie-Taubman to Marquis of Salisbury, 28 December 1885, FO 403/75 p. 198; George Taubman Goldie, "The Royal Niger Company," *The Times,* 4 January 1889, 4; Goldie, "How to Govern Uganda," 10.

186. George Taubman Goldie, "The Niger Territories," *The Times,* 21 December 1888, 14.

187. Lugard, *Dual Mandate,* 18.

188. Flora L. Shaw, "The British South Africa Company," *Fortnightly Review* 46 (1889): 668; J. R. Seeley, *The Expansion of England: Two Courses of Lectures* (London: MacMillan and Co., 1883, repr. 1895), 267.

189. Lionel Decle, "Two Years in Rhodesia: A French View of the Chartered Company," *The National Review* 27 (1896): 532; Colin Baker, "British Central Africa in 1893 and 1898: The Journeys of Lionel Decle and Ewart Grogan," *Society of Malawi Journal* 40, no. 1 (1987): 11–29.

190. Dicey, "Work of the Chartered Company," 995, 996.

191. Joseph Thomson, "Downing Street *Versus* Chartered Companies in Africa," *Fortnightly Review* 46 (1889): 177, 185; Donovan, "Figures, Facts, Theories," 45–46.

192. Cameron, "Chartered Companies," 465.

193. Lugard, *Dual Mandate,* 14.

194. Quoted in Janet McLean, "The Transnational Corporation in History: Lessons for Today?" *Indiana Law* Journal 78, no. 2 (2004): 377; Fitzmaurice, *King Leopold's Ghostwriter,* 436, 452–56.

195. *Handbook of British North Borneo,* 10.

196. Donald Read, *The Age of Urban Democracy: England, 1868–1914* (Longman, 1979 repr. Abingdon: Routledge, 2014), 351; J. Lee Thompson, *A Wider Patriotism: Alfred Milner and the British Empire* (Pickering & Chatto, 2007, repr. Abigdon: Routledge, 2016), 29.

197. Maguire, *Pioneers,* 30–62, 78.

198. Alfred C. Lyall, "Colonies and Chartered Companies," *Journal of the Society of Arts* 46, no. 2376 (3 June 1898), 634, 636, 639, 642, 643, 644.

199. George Cawston and A. H. Keane, *The Early Chartered Companies (A.D. 1296–1858)* (London and New York: Edward Arnold, 1896), vi–viii.

200. Cawston and Keane, *Early Chartered Companies*, vi, viii, 13–14, 153, 305–20.

201. Dicey, "Work of the Chartered Company," 985.

Epilogue

Epigraph: W. S. Gilbert and Arthur Sullivan, *An Original Comic Opera in Two Acts entitled Utopia Limited or, The Flowers of Progress* (London: Chappel & Co., 1893), 40.

1. F. W. Maitland to B. Fossett Lock, 10 April 1906, F. W. Maitland to Cecil Carr, 13 May 1906 and 1 June 1906, in *The Letters of Frederic William Maitland,* ed. C.H.S. Fifoot (Cambridge: CUP, 1965), 471, 475, 475n2.

2. Cecil T. Carr, *Select Charters of Trading Companies, A.D. 1530–1707* (London: Bernard Quaritch, 1913), xiv; the review is by Edward P. Cheyney in the *American Historical Review,* 19, no. 3 (1913): 605.

3. Gilbert and Sullivan, *Utopia Limited,* 49–50.

4. "Filibustering and Empire," *The Speaker: The Liberal Review* (28 October 1893), 456 ("device . . . anachronism"); *Economist* 39 (1881), 1428, quoted in John S. Galbraith, "The Chartering of the British North Borneo Company," *Journal of British Studies* 4, no. 2 (1965): 103 ("out of date").

5. J. R. Seeley, *The Expansion of England: Two Courses of Lectures* (London: MacMillan and Co., 1883, repr. 1895), 46, 249, 314; J. A. Hobson, *Imperialism: A Study* (London: J. Nisbet & Co., 1902), 265.

6. HL Deb 24 February 1908 vol. 184 c. 1278; Neal Ascherson, *The King Incorporated: Leopold II in the Age of Trusts* (Garden City, NY: Doubleday, 1964), 253.

7. *The Journal of the Society of Arts* 46, no. 2376 (3 June 1898), 644–45.

8. [James Rochfort Maguire], *The Pioneers of Empire: Being a Vindication of the Principle and a Short Sketch of the History of Chartered Companies, with Especial Reference to the British South Africa Company / by an Imperialist* (London: Methuen, 1896), 29, 58.

9. HC Deb 23 May 1887 vol. 315 c. 871; Opinion of J[ulian] P[auncefote], 14 April 1888, FO 403/76, p. 91–92.

10. "Notes by Sir James Fergusson," 22 July 1888, FO 403/76 p. 166.

11. V. Lovett Cameron, "Chartered Companies in Africa," *National Review* 15, no. 88 (1890): 470.

12. Arnold Kemball to Edward Gray, 4 July 1893, FO 2/58 fol. 170v–171r.

13. P. L. McDermott, *British East Africa or IBEA: A History of the Formation and Work of the Imperial British East Africa Company* (London: Chapman and Hall, 1895), 117–18, 121, 144, 177–78, 539.

14. F. D. Lugard, *The Dual Mandate in British Tropical Africa* (Edinburgh and London: William Blackwood and Sons, 1922), 24.

15. Arnold Kemball to Edward Gray, 20 June 1893, and "Balance Sheet," 30 April 1893, FO 2/58 fol. 126, 233; The Imperial British East Africa Company, Limited, *Report of Proceedings at the Adjourned Third Annual Meeting, Held at Winchester House, London, E.C., On 29th May 1893* (London: Doherty & Co., 1893), FO 2/58 fol. 2; McDermott, *IBEA,* 386; John S. Galbraith, *Mackinnon and East Africa 1878–1895: A Study in the 'New Imperialism'* (Cambridge: CUP, 1972), 231–34.

16. "Memorandum by Sir T. Sanderson," 20 November 1897 and "Memorandum by Mr. Ryder and Sir C. Hill," 22 November 1897, FO 881/6857X p. 3.

17. M.E.H.B., "Royal Niger Company," 21 February 1898, TNA CAB 37/46/21 f. 208.

18. "Memorandum by Sir T. Sanderson," 20 November 1897, FO 881/6857X p. 2–3; Ryder and Hill, Memorandum, 12 March 1897, FO 881/6922X p. 1.

19. "Memorandum Respecting the Claim of the Royal Niger Company," 11 August 1899, FO 881/7230; M.E.H.B. "Royal Niger Company," 21 February 1898, TNA CAB 37/46/21.
20. George Taubman Goldie to Michael Hicks-Beach, 23 February 1898, TNA CAB 37/46/22, fol. 209.
21. McDermott, *IBEA*, 384, 385.
22. "Imperial British East Africa Company v. The Queen," [1887–1898], TS 18/260; "Company number 38949: Imperial British East Africa Company, Ltd., Incorporated 1893. Liquidator's Accounts," [1896] BT 34/927/38949.
23. "Papers with respect to revocation of the charter of the Royal Niger Company," *19th Century House of Commons Sessional Papers,* Vol. 63, No. C.9372 (1899); Letters Patents, 28 December 1899, FO 93/6/22; *Extract from The London Gazette of Friday, December 29, 1899,* FO 881/7225X; "Royal Niger Company: Revocation of Charter," [1899–1900], LCO 2/2015; F.D. Lugard, *Report by Sir F. D. Lugard on the amalgamation of northern and southern Nigeria, and administration, 1912–1919* (London: HMSO, 1920), 48.
24. "The Suez Canal and the Government," *Manchester Guardian* (27 November 1875); Geoffrey Hicks, "Disraeli, Derby, and the Suez Canal, 1875: Some Myths Reassessed," *History* 97, no. 2 (2012): 182–203; Nathaniel Mayer Victor Rothschild, *"You Have It Madam": The Purchase, in 1875, of Suez Canal Shares by Disraeli and Baron Lionel de Rothschild* (London: The Author, 1980), esp. 54–55.
25. HC Deb 3 March 1931 v. 249 cc.179–81; Leroy Vail, "Mozambique's Chartered Companies: The Rule of the Feeble," *Journal of African History* 17, no. 3 (1976): 398–99, 407–10, 413–15; W. G. Clarence-Smith, *The Third Portuguese Empire, 1825–1975: A Study in Economic Imperialism* (Manchester: Manchester University Press, 1985), 103; Barry Neil-Tomlinson, "The Nyassa Chartered Company: 1891–1929," *Journal of African History* 18, no. 1 (1977): 119–28.
26. Susan Pedersen, *The Guardians: The League of Nations and the Crisis of Empire* (Oxford: OUP, 2015), 75.
27. Memorandum, 6 March 1914, CO 323/645 f. 116.
28. Arthur Berriedale Keith, *Responsible Government in the Dominions* (Oxford: Clarendon Press, 1912), III:995.
29. HL Deb 12 July 1923, vol. 54, c.1024; *The Dominions Office and Colonial Office List 1924* (London: Waterlow & Sons, Ltd., 1924), 392–93; Edward Cavanagh, "'The Unbridgeable Gulf': Responsible Self-Government and Aboriginal Title in Southern Rhodesia and the Commonwealth," in *Commonwealth History in the Twenty-First Century,* ed. Saul Dubow and Richard Drayton (Cham: Palgrave Macmillan, 2020), 93; Cavanagh, "Crown, Conquest, Concession, and Corporation: British Legal Ideas and Institutions in Matabeleland and Southern Rhodesia, 1889–1919," in *Empire and Legal Thought: Ideas and Institutions from Antiquity to Modernity,* ed. Edward Cavanagh (Leiden: Brill, 2020), 539–43.
30. F. H. Villiers to BNBC, 21 December 1900, CO 874/106 f. 284; West Ridgeway to John Anderson, 4 June 1914; John Anderson to West Ridgeway, 17 June 1914, CO 874/830 ff. 8–11; Stephenson Harwood and Co., to Harington G. Forbes, 20 July 1917, CO 874/912 pp. 1–4; West Ridgeway to G.E.J. Gent, 27 April 1922, CO 874/1007, f. 43.
31. Charles Mackintosh to Harington G. Forbes, 11 July 1921, CO 874/820 fol. 13–14.
32. "Counsel's Opinion," 23 May 1922, CO 874/411 ff. 26–27; Stephenson Harwood & Tatham to Harington G. Forbes, 9 May 1922, CO 874/411 f. 16–23.
33. "Proposals for Acquiring the Rights of the Chartered Company," T 220/472, and T 220/473.
34. D. R. Serpell to G. Whitelay, 30 May 1948, T 220/472 p. 118; "British North Borneo Company and the Secretary of State for the Colonies: Opinion," 25 June 1948, T 220/472 f. 140.
35. "In the Matter of an Arbitration," 25 February 1949, T 220/473 f. 68.
36. Private Secretary (Financial Secretary) to Private Secretary (Hugh Dalton), December 1949, T 220/473 f. 97.
37. HL Deb 12 July 1923, vol. 54 c. 1024.
38. "History of the British Central Africa Company," [1949], CO 525/208/2 [pp. 128–30].
39. J. H. E. Woods, Memorandum, [1933], PC 8/1280.
40. Frederic William Maitland, "The Crown as Corporation," in *The Collected Papers of Frederic William Maitland,* Volume III, ed. H.A.L. Fisher (Cambridge: University Press, 1911), 267.

41. G. Packer, "A Chartered Company for the Northern Territory," *Australian Quarterly* 5, no. 20 (1933): 89–89.

42. Chartered Company of Mexico to the Board of Trade, 17 August 1910, BT 58/10/COS/1192A; Memorandum, Companies Department, 24 August 1910; Earnest Cleave to Assistant Secretary, Railway Department, Board of Trade, 30 September 1897 BT 58/10/COS/1192A.

43. David Baillargeon, "'Imperium in Imperio': The Corporation, Mining, and Governance in British Southeast Asia, 1900–1930," *Enterprise and Society* 23, no. 2 (2020): 1–32; Pedersen, *Guardians*, 272–74, 485n50; Nicholas J. White, "'Ungentlemanly Capitalism': John Hay and Malaya, 1904–1964," *Management and Organizational History* 14, no. 1 (2019): 98–122.

44. [Charles Allsopp] Lord Hindlip, *British East Africa: Past, Present, and Future* (London: T. Fisher Unwin, 1905), 95.

45. British East African Syndicate Ltd., BT 34/1714/67807; *Correspondence Relating to the Resignation of Sir Charles Eliot and to the Concession to the East Africa Syndicate* (London: HMSO, 1904); Robert L. Tignor, *The Colonial Transformation of Kenya: The Kamba, Kikuyu, and Maasai from 1900 to 1939* (Princeton: PUP, 1976), 33.

46. *Report on Palestine Administration, July 1920–December 1921* (London: HMSO, 1922); Irit Amit, "Economic and Zionist Ideological Perceptions: Private Initiative in Palestine in the 1920s and 1930s," *Middle Eastern Studies* 36, no. 2 (2000): 82–102; Ronen Shamir, "Electricity and Empire in 1920s Palestine under British Rule," *Naturwissenschaften, Technik und Medzin* 24, no. 4 (2017).

47. Doy to Ferrer, 3 July 1936, CO 733/318/4 p. 10.

48. Prasenjit Duara, *Sovereignty and Authenticity: Manchukuo and the East Asian Modern* (Lanham: Rowman & Littlefield, 2003), 48–51; Yoshihisa Tak Matsusaka, *The Making of Japanese Manchuria, 1904–1932* (Cambridge, MA: HUP, 2001); Benjamin Coates, *Legalist Empire: International Law and American Foreign Relations in the Early Twentieth Century* (New York: OUP, 2016); Jason M. Colby, *The Business of Empire: United Fruit, Race, and U.S. Expansion in Central America* (Ithaca: Cornell, 2011); James W. Martin, *Banana Cowboys: The United Fruit Company and the Culture of Corporate Colonialism* (Albuquerque: University of New Mexico Press, 2018).

49. Mrinalini Sinha, "Whatever Happened to the Third British Empire? Empire, Nation Redux," in *Writing Imperial Histories*, ed. Andrew Thompson (Manchester: Manchester UP, 2013), 168–87.

50. Alasdair Pinkerton, "Radio and the Raj: Broadcasting in British India (1920–1940)," *Journal of the Royal Asiatic Society* 18, no. 2 (2008): 169–71, 173, 181–82 (quoting BBC), 183–84, 187–89; D. L. LeMahieu, "John Reith (1889–1971): Entrepreneur of Collectivism," in *After the Victorians: Private Conscience and Public Duty in Modern Britain*, ed. Susan Pedersen and Peter Mandler (London: Routledge, 1994), 195–99; Simon J. Potter, *Broadcasting Empire: The BBC and the British World, 1922–1970* (Oxford: OUP, 2012).

51. Commonwealth Telecommunications Conference 1945: Proceedings, August 1945, CO 937/11/7; Richard Collins, "The Reith Mission: Global Telecommunications and the Decline of the British Empire," *Historical Journal of Film, Radio, and Television* 32, no. 2 (2012): 168, 181n26; Jill Hills, *Telecommunications and Empire* (Urbana: University of Illinois Press, 2007), 36.

52. Collins, "Reith Mission," 168, 174–78 (quotation on 177).

53. HC Deb 11 March 1920 v. 126 c. 1622.

54. Robin D. S. Higham, "The British Government and Overseas Airlines, 1918–1939, A Failure of Laissez-Faire," *Journal of Air Law and Commerce* 26, no. 1 (1959): 4–7.

55. Qantas Empire Airways, *Facts About Qantas Empire Airways: A National and Empire Organisation* (Brisbane: Qantas Empire Airlines, 1936), SLNSW, M EPHEMERA/AVIATION/QANTAS/1920.

56. Memorandum, [14 December 1938], T 160/872; H. Wilson Smith, "Memorandum: Imperial Airways and British Airways," 16 November 1938, TNA, AVIA 2/2066.

57. HL Deb 1 August 1939 vol. 114 c. 737–38.

58. Government of India to Marquess of Zetland, 18 August 1939, IOR M/3/636 no. 5417.

59. H. Wilson Smith, Memorandum on "New Overseas Airways Corporation," T 160/872/3.

60. "Note of Meeting Held in Sir Arthur Street's Room," 22 March 1939, T 160/872/3; "Note of Meeting at Air Ministry on 22nd March," IOR L/E/9/140 ff. 439–41.

61. HC Deb 02 Apr 1958 c. 1208–09; "Sir J. Reith's New Task: Changing Imperial Airways to a New Policy, The Recent Criticisms," *The Manchester Guardian*, 15 June 1938, 12; "Airways Merger: Establishment of the Corporation," *The Times*, 27 November 1939, 3; Robin Higham, *Speedbird: The Complete History of BOAC* (London: I.B. Tauris, 2013), 7, 182–85.

62. HL Deb 01 August 1939 vol. 1939 c. 752.

63. HC Deb 11 July 1922 c. 1059.

64. "Report to the Board by the Managing Directors," December 1940, IOR L/E/8/2310 p. 11.

65. Papers of the Chairman of the United Kingdom Commercial Corporation, TNA BT 192; United Kingdom Commercial Corporation and Subsidiary Companies, T 263; HC Deb 25 November 1942 vol. 385 c. 729–30; HC Deb 2 February 1943, vol. 386, c. 728–30; "Memorandum: English Commercial Corporation," [April? 1940], IOR L/E/8/2310.

66. HC Deb 2 February 1943, vol. 386, c. 730.

67. *The Indian Annual Register, January–June 1944, Vol. I* (Calcutta: Annual Register Office, 1944), 294.

68. Cabinet Paper, 24 April 1946, IOR L/E/8/2310.

69. Joseph Morgan Hodge, "Beyond Dependency: North–South Relationships in the Age of Development," in *The Oxford Handbook of the Ends of Empire*, ed. Martin Thomas and Andrew S. Thompson (Oxford: OUP, 2018), 626.

70. W. M. Goodenough to S. Caine, 30 November 1944, CO 852/578/9/28; Geoffrey Jones, *British Multinational Banking, 1830–1990* (Oxford: OUP, 1993, repr. 2009), 308–9; Geoffrey Jones, "Competitive Advantages in British Multinational Banking Since 1890," in *Banks as Multinationals*, ed. Jones (London: Routledge, 2012), 32–33, 47, 49; Nicholas J. White, "Imperial Business Interests, Decolonization, and Post-Colonial Diversification," in *Ends of Empire*, eds. Thomas and Thompson, 643.

71. Collins, "Reith Mission," 179; Michael McWilliam, *The Development Business: A History of the Commonwealth Development Corporation* (Basingstoke: Palgrave, 2001); Sarah Stockwell, "The 'Know-How of the World Is Mainly with Private Companies': The Commonwealth Development Corporation and British Business in Post-Colonial Africa," in *The Business of Development in Post-Colonial Africa*, ed. Véronique Dimier and Sarah Stockwell (Cham: Palgrave Macmillan, 2020), 183–212.

72. Sinha, "Whatever Happened," 182–83.

73. See, for example, O. Nigel Bolland, *Colonialism and Resistance in Belize: Essays in Historical Sociology*, 2nd ed. (Barbados: University of the West Indies Press, 2003), 178, 187; Odile Hoffmann, "The End of the Empire Forestry? Issues of Land Possession in Belize, 1930s–1950s," in *Spatial Appropriations in Modern Empires, 1820–1960: Beyond Dispossession*, ed. Didier Guignard and Iris Seri-Hersch (Newcastle upon Tyne, UK: Cambridge Scholars Publishing, 2019), 52, 63–70; J. M. Powell, "'Dominion over Palm and Pine': The British Empire Forestry Conferences, 1920–1947," *Journal of Historical Geography* 33, no. 4 (2007): 852–77; White, "Imperial Business Interests," 641–42; Sarah Stockwell, *The Business of Decolonization: British Business Strategies in the Gold Coast* (Oxford: Clarendon Press, 2000), 9, 72–73, 80–81.

74. Graham D. Taylor, "Under (Canadian) Cover: Standard Oil (NJ) and the International Petroleum Company in Peru and Colombia, 1914–1948," *Management and Organizational History* 10, no. 2 (2015): 165; Vanessa Ogle, "State Rights against Private Capital: The 'New International Economic Order' and the Struggle over Aid, Trade, and Foreign Investment, 1962–1981," *Humanity* (Summer 2014): 220.

75. Amiya Kumar Bagchi, *The Evolution of the State Bank of India*, 2 vols. (Bombay: OUP, 1987–1997).

76. Kena Wani, "Remaking Capital: Business, Technology and Development Ambitions in Twentieth-Century Western India," PhD Dissertation, Duke University, 2020, 241.

77. White, "Imperial Business Interests," 645–46.

78. P. J. Cain and A. G. Hopkins, *British Imperialism, 1688–2015*, 3rd ed. (Abingdon and New York: Routledge, 2016), 619–44; Nicholas J. White, "The Business and Politics of Decolonization: The British Experience in the Twentieth Century," *Economic History Review* 53, no. 3 (2000): 544–64; White, "Imperial Business Interests," 641.

79. See, for example, Steve Coll, *Private Empire: ExxonMobil and American Power* (New York: Penguin, 2012); Nan Enstad, *Cigarettes, Inc.: An Intimate History of Corporate Imperialism* (Chicago: University of Chicago Press, 2018).

80. Hudson's Bay Company, www.hbc.com/our-company/about-hbc/.

81. Vidhi Doshi, "How the East India Company Became a Weapon to Challenge UK's Colonial Past," *The Guardian*, 6 May 2017; Rachel Rickard Straus, "East India Co Is Back, with Indian Owner," *Times of India*, 16 August 2010; Robert Siegel, "A 21st-Century Version of the East India Company," *National Public Radio*, 19 August 2010.

82. White, "Imperial Business Interests," 640, 646–50.

83. Terry Macalister, "Investors salute P&O as Dubai Takes Command," *The Guardian*, 13 February 2006.

84. D. K. Fieldhouse, *Unilever Overseas: The Anatomy of a Multinational, 1895–1965* (London: Hoover Institution Press, 1978); D. K. Fieldhouse, *Merchant Capital and Economic Decolonization: The United Africa Company, 1929–1987* (Oxford: OUP, 1994).

85. Rory Miller, "British Free-Standing Companies on the West Coast of South America," in *The Free-Standing Company in the World Economy*, ed. Mira Wilkins and Harm Schröter (Oxford: OUP, 1998), 244n3.

86. Frank H. H. King, "Structural Alternatives and Constraints in the Evolution of Exchange Banking," in *Banks as Multinationals*, ed. Jones, 93, 96.

87. Ritu Birla, *Stages of Capital: Law, Culture, and Market Governance in Late Colonial India* (Durham, NC: DUP, 2009), 25; William Goetzman and Elizabeth Koll, "The History of Corporate Ownership in China," in *A History of Corporate Governance Around the World: Family Business Groups to Professional Managers*, ed. Randall Morck (Chicago: University of Chicago Press, 2005), 149–84; Tirthankar Roy and Anand V. Swamy, *Law and the Economy in Colonial India* (Chicago: University of Chicago Press, 2016), 142–58.

88. Mircea Raianu, *Tata: The Global Corporation that Built Indian Capitalism* (Cambridge, MA: HUP, 2021), 9.

89. Vanessa Ogle, "Archipelago Capitalism: Tax Havens, Offshore Money, and the State, 1950s–1970s," *American Historical Review* (December 2017): 1443; Vanessa Ogle, "'Funk Money': The End of Empires, The Expansion of Tax Havens, and Decolonization as an Economic and Financial Event," *Past and Present* 249, no. 1 (2020): 213–49; Raymond Craib, *Adventure Capitalism: A History of Libertarian Exit, from the Era of Decolonization to the Digital Age* (Oakland, CA: PM Press, 2022).

90. Christopher Roper, "A Plan for Decolonizing the Falklands," *Tribune* 46, no. 41 (8 October 1982), 7.

91. Christopher J. Hewer, "The Falkland/Malvinas Dispute: A Contemporary Battle between History and Memory," *Global Discourse*, 3, no. 1 (2013): 146; Stephen Royle, "'Small Places like St Helena Have Big Questions to Ask': The Inaugural Lecture of a Professor of Island Geography," *Island Studies Journal* 5, no. 1 (May 2010): 10; Fritz L. Hoffmann and Olga M. Hoffmann, *Sovereignty in Dispute: The Falklands/Malvinas, 1493–1982* (Boulder: Westview, 1984, repr. Routledge, 2019), 13.

92. Martin Middlebrook, *Operation Corporate: The Falklands War, 1982* (London: Viking, 1985).

ACKNOWLEDGMENTS

Like most of the joint-stock companies detailed in this book, I have incurred so many debts over the years in writing this book that I fear I may be on the verge of foreclosure. I am also writing these words about two and a half years into COVID-19, so I have little trust that I have the memory or grace to pay my bills adequately here. First, I must begin with a perhaps unusual acknowledgment to the many scholars whose writings fill the footnotes of this book and the doubtless many more that I certainly failed to read or adequately incorporate along the way, including work that I am still discovering and seems to be emerging daily as I send this off to press. I had always planned this to be a work of synthesis and, more importantly, a tribute to both the long tradition and recent efflorescence of work on the history of colonial corporations and companies. Little could I have anticipated how much such scholarship would be a lifeline during a pandemic. Likewise, I have discussed this book so many times with so many people that any attempt to list the many generous friends, colleagues, and audiences on several continents who have had an even more direct influence on this book over the years would inevitably embarrass me both in its length and its incompleteness. I fear it may be uncharitable but I hope at least understandable if I simply leave it as: (a) you know who you are, and (b) thank you.

I am duty bound, of course, to offer a few more specific words of gratitude to the various institutions and individuals that have directly made this book possible. Support and programs funded by the Andrew W. Mellon Foundation, the Library Company of Philadelphia and the National Endowment for the Humanities, and Duke University contributed, directly or indirectly, to its research and writing. I am deeply appreciative to Sharmila Sen, Olivia Woods, and the rest of the team at Harvard University Press; Martin Schneider and Julia Kirby did especially heroic work under great pressure at the copyediting stage for which I am extremely grateful. Countless undergraduate and graduate students and faculty shaped the ideas here through courses taught at Duke as well as the Folger Shakespeare Library and a glorious week at the University of Bologna, made all the more glorious by my host Raffaele Laudani. Will Pettigrew and his team graciously invited me to spend a short residence at their center at The University of Kent some time ago as these ideas were just taking form. Much of the inspiration for this book also developed in the context of a yearlong Sawyer Seminar on "Corporations and International Law" we hosted at Duke in 2017–2018, and for that I must thank my co-conspirator, Rachel Brewster, and our team of Charlie Bartlett, Ashton Merck, Vicky Paniagua, and Ali Prince as well as (again) the Mellon Foundation, the School of Law, the John Hope Franklin Humanities Institute, and the Department of History, not to mention our many amazing guests and students over that thrilling year and some. I have also had the privilege of working with several research assistants on this and several related digital projects—Michael Becker, Sam Horewood, Lauren Jackson, Sam Kotz, Ted Leonhardt, Julia Marano, Claire Payton, Andrew Ruoss, and Helen Shears—and even if I have not done justice to all their work in the material here, their contributions shaped it nonetheless in incalculable ways. Helen deserves special mention for securing some critical late-stage materials for me in London archives, while I was grounded across the Atlantic by the pandemic. Mitch Fraas, Sasha Pack, and Owen Stanwood also generously obtained or shared documents for me at various points. And though I said I wouldn't name names, I do need to give a special "shout out," as my son might have once put it, to David Armitage, Andrew Fitzmaurice, Paul Halliday, Dane Kennedy, and Mark Peterson; each read the manuscript or parts of it at an unreasonably late stage and offered crucial feedback, of which, if you have made it this far, you will know that I clearly failed to take full advantage. Adriane Lentz-Smith, Julia Rudolph, and Robert Travers did all this and much more; in different ways, your support, advice, and, most of all, friendship got me through even the darkest days of the pandemic, writing, or both. Of course, to my family: no words can repay what I owe to Mom, Dad, Carole, and, of course, Kim, who has both put up with me and held me up through all of this. And then there is Felix, who has lived with this book in some way his whole life now and has probably read and written and illustrated a dozen of his own just in the time it has taken me to write these acknowledgments. All I can say is that this book—and more important, the fact that I am no longer trying to write it—is for you.

INDEX OF COMPANIES, CORPORATIONS, AND SOCIETIES

Aborigines Protection Society, 241, 307
Additional Sea Venture, 91
Adventure for Irish Land, 91, 93
Adventurers in the Company of Canada, 62–63, 110
Adventurers to Guinie, 19–20
African Association Limited, 282
African Direct Telegraph Company, 259
African Lakes Company, 290
African Transcontinental Telegraph Company, 288
Agence Havas, 261
Alliance British and Foreign Fire and Life Insurance Company, 211
Amazon Company, 64–66
American Company, Russian, 208, 254
American Fur Company, 204
American Trading Company of Borneo, 266
Ancient and Honorable Artillery Company, 86
Anglo-Iranian Oil Company, 314
Ashanti Goldfields Corporation, 314
Assada Adventure, 92
Assam Company, 198
Atherton Company, 98–100, 101
Austraalse Compagnie, 80
Austral Africa Exploration Company, 285
Australian Agricultural Company, 216–217, 227, 309, 316

Bank of Asia, 202, 203
Bank of Australasia, 203
Bank of British North America, 203
Bank of India, Australia, and China, 202
Bank of Jamaica, 202
Bank of St. George. *See* Casa di San Giorgio

Bank of the United States, 166
Barbados Adventurers, 103
Barbary Company, 41, 76–77, 81
Barclays Bank (Dominion, Colonial and Overseas), 314
Barclays Overseas Development Corporation, 314
Bechuanaland Exploration Company, 284, 288, 289
Bechuanaland Railway Company, 288
Bechuanaland Railway Trust Limited, 288
Beira Junction Railway (Port Beira to Fontesville) Limited, 291
Beira Railway Company Limited, 291
Belize Estate and Produce Company, 314
Berkeley Company, 57
Black River Commercial and Agricultural Company, 213
Borneo Company Limited, 266
Borneo Jute Company, 266
Brazil Companies, Portuguese, 80, 140
Brazilian Submarine Telegraph Company, 259
British Airways Ltd, 312
British American Land Company, 218–219, 230
British and Foreign Anti-Slavery Society, 241
British Broadcasting Corporation, 310–311, 313
British Central Africa Company, 290–291, 308
British Central American Land Company, 230
British Fisheries Council, 77–79, 82
British Honduras Company Limited, 257
British India Steam Navigation Company, 276

British Ladies' Female Emigrants Society, 241
British North American Association, 253
British North Borneo Company, 267–269, 276, 277, 280, 281; end of government of, 302, 307–308; North Borneo Provisional Association Limited as predecessor of, 267
British North Borneo Timber Company, 308
British Overseas Airways Corporation, 313
British Royal Bank, 266
British South Africa Company, 285–291, 297, 298, 300; comparisons to, 293; end of government of, 302, 306–307, 316
Bulama Island Association, 190–191, 195

Cable & Wireless, 311
Cable Company, 260
Caisse des Mines de Paris, 284
Calcutta & Burmah Steam Navigation Company, 276
Cambridge University, 257
Canada Company, 214–216, 219, 222, 283
Canadian Pacific Railway, 261
Canary Islands Company, 125
Canterbury Association, 240
Casa di San Giorgio, 3, 22
Central African Company Limited, 278
Central Argentine Land Company, 257
Central Argentine Railway, 257
Central Borneo Company (Limited), 274
Central Search Association Limited, 285
Charitable Corporation, 144
Charter Consolidated Ltd, 316
Chartered Bank of India, Australia, and China, 271
Chartered Company of Mexico, 309
Clergy Reserves Corporation, 214
Cockayne's Project, 75
Cockerell, Trail, & Co., 201
Collegats or the Fellowshippe of New Navigations Atlanticall and Septentrionall, 39
College, Academy, and Charity-School of Philadelphia, 153, 166
College of New Jersey, 153
College of William and Mary, 128, 153, 166
College van de Grote Visserij, 78, 79
Colombian Agricultural Association, 213
Colombian Mining Association, 213, 219
Colonial Bank, 202, 208
Colonial Development Corporation, 314
Comité d'Etudes du Haut Congo, 277
Commercial Cable Company, 260
Commonwealth Development Corporation, 314
Compagnie belge de colonisation, 232–233
Compagnie des Cent-Associés. See Company of New France
Companhia Africana, 277

Companie for the Discovery of Lands Beyond the Equinoctial, 30
Company Adventurers into the New Found Ilondes, 19
Company of Adventurers in the Mines of Real del Monte, 210–211
Company of Cathay, 31–33, 35
Company of Colonists of Vancouver's Island, 234
Company of Husbandmen. *See* Company of the Plough
Company of Merchants Trading to Africa, 185, 188, 192, 204
Company of New France, 62, 80
Company of Scotland Trading to Africa and the Indies. *See* Darien Company
Company of the Plough, 83
Consolidated Gold Fields of South Africa Company Limited, 284, 285
Council for New England, 71, 82–83, 115
Council of Assiniboia, 208
Courteen Association, 77, 92

Damaraland Company, 291
Darien Company, 120–121, 130, 133, 255; as model, 149, 184, 212, 215–216, 281–282
De Beers Consolidated Mines, 284, 288, 316
Delaware Company, 159–160
Dent & Co., 201, 267
Direct West India Company, 260
Dorchester Company, 83
DP World, 316
Dutch Margarine Unie, 316

East African Company, German, 277
East African Syndicate Limited, 310
Eastern Archipelago Company, 264–265
Eastern Archipelago Company Limited, 266
Eastern Coast of Central America Commercial and Agricultural Company, 230–232
Eastern Extension Australia and China Telegraph Company, 259, 267
Eastern Telegraph Company, 259, 311
East India Companies, 140, 170; Frisian, 80; Ostend, 140, 170; Portuguese, 80, 140; Prussian, 140; Swedish, 80, 140, 170
East India Company, American, 166
East India Company, Danish, 80, 129, 142
East India Company, Dutch, 3, 43, 46, 47, 70, 78–80, 145; as model, 53, 63, 79; *voorcompagnieën* of, 42, 43
East India Company, English, 3, 11, 44, 56, 116, 190, 212, 223, 259, 264, 265; challenges to, 46, 77, 92, 103, 109, 120–121, 136, 143, 166, 202, 204; companies laws introduced by, 256; comparisons to, 103, 148, 162, 164, 205, 211, 275; connections to other projects

of, 46–47, 59, 97, 149, 216, 220, 231; critiques of, 67–68, 131, 166, 224, 245–246, 247–248, 270, 294–295, 302, 314; defenses of, 68–71, 123–125, 195–196; diplomacy of, 47–48, 63; eighteenth-century debates over, 168–170, 173–184; end of commercial functions of, 196–198; end of government of, 248–252, 255; establishment of, 43–46; expanding trade of, 140, 185; as financier, 130–131, 139, 170; fortifications and settlements of, 51, 93, 95, 105, 108, 110, 117, 129–130; mergers proposed with, 46, 47, 92, 120, 136; as model for other projects, 86, 111, 112, 133, 166, 205, 208, 224, 228, 229, 236–238, 264, 267, 271, 275–276, 277, 281–282, 285, 289, 297–300, 302; as Mughal officeholder, 173, 176; Northwest Passage ventures of, 46–47; reliance on other companies of, 198–203; revival in 2010 of, 316; subsidiary joint-stocks of, 45, 55–56; territorial expansion of, 171–173, 185, 193–194

East India Company, French, 80, 170–171. *See also* Mississippi Company (France)
East India Company, Scottish (1617), 46, 47, 59
East India Company, Scottish (1632), 77
East India Company, Scottish (1695). *See* Darien Company
East Indian Railway, 199
Eastland Company, 41, 67, 123, 125
Edinburgh Australian Company, 227
Eleutherian Adventurers, 90, 104
Empire Cotton Growing Corporation, 313
Exploring Company Limited, 284, 285, 288, 289

Falkland Islands Company, 262–263, 270, 317–318
Family Colonization Loan Society, 241
Fife Adventurers, 49, 51, 57, 77, 79
Florida Company, 127
Frankfort Company, 107–108
Free Society of Traders, 106–107

General Mining Association, 217
General South American Mining Association, 217
German Colonization Company, 240
G.F. Angas & Co., 230
Glass Elliott, 259
GlaxoSmithKline, 316
Globe Venture Syndicate, 292
Governor and Assistants of the Cittie of Raleigh in Virginia, 39–40
Governor and Company of the English Colony of Connecticut in New England in America, 98. *See also* Connecticut

Governor and Company of the English Colony of Rhode Island and Providence Plantations in New England in America, 100. *See also* Rhode Island
Governor and Company of the New Mediterranean Sea, 107, 126
Grace Brothers & Co. *See* Peruvian Corporation
Grand Fishery of Great Britain, 137
Great Indian Peninsular Railway, 199
Great Northern Telegraph Company, 260
Greenland Company, 56. *See also* Russia Company
Gresham's College, 96
Guiana Company, 81
Guinea Company, 81, 91, 93, 103, 110
Gutta Percha Company, 259

Halifax and Bermudas Company, 260
Hanseatic Land, Mining, and Trading Company, 291
Harvard College, 85, 102, 153, 166; incorporation of, 89, 119
Hongkong and Shanghai Banking Corporation Limited, 316
Hudson's Bay Company, 11, 97, 112, 119, 139, 214, 261, 316; challenges to, 184–185, 204–205, 244–245; defenses of, 123, 125, 181; end of government of, 253–255; establishment of, 110, 112; as model, 126, 275, 281–282, 297, 298–299, 305, 307; territorial expansion of, 112, 205–208, 233–234

Ibo Syndicate Limited, 292
Illinois Company, 158, 167
Imperial Airways, 312
Imperial Bank of India, 315
Imperial British Central South Africa Company, 285
Imperial British East Africa Company, 277–278, 296, 303, 305, 309; East African Association as predecessor of, 277
imperial exhibitions, 257
India Iron and Steel Company, 198
Indiana Company, 167
Indian Broadcasting Ltd., 311
Indian National Airways, 312
Indian Trans-Continental Airlines, 312
India Rubber, Gutta Percha, and Telegraph Works Company, 260
Indo-European Telegraph Company, 260
Insurance Company of North America, 166
International Company of Mexico, 257
International Financial Society, 254
Ireland, sixteenth-century joint-stock plantation projects in, 24–28

Irish Canada Company, 235
Irish Society, 51–52, 56, 72–74, 89, 91, 95; as
    model, 148, 253; transformation into trust,
    204

Jardine & Matheson & Co., 201

Kent Island Company, 81, 88
King's College, 153

Laconia Company, 83, 86
Ladd & Co., 233
Lake of the Iroquois Company, 86
Land Bank (Massachusetts), 152
Levant Company, 55–56, 66, 86, 103, 119;
    attacks on, 69, 184; connections to other
    companies of, 43–44; defenses of, 66, 69;
    establishment of, 41–42; subsumed by
    state, 203–204
Lever Brothers, 316
Lewis Company, 78
London Adventurers for Carrying on a Trade
    (and Settling Colonies in) Terra Australis,
    142–143
London and Amsterdam Borneo Tobacco
    Company, 271
London Assurance Company, 138
London livery companies, 4, 20, 55, 56, 73;
    Haberdashers, 44; Skinners, 44; Vintners, 55
Louisiana Company, French, 155. *See also*
    Mississippi Company (France)
Loyal Company, 155

Mackinnon Mackenzie, 276
magazine companies, 56, 64, 74, 88
Marine Insurance Company, 198
Massachusetts Bay Company, 83–85, 98, 237;
    quo warranto against, 85, 115; *scire facias*
    against, 115. *See also* Massachusetts
Matabeleland Company, 288
Mauritania Syndicate, 293
Merchant Adventurers, 20; of Bristol, 20, 36,
    59, 82, 188; of England, 20, 44, 67, 68, 70,
    75, 92, 123; of Exeter, 36
Merchant Adventurers to the East Indies,
    92–93
Merchant Adventurers with Sir Humfry
    Gilbert, 35–36
Mexican Land and Colonization Company, 257
Michilimackinac (Montreal-
    Michilimackinac) Company, 204
Military Adventurers, Company of, 158
Mine Adventures Company, 144
Mineral and Battery Works, 138
Mines Royal, 138
Mississippi Company (France), 137, 139, 142,
    144, 188–189

Mississippi Company (Virginia), 155, 158
Mississippi Land Company, 167–168
Moçâmedes Company, 291
Morocco Company, 110, 125
Mozambique Company, 291–292

Nashaway Undertakers, 86
Natal Land and Colonisation Company, 283
National Colonisation Society. *See* South
    Australian Land Company
National Provincial Bank, 230
National Telegraph Company, 260
New Brunswick and Nova Scotia Land Com-
    pany, 218
New Eastern Archipelago Company, 266
New England Adventurers, 103
New England Company (1628, plantation
    company), 83
New England Company (1649, 1662, mis-
    sionary company), 97, 101; praying towns
    of, 101
Newfoundland Company, 58–63, 64, 71, 79,
    83
New London Society for Trade and Com-
    merce, 151–152, 162
New Plymouth Company (1620), 57, 74, 83,
    160
New Sweden Company, 81
New Zealand Company (1825), 217, 236–237
New Zealand Company (1841), 237–241,
    244, 246, 270; New Zealand Association
    as predecessor of, 236; New Zealand Land
    Company as predecessor of, 239
Niger Company Limited, 305
Northern Gold Fields Exploration Company,
    284
North-West Africa Company, 282–283, 292
North-West Company, 204–205, 214, 234
Northwest Passage Companies, 39, 46, 47
North-West Transportation Land Company,
    253
Nova Scotia Company, 91
Nova Scotia Mining Company, 218
Nyassa Company, 292; Nyassa Consolidated
    financing arm of, 306

Ohio Company, 155, 157, 184
Oragon Beef & Tallow Company, 233
Oriental Bank, 202
Overseas Food Corporation, 314

Pacific Phosphate Company, 306
Pacific Telegraph Company, 261
Palestine Jewish Colonisation Association, 310
Pan-Arab Corporation, 310
Peninsular & Oriental Steam Navigation
    Company, 201, 276, 316

Pennsylvania Land Company, 107, 139
Peruvian Corporation, 275
Petworth Emigration Committee, 241
Planters Bank, 202
Plymouth Company (1840), 240
Predation, joint stocks for, 40, 42
Providence Island Company, 87–89, 90, 92
Puget's Sound Agricultural Company, 233

Qantas, 312

Red Sea Telegraph Company, 258
Reuter Telegram Company Limited, 260
Ribault-Stukeley Florida project, 17, 26, 28, 30, 59
Río Tinto Commercial and Agricultural Company, 230
Royal African Company, 116, 123, 128, 140, 148, 149, 169, 187; Company of Royal Adventurers into Africa as predecessor of, 110–111; critiques of, 119, 181, 185, 188; defenses of, 125; elimination of, 185; establishment of, 111–112; opening of trade of, 119–120, 121; recapitalization schemes under James Brydges of, 139; slave trading of, 111, 136; subsidiary companies of, 111
Royal Asiatic Society, 257
Royal Colonial Society, 257
Royal Exchange Assurance Company, 138
Royal Fisheries Company, 109–110, 119, 124, 137
Royal Geographical Society, 257, 270, 280
Royal Lustring Company, 138
Royal Mail Steam Packet Company, 306
Royal Niger Company, 282, 293, 294, 295, 302, 304–305; National African Company Limited as predecessor of, 280; United African Company Limited as predecessor of, 278
Royal Society of London for Promoting Natural Knowledge, 96–97, 142, 149, 257
Russia Company, 33, 44, 69, 78, 89, 119, 123, 255; challenges to, 22–24, 35, 36, 41, 43, 46, 67, 89, 119; defenses of, 24, 46, 69, 123; establishment of, 17, 20–22; Greenland company subsidiary of, 56; investment and involvement in other ventures of, 30–31, 34, 36, 39, 46–47; as model for other ventures, 31, 34, 53, 299; plot to annex Archangelsk, 45; relations and brief merger with East India Company, 46

Santa Fe Land Company, 257
Saybrook Company, 87, 97, 160
Shashi-Mcloutsie Exploration and Mining Company, 288–289
Shire Highlands Railway Company, 290
Siemens und Halske, 260

Sierra Leone Company, 189–190, 191, 192, 194, 195, 225, 237; St. George's Bay Company as predecessor of, 186–189
Silver Bank, 152
Society for Martin's Hundred, 57
Society for the Colonization of Free People of Color of America, 229
Society for the Promotion of Christian Knowledge, 129
Society for the Promotion of Colonization, 241
Society for the Promotion of Female Emigration, 241
Society for the Propagation of the Gospel in Foreign Parts, 129, 148, 241
Society in Scotland for Propagating Christian Knowledge, 129
Society of Apothecaries, 149
Society of the New Art, 18
Somers Islands Company, 57–59, 104; *quo warranto* against, 114–115
Sons of the Clergy, 129
South Africa Gold Fields Exploration Company, 284
South Australian Association, 225–229, 238, 300; South Australian Commission as predecessor of, 225, 229
South Australian Banking Company, 230
South Australian Company, 229
South Australian Land Company, 221–225, 228
South Australian Mining Association, 240
South Manchuria Railway Company, 310
South Sea Company, 133–137, 140–141, 143, 144, 146, 149, 150, 152, 184, 204, 211
South-West Africa Company, German, 291
Spanish Company, 41, 67
Suez Canal Company, 243, 306, 315
Susquehanna Company, 158–161, 162, 167
Sword Blade Bank, 133, 139, 152
Sword Blades Company, 132–133, 138

Tana Company, 278
Tata, 317
Tati Company, 290
Telegraph Construction & Maintenance, 259, 260
Transylvania Company, 158
Trinity House, 20–21, 238
Trustees for Establishing the Colony of Georgia in America, 147–150. *See also* Georgia
Trustees of Dartmouth College, 153
Trustees of the Academy and Charitable School in the Province of Pennsylvania, 153
Turkey Company, 41. *See also* Levant Company

Unilever, 316
Union Bank of Australia, 230

Union Castle Mail Steamship Company, 306
United Africa Company, 314
United Concessions Company, 285, 288
United Fruit Company, 310
United Kingdom Commercial Corporation Ltd, 313–314

Van Diemen's Land Company, 217, 309, 316
Venice Company, 41, 42
Virginia Company, 59, 64, 68, 84, 104, 226, 237; challenges to, 60, 63, 71, 74, 77–78, 115; establishment of, 53–55; financing and subsidiary ventures of, 55–56, 57–58; lotteries of, 55, 71, 75, 79; "particular plantations" of, 56–57; promotional efforts of, 54–55; proposals to revive, 81; *quo warranto* against and dissolution of, 72, 74–76; 1606 London Company of, 53; 1606 Plymouth Company of, 53, 58
Virginia Indian Company, 127–129

Wabash Company, 167
Walpole Company, 157, 167; becomes Grand Ohio Company, 157–158
West African Company, German, 281
West African Company Limited, 278
West African Telegraph Company, 260

Western and Brazilian Telegraph Company, 259
Western Australia Company, 235
West India Agricultural Company, 235
West India and Panama Telegraph Company, 260
West India Bank, 202
West India Company, Dutch, 79, 80–81, 87, 89
West India Company (1824), 208–210, 224
West India Company (1846), 235
West India Company (1849), 235–236; West India Joint-Stock Association of, 236
West India company proposals (17th century), 87, 90–91, 92
West Jersey Society, 106, 122
Whale Fishery and Steam Communication Company, 240
Wolffs Telegraphisches Bureau, 261

Yale College, 147, 153–155, 162, 166; Collegiate School as predecessor of, 153
Yazoo Lands companies, 167
York Buildings Company, 144, 145, 149
Yorkshire and Lancashire Central American Land and Emigration Company, 230

Zambezi Traffic Company, 290

GENERAL INDEX

Admiralty, 9, 62, 126, 137, 149, 258, 265, 283
African Institution, 190
agency houses, 198, 201, 266, 274, 276
alchemy, 18, 69, 143
American Revolution, 158, 162–163, 186, 250
Archangelsk, 21, 45
Ards Peninsula, 25, 26
Argentina, 257, 262, 317
asiento, 136, 140
Assiniboia. See Red River Colony
Association (Tortuga) Island, 88
Australia, 194, 202, 203, 238, 241, 258, 261, 300, 311; companies in, 216–217, 220–230, 235, 236, 237, 240, 271, 306, 309; introduction of companies law to, 256
Australind, 235
Avalon Peninsula, 58, 59, 63
Azores, 19, 34, 42

Bahamas, 90, 104, 115, 122, 126
Baltic, 20, 41, 79, 81
Bank of England, 120, 121, 130, 136, 139, 140, 177, 203, 210–211, 216
banks, 95, 110, 132, 144, 177, 181, 198, 208, 224; as anti-Semitic trope, 245; charters for, 258; collapses and financial crises of, 139, 177, 254, 265, 283; colonial, 200–203, 230, 315; companies laws concerning, 243, 256; as company financiers, 254, 260, 271; development, 314; land, 110, 117, 151–152, 229, 253; as subsidiary company enterprises, 212, 217, 229, 257, 278, 288, 308, 310. See also individual banking and financing companies
Barbados, 76–77, 90, 92, 94, 105, 114, 202; plantation projects from, 103–104; requests corporate charter, 105

Belgium, 232, 233, 275, 277, 302
Bengal, 140, 173, 175, 176, 177, 180, 201, 237, 256, 299, 315
Berlin West Africa Conference, 275
Bermuda, 54, 57, 58, 64, 114, 115, 147, 149, 260, 317. See also Somers Islands Company
bills of exchange, 176–177
Board of Control, 169, 183, 237, 245, 247; analogies and comparisons to, 229, 236, 302
Board of Trade, 157, 184, 218, 313; assaults on charters by, 118, 122, 128, 185; establishment of, 118; petitions for charters to, 127, 142–143, 145, 264. See also Council of Trade and Foreign Plantations; Privy Council: Committee on Trade and Plantations
Bolama, 190–191
Bombay, 94, 117, 124, 140, 172, 201, 237, 315
bonds: critiques of, 226–227; in debt-for-equity swaps, 131–132, 275; as form of corporate finance, 9, 55, 130, 170, 177, 193, 212–213, 230, 263, 289, 291–292, 308; growing market in, 131; redemption for Irish lands, 131–132
Borneo, 243, 264–274, 275, 281, 308
Brazil, 17, 34, 63, 80, 140, 236, 259
Bristol, 19, 20, 58, 77, 82, 185, 188
Bristol's Hope, 59, 60
British Columbia, 254
Bubble Act, 138, 143, 150; colonial, 150, 152, 162; lax enforcement of, 140, 210, 211; repeal of, 210–211, 218, 255

Calais, 16
Calcutta, 124, 130, 173, 175, 177, 201, 202
Calvinism, 75, 154, 155
Cape Colony, 247, 256, 283
Caribbee Islands, 105

Carnatic Wars, 172
Carolina, 17, 76, 95, 128, 145, 147, 149, 158;
  Barbadian attempts at settlement in, 103;
  Carolana patent for, 76, 103, 115, 126; end
  of proprietary government in, 122; Fundamental Constitutions of, 104; joint-stock
  companies in, 104, 126, 127, 158; Lords
  Proprietors of, 104–105, 106, 115; as model
  for later companies, 222, 237; New England
  attempts at settlement in, 103; proposed
  suits against charter of, 115, 118; towns
  and urban corporations in, 104
Casa de Contratación, 21, 34
Catholics, 35, 36, 59, 62, 91, 145, 174, 292
Chancery, Court of, 55, 73, 115, 166, 193,
  210–211, 288
chaos theory, 11
chiefage, 25
Chile, 275
China, 3, 196, 201, 202, 259, 260, 265
Clergy Reserves, 214
Colonial Land and Emigration Commission,
  240, 262
Committee for the Relief of the Black Poor,
  185
Common Pleas, Court of, 55
Companies Acts, 243, 256–257, 260, 309
Congo Free State, 275, 281, 290, 302
Connecticut, 162, 165, 174, 309; assaults on
  charter of, 115, 117, 119, 161; border disputes
  with, 98–99, 101, 158–161; corporations
  from, 102–103, 151–152, 153–155, 158–161,
  162, 257; establishment of, 87; incorpora-
  tion of, 97–99; joins United Colonies, 89
conquistadores, 8, 38, 302
Council of Royal Burghs, 78
Council of Trade and Foreign Plantations,
  112–113
Crown Reserves, 214, 218
Cupers Cove, 58–59

D'Allone fund, 147
Darcy v. Allen, 67, 69
Dartmouth v. Woodward, 167, 168
debt, 45, 55, 230, 252; capacity of corporations
  to acquire, 5, 9, 50, 263, 275; companies
  in, 32–33, 45, 88, 111–112, 179, 182, 195,
  265; imprisonment for, 142, 145–146, 219;
  as means of territorial acquisition, 106, 172,
  217, 262, 263; national, 130–133, 136–137,
  139, 140–141, 170, 177, 184, 193, 215,
  227, 306. *See also* banks; bonds; loans;
  mortgages
Declaration of Independence, 163
Dominion of New England, 116–117, 152
double government, 11, 169, 194, 229, 245,
  247, 248, 250

Egypt, 306, 313
Exchequer. *See* Treasury
Exchequer, Court of, 265

Falkland Islands, 243, 262, 317–318
farman, 48, 124, 125, 172–173
fee tail-male, 148
financial revolution, 131
fisheries, 35, 38, 50, 58, 71, 80, 136, 140, 151,
  262
Florida, 17, 26, 30, 35, 76, 104, 127, 155,
  158
foreigners, as shareholders in companies, 3,
  4, 13, 46, 55, 137, 224, 246
Foreign Office, 194, 231, 232, 264, 271, 276,
  277, 282, 283, 293, 304, 305, 306
Fort Stanwix, Treaty of, 156, 157
France, 23, 59, 80, 94, 119, 125, 127, 133, 137,
  140, 150, 165, 167, 213, 226, 235, 260–261,
  262, 280, 291, 305, 306, 317; wars with,
  16–17, 26, 62–63, 110, 132, 155, 170–172,
  176, 192, 212, 304
French Revolution, 165, 167, 196

Georgia, 147–150, 186, 190, 226, 237; other
  colonial projects named, 126
Germantown, 107, 109
Gesellschaftsvertrag, 107
Glorious Revolution, 117–120, 131, 169
Guiana, 40, 63–66
guild, 3, 4, 18, 21, 41, 67, 96
Guinea, 30, 81, 91, 93, 110, 190

Haudenosaunee, 128, 156–157, 159, 160
Hawai'i, 233, 243, 261
Hebrides, 49–50, 58, 78
Honduras, British, 88, 212, 232
Huguenots, 16, 17, 36, 145
Huron Tract, 214
Hyderabad, 172
Hysperia, 254

India Act of 1784, 169
insurance, 95, 144, 181, 198, 211, 256; marine, 137–138, 142, 166, 208; as subsidiary
  projects, 133, 144, 198, 201, 310. *See also*
  individual companies
Ireland, 16, 17, 23, 76, 97, 104, 117, 316;
  Church of, 73; emigrants and settlers from,
  59, 65, 235; as model, 38, 56, 57, 59, 253;
  plantation projects in, 18, 24–29, 36, 38,
  50–52, 72–74, 77, 89, 91, 131–133. *See also*
  individual companies and projects
Iroquois Confederacy. *See* Haudenosaunee

Jamaica, 90, 94, 212, 223, 232, 235
Japan, 48, 78, 267, 307, 310, 315

Kenya, 277, 305
Kinder v. Taylor, 210
King/Queen's Bench, Court of, 69, 75, 85, 103, 114, 119, 210, 265, 289; prison, 142, 145–146

Lewis, 49–50, 78–79
Liberia, 229
limited liability, 187, 198, 217, 263
Lloyd's Coffee House, 137–138
loans, 9, 131, 152, 227, 256, 306; for development, 314; as extortion, 92, 98, 172; as means of acquiring territory, 98, 283; as means of facilitating settlement, 214, 241; as means of financing companies, 31, 45, 55, 82, 88, 111, 136, 177, 179, 197, 235, 253–254, 306; as means of securing charters and privileges, 47, 120, 130, 138, 170, 172, 213. *See also* banks; bonds; debt; mortgages
London, Corporation of, 19, 20, 32, 112, 120, 164; as adventurer, 42, 91, 127; Customer of, 44; Lord Mayor of, 31; *quo warranto* against, 108; Sheriff of, 73, 115. *See also* Irish Society; London livery companies
Londonderry, 51, 73
lotteries: as form of financing and investment, 55, 60, 79, 109, 131, 132, 144; reputations of, 28, 55. *See also* Virginia Company, lotteries of

Madagascar, 77, 92, 93, 137
Madras, 93, 108, 109, 124, 129, 153, 171–172, 174, 198, 201, 315
Maine, 53, 83, 89, 113, 118
Malvinas. *See* Falkland Islands
maps, 61, 99, 113, 127, 134–135, 159, 218; as tools of company promotion, 21, 25, 26, 33, 60, 137, 231
Maryland, 63, 76, 115, 226
Mashonaland, 285, 292
Massachusetts, 86–87, 89, 113, 115, 116, 118, 162, 165, 190
Matabeleland, 284
Mayflower, 57, 63
Mexico, 210, 235, 257, 309
middle class, 131, 203, 247, 250
mines and mining: as aspect of colonial ventures, 31, 58, 86, 87, 107, 111–112, 217, 231, 234, 253, 280, 283–284, 288, 290–291; Benjamin Disraeli as propagandist for, 219, 251; in Britain, 18, 39, 95, 138, 144; concessions for, 210–211, 217, 231, 264–265, 271, 274, 284–285, 291, 304, 305, 306, 307, 310; in Ireland, 25; as metaphor, 221, 271; of New Spain, 30; speculation in, 210, 211, 213, 240, 243, 258. *See also individual mining companies*

missionaries, 91, 97, 129, 147, 195, 196, 238, 239, 241, 277
monopoly, 7, 13; claims of companies to, 25, 29, 41, 42, 55, 105, 205, 231, 240, 244, 252, 258, 262, 264, 275, 276, 278, 280, 282, 293, 311, 312; debates over definition and defenses of, 18, 66–72, 102–103, 122–125, 128, 183, 195–196, 199–200, 203, 219, 246; failures to enforce, 46, 76, 114–115, 252; objections to, 7, 74, 119–120, 128, 169–170, 180–181, 188–189, 195–196, 199, 203, 219, 238, 244, 246, 253, 255, 259, 261, 265, 294, 304, 313
Morocco, 41, 76, 81, 110, 125, 282–283, 292
mortgages: as aspect of colonial enterprises, 202, 208, 283, 303, 310; critiques of, 227; as financing for ventures, 40; foreclosures on as means of acquiring territory, 100, 172; as form of joint-stock investment, 151; as metaphor, 179, 182; on offices, 145–146. *See also* banks; bonds; debt; loans
Mughal Empire, 47–48, 63, 116, 120, 125, 129, 131, 171–173, 176; successor states of, 171, 172, 174, 194

Napoleonic Wars, 192, 203, 212, 214–215, 245
Narragansett, 98, 100, 101
Narva, 22, 24
Natal, 235, 283
Navigation Act, 90, 118, 161
Netherlands, 57, 63, 70, 82, 89, 92, 105, 117, 133, 148, 222, 232, 267, 271; Austrian, 140; rivalry over fisheries with, 77–80; wars with, 105, 111. *See also various Dutch companies*
New Albion, 76, 106
New Caledonia (Canada), 234
New Caledonia (Darien), 121
Newfoundland, 19, 53; plantation projects in, 34–35, 38, 58–63, 79, 80. *See also* Newfoundland Company
New Galloway, 63
New Hampshire, 83, 89, 113; becomes royal colony, 113
New Haven, 87, 89, 98
New Jersey, 115, 118, 122; East, 106; West, 106
New Liverpool, 231
New Netherlands. *See* New York
New Plymouth, 57, 83, 84–85, 89, 100, 118
New South Wales, 194, 216–217. *See also* Australia
New Wales, 59
New York: acquisition of, 100–101, 105; border and trade conflicts with other British colonies, 101, 107, 155, 159; as corporate colony, 106; debates over incorporation of King's College in, 153; land companies in, 166, 204, 216; plans to surrender charter of, 115; rebellion in, 117; relation to New Jersey of, 106, 118

New Zealand, 192, 246, 247, 248, 270, 306, 311, 316. *See also* New Zealand Company (1825); New Zealand Company (1841)
Northwest Passage, 23–24, 30–34, 35, 36, 39, 41, 46–47, 55, 77, 136, 185
Nova Scotia, 59, 62, 82, 118, 136, 189

Ottoman Empire, 41–42, 258, 276, 306

Pennsylvania, 95, 126, 128; conflicts over border with, 159–161, 167; establishment of, 106–107; joint-stock companies in, 107–108, 117, 139, 156–157, 166; as model for later projects, 148, 222, 226, 230, 237; threats to charter of, 115, 122; University of, 153, 166; urban corporations in, 108–109
Pequot War, 87, 102
piracy. *See* predatory ventures
Portugal, 34, 42, 43, 65, 78, 80, 81, 306; in Africa, 190, 277, 284, 291–292; in the Atlantic, 42, 80, 140; in the East Indies, 33, 42–43, 78, 80, 140
Powhatan, 53, 54
Poyais, 212, 227, 230, 232
predatory ventures, 13, 17, 35, 40, 44, 87, 88, 136, 137, 172
privateering. *See* predatory ventures
Privy Council, 44, 67, 81, 169; challenges to companies and charters in, 25, 36, 65, 72, 74–75, 80, 105, 118, 128; Committee of Trade and Plantations of, 113; discovers Company of Cathay is not a corporation, 32–33; members of as adventurers in companies, 18, 31, 44, 45; petitions of incorporation to, 22, 30, 31, 43, 64, 84; subcommittee on New England plantations of, 85
Proclamation of 1763, 155–156, 161, 167, 176

quo warranto, 178, 245, 307; against English urban corporations, 108; against Massachusetts Bay Company, 85, 115; against Somers Isles Company, 114–115; against Virginia Company, 75, 81; recommended against use of obsolete charters, 138; threatened against various colonial charters, 115, 118, 119, 122; trusteeship as security against, 154

railways, 10, 199–200, 219, 253, 257, 271, 275, 288, 290, 291, 307, 308, 310
Red River Colony, 204, 205, 208, 233, 244, 252
regulated company, 41, 67, 69
Rex v. Dodd, 210, 217
Rhode Island, 90, 98–99, 100–101, 115, 118, 161, 166
Rupert's Land, 112, 233, 252, 254

Sagadahoc, 53, 137
scire facias, 73, 75, 114, 115, 118, 122, 138, 265
slavery, 27, 74, 87, 148, 150; abolition of, 202, 208; opposition to, 88, 148, 186, 187
slave trade, 20, 30, 65, 87–88, 91, 111, 120, 136, 140; abolition of, 190
South Sea Bubble, 139–140, 144, 169, 255; later comparisons and allusions to, 170, 174, 177, 188–189, 208, 227
Spain, 8, 19, 30, 89, 223, 262; Atlantic empire of as model, 38, 59, 116; attempted invasions of England and Ireland by, 42, 50, 299; claim to exclusive rights in Atlantic by papal dispensation, 46; colonies acquired from, 94–95, 155; diplomacy with as impediment to companies, 35, 37, 43, 53, 64, 65, 127, 267; predation on as joint-stock project, 34–35, 42, 65, 87, 133, 136; revolutions against colonial rule of as spur to company speculation, 210, 212–213, 232; rivalry with as argument for colonization, 30, 35, 40, 43, 80, 87, 121, 133, 236; trade with, 19, 41, 44, 67, 105, 136, 149, 260
Stamp Act, 161–162
Star Chamber, 73, 79, 85, 89
St. Christopher. *See* St. Kitts
steamships, 200, 253, 258, 265, 290
St. Helena, 93, 124, 317
St. Kitts, 65, 136, 150
Strongbow, 26, 38
Suez Canal, 243, 276, 306
surrender and regrant, 25, 117
systematic colonization, theory of, 10, 220–221, 228–229, 234–236

Tangier, 94, 108, 109, 110
Tasmania. *See* Van Diemen's Land
telegraphy, 200, 253, 258–261
Terra Australis Incognita, 77, 147
Treasury, 9, 84, 130, 169, 176, 186, 202, 258, 304, 311
trust and trusteeships, 3, 4–5, 51, 153, 167, 289, 305; for arbitrating dispute over Jersey proprietorship, 106; colonial laws for establishing, 256; colony of Libera established by, 229; East India Company government theorized as, 178–179, 197, 247, 251; establishment of Irish Society as, 204; for forfeited estates in Ireland, 131–132; frankpledge as form of in Sierra Leone, 186, 191; Georgia colony structured as, 146–150; for managing King's Bench prison, 146; for managing reparation payments to East India Company for first Anglo-Dutch war, 92; for managing seized assets in South Sea

bubble, 146; for managing Upper Canada clergy reserves, 214; as method of evading challenges to corporate charters, 154; reformulation of South Australian Company as, 225; for Robert Boyle's charitable endowment, 166; as strategy for distributing non-voting joint stock shares, 278, 292
Tuscarora War, 128

Uganda, 278, 296, 303, 305
Utopia, Limited, 242–243, 256, 302

Vancouver Island, 234, 244, 252–253
Vandalia, 157
Van Diemen's Land, 203, 217
Virginia, 78, 80, 94, 105, 117, 155, 165
visitation, right of, 100, 119

Western Design, 90
women: emigrant societies for, 241; as shareholders in companies, 4, 55, 56, 131, 137, 241, 246

Zanzibar, 305